THE REALITIES OF Money & Missions

KGMLF 2021

THE REALITIES OF Money & Missions

GLOBAL CHALLENGES & CASE STUDIES

Jonathan J. Bonk, Michel G. Distefano, J. Nelson Jennings, Jinbong Kim, Jae Hoon Lee, EDITORS

Available at missionbooks.org

The Realities of Money and Missions: Global Challenges and Case Studies
© 2022 by Global Mission Leadership Forum (GMLF). All rights reserved.

No part of this book may be reproduced, stored in a retrieval system, or transmitted in any form or by any means—electronic, mechanical, photocopy, recording, or otherwise—without prior written permission from the publisher, except brief quotations used in connection with reviews in magazines or newspapers. For permission, email permissions@wclbooks.com. For corrections, email editor@wclbooks.com.

All Scripture quotations, unless otherwise indicated, are taken from the New International Version (NIV), ©1973, 1978, 1984, 2011 by Biblica, Inc.™. Used by permission of Zondervan. All rights reserved worldwide. www.zondervan.com The "NIV" and "New International Version" are trademarks registered in the United States Patent and Trademark Office by Biblica, Inc.™

Scripture quotations marked ESV are taken from The Holy Bible, English Standard Version. (ESV), ©2001 by Crossway, a publishing ministry of Good News Publishers. All rights reserved.

Scripture quotations marked KJV are taken from the King James Version.

Scripture quotations marked NRSV are taken from the New Revised Standard Version Bible, ©1989 by National Council of the Churches of Christ in the United States of America. Used by permission. All rights reserved.

Scripture quotations marked (NLT) are taken from the Holy Bible, New Living Translation, copyright ©1996, 2004, 2015 by Tyndale House Foundation. Used by permission of Tyndale House Publishers, Carol Stream, Illinois 60188. All rights reserved.

Scripture quotations marked AMP are taken from the Amplified® Bible (AMP), Copyright © 2015 by The Lockman Foundation. Used by permission. www.lockman.org.

Scripture quotations marked TPT are from The Passion Translation®. Copyright © 2017, 2018, 2020 by Passion & Fire Ministries, Inc. Used by permission. All rights reserved. ThePassionTranslation.com.

Scripture quotations are marked NRSVA from the New Revised Standard Version Bible: Anglicised Edition, copyright © 1989, 1995 the Division of Christian Education of the National Council of the Churches of Christ in the United States of America. Used by permission. All rights reserved.

Published by William Carey Publishing
10 W. Dry Creek Cir
Littleton, CO 80120 | www.missionbooks.org

William Carey Publishing is a ministry of Frontier Ventures
Pasadena, CA | www.frontierventures.org

Cover and Interior Designer: Mike Riester
Copyeditor: Michel G. Distefano
Managing Editor: Melissa Hicks
Indexer: Michel G. Distefano
Translator: Soonuk Jung

ISBNs: 978-1-64508-301-6 (paperback), 978-1-64508-305-4 (epub)

Printed Worldwide

26 25 24 23 22   1 2 3 4 5   IN

Library of Congress Control Number: 2022932780

Other Titles in the KGMLF Series

Accountability in Missions:
Korean and Western Case Studies

Family Accountability in Missions:
Korean and Western Case Studies

Megachurch Accountability in Missions:
Critical Assessment through Global Case Studies

People Disrupted:
Doing Mission Responsibly among Refugees and Migrants

Missionaries, Mental Health, and Accountability:
Support Systems in Churches and Agencies

Contents

Foreword—JONATHAN J. BONK ... ix

Preface 1—JINBONG KIM ... xi

Preface 2—J. NELSON JENNINGS ... xiii

BIBLE STUDIES by Christopher J. H. Wright

1 The Integrity of Our Funding in the Eyes of God: 1 Chronicles 29:1-19 ... 1

2 Accountability in Our Stewardship of the Grace of God: 2 Corinthians 8:16-9:5 ... 7

3 The Viability of Our Ministry under the Sovereignty of God: Ecclesiastes 11:1-6 ... 13

SECTION A: Case Studies

4 Faith-Based Organizations and Investments in Mission: The Case of the All Africa Conference of Churches —BRIGHT G. MAWUDOR ... 21

RESPONSE —JEFFREY J. LEE ... 29

5 Fundraising Practices of the Mizoram Presbyterian Church —ZOSANGLIANA COLNEY ... 32

RESPONSE —SUNG-CHAN KWON ... 37

6 Missions and Money: Christian Finance in Global Perspective —GINA A. ZURLO ... 40

RESPONSE —DAESHIK JO ... 47

7 Jesus Abbey: A Case Study in "Faith Financing" —BEN TORREY ... 50

RESPONSE —INSOO KIM ... 55

8 The Structure and the Financial Management Policy of GMS from the Perspective of Credibility, Transparency, and Accountability —JINBONG KIM ... 58

RESPONSE —KAREN SHAW ... 64

9 Missions and Education —ALLISON HOWELL ... 66

RESPONSE —HYUNCHOL HONG ... 73

10 Registration of Real Estate: A Pivotal Factor in a Collaborative Effort to Establish a Seminary in Postwar Japan —J. NELSON JENNINGS ... 76

RESPONSE —JIMOON CHUNG ... 81

11 Money and Self-Support: A Challenging Principle of the Nevius Method for Korean Protestant Churches and Missions —SUNG-DEUK OAK ... 84

RESPONSE —LALSANGKIMA PACHAU ... 90

SECTION B: Workshops

12 Optimizing Missions through Organizational Financial Accountability —VALENTINE GITOHO ... 94

RESPONSE —DAE SU JUNG ... 99

13 The Core Elements of the Establishment and Development of United Theological Seminary in Kyrgyzstan —JOOHYUNG LEE, EMIL OSMONALIEV, AND SUNGBIN HONG ... 101

RESPONSE —CHARLES WEBER ... 108

14 Church Missions in the Public Sphere with a Focus on Onnuri Church's Use of Public Funds —HONG JOO KIM
111

RESPONSE —ATOLA LONGKUMER ... 117

15 Evangelicals and Structural (In)Justice—What Are We Afraid Of? —JUSTIN THACKER ... 120

RESPONSE —MINYOUNG JUNG ... 126

16	Integrity Is Illusive: Intercultural Gospel Work Needs to Be Vulnerable to Allow Indigenous Free Self-Expression —JIM HARRIES	129
	RESPONSE —C. S. CALEB KIM	135
17	Mission, Power, and Money —PAUL BENDOR-SAMUEL	138
	RESPONSE —JONGDO PARK	144
18	Global South Mission Is Possible! —ANDREW B. KIM	147
	RESPONSE —WANJIRU M. GITAU	151
19	The COVID-19 Crisis and Opportunities for Increased Community: A Local Pastor's Recommendations —MONGSIK LEE	154
	RESPONSE —SUN MAN KIM	159
20	COVID-19 and Opportunities in Mission: An Ibero-American Case Analysis —LEVI DECARVALHO	162
	RESPONSE —BYUNG SOO LEE	169
21	Mission, Fiscal Responsibility, and Care for the Environment —ALLISON HOWELL	172
	RESPONSE —BRIGHT MYEONG-SEOK LEE	178
22	Toward a Money-Missionary Relationship Model: A Grounded Theory Approach Based on the Empirical Data of Korean Missionaries —JOOYUN EUM	181
	RESPONSE —RUTH MAXWELL	190
23	The Role of Patron as Father (*Gap*) in Church Planting Efforts in Cambodia —ROBERT OH	193
	RESPONSE —SOKREAKSA HIMM	198
24	Can Any Good Be Done on a Short-Term Mission Trip? Opportunities and Pitfalls in Athens, Greece —DARREN M. CARLSON	201
	RESPONSE —CHEOL KANG	207
25	Paul Mission Training Center and Jeonju Antioch Church Mission Fund —SEUNG-IL LEE AND DONG-WHEE LEE	209
	RESPONSE —DAVID S. LIM	216

SECTION C: Testimonies

26	Have Faith in God —HAK HYUN CHO	220
27	My Testimony —SOKREAKSA HIMM	223
28	Experiencing the Faithfulness of God in Missionary Support —PAUL OGBADU	227
29	Testimony of Smyrna Church —HAKKYOON SHIN	230

SECTION D: Conclusion

30	Concluding Summary —TIMOTHY KIHO PARK	234
31	Concluding Summary —JONATHAN J. BONK	241
	Appendix: KPM's Missionary Leadership Structure and Responsibilities for Financial Policy (Accountability and Reliability) —YOUNG GEE PARK	247
	Selected Bibliography	251
	Participants	253
	Contributors	256
	Indices	266

Figures & Tables

FIGURES

Figure 4.1:	Partial View of the AACC Rental Offices, Nairobi, Kenya	24
Figure 4.2:	Partial View of the AACC Rental Offices, Addis Ababa, Ethiopia	24
Figure 4.3:	Partial View of the AACC Hotel	24
Figure 6.1:	Christians by Continent, 2020	41
Figure 6.2:	Largest Missionary Sending and Receiving Countries, 2020	43
Figure 6.3:	Percentage of World Christians vs. Income	44
Figure 6.4:	Christian Population/Income, 2020	44
Figure 6.5:	Christian Population, Christian Income, and Christian Giving, 2020	45
Figure 6.6:	Giving to Church Versus Parachurch	45
Figure 6.7:	Missions Giving vs. Ecclesiastical Crime	46
Figure 9.1:	Bediako's Model	70
Figure 15.1:	"Sauda Is One Day Old"	124
Figure 16.1:	"Free Expression" in Missionary/African Encounters	131
Figure 16.2:	"Free Expression" in Missionary/African Encounters—As It Should Be?	134
Figure 18.1:	The Comfort Zone	150
Figure 22.1:	Paradigm Model of the Impact of Money on Missionary Life and Ministry	185
Figure 22.2:	Money-Missionary Relationship Model	187
Figure 25.1:	JAC's Mission Expenses	212
Figure 25.2:	Categories of Missionaries in TPMI	213
Figure 25.3:	TPMI-FMHQ's Partnership Mechanism	213
Figure 25.4:	Missionary Training and Commissioning Process	214
Figure 25.5:	Career Paths of Missionaries after Three Years in Ministry	215
Figure 25.6:	Ministries of Recommissioned Missionaries	215

TABLES

Table 4.1:	Strategic Business Unit Results, Real Estate	27
Table 4.2:	Strategic Business Unit Results, DTCC	27
Table 4.3:	Financial Results: Total Income by Category	28
Table 4.4:	Grants from Partners Versus SBU Income at a Glance	28
Table 4.5:	AACC Property Development Strategy, 2009–2025 Flow of Funds Chart	28
Table 6.1:	Christians by Country, 1900 & 2020	41
Table 6.2:	Distribution of Annual Global Income and Wealth, 2020	44
Table 13.1:	UTS Income in $US between 2010 and 2020	106
Table 13.2:	UTS Expenses in $US between 2010 and 2020	106
Table 14.1:	ODA Matching Projects of a Better World and the Korean Government	113
Table 14.2:	Fiscal Structure of Onnuri Welfare Foundation (2019)	115
Table 14.3:	Onnuri M Mission Government Subsidy Receipt Status (2020)	115
Table 22.1:	A Conditional Matrix of the Impact of Money on Missionary Life and Ministry	183
Table 25.1:	Use of JAC's Finances	212

Foreword

by Jonathan J. Bonk

This book is one outcome of a mission leadership forum convened in Pyeongchang, South Korea, from November 9 to 12, 2021. Each chapter was presented as either a Bible study, a case study, or a workshop. For the most part, the contributors were not drawn from among the ranks of experts in the fields of investment, money management, or fund raising, but from men and women whose calling as missionaries, pastors, and administrators has brought them face to face with complex, real-life issues involving the intersection of money and ministry. Perhaps there is no greater challenge than money for, from, and in ministry. As Paul reminded his young protégé, "… the love of money is a root of all kinds of evil, and in their eagerness to be rich some have wandered away from the faith and pierced themselves with many pains" (1 Tim. 6:10, NRSV). Money sufficient to assure the viability of one's life work carries with it an insidious ethical virus that can easily undermine the integrity and accountability of its stewards.

Forum organizers and the Onnuri support team were obliged to deal with the added complications of the global COVID-19 pandemic. Pastor Jae Hoon Lee's letter welcoming presenters who participated in the forum in person or by Zoom was an apt description of the event:

> We are delighted and grateful to be able to hold the sixth Korean Global Mission Leaders Forum (KGMLF) despite the corona pandemic situation. Since 2011, Korean and world mission leaders have gathered in one place to explore a wide range of topics about mission-related challenges and accountability. The theme of the 2021 KGMLF is "Missions and Money." Money is the most complex and urgent challenge for missionary works in the twenty-first century. This challenge has profound implications for churches' faithful and effective service in a world of high material and social inequality. Money itself is a gift from God, but we can make it bad or good. Therefore,

this sixth forum will be a valuable and meaningful time to investigate, understand, and evaluate the theological, economic, and social system of donations and financial use by individual missionaries, churches, mission agencies, or organizations. Watching the preparations for the sixth KGMLF conference, held biennially, we are grateful for the many ways the KGMLF has grown and developed. Even amid the unexpected corona pandemic, God has given us time, space, and a way to gather together and share our thoughts and experiences. In his kairos time, we realize once again that everything is under God's control. Difficulties and obstacles such as distancing and travel restrictions have made this forum more technologically advanced than before. This forum will actively use a hybrid method of face-to-face and non-face-to-face gatherings to connect the world. These advances are made possible by the grace of God. In today's rapidly changing world, the mission field and the environment of the sending church are also evolving fast. Naturally, the tools and strategies for missionary work are also changing. Now, no one church or organization can overcome this situation. Churches around the world must trust God in times of uncertainty and meet more regularly to work together. Churches worldwide must meet to learn from each other, build each other up, cooperate, and help each other for God's mission in this ever-changing age. For these reasons, we believe the KGMLF has become a vital instrument and channel for the major world churches and Western churches to collaborate and discuss various missionary issues. We acknowledge and thank Dr. Jonathan Bonk, Dr. Nelson Jennings, and Dr. Jinbong Kim for their dedication and excellent work leading up to this forum. Also, we would like to recognize Rev. Jae Chul Chung of Asian Mission for providing accommodations and facilities for this sixth forum. Onnuri Church will continue to do its best to make the KGMLF a valuable forum to serve the global church.

One of the tangible results of the forum is this book. It is not a definitive examination of the complex range of issues and perspectives arising from the necessity of money in our lives and ministries, but each case study and workshop is a practical encouragement to remain resolute in making integrity, viability, and accountability paramount in our lives and ministries. Then when it is time for us to bid farewell to this life, we may truthfully say with the Apostle Paul:

> And now I commend you to God and to the message of his grace, a message that is able to build you up and to give you the inheritance among all who are sanctified. I coveted no one's silver or gold or clothing. You know for yourselves that I worked with my own hands to support myself and my companions. In all this I have given you an example that by such work we must support the weak, remembering the words of the Lord Jesus, for he himself said, "It is more blessed to give than to receive" (Acts 20:32–35, NRSV).

"And my God will fully satisfy every need of yours according to his riches in glory in Christ Jesus. To our God and Father be glory forever and ever. Amen" (Phil. 4:19–20, NRSV).

Preface 1

Be joyful always; pray continually; give thanks in all circumstances, for this is God's will for you in Christ Jesus

(1 Thess. 5:16–18, NIV 1984)

by Jinbong Kim

The fear of the COVID-19 pandemic that swept the world had a significant impact on the 2021 Korean Global Mission Leaders Forum (KGMLF), which is held every two years. The forum was held in a hybrid fashion for the first time, with over thirty-five international speakers joining online from all over the world. Thankfully, sixty Korean participants were still able to attend in person at Kensington Hotel, located in beautiful Pyeongchang, where the 2018 Winter Olympics was hosted. Dr. Jonathan Bonk, who suggested the topic "Missions and Money," was also forced to join us online while staying up all night in Canada. However, when we prayed continually with thanksgiving and faith in the Almighty God, who controls all situations perfectly, I never imagined that the crisis of the COVID-19 pandemic would be an even more amazing opportunity for blessings for our hybrid forum in Korea.

I was asked by several participants, "How was the Pyeongchang KGMLF hybrid forum able to be completed successfully?" My answer in one sentence is, "It was entirely by God's grace." However, if I were to explain in more detail, it was through the efforts of Rev. Jae Chul Chung, president of Asian Mission and Rev. Sang Joon Lee, executive director of Asian Mission, who gave great financial support and excellent cooperation. It was also possible because of the humility and support of Rev. Jae Hoon Lee, senior pastor of Onnuri Church, with all his outstanding leadership that surveys the flow of world missions in the twenty-first century. In other words, KGMLF was able to proceed because of the astonishing collaboration between the Asian Mission and Onnuri Church. Special mention should be made of the wise advice and practical help of Dr. Jonathan Bonk and Dr. Nelson Jennings, who have been my sincere academic and spiritual mentors for many years.

Faithful support provided by multiple mission departments of the Onnuri Church community under the remarkable leadership of Rev. Jae Hoon Lee, along with the extensive networks cultivated over the years through KGMLF executive members' mission and academic careers, have made it possible for our international mission forum to succeed since 2011. Praise the Lord.

We faced several challenges concerning the KGMLF hybrid forum. For example, how should we schedule the forum's events, considering the many international participants who live in different continents, and how could we avoid any technical problems? How can we simultaneously translate more than fifty different English papers into Korean and vice versa, as well as transmit them through Zoom? Many other challenges presented themselves as well. Even so, the dedication and hard work of the forty plus staff members of Onnuri Church were able to handle all kinds of challenges and difficulties. The word "unbelievable" showed up many times in the feedback we received about the Onnuri staff.

I want to express my respect for the leadership of Rev. Hong Joo Kim, the head of the Onnuri 2000 Mission Department, with whom we have had excellent cooperation since 2015 to make this work possible. To single out just two representative 2000 Mission staff members, I would like to express my gratitude to Rev. Kyung Hee Lee for his meticulous administration and service; also, Mr. Peter Ban spared no effort in his professional expertise so that more than eight hundred people could access the KGMLF 2021 website, with some of them able to participate in the forum via Zoom. I would also like to thank the Onnuri M Center staff who worked beside Rev. Kyu Suk Rho and the fifteen plus translators who worked with missionary Florence Kwon for their efforts in translating and making international communication possible in our hybrid forum. I am also grateful to Mrs. Sookyoung Han and her team for their hospitality and providing tasty refreshments to all attendees. I would also like to thank CGNTV for filming the entire forum.

As soon as the Pyeongchang KGMLF forum was over I left for Dallas, Texas, USA to attend the Mental Health and Mission Conference, which I hope will develop into a more international event. More than two hundred member care experts and some directors of various mission organizations attended, and they showed great interest in the previously published English KGMLF books I had taken and displayed. Many attendees remarked that they were grateful to learn about the Korean church and missions through the KGMLF books. They really appreciate our forum and encouraged me to continue to serve the KGMLF.

An important consideration in starting KGMLF as a new type of forum in 2011 was the publication of a well-edited book that would present the contents of the forum, a volume that could take its place, for example, in a wide range of libraries worldwide. For that reason, editing, translation, publication, and distribution are perhaps the most key elements of KGMLF.

My sincere thanks go to Dr. Soonuk Jung, who translated the English edition into Korean. And I pay my respects to Dr. Michel Distefano, who showed excellent ability in editing and revising all the English papers. Also, I express my gratitude to William Carey Publishing and Ms. Melissa Hicks, who have contributed much since the KGMLF 2015. I would also like to thank the staff of Duranno Press for its sincere work in publishing the Korean books since 2013. I especially wish to express my heartfelt thanks to all the contributors for putting in extensive time and academic effort for the KGMLF 2021 book. Finally, I am so thankful for my wife, Soon Young Jung, and my two sons, Yohan and Yoseph, who have helped and encouraged me in many ways behind the scenes.

I hope that this book will inspire missionaries, church leaders, and Jesus's followers around the world to consider afresh "Missions and Money" matters in more concrete and proactive ways. May the recent KGMLF forum and resulting two published volumes be instruments in the hands of the Lord for furthering these worthy aims! *Soli Deo gloria!*

Preface 2

by J. Nelson Jennings

Money piques most anyone's acute interest. In today's economically-driven societies almost all individuals and groups need, must somehow acquire, and necessarily administer money. Churches, mission agencies, and missionaries are no exception. The sixth biennial Korean Global Mission Leaders Forum (KGMLF), held in November 2021 at Pyeongchang, South Korea, tackled the vitally important topic of "Missions and Money." This volume carries that same theme as it comprises the forum's various presentations: Bible studies, case studies, workshops, responses, and testimonies. As with all KGMLF gatherings, each presentation was prepared well in advance so that all forum participants could read and otherwise prepare to discuss the selected topics meaningfully during the 3.5-day forum itself.

One foundational KGMLF characteristic is the interaction as equals between Korean and non-Korean participants. COVID-19 restrictions prevented most non-Koreans from attending physically, so they took part through prerecorded videos and live online discussion periods. This book's contents represent the prepared presentations, some of which were refined afterward due to interactions during the forum.

Another fundamental KGMLF value has been "accountability." This forum and resulting books (one in Korean and one in English) have thus been guided by various aspects of the subtitle, "Integrity, Viability, [and] Accountability." As broad as that threefold rubric might be, nonetheless it provides guardrails to the otherwise unwieldy topic of "Missions and Money." Who's to say how scattered and quite likely self-serving an untethered forum and book by a group of mission leaders about money matters would have turned out?

Furthermore, the combined result of the forum's penetrating Bible expositions, concrete case studies, practical workshops, and challenging responses is an in-depth panoply of essays that address poignant money-related challenges facing Christian missions today, be they Korean-initiated or otherwise. The essays do not provide easy or stock answers. Rather, they help to sharpen the questions that missionaries, those who send them, and those who receive them inevitably raise about funding sources, supporting and owning such new institutions as mission schools, financial management, justice issues, environmental implications, and cultural values.

The Korean-global mix gives this volume all sorts of hidden nuances interwoven among the topics that are examined. The contributors and their reflections have been forged in mission contexts. No matter who you or those among whom you live and serve might be, the money-related studies offered here should provide helpful pointers for navigating delicate and crucial financial issues.

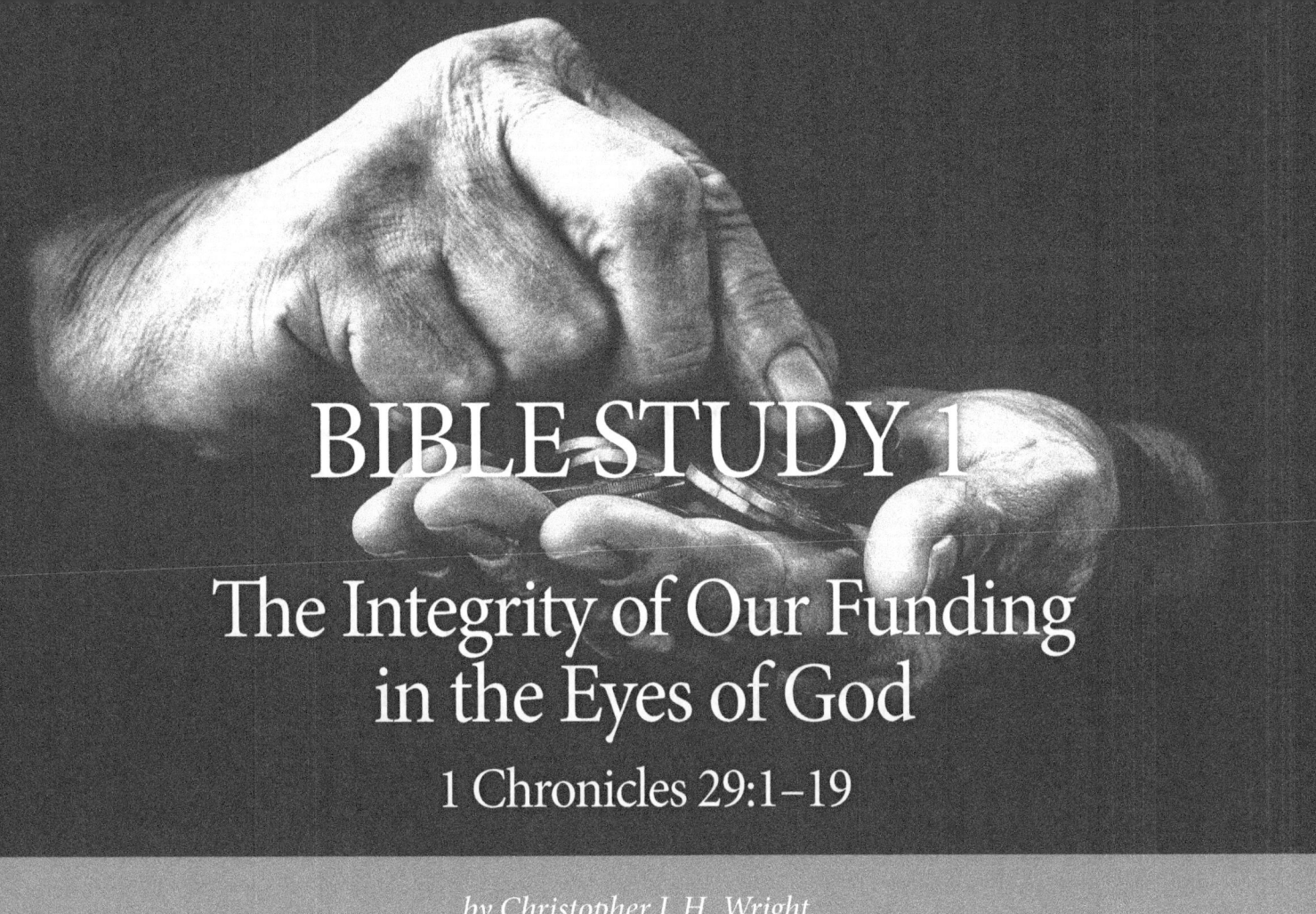

BIBLE STUDY 1

The Integrity of Our Funding in the Eyes of God

1 Chronicles 29:1–19

by Christopher J. H. Wright

Big projects need big funding, as any church or Christian mission organization knows. And big projects for the Lord God need God's people to respond from the heart, out of gratitude for God's redemption in the past and commitment to God's mission in the future. That is what happens in the story we read in this chapter.

This is, in fact, the second great fundraising moment in the Bible. And they both have the same purpose—to build a structure that would be the focal point of God dwelling in the midst of his people. The first was Moses's appeal to the people to provide all the materials needed for the tabernacle in the wilderness (Exod. 35), and this is David's appeal for all that was needed for the temple in Jerusalem, which replaced the old portable tent.

But we shouldn't think—Oh, these were just fundraisings for a building project. For who were these people, and why did God want to dwell in their midst? Answer—the people of Israel, whom God had created and called for the sake of his mission among all nations on earth, as he promised Abraham. And, as Moses pointed out to God himself, the only thing that distinguished Israel from other nations was the presence of the one true, living God in their midst (Exod. 33:16). That was what the tabernacle and the temple provided for—in a visible, tangible way. So, these were moments of providing funds in order to "enable God," as it were, to inhabit his people for the sake of their mission and God's mission in the world.

That makes it relevant to any fundraising we do for the same purpose. Why do we raise funds for our work? Not because we think God can't do anything without us. But rather because we know that God chooses to act in his world *in and through us*. We build "structures"—yes (whether physical or organizational), but not just for our own convenience, comfort, or efficiency. We do so for God to inhabit them, so that by *God dwelling in our midst* God's purposes are accomplished in the world.

So in this chapter, in vv. 1–9 we see David's heart for God as he holds a great national Gift Day, and in vv. 10–19 we hear David's great hymn of praise and humble prayer.

I. David's Heart for God (vv. 1-9)

Here's how David introduces the whole project in the previous chapter:

> King David rose to his feet and said: "Listen to me, my fellow Israelites, my people.
>
> I had it in my heart to build a house as a place of rest for the ark of the covenant of the LORD, for the footstool of our God, and I made plans to build it" (1 Chron. 28:2).

Then he goes on to say that God told him he was not the one to build it, but Solomon would. David, however, made the plans and set about raising the funds. His heart was in it—and as we'll see later, he knew very well also that God knew what was in his heart. Two things stand out in the way the event is described in the first nine verses:

The Leaders Took the Lead!

Clearly there needed to be some real generosity if the plans for a glorious temple were to be realized. But notice where that generosity started. It started with those who owned the most and controlled the most. They led by example, not just by appeal. So David sets it all in motion himself, by giving out of his own wealth. We may wonder when and how he came to be so rich (especially in view of the warnings that Deuteronomy 17:17 gives to kings!), but the point here is simply that, without boasting about it, he claims, "With all my resources I have provided for the temple of my God …" (v. 2). Only then does he appeal for others to join him: "Now, who is willing to *consecrate themselves to the LORD* today?" (v.5)—implying of course that such consecration to God would include giving to God's dwelling place among them (rather as Paul says that the Macedonian believers had first given themselves to the Lord before giving to Paul [2 Cor. 8:5]).

And then, I love verse six! The leaders of the whole community joined in—including family heads, tribal officials, and military officers. And after they did a massive accounting of all that the leadership had given, we read that "the people rejoiced at the willing response of their leaders" (v. 9), and presumably were inspired and motivated to emulate them. How often in our churches and agencies it's the other way round—the *leaders* rejoice to see how much the *people* are giving! But no, here the people rejoice to see how much the leaders had already given. Isn't that a worthwhile principle to follow? At my own home church of All Souls, Langham Place, London, when the church council decided on a major building project, the first thing they did was to ask for gifts and pledges from themselves—that is, all the council members—and only then, when that was known, did they go to the congregation. Lead by example. It's not rocket science, really, just motivational good sense and good practice. Are you able to state, with evidence, that every member of your church's leadership, or every member of your mission or ministry's board, is a committed donor to the work—that they have a personal "stake," as it were, in the vision and mission?

The Giving Was "Willingly" and "From the Heart"

You may have noticed how often the words "freely" and "willingly" crop up in this chapter (in English). It's actually the same word in Hebrew, and it occurs six times, in verses 5, 6, 9 (twice), 14, and 17. And to reinforce that, the Hebrew word for "heart" occurs five times, in verses 9, 17 (twice), 18, and 19. That's a total of eleven times that the narrator wants us to get the point: this was not a grudging or compulsory giving, out of pressure, or guilt, or duty. This was a communal outpouring of the heart—a free and willing response. Notice also that it was a response not just to David's appeal, but was a gift rooted in consecration to the Lord (as he himself put it, vv. 5, 9). David certainly set a good example. But in his appeal, he did not focus on himself ("Who is going to join *me*? Anybody up for a matching gift …?"). No, he immediately switches the focus to how the people should respond to the Lord. David's words and actions appear to have sparked a spiritual response among the whole people, such that they combined fresh commitment to God with generous giving to his dwelling place among them. That is surely something to pray for in our own fundraising efforts.

I just wonder if Paul had this very Scripture in mind as he described the way the Macedonian believers had given so generously in response to the grace of God:

And now, brothers and sisters, we want you to know about the grace that God has given the Macedonian churches. ² In the midst of a very severe trial, their overflowing joy and their extreme poverty welled up in rich generosity. ³ For I testify that they gave as much as they were able, and even beyond their ability. Entirely on their own, ⁴ they urgently pleaded with us for the privilege of sharing in this service to the Lord's people. ⁵ And they exceeded our expectations: They gave themselves first of all to the Lord, and then by the will of God also to us (2 Cor. 8:1-5).

Much in the same way, then, this great occasion of grateful fundraising among the people of Israel was led by the example of their leaders and fed by the willingness of their own hearts. So, with that brief look at the nature of the event, let's turn to David's prayer in verses 10-19.

It comes in two parts—a hymn of praise (vv. 10-13) and a humble prayer (vv. 14-19).

II. David's Hymn of Praise (vv. 10-13)

In this first part of his prayer, David celebrates *what belongs to God* (though he is willing to share it with us), while in the second part (vv. 14-19) he reflects on *what does not belong to us* (though we can give it to God).

Verses 10–13 are in poetic form, and the structure helps to show the core message. It is in a concentric shape. The outer "circle" (vv. 10 and 13) is the framework of praise and thanksgiving. Then there is an inner "circle" (vv. 11a and 12b), where the key words are *power*, along with *greatness* and *strength*. And finally, there is the center of the prayer (vv. 11b and 12a), focusing on God's reign as king and ruler:

¹⁰"**Praise** be to you, Lord,
 the God of our father Israel,
 from everlasting to everlasting.

¹¹ Yours, Lord, is the *greatness and the power*
 and the glory and the majesty and the splendor,
 for everything in heaven and earth is yours.

Yours, Lord, is the **kingdom**;
 you are exalted as head over all.

¹² Wealth and honor come from you;
 you are the **ruler** of all things.

In your hands are *strength and power*
 to exalt and give strength to all.

¹³ Now, our God, we give you thanks,
 and **praise** your glorious name.

So, the central point that David is celebrating is the affirmation of the Kingdom of God. Yahweh, God of Israel, is king and rules over all (vv. 11b-12a).

Now let's remember that David himself was speaking as a king. And his son Solomon was just about to be anointed as king (vv. 22-25). But all human kingdoms, power, and glory must bow to the Lord, the true king. Or as we say in the Lord's prayer, which is clearly based on these words of David, "Thine is the kingdom, the power and the glory." David is acknowledging a kingship above and beyond his own—as some of the Psalms also do.

This is the proper context for all our giving and our fundraising. If God reigns over all people and all things in heaven and earth, then any giving that we do has to be seen in the light of that great cosmic truth. It is not as if God is waiting for us to give him some spare cash so he can get something done in his world. No indeed. All our giving is in one sense derivative. We give in order to participate in something that is already under God's ownership and governance. All our projects and ministry funding—all of it—flows from the Kingdom of God and is for the Kingdom of God.

And that moves us on to see, in the inner circle, two things about this God who is king—what he owns and what he gives:

What God Owns (v. 11a)—Everything!

"Everything in heaven and earth is yours." The king is the ultimate owner of his domain, namely the whole created order. We easily pass over this affirmation of Yahweh's universal ownership of the cosmos without pausing to see how staggering it is. It is made in many places. For example, "To the Lord belongs the earth and the fullness of it, the world and the dwellers on it" (Ps. 24:1, my translation), and "To the Lord your God belong the heavens, the heaven of heavens, the earth and all that is on it" (Deut. 10:14, my translation).

There are vast consequences of this, which we can't go into now. But they include at least:

i) Ecology—the earth belongs to God, not to us. So, we are accountable to God for how we treat what belongs to him. It is surely impossible to claim to love God and yet trash his property, yet many Christians don't care about the environment or actively oppose environmental action in relation to the climate crisis.

The earth is created, sustained and redeemed by Christ.[1] We cannot claim to love God while abusing what belongs to Christ by right of creation, redemption and inheritance. We care for the earth and responsibly use its abundant resources, not according to the rationale of the secular world, but for the Lord's sake. If Jesus is Lord of all the earth, we cannot separate our relationship to Christ from how we act in relation to the earth. For to proclaim the gospel that says "Jesus is Lord" is to proclaim the gospel that includes the earth, since Christ's Lordship is over all creation. Creation care is a thus a gospel issue within the Lordship of Christ.[2]

ii) Mission—the earth belongs to Yahweh God, not to any other gods. Or in New Testament terms, Jesus of Nazareth is Lord of all the earth. These verses form the background also to the great affirmation and claim that Jesus makes at opening of the Great Commission: "All authority in heaven and on earth is given to me" (Matt. 28:18). There is not an inch of planet that does not belong to him. Therefore, wherever we go on mission in his name we are walking on his property. We go with confidence in the name of the owner, with no fear, affirming Christ's rightful lordship as owner of all.

So David begins with what God owns as king, namely, everything in heaven and earth. But then he also celebrates:

What God Gives (v. 12b)—Power and Strength

In the Kingdom of God, there is much that God intends to accomplish through his people. For Solomon, that meant building the temple. So God would provide the strength to do it, while the people would provide the resources (from what already belonged to God anyway). The lesson is that whatever the task, challenge, ministry, or mission, God provides the strength and resources to do it—in all of life—not just for "Christian" things. The God who owns all there is, freely gives to all who need.

The Apostle Paul makes the same point about God's ultimate gift—his own Son: "He who did not spare his own Son, but gave him up for us all—how will he not also, along with him, graciously give us all things?" (Rom. 8:32).

So as we put these two points together:
Q. What belongs to God?
A. Everything there is, which includes everything we have.

Q. What does God give?
A. Everything we need.

God owns everything we have, and God gives everything we need.

No wonder then that David begins and ends with praise and thanksgiving. For all our giving and fundraising must be done out of gratitude to God and in the service of his Kingdom. That's why it is so appropriate that before David says anything else, before he even thanks his donors (as we might put it), he gives praise and worship and thanks to God.

III. David's Humble Prayer (vv. 14–19)

We turn now to second half of David's prayer. After his hymn of praise comes this prayer of humility and petition. The focus now shifts to the people's act of giving to God—the joyful outcome of this fundraising appeal. David says four remarkable things about it: it's a privilege; it's a paradox; it's pleasing to God; and it needs to be purposeful.

It's a Privilege! (v. 14a)

David's first response, as he thinks about what is happening on this great fundraising occasion, is one of surprise. "Who am I? Who are we?" he asks. This is the same response that we heard on David's lips when God made his covenant with him and promised him an everlasting kingdom—"Who am I, Lord God, and what is my family … ?" (1 Chron. 17:16). On that occasion, he was surprised and amazed that God would *choose* him and make such a promise. This time he is surprised and amazed that God would *accept* his gifts.

Being able to give to God and God's work is a *privilege* that ought to fill us with some wonderment. It's not a chore or a duty, not something imposed or compelled, but an incredible privilege. After all, who are we that God should include us among his donors and benefactors?! It's not a matter of kudos or credit—that we should expect recognition, getting our names on donor lists, plaques or tributes, or buildings.

---

[1] Col. 1:15–20; Heb. 1:2–3.
[2] "The Cape Town Commitment," Part 1.7A, Lausanne Movement, 2021, https://lausanne.org/content/ctcommitment#capetown.

In fact, our ability and willingness to give is in itself a gift of God's grace, such that we should respond with gratitude that we are even permitted to participate in doing so. That's how the Macedonian believers thought. Paul says that "they urgently pleaded with us for *the privilege of sharing in this service* to the Lord's people" (2 Cor. 8:4).

There is a point here for the way we "message" our fundraising. It is easy to slip into a mode of congratulating people when they give—especially if they make large gifts. Don't misunderstand me—*of course* we must thank and appreciate people who take our ministry and vision to heart and give generously to the Lord's work. But somehow, we need to remind people of the enormous privilege and blessing it is to be able to do so at all, and how surprising it is that God—the God who owns and rules all things—invites us to "donate" to him!

Never lose the sense of privilege, surprise, gratitude, amazement ... at being able to serve God in any way! It is all a response to God's amazing grace and generosity toward us.

It's a Paradox (vv. 14b–16)

In my country (the UK), there is a saying you might hear around Christmas time or birthdays: "What can you give to the man (or woman) who's got everything?" It doesn't necessarily mean that the person is ultrawealthy. It just means that they seem to have comfortably all they need and it's hard to know what gift would be really welcomed and appreciated. Well, this is even harder! What can you give to the God who owns everything?

In verses 14b–16 David ponders the paradox of what he has just said about God in verse 11. It was a great day, of course. People were giving lots of stuff very generously.

But, when you think about it, what were they actually giving? Only what God already owns! "We have given you only what comes from your hand ... all this abundance that we have provided ... all of it belongs to you" (vv. 14, 16). Well, quite.

Verse 15 may seem odd, with its reference to "foreigners and strangers." It doesn't mean, "You don't know who we are." It is taken from Leviticus 25:23 and describes Israel's relation to the land God had given them to possess. It was God's land: "The land is mine," God said—just as the whole earth belongs to God.

Israel lived in the land like God's tenants. That is, they lived in it, but they did not own it. They were in the same position before God as those in their society who were "resident foreigners," that is, resident—but not owners. So, the Israelites were like tenants in a land that belonged ultimately to God.

So, says David, how can God's tenants give something to their divine landlord except what already belongs to him? It's as if you are living as a tenant in a fully furnished house or apartment that belongs to a landlord. And on your landlord's birthday, you take one of the paintings on the wall that he has provided to decorate the house for you, and give it to him as a present. What kind of gift is that? You are only giving to him what already belongs to him!

And yet, that is what God receives from us. We give to God what God already owns and has entrusted to us. That's the paradox of Christian giving. All our generosity is not only a response to God's generosity to us, it also *uses* what God has given to us in the first place.

Something of this dynamic is also present in the warning of Moses not to imagine that we generate all our own wealth for our own exclusive benefit. Don't forget the God who enabled you to do so! "You may say to yourself, 'My power and the strength of my hands have produced this wealth for me.' But remember the LORD your God, for it is he who gives you the ability to produce wealth ...'" (Deut. 8:17–18). So, our giving should never be a matter of pride, but a reflex of grace—the grace of living in God's earth, as tenants of the one who already owns everything we possess.

So, giving is a privilege and a paradox, and thirdly:

It's Pleasing to God (v. 17)

... when it is done with integrity. This verse, 1 Chronicles 29:17, was one of John Stott's favorites. I have heard him quote it often in his preaching and teaching: "I know, my God, that you test the heart and are pleased with integrity."

God is pleased with honesty and integrity, that is, when our giving reflects the truth of our hearts and our motives—not the size of our bank account. And this applies as much also to the ethics of our fundraising as to its outcomes.

Contrast Ananias and Sapphira who did give, but there was a lack of integrity between the appearance (and claim) of generosity and the truth of what they had done. And compare the widow who gave all she had with the wealthy who appeared to give so much more, but for them it was actually just a small fraction of what they actually could have given.

So, "integrity" here means not just honesty but consistency, that is, there is no contradiction between appearance and reality—between what we say and what we do, or between what we profess in church and how we behave at work or at home. It also means truthfulness in what we say or claim in our fundraising and "marketing" efforts.

The extent to which our giving is pleasing to God is not measured by the size or amount of our gift, but by the honesty and integrity of our hearts before God as we give. Fundraisers need to notice that David did *not* say, "I know, O Lord, that you (like us!) are pleased with very large gifts," but, "You are pleased with integrity, whether the gift is large or small."

We are impressed with size—God cares about honesty. We look on outward appearance ("Look at how much I am giving to God!"). God looks at the heart ("Look at how much you are keeping for yourself").

Above all, perhaps, verse 17 condemns the idea of giving to God in order to get more back in return, that is, giving in order to get rich, as in some forms of the "prosperity gospel." That kind of teaching is surely a perversion of Scripture and little more than "sanctified" greed and covetousness.

And finally, as regards our giving:

It Needs to Be Purposeful (vv. 18–19)

David finishes with a prayer for the people and for Solomon: "Keep forever such purposes and thoughts in the hearts of your people" (v. 18, ESV). David does not want the occasion to be a one-off splurge of short-term generosity in response to an emotional royal appeal, quickly forgotten as people lapse back into more characteristic selfishness. He wants such giving to the Lord to become a settled habit of the heart—a strong purposeful pattern of life and behavior. He wants the people's response to be as purposeful and planned as his own fundraising project itself.

Now that phrase, "purposes and thoughts of the heart" is the same as in Genesis 6:5, when "the Lord saw … that every inclination of the thoughts of the human heart was only evil all the time"—a bleakly negative assessment of the tendency of all human beings toward evil, including greed, self-centered pride, and competitiveness. Well, here is a powerful counterweight to that universal tendency, which is to cultivate a habit of purposeful giving. Generosity of heart and mind and hands is a very effective antiseptic to the poisonous idolatry of greed. And it reminds us of Paul's teaching that our giving needs to be systematic, proportional, regular—and cheerful!

Let me summarize and conclude:

i) David began by putting his Gift Day into perspective by celebrating the Kingdom of God. Everything in heaven and earth belongs to the God who rules over all and who owns all we have and gives us all we need to do his will.

ii) But since everything belongs to God and not to us, we need to see that even the very idea of being able to give to God is a privilege and a paradox—it is gratitude responding to grace. But when we do respond with honest hearts, it is pleasing to God and it should be purposeful as a pattern of life for as long as we live on God's earth.

May God give us grace to respond to his grace, with willing and overflowing hearts.

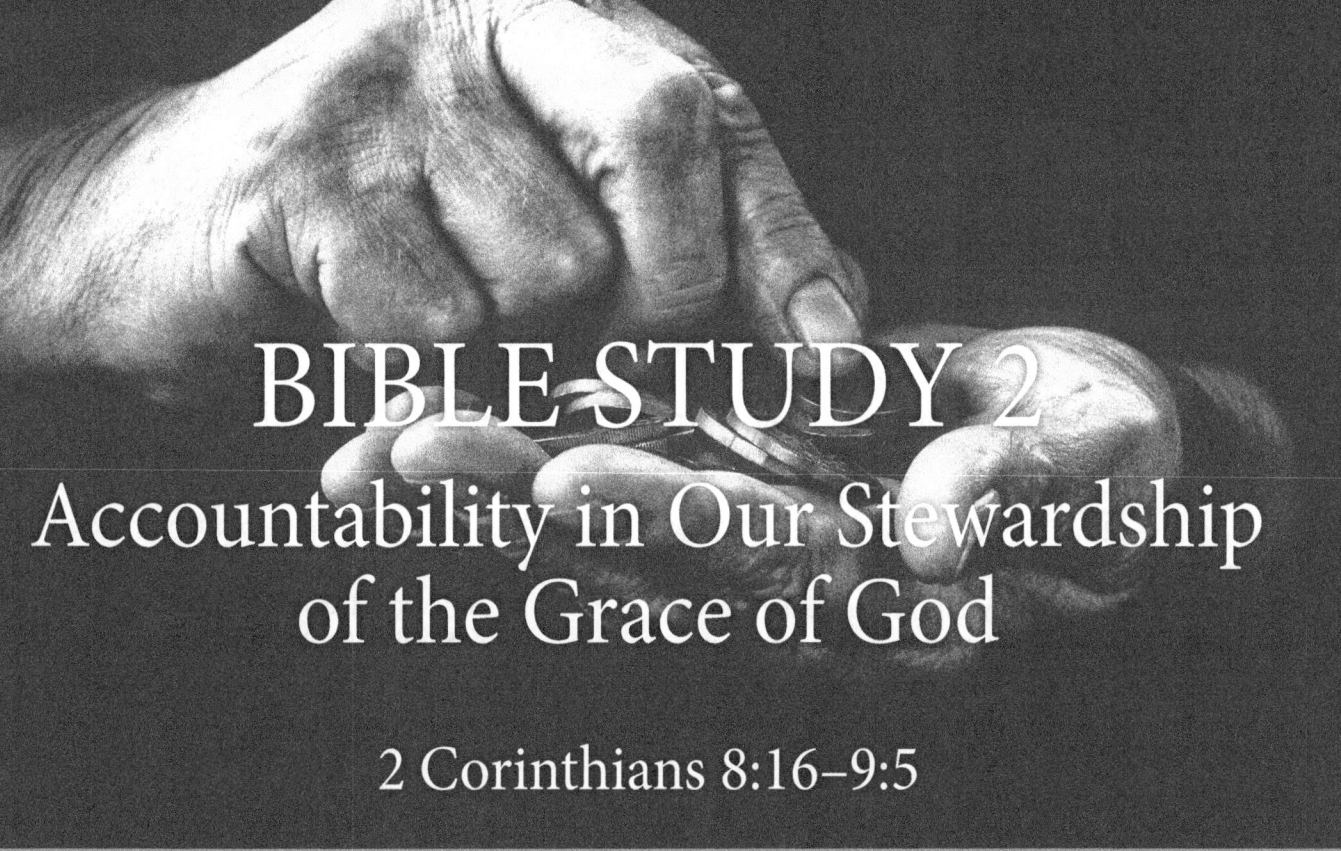

BIBLE STUDY 2
Accountability in Our Stewardship of the Grace of God

2 Corinthians 8:16–9:5

by Christopher J. H. Wright

NOTE: The substance of this address was originally delivered at a conference of the Korean Global Mission Leaders Forum, at OMSC, New Haven, CT, in 2013. It is now published as a chapter in Christopher J. H. Wright with James Cousins, *The Shortfall: Owning the Challenge of Ministry Funding* (Carlisle: Langham Global Library, 2021), and is adapted and included here by permission.

Paul's messages to the believers in Corinth and Rome about his collection of money from the Gentile churches in Greece for the impoverished believers in Jerusalem are commonly used for teaching and exhortation on Christian giving—its motivation by grace, its integral place within gospel obedience, and its spiritual outcomes. Less common, however, is to observe the lessons we learn in those chapters about Paul's meticulous care and accountability in *how he handled* this gift—a gift that he regarded as so theologically important. The main text is 2 Corinthians 8–9, but he refers to the collection also in 1 Corinthians 16 and Romans 15. From these passages we may identify at least five important principles that should guide and guard our handling of money in mission.

I. Financial Administration Is a Stewardship of Grace and Obedience

When we handle money that has been given by God's people, we are handling two things: the fruit of God's grace and also the proof of human obedience to the Gospel. That is clear in 2 Corinthians 8–9. Money that has been given as an offering to God is not just "stuff." It is not just coins and notes or online donations. It is, in fact, a deeply spiritual matter, a sacred trust. People's giving is their response to God, and the way we deal with it is our stewardship of God's grace and of their obedience. That is a lot to be entrusted with!

Three times in 2 Corinthians 8:1–7, Paul uses the word "grace" about the Macedonian believers, and a couple verses later he talks about "the *grace* of our

Lord Jesus Christ" (v. 9). This gift of the Macedonians, Paul writes, was a response to the Lord: "They gave themselves first of all to the Lord" (v. 5). Moreover, it was something that they wanted to do. They did not have to be asked to give; rather, they asked for the privilege of giving. Then Paul adds that it was because of that grace of God in them that they extended this "act of grace" to others. This is dynamic grace in action—grace received and grace passed on.

Paul then sends Titus to oversee and administer the collection. The word "So" at the start of verse 6 implies that Paul means, "Because this is such an important evidence of the grace of God and of the fruit of the Gospel in the lives of these new Gentile believers, I am sending my most trusted senior person to handle this responsibility. This is a serious matter, so we urged Titus—an important apostolic delegate in the church—to go and make sure that this "act of grace" will be properly handled and treated with the due diligence that it deserves."

This display of generosity was not just an act of grace, but also an act of obedience. Paul puts them both together when he anticipates that:

> Because of the service by which you have proved yourselves, others will praise God for the obedience that accompanies your confession of the gospel of Christ, and for your generosity in sharing with them and with everyone else. And in their prayers for you their hearts will go out to you, because of the surpassing grace God has given you (2 Cor. 9:12–14).

Why does Paul stress that their gift demonstrated gospel motivated obedience? Precisely because these were Gentiles. The Jewish believers in Jerusalem were still uncertain whether these Gentiles, who had never been circumcised and were not observing all the law, were really part of God's family. Did they really belong to the covenant people of God? Paul responds in effect, "The fact that you Gentiles have given an offering to meet the needs of Jewish believers is a proof of the fellowship that we have in Christ. Your obedience to the Gospel is in itself a proof of the truth of the Gospel—that Jews and Gentiles are one in the Messiah Jesus—former enemies now reconciled at the cross, as I've written elsewhere …" Let's not miss the profound theological significance here. Paul is talking about the spiritual heart of the Gospel, and showing how it could be modeled and authenticated in practice, in hard cash, as it were. This gift was a proof that these Gentiles understood the core meaning and reconciling power of the Gospel and were joyfully determined to obey it.

So then, we begin by noting that Paul's concern for accountability, integrity, and transparency was not just to satisfy Roman governors or any other observers. It was because he was dealing with a sacred trust: the grace of God and obedience to the Gospel. Is that how you think when you are doing your fundraising, your accounting, or your budgeting in your organization or church? It is a profoundly spiritual responsibility before God and his people.

II. Financial Appeals Require Systematic Advance Planning

Look how thoroughly Paul prepares the way for the collection to be implemented. In

1 Corinthians 16 he picks up something that he has apparently told them about before, but wants to raise again to make sure they are ready. So he says:

> Now about the collection for the Lord's people: Do what I told the Galatian churches to do. On the first day of every week, each one of you should set aside a sum of money in keeping with your income, saving it up, so that when I come no collections will have to be made (1 Cor. 16:1-3).

In his second letter, Paul shows the same concern for preparedness:

> There is no need for me to write to you about this service to the Lord's people. For I know your eagerness to help, and I have been boasting about it to the Macedonians, telling them that since last year you in Achaia were ready to give; and your enthusiasm has stirred most of them to action. But I am sending the brothers in order that our boasting about you in this matter should not prove hollow, but that you may be ready, as I said you would be. For if any Macedonians come with me and find you unprepared, we—not to say anything about you—would be ashamed of having been so confident. So I thought it necessary to urge the brothers to visit you in advance and finish the arrangements for the generous gift you had promised. Then it will be ready as a generous gift, not as one grudgingly given (2 Cor. 9:1–5).

Can you see what Paul is doing here? He does not want this collection to become debased into an emotional appeal in which everybody is urged to put their hands in their pockets, and the music goes on and on until everybody has dug deeper, and then the offering buckets are sent around again. No, Paul is purposely avoiding that type of manipulated, emotional response in giving. He does not want there to be any kind of "on the spot" pressure, or an instant response that has not been carefully thought through in advance. Paul wants his collection and the giving by the church to be something that has been considered, prayed about, and prepared for. So it should be for us.

We should encourage our donors to develop habits of systematic giving—such as Paul calls for. It should be planned (you decide what you will give and when). It should be regular (week by week or month by month, setting money aside). It should be proportionate to income (with those who have more giving more). It should be transparent (with several people overseeing it). And it should be public (announced and recorded). All of this preparation and supervision is built into the arrangements that Paul is carefully planning in advance. Clearly, Paul himself put a lot of thought into this whole project.

Accountability, then, is not just an afterthought. It is not something you try to sort out *after the event* when you realize, "All this money has come in; how wonderful! Now we'd better decide what we do with it, who is going to count it, who is going to bank it, and who will keep accounts." No, those things should all be planned beforehand. Also, accountability is not just a matter of reacting when problems or questions arise. It should be built in from the very start. Paul says in effect, "Look, here is the plan. Here is what we're asking *you* to do, and here is what *we* will then do when you have done what we ask." The whole procedure is a matter of shared responsibility. That is an important way in which he builds accountability into his financial relationship with the churches—for them and for himself.

III. Financial Temptations Call for "Safety in Numbers"

Wherever there is money, there is temptation. This is just as true for Christians as anybody else, so it is wise to protect ourselves from such temptation by having more than one person involved in handling money.

This way of working was true of Paul's ministry in general. Of course, Paul was a great individual evangelist, preacher, letter writer, and everything else. But generally, he did not operate alone. He was the leader, but he worked with teams that included people like Silas, Barnabas, Timothy, Titus, and so on. Indeed, when Paul did find himself completely alone, he was very distressed about it. In 2 Timothy 4:16, there are some heartrending words when he says that everyone had deserted him; this was terrible for him. He wanted to be in a team; he longed to work with others. That was at the heart of his concept of the church as the body of Christ, and it was carried through into his missionary practice.

That is why Paul lays great emphasis on the plurality of people involved in handling the money that his collection would raise. It is quite complicated trying to figure out who all the people were, or exactly how many, and we don't know all the names. But clearly, there was a small team of them.

Look first at 1 Corinthians 16:3-4 where Paul says, "I will give letters of introduction to the men you approve and send them with your gift to Jerusalem." So these would be people whom the Christians in Corinth trusted and chose. Paul then offers to share the task himself. He adds, "If it seems advisable for me to go also, they will accompany me." So Paul would definitely not take charge of the money by himself but would involve others in that major responsibility. This would of course add some security—a group travelling together, not just one vulnerable man with bags of money. But it also added trust—they would keep an eye on each other!

Coming to 2 Corinthians 8:16-24, there are at least three people in addition to Paul himself and those whom the church in Corinth would choose. Titus we have already heard about. But then Paul adds, "And we are sending along with him the brother who is praised by all the churches for his service to the gospel. What is more, he was chosen by the churches to accompany us as we carry the offering" (2 Cor. 8:18-19). And a little later Paul adds, "In addition, we are sending with them our brother who has often proved to us in many ways that he is zealous, and now even more so because of his great confidence in you" (2 Cor. 8:22).

Again, we don't know who this brother was, but Paul deemed him trustworthy.

So as I say, we can't be sure exactly how many people there were in Paul's party. But the point is that certainly more than one person was involved—at least three in addition to Paul himself, plus those chosen by the Corinthian believers. And they were all trusted people. They were accepted and known by everybody. They were accountable to Paul, to one another, and to church communities in at least two cities in northern and southern Greece. That's a strong level of accountability.

Now, we will want to say that as Christians we should be able to trust another Christian to be honest with money. Yes indeed, but Paul shows us the wisdom of building in safeguards of plurality, because even believers are still sinners and few things are more tempting than money. Paul is well aware that even trusted brothers and sisters can go astray. Sadly, we read about a few of them at the end of some of his letters, when he writes that some of his former companions who preferred the world and the world's ways have gone off and left him (e.g., 2 Tim 4:10). Paul knew that even the best people need the protection of relational accountability to one another.

So then, Paul insists on plurality in the handling of money. It is a very wise principle to adopt in any church or Christian organization. In my own church at All Souls, Langham Place, gift money is never counted by only one person. When the offering is brought to the vestry, there are always at least two and sometimes three or four people in the room. The door is then closed, and they count the offering together. They are a check on one another. Now of course, we all trust one another; nobody expects that anybody is going to be stealing the cash. But there is need for openness and verifiability in handling money. We need to be above suspicion.

Many Christian organizations, including my own (Langham Partnership), will not allow large bank checks to be signed by only one person; there must always be two signatures to manage the bank account and the finances. That is another wise practice.

How can this work in countries and cultures where it is quite unthinkable to question the honor and the authority of senior leaders, especially by calling them to account over money? I know that in some Asian cultures it is simply not appropriate for anybody to challenge or question leaders, especially if they are older men, and it is never done. That would be to break the relationship and cause loss of face. Christians in senior leadership seem to be routinely regarded as above questioning by anybody "beneath" them. So what can be done to ensure proper accountability?

It seems to me that the only way is for the *leader himself* (and it is usually a man, but the same would apply to a woman) to *choose voluntarily* to say to his church or organization, "Please, will you join me in this matter of financial administration? I request and insist that other people should be appointed to be with me as we arrange our financial affairs, or as we raise funds and decide how to spend them. I want other people alongside myself to see how the money is raised, spent, and accounted for. I want the rest of the congregation, or staff, or donors to be completely satisfied that all is being done transparently and honorably. And I am using *my* authority in the church or organization to set this in place and *I choose* to submit myself to such protocol and policies of accountability."

So, the person in authoritative leadership *exercises* his authority by choosing to *submit* his authority to the scrutiny of others in this matter of money. That is fully biblical. It means that the person "at the top" is leading by his own example of transparency and accountability. If leaders do this *voluntarily*, they are not saying to their staff or colleagues, "I think you don't trust me." Rather they are saying, "I want to make sure that your trust is never betrayed. I want to avoid all temptation. I want to be completely transparent, and therefore I *choose* to share my accountability with other trusted Christian brothers and sisters. And this would be to imitate the apostle Paul himself. Paul could easily have said, "Trust me. I'm an apostle. I'll take charge of this money myself." But he did not. He insisted *with apostolic authority* that there should be others alongside him to ensure it was all done honestly. Financial temptations and scandals are massively reduced by plural accountability.

IV. Financial Accountability Demands Transparency before God and Human Beings

I love the fact that when Paul has finished talking about all the people he is bringing into the team to deliver the money to Jerusalem, he actually explains why he is handling it in this plural way. Paul says: "We want to avoid any criticism of the way we administer this liberal gift. *For we are taking pains to do what is right, not only in the eyes of the Lord but also in the eyes of man*" (2 Cor. 8:20–21; my emphasis). These verses express a principle that is transcultural. That is, they provides a biblical model for us, whatever our culture or background. These verses are so challenging and necessary. I think they should be printed, framed, and hung up on the wall of any room where a Christian organization does its financial business. How about doing that?

Let's recognize that all these arrangements that Paul put in place were not only very careful, they were also probably quite costly. It would obviously cost a lot more for five or six men to travel from Greece to Jerusalem than for Paul to go there by himself; travel was not cheap in those days any more than today. So, the arrangements Paul was building up around this gift could have aroused resistance. People could have criticized and said, "Why send so many people? You are going to waste some of the gift on these "overhead expenses" (just as we complain about the cost of auditing our accounts). But Paul says in effect, "It's worth that cost because I don't want to be vulnerable to any accusation of fraud or misappropriation of this precious gift; I want to be completely transparent before God and people so that nothing we do can be open to criticism later."

I would love 2 Corinthians 8:21 to become a motto for each of us as Christ's followers, to be something that we could take to heart: "We are taking pains to do what is right, not only in the eyes of the Lord [we all want to do that] *but also in the eyes of man*." What a difference it would make if all Christian organizations were totally committed to Paul's fundamental principle here, and how it could help to prevent some of the tragic scandals of fraud and theft and mismanagement within Christian organizations. Vertical and the horizontal accountability are both needed. We should be able to trust one another in the Lord, but we want to do what is above criticism in the eyes of the watching world as well.

V. Financial Trustworthiness Is an Apostolic Honor to Christ

Think for a moment about upward and downward accountability. We tend to think that we are *upwardly* accountable to bodies such as boards, funding foundations, donors, and the government and legal authorities, and that we are *downwardly* accountable to our beneficiaries, that is, to those who actually receive from our ministry, those whom we are serving "in the field" as we say.

Actually, however, the direction of our accountability is the reverse. Jesus said, "Truly I tell you, whatever you did for one of the least of these brothers and sisters of mine, you did for me" (Matt. 25:40). Our *upward* accountability is to Jesus, and therefore to those who occupy the position Jesus was referring to. Whatever we do for our "beneficiaries" we are doing for Jesus. It is those whom our ministry is serving who actually are Jesus to us. Therefore, our accountability to *them* is really our accountability to *him*—which is "upward." When we serve others in our ministry, we are serving Christ. We are honoring him in serving them. That is our primary accountability.

Now think of those who serve as administrators of our finances, those who handle money. Paul says in several passages that doing this in a trustworthy manner is *an honor to Christ,* not just a matter of transparency before people. Of course it is important to do the job with honesty and integrity. But even more, it is important to do it for the honor and glory of Christ.

Look first at 2 Corinthians 8:18–19. Who were these people who were administering the gift? Paul says, "We are sending … the brother who is praised by all the churches for his service to the gospel. What is more, he was chosen by the churches." This man, then, was an honored person whose life was already seen to be honoring to the Lord and honoring to the Gospel. For that reason, Paul and the Corinthians could trust him with their money. And the way he would handle the money would also be honoring to the Lord and to the church. Honest finances are honoring to Christ (with the obvious implication that dishonesty dishonors Christ).

Paul then makes the point even more explicitly: "As for Titus, he is my partner and co-worker among you; as for our brothers, they are representatives of the churches and *an honor to Christ*. Therefore show these men the proof of your love and the reason for our pride in you, so that the churches can see it" (2 Cor. 8:23–24; my emphasis).

The Greek word translated "representatives" is actually *apostoloi,* "apostles." It is used in the weaker sense that occurs several times in the New Testament to refer to others beyond the twelve apostolic pillars of the church: the twelve disciples, minus Judas Iscariot and plus Matthias in the book of Acts, and then the apostle Paul. In this slightly looser sense, the word *apostolos* meant someone who was an emissary or a trusted delegate of a church. There seem to have been a number of these apostolic delegates going around the churches—Titus, Timothy, Barnabas, Andronicus, and Junia (Rom. 16:7), and others. Paul says these *apostoloi*, these chosen delegates of the churches who are being entrusted with this large financial gift to Jerusalem, are "an honor to Christ" (2 Cor. 8:23).

What a commendation! What a way to speak of an accountant or a treasurer! These people are entrusted with money. And by being faithful in that trust, they are not only an honor to Christ, but also they should have church approval: "Show these men the proof of your love and the reason for our pride in you, so that the churches can see it" (v. 24).

Another example is Epaphroditus. Look at how Paul speaks about him in Philippians 2:25–30. He says, "I think it is necessary to send back to you Epaphroditus, my brother, co-worker and fellow soldier, who is also your messenger, whom you sent to take care of my needs" (Phil. 2:25). The Greek word translated "messenger" here is *apostolos* again. Now, Epaphroditus was not an apostle in the sense that Paul was, but he was the emissary, the representative, the trusted messenger of the church, and hence "apostolic." Later Paul says, "I have received full payment and have more than enough. I am amply supplied, now that I have received from Epaphroditus the gifts you sent. They are a fragrant offering, an acceptable sacrifice, pleasing to God" (Phil 4:18). What Paul is describing is Epaphroditus's handling of the financial and material gift that the Philippian church had made to Paul when he was in need. And Paul means that Epaphroditus's service was a work of the Gospel. It was a work born out of love for Christ and for his church. Actually, Paul tells us, Epaphroditus nearly died doing what he did for his church and for Paul, so therefore Paul says, "Honor him. He did what he did for Christ's sake."

Epaphroditus's role then, says Paul, was *an apostolic honor*: serving God and serving Christ by serving the servants of God. People like Epaphroditus who handle the church's gifts are deserving of honor and respect because they are an honor to Christ himself. In short, to administer financial affairs with trustworthiness, honesty, and diligence, like Epaphroditus and others in the New Testament, is a Christ honoring thing to do: we do it for him. That puts accountability into a wonderfully relational perspective—our relationship not just with our church or organization or donors or beneficiaries—but with Christ himself.

Let me finish with a personal memory. When I was the principal of All Nations Christian College near London, there was a time when issues arose that affected me personally. I was required to give account of some aspects of how I was running things and decisions that had been made. That was not easy; it is not comfortable to have people poking into everything that is going on. That is true even if you have nothing troubling your conscience. I knew that in relation to the college, I had done nothing wrong, but still I had to accept the questioning, even though I did not like it.

At that time the chairman of the college board of directors was a very wise, godly brother whom I greatly respected. At one point, he came privately to my office and said to me, "Chris, accountability is not a burden; it's a gift. It's a gift that we as the board give to you as our principal. We hold you accountable, and that is for your good; it's for your protection. It's not something we are imposing upon you. It's something we are giving to you because we love you, because you are a brother in Christ, and we want to affirm your integrity by expecting proper accountability."

I thought that was a very helpful, positive way for me to look at the demanding challenge of accountability. I learned to see accountability not as a threat or an insult or something "beneath my dignity to be questioned," but rather as something that was honoring to me and also, of course, to God.

May we all pray for God to grant us the courage to live and work with complete integrity, and may we honor one another by expecting—and giving—accountability to one another and to the Lord.

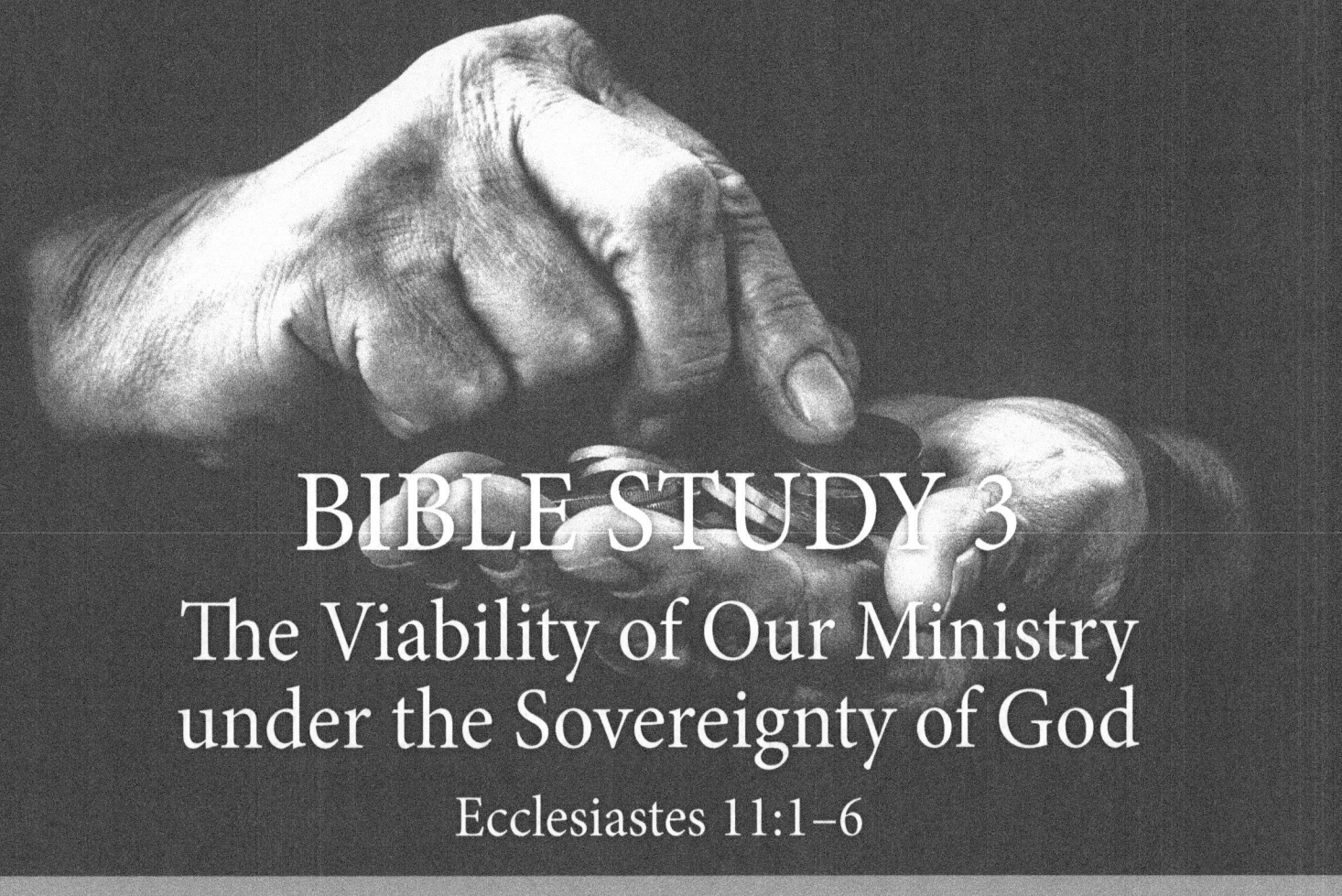

BIBLE STUDY 3
The Viability of Our Ministry under the Sovereignty of God
Ecclesiastes 11:1–6

by Christopher J. H. Wright

A few years ago I wrote a book called, *The God I Don't Understand*. I think that an appropriate title for the book of Ecclesiastes could be, *The World I Don't Understand*. In fact, that *is* the title of a book that I've been working on, combining Ecclesiastes and Habakkuk, who both find the world a baffling and agonizing place, for different reasons.

The author of Ecclesiastes (the narrator of the frame at the beginning and end) introduces us to someone whom he calls "Qoheleth"—which is hardly a personal name, more like a job description or role, like teacher, philosopher, guru, or consultant. And Qoheleth is a very conflicted man. He is an Israelite who lives within the framework of confessional faith in one true, living God. He is also one of "the wise"—an inheritor of the wisdom tradition such as we find in the book of Proverbs. And yet he struggles to reconcile the truths he *knows* in his heart with the realities he *sees* in the world around him.

In fact, "struggle" is too weak a word. He finds himself utterly baffled and frustrated as he tries to find the meaning of life. He sets out on a long journey of enquiry, but all his efforts keep ending in futility and apparent pointlessness: *hebel* (הֶבֶל)—the word that echoes through the book, with flavors varying from meaninglessness (there simply is no meaning to life), to transience (like a whiff of smoke, nothing lasts), to absurdity (some things are just crazy!), to enigma (there must be a meaning somewhere, but I can't find it).

But he cannot abandon his scriptural faith in the living, creator God and the conviction that it was not meant to be like this. Things are not what they should be in this world, yet God is still there and still somehow in charge of it all. Basically, Qoheleth is living in the tension between Genesis 1–2 and Genesis 3–11.

Genesis 1–2 gives him the robust conviction that, fundamentally, life is good and the creation gifts of God are to be enjoyed as good things—life itself, work, sex, and food and drink. Indeed, he is so convinced of this, that he affirms it seven times in the book, with increasing passion. And we should not interpret those passages, which make that point again and again, as sheer *hedonism* (let's eat, drink, and be merry, because pleasure is actually the meaning and point of life itself). Nor are they *cynicism* (we might as well eat, drink, and be merry, for tomorrow we die). They are simply affirmations by faith of the truth of the world as created in Genesis 1–2. Life *is* good, and God approves our enjoyment of it. And Qoheleth believes it.

But at the same time, we live in the world of Genesis 3–11, riddled with the effects of human sin and satanic evil infiltrating every dimension of human personhood, escalating through the generations of history, poisoning society and culture, and harming creation. And that is the world that Qoheleth cannot fathom. Not only is there so much that is futile, absurd, unjust, and enigmatic, but also at the end of it all awaits the ultimate reality (as far as he can see) of death, which seems to render pointless all the joys and achievements of life.

Don't we resonate with Qoheleth, if we're honest? Even when we add together our faith in the goodness of creation (which we share with him), with the additional New Testament glory of Christ's death and resurrection and our future hope of triumph over death and the destruction of all evil, we still have to live, now, in this fallen world. How can we carry on any business or work with confidence when so much seems ambiguous, unpredictable, flawed, and, in the light of history, often rather transient and provisional? And that includes so-called Christian work, in ministry and mission. Will what we try to accomplish through all our projects last? Will they bear fruit that lasts? Can we be sure of success? Do our efforts in mission have any lasting viability? I think that these are, at least in part, the questions that Qoheleth tries hard to answer as best he can as he comes toward the end of his journey in this book, in chapters 10–12.

Now remember, as I said a moment ago, that Qoheleth stands in the tradition of Israel's Wisdom literature. And running through that whole tradition is a fundamental duality. There is a dichotomy between three fundamental opposites that are constantly put before our eyes in the wisdom tradition, and we are urged to choose between them:

- Wise   Foolish
- Righteous   Wicked
- Godly   Ungodly

And these three polarities are all connected with each other—the *intellectual, moral,* and *spiritual* dimensions of human life. The Israelites did not split apart, as we so easily do in the modern world, academic learning, ethical behavior, and religious faith. No, the *wise* person will choose the ethically *right* path because they are humbly seeking to obey *God*. Conversely, the one who rejects God will choose the path of wickedness, which is ultimately an act of lethal stupidity.

That is why "the fear of the LORD is the first principle of wisdom." For it is in our proper relationship with the living God that we receive God's guidance in all three areas. The fear of the Lord will shape our lives into the ways of wisdom, righteousness, and godliness, and help us to avoid the ways of folly, wickedness, and ungodliness.

Now Qoheleth knows and broadly accepts that worldview. And he knows many proverbs that express it, such as we find in abundance in the book of Proverbs. But he cannot help commenting that when you honestly look at life, it often seems to undermine those simple binary opposites, or shows that things can be more complicated and uncertain than those polarities suggest. And so there is confusion and enigma still, right to the end of the book, even when we accept the basic fundamental truths of wisdom, righteousness, and godliness.

So in 9:17–10:20, Qoheleth gives us, on the one hand, a mixture of traditional proverbs that mostly reflect the "two ways" wisdom worldview. But then, he intersperses among them a number of comments (his own "alternative facts" we might say), which force us to hang a few question marks around what seems obvious or certain. Life just doesn't always work out like it's supposed to. We know which of the "two ways" we ought to choose. Yes, but sometimes … sometimes stuff just happens.

Stuff Happens (9:17–10:20)

Sometimes Folly Rules (9:17–10:7)

¹⁷ The quiet words of the wise are more to be
  heeded than the shouts of a ruler of fools.
¹⁸ Wisdom is better than weapons of war,
  but one sinner destroys much good.
10 As dead flies give perfume a bad smell,
  so a little folly outweighs wisdom and honour.
² The heart of the wise inclines to the right,
  but the heart of the fool to the left.
³ Even as fools walk along the road,
  they lack sense
  and show everyone how stupid they are.
⁴ If a ruler's anger rises against you,
  do not leave your post;
  calmness can lay great offences to rest.
⁵ There is an evil I have seen under the sun,
  the sort of error that arises from a ruler:
⁶ fools are put in many high positions,
  while the rich occupy the low ones.
⁷ I have seen slaves on horseback,
  while princes go on foot like slaves.

We begin with an obvious truth in 9:17–18a, on which we'd all agree. But then, 18b and 10:1 are equally obvious. "There's always one!" we say, when some idiot (we think) messes up everybody else's good work. So much wisdom and patience can be destroyed by one stupid action, or one daft fool, or one hurtful or confidence-breaking word, or one lying politician … A tiny bit of folly can undo a huge amount of good work.

Right and left (10:2–3) are clear binary opposites, illustrating the "two ways." And the fool is somebody who habitually chooses the wrong one and shows everybody what a fool he or she is. Once again, we can all nod in agreement.

But then, things may not be so clear in the political world. Even if "Keep Calm and Carry On" sounds like good advice (v. 4), we may end up being governed by fools (vv. 5–6)—and how true that sounds in today's world in several countries. And a mere reversal of the system (perhaps by revolution) may only pile absurdity on top of injustice (v. 7). And there are modern examples of that too.

So, we may all agree on the benefits of standard wisdom. But when folly comes to dominate the key levers of political life, you see some pretty strange and unwelcome sights.

Sometimes Accidents Happen (10:8–15)

⁸ Whoever digs a pit may fall into it; whoever
  breaks through a wall may be bitten by a snake.
⁹ Whoever quarries stones may be injured by
  them; whoever splits logs may be endangered
  by them.
¹⁰ If the axe is dull
  and its edge unsharpened,
  more strength is needed,
  but skill will bring success.
¹¹ If a snake bites before it is charmed,
  the charmer receives no fee.
¹² Words from the mouth of the wise are gracious,
  but fools are consumed by their own lips.
¹³ At the beginning their words are folly;
  at the end they are wicked madness—
¹⁴ and fools multiply words.
  No one knows what is coming—
  who can tell someone else what will happen
  after them?
¹⁵ The toil of fools wearies them;
  they do not know the way to town.

Verse 8 is a traditional proverb stating the law of "acts and consequences." Digging a pit was probably a metaphor for planning evil. Breaking through meant burglary of someone else's house. So, the proverb warns that both may rebound on the perpetrator with unforeseen disaster to themselves. Some kind of punishment will follow the crime, even if not delivered by a judge in a human court.

But then the following verses seem to imply that unforeseen bad consequences don't follow only *bad* actions. Even doing *good* ordinary jobs that are perfectly legitimate (v. 9) can lead to accidental injury too, which is not at all deserved. And even expertise (like a snake charmer's), though it can lead to success, won't necessarily save you from harm; things can always go wrong, sometimes fatally (vv. 10–11). We really don't know what's coming round the next bend to hit us (like a flying stone or axe-head, v. 9), or what will happen after we've gone (v. 14b). Stuff happens. Get over it.

Sometimes Money Talks (10:16–20)

¹⁶ Woe to the land whose king was a servant
  and whose princes feast in the morning.
¹⁷ Blessed is the land whose king is of noble birth
  and whose princes eat at a proper time—
  for strength and not for drunkenness.
¹⁸ Through laziness, the rafters sag;
  because of idle hands, the house leaks.
¹⁹ A feast is made for laughter,
  wine makes life merry,
  and money is the answer for everything.
²⁰ Do not revile the king even in your thoughts,
  or curse the rich in your bedroom,
  because a bird in the sky may carry your words,
  and a bird on the wing may report what you say.

These verses are mostly about the benefits of wise and honest government by people who take their responsibilities seriously (16–17). In such a culture, you can work hard and avoid the perils of laziness (18). So far, so good.

But then, after two lines of jollity, comes the last line of verse 19: "Money is the answer for everything." Unless this is just an innocent comment that it's always good to have a bit of cash handy, it is surely astonishingly cynical! It fits with Qoheleth's observations throughout the book that you'll find corruption everywhere. People with enough money can get whatever they want. Everyone has their price. That's certainly a fact of life in politics and in much of the rest of life.

So then, what's the point in praising good sober government and honest hard work if, in the end, it's the rich and the cheaters who get all the benefits anyway? It's still a very relevant question that many of us ask in frustration, anger, and disgust, even if the most prudent thing is just to keep quiet (v. 20).

Stuff happens, then. We live in a word of unpredictable accidents and willful folly. So what to do? Qoheleth is coming to the climax of his book and wants to end on a positive note. So in these last two chapters, he first of all commends what we might call godly opportunism, and then embraces that within strong encouragement to rejoice in the goodness of life that he still commends, while remembering God as both our creator and our ultimate judge. And that seems to me a sound matrix within which to entrust the viability of our own efforts in ministry and mission—a matrix to which, of course, we can readily add more familiar motivations and assurances from the New Testament.

Godly Opportunism (11:1–6)

¹ Ship your grain across the sea;
  after many days you may receive a return.
² Invest in seven ventures, yes, in eight;
  you do not know what disaster may come
  upon the land.
³ If clouds are full of water,
  they pour rain on the earth.
  Whether a tree falls to the south or to the north,
  in the place where it falls, there it will lie.
⁴ Whoever watches the wind will not plant;
  whoever looks at the clouds will not reap.
⁵ As you do not know the path of the wind,
  or how the body is formed in a mother's womb,
  so you cannot understand the work of God,
  the Maker of all things.
⁶ Sow your seed in the morning,
  and at evening let your hands not be idle,
  for you do not know which will succeed,
  whether this or that,
  or whether both will do equally well.

These are familiar verses, much loved by entrepreneurs. Indeed, my friend Pieter Kwant, the programme director for Langham Literature and a publisher himself, says they are among his favourite words of Scripture.

Verse 1 is most probably a maritime trading metaphor, as the NIV, 2011, translates it, since the traditional, "Cast your bread upon the waters" (ESV, etc.) sounds like feeding ducks on a river. The point is: make your investments, take the risks involved, diversify if you can (v. 2a), and in the end you ought to get a good return. So far, so good.

But then, still in the mood we found in chapter 10, the rest of the section paints a series of pictures of the randomness and unpredictability of life in general. Some things you can be sure of (like clouds and rain, v. 3a). But other things you just can't know for sure, such as whether, when, and where a tree will fall, how and where the wind will blow, etc. (vv. 3b–4).

That leads Qoheleth in verse 5 to a crucially important theological point. He has already proved beyond doubt all through the book that there are limits to our human knowledge. There are things we simply can never know for sure. And here he illustrates it yet again from our ignorance of the path of the wind or how human babies grow in a mother's womb (v. 5a; let's remember he was writing before advances in meteorological science and obstetrics). But now he wants to affirm that these very things that *we* cannot understand (including randomness and unpredictability) are nevertheless things in the hands of *God*. They are all part of "the work of God," the God who is "the Maker of all things" (v. 5b).

Now this is a great and positive thing to say. The whole world, life, the universe, and everything originate in God. So even if God's ultimate purposes are hidden from our understanding (as they are), we can trust that God is somehow there, present, involved—even in things that seem irreducibly random and unpredictable to us. And with the security of that confidence, we can throw ourselves into life and work as Qoheleth advocates, trusting God with the outcomes.

The strong affirmation of "the work of God" in verse 5 means we can turn life's unpredictabilities, not into paralysis, but into opportunities (v. 6). Live adventurously! Don't be idle. Be active, bold, and busy. Make your investments ("sow your seed"). You don't know if this will succeed, or that, or both or neither, but go for it anyway.

Clearly, Qoheleth has moved on somewhat from the nihilistic fatalism of earlier reflections about the uncertainty of the future to a more robust opportunism. Whereas in his earlier pessimistic mood he complains, "We don't know what will happen, so there's no point doing *anything*," now he's encouraging us with, "We don't know what will happen, so get on and do *something*."

So, in applying this unusual text to our personal commitment to serving God in leading a whole variety of Christian agencies in ministry and mission, we need to take verses 5 and 6 together. We can never be 100 percent certain of the outcomes of all our efforts (v. 6). But we can be certain of God's sovereignty as "the Maker of all things" (v. 5). As the one whose commitment to his own missional purposes for his church and the world cannot be thwarted, God will do what God will do. Our place is to do whatever "shipping" (v. 1) and "sowing" (v. 6) we prayerfully plan and have the power to carry out—and then leave the outcomes and returns in his hands.

And it is only fair to add that there is a right kind of *Christian* opportunism and pragmatism too. Jesus admonishes his disciples to be ready at all times to respond when the master "knocks" (Luke 12:35–48). Paul speaks with the voice of the wisdom tradition: "Be very careful, then, how you live—not as unwise but as wise, making the most of every opportunity, because the days are evil" (Eph. 5:15–16). Quite, nods Qoheleth. And a pastor and preacher has to be "prepared in season and out of season"—that is, ready to do their work whenever the opportunity arises (2 Tim. 4:2).

Finally, since God is indeed "the Maker of all things" (v. 5), then the only place to turn, ultimately, is to God—which is what Qoheleth does from here to the end of the book. With the sovereignty of God in mind, both as our creator and our ultimate judge, he counsels us to rejoice and remember.

Rejoice and Remember (11:7–12:7)

For the seventh and last time, he returns to the running theme of the goodness of life in God's world—in spite of all the baffling evil and chaos, and the looming and unavoidable approach of death. Enjoy life, he says, but do it responsibly, with your eyes on what lies ahead.

Enjoy Life Responsibly (11:7–10)

> ⁷ Light is sweet,
>   and it pleases the eyes to see the sun.
>
> ⁸ However many years anyone may live,
>   let them enjoy them all.
>   But let them remember the days of darkness,
>   for there will be many.
>   Everything to come is meaningless.
>
> ⁹ You who are young, be happy while you are young,
>   and let your heart give you joy in the days of your youth.
>   Follow the ways of your heart
>   and whatever your eyes see,
>   but know that for all these things
>   God will bring you into judgment.
>
> ¹⁰ So then, banish anxiety from your heart
>   and cast off the troubles of your body,
>   for youth and vigor are meaningless.

These verses are strongly positive, even if tinged with the darkness and apparent meaninglessness of death (v. 8b). Life now is to be lived with joy, and by following what our heart desires (v. 9a). This is not urging a free-for-all license to live any way you want. Rather, it recognizes that we have individual giftings, talents, vocations, and preferences. Follow your heart. Go for what you love!

Don't give in to pessimism and anxiety (v. 10). It sounds like he's preaching to himself, since he has done a lot of that on this journey! In the end, youth and strength are enigmatic in themselves, in the sense that they are transient and sometimes regretted in later life. But while you *are* young, enjoy all the blessings it brings and the opportunities it gives. Youth is a "time," in the sense of his poem in 3:1–8. It is a time "for" something, something valuable, even if it is not permanent nor an end in itself. Youth is to be valued, but not idolized in a hollow "cult of eternal youth."

So then, most of these verses are resonant of the advice given to young people in the traditional wisdom way, as we see repeatedly in Proverbs 1–9. But then Qoheleth injects a sobering consideration. In all of this enjoyment of life, remember that you are accountable to God. "For all these things God will bring you into judgment" (v. 9b). God's judgment lies ahead. Be prepared. Enjoy the present moment, but keep your eyes on the future. Prepare to meet your God, as Amos said, but in such a way that you have nothing to fear.

This is a key point, and it is crucial that Qoheleth states this conviction before he ends his discourse. For this is very different from his bleak musings back in 9:1–3. Those verses are probably the lowest point of his journey. Listen to his despair …

> So I reflected on all this and concluded that the righteous and the wise and what they do are in God's hands, but no one knows whether love or hate awaits them. 2 All share a common destiny— the righteous and the wicked, the good and the bad, the clean and the unclean, those who offer sacrifices and those who do not.
> As it is with the good, so with the sinful; as it is with those who take oaths, so with those who are afraid to take them.
> This is the evil in everything that happens under the sun: The same destiny overtakes all.

Does it really matter how we live? he is asking. Does it make any difference in the end whether you lived wisely, religiously, or morally? Will there ultimately be any distinction between the righteous and the wicked? Will there be justice in the end? Back then in chapter 9, Qoheleth left the questions just hanging in the air, with a shrug and a "nobody knows."

But now, he asserts his faith conviction: *Yes, it does matter.* Those distinctions are real and have real consequences. God will be the final judge, and all our life, work, and enjoyments must be lived in the light of that long-range truth.

However, we should not take this in a negative way. Qoheleth is not back to his old cynicism here. This is not a kind of "spoilsport" twist. He is not sneering at the young person, "Go on kid, have your fun now, but you'll pay for it later …" No, he is simply calling for a life lived to the full, with maximum enjoyment of every moment of the present, but also for a life lived with an eye on the reality of God's presence here and now, *and* into the ultimate future—even beyond death. God is the final auditor and judge. Live life under God. That is not to spoil our lives, but to enrich and ennoble them.

And once again, we can say that this note of hearty joy in life and work, lived with full awareness of God, is consistent also with New Testament teaching. Paul seems to echo Qoheleth, with a Christ-centered touch, when he tells the Colossians, "Whatever you do, whether in word or deed, do it all in the name of the Lord Jesus, giving thanks to God the Father through him … Whatever you do, work at it with all your heart, as working for the Lord, not for human masters" (Col. 3:17, 23; cf. Eccles. 9:10). Enjoy life and banish anxiety, says Qoheleth. "Rejoice in the Lord always," says Paul, "Do not be anxious about anything …" (Phil 4:4–7; cf. 1 Thess. 5:16–18).

Qoheleth's advice, however, is not merely to "remember the future," as it were, but also to remember the past—the past in the great story of the Bible, from the very beginning.

Remember the Story You Are In: The Beginning and the End (12:1–7)

"Remember your Creator in the days of your youth" (12:1) is a familiar verse. But it is not meant as an excuse for forgetting him in your old age! The point is that remembering who created the world and gave us life within it should shape our lives from our earliest moments until—well, until the end. The poignant poem that follows those words probably describes the slow process of aging and the inevitable moment of personal death. But by speaking here of our creator and having just spoken of God as our judge, Qoheleth has set our short human life span within the great biblical narrative with its beginning and ending in God himself, the Alpha and the Omega, the Beginning and the End, as the risen Christ says. That is a perspective that Qoheleth does not really pause to explore or expand further—exhausted as he seems to be from the intensity and inscrutability of his quest. But for us who have the far greater vista of the whole canon of Scripture, it is the most reassuring perspective of all.

We may not be able to guarantee all the outcomes of our efforts for the Lord, even over a whole lifetime. We may have to live with the adventurous optimism of Ecclesiastes 11 in the midst of this unpredictable world. But we ship our grain and sow our seed knowing that we do so under the sovereign governance of "the Maker of all things," the God who in the beginning created the world and who in the end will bring all things under his just and merciful judgment. That is the story we are in, the story in which God calls us to participate for his glory.

And so we can pray, with the ancient prayer for guidance in the Book of Common Prayer:

> Direct us, O Lord, in all our doings with thy most gracious favour, and further us with thy continual help, that in all our works *begun, continued, and ended* in thee, we may glorify thy holy Name, and finally, by thy mercy, obtain everlasting life; through Jesus Christ, our Lord. Amen.

SECTION A: Case Studies

Chapter 4
Faith-Based Organizations and Investments in Mission:

The Case of the All Africa Conference of Churches

by Bright G. Mawudor

Church Related Organizations (CROs), especially in developing countries, continue to face numerous financial crises due to declining financial support from their traditional funders. The net worth of most of these organizations is shrinking, a factor accompanied by chronic, unmanageable budget deficits. The reduced funding has been attributed to the worldwide economic recession and to changing domestic and international priorities in the North, which in turn have affected the volume and nature of available aid.

Even CROs that had established successful local fundraising strategies can no longer be complacent due to the pressing demands of poverty and the need for local fundraisers to attend to social needs.

Research conducted by the Christian Organizations Research Advisory Trust (CORAT), a Pan-African Christian research and consultancy body, on the "Sustainability of the Social Ministry of Churches and Church Related Organizations in Africa" revealed that of the seventeen CROs interviewed, 18 percent claimed to be fairly sustainable while 82 percent claimed to be in a survival mode or moving toward a crisis, demonstrating that sustainability for many CROs is a priority issue.[1]

In 1996, the All Africa Conference of Churches (AACC), in response to calls from its 173 member churches, organized an international symposium on the "Sustainability of the Church in Africa" in which delegates called for a determination to overcome the dependency crisis in the Church. The AACC further called for church leadership in Africa to "conceptualize the insight and articulate the stroke which will cut the Gordian knot inhibiting Church financial growth in Africa."[2]

---

1 CORAT – Africa, *Sustainability of Church Related Organisations* (Kenya: CORAT – Africa Library, 2008).

2 AACC, *Church Leaders Conference on Sustainability of the Church* (Kenya: AACC, 1996).

In 2009, the mega-rich Trinity Anglican Church in New York commissioned six African Anglican bishops to explore the possibilities of rendering the Anglican Communion in Africa financially sustainable.

Meanwhile, as the twenty-first century wears on, churches and their related organizations in Africa are faced with enormous challenges that call for more financial resources, thus acknowledging socioeconomic and political developments that leave some aspects of society in poverty, drought, and suffering from HIV/AIDS.

In the author's twenty-five years of working with the church and its related organizations at national and continental levels in leadership development and stewardship of resources, he has always been troubled by the fact that African churches depend heavily on external funding for any semblance of sustainability. This dependency has more or less reduced bishops and other leaders to the status of ecumenical beggars. During visits to churches across the continent, incidents of funding cuts were observed, resulting in pain and despondency followed by the loss of jobs in projects hitherto supported by donors.

The question one may ask is: How is it that some churches are able to sustain themselves while others cannot? The African continent has enormous potential, but it remains a potential that has never been translated into prosperity. Abject poverty, not riches, characterizes Africa in its struggles.[3]

In response to these challenges, some churches in Africa are turning to new sources of income generation, giving importance to their social ministry and economic development among the faithful. In the absence of such initiatives, it will be difficult to proclaim Christ to people who are daily becoming poorer.[4]

Already, churches like the Anglican Church of Kenya and the Methodist Church of Kenya are embarking on social entrepreneurship initiatives like real estate developments and guest houses. Christian managers of small enterprises see participation in business as an opportunity to "incarnate" Christian values into every aspect of business.

The current option for many African churches and their related organizations is "change or perish."

The reality, which is deemed changeless and absolute, is in fact constantly changing. The time has come to take a serious look not only at what we are doing, but also—and more importantly—at how, and why we do what we do.

The statistics of most mainline denominations clearly indicate that something is wrong. Churches are losing members. Churches are struggling financially. Church attendance is down. Mission giving is waning. What worked well in the past is not working today.

The fact is that the funding landscapes of local churches—both in Africa and the Western world—have changed dramatically in the last fifty years. Whereas the world is changing at lightning speed because of competition from new emerging economies, globalization, and technology, the maps that define churches, and the related financial practices including budgeting, pledging, and tithing have not kept pace with these changes."[5]

What Is the AACC

The All Africa Conference of Churches (AACC) was established in April 1963 during the second meeting of the Assembly of African Churches held in Kampala, Uganda. One of the key objectives of the delegates was to accompany the people of Africa in what was then a revolutionary moment on the continent, as many countries were gaining independence and shedding the shackles of colonialism. It was a time when many African people were still fighting for their freedom and were struggling for self-determination and dignity as a people.

The AACC has developed over many years to become the largest ecumenical movement of Christians on the continent. It is the largest association of Protestant, Anglican, Orthodox, and indigenous churches in Africa representing more than 140 million Christians. It has 193 members comprised of churches, national councils of churches, theological and lay training institutions, and other Christian organizations in forty-two African countries.

The organization has also grown its program portfolio to include Gender, Women and Youth; Peace, Diakonia and Development; Advocacy at the African Union; and Theology, Interfaith Relations and Ecclesial Leadership Development.[6]

---

3 J. N. K. Mugambi, *The Church and the Future of Africa: Problems and Promises* (Kenya: AACC, 1997).

4 Catholic Bishops Conference, *The Future of the Church in the 21st Century* (Kenya: AACC Library, 2002).

5 W. Dick, *Sustainability of the Church in the 21st Century* (UK: 2010).

6 "AACC Programmatic Pillars," Programmes: Our Focus, All Africa Conference of Churches, 2019, http://aacc-ceta.org/en/programmes.

Dependency of the AACC

It took a long time for AACC to start thinking about financial self-sustenance. For nearly sixty years after it started operations, the AACC relied heavily (almost 80 percent) on grants from its overseas partners for its program delivery, with little built-in mechanisms or strategies for financial independence.

Inevitably, this dependence would lead to major problems for AACC. By 2002, the organization was in financial crisis for various reasons including: weak financial management/strategy, dwindling donor funding, weak delivery of programs, waning loyalty to the AACC as a brand, lack of innovation, etc. It became clear that the organization had no option but to drastically change the way it operated, or face collapse. Further, the organization had to act urgently.

AACC Turnaround Strategy

The leadership of the AACC acted quickly. By 2003, the organization had developed a "Turnaround Strategy" based on the following pillars:

Rebranding the Organization

AACC needed a new face to refresh its image among its members, partners, and members of the public, whose confidence had fallen so much that their value for the organization had waned or disappeared altogether.

Developing a Financial Sustainability Strategy

This was at the core of the turnaround strategy, as the renewal and rejuvenation of the AACC was completely dependent on its capacity to provide consistent and reliable membership services via its programmatic work.

Reducing Dependence on "Partner" Funding and Covering Core Overhead Costs

Developing capacity for funding of programs for Faith Based Organizations (FBOs) would give them stability in their programmatic work and enable it to proceed smoothly and consistently.

Developing an Ambitious Plan to Make the Organization a "Donor" Organization by 2025

The body's leaders felt that the AACC, being an apex organization, should have the capability of supporting its members in their work by being a donor. This philosophy was embedded in the growing ecumenical thinking at the time that FBOs needed to change their thinking and generate their own resources. Further, this was in line with the growing movement on the continent to "break the chains" of dependency and become truly free.

AACC Recovery Roadmap

With the pillars of the turnaround strategy having been developed, the AACC came up with a roadmap to guide the organization toward its goal. The hard work of restoring the AACC back to its former glory and preparing it for the future as a self-reliant ecumenical organization playing a central part in the continent's development had begun. The following actions were undertaken:

Undertook an Organizational Audit and Health Check

The organization underwent a comprehensive "blood screening" in which a review was done of its governance structures, mandate, organizational systems and structures, resources, asset mapping and valuation, and management, among other parameters, to determine what was ailing it. After this exercise it became clear that the traditional donor approach, where donors "fix the problems for them," had shifted to a facilitative approach, where donors empower them. The key objective of the AACC then was to develop effective, strategic financial sustainability plans and implement them to achieve financial independence in the wake of this fundamental shift.

Reviewed Systems and Developed Policy Manuals

How were the existing systems a hindrance to the growth and well-being of the AACC? New policy manuals covering the entire governance structure of the AACC—financial regulations and procedures, procurement, and human resources, among others—were developed.

Developed a Business Continuity Plan

The AACC was looking for long-term sustainability and needed a plan that showed how this could be achieved.

Generated a Budget and Cashflow Forecast

This was in line with developing a business model for the organization's business and investment ventures, as well as managing its targets.

Developed a Roadmap to Financial Sustainability via Asset Development

Because the organization has a huge asset base in terms of land and buildings, the leadership decided to focus on the development of these assets, as seen in table 4.3. It was envisaged that the organization would become a donor organization by 2025.

Establishing a "Strategic Business Unit" (SBU) to Become the Investment Wing of the AACC

It was thought that a strategic business unit whose mandate would be clearly commercial to invest and run businesses on behalf of the AACC was the best model for the organization. The advantage was that it would develop its own capacity and strength in business and investments and be run on commercial principles, as this offered the most viable way to achieve AACC's self-sufficiency goals in the long-term.

The SBU is comprised of two units:

i. *Real estate.* This is made up of a seven-story, sixty-five thousand square foot capacity rental office, five stand-above bungalows in prime areas of the city, and four apartments. The initial value of these assets in December 2002 was US$1.8 million. By September 2009, the market value stood at US$3.5 million, with additional rental offices in Togo (West Africa) and a four-story building in Addis Ababa.

Figure 4.1: Partial View of the AACC Rental Offices, Nairobi, Kenya

Figure 4.2: Partial View of the AACC Rental Offices, Addis Ababa, Ethiopia

As can be seen in table 4.1, the real estate contributed about US$1.5 million to support the mission work of the AACC from January 2013 to September 2019.

Figure 4.3: Partial View of the AACC Hotel

ii. *DTCC/Hotel.* The Desmond Tutu Conference Center is a 106-room hotel. It was originally a student dormitory. What the leadership did was sell one of its landed properties and invest the proceeds to convert the dormitory initially into twenty-three self-contained rooms and one conference hall in 2005. When the first two years proved successful, the organization took out a US$200,000 bank loan to expand the guest house to forty-two rooms with two additional meeting halls. After ten years of operations, what was initially conceived as a guest house is now a three-star hotel comprising 106 self-contained hotel rooms, a one thousand-person capacity conference hall, five fifty-person capacity conference halls, three break-away rooms, a gym, a restaurant with a sitting capacity of four to five hundred guests, and a state-of-the-art videoconferencing facility. It is named after one of the past presidents of the AACC, Archbishop (Emeritus) Desmond Tutu, for his distinguished service as a peacemaker on the continent. The hotel has a staff of fifty-two. The management reports to the board of trustees via the finance committee. The profit generated from its operations is used to support the core mission and programmatic work of the AACC. As can be seen from table 4.2, between 2013 and September 2019 the hotel supported the programmatic work of the AACC with the sum of US$404,000.

Registration of "AACC Investment Trust Limited" to Run the Investment Wing (SBU) with Its Own Board

To create a Chinese wall between the commercial wing of the AACC and its ecumenical work, the leadership felt it was necessary to separate the two mandates and have each run independently. That way, the mission work of AACC would not in any way be affected or influenced by commercial imperatives.

Launched a "Campaign for African Dignity"—"One Dollar Per Member"

This is another attempt at making the AACC financially less dependent on donors. Under this scheme, member churches are encouraged every year to raise $1.00 per congregation member toward the mission work of the organization. The funds raised are put into a special interest earning bank account and reported on to the finance committee every six months. We have so far raised US$200,000 from this endeavor.

Donor Grants Versus SBU

The net effect of the turnaround strategy and the AACC's venture into real estate and hotel businesses can be seen in tables 4.3 and 4.4, as dependency on grants from partners reduced from 76 percent (2013) to 38 percent (September 2019).

One can only give glory to God for taking this continental giant this far. The vision of making the AACC a donor organization is still alive.

Guiding Principles

As an FBO, AACC wanted to ensure that its commercial activities were run to the highest levels of ethics and probity. It had to be seen to be leading by example by following its own teachings on morality and integrity. It, therefore, formulated four parameters that would guide its businesses and investments. These guiding principles remain the basis of AACC's business and commercial ventures up to today.

Regular Risk Mapping and Analysis

AACC had to remain vigilant against reputational risk that came with running commercial enterprises. This it could only do by regularly evaluating emerging risks and taking countervailing measures to mitigate them.

The "3Es" Concept

The organization developed what came to be known as the "3Es" concept to generate maximum economic value. These are:
- Economy—prudence of minimizing costs at all opportunities
- Efficiency—resources achieving maximum results with minimal waste
- Effectiveness—the organization meeting its objectives as completely as possible

Ensuring the "Value for Money" Concept in All Expenditures

The limited resources available were used to generate the best value possible for each dollar spent. Prudence was to rule every cent utilized.

Transparency

This was the bedrock in ensuring that AACC business and investment dealings were run openly. There was nothing to hide.

Challenges

Changing the Mindset of the Top Leadership/Governing Bodies of the Organization That Strategic Investment in Missions Is Possible

For an organization that had become almost entirely dependent on donor funding for its very survival, getting people to start believing and moving in the direction of becoming responsible for their own self-sustenance required a quantum leap of faith. There was skepticism, uncertainty, and maybe even fear of the unknown among the top leadership.

How to Separate and Run the Investment Wing from the Normal Programmatic Work of the AACC

Running a commercial enterprise required its own set of skills and focus. Yet this had to be undertaken without distracting or undermining the AACC's core business. To overcome this, a capacity building seminar was organized for members of governing bodies to sensitize them.

Management of Businesses and Operational Risks Associated with Running the Investment Wing (SBU)

Even as the commercial wing ran independently, the organization's top leadership had to be kept fully abreast of everything the SBU was doing. There is always the risk of business scandals from unethical behavior; even inadvertent engagement can result in an image crisis for AACC.

Ensuring Ethical Values in Investments While Maintaining a High Rate of Return on Investments

As an FBO, all of AACC's commercial ventures must be governed by the highest levels of integrity at all times. How you do this even as you go for the highest possible rates of return, as per the guiding principles, remains a perpetual challenge of the SBU.

Lessons Learned

We have learned some basic but very powerful lessons from our six-year journey in business and investment:
- Doing business with a human face is possible. Business can still be done in a humane manner, and still provide high returns.
- The AACC's experience demonstrates how an FBO can do investment with religious values as well as economic values for a better world, that is, to help the economy to serve the common good.
- Between 2013 and 2019, total support from SBU to programs was almost US$2 million.
  The organization's mission with the SBU has been a huge success.

Future Strategy and Expectations

AACC's four guiding principles remain its pillars, and the SBU Board continuously reviews its operations using them as a basis. In the short and long terms, AACC has several business and investment plans:
- Install solar panels in rental properties to cut electricity cost by 50 percent.
- Seek partnerships to develop our properties in Nairobi.
- Reduce donor dependency to zero, but partner with donors on programs of mutual interest.
- Channel a substantial part of surplus funds into poverty reduction and social impact programs in Africa.
- Be a role model for churches in Africa of investments as a driver to missions.

Conclusion

The twenty-first century is characterized by reengineering of organizations in order to make them more relevant to the challenges of the times. Today we know that in many areas of life we cannot guarantee more of the same, be it work, money, peace, freedom, health, or happiness.

Well into the twenty-first century, it has become clear that financial independence with a predictable cash flow is essential for FBOs to keep their course and to withstand the challenges of donors whose attitudes could suddenly change due to their own domestic or internal challenges. Financial stability and independence, as well as strong roots in society, are necessary so that an FBO can better deliver on its core mission and promote public interest.

Today, most FBOs are facing the challenges of an economic downturn due to societal changes, competing players in the traditional fields, dwindling donor support, and donor fatigue, among others. This progressive squeeze of the church's ability to sustain its mission calls for new thinking in the way the church is funded, new theological thinking, and growth strategies for maximizing internal strengths and resources to sustain its mission.

In this chapter I have focused on the use of assets of the AACC, in real estate and the hospitality industry. The result is one that can be recommended to FBOs in Africa. It is common knowledge that FBOs in Africa have vast tracts of land that are lying idle for development. If FBOs can strategize to maximize the economic use of the land at their disposal, they can be sure to end the age-old mentality of "not having" the resources to do their mission work, and reduce dependence on their founding or mother churches in Europe and North America.

The case of AACC provides ample evidence. The fact is that overdependency on foreign funding violates the three self-principles of moral philosophy: self-sustenance, self-propagation, and self-governance. It also reflects a deficiency of creativity and innovation on the part of the receiver. FBOs have enormous potential to reduce dependency by diversifying their income base, by undertaking economic empowerment programs for wealth creation, and by encouraging entrepreneurship among members as well as others on the continent. All that is needed is the will to do it.

Table 4.1: Strategic Business Unit Results, Real Estate

YEAR	INCOME KES	EXPENDITURE KES	OPERATING SURPLUS KES	SUPPORT TO MISSIONS AND PROGRAMMES KES	NET SURPLUS KES
2013	76,841,784	(25,735,822)	51,105,962	(9,433,586)	41,662,376
2014	72,460,089	(23,702,825)	48,757,264	(18,689,730)	30,067,534
2015	76,732,195	(23,899,515)	52,832,680	(36,283,213)	16,549,467
2016	83,534,609	(32,707,080)	50,827,529	(49,535,787)	1,291,742
2017	89,815,698	(41,588,125)	48,227,573	(38,263,238)	9,964,335
2018	91,790,642	(30,898,862)	60,891,780	(48,713,424)	12,178,356
2019 (8 months unaudited)	72,142,550	(23,560,605)	48,581,945	(29,190,879)	19,391,066
CUMULATIVE TOTAL	399,384,375	(147,633,367)	251,751,008	(152,215,554)	99,535,454
Equivalent in US$	3,993,844	(1,476,334)	2,517,510	(1,522,156)	995,355

Source: AACC audited financial statements

Table 4.2: Strategic Business Unit Results, DTCC

YEAR	INCOME KES	EXPENDITURE KES	OPERATING SURPLUS KES	SUPPORT TO MISSIONS AND PROGRAMMES KES	NET SURPLUS KES
2013	107,761,105	(73,152,002)	34,609.103	(2,360,897)	32,248,206
2014	118,675,043	(86,974,109)	31,700,934	(4,672,432)	27,028,502
2015	125,147,472	(97,771,155)	27,376,317	(9,070,803)	18,305,514
2016	115,216,482	(100,760,405)	14,456,077	(12,383,947)	2,072,130
2017	103,529,183	(88,812,711)	14,716,472	(9,565,810)	5,150,662
2018	85,451,244	(89,873,413)	(4,422,169)		(4,422,169)
2019 (8 months unaudited)	80,492,917	(71,100,005)	9,392,912	(2,348,228)	7,044,684
CUMULATIVE TOTAL	736,273,446	(608,443,800)	127,829,646	(40,402,117)	87,427,529
Equivalent in US$	7,362,734	(6,084,438)	1,278,296	(404,021)	874,275

Source: AACC audited financial statements

Table 4.3. Financial Results: Total Income by Category

SOURCE OF INCOME	2013 KES	%	2014 KES	%	2015 KES	%	2016 KES	%	2017 KES	%	2018 KES	%	2019 KES	%
Partner Grants	232,690,206	76%	133,114,476	71%	109,407,325	58%	112,890,632	65%	129,175,820	40%	147,284,810	43%	96,981,890	38%
Membership contribution	2,871,805	2%	2,822,028	2%	2,917,555	1%	2,306,454	1%	2,963,365	1%	4,364,333	1%	1,716,645	1%
Strategic Business Unit	184,602,889	17%	191,135,132	18%	201,879,667	28%	198,751,091	33%	193,344,881	59%	177,147,548	52%	152,636,467	60%
Other income	11,107,698	2%	1,174,045	9%	1,553,411	13%	1,140,397	1%	699,520	0%	11,516,363	3%	1,364,507	1%
TOTAL INCOME	431,272,598	100%	328,245,681	100%	315,757,958	100%	315,088,574	100%	326,183,586	100%	340,313,054	100%	252,698,510	100%

Source: AACC audited financial statements

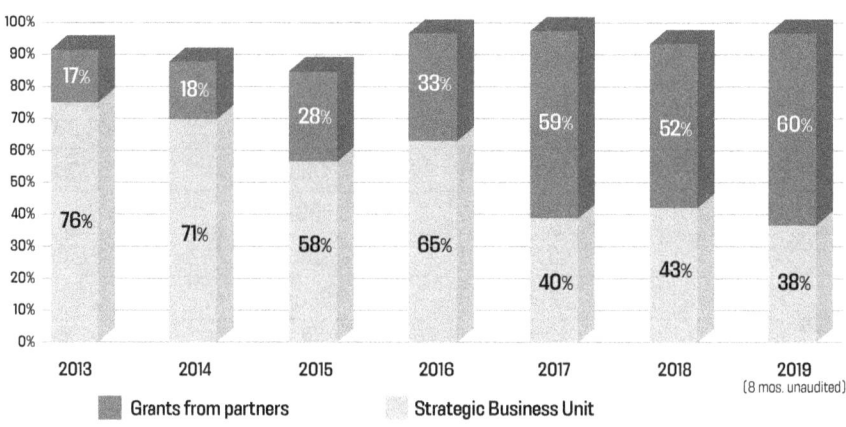

Table 4.4: Grants from Partners Versus SBU Income at a Glance (Percentage of Total Income)

Source: Report of AACC Board of Trustees

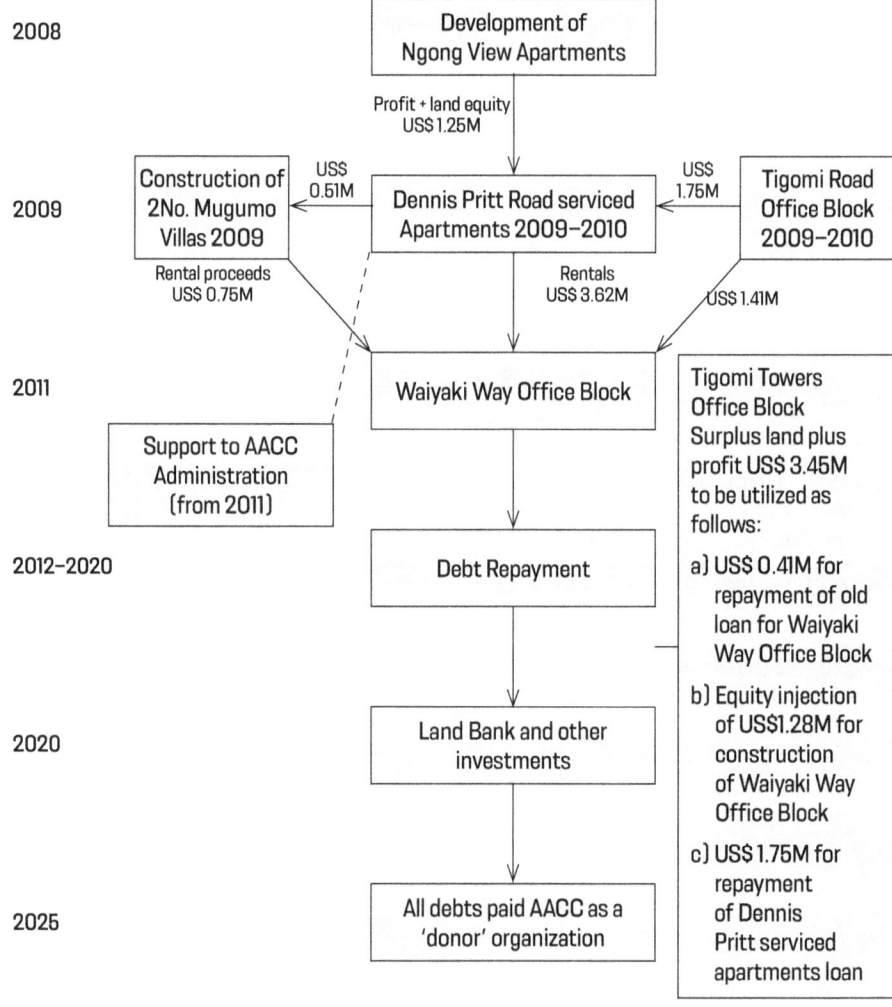

Table 4.5: AACC Property Development Strategy, 2009–2025 Flow of Funds Chart (currently under review)

Source: AACC business plan 2008 (revised)

Chapter 4 Response

by Jeffrey J. Lee

The Problem of Dependency

> Give once and you elicit appreciation;
> Give twice and you create anticipation;
> Give three times and you create expectation;
> Give four times and it becomes entitlement;
> Give five times and you establish dependency.
> —Bob Lupton[7]

My wife and I lived and worked on the African continent for eight years. In our experience, it was evident that dependency was prevalent in foreign aid, international development, and even mission-based business work. But dependency is a form of bondage. It leads people to think that their situation is hopeless without charity and that they cannot do anything to change it. This is unfortunate in light of God's will, which has set us free from all kinds of bondage through Jesus Christ.

While Lupton's observations on aid concern people in poverty, they are also relevant to middle-class people. Due to the impacts of COVID-19, many Americans have received free stimulus checks along with unemployment benefits. As the *Wall Street Journal* reports, "The unemployment benefits are so generous that in many places, workers are telling their bosses they'd rather be unemployed than return to their jobs."[8] How sad that charity is demotivating people from working because aid is worth more than what they can earn from their jobs.

---

[7] Robert D. Lupton, *Toxic Charity: How the Church Hurts Those They Help and How to Reverse It* (New York: HarperCollins Publishers, 2011), 130.

[8] Eric Morath, "Coronavirus Relief Often Pays Workers More Than Work," *The Wall Street Journal*, April 28, 2020, https://www.wsj.com/articles/coronavirus-relief-often-pays-workers-more-than-work-11588066200.

Highlights of the AACC Case Study

The All Africa Conference of Churches (AACC) case study was delightful to read because the leadership identified the issue of dependency correctly and tackled it decisively. My deep interest in the AACC case study stems from it being ultimately about self-sustenance. This is an essential objective that our organization, Synergy for the Kingdom (SfK) Network, strives to cultivate in the missional businesses we serve.

Additionally, the AACC's work exhibits the holistic transformation that we encourage missional businesses to pursue through their own work—improvements not only in economic life, but also in dignity and hope. The points that most warmed my heart while I was reading the case study were as follows:

1. Awareness and Action

The AACC leadership realized the serious nature of dwindling external support and the dire need to stand on their own two feet. Moreover, the AACC took decisive action, and action presents an opportunity for result. As stated by a Japanese proverb, "Vision without action is a daydream, and action without vision is a nightmare."

2. Motivation and Participation

The leadership did more than just devise action plans; they also were able to convince and motivate their stakeholders through workshops. This took a clear vision and a persuasive roadmap of their mission. While motivation without resulting participation could be ineffective, the AACC proceeded to launch the "Campaign for African Dignity," with the aim of raising $1.00 per congregation member. This is truly remarkable.

3. Partnership and Governance

When things are going well, people tend to choose to go alone, but the AACC chose to pursue synergy among the new and existing organizations. They also established a clear division between the management of their traditional faith-based organization (FBO) and their business wing or strategic business unit (SBU), with the SBU run by an independent entity and board. Without strong and disciplined governance, many good intentions result in mediocre outcomes. I am certain that they faced resistance and criticism during the implementation phases, and yet they were able to overcome them.

4. Fruitfulness

The outcomes proved the leadership's initial conviction to be right and it bore fruit, including uplifting the "can-do" spirit of church leaders and congregation members, completing many good works in Christ's name, and restoring hope and dignity among all stakeholders. More than anything else, the AACC set an example of FBOs having been liberated from the bondage of well-intended, but "toxic charity" as described by Lupton.

Areas of Further Inquiry

While the aforementioned highlights were notable, I have identified a few aspects that I felt could have been included or elaborated on in the case study:

1. The Multifaceted Meaning of Work

Spiritual work involves more than just labor; it also includes worship and service. The word "work" appears in Genesis 2:15, when Adam was called to work (in the garden) and take care of it.[9] The Hebrew root for "work" is 'bd (עבד), and means *labor*. This points to our typical understanding of what it means to work.

However, 'bd also appears in Exodus when Moses was conveying God's message to Pharaoh to let his people go so that they may worship him;[10] here 'bd is translated as *worship*.

It also appears in the well-known passage Joshua 24:15,[11] where 'bd is translated as *serve*. God is always at work, and Jesus too worked like God the Father (John 5:17).[12] As followers of Jesus, we should follow his footsteps, working in worship and service as well.

If this more nuanced understanding of spiritual work was better understood, the sacred-secular divide still existing in churches could have been avoided.[13] As a more all-encompassing approach to work as worship and service, I offer Business as Mission (BAM) or missional businesses that worship and serve God in their work. Missional businesses not only serve people by producing jobs as well as goods and services, but also manifest God's goodness in the process of doing so.

2. Following a Calling in Various Forms

People tend to think that having a calling must involve holding a clergy or ministry-related vocation. This notion is also deeply rooted in the dualistic worldview of the sacred-secular divide. But God's universal calling for his people is to worship and glorify him in whatever they do.[14]

For example, take the case of Joseph. First, he was called to be a slave, an unexpected role that he definitely did not want. Next, he was called to be Potiphar's personal attendant, later a prison warden's assistant, and finally the prime minister to govern under Pharaoh. In whatever situation he was called into, he honored God in what he did. He was faithful to God's primary calling to honor him in many different roles, whether he chose them or was thrown into them.

3. Intentional Integration

We worship a triune God who encompasses the Trinity of the Father, the Son, and the Holy Spirit, while being one God in essence and in nature. God demonstrates the possibility of maintaining both

---

9 "The LORD God took the man and put him in the Garden of Eden to work it and take care of it" (Gen. 2:15).

10 "Then say to him, 'The LORD, the God of the Hebrews, has sent me to say to you: Let my people go, so that they may worship me in the wilderness. But until now you have not listened'" (Exod. 7:16).

11 "But if serving the LORD seems undesirable to you, then choose for yourselves this day whom you will serve, whether the gods your ancestors served beyond the Euphrates, or the gods of the Amorites, in whose land you are living. But as for me and my household, we will serve the LORD" (Josh. 24:15).

12 "In his defense Jesus said to them, 'My Father is always at his work to this very day, and I too am working'" (John 5:17).

13 "Role of the Church in Wealth Creation," Lausanne Movement, September 12, 2017, https://lausanne.org/content/role-church-wealth-creation.

14 "So whether you eat or drink or whatever you do, do it all for the glory of God" (1 Cor. 10:31).

three persons (diversity) *and* the singular integrity of his deity (unity).

It was commendable that the AACC took preventive measures to avoid unwanted interference by the governance and management of the SBU. But to exhibit organizational maturity, the separation should evolve to intentionally integrate the church and the business ministry.

If the AACC chooses to keep the two ministries separated long term or perhaps forever, it risks perpetuating the mistaken notion that work is separate from worship and service. These should be united to overcome the sacred-secular divide. This is an artificial byproduct of human invention, whereas God's design is holistic and integral.

The Need for Continuous Change

As a Greek philosopher Heraclitus of Ephesus said, "The only constant in life is change."[15] It was true in ancient times, and it is still true now. Change is inevitable in every facet of life, and nothing can stop it. It is necessary for organizations, including FBOs, to respond to change—not just to *survive*, but to *thrive*.

The AACC saw changes in the behaviors and patterns of charity, realized the need to be liberated from external aid, and took decisive action toward self-sustenance. With continued growth in understanding and action taken, I trust that the AACC will continue to provide good examples for FBOs that seek self-sufficiency. And I pray that the Lord will bring forth more examples of FBOs that achieve self-sustenance in and through missional business models.

---

15 *World History Encyclopedia*, s.v. "Heraclitus of Ephesus," by Joshua J. Mark, July 14, 2010, https://www.worldhistory.org/Heraclitus_of_Ephesos/.

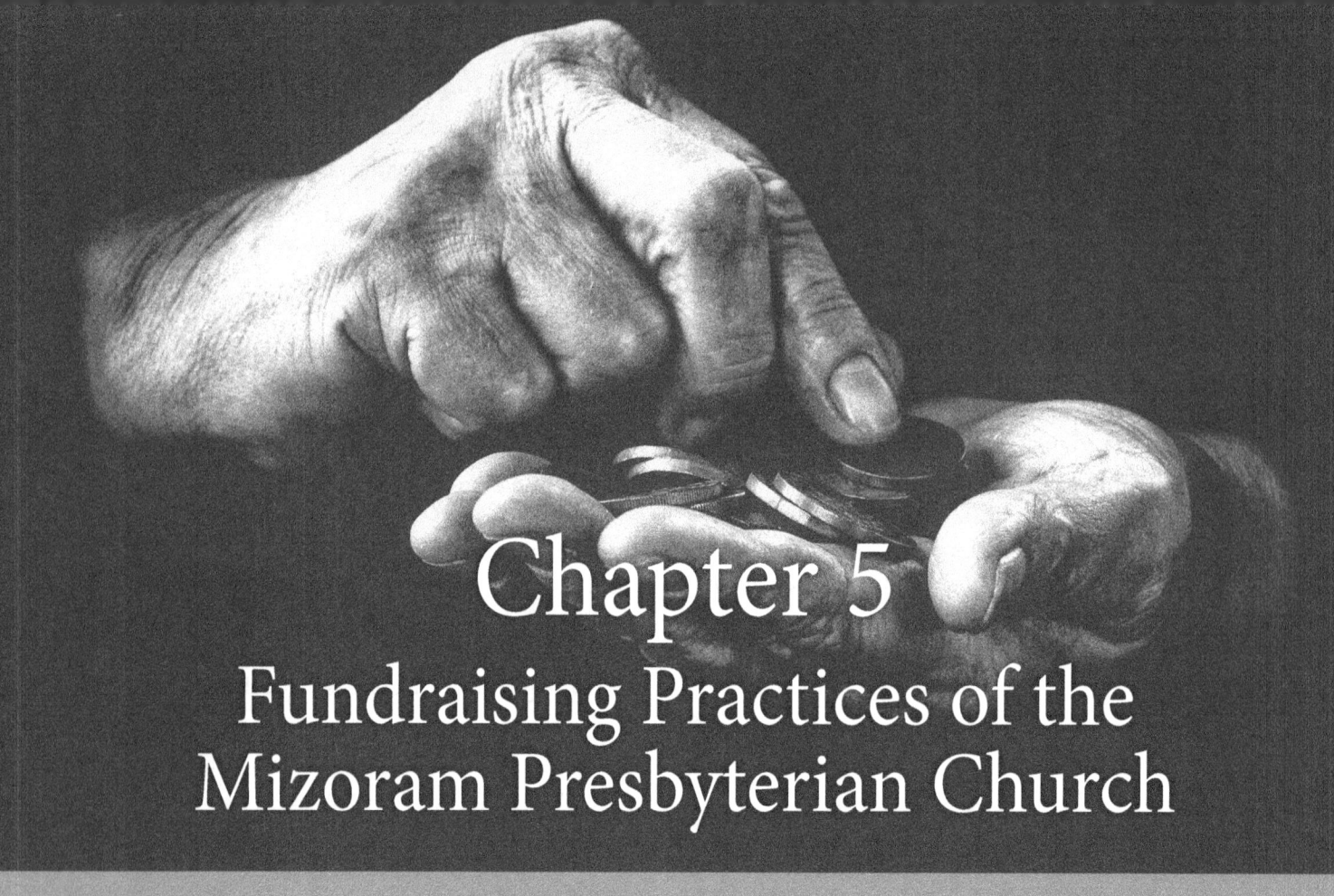

Chapter 5
Fundraising Practices of the Mizoram Presbyterian Church

by Zosangliana Colney

In response to the question of Dr. Jonathan Bonk,

"How can such a poor church provide for so many missionaries?"[1]

The Land

Perched on the tip of the northeastern border of India, the beautiful, mountainous state of Mizoram is geographically, economically, and culturally isolated from much of the rest of India, which considers Mizoram "industrially backward." Despite having the second highest literacy rate in the country, most of the Mizo populations live in poverty. Electricity and decent roads are in short supply.[2] Mizoram is the twenty-third state of the Indian Union, situated in the northeastern corner of the country bordering with Myanmar in the east and south, Bangladesh in the west, and Assam and Manipur States of India in the north. Mizoram occupies 21,087 square kilometers with a population of only 1,097,206 (2011).[3] It has a pleasant moderate climate with temperatures ranging from twenty to thirty-one degrees Celsius.[4]

The People

J. H. Lorain, one of the first two missionaries to the Mizo writes, "The Lushais [Mizos] are a fine intelligent tribe of Mongoloid hillmen inhabiting parts of the wild forest-covered mountainous region forming the watershed between India and Upper Burma [now Myanmar]. Their ancestral home would appear to have been somewhere in the neighbourhood of Southeast Tibet and Western China, whence, by slow degrees, through the centuries, they have pressed southward

---

1 Jonathan J. Bonk, "Good News from a Distant Land," *The Hearth: A Newsletter for the Friends of OMSC* 16 (Fall 2004):1.

2 Russ Bravo, ed., *Inspire* (London: Christian Publishing & Outreach, 2006), 19.

3 Directorate of Economics and Statistics, *Statistical Handbook of Mizoram 2018* (Aizawl: Government of Mizoram, 2018), 1.

4 *Statistical Handbook*, 18. Mizos were known formally as Lushai (Lusei, the largest subtribe of the Mizos) by Westerners.

and westward to their present habitat. Their speech belongs to the Assam-Burma branch of the Tibeto-Burmese family of languages.

Until the annexation of their country by the Indian Government in 1890 they were only known to the outside world as a race of daring headhunters, whose periodic raids were a source of terror to their more peaceable neighbours in the lower hills and plains of Eastern Bengal and Assam."[5] Mizos were first known by outsiders for their savagery. They often raided the people in the adjoining plains of their habitation. In one of their head-hunting expeditions on January 27, 1871 they killed Dr. James Winchester, manager of a Tea Garden at Alexandrapore in Cachar District of Assam State, and then took his five-year-old little daughter Mary as a captive. On hearing about this incident, the British Government sent its troops to rescue Mary, suppress head-hunting, and establish law and order in the land of the Mizos.

Entry of Christianity

The British expeditions paved the way for the coming of Christian missionaries to Mizoram. Rev. William Williams, the Welsh Presbyterian (then Welsh Calvinistic Methodist) missionary, visited Mizoram in 1891. He was the first Christian missionary who sowed the seed of the Gospel in Mizoram. He wrote to the assembly of his church recommending adopting Mizoram as a mission field. He himself longed to return to work among the Mizos. The assembly resolved to accept his proposal and selected Rev. Williams to work in Mizoram. But unfortunately, Rev. Williams died on April 21, 1892.

Remarkably, a devout millionaire in Leeds, Mr. Robert Arthington, set about fulfilling the dreams of Williams. With a great burden for lost souls he set up the Arthington Aborigines Mission to send missionaries to northeast India. Its first missionaries, Rev. James Herbert Lorrain and Dr. Fredrick William Savidge, arrived in Mizoram on January 11, 1894.[6] They became the first Christian missionaries who settled in Mizoram, but left in 1897.[7]

---

5 J. H. Lorrain, *Dictionary of the Lushai Language* (Kolkata: The Asiatic Society, 1940), v.

6 Chhangte Lal Hminga. *The Life and Witness Of The Churches In Mizoram* (Lunglei: The Literature Committee, Baptist Church of Mizoram, 1987), 48.

7 Hminga, 52.

The Church

In 1897 the Presbyterian Church of Wales sent Rev. David Evans Jones in the place of Rev. William Williams to work among the Mizos. He entered Mizoram on August 31, 1897, joining the first two missionaries and working alongside them for a short time. Rev. Lorrain and Dr. Savidge left Mizoram in late 1897. Rev. D. E. Jones was the founder of the Mizoram Presbyterian Church. The first two Mizo believers were baptized on June 25, 1899. By 1951 the Christian population in the region was 83.01 percent. Now the percentage of Christians in Mizoram is about ninety.

The Mizoram Presbyterian Church (MPC) Synod, a unit of the Presbyterian Church of India, is now the biggest church denomination in Mizoram with 612,804 members, which is more than half of the total population of Mizoram State.

Insurgency broke out in 1966 driving western missionaries out of Mizoram, and all foreign missionaries left by 1968. Subsequently, the indigenous ministers and pastors began to administer the needs and requirements of the churches. As soon as the Mizo accepted Christianity they were quick to take the burden of spreading the Gospel into their neighboring states and beyond their national boundaries. The work of administering the local churches and spreading the gospel beyond Mizoram has continued side by side.

The MPC adopted its indigenous practices of fundraising in its different local units. This church had 431,056 communicant members with a total membership of 612,804 in 2018/19. The average per capita annual contribution of each communicant member of the church was then Rs. 1224/-.

1. The Mizoram Presbyterian Church is what we call a "three-self church" in the sense that it is financially self-supported, self-administered, and self-propagating. It is financially self-supported in that the total expenditure of the church of Rs. 3,33,82,18,277 was exceeded by the income of Rs. 4,01,20,03,571 in the fiscal year 2019/20. The church is self-administered by its own 585 ordained ministers and 3,940 other workers employed (paid) by the church itself. The church is self-propagating in that it has its own mission with 2,741 workers in and outside of India with no outside funding support. Let us see how this church has managed such an achievement in God's ministry.

Fundraising Practices

The late Rev. Saiaithanga once said, "From the very beginning our missionaries taught us to be self-supporting. They taught and introduced the 'Kingdom of God (*Pathian ram*) contribution,' which was used for the support of local evangelists."[8] Moreover, Mizo community is a giving and generous community. "One of the principles of Mizo society is '*Sem sem dam dam, ei bil thi thi*' which means 'equal share for all to survive, curse to death who deviates from it.'"[9] Thus, Mizos received the teaching of generous giving both from their missionaries and their forefathers. Talking about the history of the church in the early twentieth century Rev. J. Meirion Llyod writes, "The number of paid and church-appointed workers was slowly growing. Pastors and evangelists generally gave devoted service and worked on very meager salaries of which they invariably gave a tenth to the collection known as the 'Kingdom of God Collection,' the main support of the Church."[10] Donald Chapman, Vice President of Mission India USA, reported in 2007 that the "Mizoram Church is a poor Church considering the average per capita income for the state at $150 per year. But this is not a church comprised of rice Christians, always with a hand outstretched like the beggars lining the streets in every major city in India. The Mizo people do not follow Jesus because of what they can get. Even though very poor, they have avoided becoming crippled with foreign finance. It is not a welfare church. They consider themselves abundantly blessed and generously give and share as demonstrated at each and every meal in every home. These are not rice Christians but Christians who share their rice, the food staple that keeps them alive."[11]

1. Tithe or One-Tenth

The organizational set up of the church is a centralized administration in terms of ministry and finance. Mizo Christians are giving Christians in that most of the church members give a tithe, one-tenth of one's total income. The process of giving is done systematically. A member is free to split up his or her tithe into three selected ministries—pastoral ministry, mission (ministry of evangelism), and local church ministry. The distribution ratio recommended by the church in these three fields is 5:3:2, meaning that one must give about 50 percent of his tithe to pastoral ministry, 30 percent to mission, and 20 percent to local church ministry. The local church retains only the 20 percent that is meant for its local ministry. Both the pastoral and mission funds amounting to 80 percent are sent to the synod headquarters office. In the 2019/20 financial year the total amount received toward pastoral ministry was Rs. 1,43,93,62,700, and toward mission (ministry of evangelism) was Rs. 90,23,12,901.[12] In addition to members' contributions from tithes there are many more fundraising practices exercised by the Mizo Christians such as missionary support, collection of handful of rice, etc. Some of these practices will be explained briefly as follows.

2. Handful of Rice Collection

This is purely an indigenous fundraising practice. Mizos generally eat two rice meals a day. When the rice for family consumption has been measured into the cooking pot, as large a fistful as one can is taken out and put aside into a special bin. The rice thus set aside is collected once a week and presented to the church to be sold. The proceeds from the sale of handful of rice collected and submitted to the synod headquarters amounted to Rs. 189,124,196/- in the 2019/20 financial year.[13] The Mizoram Presbyterian Church celebrated the centenary of this method of fundraising. The Mizo church began this practice of fundraising in 1910 when they needed funds for the church building at Mission Veng. The Women's Fellowship started collecting the handful of rice collection, sold out, and the sale proceeds were submitted to the church in support of construction of the building.[14] To this day the management of this fundraising practice (i.e., the collection, selling,

---

8 Rev. Saiaithanga, *Kohhran chanchin* [History of the church] (Aizawl: Mizo Theological Literature Committee, 1993), 35. Translation mine.

9 C. Lalkima, *Social Welfare Administration in a Tribal State: A Case Study of Mizoram* (Guwahati: Spectrum Publication, 1997), 138.

10 J. Meirion Lloyd, *History of the Church in Mizoram: Harvest in the Hills* (Aizawl: Synod Publication Board,1991), 215.

11 Donald Chapman, "Rice Churches" (unpublished reports of his visit to Mizoram, 2007).

12 Synod Finance Committee, *Annual Statement of Accounts 2019–2020* (Aizawl: Presbyterian Church of India, Mizoram Synod, 2020), 1.

13 *Annual Statement*, 1.

14 Lloyd, *History of the Church*, 145.

accounting, etc.) is in the hands of the women's fellowship of the church. Rev. J. M. Lloyd writes, "In 1913 this (handful of rice collection) provided funds to enable them (Women's Fellowship) to appoint the first Bible woman (Woman Evangelist)."[15] In this indigenous practice of handful of rice Mizo Christians say, "As long as we have something to eat every day, we have something to give to God every day." Rev. Dr. Donald Chapman wrote an eyewitness account of the collection of handful of rice when he visited Mizoram: "After the service we visited several homes. I wanted to see and understand how this poor church in a tiny state in North East India could send so many missionaries and be so generous. In the first home, the lady of the house showed us a 2 gallon plastic bucket. There was a label stuck on the outside. It read 'The Lord's Share,' but in the Mizo language. At every meal, the woman of the house sets aside a portion of rice considered 'The Lord's Share' in this plastic bucket. It might be as small as a handful. It can be much more depending on the financial status of the family. But in every home, at every meal, the Lord gets His share. Then on Saturday morning, volunteers collect the rice from each family. A woman volunteers for a month of Saturdays and visits each of 10–12 homes assigned to her, records the amount the family gives in a ledger, and carries the rice on her back in a basket strapped around her forehead. She then brings it to a collection point. Many exist throughout the city. In the Presbyterian Church alone, more than 5 million kilograms of rice are collected each year. That is 5,500 tons of rice!"[16]

3. Missionary Support Fund

Members are encouraged to support a missionary at the rate of Rs. 1000/- per month. The total income from the missionary support fund amounted to Rs. 385,186,429/- during the last financial year (2019/20). Individuals, families, groups of individuals, and Christian Fellowship are supporting missionaries under this policy. The funds under this heading are meant for mission and evangelism departments, particularly for the salary of missionaries. The five local churches supporting the most missionaries with the numbers of missionaries supported are listed here:

Chhinga Veng Church	700
Chanmari Veng Church	580
Bungkawn Church	525
Khatla Church	500
Zarkawt Church	465

4. Mission Garden/Farm

Many local churches have gardens or farms usually called *Ramthar Huan*, "Mission Garden," in order to support the mission and evangelism ministry. Prof. Jonathan J. Bonk acknowledged that "Mizoram churches in rural areas frequently dedicate entire gardens, farms, and teak plantations to missions."[17] These gardens/farms mostly produce various local cash crops—banana, orange, ginger, tea, teak, grape, paddy, and many others. The proceeds from the sale of these crops go to the mission fund. Clearing and monitoring of the gardens are managed by the church through its mission committee, which mostly organizes social works whenever necessary. For instance, the Kulikawn West Presbyterian Church has a mission garden three miles away from the city. The garden's land was donated by Mrs. Siamkungi, a widow member of the church. Mr. Hrangkhama looked after the garden voluntarily for sixteen years until he retired from it at the age of eighty. The garden is beyond the reach of any kind of motor vehicle. Mr. Hrangkhama used to carry the products home on his back using a yoke he made himself. Many local churches have this kind of garden in support of mission work. The meager income derived from these gardens and farms goes to the mission support fund.

5. Missionary Firewood

Firewood is the main cooking fuel in rural areas. Collecting firewood from the forest is mainly the responsibility of women. On the way home they are expected to donate sticks of firewood in the place that the church prepared at the entrance of a village, to await the monthly sale. Referring to this practice Rev. Dr. Zairema said, "Another form of raising funds without anybody feeling the pinch is called missionary firewood,"[18] since collecting firewood from the forest needs no capital outlay. The mission committee of

---

15 Lloyd, 163.
16 Chapman, "Rice Churches," 3.
17 Bonk, *Good News*, 3.
18 Rev. Zairema, *God's Miracle in Mizoram* (Aizawl: Synod Publication Board, 1978), 34.

the local church is responsible to sell the collected firewood to support the mission work of the church.

6. Missionary Chickens

Traditionally most Mizo village families own poultry. It is very common among the missionary-minded members of the church to identify some chickens as "missionary chickens" as soon as they are hatched. When these chickens are full-grown, they are sold and the amount goes to the church in support of its mission projects. I remember a childhood experience when a woman approached my mother about selling a missionary chicken. We knew that whatever price we paid would go to the mission fund, so my mother gave a higher price than the chicken deserved. My father who was in the receiving and counting team of the mission fund confirmed that the exact amount my mother gave for the chicken was received from the woman who sold the chicken to us. Another approach to missionary chicken practice in some churches is to distribute eggs to members of the church at the beginning of the year and to collect grown-up chickens at the end of the year, expecting all along that some eggs would hatch and chickens would grow for a year!

7. "For Missions" Box

Mission committees of some local churches keep a box or container labeled "For Missions" at the "Government Fair Price Shop," where every family receives their rations of rice, sugar, etc. from the government at a low price. Here, willing persons may donate a little amount of rice out of their share, and the sale proceeds go to the mission fund.

8. Setting apart of Land and Plants

Farmers set aside a portion of their land for missions. The produce from such designated areas is kept exclusively for mission work. Likewise, gardeners set apart certain fruit plants (e.g., oranges) for missions. The produce from such plants is set aside for mission work. Many gardeners who have tended to particular mission plants have said that these plants always bear more and better quality fruit than other plants in the same garden!

9. Giving Sunday Salary or Meal

Some local churches encourage their members, particularly government servants, to donate Sunday salary. Such a donation is collected in a box at the door of a church. Similarly, some families donate their Sunday meal or Sunday meat (having Sunday lunch without meat so that the price of the meat is donated to the mission fund). This system is not a regular, ongoing means of collection. It is used mainly for particular projects on the mission field such as construction of church buildings and so on.

10. Multiplying Talents

Willing members of the church take certain sums of money from the treasurer for multiplication for mission support. At an appointed time they return the original amount along with a surplus. The capital is returned to the treasury and the surplus or interest goes to the mission fund.

11. Imaginary Mission Field Visit

Members gather in the church premises or the house of a member family for an imaginary mission field visit, mainly during the night after usual working hours are over. They are expected to bring enough money for the expenditure to visit a certain mission field. Some mission fields are far from Mizoram, viz. Delhi, Lucknow, Patna, etc., whereas some fields are near, viz. Barak, Tripura, etc. Those who would like to visit far away fields are expected to give more, perhaps the amount for return airfare and so on. The money collected goes to the mission support fund. Some generous members give not only the conveyance charge but also the cost of lodging and food for the imaginary visit.

12. Hosting of Missionaries

There is also an imaginary hosting of missionaries by members of the church. A willing family is assigned to host a missionary or missionaries for several days. Travel expenses, daily food allowances, and the cost of lodging a missionary for a few days are collected from the host family or individuals. The sum of money offered by the host goes to the support of mission work.

13. Roaming Box

Roaming box or visiting box (*Bawm inleng*) is a box with the label, *Ka lo leng e, thlarau bo chhandam nan engzatnge min pek ve theih dawn le?*, which means, "Hello, I am visiting you. How much will you give me in order to save the lost soul?"[19] A freewill offering

---

[19] S. Nengzakhup, *Amazing Mizo Missions* (Bangalore: SAIACS Press, 2012), 58.

is cast into the box and is passed on from house to house. When the roaming or visiting is completed the box is opened and the amount received is given for the support of mission work of the church.

Conclusion

Although I could describe many more fundraising systems and practices of church members in Mizoram, time and space do not permit. What I would like to emphasize is that if we are willing at all to give to the One who gave his life for us, then poverty is not a valid excuse for not serving the Lord by giving. Rev. Canon Chye Ann Soh, the EURASIA Director of the Church Mission Society, commented on the generous giving of the Mizo Christians: "Though they are poor, they always set aside 10 percent of whatever they have to support missions: rice, firewood, food. They go without so that the Gospel can be shared."[20] It is neither poverty nor richness that motivates people to serve the Lord but the willingness to reciprocate the love and gift of the Lord.

Discussion Questions

1. Can this Mizo model of fundraising be replicated elsewhere, or is it culture-specific?
2. What are the strengths and weaknesses of this fundraising model?

---

20 Bravo, *Inspire*, 20ff.

Chapter 5 Response

by Sung-Chan Kwon

Thank you for sharing this great example of successful mission fundraising by the Mizoram Presbyterian Church (MPC). I believe this is an exemplary story that all churches should listen to, whether they are in the traditionally labeled "sending" countries or on the "receiving" end. As Rev. Colney emphasized, "poverty is no excuse for not serving the Lord by giving" and, "it is neither poverty nor richness that motivates people to serve the Lord but the willingness to reciprocate the love and gift of the Lord." The presentation was effective at pinpointing the keys to success. In my response, I will briefly summarize the presentation, look at the resulting factors, and suggest a few additional ideas that we need to reflect on.

Summary

According to the presentation, the success of the MPC's mission fundraising was based on the integration of three significant factors:

First, the three-self theory direction that missionaries took led to the successful fundraising. Missionaries who went to Mizoram taught the local believers (Mizos) to be self-supporting from the very beginning. As the author explains, "The Mizoram Presbyterian Church is what we call a 'three-self church' in the sense that it is financially self-supported, self-administered, and self-propagating." In 1890, John L. Nevius, a missionary in China, was invited to Korea to share his three-self method and the missionaries adopted it, which was later called the "Nevius method." As a result, the early Korean churches went through similar experiences as the Mizo churches.

Second, the giving and generous culture of the Mizo people augmented what they had learned from the missionaries. The self-supporting principle introduced by the early missionaries was well received by the Mizos because of their culture of hospitality.

Rev. Colney pointed out that the "Mizos received the teaching of generous giving both from their missionaries and their forefathers." Even though the community is less affluent than the outside world, the Mizo Christians shared what they had for the expansion of the Kingdom of God.

Third, the contextualized method of the fundraising was a key factor to success. Rev. Colney introduced thirteen different mission fundraising methods practiced by the Mizo Christian community, adding that he could go on describing more. The variety of different methods practiced by the MPC members represented not only their creativity but also their commitment to the Kingdom of God. These were well contextualized for the members to put into practice.

Analysis

I will now evaluate the above factors from a contemporary perspective. The reason that missionaries bring money from their home country or other external sources is not because they do not know the self-supporting principle. Rather, they think that current conditions on the field do not warrant the application of the principle. They insist on the need of priming the water before they apply the rule. It takes courage to adhere to and practice the principle in such a situation. It is only possible when missionaries understand the proper long-term direction of mission rather than focusing on the achievement of visible tasks. I salute the early Mizoram missionaries who were able to achieve this.

The same was true of the Mizo people. When they received the Good News at the early stage, it was natural to lean on outside sources to fund the ministry. It was difficult to recognize that spreading the Good News and supporting ministries were their own responsibility. A few years ago, I met the archbishop of the Solomon Islands to discuss the implementation of the Bible translation project in the region. He told me that his congregation believed that mission was something outsiders did on their behalf, and that unless his congregation's understanding of mission changed, any additional mission projects done by outsiders would not add much significance to the mission work in his country. Even though the Mizo community has a giving and generous culture, it would have been easy to accept funds from missionaries who came from more affluent countries. Nevertheless, the Mizo Christians took responsibility for the Kingdom of God. Their action deserves praise.

I believe that these contextualized fundraising methods practiced by MPC members were made possible by the principle-based direction of the early missionaries and the willingness of the Mizos. One of the popular methods for outside donors to encourage local participation in fundraising is called the "matching fund." When the method is used prematurely without local readiness, it can produce the side effect of members lending money to each other or borrowing money from friends to receive the maximum amount of external funding. In the MPC's case, the members' willingness to give permeated those practices. The fact that individuals have the freedom to allocate their tithes to different ministries such as pastoral ministries, evangelism, and/or local church ministry demonstrates their self-initiative and voluntary participation. There surely are many lessons to be learned from Mizoram's case, not just from the methods utilized by them, but from how fundamental principles were contextualized in their situation.

Further Questions and Reflection

The integration of three important factors led the MPC to succeed in their mission fundraising: the proper direction and perseverance of the pioneer missionaries, the willingness of the Mizo people to give, and the use of contextualized methods based on the locals' willingness.

The author questions whether the Mizo model of fundraising can be replicated elsewhere or is culture-specific. Before answering the question, I'd like to view the Mizo case from a different perspective by asking another question: Is their fundraising model sustainable? If yes, what makes it sustainable? Is it sustainable based on the generous culture of the Mizo community? Although I pointed out three factors of success, those factors are not necessarily permanent ones. The early missionaries have passed away and we do not expect the Mizo community to keep receiving missionaries. Their generous culture is not necessarily permanent either—it could be different in successive generations. Future economic growth could have an impact on their culture as well. In such situations, their contextualized fundraising methods may no longer work. That is exactly what we, the Korean church, have experienced. As the Jewish exiles remembered Jerusalem by the rivers of Babylon, we miss the time when our forefathers brought us what they had for the Kingdom of God.

At this point we have to think of another principle that truly makes the three-self principle possible, the fourth self that Paul Hiebert called "self-theologizing." I will limit the discussion of this phrase to the question that Hiebert first asked: "Do young churches have the right to read and interpret the Scriptures for themselves?"[21] In order for the successful case of MPC to be sustained by the integration of mission, culture, and contextualized methods, it is necessary not only to be self-governing, self-supporting, and self-propagating, but to have the ability to read God's Word on their own so that they can continuously participate in God's mission.

The author asks about the strengths and weaknesses of this fundraising model. I believe that MPC members should ask themselves if these practices are based on their own reading and interpreting of the Scriptures. Are their practices the result of their deep understanding of God's mission based on the Bible and their willingness to participate in it? If they answer yes, this is one of the absolute best cases of fundraising practices. If they hesitate to answer, then the model might only be valid as long as the same culture and conditions exist.

Rather than being remembered as an example where MPC once succeeded in mission, including mission fundraising, I pray that it will continue to participate in God's mission until the day the Lord comes and become a living church that challenges the church worldwide.

---

21 Paul Hiebert, *Anthropological Insights for Missionaries* (Grand Rapids: Baker Book House, 1985), 196.

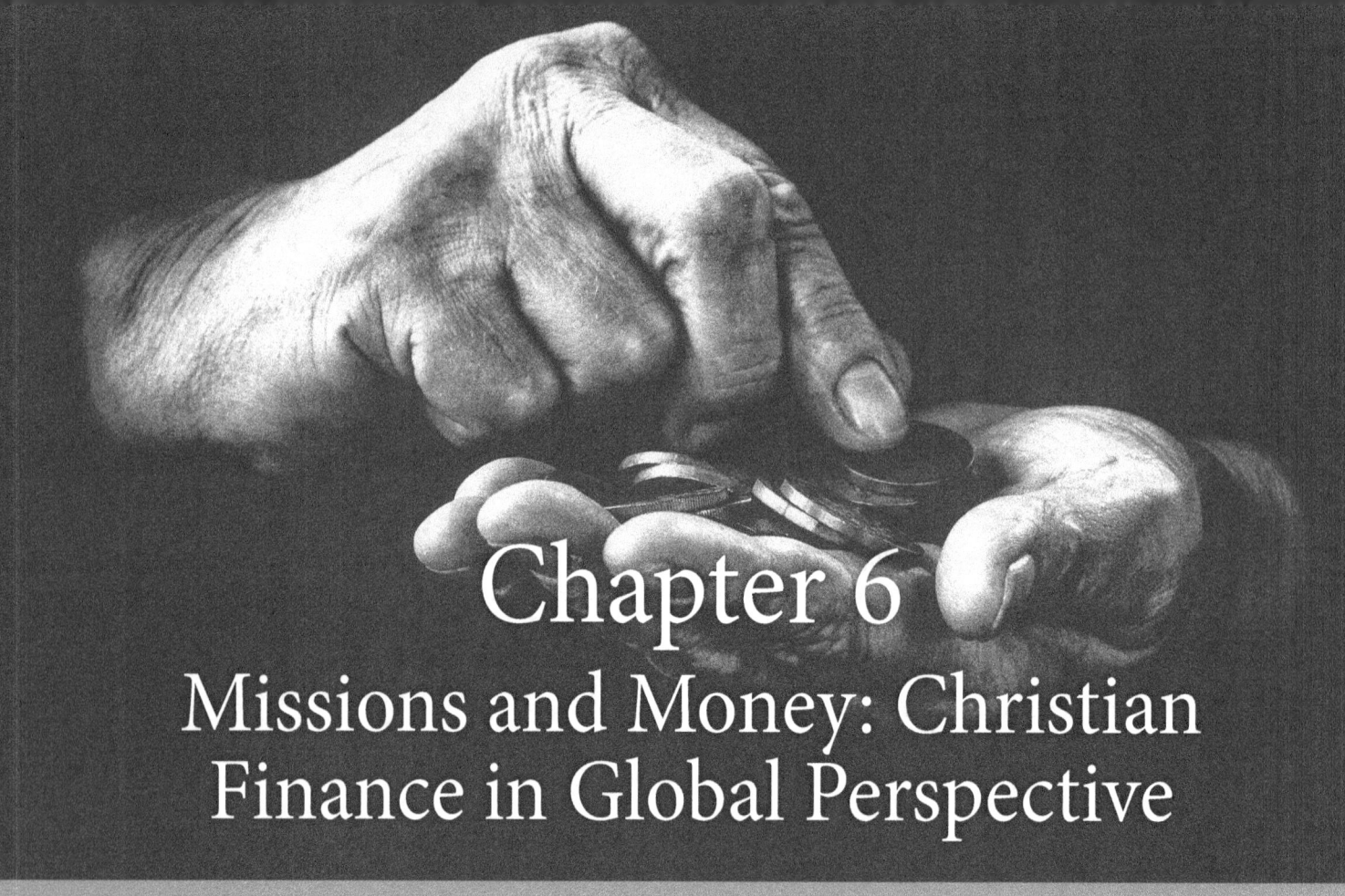

Chapter 6
Missions and Money: Christian Finance in Global Perspective

by Gina A. Zurlo

If one hundred Christians represented all of World Christianity (2.5 billion Christians in 2020), nineteen would live on more than US$100 a day; sixty-three would live on $10–$100 a day, and eighteen would live on less than $10 a day. Total Christian income in 2020 was US$32.5 trillion, and the highest concentration of Christian income was in Europe (36.5 percent), with Northern America close behind (29.7 percent). However, there exists a deep inequality in the global Christian family as it relates to money, since Europe and North America are home to only 33 percent of the world's Christians, with the majority living in Asia, Africa, Latin America, and Oceania. That is, the North has the money, but the South has the Christians. Utilizing findings from the *World Christian Encyclopedia*, this case study provides an overview of global Christian finance, including how Christian wealth is distributed around the world, what Christians spend their money on, and how this potentially impacts the missionary movement worldwide. In particular, significant questions arise concerning missions and money with the shift of missionary sending from the North to the South. What does it mean for "reverse mission" if most Christian resources are not shifting with it?

Global Christianity 1900–2020

The shift of Christianity from the Global North to South is well-documented and one of the main findings of the *World Christian Encyclopedia*. Although Christianity maintained nearly the same proportion of the world's population over the twentieth century (34.5 percent in 1900 and 32.3 percent in 2020), its internal makeup changed dramatically.[1] In 1900, 82 percent of all Christians lived in the Global North, the historic areas of "Christendom" in Europe and North America. By 1970, the percentage of Christians in the North had fallen to 57 percent and it dropped below 50 percent

---

1 This section is adapted from Todd M. Johnson and Gina A. Zurlo, *World Christian Encyclopedia*, 3rd ed. (Edinburgh: Edinburgh University Press, 2019), 4–32.

Missions and Money: Christian Finance in Global Perspective

Figure 6.1: Christians by Continent, 2020

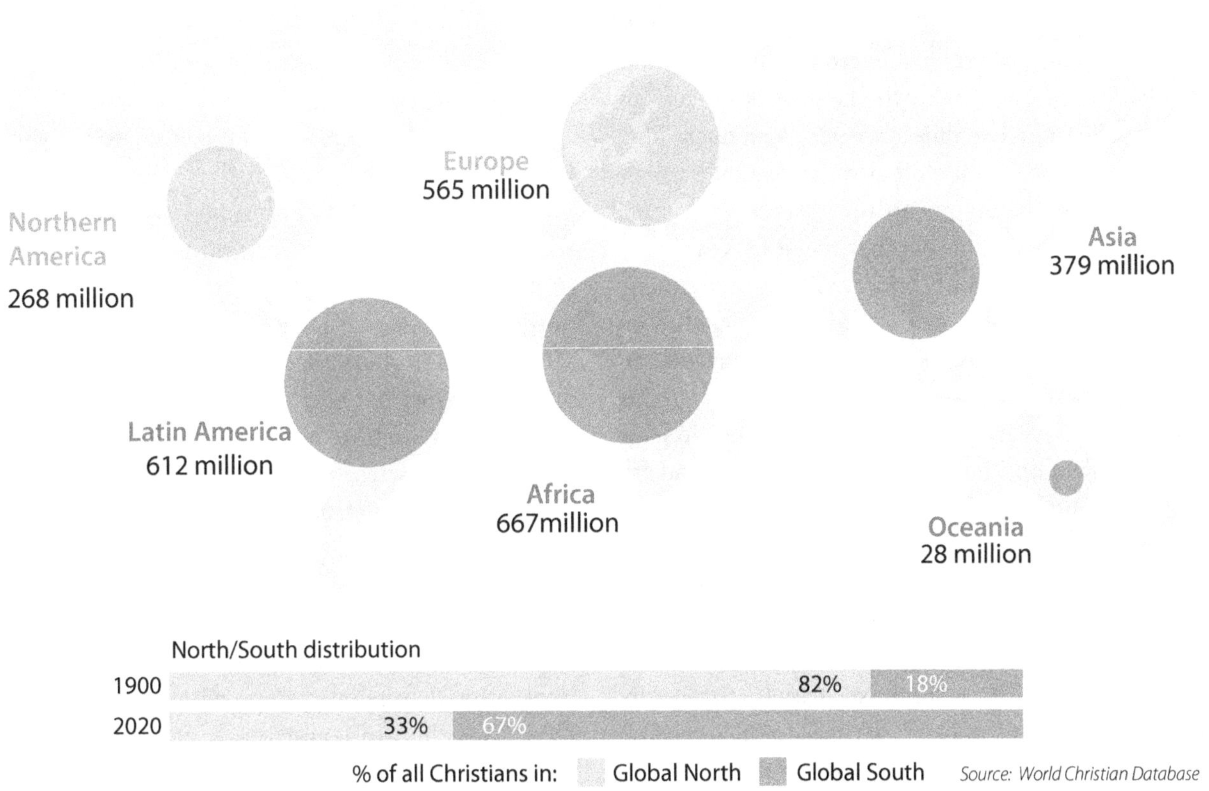

Northern America
268 million

Europe
565 million

Asia
379 million

Latin America
612 million

Africa
667 million

Oceania
28 million

North/South distribution
1900   82%   18%
2020   33%   67%

% of all Christians in: Global North   Global South   *Source: World Christian Database*

Source: Todd M. Johnson and Gina A. Zurlo, "World Christian Database," 3rd ed. (Edinburgh: Edinburgh University Press, 2019), 4.

sometime around 1980. In 2020, Christians in the Global South represent 67 percent of all Christians in the world, projected to reach 77 percent by 2050. It is also important to note that the Global South has a much larger overall population than the North: over 6.2 billion versus nearly 1.1 billion.

From only 1.7 percent in 1900, by 2050 an estimated 39 percent of all Christians in the world will live in Africa. Africa is also the continent with the most Christians, surpassing Latin America in 2018 (which surpassed Europe in 2014). In 1900, the ten countries with the most Christians included only one in the Global South: Brazil. In 2020 the picture is much different, with eight of the ten countries with the most Christians in the Global South.

Table 6.1: Christians by Country, 1900 & 2020

Country	Christians 1900	Country	Christians 2020
United States	73,712,200	United States	244,312,534
Russia	62,544,600	Brazil	193,859,446
Germany	41,533,000	Mexico	128,229,027
France	40,731,100	Russia	117,847,582
UK	37,125,000	China	106,030,000
Italy	32,903,000	Philippines	99,576,796
Ukraine	28,501,000	Nigeria	95,357,701
Poland	22,049,500	DR Congo	85,120,101
Spain	18,794,670	Ethiopia	67,491,215
Brazil	17,319,000	India	67,356,000

Source: Todd M. Johnson and Gina A. Zurlo, eds., "World Christian Database" (Leiden/Boston: Brill www.worldchristiandatabase.org). Used by permission.

The shift to the Global South is not just a demographic one. The languages of Christianity are changing. Already by 1980, Spanish was the leading language of church membership around the world due to Latin America and today the languages spoken by the most Christians include Brazilian Portuguese and Mandarin Chinese. This shift also means that there is increased potential for positive interactions between Christians and adherents of other religions. Churches in North America and Europe are experiencing an increase in religious and ethnic diversity due to migration, which sometimes leads to misconceptions and fears of people of other religions. Christians in the Global South have lived in religiously diverse contexts for generations and have the opportunity to lead by example of how to show hospitality to neighbors of other religions. At the same time, the spread of Christianity in the south sometimes clashes with other religions, such as across the Sahel in Africa, where Islam in the north meets Christianity in the south. This contrasts with the relative security Christians in the North live with, but hearkens back to the reality of persecution experienced by the early church.

The human needs of Christians are also shifting. The rapid growth of Christianity in the twentieth century has occurred in places that, overall, have a lower quality of life. Looking at data related to socioeconomics, health, and gender reveals the chasm between Christians in the North versus South. Much of the Global South deals with serious issues related to poverty and proper health care. Countries that have been hardest hit by HIV/AIDS such as Botswana, Zimbabwe, and Eswatini are also countries where Christianity is flourishing. The growth of Christianity in poorer regions implies not only a different reading of the Bible, but a different experience of the Bible. An emphasis on the Holy Spirit, healing miracles, and deliverance from demonic powers is common in many churches in the South. While many Christians in the North live in in relative affluence and safety, many in the South live on the edge of existence. Meeting the social needs of people is integral to Christian witness, theology, and ministry.

Global Christianity would not exist without Christian mission, and that is shifting as well. The concept of who is a missionary has evolved substantially since the beginning of the twentieth century, making it much more difficult to assess how many missionaries there are in the world. The sending of long-term missionaries from the West is on the decline, but since the 1980s and 1990s there has been a dramatic explosion in the number of short-term "missionaries," particularly youth, who spend as little as a week outside their own cultural context performing an array of service-oriented projects. Missionaries here are defined as Christians of all traditions who cross national borders for a period of two years or more. Not included are short-term international missionaries or national workers who serve in their own countries. A prominent trend in missions today is the increase of national workers, many of whom are often working cross-culturally in their own countries. Africa and Asia are home to nearly two million national workers each, and Latin America to more than nine hundred thousand.

North America (143,000 missionaries) and Europe (80,900 missionaries) continue to send the bulk of foreign missionaries today (53 percent), but Brazil, South Korea, the Philippines, and China each send large numbers as well. This is partly because of more resources available in the North versus the South for investment in foreign mission, and because of the longer history of the foreign missionary movement in the West. Brazil, however, is an exception; most of its missionaries are Catholics working in Latin America, the United States, and Europe.

Figure 6.2: Largest Missionary Sending and Receiving Countries, 2020

Source: Todd M. Johnson and Gina A. Zurlo, "World Christian Database," 3rd ed. (Edinburgh: Edinburgh University Press, 2019), 32.

Christian missionaries are sent from everywhere to everywhere, but the map above shows a pattern of predominantly Christian countries receiving the most missionaries. Indeed, the countries with the most Christians receive the largest number of missionaries. This makes some sense if one considers that invitations are a major avenue for missionary sending. Sponsorships are also more likely in places with large Christian populations. However, there remains a contradiction from the standpoint of introducing Christianity to people of other religions. One dramatic example is Brazil (a majority Christian country), which received a total of twenty thousand missionaries, whereas Bangladesh (a majority Muslim country) with as many people, received only one thousand missionaries.

The Global South is home to the new "centers" of World Christianity while the gradual decline of Christianity in the West continues. The shift of Christianity to the Global South raises an important question about the state of Christian resources. Are they also shifting?

Global Christian Finance

A basic resource for any Christian activity is money.[2] Christians often account for money with greater precision than for any other resource. Money plays an important role in denominations, churches, mission, and evangelism. Table 6.2 includes data on overall population, income, and wealth and Christian population, income, and wealth by globe, continent, and United Nations regions. Christian income is calculated by multiplying a country's Gross National Income per capita by the number of Christians. In 2020, the total income of World Christianity was US$48.6 trillion. The highest concentration of Christian income was in Europe (36.5 percent, home to 22.4 percent of all Christians worldwide) with North America close behind (29.7 percent; home to 10.6 percent of all Christians worldwide). Africa, home to 26.5 percent of all Christians in the world, held only 4.9 percent of all Christian income.

---

[2] This section is adapted from Todd M. Johnson and Kenneth R. Ross, *Atlas of Global Christianity* (Edinburgh: Edinburgh University Press), 296–297, and Johnson and Zurlo, *World Christian Encyclopedia*, 941.

Table 6.2: Distribution of Annual Global Income and Wealth, 2020

	Population (monetary values in Billions $US)						Christians (monetary values in Billions $US)						Ecclesiastical crime $US p.a.
	Population	%	Income	%	Wealth	%	Christians	%	Income	%	Wealth	%	
Africa	1,352,622,000	17.4	6,022	5.1	2,654	0.8	667,169,000	26.5	2,404	4.9	1,149	0.7	1,824,613,000
Eastern Africa	457,440,000	5.9	910	0.8	228	0.1	303,183,000	12.0	601	1.2	146	0.1	508,606,000
Middle Africa	178,959,000	2.3	475	0.4	192	0.1	149,426,000	5.9	395	0.8	165	0.1	225,792,000
Northern Africa	246,049,000	3.2	2,317	2.0	1,085	0.3	11,672,000	0.5	109	0.2	23	0.0	64,345,000
Southern Africa	67,595,000	0.9	782	0.7	858	0.3	55,818,000	2.2	641	1.3	705	0.4	404,733,000
Western Africa	402,579,000	5.2	1,539	1.3	291	0.1	147,070,000	5.8	657	1.4	109	0.1	621,137,000
Asia	4,623,454,000	59.3	57,531	48.8	107,953	33.6	378,735,000	15.0	4,998	10.3	9,074	5.6	4,234,800,000
Central Asia	73,821,000	0.9	786	0.7	226	0.1	5,609,000	0.2	114	0.2	19	0.0	106,523,000
Eastern Asia	1,663,619,000	21.3	29,913	25.4	90,222	28.1	128,787,000	5.1	2,440	5.0	7,281	4.5	1,812,092,000
South Asia	1,935,616,000	24.8	12,513	10.6	7,196	2.2	76,147,000	3.0	489	1.0	318	0.2	362,699,000
Southeastern Asia	669,016,000	8.6	7,407	6.3	4,978	1.5	153,102,000	6.1	1,555	3.2	1,041	0.6	1,547,856,000
Western Asia	281,382,000	3.6	6,912	5.9	5,331	1.7	15,090,000	0.6	399	0.8	415	0.3	405,630,000
Europe	743,390,000	9.5	24,072	20.4	86,044	26.8	565,416,000	22.4	17,737	36.5	60,601	37.5	18,896,314,000
Eastern Europe	290,776,000	3.7	6,306	5.4	4,756	1.5	244,778,000	9.7	5,259	10.8	3,870	2.4	3,909,715,000
Northern Europe	105,863,000	1.4	4,452	3.8	20,695	6.4	74,184,000	2.9	3,148	6.5	14,397	8.9	4,708,376,000
Southern Europe	151,553,000	1.9	4,671	4.0	20,366	6.3	120,547,000	4.8	3,739	7.7	16,243	10.0	3,457,099,000
Western Europe	195,197,000	2.5	8,644	7.3	40,227	12.5	125,908,000	5.0	5,591	11.5	26,091	16.1	6,821,123,000
Latin America	664,474,000	8.5	9,054	7.7	8,054	2.5	611,964,000	24.3	8,330	17.1	7,410	4.6	5,192,427,000
Caribbean	44,679,000	0.6	391	0.3	208	0.1	37,719,000	1.5	327	0.7	173	0.1	282,718,000
Central America	184,127,000	2.4	2,676	2.3	2,326	0.7	176,298,000	7.0	2,560	5.3	2,226	1.4	1,524,064,000
South America	435,667,000	5.6	5,987	5.1	5,519	1.7	397,947,000	15.8	5,443	11.2	5,011	3.1	3,385,645,000
North America	369,159,000	4.7	19,849	16.8	108,057	33.6	267,944,000	10.6	14,450	29.7	78,714	48.7	21,234,162,000
Oceania	42,384,000	0.5	1,318	1.1	8,842	2.7	27,606,000	1.1	730	1.5	4,802	3.0	1,209,836,000
Australia/New Zealand	30,233,000	0.4	1,271	1.1	8,797	2.7	16,363,000	0.6	688	1.4	4,761	2.9	1,139,825,000
Melanesia	10,909,000	0.1	41	0.0	39	0.0	10,069,000	0.4	36	0.1	35	0.0	59,631,000
Micronesia	541,000	0.0	3	0.0	2	0.0	501,000	0.0	2	0.0	2	0.0	3,975,000
Polynesia	701,000	0.0	4	0.0	4	0.0	673,000	0.0	4	0.0	4	0.0	6,404,000
Global total	7,795,482,000	100.0	117,847	100.0	321,604	100.0	2,518,834,000	100.0	48,648	100.0	161,751	100.0	52,592,000,000

Source: Todd M. Johnson and Gina A. Zurlo, "World Christian Encyclopedia," 3rd ed. (Edinburgh: Edinburgh University Press, 2019), 941.

Christian wealth is an application of the World Institute for Development Economics Research of the United Nations University measurement of net worth, or household wealth. Net worth per capita by country is multiplied by the number of Christians in the country, giving an overview of the current assets held by Christians as a whole in the country. North America is home to nearly half of all Christian wealth (48.7 percent), with Europe at 37.5 percent. Africa holds just 0.7 percent of all Christian wealth, Asia 5.6 percent, and Latin America 4.6 percent (see chart below).

The income and wealth distribution of Christians around the world is very unequal. While the majority of Christians are coping or well off, a significant minority are poor, with some living in absolute poverty. Some 325 million Christians live in the world's twenty-nine poorest countries; of these, 97 percent live in Africa. The pair of graphs below illustrate the inequality of Christian presence versus Christian income in the world.

Figure 6.3: Percentage of World Christians vs. Income

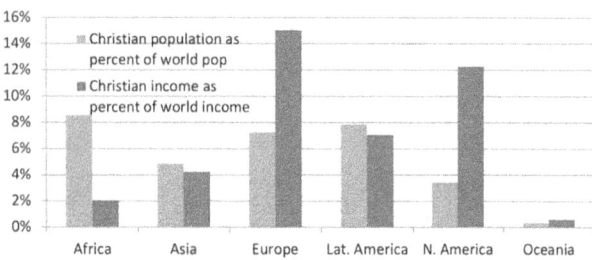

Source: Todd M. Johnson and Gina A. Zurlo, eds., "World Christian Database" (Leiden/Boston www.worldchristiandatabase.org).

Figure 6.4: Christian Population/Income, 2020

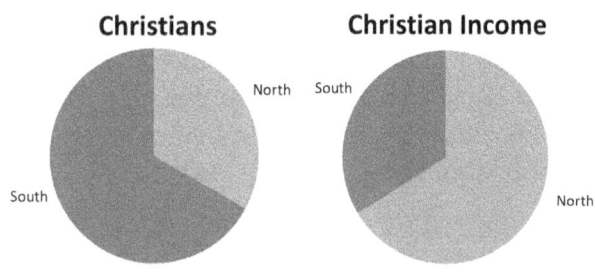

Source: Todd M. Johnson and Gina A. Zurlo, eds., "World Christian Database" (Leiden/Boston: accessed January 2021, www.worldchristiandatabase.org).

Despite such great differences in the incomes of Christians, the church is largely financially self-supporting, relying on the local resources of its members. The personal incomes of the poorest Christians average roughly US$1,300 per year, but their churches operate with a combined income of US$1.8 billion per year, running ministerial and relief programs of all kinds. Of course, uneven distribution of personal wealth exists not only between countries, but also within countries. Poor Christians are citizens of countries that are also home to relatively affluent fellow Christians.

Calculating Christian income and wealth naturally leads to investigating what Christians do with their financial resources: potential versus actual Christian giving.[3] Potential giving is defined here as a 10 percent tithe of Christian income. Data on giving patterns of Christians to secular causes, churches, denominations, and parachurch organizations are not available from organizational financial records, so the percentage of Christian income donated is estimated. Using 2.3 percent of Christian income as the estimate for donations to Christian causes in the United States, each country is assigned a higher or lower percentage, with the lowest percentage set at 0.5 percent.[4] Doing these calculations allows for comparison between Christian population, income, and giving, seen by continent below. For example, Asia is home to 15 percent of the world's Christians, who earn just 10 percent of global Christian income and contribute 6 percent of all Christian giving. Among wealthier continents, Oceania and North America represent larger shares of global Christian giving than of income, while Europe's share of total giving is less than its share of Christian income.

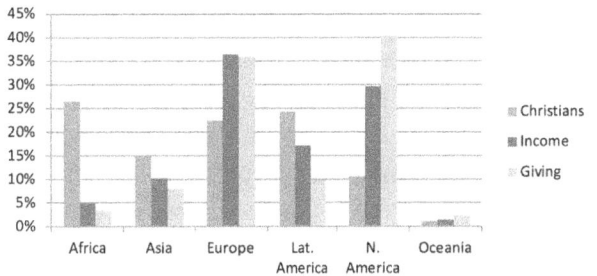

Figure 6.5: Christian Population, Christian Income, and Christian Giving, 2020

Source: Todd M. Johnson and Gina A. Zurlo, eds., "World Christian Database" (Leiden/Boston: accessed January 2021, www.worldchristiandatabase.org).

Most (perhaps upward of 80 percent) Christian expenditures are dedicated to the pastoral ministries of the churches in the home countries of the givers. A much smaller amount is spent on home missions or parachurch organizations in those same countries, with about the least amount given to foreign missions. Much of this money, however, is spent on work among Christians (in the case of foreign missions) or in affluent countries that already have large Christian populations (in the case of home missions). As a result, a very small proportion of total Christian expenditure is actually directed toward people without access to the Christian message. This finding pairs with that related to missionary sending and receiving above. The countries with the most money and the most Christians receive the most resources (money and personnel).

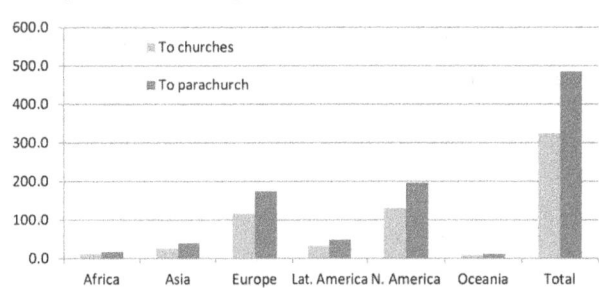

Figure 6.6: Giving to Church Versus Parachurch

Source: Todd M. Johnson and Gina A. Zurlo, eds., "World Christian Database" (Leiden/Boston: accessed January 2021, www.worldchristiandatabase.org).

The last variable that is sadly connected to missions and money is financial fraud.[5] Nonprofit organizations, especially those that begin as small, under-resourced volunteer run organizations, face tough challenges in combating financial fraud, which is a well-documented

---

[3] See Todd M. Johnson, Gina A. Zurlo, and Albert W. Hickman, "Embezzlement in the Global Christian Community," *The Review of Faith and International Affairs* 12, no. 2 (2015): 74–84.

[4] "Giving USA 2012: The Annual Report on Philanthropy for the Year 2011: Executive Summary," GUSA (Giving USA Foundation), 2012, accessed March 23, 2015, http://www.jjco.com/resources/pdf/2012_Giving_USA_Report.pdf. GUSA (Giving USA Foundation). 2012. Countries that are not in the index are allocated weighted averages for their respective United Nations regions, except countries in Oceania, which are allocated the continental weighted average.

[5] Johnson, Zurlo, and Hickman, "Embezzlement."

global problem. These organizations are so myopic in their mission focused vision that they neglect basic financial concerns. Nonprofits also tend to be more trusting of their employees, assuming that they share the organization's philanthropic goals. Charities that experience embezzlement try to handle it quickly and quietly to avoid ruining their reputation. Most nonprofit fraud goes unreported. Fraud also happens in churches, both large and small. Christians are particularly susceptible to affinity fraud that exploits the trust that exists within their shared faith community. Often in these cases, a trusted pastor or other leader makes a case for using money in particular ways that might seem like a "grey area," but members of the community want to avoid confronting their respected leaders, so it goes unchecked. If we apply findings from the Association of Certified Fraud Examiners to Christian giving, the estimated annual total of US$52.6 billion embezzled exceeds the worldwide church's foreign missions expenditures of US$46.9 billion. Most cases of embezzlement are kept private or swept under the carpet, but each year many thefts of over US$1 million each are uncovered and publicized in the media. Of the top recent massive embezzlements of Christian funds, many occurred in the United States and Europe by presidents, officials, treasurers, and pastors of various church and parachurch organizations. There have also been an alarming number of Ponzi schemes involving Christian leaders, both as perpetrators and as victims. That more money is stolen from Christian organizations than is given to Christian missions has been the reality for many decades and appears unlikely to change.

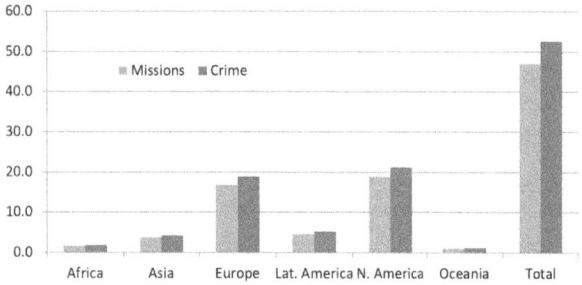

Figure 6.7: Missions Giving vs. Ecclesiastical Crime

Source: Todd M. Johnson and Gina A. Zurlo, eds., "World Christian Database" (Leiden/Boston: accessed January 2021, worldchristiandatabase.org).

"Reverse Mission" but Not "Reverse Finance"

World Christianity is rife with uncomfortable realities. The stability of Christians in the North is contrasted with serious needs of Christians everywhere else in the world. Christians in Africa, Asia, and Latin America have fewer physicians, higher infant mortality rates, lower life expectancies, and higher rates of HIV and malaria than Christians in Europe and North America. Women in Africa, for example, are often disadvantaged in education, the labor force, and access to health care. China and India are ramping up their economic power, but Asian cities are some of the most polluted in the world. Christians in the Middle East have left the region in droves in the twenty-first century due to war and conflict. Poverty in Latin America is rampant; Haiti, a majority Christian country, ranks the lowest on the Human Development Index in the Western Hemisphere. Christians in island nations in Polynesia, Melanesia, and Micronesia have very real fears related to climate change and rising sea levels, which threaten their way of life. Deep imbalances around the world in opportunities for Christians and choices available to them are going to remain a challenge for the global Christian community.

The most personal assets of Christians around the world are primarily held by North American and European Christians despite the shift of Christianity's population to the Global South. This reveals yet another deep inequality in the global Christian family. What are churches in the North supposed to do with their money? Simply sending it to the South surely is not the answer. Twentieth century styles of missionary engagement are also surely over. Christians in the Global South are taking up the mantle of missions and bringing the Gospel to the least reached places (e.g., East Asians in Central Asia), while others are bringing a renewed faith back to old colonial masters (e.g., sub-Saharan Africans in Western Europe). Diaspora is also changing the face of mission and blurring the lines of who is and who isn't a missionary. If "reverse mission" (a term that does not quite make sense if mission is "from everywhere, to everywhere") is the latest twenty-first century trend in mission, we are certainly not experiencing "reverse finance" along with it. Can missions be done without substantial financial resources? As Christianity continues to move southward and into poorer areas, churches must develop mechanisms for global sharing that do not distort local, national, and regional initiative and responsibility.

When I was teaching mission and global Christianity courses at an evangelical undergraduate institution in the United States, I asked my students to do a brain storming session on "who is a missionary." What is the difference, I asked, between a Christian working for an organization overseas—indeed, out of their Christian conviction—and a missionary proper? After deconstructing colonialism, imperialism, racism, and all other "-isms" related to global missions, one student blurted out, "It's the money!" The class went briefly silent and then a chorus of agreement rang out. They largely concluded that a Christian is a missionary if they raise full-time support to go overseas and "do ministry." This is a largely white, Western twentieth century way of understanding mission. But is there still truth to it? Is it really all about the money? Or does Christian history give us other models of cross-cultural ministry that actually fit better with the makeup of World Christianity in the twenty-first century? All Christians were Asian at the time of Christ, and the Global South was home to over half of all Christians from the beginning of Christianity until the year 923. For over one thousand years after that, Christians in the North dominated Christian demographics. By the time of the sixteenth century reformations, 92 percent of all Christians were Europeans. In the twentieth century, a dramatic turnaround resulted in the majority of Christians, once again, living in the Global South—just like during the time of Christ.[6] As this trend continues, perhaps we need to turn to Christianity's ancient past to help us understand the future.

Discussion Questions

1. What are some ways forward to recognize and respond to the growing inequality of financial resources that exists in World Christianity? What are some theological, missiological, and practical responses to this growing problem?

2. How do the meaning and methods of mission change if the missionary endeavor is not backed by huge financial resources, as has been the pattern in Western missionary sending?

3. Christian financial giving to missions is generally very low, with more money stolen from churches than given to missions. Although this is striking, does it matter? Must mission be inextricably tied to money? Is there mission without money?

---

6 Johnson and Zurlo, *World Christian Encyclopedia*, 4.

Chapter 6 Response

by Daeshik Jo

Overall Opinion

Gina's presentation helped us see the big picture for global Christian finance, and how it trended during a mid to long-term period. In particular, the data by continent spanning 120 years showed us the reality of the uneven distribution of global Christian wealth, in a very meaningful analysis.

The statistical data on the number of Christians, wealth, and giving compared across continents were helpful. The information on fraud and abuse in church and mission finances was revealing. The questions about "reverse mission," "reverse finance," and changes in the concept of who a missionary is were timely.

Building on Gina's analysis, I believe the following issues require further consideration in the future:

Global Christian Population and Wealth Trends

The wealth and Christian population imbalances and gaps between the Global South and Global North might be considered inevitable concomitants because the gaps in Christian wealth are a natural result of the gaps between the total wealth of the nations within their respective groups. To analyze the future trend of Christian finances, I think three additional variables are needed.

The first one is the change in giving across generations. When members donate, older generations concentrate their donations on churches and missions agencies, whereas younger generations tend to disperse their donations. Younger generations tend to make donations to NGOs and social causes in the world. Some of the funds donated by church members are moving to NGOs and civilian society organizations outside the church.[7] Such changes have been observed for more than ten years now. This is supposedly due to the change in values of the younger generation and their low confidence in the financial transparency of churches and missions organizations.

The second variable is the change in the method of solving the poverty and inequality problems in the international community. Since the 2000s, the international community's response to global issues has become more integrated, centered around the United Nations (UN), which contrasts with the past methods where individual countries chose their own way to respond. The nations are working toward common goals set by the UN since 2000, in fifteen-year terms (Millennium Development Goals, 2000–2015; Sustainable Development Goals [SDGs], 2015–2030). Some of these UN goals overlap with the service and charity activities of missionary work, and this has a profound impact on traditional missionary work, both directly and indirectly. Therefore, Christian giving and service that does not take this variable into account will lose significance.

The third variable is the increase of social welfare finances in the public sector. In Korea, as the government and public sector social welfare finances are increasing rapidly, the proportion of traditional religious institutions and NGOs is decreasing. In recent years, Korea's welfare sector expanded to account for one-third of the annual national budget. (During 2018–2019, the government's annual budget totaled approximately ₩500 trillion, and the welfare sector reached approximately ₩150 trillion.)

Financial Changes Since the COVID-19 Pandemic

Whether for Christians or the nations, the gap between the Global South and the Global North is a problem that cannot be resolved in a short period. To make things worse, the COVID-19 pandemic is slowing down the pace of resolving the gap, according to the recent UN agency UNDP analysis.[8]

Change in the Concept of a Missionary

Who is a missionary? This question from Gina's chapter is related to the issue of where to turn to for the finance needed for missions and its procurement. The traditional, Western, white-centered concept of a missionary, who relies totally on fundraising for his or her finance, is already changing in Korea. This change is taking place along with the discussions of bivocational ministry and self-supporting ministry. And there is a growing recognition that the existing mission model, which relies entirely on churches or church members for its finance, is no longer applicable.

Since the 2000s, many churches in Korea have established church-based NGOs, which is evidence of a tendency to deviate from the model of relying entirely on church members for missionary finance. Although the financial aspect is not the only reason for this phenomenon, it nevertheless reflects the limitations and shifts of finance. As NGOs are emerging as an important tool to handle the needs of this world, their importance is increasing as a major instrument of mission. For example, the total funding for international development cooperation NGOs in Korea amounted to ₩1.7 trillion in 2019, an amount comparable to the overseas grant assistance awarded by the Korean government.[9]

---

7 In Korea's case, the total amount of donations in 2017 was ₩13 trillion (₩8 trillion for individual donations, ₩4.600 trillion for corporate contributions (*National Tax Service Statistical Yearbook: 2008–2018*). There are no accurate statistics for churches and missions agencies.

8 "Combining the conservative scenario of the impact on school attendance (50 percent) with the moderate scenario of the impact on nutrition (25 percent), the simulations indicate that the aggregate global MPI [Multidimensional Poverty Index] across the 70 countries could increase from 0.095 to 0.156 in 2020, which is the same value as around 2011. So, the increase in deprivations because of COVID-19 may set poverty levels back by 9.1 years, with an additional 490 million people falling into multidimensional poverty across the 70 countries" (Sabina Alkire et al., "Charting Pathways out of Multidimensional Poverty: Achieving the SDGs," The United Nations Development Programme and Oxford Poverty and Human Development Initiative, 2000, 15, http://hdr.undp.org/sites/default/files/2020_mpi_report_en.pdf).

9 KCOC Policy Education Center, ed., *2019 Korean International Development Cooperation CSO Statistics Handbook* (Seoul: Korea NGO Council for Overseas Development Cooperation, 2020), 7.

Increased Demand for Transparency from Churches and Nonprofit Sectors

Regarding accounting corruption and fiscal transparency issues in Korea, negative cases of mission organizations or missionaries in churches are exposed less frequently than those of secular organizations. Gina's analysis, that the community tends to not raise issues regarding fiscal abuse "to avoid confronting their respected leaders," might also apply to situations in Korea. However, the society's trust in the church is very low in Korea.

On the other hand, accounting fraud cases of secular, nonprofit organizations have been exposed at high frequency in recent years. The public's negative perception of churches and missions organizations also increases whenever such fraud cases are exposed. As a result, there is a growing demand to strengthen transparency across the nonprofit sector, and accordingly, the government is strengthening its regulations. These stricter regulations for the nonprofit sector naturally require fiscal transparency from the church.

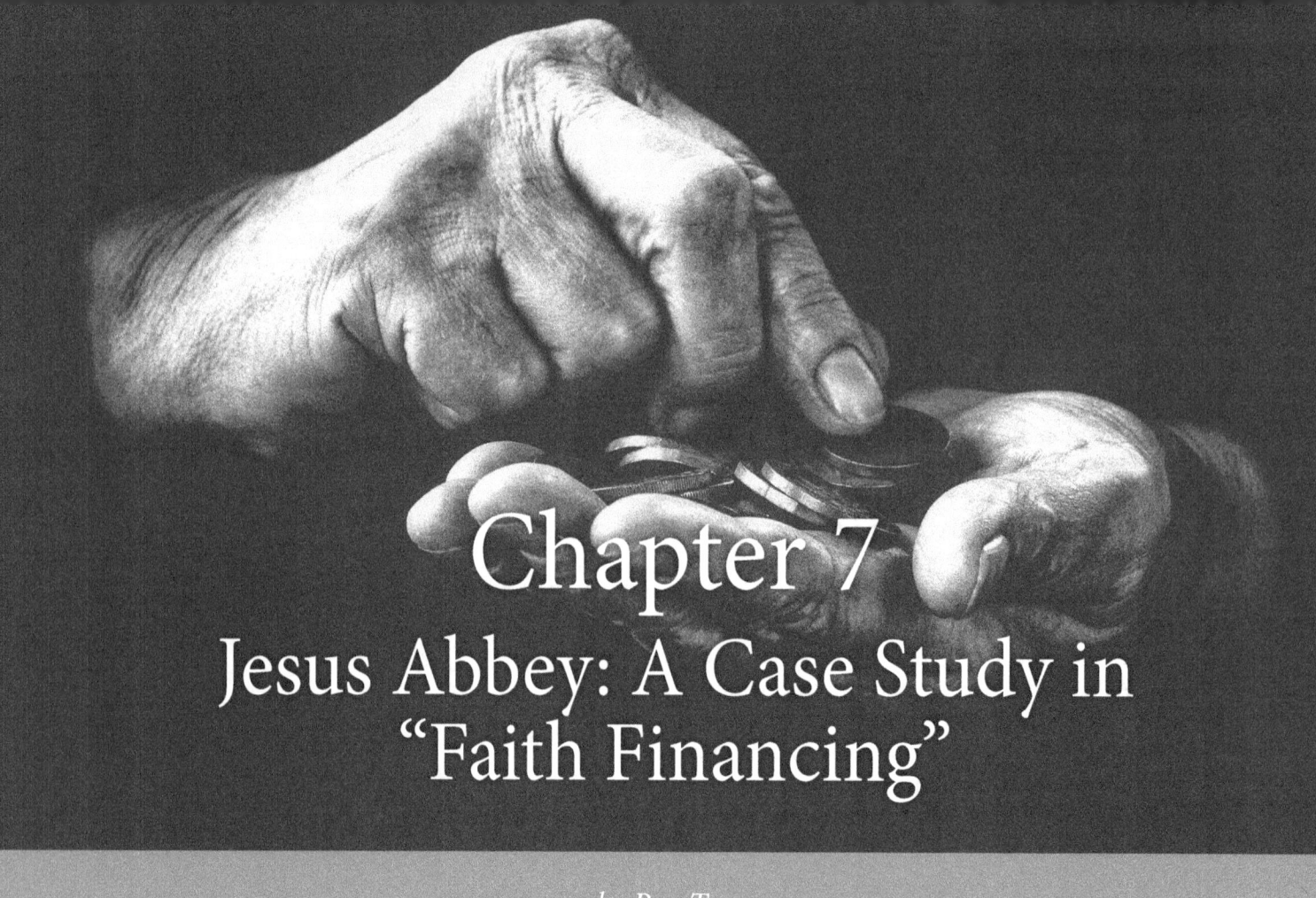

Chapter 7
Jesus Abbey: A Case Study in "Faith Financing"

by Ben Torrey

This chapter is an exploration of the concept of "faith financing," a direct translation of the Korean term used at Jesus Abbey, *mideum jejeung* (미듬재정).[1] We will look at what it means and how it is understood by the community of Jesus Abbey, its origins, how it is currently practiced, and the results.

Jesus Abbey is an intentional Christian community established to be a laboratory of Christian faith and life and dedicated to intercessory prayer. It is located in Taebaek City in the Taebaek Mountains near Korea's east coast. It was established in 1965 by Fr. Archer Torrey (Reuben Archer Torrey III), an Anglican priest, with his wife, Jane, their children, and a number of Korean men and women. Ben Torrey, the author of this chapter, is the son of the Torreys. He was involved as a teenager at the beginning and returned with his wife, Liz, in 2005. Ben and Liz Torrey are members of Jesus Abbey.

The information used is from Jesus Abbey documents and brochures, the writings of Fr. Archer Torrey and of Jane Torrey, and personal recollections by the author of conversations and experiences.

Faith Financing: The Concept

The concept of faith financing is generally understood by the members of Jesus Abbey to be a way to live life trusting in God for material provision without asking the help of others or any sort of fundraising. This is both personal and corporate. Before approving a membership request, which must be approved by a two-thirds majority of a members' meeting, the applicant's commitment to living this way is examined. Faith financing does not exclude earning money or receiving gifts, either personal or corporate. Funds received by members for speaking, teaching, or working go into the community's common fund. Gifts to individuals may be kept by the individual.

---

[1] In his English language writings, Fr. Archer Torrey used the term "faith mission."

When Fr. Torrey established Jesus Abbey, he intended it to be, among other things, a laboratory of Christian living. In an early brochure he wrote, "Jesus Abbey was founded in 1965 to be a house dedicated to intercessory prayer [and] … A training center—to teach '3D Theology' (Scripture, Tradition, Life) in these three scientific laboratories. (1. The individual and God. 2. The individual and the Christian community. 3. The community and the world)."

The intent of the first laboratory is to test the hypothesis that the promises of Holy Scripture referring to an individual's dependence on God may be trusted. Faith financing is an important aspect of that. There are several passages of Scripture that are considered fundamental to this laboratory. In the *Jesus Abbey Community Principles and Customs*,[2] we read the following:

> As a goal-oriented community we believe that there are effective methods for systematically engaging in economic living, but this is not our primary interest. Our primary interest is to do the will of God and to seek his kingdom and his righteousness (Matt. 6:33; Luke 12:33). If we participate in God's enterprises, then God will provide for us a place to live, clothing, education, and all other practical necessities.[3]

The above references Matthew 6:33, which ends an exhortation by Jesus beginning at verse twenty-five (a passage too long to quote here) calling on his hearers to trust God for their physical needs. The whole passage is fundamental to the Abbey community's perspective on faith financing. The statement about "effective methods" above refers to income producing activities.

Faith financing is the attempt to live out this and similar passages of Scripture by, as indicated above, seeking God's provision in all things rather than asking help from others.

Faith Financing: Its Origins

Faith financing as applied at Jesus Abbey developed from the teachings of Fr. Archer Torrey and his desire to see the concept tested in the first of the "three scientific laboratories" referred to above. The concept grew out of his own background and experience—both within his family legacy and in his own life. In his autobiography, "The Way of a Pioneer," he wrote:

> Both families [the families of his maternal grandfather, Francis Lorain Mallary, and paternal grandfather, Reuben Archer Torrey Sr.] knew how to live by faith. Both had, at various times, experiences of being suddenly penniless and having to choose between going into debt, going into a line of work that God had not authorized, soliciting funds, or simply depending on God to supply their daily bread.[4]

His grandfather, R. A. Torrey Sr., had been heavily influenced by George Mueller. Having read Mueller's book, *Life of Trust*, he "became personally convinced in the fall of 1888 that he should trust God directly for all of the needs of himself and his family… the venture was marked by intense conflict."[5] Torrey Sr. resolved never to borrow money for his needs or his work nor to ask for funds from anyone.

Archer Torrey began his journey of dependance on and obedience to God in college where he conducted an experiment for over two years to prove to his own satisfaction the existence of God. This story is detailed in "The Way of a Pioneer." He also lived it out in his marriage and ministry:

> Soon after this I lost my job because of the political situation and we lived like Elijah of old, being fed by the ravens. The "ravens" whom God used to feed us were black skinned brothers and sisters who accidentally heard about our situation. Our rich friends never knew we were in trouble. We never went hungry. Jane says that was her training for all the years since that time in which we've had to trust our faithful God for everything.[6]

---

2 This is a document developed and applied by the members as authoritative concerning how life at the Abbey is to be lived.

3 예수원 공동체 원칙과 습관 [*Yesuwon Gongdongchae Wonchik-gwa Seupgwan*; Jesus Abbey Community Principles and Customs], Section 3: Main Principles of Community Life; Sub-section C. Group Finances, fifth paragraph (unpublished translation by Deberniere Torrey). Hereinafter referred to as *Principles and Customs*.

4 Archer Torrey, "The Way of a Pioneer," (unpublished English manuscript), 4. Published in Korean as 대천덕 자서전: 개척자의길 [*Dae Cheon Duk Jaseojeon: Kaechukja-ui Gil*, Dae Cheon Duk's autobiography: The way of a pioneer], trans. Hye Won Yang (Hongsongsa, Seoul: 홍성사, 1998).

5 Roger Martin, *R. A. Torrey: Apostle of Certainty* (Murfreesboro, TN: Sword of the Lord Publishers, 1976), 77.

6 Torrey, "The Way of a Pioneer," 105.

His experience through the years, those he wrote about, and incidents retold in the family as well as experienced by the author, convinced him that if he were obedient to the will of God, God would provide for his needs. He wanted to test this in the greater context of a community of individuals beyond his own immediate family. This is what he sought to do through establishing Jesus Abbey.

In his autobiography, he details the process that led to the establishment of the Abbey, including a time of testing concerning obtaining the land on which it now stands. After relating the remarkable circumstances involved in getting the land, he wrote this:

> From that time to this our life has been a series of miracles. We have never asked for money or told people we were in need but the Lord has supplied.[7]

In describing the Abbey's life of prayer and God's provision of people as well as finances, he writes of an initially enthusiastic young man who could not stay the course:

> As the young man turned a bend in the road and disappeared from sight I saw another person coming up the hill to our camp. Sure enough, when he got to where I was standing he greeted me and said, "I've come to work." How I praised the Lord! That pattern has continued until now. Whenever anyone leaves, no matter how irreplaceable we think that person is, the Lord sends someone to take his place.[8]

Learning the Way of Faith

Setting up an experiment to test the concept of faith financing is one thing. Actually, carrying it out is another. From the beginning, the Abbey operated on a cash basis, trusting God to provide day to day in the spirit of collecting the manna in Exodus 16.[9]

Fr. Archer Torrey's practical application of faith financing included sharing publicly in newsletters and prayer letters how God had provided for the Abbey through the years, making it clear that the provision was in response to prayer. He expressed in an early newsletter that, while not advertising needs, he did respond to direct requests for information with specifics, but he asked people to seek the Lord's guidance as to whether or not to contribute.[10]

In newsletters and brochures, information was always provided on how to make financial contributions to Jesus Abbey. Another important principle of faith financing for him was that prayer for specific needs was an important way of gaining guidance from the Lord. He would pray for exact amounts required for various needs. Based on what came in, he would allocate the funds to these various needs.

This dependence upon God for provision had to be learned again and again. The principles as laid down in various documents and letters were learned the hard way. Jane Torrey relates one difficult lesson in *At the Table in the Wilderness: The Story of Jesus Abbey*. Excerpts from chapter 12, "Reprimand," follow:

> … the people in the village wanted to work with us and help us build our house … they said, "We don't care when you pay us." To enable them to work we had to have building material, and we borrowed money to buy it. Month after month, on the last day, we were able to pay our debts—it seemed. But then on [a] Saturday night in December 1968, the fact was laid bare that several months had gone by without squaring away our debts.
>
> How had we let this happen, when we knew from the beginning that God had said, "Let the funds available guide your actions, and don't get into debt"?
>
> Puzzled and disturbed, we searched Archer's journals to find out how the tide had turned and to find out when the debts had begun to pile up… It was a shock to realize, through this research, that every time we had made a bad move toward getting into debt, every time we had let ourselves be talked into borrowing money, some freak accident had happened in the barn …
>
> It seemed that God had been trying to warn us through these most unlikely accidents and we had been treating them as "mere, but costly coincidences," and not taking notice. Now we saw full well our mistake … It was merciful of God to take out his displeasure on the cattle, as it were, and not on the people. Now it was vital that we reckon with our errors and change course. We decided, from the next day, to charge nothing. We decided to buy only what we had money in hand for.[11]

---

7   Torrey, 120.
8   Torrey, 121.
9   *Principles and Customs*, Group Finances.
10 Read by the author within the past three years but now lost.

11 Jane Torrey, *At the Table in the Wilderness: The Story of Jesus Abbey* (Xlibris, 2005), 60-61. Published in Korean as Hyun Jae In, 에수원 이야기: 광양에 마련된 식탁 [*Yesuwon Iyagi: Gwangya-ae Maryeon-doen Shiktak*, The story of Jesus Abbey: The table provided in the wilderness], trans. Hye Won Yang (Hongsongsa, Seoul: 홍성사, 1999, 2004).

She goes on to relate how their commitment to this course was tested the very next day. However, as they remained true, funds came in, often from completely unexpected sources, and often just in the nick of time. They received enough to pay off the debts and enable the family to return to the US when Jane was taken ill. Reflecting on this discovery, Archer wrote in his journal on January 4, 1969 the following:

> One thing seems to me clear—I missed my guidance about the budget for 1968. I believed the Lord was telling me to expect great things of him and budgeted 19,000 "regular" income and 10,000 special income for a total of $29,000 US. The previous year's income had been over 17,000. This year we took in only $15,000—about 12% down from last year's total and just about 50% of what I expected. We are just about that much in the hole because I stuck my neck out on what I thought was "faith."
>
> Lesson No. 1. Go back to the original faith basis—no credit. If I had stuck to my guns on this from the very beginning we might have had revival 2 years sooner. We would have survived very handily and would have no debt now.
>
> Lesson No. 2. I was so sure we needed—just had to have all this extra building. Well, we are hardly using it at all. The studio attic could have served for what we have used the workshop attic for.
>
> Lesson No. 3. I also missed my prophecy that we would be 50 people by New Year's. If Bro. Albert had not steered us in the other direction I probably would have had 50 people and a catastrophe—both spiritually and financially—on my hands.[12]

A few days later he wrote:

> Jane and I talked over the financial situation after I got home. Since the Lord didn't bail us out by the end of the year, I have to conclude I got my guidance wrong.[13]

There were many remarkable examples of God's provision through the years, too many to list here but well recorded in Jane Torrey's *At the Table in the Wilderness* as well as in a book by Dr. Zeb Bradford Long, *Growing in Friendship with Jesus, Book 1: Jesus' Friend and Co-Worker, Reuben Archer Torrey, Founder of Jesus Abbey, South Korea*.[14] The Abbey community continued to grow in dependence on God, enjoying his many blessings; yet, it was all too easy to slip into patterns that were not of him as attested time and again in Fr. Torrey's journals.

Not only were there lessons to be learned about trusting God for provision and resisting the temptations to go against his will in the areas of buying on credit or contracting debt, but there were fundamental principles that applied directly to Jesus Abbey's calling. From the beginning, Fr. Torrey intended the community to be self-supporting and to support missionaries and other works out of its abundance. However, things did not turn out that way. While tithes are scrupulously set aside and given for other works and needs, there has not been the financial abundance anticipated that would allow them to support missionaries fully or other works. The community has continued to live by day-to-day provision. Fr. Torrey came to the conclusion that the primary work of the Abbey was prayer, not self-support as explained in *The Way of a Pioneer*:

> I pointed out that God had called us to be a house of prayer and that, while we should do what we could towards self-support, we should trust God for our support for now and get on with the primary task, which is the task of prayer and intercession. When it became clear that this was going to be the official line, we lost a number of very good men. We hated to see them go, but we were convinced that we could not retreat on the matter of prayer being the primary task.[15]

The Present and the Future

Archer Torrey went to be with the Lord on August 6, 2002, Jane Torrey on April 5, 2012. Jesus Abbey has been in something of a transition ever since, yet it has sought to continue to be faithful to the principle of faith financing throughout the years. It has continued to function quite well under this policy even though members have struggled with it both individually and communally.

---

12 Archer Torrey, *Unpublished Journals*, 8, entry for January 4, 1969.

13 Torrey, *Unpublished Journals*, entry for January 9, 1969.

14 Dr. Zeb Bradford Long, *Growing in Friendship with Jesus, Book 1: Jesus' Friend and Co-Worker*, Reuben Archer Torrey, Founder of Jesus Abbey, South Korea (Black Mountain, NC: Presbyterian and Reformed Ministries International, 2003).

15 Torrey, *The Way of a Pioneer*, 131.

A Challenge

From the earliest days the Community acquired a ministry to guests that had been completely unforeseen. In the spirit of the *Rule of St. Benedict*,[16] the Abbey has sought to welcome all guests as Christ. During the Abbey's second year a group of reporters were travelling to a large cavern in the area. They saw the author as a teenager walking along the road carrying a load. One of them inquired and heard that a group of foreigners and Koreans were living together up the remote valley where the Abbey was located. He came by some time later, interviewed Fr. Torrey and published an article in a national daily newspaper. That started a stream of guests coming to the Abbey. Later on, guests continued to come because of Fr. Torrey's published writings and speaking engagements. At the peak in the 1990s as many as 10,000 visitors came each year to stay for visits of three days or more.

Despite not charging to receive guests, they became a major source of income; in many years, the primary source of income for the community. There is a donation box in the Guest Department office where guests receive an orientation upon arrival. They are not asked or encouraged to make donations but often want to. The box is provided for their convenience. It is opened on Saturdays and contributions received during the week are counted and then offered on the altar at the Sunday morning Eucharist service.

Over the years this cash inflow from guests has presented the community with a particular challenge: How much are we trusting God to provide and how much are we looking to guests? There were times when it seemed that trusting God had given way to deliberately trying to increase the flow of guests or to despairing at the drop in numbers. At other times, the ministry to guests became a burden to community members and some aspects of the Abbey life. There were also times when the Council (selected annually to manage operations) appeared to come into conflict with the rest of the community over the issue of guests. However, the year 2020 seems to have changed these dynamics radically. Whether this will be a long-term change or not remains to be seen.

No Guests

With the COVID-19 pandemic, Jesus Abbey stopped receiving guests altogether beginning in March, 2020. One very positive effect is that the children of the community[17] have become much more engaged in the prayer and work life of the Abbey. In the past, they were simply overwhelmed by the constant presence of numerous guests and tended to keep to themselves. The overall atmosphere of the house has become much more intimate and less institutional.

Another positive effect is that community members are spending more time in prayer either individually or in small groups as well as in the regular corporate prayer and worship schedule. This has come about as people have experienced more free time without having to care for or interact with the steady stream of guests.

Finally, appearing to justify the community's commitment to faith financing, the lack of guests has had little impact on the overall economics of the community. While there were no guests to provide contributions through the year and few sales of items from the bookstore, the community has had all the funds needed for food, daily operations, utilities, and even some expensive repairs. It seems that God is interested in keeping the Abbey afloat financially without using guests as a means to do that.

Looking Ahead

As the pandemic ends, there will once again be a stream of short-term guests coming to Jesus Abbey for personal retreat and spiritual renewal. Whether or not that stream will be as large as in the recent past only time will tell. If it does not grow appreciably, it may have little impact economically but, if there is a large influx, it may well present the same challenge to faith as in the past. The members themselves hope that these positive changes in the culture of the community, particularly in relation to the families with children, will survive once guests start returning.

The ideal and culture of faith financing, originally articulated by founder Fr. Archer Torrey over fifty years ago, has become deeply embedded in the hearts and minds of the membership. In the author's estimation, this is not likely to change in the foreseeable future.

---

16 *The Rule of St. Benedict* was one of several community rules that Fr. Torrey used as guides or inspiration when establishing Jesus Abbey. The reference to guests is from chapter 53 of the *Rule*.

17 The Community of some thirty members and a few novices includes single adults and families with children, from toddlers to teenagers.

Chapter 7 Response

by Insoo Kim

The faith financing of Jesus Abbey is widely known in the Korean church. This principle of faith financing also inspired me in my service at Dandelion Community. I am thrilled to read and comment on this excellent article by Fr. Ben Torrey, son of Fr. Archer Torrey who founded Jesus Abbey. In a time when the authenticity of Christians and churches is sought, this article challenges us by showing that dependence on God is practical. It is a great comfort to read about Jesus Abbey's adherence to the principles of faith financing and their experiences, which show that God is alive and show the clear path of true discipleship, even in an era of aggressive capitalism.

Fiscal Policy Suitable for Calling

Christian ministers and institutions should find financial principles that fit their calling and internalize those principles. One such principle is faith financing, which was practiced by Hudson Taylor, George Mueller, and Jesus Abbey (to the present). Another is the tentmaking model, practiced by the apostle Paul, the Moravian community, and recently by BAM (Business as Mission).

The question of which fiscal policy is best depends on one's confession of faith and the content of one's ministry. Still, I think the most important thing is establishing and implementing financial principles according to God's calling and the development of that call. In this regard, I believe that Jesus Abbey practiced its faith financing according to its calling. It is fascinating to learn that they took a scientific approach to faith and relying on God alone in a remote location where people and resources were scarce, and to hear about the profound possibilities and results of their laboratory investigations. It also gives us a good lesson on practical Christianity. Their ardent experimentation and their conclusions on the fundamental topics of Christian faith (the individual and God, the individual and the Christian community, and the community and the world) are a gift to Jesus Abbey and to all believers.

Driving forces behind the simple, yet honest question of how to live by faith were the prayers and life of the founder of Jesus Abbey, and a tradition handed down from the ancestors of the faith. Calling in Christian ministry is not attested by external business growth and financial performance, or the number of employees, or statistically proven achievements. The key element is how much of God's intervention and grace was present in the ministry. In this regard, Christian ministry should hold fast to traditional attitudes about financial principles, that is, it should prioritize the evidence of God's presence, however slow it may appear, and keep relying on God himself, as opposed to trying to work with money and making work more efficient by using money.

Jesus Abbey had initially intended to attain self-sufficiency with which they would support missionaries and do other ministries. Later, however, they realized that their primary ministry was prayer. I think they made the right decision to limit themselves to that calling of prayer.

About Debt

Even though Jesus Abbey did not intend to, they accrued debt during the construction process, and God had warned them of this. When they realized that it was never God's intention for them to work and live under debt, they started to rely on God himself again instead of depending on credit. They testified that ever since, their financial difficulties were resolved. In modern society, it is natural to take on debt. The systemic problem underlying the current collapse of the Korean church is the excessive debt that was built up while pursuing external expansion. This is because the church was optimistic about the growth of its membership and their offerings and the repayment of debts. To preserve the purity of our ministry, we should live a simple lifestyle within the means given to us rather than maintaining an attitude of expecting God to give us money and make us rich if we have faith. The act of taking on debt stems from the self-confidence that we can be optimistic about the future and the self-centered attitude that we have control over the future, which can eventually lead to the breakdown of faith itself.

The modern state and the church have been pursuing the supreme goals of coexistence and co-prosperity. However, the time has come to turn to a life of communal joy, a lifestyle of living together even in poverty. Churches and Christian institutions would have to turn away from a life of accruing debts and bring about a life of jubilee that pays off the debts of the poor.

From Faith Financing to the Life of Faith

I hope that the "faith financing" experiment at Jesus Abbey will pave the way for daring brothers and sisters to move on to "faith living." I hope that there will be a movement of genuine, living faith that depends on God.

In order to move from faith financing to faith living, firstly, missionaries and ministers must recognize that it is wiser and vital to build a stable community that relies on the steady productivity of the cooperative life of the community. We need to realize that our true security does not lie in the excessive possession of money and means but in building a community of faith where we can live together with trust. We need to go beyond faith financing to create faith living. In that sense, community life in a rural area based on the soil will be more stable in the long run than in a city dominated by capitalism and meritocracy.

At Dandelion Community where I serve, we live in pursuit of self-reliance in five central areas—food, economy, energy, education and culture, and faith and conscience. In a mountain village such as Jesus Abbey, it may be possible to consider a more creative and innovative community enterprise that embodies spirituality.

Secondly, we must build a community in which the positive influence of the poor steadily increases. Whether it is a church, a mission field, or a community, the growing influence of the poor among its members can be considered a very healthy sign. This is because, like Jesus, we become friends with the poor and live a life of preaching the Gospel to the poor. Kwasizabantu Mission in South Africa is a fine example of this.

Third, the public nature of communities and institutions must be strengthened to move forward from faith financing to faith living. Churches, missions agencies, and Christian institutions should have clear visions, goals, and documented guidelines to achieve transparent financial management, the reliable performance of duties, and effective communication and governance. Many religious institutions are built with spiritual fervor at first. But, later on they become secularized and collapse when they keep pursuing their private interests only. To live by faith means depending on God for everything we need for our daily use, but in the process we must hold onto the heart and hand of a just, fair, and merciful God.

Fourth, to move from faith financing to active faith living we need to expand our understanding of labor. Apostle Paul said that he constantly remembers the "work of faith" together with the "labor of love" and "perseverance of hope" before God the Father (1 Thess. 1:3). Faith, love, and hope are the most precious and spiritually meaningful values pursued by believers. Still, the words attached to faith, love, and hope are "work," "labor," and "perseverance." These terms carry the physical connotation of hard work, intense labor, and lengthy perseverance.

Above all, the life of faith is accompanied by the work (labor) of faith. Although modern Christianity has fallen into the habit of Neo-Gnosticism that emphasizes spirituality in everything, true life can only be found in the perfect unity of faith and life.

Lastly, as we move from faith financing to faith living, we must also respect the element of prophecy, the encouragement of God's word. Sometimes a calling may require doing the same work at any given time, but most callings develop, expand, and sometimes change. The calling changes with the growth of the individuals and the communities who put the calling into practice. When this happens we should discern prophecies, be cautious, and confirm them with faith. Prophecy, like the rudder of a ship, can play a very decisive role in guiding the direction of the community of faith.

Conclusion

Community life based on the faith financing of Jesus Abbey is a practical example of life made possible by trusting in God in an extreme capitalist society, where money makes money, and in an age of materialistic idolatry, which says life is not possible without money. This is a testimony that makes faith mission possible in the church and on the mission field. The financial structure of a ministry is directly related to the calling of that ministry, and it is necessary to find a financial principle and management plan suitable for that calling. A calling-based financial principle will lead us to a calling-based life.

In this regard, debt can lead us to the false belief that we have control over the future, by precluding God's guidance as the only principle we can trust, which may, in the end, lead us to forsake both God and the church

Following the tradition of Jesus and his disciples who preached the Gospel to the poor, it is time for us to respect the lifestyle of the poor and learn the value of a simple and unpretentious life and manual labor. Above all, we look forward to the emergence of a Christian community that pays off the debt of the poor, instead of living in debt.

I believe that Jesus Abbey's practice of faith financing has challenged us to move on from "faith financing" to "faith living" in our time.

Chapter 8
The Structure and the Financial Management Policy of GMS from the Perspective of Credibility, Transparency, and Accountability

by Jinbong Kim

When the 1910 World Missionary Conference took place in Edinburg a century ago, Korea was a small hermit kingdom in East Asia, and the Korean church was frail in her capabilities. But a series of events including the Wonsan Revival Movement of 1903, the Great Pyongyang Revival of 1907, and the Million Souls Movement that began in 1909 prepared the Korean church to eventually become a globally recognized, missions-oriented church. At KGMLF 2017, Dr. Andrew Walls described some aspects of the early Korean churches' preparation.[1]

Now, a century after the stunning revival of the early Korean church, more than twenty thousand Korean missionaries are working around the globe.[2]

The explosive increase of Korean missionaries is closely linked with the growth of the Korean church. Also important were the efforts of the mission societies in various church denominations as well as the missionary organizations. For instance, the General Assembly of the Presbyterian Church in Korea (GPCK), established in September 1912, began sending missionaries from its early years. The Global Mission Society (GMS), an affiliate of GPCK, is now in charge of missionary activities within the denomination, with 2,574 missionaries in 101 nations (as of January 2021). This chapter discusses the brief history of GMS and its organizational and financial structure, followed by a deeper review of its financial operation from the viewpoint of transparency, credibility, and accountability. Recommendations for GMS regarding its structure and financial management policies are presented based on surveys of the GMS missionaries around the world.[3]

---

1 Andrew Walls, "Migration in Christian History," in *People Disrupted: Doing Mission Responsibly among Refugees and Migrants,* ed. Jonathan Bonk and Jinbong Kim et al. (Littleton: William Carey Library, 2018), 36.

2 Steve Sang-Cheol Moon, "The Protestant Missionary Movement in Korea: Current Growth and Development," *International Bulletin of Missionary Research* 32, no. 2 (April 2008): 59.

3 See GMS website, https://gms.kr and "Articles of Association Management Regulations Headquarters Bylaws of GMS (2018) and "2020 Reports of the Board of Directors and the General Assembly."

A Brief History of GMS

The Missions Society of the Denomination Prior to GMS

By 1969, GPCK had commissioned eighteen missionaries without a permanent organization in charge of missionary activities. At the 66th General Assembly of 1981, however, the Mission Department was established as a permanent institution, the Mission Society, and became the leader of pioneering mission administration. At the 75th General Assembly of 1991, a decision was made to establish the Overseas Missionary Society of the General Assembly of the Presbyterian Church in Korea (OMSGAPCK) under the Mission Department. Reverend Seung Sam Kang, a former SIM missionary to Nigeria, was appointed to lead the organization. Member missionaries of OMSGAPCK increased from 168 in 1991 to 734 in 1995. The mission budget at OMSGAPCK increased from US$755,000 in 1991 to more than US$943,400 in 1995. The sources of the fund were the offerings as well as the dues gathered from the members in the Mission Department and the sending churches. In 1994, fifty-three senior missionaries convened to revise the General Assembly mission policy. Although the Mission Department existed within the General Assembly, it was in name only; it was OMSGAPCK that managed the missionary activities during this period.

The Launch of GMS: The Organization and the Board of Directors

In 1998, at the general assembly of the denomination, resolutions were made to unify mission organization, and to extend the denomination's Mission Department to form the Global Mission Society of the Presbyterian Church (GMS). GMS has a board of directors and the headquarters. The Headquarters is a permanent organization whose purpose is to manage practical affairs such as missionary sending, management, welfare, church support development, presbytery management, mobilizing regional church missions, etc. The headquarters is a place for selection and training missionaries, for missionaries who take temporary leaves, for meetings related to mission, and as a residence for retired missionaries.[4]

An important change that came with GMS was the introduction of the board of directors. The board of directors was composed of the sending church directors and the sending presbytery directors. The board of directors is the top decision-making body, and it has the legal power to represent GMS. That is, the board of directors decides on all missionary policies, and not only oversees the missionary work of the church, including execution and supervision, but also establishes, executes, and settles necessary budgets. It also has the power to review and approve the budget and the financial statements. Yet, it is regrettable that the missionaries are not included at the General Assembly of the Board of Directors in which important decisions on GMS missionary work are made.[5]

Finances of GMS and Finances for the Missionaries

The two key elements of the finances of GMS are fundraising money by the missionaries and the administrative expenses for running the headquarters. The total fund for GMS missionaries is over US$40 million per year, out of which US$2.7 million is used for administrative expenses.

(1) Missionary finances. To be commissioned by GMS, missionaries are required to raise money to cover their basic living finance and basic ministry finance as determined by GMS. Because it is the responsibility of the missionary to fundraise, the commissioning can be difficult if the required funds are not enough. For instance, I (Jinbong) was required to raise up to US$2,400 per month for my family of four (including two children) to work and live as a GMS missionary in Africa in 1994. As the offerings at churches are shrinking due to COVID-19, the supporting money for missionaries is also decreasing. Yet, GMS policy holds the missionaries primarily responsible for the fundraising of their mission work. The fundraising money for the missionaries is first wired to the bank account of GMS Headquarters (via virtual account number for each missionary) and then transferred to each missionary. A portion of the fundraising money is set apart for various funds and is managed by the headquarters.

(2) Administrative expenses for GMS. The administrative expenses for GMS, which are about US$2.7 million, are covered by three sources of income: the dues of the directors, the dues of the missionaries,

---

[4] For further information on GMS, see their website at https://gms.kr.

[5] At the GMS General Assembly in 2001, the Board of Directors removed the missionary membership from the General Assembly.

and the support funds from the general assembly and other donations. The dues paid by the missionaries amount to over US$1.4 million per year, which covers over 50 percent of the administrative expenses (based on the twenty-third accounting term from September 2019 to August 2020).[6] The dues paid by the members of the board amount to around US $660,370 annually.

Unlike the dues of the missionaries, the dues of the directors are not mandatory; only about 40 percent of the dues of the directors are collected. Out of the US$660,370, US$188,670 is used to cover the expenses of the chairperson of the board and the expenses for retreats, conferences, and the annual meeting. Thus, the net contribution to the administrative expenses from the dues of the directors is US$471,700, which is about one-third of what the missionaries contribute. Yet, GMS structure excludes the missionaries from the very process where decisions for budget, execution, and financial reporting are made. The problem regarding the structure of the GMS board of directors is pointed out by many missionaries.

The Korean government has enforced The Improper Solicitation and Graft Act (colloquially, Kim Young-ran Act) since September 2016.[7] The purpose of this law is to make society more transparent and fairer. If that is so, Christian communities and organizations, as the light and the salt of the world, should strive even more to be transparent and fair.

(3) Missionary welfare finances (reserve funds). Out of the supporting money by the missionaries, a certain portion is set apart for various reserve funds for the missionaries that are managed by the headquarters. The total amount of the reserve funds is over US$28 million, which is composed of Silver Reserve Funds (US$10 million), Retirement Reserve Funds (US$12.5 million), Sabbatical Traveling Reserve Funds (US$3.2 million), Welfare Funds (US$1.2 million), and Common Funds (US$94,000). Common Funds are interest accumulated from the Traveling Reserve Funds that are not distributed to each individual and are used for providing interest-free loans to the missionaries in need. Welfare Funds are used for supporting medical needs and other emergencies of the member missionaries. Sabbatical Traveling Funds can be used for travel and other emergencies during the sabbaticals of the missionaries. Silver and Retirement Reserve Funds, a monthly deposit plan required for postretirement benefits of the missionaries, had been managed by the board of directors until February 2011 when it was transferred to one of retirement pension funds operated by Hana Bank. In August 2017, however, the bank refused the payment of the retirement pension fund. After a 3.5-year long lawsuit, the decision was made in favor of the missionaries.

As mentioned earlier, GMS is one of the largest missionary organizations not only in Korea but in the world. Based on the total number of the missionaries sent, GMS would probably be the second largest missionary organization in the world after The International Mission Board (IMB) in the USA.[8] But the number of the missionaries and the size of the budget are never a guarantee that God is delighted with the organization. Therefore, the structure as well as the financial management of GMS is discussed in the following section from the viewpoint of credibility, transparency, and accountability as highlighted in the Bible.

Credibility, Transparency, and Accountability of GMS

At KGMLF 2019, Dr. Brent Lindquist, the president of Link Care, USA, pointed out the six characteristics of a healthy organization as follows:

> First, an environment of trust. Second, communication. Third, connected and empowered team members. Fourth, a focus on priorities and purpose, not just policy. Fifth, wellness and balance. Finally, evaluation and change.[9]

An organization must be healthy to keep growing while keeping abreast of the fast-paced changes in the twenty-first century. For a large missionary organization like GMS to maintain its health, it is even more important to be equipped with credibility, transparency, and accountability.

---

6 The dues of GMS missionaries are withheld from their supporting money: single (US$62), couple (US$87), and couple with two children (US$118). In 1999 the dues of one couple with two children were only US$36.

7 See Wikipedia, s.v. "Improper Solicitation and Graft Act," last modified August 3, 2020, 09:44, https://en.wikipedia.org/wiki/Improper_Solicitation_and_Graft_Act.

8 IMB is a Baptist Christian missionary society affiliated with the Southern Baptist Convention. For further information on IMB, see "Fast Facts," IMB, 2021, https://www.imb.org/fast-facts/.

9 Brent Lindquist, "Organization-Centered Member Health," in *Missionary Mental Health and Accountability: Support Systems in Churches and Agencies*, ed. Jonathan Bonk and Jinbong Kim et al. (Littleton: William Carey Publishing, 2019), 199–200.

Credibility of GMS

Dr. Lindquist pointed out an environment of trust as the first characteristic of a healthy organization. The credibility of an organization refers to both the people who manage the organization and the process by which the organization is managed. For instance, in 2011, GMS misappropriated US$940,000 from Sabbatical Travel Funds to purchase real estate for a liaison office in the USA, which was obviously not the purpose of the fund.[10] This problem is related to the process by which the organization is managed. It is regrettable that the incident produced a lawsuit between the missionaries and the directors who were involved in the decision. This incident revealed the mistrust against the managers who are in charge of GMS. Such misappropriation could have been avoided if the missionaries were involved in the decision-making process. Dr. Christopher Wright, in his letter of recommendation for a publication of KGMLF, advises the leaders in the church and the missionary community as follows:

> We call on all church and mission leaders to resist the temptation to be less than totally truthful in presenting our work. We are dishonest when we exaggerate our reports with unsubstantiated statistics or twist the truth for the sake of gain. We pray for a cleansing wave of honesty and the end of such distortion, manipulation and exaggeration.[11]

In the survey conducted for this chapter, GMS missionaries were asked regarding the credibility of GMS, to which 52 percent of the respondents replied, "Strongly negative," and 20 percent replied, "Negative." Seventy-two percent of the respondents did not find GMS credible.[12]

In the Old Testament, Samuel delivers his farewell speech in front of the Israelites at the end of his ministry as a prophet and judge. He asks, "Whose ox have I taken? Whose donkey have I taken? Whom have I cheated? Whom have I oppressed? From whose hand have I accepted a bribe to make me shut my eyes?" (1 Sam. 12:3). The Israelites reply, "You have not cheated or oppressed us. You have not taken anything from anyone's hand" (1 Sam. 12:4). This scene exhibits the complete trust of the Israelites in the servant of God.

In order to restore its credibility, GMS must quickly change the way it manages the organization. As Dr. Lindquist mentioned, the communication between the Directors and the missionaries should not be based on a top-down, hierarchical relationship but based on the attitude of a humble servant as the Lord taught us. A democratic communication channel should be set up. One of the best ways to make it happen is to have the same number of directors who represent the missionaries as those who represent the sending churches in the board of directors. It also should be clearly mandated in the GMS policy that the financial operation be transparent and open to the missionaries. Also, the missionary funds should be professionally managed by third-party experts (organizations) with approval from all involved parties. These changes would help GMS restore its credibility.

Transparency of GMS

Transparency means having nothing to hide, thus being honest, credible, and trustworthy in the eyes of other people. There is much to learn from the transparency of Samuel who served before the Almighty God from whom nothing can be hidden as well as in front of the eyes and the ears of the people of Israel throughout his life.

The financial budget of GMS is the largest among Korean missionary organizations. The budget of over US$40 million is approved and executed through the decisions at the annual meeting of the board of directors. We can only imagine how much temptation of bribery Samuel would have been exposed to in his lifetime as the most influential person in the nation. The tempting power of money is also shown in the story of a rich young man who wanted to follow Jesus but ended up turning away in sadness (Matt. 19:22). Dr. Wright highlights the importance of financial transparency for the leaders in church and missionary organizations as stewards of the resources entrusted by God. First, financial temptations call for "safety in numbers." Second, financial accountability demands transparency before God and man. Third, financial trustworthiness is an apostolic honor to Christ.[13]

---

10 For further information see Jeonghoon Baek, "GMS Executives' Association Dedicated to the Sabbath Fund Implementation Ignoring Procedure: A Problem with the Perception That Certain People Can Do Whatever They Want," News & Joy, April 17, 2012, www.newsnjoy.or.kr/news/articleView.html?idxno=37511

11 Jinbong Kim et al., eds., *Megachurch Accountability: Critical Assessment through Global Case Studies* (Pasadena: William Carey Library, 2016), x.

12 For further information about the survey, see section III below.

13 Christopher J. H. Wright, "Paul, A New Testament Model: His Collection for the Poor in Jerusalem," in *Accountability in Missions: Korean and Western Case Studies*, ed. Jonathan J. Bonk (Eugene, Wipf and Stock Publishers, 2011), 44–52.

It is true that there has been a lot of noise about the financial management of the board of directors since GMS was launched. An exemplary case, in contrast, is that of the 100th Anniversary Memorial Church. The church, well-known for its clean financial management, has fully opened its monthly financial reports to the public as well as the church members since 2005.[14] GMS, with an annual budget of more than US$40 million, should also open its financial reports transparently, following the example of this church. Like Samuel, GMS should have nothing to be ashamed of before God and people.

Accountability of GMS

The parable of the talents in the Bible (Matt. 25:14–30) describes what accountability is. In this section of the chapter, an exemplary response made by GMS regarding the COVID-19 pandemic is highlighted. Also, we will discuss several urgent issues that GMS should be held accountable for by the missionaries.

(1) The operation of the COVID-19 Emergency Situation Center. Facing the COVID-19 pandemic, GMS launched the COVID-19 Emergency Situation Center on April 2, 2020. The activities of the operation were documented in a 9,000-page report by Jung Han Kim. Key points are as follows:[15]

- Out of 4,909 overseas GMS missionaries and their children, 940 members returned to Korea. Self-quarantine facilities were provided for 377 members. Three hundred forty-one sets of care packages were provided. A one-time gift of US$100–300 each was offered to 1,400 units.

- Three hundred forty-one sets of emergency kits and self-testing kits were quickly deployed for the needs of the missionaries in the field. The total amount of donations from churches, organizations, and individuals was US$540,000.

The report shows the dedication of many churches and believers as well as the beautiful results of accountability shown by the GMS directors and the headquarters staff as they gave their best efforts to handle the COVID-19 crisis since April 2020.

(2) Accountability for missionary kids. GMS has been exemplary in their faithful accountability regarding the COVID-19 crisis. In contrast, there is no active group within GMS for missionary kids (MKs) who are more than three thousand in number within GMS. These MKs are paying monthly dues that amount to around US$3,000 per person in ten years. A missionary asked for an honest accountability for the MKs, saying, "The amount of money is not the issue. We need to do more than just talk about the MKs. We really need to think the whole thing over."[16] When the COVID-19 crisis is over, the COVID-19 Emergency Situation Center will no longer be needed. But we desperately need measures to help GMS MKs who are going through unutterable difficulties that might lead even to suicide (there were two cases in 2020). In a paper on "Third Culture Kids (TCKs)," Soon Young Jung writes as follows:

> Like other TCKs, MKs experience a variety of difficult challenges. Their depression and suicide rates increase after their first year of returning home to their passport country. Issues related to identity crisis, feelings of marginality, loss, and grief, and a sense of rootlessness are associated with a cross-cultural upbringing and the high mobility characteristic of MKs and TCKs.[17]

At KGMLF 2019, Young Ok Kim also pointed out that Korean churches and missionary organizations have been focusing too much on the number of missionaries sent. She emphasized the need for the investment of resources and time for the development of missionary member care.[18] Thus, GMS directors should be accountable for the MKs by employing practical measures through experts and proactive investment, instead of merely setting up a nominal structure.

(3) Accountability for the retirement of missionaries. In a recent survey missionaries were asked, "Are you satisfied with your expected postretirement financial income?," to which 35 percent of respondents replied,

---

14 See "100th Anniversary Commemorative Church for Christian Missions in Korea Reveals Monthly Budget Execution for 10 Years … 'Clean Finance,'" KMIB, last modified January 14, 2016, http://news.kmib.co.kr/article/view.asp?arcid=0923393909.

15 Jung Han Kim, personal interview by author at GMS headquarters, January 20, 2021.

16 Ji Seong-gu, "Voice of the Margin: Is the Monthly Membership Fee for the Missionary Child Good?," GMS Mission Society, October 9, 2020, http://pf.kakao.com/_Mxjeaxb/57449917.

17 Soon Young Jung and Donna Kaiser, "Transcultural Kids: Implications for the Care of Missionary Children," in *Family Accountability in Mission: Korean and Western Case Studies*, ed. Jonathan Bonk et al. (New Haven: OMSC Publications, 2013), 275.

18 Young Ok Kim, "God's Wounded Servants: Exploring the Lived Experience of Trauma," in *Missionary Mental Health and Accountability: Support Systems in Churches and Agencies*, ed. Jonathan Bonk and Jinbong Kim et al. (Littleton: William Carey Publishing, 2019), 166.

"Not at all," and 35 percent replied, "No." That is, at least 70 percent of the missionaries are expecting their postretirement life to be difficult. It is fortunate that GMS is preparing housing facilities for single missionaries at Wolmoon-Ri. But GMS should also be accountable for the retirement of over 2,500 missionaries. What is needed is a permanent organization dedicated to the cause of the missionary retirees. Also called for is accountability regarding the transparent and credible reporting on Retirement Funds.

GMS as Seen Through the Survey of the Missionaries

The views of the missionaries on the structure and the financial management of GMS were collected through an online survey using Google Forms. Two hundred fourteen respondents gave their answers during the three-month period from December 15, 2020, to January 25, 2021. To the question, "Do you have trust in the structure and the management of GMS board of directors?," 53 percent answered in the negative. Seventy-five percent thought that the opinions of the missionaries are not adequately reflected when the policies are determined. Eighty-nine percent replied that the participation of missionaries is needed at the annual meeting of the board of directors. Seventy-two percent thought that the financial policies and its management are not transparent. Seventy percent were dissatisfied with how the missionary funds were being managed. Eighty-seven percent said that the GMS missionary fund should be managed by experts. Finally, to the question asking whether the GMS financial report should be open to the missionaries, 64 percent answered, "Strongly agree," and 30 percent answered, "Agree." GMS directors and the general assembly, to which GMS belongs, should give serious consideration to this response that 94 percent of the missionaries think the financial information should be transparently open to them.

Conclusion and Recommendations

In 2018, Dr. Bonk, who was an invited speaker at the GMS mission conference commemorating its twentieth anniversary, was shocked to see the organizational chart of the GMS board of directors shown on a bulletin board at GMS headquarters. He could hardly understand how senior pastors without missionary field experience could make decisions on the mission policies and the budget on behalf of more than 2,500 missionaries in the organization. A fundamental change is called for at GMS. The organization should throw off its top-down, hierarchical management style and work on mending its lack of straightforward, open communication. The teachings of the Bible are clear on this. We should take on our accountability with transparency and integrity as Samuel did. By doing so, GMS will recover its credibility.

Conclusively, recommendations for GMS are as follows:

A. The communication between the directors and the missionaries should not be based on a top-down, hierarchical relationship but based on the attitude of a humble servant as the Lord taught us. Also, representatives of the missionaries should be included at the general assembly of the board of directors in which important decisions on GMS missionary work are made.

B. It should be mandated in the bylaws of the organization that transparency be maintained throughout the process of determination, execution, and settlement of the budget, and that audit reports by third-party experts be open to all missionaries.

C. The unreasonableness in the financial structure for administrative expenses should be corrected. Unnecessary expenses should be cut back. Seventy percent of the administrative expenses should be covered by the dues of the directors and the support funds while reducing the dues of the missionaries.

D. The missionary reserve funds should be managed by third-party experts and the missionaries should participate in the management process. Also, the salary of the GMS staff members should be transparently open to the missionaries for the sake of credibility.

E. Preparation teams should be set up for specific purposes such as an MK support team and a retirement support team. The teams should include representatives of the missionaries. They should determine and execute the top priorities for the accountability of GMS.

F. A "Committee for Assessment and Development of GMS" should be launched with representatives from the directors, the missionaries, the headquarters staff, and third-party experts. The committee should plan for the transformation and growth of GMS in the ever-changing global mission environment.

A regular forum should be created so that field leaders, experts from home and abroad, ministers, and missionaries could assess the ministry of GMS from their objective viewpoints and thus accelerate the global development of GMS. Also needed is a special team for archiving and publication.

Chapter 8 Response

by Karen Shaw

Reading this chapter brought back memories for me. When my husband Perry and I first went to the Middle East with Middle East Christian Outreach (MECO) in 1990, we went under a system very similar to the one described in Jinbong Kim's chapter, "The Structure and the Financial Management Policy of GMS from the Perspective of Credibility, Transparency, and Accountability." Funds were pooled and all were required to raise the same support sum, but workers at the head office and in the home countries were only required to raise 60 percent of their support, while field missionaries were required to be 100 percent supported. In our first year our allowance was cut seven months out of twelve, even though we were well over 100 percent supported, and one of those months we received nothing, while the home workers and those in the head office received full salaries. Sometimes missionaries would have to leave the field because they were undersupported, while home workers could stay on and on drawing upon the missionaries' fundraising. Without any real accountability for the effectiveness of their work they became a drain on the missionaries as much as an asset. As you can imagine, this was a cause of considerable resentment.

About fifteen years later, new leaders presented a strong case for changing the financial structure of the mission. They argued that the extant structure was both unfair and inefficient. MECO was restructured, with missionaries raising money that went into designated funds from which they drew as need arose. The amount missionaries needed to raise would depend upon the lifestyle they chose and the needs of their ministries. Home office took 10 percent and international office took 5 percent to pay for basic operating costs, but the salaries of home and international office workers had to be paid out of administration fees, personal support raised by these staff workers, the occasional legacy, and other exceptional sources. Field missionaries were not responsible to cover international office and home workers' shortfalls. The leaders taught home and international office personnel how to raise money not only for themselves but for missionaries, to augment what they had raised. The result? Happy missionaries, yes, but also the failure of some home offices to survive and the eventual absorption of MECO into a larger organization.

Thank you, Jinbong Kim, for sharing with us this difficult time in GMS and for the work that you did in determining the degree of the breakdown of trust that stemmed from the decision-making and economic policies of the mission.

My first response is academic. I would like to know more about how this survey was conducted. Of course, word count restrictions limited what could be written, but it would have been helpful to know how the survey was introduced to those who were surveyed, the methodology used, and the way in which the analysis was conducted.

My second response is cultural. Korea is known to be a vertical society. Dr. Kim has advocated for a flattening of the decision-making and economic structures of the mission. To what degree do these changes reflect changes in the culture of Korea? That is, to what degree will these changes be understood and accepted by the people who will fund, pray for, and support in other ways the work of the mission? On the other hand, to what degree will such changes be understood in recipient countries? Obviously, the mission cannot cater to the concerns of every country and culture among which its missionaries serve, but this should be taken into account as missionaries and mission leadership work together to ensure that national church leadership in recipient countries can understand and work with the mission in a meaningful way.

My third response is one of suspense. Dr. Kim's chapter was written months ago. I would love to know what has happened as a result of the survey.

My final response is pastoral and missiological. A man came to Jesus and said, "Tell my brother to divide the inheritance with me." Jesus didn't argue that this plea for justice was unfounded. Instead, Jesus warned the complainant to "be on your guard against all kinds of greed."[19] Dr. Kim's chapter is essentially about power and money, two of the most divisive factors in any organization or relationship. They can be both tools of the Kingdom of God or of Satan. Paulo Freire's observation is so true it has become cliché: "The oppressed, instead of striving for liberation, tend themselves to become oppressors."[20] I invite the missionaries of the GMS to ask themselves if they are willing to be held to the same standard of accountability to which they are holding their directors. After all, mission is not primarily about missionaries but the work of the Kingdom. Let me give two examples.

First, I heartily concur that decisions should be made by people who understand the work from experience. Nevertheless, I am concerned that there not be an overreaction. I suspect that one of the reasons pastors and presbyters were chosen to comprise the board of directors of the GMS was to ensure that the church be involved with the mission, that there be true buy-in and answerability from the missionaries to the home churches that fund them. One pastor cynically described the attitude of some missionaries toward the churches as, "Pay, pray, and get out of the way."[21] If the locus of the mission's decisions is moved away from the sending churches, how responsible will the missionaries be for educating Korean churches in mission and for keeping the pastors passionate about God's mission in the world? Also, to whom will missionaries be responsible in a meaningful way?

Secondly, when it comes to money, are the missionaries willing to be as credible, transparent, and accountable to the church on the ground as they wish their directors were with them? To what degree will churches in the areas that are recipients of mission have a say in how the money designated to the missionaries and their projects is used? Will missionaries be sensitive to the effects their lifestyles have on the perception of righteousness (or lack thereof) among local people?[22] It is missiologically and spiritually important that missionaries' cries for justice be strategic for the Kingdom of God and not simply be a plea for a bigger slice of the pie, however well justified.

I want to conclude with hearty congratulations to Dr. Kim and those in GMS responsible for permitting and contributing to this valuable research. Would that more agencies around the world engaged in such soul-searching self-examination! The questions I have raised for reflection are not so much a critique of Dr. Kim's work, but an expression of hope that the GMS and other missions will benefit by it and commit themselves to ongoing assessment for the sake of unity and effectiveness in serving the interests of our Lord and Savior, Jesus Christ.

---

19 Luke 12:13-14.

20 Paulo Freire, *Pedagogy of the Oppressed*, trans. M. B. Ramos (New York: Continuum, 1982), 45.

21 Rick and Kay Warren, Saddleback Church newsletter, accessed 2007, since removed from the Saddleback website, http://www.saddleback.com/peaceplan.

22 For more on this topic see Jonathan Bonk, *Mission and Money: Affluence as a Western Missionary Problem* (Maryknoll: Orbis, 1991), especially 45-58 and Karen Shaw, *Wealth and Piety: Middle Eastern Perspectives for Expat Workers* (Littleton: William Carey, 2018), especially xix-xx, 70-72, 84-86, 99-102, 117-120, 134-137, 148-150, and 172-182.

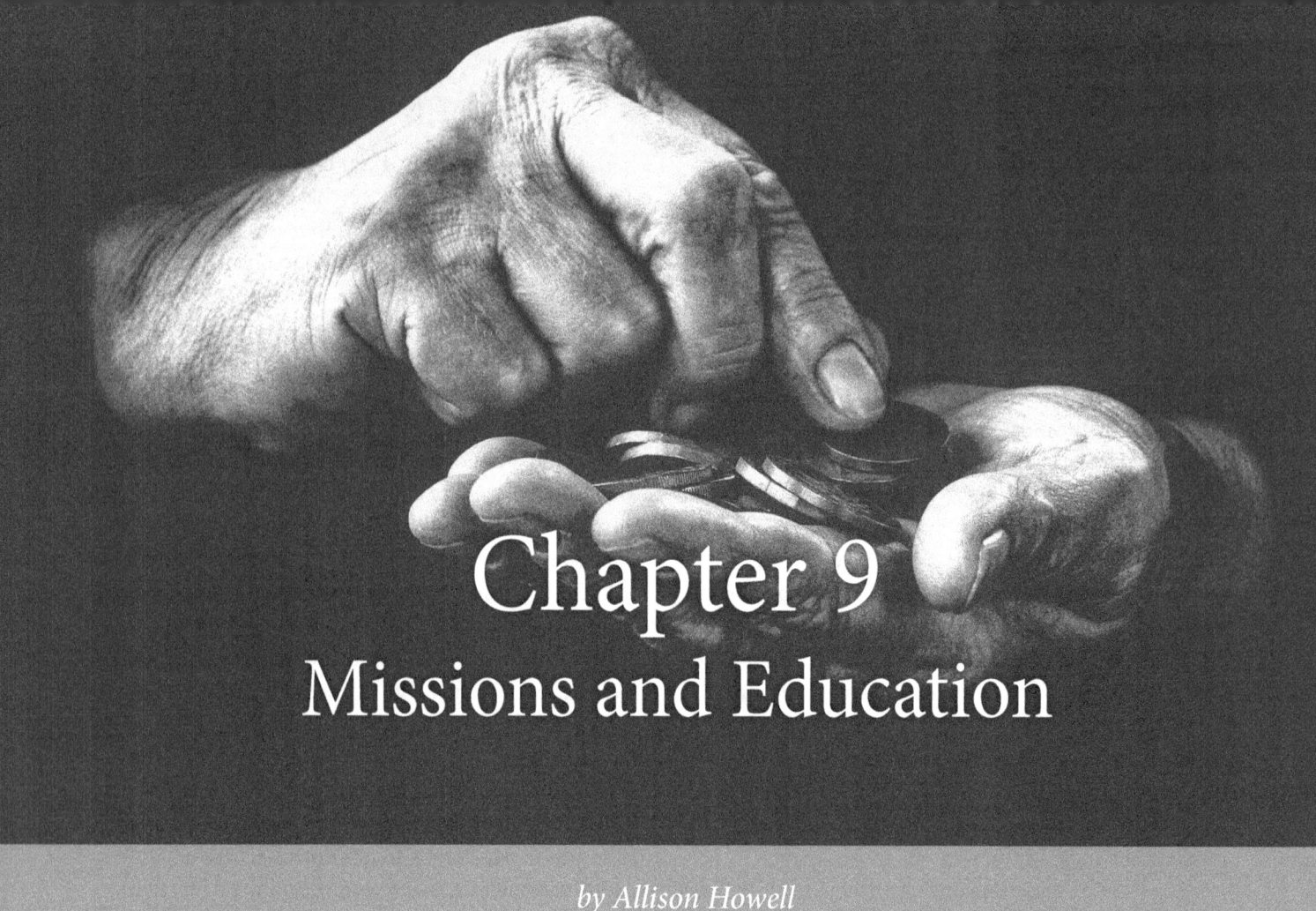

Chapter 9
Missions and Education

by Allison Howell

The word "education" often connotes a structured school setting where children, teenagers, or adults gather to receive formal instruction. Throughout the history of Christian mission, schools have been established to provide both informal and formal learning. Today, missions and churches continue to establish and manage various educational institutions. These include early childhood centers, primary-, high-, and tertiary-level institutions, training centers focussing on technological, vocational, computing, or skills development, language learning centers, Bible schools, theological colleges, and seminaries. Some missionaries are also involved with theological education by extension. In the Korean church and mission the role of "School Ministries" is considered crucial.

For over thirty-eight years in Ghana, I witnessed the establishment of two educational institutions and taught in both. The first, a "Bible Training Centre" (BTC), is a basic-level institution founded by SIM (Serving in Mission) missionaries working with the Good News Bible Church in northern Ghana. The second, Akrofi-Christaller Memorial Centre for Mission Research and Applied Theology in southern Ghana, is a tertiary institution founded by a Ghanaian theologian, Rev. Professor Kwame Bediako. It became the Akrofi-Christaller Institute of Theology, Mission and Culture (ACI) in 2006, when it gained full accreditation as a theological university awarding postgraduate degrees. Both institutions continue to function today, although at different levels and capacities.

This chapter presents a case study on "Missions and Education" and creating viable, sustainable, and useful educational institutions. Rather than focussing on a single institution, I have drawn from my own missionary experiences and observations in theological education, famine relief, establishing a primary health care program, water supply and sanitation projects, and attempts at reafforestation, as well as insights from others in education in Ghana and elsewhere.[1] No procedure manuals existed for any of these ministries. As missionaries in unfamiliar contexts, we largely muddled through things. Some efforts worked while others failed. However, some of the principles and lessons learned from these ministries have important implications for the creation of viable, sustainable, and useful educational institutions.

This case study highlights some challenges in establishing educational institutions and addresses the important questions: Why? What? How? Some of these responses are pertinent to all institutions. However, I will indicate where procedures differ in establishing Bible/theological colleges. My conclusion will examine the limitations and strengths at various levels of mission/church involvement in education and present some discussion questions.

Challenges

Where missionaries think that formal education is lacking, the temptation is to "do something" quickly to "meet the need." Moreover, I have frequently observed missionaries pressured to report positive results rapidly to their home church or mission agency. Expeditiously establishing a school or Bible school for training Christian leaders may appear sensible. So, they appeal for funds, build structures, and search for teachers. Because of a lack of appropriate teachers, the "founder" may employ expatriates who have no or little knowledge of the language(s) and culture(s) in which they teach.

The lack of judicious preparation and awareness of government regulations related to land (as occurred with the BTC) or education can result in unviable institutions that are difficult to sustain and disadvantageous due to the type of curriculum introduced in the institution. The mission/missionary may even find themselves "owners" of the educational facility. If they leave the field suddenly or retire, there may be myriads of complications controverting the educational facility's viability, sustainability, and usefulness.

Missionaries' perceptions about the type of training they think people "need," as well as the methods, content, motives, and outcomes of education, may be based not only on their personal experience but also illustrate a view of "education" that ultimately promotes a consumerist worldview. Their preferred model and content reflect one of Western consumer education.

Some evangelical missions in the past only set up primary schools because they did not think it necessary to offer high school level training. Others discouraged women from going beyond basic-level education because of their cultural view of the woman solely as a "homemaker" and incapable of pursuing higher education. Contrary to this perspective, I was encouraged to observe, at ACI's January 2021 graduation, women graduating in all levels of degrees, many with distinction.

For any institution to be *viable* it needs to be feasible, started successfully, and able to survive. Its *sustainability* will depend on its setup, longevity, and capacity to be financially autonomous. To be *useful* it must be beneficial to the country or group for whom it is set up. More importantly from the perspective of Christian mission, it must relate to the overall task of the Gospel and lead to transformation in the learners' lives.

Why?

Schools/School Ministries

My observations identified a variety of reasons why missions/churches begin and run schools:

1. To meet a need in a country because they consider existing schools inadequate
2. To evangelize or establish a Christian school where this is a legal option in a country, since both Christians and non-Christians will send their children to the schools
3. To initiate a "development" project or social intervention in the context by providing respectable employment for people in the community, including Christians
4. To create income for the mission and/or church as a "commercial" venture
5. To develop specialized areas of instruction such as early childhood education, language teaching (such as English in a French-speaking country), and technical and skill-based training such as agriculture, carpentry, masonry, computing, hair dressing, and so on. Often Christian teaching is incorporated in the learning.

---
[1] I am grateful for insights from several friends in email messages to the author from Mrs. Bethany Kapezya (DR Congo, November 24, 2020), Mrs. Annette Levy (Japan, December 30, 2020), and Professor Stephen Adei (Ghana, December 31, 2020) and WhatsApp messages to the author from Rev. Francis Kupoe (Ghana, December 7, 8, 11, 14, 15, 28, 2020) and Rev. Vasco Pwakechega (Ghana, December 16, 24, 27, 28, 29, 2020).

Besides the above reasons, what is the rationale for creating schools in Christian mission?

Education is a basic human need. Most parents want their children to be educated, especially if they did not have the opportunity themselves. Education can also be considered a step toward better employment.

If a mission/church/founder's understanding of God's mission includes responding to human need by loving service, then developing schools are a vital aspect of the Gospel of Jesus Christ. Where permitted by law, establishing a Christian school provides an opportunity to openly proclaim the Good News of Jesus Christ and to nurture Christian faith and disciple students as part of the overall ethos and curriculum of the school. The aim is to reflect Christ in all the activities in the school from pedagogy to play on the fields while promoting a high academic standard so that students develop good morals and godly character.

In countries that do not permit open proclamation of the Gospel, a mission's involvement in developing schools may still provide an opportunity to model godliness in education.

Bible and Theological Education

Developing Bible/theological education is important when people respond to the Gospel, as they need to be taught by consistent, courageous, and committed leaders trained to function effectively and equipped to serve the growing church ministries. This entails the academic and spiritual formation of men and women who will advance the Gospel, contribute to church growth, have a vision to respond to human need with loving service, are willing to speak prophetically against injustice, and see caring for God's creation as part of God's mission.

What?

These "What?" questions are closely linked with "Why?" What is the mission/church/founder trying to accomplish by establishing a school/seminary? What is the overall strategy for a country, church, or community? What is involved in setting up an institution?

The viability of an educational institution depends on a number of key factors. A mission/missionary/church needs to research and consider these important points with potential associates before establishing the institution:

1. **Ethos, Vision, and Mission of the Institution/School**

   What will be the ethos, vision, and mission of the institution? How will it be maintained, particularly when mission/missionaries have left?

2. **Governing Board/Council**

   As custodians of the ethos and vision of the school/college/seminary, they need to be like-minded people who understand their role, not as micromanagers, but in helping to set its vision and direction. How can its members sustain this vision? Will it involve training them?

3. **Ownership of the School/Property/Infrastructure**

   Who "owns" the school/buildings? This must be well understood and defined from the outset in accordance with the laws of the country. The relationship between the school/college and the founder(s) needs to be clearly articulated in the articles of incorporation. Otherwise, complications may arise if the school becomes successful.

4. **The Current Education System in the Country**

   What are the laws of the country with respect to education? Every country has a system of education structured on an established curriculum, calendar, final/qualifying exams, and certificates/diplomas. It may also entail a choice between offering a national school curriculum that prepares children for entry into the country's tertiary system and an international curriculum that enables children to access tertiary education outside their country. What regulations govern Bible/theological institutions in the country?

5. **Target Population of the School/College/Seminary**

   What will be the target population of the institution? If it is the community, what are the number of preexisting schools, their locations, and the community's view toward education? If it serves a peculiar clientele, such as middle-class and elite, how will a Christian school be more attractive than other schools that provide for this group? If it is a Bible/theological institution, what others exist and how will this institution be distinctive?

6. **Resources**

    a. *Land acquisition.* Who are the landowners? The aim is to acquire sufficient land to allow for expansion, consult relevant government bodies to secure the land, and to register it. This involves getting the required written documents and an official site plan properly signed between the one(s) establishing the school, the landowner(s), and other relevant parties so that in future the children of landowners may not cause trouble. In the case of the BTC, missionaries did not understand the process for registering land and obtaining title. The church has been left with complex problems and huge expenses sorting out legal rights to the land.

b. *Infrastructure*. What buildings are required for the school? What existing structures could be used or new structures built? ACI started from the old, dilapidated remains of the first Basel Mission Seminary in Ghana.

How can buildings be designed to incorporate the environmental conditions of the context? This requires involving people in the community and building sustainable structures that will endure.

What facilities, furniture, teaching materials, computing resources, and games equipment will be provided to attract people to send their children to the institution?

c. *Human resources*: identifying relevant people who will be involved in running and sustaining the institution.

Teaching staff. How many are needed and where will they come from? How will Christian teachers be assessed? Where will qualified staff be sourced for a higher-level theological institution? Teachers need to be committed to the Lord, to giving quality education, and to selfless service. Every staff member is in this sense a "chaplain" in their care for the students.

Administrative staff. How many are needed and what competencies are required in them?

7. Finances

Finances are needed for land acquisition, buildings, furniture, computing materials, internet access, recruiting, and paying staff. What are the legal obligations to pay staff social security? If a Christian institution has the attitude that staff are "working for the Lord" and pays low wages, this can be counterproductive as it may be difficult to employ well-qualified staff or even abusive if staff find it difficult to survive on their salaries.

A school is a long-term project and its viability in a country with few resources will depend on how the school is financed. In some contexts, people in the community may wait to see the progress of a new school before they send their children there.

Sources of financing to establish an institution and sustain it in the long-term include:

a. Support from others within or outside the country. Bank loans may be possible from within the country, especially as an institution cannot depend on foreign support as missionaries come and go as occurs in SIM.

b. Students' fees. Ideally, an institution should aim for students' fees to cover 100 percent of the running costs. This is possible if student numbers are high. If the numbers are small, sustaining a school becomes a challenge. This is a particular concern for Bible/theological institutions as they may charge higher fees to cover costs. The risk however, which ACI faces, is that students may prefer other institutions in the country that offer programs at lower costs.

c. Alumni. They are a possible source of finance for sustaining an institution and can work to raise funds.

d. Churches. If a school is linked with a church denomination, its churches may raise funding for the school.

e. Renting out the facilities. This may provide some revenue to complement students' fees.

8. Administration

What personnel are needed to properly administer the institution daily and to manage the grounds and buildings? If missionaries are working in the institution, are they established well enough in the language and culture to know what is going on in a typical work environment?

9. The Approach to Teaching (Pedagogy) and Learning

What will be the approach to teaching and learning? What understanding is there of indigenous methods of learning? Teaching must reflect the best of what is at the cutting edge of the profession and be thoroughly Christian in approach, focussing on the learning and well-being of the learners. Mobile phones, computers, and internet access are now widely available and considered a part of a global teaching and learning approach. ACI was forced to embrace online learning because of COVID-19.

10. Curriculum

Primary and high schools. What is the national curriculum for schools? The school would be required to comply with it. Some schools may also cater to an international curriculum. A Christian school, however, must have components that reflect their core mission and a Christian worldview integrated within the curriculum. Much work is required to integrate a Christian perspective into a course. More than just dropping biblical verses into subjects, it demands an awareness of Christian concepts that relate to particular subjects without promoting a consumer mentality. The timetable may include morning devotions/worship, a mentorship/discipleship session each week, and so on.

Bible/Theological training. The type of Bible/theological institution and its curriculum depend on the context, circumstances, and level of training appropriate to the mission/church context. Will it be residential full-time/part-time, online, or theological education by extension? Will the courses be accredited for a certificate, diploma, or degree? If so, by whom?

One problem with the Bible/theological content that missionaries introduce in cross-cultural contexts is their attempt to reproduce the type of training they received or what their home church recommends. Thus, assuming that theology is "fixed" and unchanging, they "import" courses designed and taught in their home countries. With many courses now being offered online, it is easy to fall into this trap.

Kwame Bediako at ACI developed "a model for new African theological and Christian formation for mission"[2] to help redesign curriculum for theological formation. Prior to his article, Bediako was already using this model to guide ACI lecturers in developing courses and new programs. The MA in Theology and Mission, for example, was developed, first, to equip Christian professionals for ministry, and second, as a bridging program for those who wanted to pursue higher studies in theology. As an educator, missionary, observer, and critic of education in Ghana, I realized from the outcomes and impact of this model on students that not only is it generally applicable to schools, but it also has a universal relevance beyond just the African context. Its four key overlapping components, depicted as four overlapping circles, are crucial in designing courses:

a. *Discerning the signs of the times* so that teachers and students grasp the significance of the time in which they stand and their part in it. One sign of these times is that as the most invasive, destructive, and rapacious of all the world's species, humans are consuming the world's resources at an unsustainable level.

b. *History and tradition,* as tools for understanding the signs of the times, enable students from diverse contexts to understand their story as part of wider Christian history, connected with both early Christian history and more recent Christian history.

c. *Context* allows for "contextualization," but not as an independent and dominant goal. Rather than writing artificial and abstract "contextual" theologies, it seeks to develop a deep understanding of the relationship between Gospel and culture where Scripture is the interpreter of culture and tradition.[3]

d. *A mind for mission and transformation* takes a student beyond simply "getting a degree" and breaks the dichotomy of "ministry" versus "mission." For a student, pastoral work involves full participation in God's mission to build up God's people in the church, to equip them to be witnesses in their families and communities, and to enable them to sustain God's creation as partners with God and not consumers.

Bediako suggests that these four key areas are superimposed on three core essential features of theological education: *the living God, the Bible,* and *faith and spirituality.* Bediako's model can be depicted as follows:

Figure 9.1: Bediako's Model

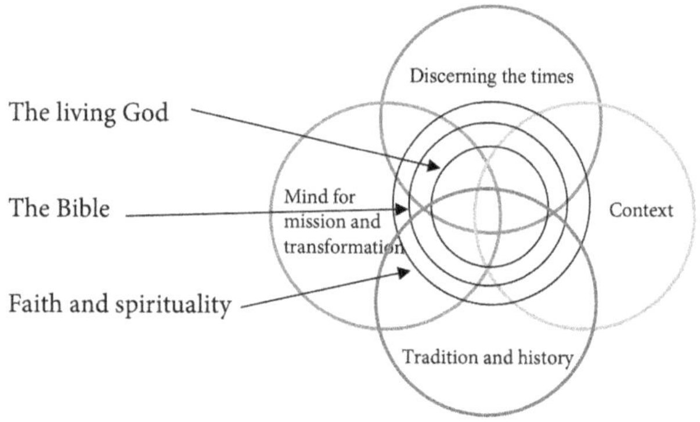

---

2 Kwame Bediako, "The African Renaissance and Theological Reconstruction: the Challenge of the Twenty-first Century," *Journal of African Christian Thought (JACT)* 4, no. 2 (December 2001): 29–33.

3 Kwame Bediako, "Scripture as the Hermeneutic of Culture and Tradition," *JACT* 4, no. 1 (June 2001): 2–11.

How?

If background preparation is important to start an institution, how then can school ministries and Bible/theological training be established? They may be established through a

- church,
- church community,
- group of passionate Christians,
- passionate individual, or
- mission already established in the country.

They can also be established as a

- nonprofit organization, or
- development project (again, nonprofit).

Whatever the case, establishing a school/college/seminary needs to be a cooperative effort between missionaries/founder(s), government authorities for legal registration, people in the proposed host community, and the board/council that will govern the institution. This will require building relationships and trust with people.

Prayer is critical in beginning an institution and throughout the stages of its development. Background research is vital. Schools/colleges/seminaries can start small and informally without requiring large finances, while missionaries/founder(s) and their partners seek resources to establish a more formal institution.

Hiring staff is also part of its sustainability. Because hiring the right people takes time, it is critically important to do thorough background checks on candidates. This may save time and heartache later on. Periodic staff training is important for refreshing their commitment to the school's ethos and vision.

If a school/college/seminary is in a culturally diverse city or has multicultural staff and/or students, intercultural intelligence becomes indispensable. Staff and students need to relate well to others. This impacts the effectiveness and sustainability of the institution.

In my observation, as an institution develops, certain procedures need to be put into place for:

- Quality assurance of programs and staff
- Accountability through timely communication, reports, and accreditation
- Safety and protection so that children/students are not abused by staff. This is necessary for Bible/theological institutions as well.
- Conflict resolution, restorative justice, fairness, and emotional intelligence to help staff and students positively manage emotions and diffuse disputes
- Environmental/ecological intelligence and renewal where staff and students become aware of their responsibilities in caring for creation

Limitations and Strengths

In general, there are limitations related to creating viable, sustainable, and useful educational institutions. One is where a government restricts Christian/mission involvement in education. Another occurs when the national curriculum promotes prosperity and consumerist ideals that further destructive attitudes toward the world's resources. Many, however, arise because of inflexible, ambiguous, and incomprehensible mission/founder's policies; poor human relationships; failure to consult relevant authorities, community, and church members; and cultural differences. When missionaries do not culturally adjust, host people conceive their actions as inappropriate.

These problems can escalate and result in the emerging church being angry and frustrated because their hopes are unfulfilled, especially if they expected the mission/founder to continue to financially sustain and run the institution. I observed this outcome in the BTC.

Other limitations are caused by pastors/missionaries being so driven that they "appropriate" the school—it is entirely about them and when they leave or die, the school collapses; "Christian/church schools" having a purely commercial motive; fees being lowered for the "church" and costs not being covered; external bodies "donating" money on the condition of diminishing the Christian emphasis; or institutions employing unsuitable teachers and not retraining them. I have observed institutions ending up having negligible Christian influence or even unwholesome impact, with a veneer of Christianity but no Christian essence. It reflects a lack of clear vision and transforms a Christian school into a nest of trouble.

When the methods, content, motives, and outcomes of education promote a consumerist gospel and Western consumer education it severely limits the viability and usefulness of Christian education. When a Bible College introduces courses or degrees in business or management solely to attract students and increase income, the Christian or theological components can end up being sidelined because no thought goes into how the Gospel interprets these subjects.

Conversely, as a valid aspect of God's mission, mission involvement in education has its strengths. Its long history illustrates the significance of education in the spread of the Gospel, the growth of the church, and increased self-confidence and awareness in those trained in Christian schools and theological institutions. A Christian school provides a valuable opportunity to inculcate in students a Christian worldview and to support the perspective of Christian parents. It projects the quality of education where teachers as educators do their work for the Lord and subscribe to the vision of Christian education. Students have the opportunity to experience life in a Christian community. In aiming for excellence even non-Christians see value in sending their children to a Christian school.

Whatever the strengths and weaknesses of educating children in a Christian school or training adults in a theological college, it is a privilege and a huge responsibility. God gives children to families, not to schools. A school has a moral contract with a family to partner with them in educating their children. Schools are an excellent opportunity for mission beyond the children. Students in theological training are potential partners in the work of God's mission.

The mission of establishing an institution is ultimately not just about the children or Christian leaders it serves. It is about rethinking methods, motives, and outcomes of education. It is about discipleship and serving God in the context of his mission in education. This requires a living faith in God the Father, the Lord Jesus Christ, and the Holy Spirit, as well as a total commitment to God's mission.[4] Thus at ACI, the curriculum is not only designed to produce such outcomes in the students, but the faculty and other staff are frequently reminded that they are part of a growing, transforming, serving, and worshipping community of God's people in mission.

Discussion Questions

1. What challenges and limitations do you perceive in mission involvement in creating educational institutions?

2. In considering the questions why, what, and how, what features do you consider important for creating a viable, sustainable, and useful school/college/seminary?

3. How does Bediako's model help reshape the motives, methods, and outcomes of education and so lessen the likelihood of students graduating with a consumerist perspective on life?

4. What features would you include in the overall curriculum and activities of a school, college, or seminary that would enable students to become responsible contributors to the spiritual and physical renewal of this earth?

---

4 See Andrew F. Walls and Cathy Ross, eds., *Mission in the Twenty-first Century: Exploring the Five Marks of Global Mission* (Maryknoll, NY: Orbis, 2008) for a discussion on the five marks of God's mission.

Chapter 9 Response

by Hyunchol Hong

I would like to express my deep gratitude to Dr. Allison Howell for considering important issues in educational mission work. I hope that this case study, based on her vast missionary experience, will greatly benefit the field of educational mission work.

There is a high possibility for missionaries to be associated with teaching, regardless of what kind of missionary works are being carried out in various mission fields. Mission work in establishing educational facilities requires a considerable amount of preparation and financial support. Along with these, sustainability should also be considered as one of the most fundamental requirements.

Howell provides a blueprint for designing educational institutions from the perspective of sustainability. Despite all of the difficulties on mission fields, this study shows that educational mission work is of strategic value to indigenous students and their families, and that it also holds a strategic position in view of God's Kingdom.

In the following two categories, I would like to add my thoughts to what Dr. Howell has discussed.

Considerations for Establishing Educational Institutions

Howell points out that missionaries are tempted to establish educational institutions expeditiously, and are often pressured to report positive results rapidly to their home churches or mission agencies, which may result in negative consequences.

Though there are many positive examples of Korean missionaries who establish educational facilities, there are some who try to make rapid progress by considering only the potential of educational mission work. However, such a hasty process often leads to failure when they do not spend time preparing for indigenization, which poses challenges to the sustainability of local schools when missionaries leave the field. Therefore, the importance of checking the following aspects can never be overemphasized—the reasons that missional ministries should be initiated and how indigenization in educational mission work is carried out.

After this, the "genuine needs" must be considered as well. When the needs of a missionary rather than the genuine needs on the field are considered the main motivation, the missionary will encounter deep troubles in the long run. As this study indicates, the genuine needs are the essential educational values that could influence the whole lifetimes of the students, and these genuine needs are not to be scaled by the mere principles of supply and demand but to be driven by missional values. This is well-reflected in the 2014 educational mission report in Korea that was written by Dr. Steve Sang-Cheol Moon. In this report, 62.5 percent of representatives and administrators of Korean missional institutions gave the following response—they consider that the most positive part in educational missions of Korea is the education of students who don't have access to the benefits of education.[5] This response reflects the values of holistic mission, which are not centered on the principle of economic consumerism but on the genuine needs on mission fields.

Evaluating Sustainability

It may not be easy to maintain the early founding visions and policies of educational institutions in

---

5 Sang-Cheol Moon, 한국교회의 교육선교 현황과 발전방안 [*Hangukgyohoeui gyoyukseongyo hyeonhwanggwa baljeonbangan*, Current status and development plan of the educational mission of the Korean church] (Seoul: GMF Press, 2014), 60; also available at https://krim.org/report-2014.

a cross-cultural field. Numerous problems arise unexpectedly in other cultures, and these problems could continue to occur when dealt with improperly, which would weaken sustainability. On the other hand, when missionaries rely on temporary methods for the sole purpose of smooth operation (rather than following the early policies and visions) due to the many restrictions, financial burdens, and operational difficulties in other cultures, there is a high possibility that it will blur the early spirit and vision of the establishment. Therefore, regarding sustainability, efforts should be made in maintaining the early spirit of the establishment. In this regard, the following issues need to be vigorously addressed from the very beginning of the establishment of an institution:

Financial independence. Many representatives and administrators of Korean educational mission agencies cite lack of financial independence as one of the most negative aspects of the educational missions of Korean missionaries. They replied that the best counterplan is "operating schools at reasonable sizes by grasping their appropriate educational demands in the mission fields."[6] This indicates that if a school is operated without considering its financial independence, it will not only weaken its sustainability but will gradually yield the early vision and spirit of the establishment when it cannot raise sufficient funds.

Recognizing the limitation of legal and government regulations. By providing the example of Bible Training Centre in Ghana, Howell notes that the "lack of judicious preparation and awareness of government regulations related to land (acquisition)" became sources of high expenditure. When missionaries establish educational facilities in mission fields, they tend to focus on the validity and positive prospect of their missionary work rather than focusing on the limitations. For this reason, they often emphasize only the bright side of the missionary work (whether intentionally or unintentionally), which causes their sponsors or mission headquarters to overlook the weakness and limitations of their plans. There are many limitations when missionaries establish educational facilities in foreign mission fields, such as those posed by the local laws or education law. Furthermore, if missionaries only rely on local assistants or partners to proceed with contracts, they may be negligent in following the policies and laws of the local region and the country, which will cause further problems.

Importance of the community environment that preserves a school's vision. While agreeing with Howell's emphasis on experiencing Christian life through curriculums with a Christian worldview, designing a community capable of maintaining close relationships with the students, rather than relying solely on curriculums, is crucial for educational projects to endure as strategic forms of mission work. A community where these close relationships form creates opportunities to share the Gospel.

In countries with restrictions on missionary work, it is very important to create a community environment based on such relationships to influence students with a Christian worldview. However, establishing such a community environment requires as much effort as developing a curriculum, and perhaps it could be accounted even more valuable than the curriculum. Thus, missionaries, teachers, indigenous coworkers, students, and families will have to put a lot of effort into creating a community environment that shares the vision and the spirit of the school.

Who is going to keep leading? "Who will continue to run this institution after a long time?" This is both a matter of sustainability and leadership succession, and we should not forget that the higher the degree of dependence on missionaries, the more difficult the problem of leadership succession becomes.

For long-term sustainability, it is necessary to look beyond the point of view that focuses only on recruiting teachers that are needed right away. In the long run, the task of how to train local education leaders may be more important than focusing only on immediate recruitment. Consequently, when considering leadership succession and the sustainability of an establishment, it is important to enable the active participation of the indigenous population from the beginning.

Howell notes the need for cultural sensitivity (intercultural intelligence) in school operations that work with local people, as well as systematic preparations to resolve cultural conflicts. What I would like to add to the point is that it is essential to involve native people in these intelligences and preparations as well. Especially, it is necessary to check if local voices were taken into consideration regarding important decisions of the school, through

---
6 Moon, 61.

reflective examination of the management system. This is because missionaries should always guard against falling into ethnocentrism and paternalism.

Accountability. This case study mentions several administrative responsibilities in the course of institutional development, and in my opinion it seems necessary for them to be further dealt with in depth from the point of view of mutual accountability. Problems such as leadership succession, fundraising, and ownership should be resolved from the perspective of accountability with mission agencies and home churches rather than from a missionary's individual perspective. The mission agency should evaluate the missionary plan more carefully in terms of sustainability, with mission agencies, missionaries, and sponsors sharing accountability rather than facing difficulties by proceeding from only a single missionary's perspective.

It is necessary to share responsibilities for education in the mission field with stakeholders (local leaders, churches, and families), not only for finances but curriculum designs as well. Here, missionaries should try to create a model that reflects holistic education and a biblical perspective rather than listening only to the needs of local consumers. In this respect Kwame Bediako's model, which Howell introduces in her discussion of "Bible/Theological training," provides appropriate help. Additionally, it is also important to develop an evaluation system based on such a model.

Conclusion

Missionaries who establish educational institutions need to take responsibility and a reflective approach toward their mission work. This is because despite the problems mentioned above, commitment to this field is, as Howell said, a commitment to education with Christian values: "Whatever the strengths and weaknesses of educating children in a Christian school or training adults in a theological college, it is a *privilege* and a *huge responsibility*" (emphasis mine).

I hope that there will be more critical and multidimensional assessments of the establishment of institutions for educational missionary work, such as Dr. Allison Howell's study, and I look forward to future research and discussions on what needs to be improved.

Chapter 10
Registration of Real Estate: A Pivotal Factor in a Collaborative Effort to Establish a Seminary in Postwar Japan

by J. Nelson Jennings

Imperial Japan's defeat and the subsequent US-led Occupation presented new opportunities and challenges to both Japanese churches and Christian mission agencies. Churches in Japan faced daunting realities of widespread poverty and of renewing their own multigenerational histories in the wake of their mixed wartime legacies. Western mission organizations strategized how to reconstruct Japan spiritually, politically, and economically.

It was within that volatile setting that a crisis erupted over the registration of a new seminary's real estate.

Deciding to Establish Tokyo Christian Theological Seminary

The multiple backgrounds of the crisis lay in the histories of the three entities that partnered to establish the new Tokyo Christian Theological Seminary.

No Protestant congregation in Japan had a longer history to renew than the Yokohama Kaigan Church, having been established in 1872. Led by Pastor Watanabe Renpei, in late 1948 the church voted to leave the wartime government-shaped *Kyodan* (United Church of Japan). Watanabe soon contacted Hasegawa Shintaro about establishing a "new Presbyterian church faithful to the Bible."[1]

Coming from a *Mukyokai* (Non-church) home, during his 1936–1946 US sojourn Hasegawa graduated from Faith Theological Seminary (FTS) and joined Presbyterian circles. In April 1949, the student ministry Hasegawa had been leading out of his father's house in Horinouchi, west Tokyo[2] became the Horinouchi Christian Church.[3] Approached by Watanabe and with young converts needing ministerial training, Hasegawa contacted his fellow FTS graduates in the Japan Mission of the

---

1 Yamaguchi Yoichi, 『東京基督神学校　草創期史』 [Tokyo Kirisuto Shingakko Sosokishi, Early history of Tokyo Christian Seminary], comp. Shimokawa Tomoya (Chiba, Japan: Tokyo Christian University, 2003), 6–7. This and subsequent translations mine.

2 Yamaguchi, 4.

3 Yamaguchi, 5.

Independent Board for Presbyterian Foreign Missions (IBPFM) about establishing a new seminary.

The IBPFM was established in 1933 by churchmen opposed to the infiltration of "modernism" into both the Presbyterian Church in the USA and its Board of Foreign Missions.[4] The Orthodox Presbyterian Church (OPC) and Bible Presbyterian Church (BPC) began soon thereafter. FTS was one of several BPC-associated agencies, all characterized by independence from official ecclesiastical control and separation from apostasy.

J. Gordon Holdcroft, former missionary for thirty years in Korea (1910–1940)[5] under its Japanese Occupation, was General Secretary of the IBPFM when its missionaries Phil and Jane Foxwell first arrived in south-central Japan (Mie Ken) in February 1948. Within one year five other IBPFM missionaries had joined them, including John and Jean Young. Like Holdcroft, John Young had lived many years under Japanese rule, namely in Korea, Japan, and Manchuria.[6] These missionaries constituting the IBPFM Japan Mission spent their early months in language learning, starting up children's ministries, considering alternative locations,[7] and looking into establishing a new BPC Japan (YC).

The IBPFM Japan Mission also searched early on to partner with existing Reformed and Presbyterian churches that would meet the IBPFM's (especially Holdcroft's and Young's) firmly held criteria of separation from apostasy, biblical inerrancy, and full repudiation of shrine worship. The new *Kaikakuha* (Christian Reformed Church of Japan [CRCJ]), per Young's description "composed of ministers and churches, about 20 in all, who have withdrawn from the Kyodan, … the large apostate organization" (YC), was the earliest leading candidate (YC).

Unexpectedly, however, the ministry partnership that took center stage for the IBPFM missionaries came through fellow Faith Seminary graduate "Roy" Hasegawa (as Shintaro was known by his English-speaking acquaintances). In September 1949, the IBPFM Japan Mission decided "to cooperate in establishing an independent seminary on the basis of the Westminster standards" and, starting with the Youngs, move to Tokyo as soon as possible (YC).

Attempting to Establish Tokyo Christian Theological Seminary

The leadership of Yokohama Kaigan Church and of the Horinouchi Christian Church, Young, and Foxwell soon met in Horinouchi and decided on the new church's (denomination's) name (apparently per Watanabe's suggestion [YC]): Christian Presbyterian Church of Japan (CPCJ). The Japanese held more planning meetings for the church's establishment over the next two weeks.

Disappointingly to the Japanese, soon thereafter Young conveyed that the missionaries were not going to join in with the new church.[8] Undeterred, on Sunday November 20 the Japanese church leaders gathered at the Kaigan Church and established the new CPCJ. Pastor Watanabe's summary remarks noted, "The new church's position is Bible-centered, Presbyterian in government, Calvinist theologically, and emphasizing evangelism. However, the church will never hold to a narrow denominationalism." Also, the new CPCJ adopted a revised version of the prewar Japan Christian Church (CCJ) constitution.[9]

In parallel fashion, basically the same group of people (including the missionaries) planned and established, one month earlier on October 16, the new Tokyo Christian Theological Seminary (TCTS) in the Hasegawa house in Horinouchi.[10] The TCTS "Founding Purpose" included "to raise up evangelists" who would be faithful, uncompromising with the world, and teachers of "the exact meaning of the Bible through its original languages"; be founded on the Westminster

---

4 Edward H. Rian, "The Independent Board," chap. 6 in The Presbyterian Conflict (Committee for the Historian of the OPC, 1992). Available online at The Orthodox Presbyterian Church, accessed December 7, 2020, https://www.opc.org/books/conflict/ch6.html.

5 Keith Coleman, "Missionary-Statesmen of the Bible Presbyterian Church," WRS Journal 11, no.1 (February 2004): 15–16, accessed December 28, 2020, accessed December 28, 2020, https://www.wrs.edu/assets/docs/Journals/2004a/Coleman%20-%20Missionary-Statesmen.pdf..

6 "Biographical Sketch," John M. L. Young Manuscript Collection #042, PCA Historical Center, accessed January 6, 2021, https://www.pcahistory.org/mo/youngjml.html.

7 John M. L. Young to IBPFM General Secretary J. Gordon Holdcroft, January 18, 1949; Letter 2, File 340-30, John M. L. Young Manuscript Collection, PCA Historical Center, St. Louis, Missouri (hereafter "YC"; details for all YC references available from the author).

8 Yamaguchi, 『草創期史』[Early history], 7.

9 Yamaguchi, 17–18.

10 Yamaguchi, 12–15; Anne E. Wigglesworth, "The History of the Japan Christian Theological Seminary," The Bible Times 10, no. 1 (1960): 16–17.

Standards; and have an independent board. Watanabe was board chairman, with other board members being Hasegawa, Kaigan Church elder Omura Haruo, Young, and Foxwell. Hasegawa was the school president.[11] As for the faculty Young explained to Holdcroft, "The Trustees and faculty are the same now for there is simply no one else we feel we can fully trust to work with us on its formation" (YC).

Central to this case study was how fundraising in the US for the seminary began with the Japan Mission's decision to move to Tokyo. That fundraising and searching for land purchases continued over the coming months (YC).

The First, Two-Part Rupture

Cracks in trust among TCTS's three founding entities soon opened into a twofold break: by the spring the Kaigan Church's Pastor Watanabe and Elder Omura were no longer part of the seminary (YC), and the new CPCJ had dissolved.[12] Hasegawa, who became the seminary board chair after Watanabe's departure, and his Horinouchi Christian Church quickly joined with another new church and effectively reestablished a slightly renamed[13] Christian Presbyterian Church of Japan (CPCJ).[14]

The most straightforward explanation for the two-part rupture lay in the relationship and theological differences between Watanabe and the seminary, particularly John Young.[15] The missionaries' decision not to participate in the new CPCJ must have raised questions for Watanabe; similarly, Watanabe and the Kaigan Church's (as well as Hasegawa's) participation in the Japan Protestant Federation, established in May 1948[16] and not as separatist as the BPC, must have raised questions for Young and the IBPFM. The contrasting emphases in the founding purposes of TCTS and CPCJ—the former stressing the Westminster Standards, the latter a less specific Calvinist stance and continuation of the prewar CCJ—revealed the two strong leaders' contrasting theological convictions as well.

Young wrote to Holdcroft, "I feel that it is very much of the Lord, and a cause of real gratitude to him, that Mr. Watanabe is off our Seminary Board and faculty since he wouldn't come around to our position" (YC). Holdcroft responded similarly (YC). In Watanabe's case, as the differences in viewpoints came more fully to light through his being pressed by fellow seminary board and faculty members (the missionaries), and in his "hoping that the Kaigan Church traditions of living and evangelism would continue," he concluded it best to "wipe the slate clean" and "call the whole thing off" with the seminary. That would have to be true of the new CPCJ venture with the Horinouchi Church as well (the rupture's second part), since apparently they thought like the seminary.[17]

While real estate registration was not directly related to this first TCTS rupture, the stage was set for what unfolded immediately thereafter.

The Second Rupture and Real Estate Registration

No sooner had TCTS and Watanabe/Kaigan Church parted ways than Young began raising concerns about Hasegawa, the single most central figure in the TCTS enterprise and then new board chair: "We have a problem to work out with Roy [Hasegawa] yet as to the exact relation between himself and our Mission in the direction of the seminary and gathering of funds for it" (YC). Over the ensuing months Young and Holdcroft increasingly expressed a plethora of additional concerns, including Hasegawa's changeableness, fits of anger, and nationalism (YC). They perceived Hasegawa as desiring, including for fundraising purposes, to keep his US and Japan church relations wider than IBPFM's preferred separatist circles, thus holding Hasegawa back from taking a clear enough stand condemning shrine worship (YC).

With specific regard to TCTS, there was no more inflammatory point than in whose name the seminary's land and buildings would be registered, as well as how that decision would be made (YC). On the IBPFM side, who raised the funds was a crucial factor for deciding the registrant's name (YC). Because the bulk of funding for seminary land and buildings was being raised from US donors (often as designated gifts) by IBPFM personnel, the IBPFM US home office

---

11 Yamaguchi,『草創期史』[Early history], 12–15.

12 Yamaguchi, 18–20.

13 Yamaguchi, 12–15; Anne E. Wigglesworth, "The History of the Japan Christian Theological Seminary," *The Bible Times* 10, no. 1 (1960): 16–17.

14 Yamaguchi,『草創期史』[Early history], 20;[*Kyokai Enkaku*, Church history],[Horinouchi Christian Church], accessed January 5, 2021, http://horichurch.main.jp/enkaku.html.

15 Yamaguchi,『草創期史』[Early history], 18–20.

16 Yamaguchi, 21.

17 Yamaguchi, 19.

and its Japan Mission together assumed and exercised decision-making authority over the funds' specific use as well as over how the real estate purchased would be registered, specifically in the IBPFM Japan Mission's name (YC). That multifaceted matter, which coalesced in September 1950 (as described next), eventually led to the spring 1951 rupturing of the collaborative TCTS venture between the IBPFM Japan Mission and Hasegawa.

From June to November 1950 Hasegawa was away from Japan, mainly in the US for fundraising. Soon after he had left Japan, the TCTS Faculty voted to establish a preparatory Tokyo Bible College (YC), an idea to which Hasegawa had always been opposed (YC). In early September the TCTS Board and Faculty, in coordination with the IBPFM Japan Mission, went ahead and decided to build a seminary dormitory and register it in the mission's name—agreeing as well to "discuss whether to register it in the name of the Seminary Board or not" after Hasegawa returned (YC). Upon learning of these decisions from a late September meeting with Holdcroft, Hasegawa immediately wrote to the missionaries that the seminary was to be "a united effort" (YC)[18] for the sake of the indigenous Japanese church. Hasegawa's conviction was that, while independent from ecclesiastical control, TCTS should have its real estate holdings in the name of the CPCJ, not that of the (foreign) IBPFM Japan Mission (YC). However, Young's letter to Holdcroft regarding Hasegawa's request "to delay building the seminary dorm until he had worked out a satisfactory arrangement, of ownership I assume, with you" was clear: "It is too late to delay now, and besides I see no point to it at all…. If our Board raises the money for the building what is more reasonable than that it should be registered in our name?" (YC).

Hasegawa–IBPFM relations deteriorated over the next several months. Holdcroft stressed the confusion caused by there never having been a written agreement regarding responsibilities for TCTS, including for property holdings (YC). In November Hasegawa returned to Japan deeply convinced of the dictum, "Evangelism of Japan by Japanese hands"[19]; put differently by Young, "When Roy got back he came in a different mood" (YC). Just as Young and Holdcroft had questioned his alleged changeableness, Hasegawa questioned the IBPFM's alleged changes in policy about control of new churches and of TCTS—to the point of rhetorically asking Holdcroft, "Do you really wish to help establish an indigenous institution and help it grow? Or do you (as your recent letter indicates) wish to establish a puppet organization 'under the auspices of the Board completely'?" (YC). The IBPFM Executive Committee began to "feel that there was little or no possibility of conducting a school in which [Hasegawa] was a partner [and] that [TCTS] had better be, and could only be, under the control of the [IBPFM] Board" (YC). Young, having concurred with Hasegawa's initial appeal that "the seminary … could not be started without us [the Japan Mission]," also came to believe, "It is perfectly obvious that it can operate without him" while expressing the concurrent desire, "but we dont [sic] want that. We want a harmonious cooperation in which together we advance this work" (YC).

All along "in the background" was the crucial reality—all too evident to the students, faculty, and other Japanese aware of US-supported schools like TCTS—that silently nudged the IBPFM to assume primary control of what had begun as a Japanese initiative: "the magnitude of the [financial] support from the US."[20] That support was true of the Occupation in general, the context within which the IBPFM Japan Mission, relatively non-affluent as it was, could envision constructing "a real seminary building [with] class rooms [sic], dining hall and kitchen…, 2 rooms for dean and wife…, [and] library…." (YC). The financial disparity between the US-based IBPFM and postwar, poverty-stricken Japanese Christians—including Hasegawa, despite his financial connections in both Japan and the US—also enabled the IBPFM to appeal to its commitment to "build up 'indigenous' institutions" in two different ways. On the one hand, IBPFM's stated goal for TCTS was to have it owned and governed by Japanese. However, simply to give funds and property to the CPCJ (by then minus the large and historic Kaigan Church) would violate "a really indigenous work [being] self-supporting" (YC)[21] and "would simply be to turn it over to Roy and let him control it" (YC).

---

18 Emphasis original.
19 Yamaguchi,『草創期史』[Early history], 22.

20 Yamaguchi, 28.
21 Emphasis original.

At the May 16, 1951 TCTS faculty meeting Hasegawa announced, "I cannot continue to teach under the current faculty."[22] Over the next two days, votes by the TCTS Faculty, IBPFM Japan Mission, and TCTS Board resulted in:

- A reconstituted seminary board of Rev. Fujii Shigeaki,[23] Young, and Foxwell;
- The closure of TCTS and TBC;
- The immediate establishment of the Japan Christian Theological Seminary (JCTS) and Japan Bible College (JBC), both of which would use the facilities (1) registered in the IBPFM Japan Mission's name and (2) heretofore had been used by the seminary and Bible college.

Moreover, on May 23 Hasegawa began a new Tokyo Theological Institute, operating out of his father's house in Horinouchi. The JCTS and JBC faculties continued (minus Hasegawa) from TCTS and TBC, while students were divided as to where they would continue their studies.[24]

The Ruptures' Summary and Analysis

Some analysis of, effects from, and reactions to the first rupture have already been mentioned. Important to reemphasize is how the significant Watanabe/Kaigan Church departure from TCTS severely weakened the Japanese composition of the seminary's board, faculty, and wider support. That weakness directly contributed to the second rupture, namely between Hasegawa and others in TCTS, by leaving Hasegawa practically alone in dealing with the IBPFM Japan Mission, particularly regarding TCTS real estate registration.

While Hasegawa's and Young's similar convictions about "strict biblical faith" held them together in supporting Watanabe's separation from TCTS, several differences emerged between Hasegawa and the IBPFM Japan Mission. Per Young's public explanation, Hasegawa was opposed to starting a Christian college, and he criticized TCTS's lack of independent status due to the board having a majority of missionaries. The missionaries, on the other hand, had emphasized the Shinto problem and stood for BPC-type separatism. One insightful analysis points out that, alongside such an explanation, the core issue was the "antagonism" between Young and Hasegawa. Young was a "champion" of BPC "separatism, anti-modernism, and anti-communism," with the added element in Japan of anti-idolatry (State Shinto),[25] all of which pushed Hasegawa further than he wished fully to identify himself.

What this case study shows is that, interconnected with the issues just summarized, the several facets of registering TCTS real estate are what inflamed tensions between Hasegawa and the IBPFM Japan Mission enough to result in a formal separation.[26] As part of its "strong, militant, daring testimony on a world level" (YC), IBPFM had come to Japan "still a pagan, feudalistic nation" in their eyes (YC) with clear, uncompromising positions but without a clear strategy to implement them. Pastors Watanabe Renpei and Hasegawa Shintaro, leaders of the new Christian Presbyterian Church of Japan, offered the newly arrived IBPFM Japan Mission both a clear strategy and Japanese partnership for implementing IBPFM's testimony. When Watanabe, then Hasegawa, did not fully align with the IBPFM's clear and uncompromising positions, the missionaries realized they did not "fully trust" Watanabe, then Hasegawa, after all. The mistrust between Hasegawa and IBPFM arose and grew over questions about seminary control, especially property ownership.

Particularly important was how the Japan Mission's access to US–IBPFM funding, greater than Hasegawa could raise, for TCTS real estate holdings translated into a gradual transfer of shared control of TCTS to IBPFM control-cemented by the decision to register the first new TCTS building in the name of the IBPFM Japan Mission. The missionaries believed, and tried to explain to Hasegawa, that the new dormitory "was an <u>absolute must</u>," that it was to be "loaned to the seminary" by IBPFM, and that the other Japanese involved had been "urging it and pushing it" (YC).[27] Even so, the Japan Mission's genuine intentions of helping to establish an indigenous seminary in support of an indigenous Presbyterian church were stifled, at least temporarily, by the financial and legal control the IBPFM and its Japan Mission exercised over new TCTS real estate.

---

22 Yamaguchi, 30.

23 Fujii was a CRCJ pastor who had moved from Mie Ken to Tokyo as Young's "helper and interpreter in teaching for each of our Mission" (YC).

24 Yamaguchi,『草創期史』[Early history], 30–31.

25 Yamaguchi, 31–32.

26 The depth and scope of Young's unfavorable opinion of Hasegawa emerges in response to Hasegawa's objections to the September 1950 decision to construct the dormitory and register it in the IBPFM Japan Mission's name (YC).

27 Emphasis original.

Epilogue

JCTS completed its first three buildings between December 1950 and November 1953, all registered in the IBPFM Japan Mission's name and each publicly named after US donors.[28] In 1952 the IBPFM Japan Mission decided, voluntarily and particularly for tax-related purposes, "that constitution for incorporation under the new [1951] religious boides [sic] law[29] be accepted" (YC). In 1960, at "THE INITIAL RECOMMENDATION of the Japanese government official … concerned with our conformity to their laws," (YC)[30] the Japan Mission changed its incorporated name to the "Japan Presbyterian Mission" (JPM). The corporation's constitution was also changed to make the board members self-perpetuating instead of also requiring outside, i.e., IBPFM, representation.[31] These constitutional changes were made during the Japan Mission's separation from IBPFM (due to a painful split in the BPC) and related tug-of-war over the JCTS real estate. While the changes drew the ire of the IBPFM and its sympathizers,[32] the missionaries suggested parenthetically, "(Perhaps a hundred years from now we will be able to say that this was a most unusual providence put forth to contiune [sic] the testimony in Japan without injury)" (YC). The increased antagonism between the IBPFM Board and the missionaries, plus the legal assurance of the seminary's ongoing ministry in Japan, also once again demonstrated the vital importance of the decision process and name selected for a mission's real estate registration.

One final and important note is that the missionaries' goal of an indigenous seminary was gradually realized. Japanese board and faculty members, largely trained at JCTS or in the US, increasingly assumed leadership during the 1960s and 1970s. Moreover, in 1978 the Kyodan Holiness Flock bought the JCTS portion of JPM's property, and JCTS moved to a different campus.[33]

Discussion Questions

1. How did the histories of all three collaborating founding entities of TCTS contribute to the struggles that arose in connection with TCTS real estate registration?

2. What could, or should, any of the three entities have done differently to avert the rupture that took place in connection with TCTS real estate registration?

3. Could, or should, the TCTS real estate registration have been handled differently? If so, how?

---

28 Wigglesworth, "The History," 17–18.
29 "Religious Corporations Act," accessed January 5, 2021, http://www.japaneselawtranslation.go.jp/law/detail_main?re=02&vm=02&id=2084.
30 All capitals original.
31 JPM Archives, Chiba, Japan.
32 J. Philip Clark, "To Answer Your Questions on Japan," *The Free Press*, October 19, 1961, 6–9.
33 三交沿革史編纂委員会 [Three Schools Historical Development Compiling Committee], 『東京キリスト教学園のあゆみ』 [*Tokyo Kirisutokyo Gakuen no Ayumi*, The life of Tokyo Christian Institute] (Chiba, Japan: Tokyo Christian Institute, 1989), 111–113.

Chapter 10 Response

by Jimoon Chung

I am so privileged to give a response to Dr. Nelson Jennings's very meaningful case study on TCTS real estate registration, which resulted in ruptures between Japanese church leaders and a North American mission group. In this study, Dr. Jennings analyzed the main reason for the clashes between three collaborating, founding entities of TCTS. I fully agree that the reason was the matter of trust between those groups, along with the lack of a proper written agreement to clarify the responsibilities of each group.

I was deeply reminded of how important it is to trust colleagues in ministry and life, including one's spouse. And I simply find that we need a long time to build up trust in human relationships. Registration is not just a matter of names, but of trust. Lack of trust resulted in the conflict of hegemony. We need much grace from God and much patience to affect synergy between team members instead of judging each other on our differences. And, Dr. Jennings also pointed out that it caused distrust between the groups when there was no written agreement to clarify each group's responsibilities.

There were three collaborating entities involved in establishing TCTS. The first one was Kaigan (海岸) Church, which was the first Protestant church in Japan. Kaigan Church left *Kyodan* (教団), the denomination formed by the Japanese military government during World War II when they forced all denominations to unite. I understand why Pastor Watanabe and Kaigan Church parted from TCTS. Pastor Watanabe was imprisoned for refusing to hand over a large church bell for making weapons in the war effort. The church bell had been presented to Kaigan church by Christians in the United States. He took a very courageous stance—he did not want to repay the generosity of American Christians with enmity. Kaigan Church and its pastor wanted to preserve their tradition as the first Protestant church in Japan.

The second entity was Pastor Hasegawa, who stressed the "evangelism of Japan by Japanese hands." He had a *Mukyokai* (Non-church) background. He was from Faith Theological seminary and joined Presbyterian circles. He was leading students in his father's house, which became the Horinouchi Christian church. The leading pastors of the next generations in the Japanese churches, including pastor Oyama Reiji (尾山玲二), were from that church.

The third entity was IBPFM, which emerged from a militant background with emphasis on anti-modernism and anti-communism, clearly rejecting State Shinto. IBPFM put emphasis on biblical inerrancy and separation from apostasy. They wanted to establish Bible Presbyterian Church. Two Japanese churches (Kaigan and Horinouchi) agreed to launch TCTS and asked IBPFM to join them. IBPFM had a good testimony, standing for truth. On the other hand, the two Japanese churches had clear strategies, and the personnel. It seemed that they complemented each other well. But there were theological differences and different opinions about in-depth training of full-time workers. Above all, there was mistrust between Young and Hasegawa, which resulted in painful ruptures in the end. God blessed each group in building up his Kingdom. But they were not successful when they worked together for a single purpose. They could not trust each other, even though they trusted God. How much should we trust God, who called us together for his purpose, is faithful, and will carry out his purpose to call us as teams? When I reflect on my missionary life, during a church plant eight years ago I could not overcome the different opinions between missionaries. I chose to work on my own instead of becoming part of a missionary team to complement each other.

It looked like it was off to a very good start when two Japanese pastors agreed to build TCTS to train full-time workers. It was ideal that Japanese Christian leaders took the initiative and asked missionaries to join them. But reality was different. In Acts 15, there was a rupture between Paul and Barnabas in the matter of forming a mission team that included Mark. It seems that we can't avoid such conflicts in building his church. God causes everything to work together for the good of those who love God (Rom. 8:28). Later Paul wrote to Timothy, "Get Mark and bring him with you, because he is helpful to me in my ministry" (2 Tim. 4:11). If IBPFM had had such an attitude—to be helpful to the Japanese church instead of asserting their position—they might have averted the ruptures.

I feel that trusting relationships are more essential than carrying out projects. In general, we need a long time to build up trusting relationships. Without healthy relationships, projects can be very fragile. If there had been mutual trust between them, TCTS might have had a different history. As Dr. Jennings mentioned, a core issue was the antagonism between Young and Hasegawa. Young was a champion of BPC (anti-idolatry, anti-modernism, anti-communism, and anti-separatism). Young could not trust Hasegawa because he did not take a clear stance against shrine-worship, and he was also too changeable and easily angered in person. If they had taken more time to seek his way together, for several days or on a weeklong retreat, they would have found wonderful points of contact with each other, and there would have been a different story.

When we trust each other under the flag of lordship, it is easier to die to our rights to be right before God. In fact, we cannot succeed in team ministry unless we die to ourselves with Christ on the cross.

Because IBPFM collected most of the funds, they thought that it was very reasonable to register TCTS in their name. Missionaries even thought that registration in the name of IBPFM was helpful to the indigenous Japanese church.

On the other hand, Pastor Hasegawa should have conceded that TCTS be registered in the name of IBPFM, on the condition that it be for a temporary period, either five or ten years. It seems contradictory that Pastor Hasegawa insisted on the evangelism of Japan by Japanese hands, but also received the funds for TCTS from the US. I remember that unordained, professional missionaries came to Korea, at a time when Korea was not widely recognized by Western churches. So, there was at least some support from Western churches compared with Japan. Missionaries emphasized self-support from the earliest stage and taught Korean Christians to sacrifice for building up churches. Ironically, in God's hands poverty became a great blessing to build up churches in Korea.

In conclusion, I am so grateful to Dr. Jennings for his case study that makes us think deeply about the matter of trust. I am reminded of Philippians 2:3–5 for the work of the Lord: "Do nothing out of selfish ambition or vain conceit. Rather, in humility value others above yourselves, not looking to your own interests but each of you to the interests of the others. In your relationships with one another, have the same mindset as Christ Jesus." I would like to remind us that we are called to serve the Lord and others; in other words, we are called to make others successful in following the Lord and to be helpful to national churches. We see many conflicts between Christian workers in the mission field. We cannot avoid ruptures unless we deny our rights, trusting in our faithful Lord. When there was quarreling between Abram's and Lot's herdsmen (Gen. 13), even though Abram could have chosen first (either the land of Canaan or the plain of the Jordan), he gave up his right and let his nephew Lot choose first. Abram trusted God. He wanted to avoid quarreling before the world. He chose the testimony of God, and that became his inheritance.

Chapter 11
Money and Self-Support: A Challenging Principle of the Nevius Method for Korean Protestant Churches and Missions

by Sung-Deuk Oak

This chapter discusses the Nevius Method (hereafter NM) in Korea in the context of its historical development from 1879 to 1920 and its missiological and academic interpretations from 1930 to the present. It focuses on the issue of self-support, the first among the three-self principles (self-support, self-propagation, and self-government). The chapter highlights the indigenization of NM in Korea by examining controversies between Seoul (Underwood) and Pyongyang (Moffett) over the revision of NM. After evaluating major interpretations of NM, it concludes that self-support is an enduring principle that can be applied to contemporary declining Korean Protestantism.

History and Genealogies

The first section of history searches for the original meanings of the principle of self-support of the NM. Here we need to study four genealogies of the NM and its method of self-support. Genealogy 1 describes the Nevius Method in Shandong, China, 1880–1890, and the Ross Method in Manchuria, 1872–1910. Genealogy 2 describes the Underwood Method in Seoul, 1885–1910, and the Moffett Method in Pyongyang, 1894–1910. Each genealogy preserved the DNA of self-support, yet modified it in the process of its application.

Genealogy 1:
Nevius-Ross Method in China, 1880–1890

Unlike the conventional historiography of the NM, this chapter uses two coined terms—the Ross Method (hereafter RM) and the Nevius-Ross Method (hereafter NRM), for John Ross applied the NM in Manchuria and developed a new, synthesized version—the NRM. The NRM was introduced to northwestern Korea before the NM was transferred to Seoul in 1890.

Self-Supporting in the Nevius Method in Shandong

John Livingston Nevius (1829–93) advocated Christ instead of civilization. Nevius thought that mission work passed through three stages. In the second stage when a small church was gathered, a missionary's "special business was to plant independent, self-supporting Christian institutions, and to raise up a native ministry." The final stage was "real conversions from heathenism, and the establishment of native Christian churches."[1] The goal of NM was to make a speedy evangelization of a region or a nation through planting indigenous churches. He tried to make the work "independent and self-supporting from the first. Rural Christians provided their own places of worship—generally a large, decent room in some house; and everywhere aggressive work is being done in the regions around, entirely on the voluntary principle."[2] In 1880, he summarized the new revolutionary system with ten points. The first one was, "Its most important nature is the 'voluntary system' in contrast to the 'employment system.'"[3]

Nevius presented a series on mission methods in *The Chinese Recorder* in November and December of 1885.[4] They were reprinted in 1886 with a supplement as *Methods of Mission Work*.[5] The new system had the same aim as the old one—"the evangelization of China by the Chinese." The famine relief work in 1876–78, which distributed more than $20,000 and helped more than seventy thousand people, left the impression that foreigners had an abundance of money. The old employment system tended to excite a mercenary spirit, increasing the number of rice Christians and halting the voluntary work of unpaid agents.

The Ross Method in Manchuria

John Ross (1842–1915), the founder of the Protestant mission in Manchuria in 1872, was not only the initiator of the Korea mission, but also an architect of the Presbyterian mission method in Korea. He was a practitioner of the three-self method in Manchuria, which was introduced to Korea in 1879. He began to translate the Scriptures into Korean after the publication of *The Corean Primer* in 1877 for future missionaries to Korea. Ross was the first translator, publisher, and distributor of the Korean Gospels. He completed the whole Korean New Testament in 1887. RM or NRM had strong elements of vernacularism and self-propagation through Korean colporteurs' distribution of the Korean scriptures.

Most studies have not recognized the close relationship between Nevius and Ross. In 1898, Ross wrote to the editor of *The Chinese Recorder* and confessed that he learned his own method from Nevius and his writings.[6] Ross visited Nevius to learn his method in September 1887, during his visit to see the first organized Korean Presbyterian Church in Seoul.

Ross published *Mission Methods in Manchuria* in 1903. In it he explained the principles and the methods by which the Manchurian church began with three baptized men in 1874 and grew to more than thirty thousand church members after thirty years. In its second edition in 1906, Ross stressed that the Diocletian persecutions during the Boxer uprising tested and justified the legitimacy of the three-self principles. Ross believed that the case of Mukden could be used as an example "for the speedy evangelization of the world."[7]

Ross recommended a form of itinerancy whereby a mission settled in a larger city as strategic center. Missionaries could superintend a large circuit of many hundred square miles and travel several times a year to as many as twenty substations. Each substation had its own paid Chinese evangelist. As Ross put more emphasis on self-propagation, he employed more paid evangelists than Nevius. Ross could hire good helpers with lower salaries. The minimum concentration of foreign missionary force, and the maximum extension of Chinese evangelism was their basic principle.

Genealogy 2:
The Underwood-Moffett Method in Korea, 1885–1910

NM and NRM in China developed into the Underwood-Moffett Method in Korea from 1885 to 1910. Underwood said in 1900, "The system as now followed by our mission is not exactly what we

---

1 J. L. Nevius, *China and the Chinese* (New York: Harper & Brothers, 1869), 336, 352–353, 370.

2 Helen S. C. Nevius, *The Life of John Nevius* (New York: Revell, 1895), 381–382.

3 J. L. Nevius, "Mission Work in Central Shantung," *The Chinese Recorder* 11 (October 1880): 357–364.

4 J. L. Nevius, "Principles and Methods Applicable to Station Work, Letter I," *The Chinese Recorder* 16 (November 1885): 421–424; Nevius, "Letter II," *The Chinese Recorder* 16 (December 1885): 461–467.

5 First edition, *Methods of Mission Work* (Shanghai: Presbyterian Mission Press, 1886); second edition, *Methods of Mission Work* (New York: SVM, 1899); third edition, *The Planting and Development of Missionary Churches* (New York: BFMPCUSA, 1899); fourth edition, *Planting and Development of Missionary Churches* (Philadelphia: Presbyterian and Reformed Publishing Co., 1958).

6 John Ross, "Missionary Methods," *The Chinese Recorder* 29 (May 1898): 247.

7 Ross's Reply (#164) to the Questionnaire of the Commission I, The World Missionary Conference, 1910 (Day Mission Collection, Yale Divinity School Library).

originally knew as the Nevius system."[8] When inexperienced young missionaries—Allen, Underwood, Heron, and Miss Ellers—arrived in Seoul in 1884 and 1885 and argued over the policy to deal with the prohibition of evangelism by the government, they sought advice from Dr. Frank F. Ellinwood, the secretary of the board in New York, and the seasoned missionaries in the neighboring stations in China and Japan. Thus, John L. Nevius in Shandong across the Yellow Sea, John Ross in Mukden across the Yalu River, and Dr. James C. Hepburn (1815–1911) in Yokohama across the Korean Strait became their mentors.

Self-Support in Underwood's NM in Seoul

Rev. Horace G. Underwood (1859–1916), the first Presbyterian clerical missionary working in Seoul from 1885, was an enthusiastic evangelist. He clashed with Dr. Horace N. Allen (1858–1932) over mission methods. Allen, who transferred from Shanghai to Seoul in September 1884 as the first resident Protestant missionary, cured Min Yŏngik, Queen Min's nephew, seriously wounded at the Kapsin Coup in December 1884. Allen was appointed to the head of the Government (Royal) Hospital in April 1885. Allen opposed the illegal direct evangelism of Underwood and Dr. John W. Heron.

When Underwood organized the first church in Seoul with fourteen members on September 27, 1887, he invited Dr. Ross to find a solution for the conflicts in mission policy and method. The fourteen Koreans, except for Ro Ch'un-gyŏng, were converted through Ross's teaching and Sŏ Sang-nyun's distribution of the Ross's translation of the Gospels of Luke and John. After meeting Ross, Underwood studied the NM and read *Methods of Mission Work* (1886) to train Korean evangelists.[9]

Underwood invited Mr. and Mrs. Nevius to Seoul in June 1890. The couple advised seven young missionaries for two weeks. The Korea Mission of the PCUSA adopted the NM in its "Standing *Rules and By-Laws*" in February 1891. Since then, the board presented every outgoing new missionary to Korea with a copy of Nevius's little book, *Methods of Mission Work* (1886), retitled *The Planting and Development of Missionary Churches* (1899). The rules of the Korea mission were more thoroughly self-supporting than the plans laid out by Nevius. In 1893, the Council of the Presbyterian Missions (consisting of four missions) adopted the modified NRM. The "native" workers' contribution to the growth of the church was more significant in Korea than in China and Japan.

A good example of self-support was the church building in Sorae, Hwanghae Province, in 1894. A widow donated the lot; a yangban woman caught seashells and sold them; some donated timbers, ox to haul them, or grain for the workers, and others volunteered for labor.[10] The first Christian chapel in Korea was built solely by self-support. Following the example at Sorae, Koreans in Chŏngdong, Seoul, began to build a chapel in 1894. Young members of the church volunteered to work as the "Red Cross Cholera Corps" at the Underwood Shelter, used as a temporary government cholera hospital. The government paid them wages, which they offered for the church building. Koreans paid all the cost except for the lot and the roof.

The Moffett Method in Pyongyang

Rev. Samuel A. Moffett (1864–1939), who arrived in Seoul in January 1890, decided to move to Pyongyang to open a new station for building indigenous churches in the northwestern provinces. He was unsatisfied with political entanglement and missionary infighting in Seoul. After meeting with Dr. Nevius in June 1890, Moffett visited Dr. Ross in 1891 in Shenyang (Mukden), with James S. Gale (accompanied by Sŏ Sang-nyun to Ŭiju and Paek Hong-jun to Shenyang), and learned the Ross method.[11] Moffett opened a new station in Pyongyang in 1894 with seven baptized Korean members and made it one of the most indigenous mission stations (with Korean style buildings) in the world.[12] More than one thousand members began to erect the Central Presbyterian Church in Pyongyang in 1898. Rev. Graham Lee supervised Korean carpenters and completed the church building of one thousand five hundred seats in 1901. Koreans raised two-thirds of the cost of the mission, while missionaries and their

---

8 H. G. Underwood, "The Working of Self-Support in the Fields: Korea," *Ecumenical Missionary Conference, New York, 1900*, vol. 2 (New York: American Tract Society, 1900), 301.

9 H. G. Underwood to F. F. Ellinwood, July 10 and August 25, 1888, Letters and Reports of the Korea Mission, PCUSA, Presbyterian Historical Center, Philadelphia.

10 Underwood, "The Working of Self-Support," 303.

11 S. A. Moffett, "Evangelistic Tour in the North of Korea," *Church at Home and Abroad* 5 (October 1891): 330; Moffett, "An Evangelistic Tramp through North Korea," *The Herald and Presbyter*, January 13 & 20, 1892.

12 J. Hunter Wells, "Northern Korea," *The Assembly Herald* 7, no. 5 (November 1902): 442–443.

friends in America donated the remaining one-third. This became the usual practice for larger churches in the cities.

In 1909, Moffett stated that "the seed thoughts of two great principles in our work—the Bible Training Class system and self-support" came from Nevius. "In the development of these ideas," Moffett continued, "local conditions and our experience in adapting the methods to meet different circumstances have led to great modification."[13] As Underwood mentioned, the methodology of the Korea Mission did not impose a completely organized church on the Koreans, and planned church architecture in accordance with the ability of the natives to build and the styles of houses generally used. Self-support, with flexible church organization and Korean-style church buildings, became "the cornerstone of the indigenization."[14] The whole system of the Nevius method in Korea was, therefore, closer to the congregationalism of Rufus Anderson (1796–1880) than the moderate Anglicanism of Henry Venn (1796–1873). Yet NRM—a combination of Scottish Enlightenment mission theory and NM—supplemented this local church centeredness and individual salvation priority.

NRM had some distinctive Korean features. A major objective of the self-supporting principle was building local churches without the mission's support. So, most early chapels were small, thatched houses or tiled roof houses. Some churches, when enlarged or newly constructed, were built in an "L" shape, so that one wing was occupied by men and the other by women.

NRM's motto, "Maximum natives, and minimum missionaries," could be realized with well-trained church members as volunteer evangelists, and one of its most effective means was the system of the Bible Training Class (BTC). At the BTC in Pyongyang in January 1907, the great revival started and swept through all the churches in Korea in a year, and spread out to Manchuria and China. In addition, a voluntary dawn prayer meeting was started by Koreans at BTC in Hwanghae province 1898, and Kil Sŏnju made it a voluntary church program in 1909 when the revival fever receded.[15]

---

13 S. A. Moffett, "Evangelistic Work," *Quarto Centennial Papers Read Before the Korea Mission of the PCUSA* (Pyeng Yang: 1909), 18.

14 George Paik, *The History of Protestant Missions in Korea* (Pyongyang: YMCA Press, 1929), 151–152.

15 Sung-Deuk Oak, *The Making of Korean Christianity* (Waco: Baylor University Press, 2013), 292–293.

Controversies over the Modifications of the NRM in Korea, 1897–1920

Underwood, however embraced Hepburn's Christian civilization theory and merged it with the NRM, as seen in the following three controversies over the revision or maintenance of the NM. The first one was the "newspaper question." Underwood published *The Christian News* in 1897 and included topics like business and politics, even tabaco farming, for the enlightenment of the people. The government subscribed to it and sent copies to magistrates and officials. Moffett opposed such a secular newspaper and planned to publish a Christian one for evangelism. James S. Gale, a friend of Moffett, became editor of *The Christian News* as a compromise in 1902.

The second controversy between Underwood and Moffett was the "hospital question." In 1900 Underwood supported Dr. Olive R. Avison's plan to establish a union hospital with more than two missionary doctors, which could compete with Japanese hospitals. It was built in 1904 as one of the best modern Christian hospitals in East Asia, with the donations of Mr. Louis H. Severance of New York and by the supervision of a Canadian architect Henry D. Gordon. Mr. Gordon built many mission buildings, including John D. Wells Academy and missionary houses. These buildings and institutions represented the Underwood-Avison Method, a revised version of NM, accommodating to the modernizing capital city. It accepted the civilization theory and institutionalism in educational and medical works in Seoul and maintained NM in the evangelistic work in the rural area.

This metamorphosis was accelerated by the Methodists joining in the union medical work at Severance Hospital and Medical College from 1909, and in the establishment of the Chosen Christian College in 1915–16. Presbyterian missionaries engaged vigorously in the "college question" in the 1910s. The issue was the location of the single union college—Seoul or Pyongyang—and the nature of college education. Underwood and Avison established the college in Seoul with the help of Mr. Arthur L. Becker, a Methodist and the vice-principal of Soongsil Union College in Pyongyang, and support from the Presbyterian and Methodist mission boards in New York, whose missiology evolved into the modern view of education for urban young people. Their goal was to produce national leaders and Christian elites through Christian liberal education.

In contrast, missionaries in Pyongyang—represented by William M. Baird in education, Dr. J. Hunter Wells in medicine, Graham Lee in architecture and spirituality, and S. A. Moffett as their leader—and the majority of Presbyterian missionaries advocated indigenous style church buildings, a newspaper for Christian homes, a one-doctor small-scale mission hospital focusing on evangelism, mission schools for Christian children, and a Christian college for church leaders. They maintained NRM and self-support up to 1920.

Interpretations

Four missiological and academic schools competed in the interpretations of NM in Korea from 1930—conservative Presbyterians' triumphalism over Methodist institutionalism, liberal Presbyterians' criticism of the lack of self-government, political historians' nationalism, and economic historians' connecting capitalism with self-support.

Conservative Presbyterians: Triumphalism over Methodist Institutionalism in the 1930s

The first missionary interpretation of NM appeared in the 1930s–1940s. It focused on denominational differences—Presbyterian success and Methodist failure. Charles A. Clark, a Presbyterian from Pyongyang, argued that NM had produced Presbyterian dominance. He criticized the methods of nationalism, liberal theology (social gospel), and syncretism (indigenization), which were connected with the Methodists.[16] His revised edition of *The Nevius Plan for Mission Work* strongly confirmed his arguments, for the members of Presbyterian churches numbered five times more than the Methodists' in 1936.[17]

In 1947, Rev. Charles D. Stokes, a Southern Methodist missionary scholar, analyzed the reasons why Methodists recorded such modest growth compared to the Presbyterians, and argued that the decline of the Methodists from 1910 to 1930 resulted from their overemphasis and overinvestment in educational, medical, and woman's works at the expense of direct evangelism, and the lack of the support for these institutional works from the boards.[18]

Liberal Presbyterians: Criticism of the Lack of Self-Government

Chun Sung-chun insisted that the policy of maintaining a lower level of education of Korean pastors produced "isolationism" of the Korean Church.[19] Put differently, ill-educated Korean pastors ruled the churches with ecclesiastical authoritarianism, and such hierarchical clericalism resulted in church schism.

First, the standard of theological education in Korea was not lower than in any other mission field that had a similar policy, like the comity (territorial division), adopted by the Foreign Mission Conference of North America in 1897[20] and world missionary conferences from 1900 to 1910. Secondly, the Presbyterian Church did not have any ordained Korean elders until 1900 and no ordained Korean minister until 1907. However, this does not necessarily prove the absence of self-governance. Local churches and groups expanded rapidly beyond missionaries' capacity for proper care. Since they could only visit them once a year, they had to appoint a Korean leader (unordained elder) for a local church and a helper (unordained minister) for a circuit of twenty to thirty churches and groups. These leaders and helpers had self-governing rights to preach and minister to their congregations.

Political Historians: Nationalism and the Nevius Method

Under the metanarrative of Korean nationalism since 1945, Wi Jo Kang, Chungshin Park, and Jacqueline Park have emphasized the contribution of NRM to nationalism in the Korean churches.[21] However, their representative nationalist, Ahn Ch'ang-ho, opposed the revival movement in 1907. His organizations in San Francisco and in Pyongyang had nothing to do with NM. And, Presbyterian polity in Korea up to

---

16 Charles A. Clark, *The Korean Church and the Nevius Methods* (New York: Revell, 1930), 234.

17 C. A. Clark, *The Nevius Plan for Mission Work*, 2nd. ed. (Seoul: Christian Literature Society, 1937).

18 Charles D. Stokes, "History of Methodist Missions in Korea, 1885–1930" (PhD diss., Yale University, 1947).

19 Chun Sung-chun, "Schism and Unity in the Presbyterian Churches of Korea" (PhD diss., Yale University, 1955), 71.

20 "Native converts should be discouraged from coming to Europe and America for education" (Foreign Missions Conference of North America, *Report of the Meeting of the Conference of Foreign Missions Boards in Canada and in the United States*, vol. 5 [New York, 1897], 13.)

21 See Wi Jo Kang, *Christ and Caesar in Modern Korea* (New York: State University of New York Press, 1997), 30; Chung-shin Park, *Protestantism and Politics in Korea* (Seattle: University of Washington Press, 2003), 4; and Jacqueline Park, "Cradle of the Covenant: Ahn Changho and the Christian Roots of the Korean Constitution," in *Christianity in Korea*, ed. Timothy S. Lee and Robert E. Buswell, Jr. (Honolulu: University of Hawaii Press, 2005), 128.

1907 was similar to Andersonian congregationalism that gave more autonomous (self-governing) rights to local churches and their leaders. The relationship between NRM and Christian nationalism was not causative but correlative.

Economic Historians: Capitalism and the Nevius Method

Albert L. Park argued that "Western missionaries contributed to the cultivation of new forms of economic thought and practice [capitalism] through the establishment of ideological and physical structures between 1885 and 1919."[22] By "ideological structure," he meant the "self-supporting" principle of NM, which made church members stakeholders who were required to contribute money constantly. He argued that this practice promoted a view of "money as a form of productive capital" and a definition of labor as a positive activity for the accumulation of money. By "physical structures," Dr. Park meant the Industrial Education Departments (IEDs) of Christian schools.

Church members had a duty to give offerings, especially the tithe. In many cases, however, a rich person or a widow donated the land for a chapel or a house for a church building at the beginning of a local church plant. When the church grew, the members adopted a three-year subscription plan for a larger building. Wealthy people were major donors. In rural areas, a few rich people's donations sustained a local church of poor farmers and tenants. In short, the self-supporting principle of NRM had created neither a new idea of money, nor a new social class for capitalism.

Furthermore, earlier IEDs were developed by Methodists who had not adopted NRM—at the Paejae School in Seoul in 1888 and the Anglo-Korean School in Songdo in 1906. IEDs were also a part of general mission policy in other mission fields where the Nevius method was not practiced. In fact, in 1918 the "only instance of Christian industrial training *per se*" in Korea was at the YMCA of Seoul,[23] which was not necessarily related to NRM. Park quotes Yun Ch'iho and his school several times to support his argument. But, Yun's school belonged to the Southern Methodist mission, and he did not support NRM.

NRM in Seoul began to change from 1897, and its focus gradually shifted from planting indigenous churches to promoting Christian civilization through institutions. The churches in Seoul in the 1910s were not under the Nevius method *per se* any longer. It is true that NRM, Protestant ethics, and Christian civilization theory have contributed to the rise of capitalism in early modern Korea. Yet there were more diverse factors at play than just a mission method. It is difficult to directly connect the self-supporting principle of NRM with the rise of early Korean capitalism and industry.

Conclusion

This chapter emphasized the diverse genealogy of the Nevius Method in Korea, its indigenization, regional differences, and their evolution in the changing political and ecclesiastical context. A mission method needs to be contextualized, for its life span is temporal. At the same time, there are unchanging principles of NM. The first principle of self-support (financial independence) has been foundational for indigenous local churches. With financial independence, a church can grow and its leadership can be trained.

Today, small churches (with less than fifty members) make up more than 80 percent of the churches in the more than 350 Protestant denominations in Korea. Their struggle for survival is one of the most serious "church-centered" issues today. In front of the glittering gates of the megachurches, there are poor ministers who have to work two or three different jobs to survive. Self-support of NM was a "church-centered" mission method. Today, small churches have become a mission field that cries for financial independence. Like Nevius in 1880s, we need to invent a new "mission-centered" church method that promotes a healthy ecosystem where missions and churches are interdependent, and small churches and megachurches are in the relationship of coexistence and co-prosperity.

---

22 Albert L. Park, "A Sacred Economy of Value and Production: Capitalism and Protestantism in Early Modern Korea (1885–1919)," in *Encountering Modernity: Christianity in East Asia and Asian America*, ed. Albert L. Park and David K. Yoo (Honolulu: University of Hawaii Press, 2014), 19.

23 Horace H. Underwood, "Industrial Training in the Far East," *Missionary Review of the World* 41 (September 1918): 677.

Chapter 11 Response

by Lalsangkima Pachuau

In this historically rich and theoretically profound study of missionary schemes and methods surrounding the famous method of John L. Nevius, Prof. Sung-Deuk Oak takes us on a journey through Protestant missionary thoughts in Korea and China. The chapter is intended for knowledgeable readers and clearly presumes a general knowledge of the history of Korean Christianity, John L. Nevius, and his famous method to provide its interpretation. Such a presumption does cause a lack of clarity in several places. To attempt a meaningful response, I will have to return (below) to some secondary sources for simpler descriptions of the method.

For one who has a general knowledge about the life and work of John L. Nevius, how his ideas were implemented successfully in missionary work in Korea, and how they were supplemented by others including John Ross, this chapter helps further that knowledge and shows its complex history. By calling the different lines of development "genealogies," the author traces two sets[24] of development of the missionary principle surrounding John Nevius that prioritized planting a native, independent, self-supporting church and showed how the principle came to produce Korean Protestantism. Although the title says "Nevius Method," the discussion does not give any longer treatment of Nevius's method itself than the others. However, in discussing the other "genealogies," Nevius's method features as a major influence. In other words, the discussion gives good treatment to the supplementing method of John Ross and how two early Presbyterian missionaries, Horace G. Underwood and Samuel A. Moffett, modified and implemented the method in Seoul and Pyongyang, respectively.

Through works by Charles Allen Clark[25] and others, the Nevius Method has been well-known in mission study circles even outside of Korea. By highlighting its four major points, mission historian Stephen Neill provides a precise and helpful explanation of the method, which in fact became an influential understanding at a more popular level. Neill's points are: first, every Christian should be taught to be a witness in his or her original place; second, the church's machinery and method should be developed only in accordance with the ability of the native church; third, the church itself should select its workers as it is able to support; and lastly, churches should be built in native style by native Christians with their resources.[26] While early studies did not popularly relate Nevius's method with the works of John Ross, recent scholars have combined it, and thus, the name "Nevius-Ross Method" is becoming popular. Prof. Oak's chapter most helpfully explains the relation between the methods of Nevius and Ross and how the latter learned and adapted from the former. However, when it comes to their works in Korea, Ross preceded Nevius. The chapter tells us that missionary Underwood had invited Ross in 1887 to Korea to help resolve conflicts in missionary policies and methods. Ross's visit took place three years before Nevius came to teach his method to the Protestant missionary community in Korea. However, it was Nevius's teaching that made a

---

24 Whether the genealogies named are two or four is a bit confusing. While it says "four genealogies," only two are named. It appears the four are classified into two sets.

25 Charles Allen Clark, *The Korean Church and the Nevius Methods* (New York: Flemming H. Revell, 1930); "The Nevius Methods," *International Review of Mission* 24, no. 3 (1935): 229–236.

26 Stephen Neill, *A History of Christian Missions*, 2nd ed., rev. Owen Chadwick (London: Penguin Books, 1986), 291.

lasting impact on the missionary work in Korea. One difference highlighted between Nevius's method and Ross's is in the emphasis. While Nevius prioritized the independence and self-support of the new indigenous church, Ross stressed self-propagation by employing more paid evangelists than Nevius.

In the second set of genealogies, Oak deals with the works of two pioneering Presbyterian missionaries, Underwood and Moffett, by showing how the two furthered the method drawn from Ross and Nevius for Korea. It was Underwood, according to Oak, who invited both Ross and Nevius and was thus responsible for organizing the Korean missionaries' quest for good plans and methods of the mission. Although the chapter does not show how the name changed from NM (adopted in 1891 by Presbyterians) to NRM (adopted in 1893), and how the two differ, one can suspect a much more active role played by Underwood and other missionaries in Korea in the creation of NRM. Is this what Oak is trying to show? The chapter is unclear on this point. Is NRM really NRM? Or, is it a product of missionaries in Korea using the works of Nevius and Ross under the leadership of Underwood?

Underwood, in Oak's presentation, seemed to have changed from being critical of importing the Western system and institutionalization to utilizing them. If there was a gradual abandonment of indigenization, Samuel Moffett's work in Pyongyang contrasted it. Like Underwood, Moffett took great effort to learn Nevius and Ross and "built one of the most indigenous mission stations in the world," which grew to become the largest station. If Underwood drifted toward a civilizing mission, Moffett seemed to have stuck with the basic elements of the Nevius-Ross method. The difference seems minor, especially in view of its great product of self-supporting, independent, and vital indigenous churches.

The second half of the chapter consists of four major interpretations, which he called "academic schools" beginning in the 1930s. Although Oak does not mention why such interpretations began to come from that period and why the 1930s were particularly "eventful," one wonders if it may have to do with the golden jubilee of Korean Protestant missions and the Nevius-Ross method. The first of the four "academic schools" is the conservative Presbyterians who made a triumphal claim of the Nevius method (not the Nevius-Ross method?) as their reason for success against the Methodists' (relative) failure due to investments in developmental aspects rather than direct evangelism. The second interpretation is a critical assessment by liberal Presbyterians who argued the low-level education of pastors from the beginning resulted in schisms and disunity of Korean Christians. Oak persuasively made a case against such an assessment showing that in the context where Korean Christians outgrew the number of missionaries, it was inevitable for local unordained leaders to lead the budding congregations. Political historians, the third school, "emphasized the contribution of the Nevius-Ross Method to nationalism in the Korean churches." Oak, with a rather unclear argument, rebutted this theory by saying that the relationship "was not causative but correlative." The fourth school, economic historians, offers a socioeconomic interpretation, saying the Nevius method helped to educate Christians toward a capitalist economy.

To conclude, let me offer a few critical observations. First of all, the chapter certainly unearths the complex development of the Nevius and/or Nevius-Ross Method, its understandings, interpretations, and influence. For an occasional reader of the method through secondary sources, this brief chapter is worth the attention for its in-depth treatment of the topic. On the negative side, clarity is lacking as it presupposes a good knowledge of the topic. In addition to the few we have mentioned, we encounter unexplained phrases and descriptions throughout the chapter such as "the new system" and "the old," and "the Diocletian persecution during the Boxer uprising" (in China). The author seems to try to fit a much larger thought than could be fit into the given space.

One difficult issue throughout the chapter for this reviewer is the relationship between NM (Nevius Method) and NRM (Nevius-Ross Method). While Oak showed the differences between Nevius and Ross, the differences between NM and NRM are difficult to determine. How do they differ? How much of NM continued in NRM? The author, at times, differentiates them clearly and, at times, seems to be using them interchangeably. After reading the chapter, I came away thinking that the method, as used in Korea, was an amalgamation of the works of Nevius, Ross, and the missionaries in Korea. In other words, we can think of the method as employed in Korean missions to be one unified entity, not two or three, to which Nevius, Ross, Underwood, Moffett, and other missionaries contributed. Of course, Nevius's contribution may be relatively more important than the others. Although much effort has been made in recent years to include the contribution of Ross, the contributions of the missionaries in Korea in adapting, rewriting, and perhaps, repurposing the theory have not been acknowledged. Their hard work and genius in drawing on, combining, modifying, and putting it into practical use made the system work.

In addition to "four genealogies," Oak identified "four academic schools" who, he said, "competed in the interpretation" of the method. He explained each and strongly rebutted two (the liberal Presbyterian and political-nationalist interpretations) and cast doubts on the last (the socioeconomic interpretation). In the end, only the conservative Presbyterian interpretation seems to stand. Instead, I wonder if we may look at these four interpretations inclusively as the different—direct and indirect—outcomes of the method. They may not need to be seen as competing, but as complementing.

SECTION B: Workshops

Chapter 12
Optimizing Missions through Organizational Financial Accountability

by Valentine Gitoho

Advances in technology and technologically savvy youth demand that organizations stay on top of their money flows internally and externally. Moreover, should there be a leak in any form of financial impropriety, the risk of losing credibility is higher than ever before as social media spreads the word. One is judged and condemned even before they can stand trial. Worse still, the name of God is maligned making it a continual uphill task for the rest of the body of Christ to uphold public trust.[1]

This calls for strong organizations that can maintain continual growth in impact and scope of their vision and mission as called by God. We formed the African Council of Accreditation and Accountability (AfCAA)[2] for this reason in 2015, to come along Christian organizations by holding each other accountable through accreditation based on a set of standards that bring about public trust and optimize mission. Matthew 5:16 is the overarching scripture where we see Africa's potential will be unlocked through adherence to these biblical standards. To enhance this peer accountability movement globally, Global Trust Partners[3] was formed in 2019 to bring organizations like AfCAA together to learn and grow from one another and help form new ones, among other objectives.

I will share some suggestions of how we can optimize missions through financial accountability using AfCAA standards. But first, let us have a common understanding of the terms used in the topic.

Definitions and Contextual Explanations

Optimizing: *to make as perfect, effective, or functional as possible.*[4] From a biblical perspective, a combination of faithfulness and fruitfulness describes the optimization of missions through financial accountability, as found

---

1 Rufus Harvey, "Fraud in Ministries: Real Examples and Red Flags," Financial Management, ECFA: Enhancing Trust in Ministries, 2021, https://www.ecfa.org/Content/Fraud-in-Ministries-Real-Examples-and-Red-Flags.

2 Home page https://afcaa.org.

3 Home page https://www.gtp.org.

4 *Merriam-Webster*, s.v. "optimize," accessed February 18, 2021, https://www.merriam-webster.com/dictionary/optimize.

in Luke 16:10–13 and John 15:16–17. In summary, Matthew 25:19–21 demonstrates what the Lord expects of us in optimization:

"After a long time the master of the servants returned and settled accounts with them. The man who had received five talents brought the other five. 'Master,' he said, 'you entrusted me with five talents. See, I have gained five more.' His master replied, 'Well done, good and faithful servant! You have been faithful with a few things; I will put you in charge of many things. Come and share your master's happiness'" (NIV, 1996).

Missions: *a body of persons sent to perform a service or carry on an activity.*[5] We have been sent by our Lord to make disciples in all nations through the Great Commission in Matthew 28:18–20. Therefore, every Christian is on mission wherever they are. However, we cannot make disciples unless we are his disciples. We are his salt and light in the world. Matthew 5:13–16 demonstrates how we should carry out our mission with the emphasis that "they may see your good deeds and praise your Father in heaven" (NIV 1996), not us.

Financial Accountability: *responsibility for the way money is used and managed.*[6] Examples of various facets of organizational financial accountability in the Bible include: 2 Kings 12:1–16; Luke 14:28–30; Matthew 25:14–30; 1 Corinthians 16:1–4; and 2 Corinthians 8:21. Second Corinthians 8:20–21 summarizes financial accountability as, "We want to avoid any criticism of the way we administer this liberal gift. For we are taking great pains to do what is right, not only in the eyes of the Lord but also in the eyes of men" (NIV 1996).

Organizational Financial Accountability

Financial accountability is crosscutting in the organization. It requires more than good accountants. It tells the world how we use money to carry out our mission.

Organizations in this context include churches, Christian nonprofits, and Christian-owned businesses. However, AfCAA standards can be applied in a family setting in communities or in any organization (definition being, "where two or three are gathered").

Let us now look at some of the challenges of Christian organizations in financial management and how these can be overcome through the seven AfCAA standards of accountability. Hopefully, these will trigger proactive steps to review and implement changes on the financial accountability continuum.

Doctrinal Foundation

The doctrinal foundation of an organization is stated in their statement of faith.

As a Christian organization, the Bible is our final guide in all we do. We believe the Bible is the only inspired, true, and infallible Word of God (2 Tim. 3:16). We believe it is the supreme and final authority and without error in what it teaches and affirms (John 2:22; 1 Cor. 15:3–4; 1 Pet. 1:10–12). The statement of faith should be agreed on and signed by all staff, board, and other key partners. The core values of the organization should be in line with the statement of faith. This holds everyone to account in case of any dispute, including financial impropriety.

I recall an incident where a donor was giving designated funds that were greatly needed for some work in a nonprofit. But there was a clause in the agreement that was especially important to the donor that went against the statement of faith. This brought contention to the organization because of the desire to do, driven by compassion, against the desire to have financial integrity with our Lord. Unfortunately, those with the desire to do won the day. It did not take long for the organization to start falling apart, and sadly, this was a global organization that affected various nations. The Lord watches over his Word. He is the source of all finances. Do not limit God by putting our trust in man (Jer. 17:5, 7).

Leadership and Governance

Leadership refers to the chief executive officer and governance refers to the board (with committees) or their equivalent. They have a higher calling of accountability as stated in Titus 1:7–9. They are Christian role models who are trustworthy, humble, diligent, and servant leaders as modeled by Christ. Other specific aspects of their suitability include their alignment to the organization in terms of their capability, competence, commitment, and compatibility to the vision and mission of the organization.

Their independence demonstrated through the signing of a statement of conflict of interest is of great importance, especially in decisions that include

---

[5] *Merriam-Webster*, s.v. "mission," accessed February 18, 2021, https://www.merriam-webster.com/dictionary/mission.

[6] *Cambridge Dictionary*, s.v. "financial accountability," accessed February 18, 2021, https://dictionary.cambridge.org/dictionary/english/financial-accountability.

finances such as procurement. This enhances financial accountability.

Their induction, training, and development keep them relevant to the organization's needs so that they can also contribute to its growth and make informed decisions in every aspect of the organization, including financial decisions.

Having a fixed tenure that allows continuity and yet relevance in changing seasons is also a safeguard to financial mismanagement due to familiarity.

For clarity in organizational roles and responsibilities, it is important to have documentation that guides them in their operations, such as the governance and policies manual with the skills matrix, the signed minutes and resolutions, strategic plans and budgets, and other operational manuals that will be used by staff. This makes it easier to hold each other accountable in case of any financial impropriety. The documentation should be updated periodically for relevance.

The leadership and governance should not only sign the statement of faith but also the conflict of interest and confidentiality statements at a minimum, holding them accountable to all the operations of the organization.

Governance has a duty to safeguard the vision and mission as it is God-given, and the Lord will hold them accountable for any mission drift. They also provide the strategic direction financial oversight, safeguarding assets and legal compliance, among other duties.

Poor stewardship of financial resources at the governance and leadership level and mission drift are the two largest culprits of financial mismanagement. Poor stewardship mostly occurs when governance interferes with day-to-day management (e.g., in procurement) leading to conflict of interest and financial impropriety. Mission drifts occur mainly due to availability of funds. Lack of funds may lead to the decision to divert funds away from the mission toward other activities that are more lucrative in order to make money to help achieve the mission. It becomes more complex when the leadership and governance lack integrity and accountability, compounded with conflicts of interest, or they are not committed and diligent.

The face of an organization to the world is its leadership and governance. So, when they are not faithful in their roles there is loss of credibility of the organization. This hurts the body of Christ because when one part suffers, we all suffer (1 Cor. 12:26).

It stifles the growth in mission. That is why at AfCAA peer accountability is important to us, as we have equal concern for each other as accredited members (1 Cor. 12:25).

Talent Management

Talent management is all about the staff. Staff are our first disciples in an organization, our Jerusalem. How we hire them, their talents vis-à-vis their assignments, how we pay them, treat them, motivate them, train and develop them, and care for them and their families is particularly important (Col. 4:1; 3:23–24; 1 Tim. 5:18; 1 Pet. 5:1–5). They are also the ones who will be our organizational disciples to the rest of the world. They are even more important than those we serve. It is crucial to have human resource polices and manuals that cover areas such as recruitment policies and procedures in compliance with legal requirements, compensation and benefits, performance management, work environment, conflict resolution, and separation with dignity, among others.

From experience, one of the areas where Christian organizations fall short in financial accountability is hiring the right accounting staff. The argument is that they are expensive, but the decisions made from inaccurate financial information will cost the organization more. Another area that causes strife and loss of credibility in and outside the organization is when staff deductions for various long-term benefits, such as pensions and loans, are made and not remitted to the relevant institutions due to poor cash flows, and the staff is unaware. A serious case I came across was where staff had retired and when they went to collect their pension funds, they found some of it had not been remitted. Not only did the organization lose a disciple, but it was also discredited in the family of the staff member and in the other institution, not to mention the personal loss and possible litigation loss.

Learning and Innovation

To optimize and widen impact and scope in missions there is the need to be a lifelong learning and research organization (Hos. 4:6), especially in this fast-paced era of technological changes that improve efficiency, excellence, competence, and effectiveness. Space for critical thinking and dialogue and best practice and technical upgrades, among others, should be created across all levels of the organization up to governance. Therefore, having a knowledge management policy and implementation plan as part of the strategic plan that is cross-cutting in the organization is key. A continuously updated risk management policy and implementation plan should be made and adopted to mitigate any financial management and credibility risks, among others. It may be worth considering having internal auditors to mitigate risks.

The COVID-19 season has forced organizations into this learning space to enable them to continue their operations.

One of the challenges I have found is the lack of competent staff who understand innovation and can manage it and sign off before purchase so there are no hidden costs or hitches. Relying on outsourced services for everything can prove expensive and may also interrupt the smooth running of operations. The choice of outsourced services should ensure diligence, accountability, and sustainability just in case anything happens that would disrupt operations.

Another challenge I have seen has been not ensuring that there are security checks and balances in financial gateways, especially now when online donor giving is easily available across nations, continents, and the globe. There should be an audit trail with proper internal controls for staff to regularly check with the banks and other recipients. Credit card giving can also be abused. In other words, be on top of checking all money flows and charges for good stewardship and optimization of funds.

Cultural Differences, Acceptance, and Interdependence

Christian organizations foster life giving relationships of the love of God and of one another through celebrating and valuing cultural diversity and ensuring there is no discrimination due to gender, ethnicity or race, age, origin, disability, or any other difference (1 John 4:19–21; Gen. 1:27; Col. 3:11). This should be demonstrated through policies and procedures and cultural representation from the governance to the staff to external relationships.

In my experience, I have seen that stereotypical thinking can have negative financial consequences, especially for donors and recipient organizations. Funding and strategies imposed to align with what a donor requires, yet that do not fit the operations and cultural situation of the organization and those it serves, create strife in implementation, and at times do not meet expectations. Organizations need to be strong and state what works best to fit their mission. In one organization, I saw this positively where the leadership in an organization declined funding that would cause a dependency culture because their mission was about empowerment.

May Christian organizations be the example of cultural acceptance to the rest of the world. As we do this, we will be able to grow our mission significantly as we are divinely connected by the Holy Spirit, thereby growing our funding and reach in our mission to the ends of the earth.

Financial Management and Disclosure

To financially manage an organization effectively, strategic plans and budgets, accurate financial statements with adequate policies, and procedures for safeguarding assets need to be in place. It is vital that management, financial statements, and internal controls are reviewed regularly throughout the year by management and periodically by governance, while ensuring tax compliance and other legal requirements in the country. Compliance with the constitution that formed the organization is also important. Romans 13:1–7 requires us to submit to the governing authorities. May we not bring disrepute to our Lord nationally. Financial management policies and procedural manuals should be in place to address these issues, including procurement management, grant management, and investing based on biblical values.

Financial oversight is the role of governance as mentioned above. Monitoring the accuracy and alignment to the mission and timely implementation and evaluation of the strategic plans, budgets, and financial statements is key. Having a competent independent finance committee, audit committee, and internal auditors with clear terms of reference enhances financial accountability in the organization in performing these tasks. Some committee members should be licensed professionals who are up to date with the standards of their various professions to ensure compliance.

Financial disclosure to constituents according to relevant accounting standards adds credibility and accountability. It is also a great way of resource mobilization. When highlights of financial statements are made available to the public, this truly enhances accountability and public trust. It is walking in the light and can result in the growth of the mission beyond what you ever thought or imagined. Like-minded people in different facets of life that the organization needs will be attracted to you. Indeed, "when we walk in the light, we have fellowship with one another," and we are purified from financial misappropriation (1 John 1:7).

Compliance to tax and legal requirements is one of the challenges that I have found in Christian organizations. This is either because of lack of competent staff in accounting, or lack of leadership that understands the importance of compliance when going through cash flow challenges.

Another area of concern I have found in financial management is having an audit done by competent, licensed external auditors of good standing and following through on the management letter action points. I have come across accounts that have been given a clean audit opinion and yet there was important information not brought to the attention of governance and external users. The main reason for this I have found is that Christian organizations want to keep their costs low so the audit firm uses junior audit staff who may not be as competent.

Resource Mobilization

Whom we raise funds from, how we raise and use them, and how we communicate in the resource mobilization cycle is particularly important in financial accountability (Matt. 24:45–50; 1 Tim. 6:10; Ps. 24:1). A resource mobilization policy and plan should have this information for implementation and accountability. A governance committee should have oversight especially where grants are the main source of funds for an organization.

Global giving has become easier. Platforms for raising money have grown from local to global, like TrustBridge Global.[7] The risk of a substantive donor derailing the vision and mission of an organization has become greater. The wolves in sheep's clothing are ever increasing within and without organizations.

One of the challenges I have seen is an organization being unable to continue the fulfillment of its operations when a major donor withdraws for their own internal reasons. It is therefore important to have multiple givers, encouraging them that "it is more blessed to give than to receive," says the Lord (Acts 20:35). It is also important to work on a financial sustainability plan that at least meets the fixed and overhead costs that are a necessity for the organization to continue. We have been given a trust by the Lord; may we do all we can as he leads us to optimize on this so that we do not lose financial credibility.

Another challenge I have found is use of designated funds either knowingly or unknowingly for other purposes. This creates distrust in financial management. Compliance with the grant agreement, discussion, and getting the necessary written approvals, should there be a deviation from what was originally agreed, enhances accountability and relationships and opens doors for more funding.

Conclusion

Financial accountability ranks extremely high in how successful our missions will be. The reputation and credibility risks alone have such a great impact on our work and testimony in making disciples. All the other risks—financial, operational, organizational, and any others that are important to an organization—have an impact on reputation and credibility risks. May we truly be faithful in the way we financially manage all aspects of an organization, as the internal impact will reflect externally.

Where is your organization on the financial accountability continuum of the seven standards, on a scale of 1 to 10? What are the three top financial accountability constraints that arise from the continuum? What are the key changes that you could make immediately that would unlock the constraints? These could be personal constraints like dealing with issues of the integrity, in word and deed, of the leadership and governance on whom the financial oversight falls. Remember, no organization can move beyond the constraints of leadership or the constraints in the processes, policies, systems, or procedures.

What has been the influence of your giving on the strategy and hence the vision and mission of the organization? Has your giving caused a mission drift or curtailed growth in the work? What do you have to do to understand the organization and build on their mission together as brothers and sisters in Christ?

What are you doing: (1) to motivate youth to influence the future of your mission, and (2) to learn from them about technology, social media, and culturally relevant ways?

Ask the hard questions on the constraints and face them, God being our helper. It is his mission, and we are his privileged chosen vessels called to fulfill it, being fully accountable to him and no other.

---

7 Home page https://www.trustbridgeglobal.com.

Chapter 12 Response

by Dae Su Jung

The Importance of Financial Accountability in International Mission Organizations

Proper financial management is very important for international mission organizations. The points suggested by Mrs. Gitoho are important ones that all leaders and supporters of missionary organizations should always refer to and follow.

The most important point she makes is that the leaders of all mission agencies should have a comprehensive biblical concept of organizational management. This should be especially true of the CEO and the directors—they must abide by biblical teaching about management, and in no case should they think they are exempt from that teaching and make unruly decisions. Moreover, starting with the leaders, all parts of the organization must be aligned with the overall mission of disciple-making. Such thorough organizational commitment to the mission is in line with her point that special care should be taken to prevent a large donor from having an excessive influence on the ministry of the organization.

In general, when electing top leaders many members of mission organizations pray and seek God's will very carefully. But organizations should also be very careful when hiring middle managers, since they are more exposed to the outside world than the CEO or the directors, plus they have great influence by setting directions and examples both to other coworkers and subordinates.

Mrs. Gitoho also emphasized the importance of the transparency of financial management and of preventing the misuse of designated funds. In order to strengthen these two accountabilities, first I recommend that all mission and Christian organizations adopt double entry bookkeeping. Many institutions may already be using this system, but as far as I know there are still many others that do not; they keep using a simple cash book such as an Excel file. Some people may be reluctant, thinking that the double entry bookkeeping system is too big and complicated. Actually, though, double entry bookkeeping can be easy and simple if the number of accounts is minimized. In other words, if the chart of accounts is kept short enough, according to the size of the organization, the workload will not increase much. Double entry bookkeeping will, however, prevent inadequate or delinquent uses of funds by making them easily visible. As a result, this approach will enhance transparency and designated uses of financial resources.

Secondly, it is also very important that an organization's leaders hire financial managers with the right skills to properly perform the job, even if it may cost more in the beginning. Mission organizations should be able to manage their finances while keeping pace with the ever-evolving and globalizing financial systems. It is a great blessing if an organization can hire a financial manager who is already a disciple of Jesus, since the most influential way that Christians' behaviors affect nonbelievers is how they handle money.

Making Disciples by Saving Souls

However, it is in fact quite difficult for mission organizations to find a disciple with sufficient financial skills. Should organizations hire a disciple with insufficient financial experiences and then provide training, or should they hire someone with enough financial skills who is not against Christianity and pray and help him/her to be born again? In most cases, organizations will very likely end up with the latter.

Then, the original goal of missions becomes important. A financial manager's competencies include understanding the job, management skills, and communicating honestly with superiors. However, "not yet born-again" means that they do not yet have enough ability to behave ethically, voluntarily, and honestly, and their ability to fully communicate with mission leaders is also limited. In other words, given the opportunity, there is a very high chance that those in charge of the money box, like Judas Iscariot, will act selfishly if undetected.

The Bible is consistently very strict about greed for money. It doesn't present the case of Judas Iscariot only, but also of Achan during the conquest of Jericho, Gehazi, Elisha's servant, Ananias and Sapphira in Acts, and others. All of these financial offenders were strictly punished, without exception, because they deliberately tried to deceive the Holy Spirit by coveting wealth. Therefore, it is very important to properly install and operate various checking systems, including mutual checks such as the ones designed and implemented by Mrs. Gitoho. The better these devices are, the less chance there is of being seduced. Therefore, the financial management system that oversees the financial managers should also be as elaborate as possible.

However, even the most perfectly designed systems cannot perfectly deal with all the deception of human sin. Sinful financial managers can find many ways of cheating, and the greater their competency, the more their shrewdness and treachery.

The first and most effective way to manage financial managers is through intercession. Most mission agencies pray a great deal, but we should pray not only for our ministries but also for all the servants in charge of the ministry, especially those who have important financial responsibilities. Just as with sexual temptations, anybody can easily fall into the strong temptations of wealth.

Secondly, because no system can completely prevent crimes from happening, a good governing system of discipline should be in place. Such a system provides guidelines for what to do if the corruption of a financial manager is revealed. Reprimanding, dismissing, and hiring a replacement is a common method used in the world—but that would be a sham for a mission agency. The ultimate purpose of a mission organization is to spread the Gospel to nonbelievers and help them to be converted and grow as disciples. This purpose includes, of course, unbelieving local staff as well. When an unbelieving staff member commits a sin, and when it is revealed, paradoxically it could be the best opportunity for the Gospel to enter. The exposed offender cannot deny that he/she is a sinner. The leaders' task is to guide that staff member toward heartfelt confession and repentance, then graciously to forgive without destroying the offender's soul. Through all these processes, the leaders can share with the sinner about Jesus Christ, who died for sinners, and provide the best chance for the Holy Spirit to save the transgressor for whom Christ has died and risen.

Financial managers who have deeply repented and are born again will find it difficult to commit similar crimes again. Increasingly, not because of the supervisory system but because of their inner honesty, they will be more able to resist the temptation to sin. They will voluntarily and joyfully observe all the regulations, not because of fear of the strict rules, but because of the joy of working together and because of their new identity as a people of God and disciples of Christ. They will no longer work like a slave but will be able to work according to God's calling. In short, we will have a colleague, a disciple of Christ who is genuinely capable of financial management to help optimize the organization's mission.

Conclusion

Mrs. Gitoho pointed out seven financial accountabilities that mission agencies must assume in order to optimize their mission work. She has also set a practical example for theorists, not just asserting and exhorting but actually implementing the standards through AfCAA. I would suggest a few additions:

- Mission organization leaders must familiarize themselves with financial, accounting, and managerial skills.
- International mission organizations should implement a double entry bookkeeping system.
- Mission organizations need systems of discipline for handling financial offenses, including forgiveness, confessing faith in Jesus Christ, and job restoration.

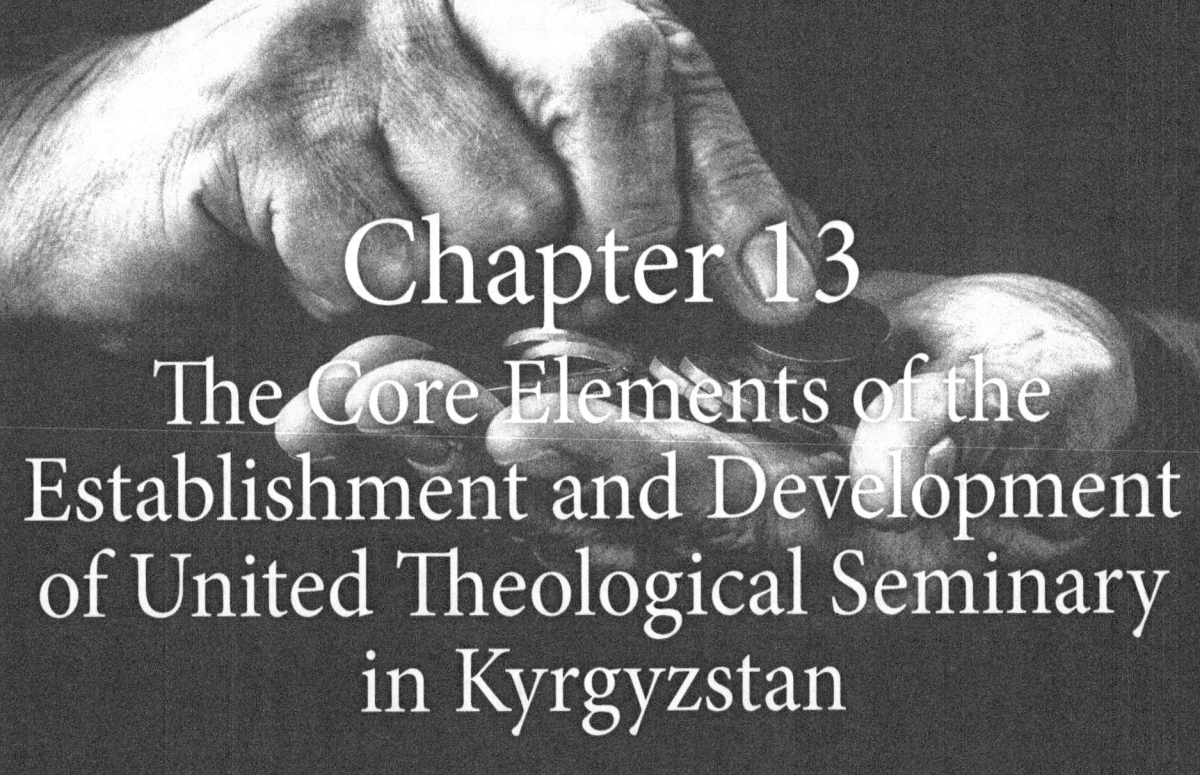

Chapter 13
The Core Elements of the Establishment and Development of United Theological Seminary in Kyrgyzstan

by Joohyung Lee, Emil Osmonaliev, and Sungbin Hong

Under the main theme of KGMLF 2021, "Mission and Money," we presented a workshop about United Theological Seminary (UTS) as a case study, at the institutional level, of how a seminary in the mission field was established, developed, and transferred to local leadership with a focus on self-support.

A Brief History of The Establishment of UTS

There were several seminaries in Kyrgyzstan in 1996. A seminary was established by Russian Baptists in 1992 and two seminaries were founded by two Korean missionaries in 1993. With the addition of two more, there were a total of five seminaries. Nevertheless, most of the Korean missionaries were not satisfied with the seminaries that did not have the spirit of unity and a self-supporting vision, so Dr. Lee started convincing other missionaries to establish UTS.

In the initial stages, a few people gathered and discussed ideas about establishing UTS. Dr. Lee was encouraged to develop those ideas, and he poured out his heart and soul on this project all summer of 1996. At that time, eighteen long-term Korean missionaries were in Kyrgyzstan. Dr. Lee met with each of them, explaining the historical significance of the establishment of UTS in Kyrgyzstan and appealing to them to join this endeavor.

In the end, a total of eight Korean missionaries came together to initialize the establishment of UTS. Due to the main visions of UTS, which were to have a spirit of unity and to become self-supporting, they began by renting a place at an affordable price, considering the financial situation of churches in Kyrgyzstan. To avoid dependency, the founding members decided to operate UTS with missionaries' offerings that were set to US$600 per year per family. Also, churches that sent students were required to subsidize certain living expenses while the students were studying, and to pay a certain amount each month to the seminary for books. Lunch and dormitories were provided for free at the seminary.

Master Plan of UTS

UTS decided on these significant resolutions in 1998:

a. First, a schedule for handing over leadership of UTS was planned. The transfer to a local principal would be completed by 2010. Following are the preparatory factors to successfully achieve the transfer:

- For self-support, the local churches are encouraged to take ownership of the operations in the seminary and donate 5 percent of the finances of churches to the seminary.
- Raise local lecturers through apprenticeship.
- Raise administrative personnel including the director.

b. Second, the curriculum of UTS is to be primarily focused on fostering evangelists. In addition, the theological foundation must be strengthened, and in efforts of doing so, a graduate school would be established in the future.

c. Third, for the development of UTS, it will not be encouraged to expand without specific purpose or to open another department under the premise of self-support.

Expansion of UTS
(from Korean to Western Missionaries)

From June 1998, in connection with Interserve and WEC, the board invited missionaries who were willing to serve as lecturers at UTS, emphasizing the Master Plan. With deep empathy, several people joined, including British Baptist missionary couple I and F, and Presbyterian missionaries D and E from the United States. Afterward, New Zealand Presbyterian missionary E joined, and missionaries from Germany, Hong Kong, and Philippines joined. As a result, 70 percent of the lecturers were comprised of missionaries from various countries in 2001. In particular, missionary E from New Zealand earned a doctorate under the title of "Theological Seminary Curriculum Desirable for Missionary Places," which led to the advancement of the curriculum at UTS. Given the situation in Kyrgyzstan at the time, subjects such as discipleship training and evangelism training were added to foster evangelists. Korean missionaries who were pastors taught theological courses and other missionaries were involved in various teaching ministries.

Campus Building And Improvement Of Self-Support

UTS did not have its own building until the year 2000. After moving between two locations that year, the board decided to pursue an independent building since the current facilities could not meet the increasing enrollment and other demands necessary to operate as a seminary. Accordingly, 1,983 square meters of land in the center of the city was purchased and the campus was built. While discussing how to fund the construction, churches and individuals in Kyrgyzstan decided to make a commitment first. Starting with the board members, various churches and individuals made donations. In addition, around one hundred individuals, organizations, and churches from outside donated. The total amount summed up to $64,877. The construction of the UTS main campus was completed in 2001 and a dormitory for students from Osh was prepared as well.

In 2002, a one-year certificate program was organized in response to a request for a branch school for churches in the southern city of Osh. This branch school was reorganized into a three-year course program in 2013. In 2002, in relation to the financial situation of UTS, about 15 percent of the finances were offerings from local churches' 5 percent financial commitment for UTS. Rental fees covered about 20 percent of UTS finances and 65 percent was covered by board members. These financial trends continued into 2008. It seemed that the preparation for leadership transfer to a local leader went well, but the offerings from local churches were status quo. The reason behind that seemed to be the stagnant growth of the churches in Kyrgyzstan.

In June 2008, principal E from New Zealand was deported due to a conflict with the local government. Despite the sudden incident, the chairman of the board and the board members were able to appoint Dr. Lee, who had been deported from Afghanistan, as principal, and commissioned him to prepare for the leadership transfer to a local pastor in June 2010. In June 2008, 20 percent of faculty members at UTS were composed of local teachers, 10 percent were Korean missionaries, and the rest were other international missionaries. Thus, it had an international spirit of unity.

Dr. Lee asked for expanded cooperation from churches so that UTS could maximize its financial self-support rate before the transfer of leadership planned within the next two years. Looking at the financial income analysis during the leadership transfer in 2010, 25 percent was board membership contributions, while 40 percent came from external sponsorships. Twenty percent was from rental income on Sundays and weekdays, but only 15 percent was from church contributions. So, the board of UTS decided to reduce external support as much as possible by 2020, and to persevere during those ten years. Thirty-five percent of the expenditure was for personnel expenses for staff, 25 percent for maintenance and operations, and 40 percent for local instructors' tutoring fees and the welfare of students. About US$150,000 was donated by Youngnak Church in Toronto, Canada, for building renovations in 2008 and 2019.

Transfer To Local Leadership And Improvement Of Self-Support

In January 2010, a local administrative director was appointed and a new local principal was elected in March 2010. The new principal, Rev. Kairbek, who was elected for his first three-year term, previously served as an instructor at UTS and was very influential among Kyrgyz churches. The previous principal, Dr. Lee, was asked by the board to assist the new principal for six months so that he could be fully functional. When Rev. Kairbek was inaugurated in June 2010, there were eight local and eight foreign board members. Rev. Kairbek served for nine years, and during his term several changes were made.

Foremost, Rev. Kairbek made changes in the academic programs. First, he developed an intensive course that was mainly for local ministers. Once every two months they studied intensively at the seminary for two weeks, and then studied independently for the rest of the time. The response to this program was exceptional, and ten years later, it has become one of the most popular academic programs at UTS. Secondly, he opened an evening course. This course was for those who worked in the capital and surrounding areas or attended other universities during the day. Thirdly, the regular full-day program was reduced. While the regular program was free of charge, students paid tuition for the intensive and evening courses. Nevertheless, the number of regular course students decreased, while the number of intensive and evening course students increased as the courses became more popular. As the dorms gradually emptied out, it was natural to consider minimizing the regular course. The principal repeatedly proposed to the board to close the regular full-day program, but the opposition of foreign lecturers was strong, so it was denied. Eventually the program ended in September 2019.

Additionally, Rev. Kairbek made significant efforts for UTS to become a self-supporting seminary. He acknowledged the difficulty of asking local churches to support UTS since the churches in Kyrgyzstan were facing financial difficulties as well. Thus, UTS rented two dormitories to cover expenses. Also, local board members were encouraged to pay their membership fees. Since 2014, intensive course students began to pay their own tuition and later, starting in 2016, the evening course students began paying. The tuition fees were used for students' lunches and textbooks. Through these efforts, UTS's financial status had been improving since the beginning of the principal's second term. There were six foreign and twelve local board members in 2020.

Status after Transfer to Local Leadership (June 2010–June 2019)

When Dr. Lee visited churches served by UTS graduates, he was deeply concerned about their ministries. The preaching and pastoral ministry in the churches were shallow. It appeared that they had no clear pastoral philosophy. Dr. Lee felt the need to open a course specifically for pastors. After several years of searching for a suitable seminary to partner with, Dr. Lee connected with Miami International Theological Seminary in the US, which was founded in 2001 for theological training of native pastors and leaders from the mission field. This program accepted students who graduated from UTS and other colleges. The Master's program consisted of twenty subjects and eighty credits to be completed within five years along with a final thesis. If students were not able to finish the program within seven years, they received a certificate.

UTS continued to acquire accreditation since 2016 and became a regular member of the Euro-Asian Accrediting Association (EAAA) in 2019. As a result, UTS was reorganized as a three-year and four-year program. The graduates received an EAAA diploma in addition to that of the Ministry of Education in Kyrgyzstan. Furthermore, through contact with other international accreditation bodies, UTS was recognized as an exemplary case of leadership transfer from foreigners to locals along with its development process. Rev. Kairbek was elected as chairman of the board in April 2020. Thus, UTS was transferred to the local leadership in every form.

Financial Analysis of UTS After Leadership Transfer

One of the founding members of UTS, Dr. Lee, who had been very influential in the operation of UTS, articulated that UTS leadership transfer was completed in 2020. He affirmed that all the responsibility and authority of operation of UTS belonged to local leadership, not to foreigners. From the perspective of the main topic of KGMLF 2021, which is "Mission and Money," we need to analyze and evaluate the financial status of UTS, in particular, the self-supporting aspect, to evaluate the sustainability and future development after leadership transfer from foreigners to locals.

Here we present a brief financial report for the past ten years (2010–2020) of UTS along with analysis, evaluation, and some practical recommendations.

I. Income (See Table 13.1 on page 105.)

The fiscal year of UTS begins in July every year and closes in June the following year. As shown in table 1, the income items are board membership fees, support from foreign countries, lease (rental fees), support from local churches, individual support, tuition, and miscellaneous.

a. Board members. There were twelve local and six foreign board members in 2020. A local board member pays about US$100 and a foreign board member pays about US$650 yearly for the membership fee. The portion of board membership fees is about 11.4 percent of total income for the past ten years.

b. External support. This is support from outside of Kyrgyzstan. Until now, six churches have been supporting UTS financially, all of them Korean. As seen in table 1, since 2010, the year of leadership transfer, the external support gradually decreased. This external support is about 49.5 percent of total income.

c. Lease. The auditorium and rooms are rented by the international church and other churches for their regular worship gatherings. Additionally, UTS charges a rental fee for any gathering, adding to the lease income. The lease fee is about 14.6 percent of total income.

d. Local church. Churches in Kyrgyzstan support UTS financially. Dr. Lee encouraged local churches to support UTS with 5 percent of their yearly offerings, which was a practical suggestion he made during the transfer of leadership. Through their support, local churches had been sensing their ownership of UTS. Until now, thirteen churches supported UTS financially. As we see above, it is confirmed that the portion of local churches' support has been decreasing since 2010. According to an accountant at UTS, this decrease is due to a decline in the number of churches in Kyrgyzstan since 2010. One of the main reasons that local believers in Kyrgyzstan had been decreasing was a new religious law was introduced in 2009. Here we refer to an analytical article that evaluated the new religious law of Kyrgyzstan. According to a report by the Norwegian Helsinki Committee in 2012, the new religious law in Kyrgyzstan restricted and infringed the freedom of religion.[1] The portion of local churches' support is about 5.6 percent of total income.

e. Tuition. This is the tuition fee paid by the students. The peculiarity is that tuition fees were not paid during 2010–2013, but from 2014 on, generating income for the seminary. The tuition fee was adjusted to 5,000 som ($58) from 2014 to 2016, 7,000 som ($100) from 2017 to 2019, and 10,000 som ($125) from 2019 onward. Accordingly, it can be seen that the seminary's income gradually increased due to the tuition increase. Students' tuition fees account for approximately 3.5 percent of the total income.

II. Expense (See Table 13.2 on page 105.)

Expenditures of UTS can be largely divided into education, employee salary, administrative expenses for school management, and other items. A summary analysis of each item is intended to help understand the expenditures of UTS.

a. Education. The education fee includes lecture fees for local teachers, translating fees, scholarship, and practicum fees. UTS pays local teachers while foreign volunteer instructors are not paid. The education fee is about 30 percent of the total expenditure.

---

[1] "According to a recent report by the non-governmental organization Open Viewpoint, Freedom of Religion or Belief in the Kyrgyz Republic: Overview of Legislation and Practice, no religious institutions except those affiliated with the Orthodox Church or Spiritual Board of Moslems have been registered since January 2009. In conclusion, the 2009 Religion Law's requirement of minimum 200 members in order to register has proved to be an effective barrier of registration and achieving legal status for other religious groups," Norwegian Helsinki Committee, "Law on religion in Kyrgyzstan should be amended in an open and inclusive process," April 25, 2012, https://www.nhc.no/en/law-on-religion-in-kyrgyzstan-should-be-amended-in-an-open-and-inclusive-process/.

b. Salary. This is a monthly salary paid to all administrative staff, such as the dean and director of UTS. It can be seen that salary expenditure is gradually decreasing, and this is related to the reduction in the number of employees. The increase in monthly salary expenditure in 2018–2019, while maintaining an overall modest decrease, reflects the payment of severance pay for the retirement of two long-term employees. Employee salaries account for about 42.5 percent of all expenditures.

c. Administration. This category includes expenses necessary for operations, including office supplies, taxes, and utility expenses. It accounts for about 21.5 percent of all expenditures.

d. Miscellaneous. Building repair expenses, administrative agency-support expenses, etc. are included, and this cost is about 5.8 percent of the total expenditure.

Accountability for Finances of UTS

UTS financial audits were conducted by Dr. Lee until the fiscal year 2019. After Dr. Lee's departure, the audit was delegated to one of the board members, but the treasurer voiced the concern that the audit was not being conducted properly. In response, the board should be actively involved in carrying out the duty of auditing the financial accounts of UTS. We believe that there is a need for institutional financial audits to ensure transparency and the sound use of finances.

Sustainability Analysis of UTS Operations

Looking at the income category of UTS finance, it can be seen that dependence on external sponsorship is close to 50 percent. Although the leadership of UTS was handed over to locals in 2010 and self-governing is taking place, it is somewhat difficult to conclude that financial independence has been achieved. We think that the next ten years will be a vital time in increasing the financial independence of UTS and the sustainability of its operations. Considering the various challenges of Kyrgyzstan at home and abroad, and the changing situation of the mission field, a blueprint for how to build a sustainable UTS should be prepared. It can be said that the remaining tasks of the local leadership (dean, director, and administrative staff) are imperative.

Recent Challenges of UTS

UTS was fully recognized by the government as a religious educational institution and has received accreditation for a diploma program from EAAA, and is in the process of getting an accreditation for a bachelor's program. The seminary has a good reputation among many churches, especially Kyrgyz speaking churches. Many faithful Christian ministers including pastors, teachers, and workers in different mission organizations have graduated from UTS. At the same time, there have been some challenging trends observed in recent years.

First, the 2019–2020 academic year was the first year in the history of the seminary when it had to stop the full-time program. It shows that the interest in studying at the seminary has decreased over the past years. One possible explanation for this tendency is that the churches in Kyrgyzstan stopped growing due to the increased migration of Christians to other countries, which is safer for Christians and more stable from an economic viewpoint. In addition, theological education is not attractive because, compared to secular education, it does not give financial security and stability for the person after graduation.

Second, there is a pressing need for well-trained theological educators in the Kyrgyz language, because there is an evergrowing number of people in our country who do not know Russian very well.

Third, research should be conducted in the area of cultural anthropology about unique ways to reach out to the Kyrgyz nation. The Western, Far Eastern, and Russian ways of reaching out to people were effective in certain periods, but now we have to investigate new ways of, so to say, touching the hearts of our people.

Lastly, there is a pressing need for high-quality theological literature in Kyrgyz. We recently investigated our library. It has 12,630 volumes, but there are only 404 copies (about sixty titles) of literature in the Kyrgyz language. These are motivational types of literature, mainly written for new believers. The total number even includes small brochures and small books for beginners. Although there are a few academic books on theology, commentaries, theological dictionaries, and books on homiletics, hermeneutics, Christian psychology, consulting, etc. in the Kyrgyz language, they are almost nonexistent.

The Realities of Money & Missions

Table 13.1: UTS Income in $US between 2010 and 2020

Item	2010-2011	2011-2012	2012-2013	2013-2014	2014-2015	2015-2016	2016-2017	2017-2018	2018-2019	2019-2020	TOTAL
Board	5,000	6,100	4,111	4,600	6,247	7,973	6,907	7,350	7,482	3,550	59,320
Foreign support	39,244	29,829	36,547	26,051	23,920	23,321	17,796	20,920	18,680	21,249	257,557
Lease	5,382	5,766	6,104	7,072	7,305	6,171	9,618	10,187	8,793	9,713	76,111
Local church	4,325	4,629	3,680	2,948	2,969	1,924	2,355	2,326	1,793	2,330	29,279
Individual support	0	0	0	0		348	385	421	34	0	1,188
Tuition	0	0	0	0	929	1,494	2,542	3,980	6,336	3,003	18,284
Miscellaneous	2,538	5,861	2,543	1,725	3,543	2,064	2,343	4,300	2,517	5,515	32,949
Flat										45,000	45,000
Total	56,489	52,185	52,985	42,396	44913	43,295	41,946	49,484	45,635	90,360	519,688

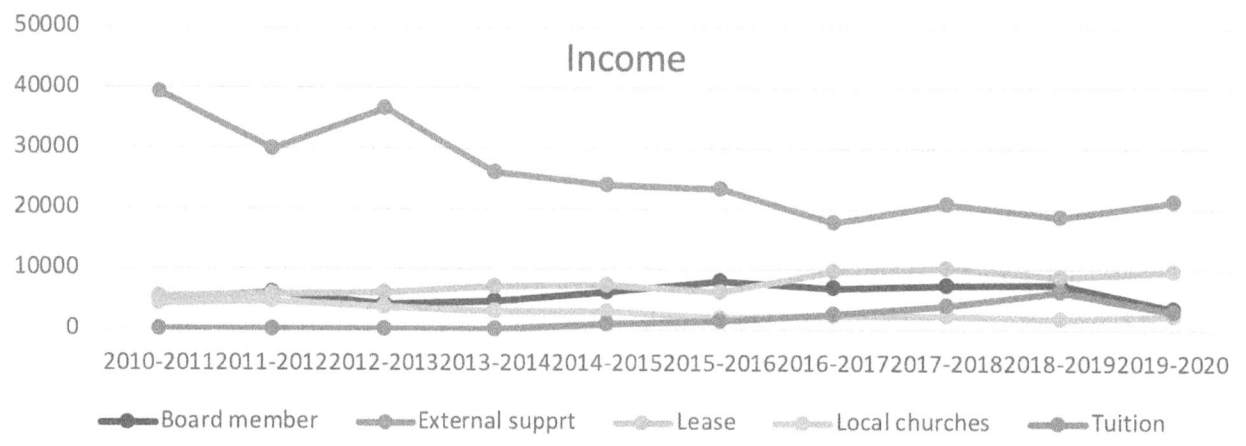

Table 13.2: UTS Expenses in $US between 2010 and 2020

Item	2010-2011	2011-2012	2012-2013	2013-2014	2014-2015	2015-2016	2016-2017	2017-2018	2018-2019	2019-2020	TOTAL
Education	14,015	15,501	17,366	12,592	15,821	12,158	9,462	16,698	13,710	15,936	142,259
Salary	24,829	23,317	20,877	20,455	21,328	15,954	17,770	19,093	23,108	15,000	201,731
Administration	18,821	13,820	11,000	8,777	8,320	6,000	7,093	8,926	11,210	7,532	102,147
Miscellaneous	2,686	4,274	1,007	1,288	1,143	1,183	1,060	7,418	5,795	2,014	27,868
Total	60,351	56,912	50,250	43,112	46,621	35,934	35,385	51,135	53,823	40,482	474,005

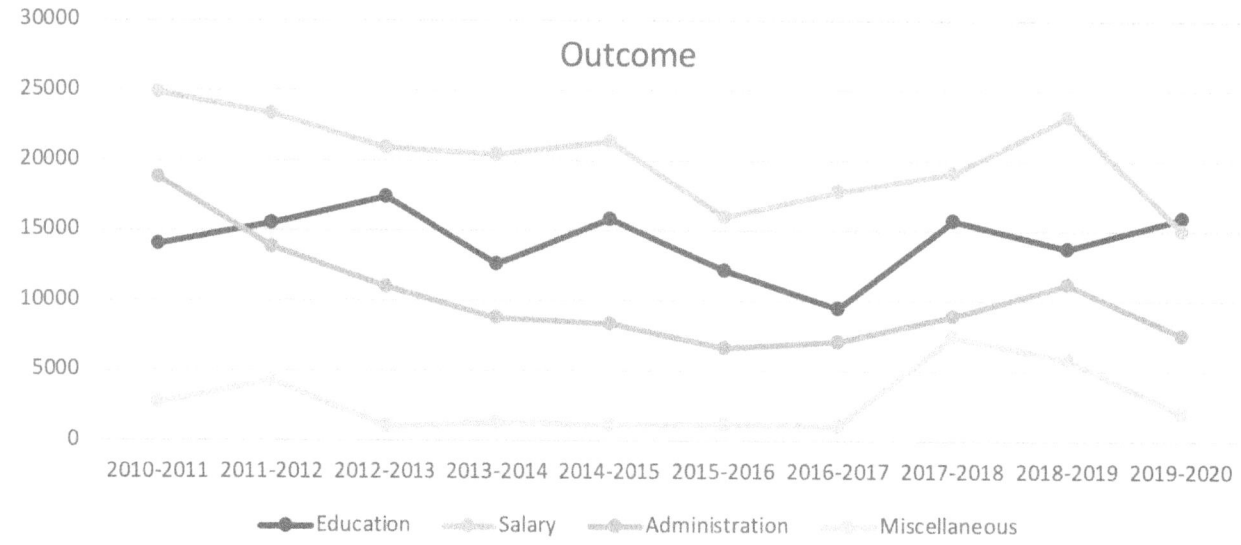

Last year was particularly difficult for our seminary because of the COVID-19 pandemic, but thanks to our Lord we were able to transform our activities and continue the educational process online. We conducted several seminars on developing online courses for our teachers last summer and in January 2021. In the beginning, most of the people in our country were very discouraged during lockdown and the overall mood influenced our faculty too. Surprisingly, we experienced some unexpected things such as reaching out to the Kyrgyz population whom we could not have reached otherwise. Today, we have three students in our seminary who work in South Korea. Two of them are our citizens, and one is from Kazakhstan. In addition, there are four students from a remote village in Kyrgyzstan. There is also one potential enrolment from Georgia who is very interested in studying at UTS.

Future Development of UTS

Recent events revealed to us possible opportunities for developing a new strategic plan for the next five years. First, UTS will concentrate on developing online programs for those living in remote areas of Kyrgyzstan, for whom it would be too difficult to leave their jobs and families to attend courses in the capital. These programs will also target those who are working in other countries, particularly in Russia, South Korea, and Turkey (experiences from last year showed that there could be an interest in theological education among them). Second, the next area that we have to concentrate on is translating theological books into the Kyrgyz language, and encouraging local Christian authors to start writing Kyrgyz theological books. This would help establish a Kyrgyz theological vocabulary, which is undeveloped and has not undergone unification between different Christian denominations. As mentioned above, good theological books are practically nonexistent in the Kyrgyz language. So, we could say that this is the pressing need for our country—to have good Kyrgyz theological books, which would help develop a Kyrgyz-speaking Christian academic society.

Discussion Questions

1. Was the self-supporting plan prepared by UTS too ideal? In what way should it be considered? Also, how appropriate is it to make a self-supporting master plan for a seminary that begins on the mission field?

2. How desirable is it for missionaries to withdraw financially after the leadership transition to locals? What are the best practices?

3. Dr. Bonk says, "It is a hopeful sign when Western mission agencies begin to move away from the traditional Western stresses on independence, autonomy, and self-sufficiency, restructuring along lines more consistent with biblical teaching on the church as the Body of Christ."[2] UTS is one of the seminaries in mission fields around the world. It is a seminary that has been transferred from missionaries to local leadership. When a seminary is transferred to local leadership, what are the principles for financial independence that local leadership must have, and what are the things that local leadership must keep in mind in order to become a sustainable seminary?

---

2 Jonathan J. Bonk, *Missions and Money: Affluence as a Missionary Problem ... Revisited*, rev. and exp. ed. (Maryknoll: Orbis Books, 2006), 181.

Chapter 13 Response

by Charles Weber

This chapter analyzes the beginnings, the philosophy, and development of a recent, Korean-initiated seminary in Kyrgyzstan, written by three educators integrally involved with the school. They provide perceptive insights into the seminary's purposes and history, along with issues confronting it.

The larger sociopolitical context for UTS provides an understanding of the environment in which it developed and operates. To begin with, Kyrgyzstan is notable for its indigenous Korean ethnic population, especially around its capital of Bishkek. This Korean population, known as Koryo-saram or Koryoins and numbering about fifteen thousand people, originated from a forced migration by Stalin in the 1930s of Koreans from the Russian Far East to keep them from identifying with Japan, which had colonized Korea at the time. These new settlers became successful farmers and have created a heterogeneous, marginal group in Kyrgyz society. However, they also provided an entry point for Korean missionaries in the late twentieth century. In addition, they maintained a culture that preserved traits of Korean customs and folk religions.[3] Still, they served as an initiation for Protestant Christianity and a base for the establishment of UTS, although it has not confined itself to the Korean community but has actively reached out to the Kyrgyz people.

Kyrgyz Christians are a distinct minority in a population of about 6.3 million people. The vast majority of the population (about 87 percent) are Hanafi Sunni Muslims, whose faith is generally a loosely held cultural overlay. The Christian community is diverse and includes about seventeen different groups and 4.4 percent of the population. While difficult to estimate, Protestants and independents are under 1 percent and number around forty thousand adherents. Thus, UTS provides a significant input for this community, which has increased markedly since the country's independence in 1991.[4]

The Master Plan of UTS is clearly modeled after the three-self mission strategy developed by Henry Venn and Rufus Anderson but implemented in Korea by John Livingston Nevius in the late nineteenth century. This "Nevius Plan is the most frequently cited factor in the outstanding growth of the Korean Church" and provides a pattern for the goals of UTS.[5] A recent article by Robert Reese postulates that the three selfs, namely self-government, self-propagation, and self-support, are still relevant today because it takes "seriously the autonomy of the indigenous church." He also references Paul Hiebert's advocacy for "self-theologizing" as a fourth self and this is also relevant for UTS's approach to ministry.[6]

---

3 See Weonjin Choi, "Korean Baptist Missions in Kazakhstan," *East-West Church and Ministry Report* 18, no. 3 (Summer 2010): 6–8, https://eastwestreport.org/36-english/e-18-3/287-korean-baptist-missions-in-kazakhstan. This article explains the common ethnic, linguistic, and cultural ties among Central Asians and Koreans based on their Mongol-Altaic background.

4 Todd M. Johnson and Gina A. Zurlo, *World Christian Encyclopedia*, 3rd edition (Edinburgh: Edinburgh University Press, 2019), s.v. "Kyrgyzstan," 460–462.

5 Everett N. Hunt, "The Legacy of John Livingston Nevius," *International Bulletin of Missionary Research* 15, no. 3 (July 1991): 120–124, http://www.internationalbulletin.org/issues/1991-03/1991-03-120-hunt.pdf.

6 Robert Reese, "The Surprising Relevance of the Three-Self Formula," *Mission Frontiers* (May–June 2021), http://www.missionfrontiers.org/issue/article/the-surprising-relevance-of-the-three-self-formula1.

Chapter 13 Response

Let's investigate the selves as related to UTS's program. Regarding self-government, UTS leadership has intentionally transitioned largely from foreign, namely Korean and Western missionaries to Kyrgyz leaders. In fact, "international accrediting bodies" recognized UTS as exemplary in this "transfer from foreigners to locals," culminating in Rev. Kairbek being elected chair of the board in April of 2020. This accomplishment of Kyrgyz leadership of UTS, and the churches affiliated with it, is looked favorably upon by the Kyrgyzstan government, which provides some protection for these churches under the vicissitudes of changing governments and the political relationships to various religious entities in the country. In addition, UTS's Master Plan specifically calls for developing indigenous lecturers and administrative personnel and thus for weaning the school from its early association with Interserve and WEC.

From UTS's very beginning, self-propagation was a high priority. Its purpose was to train Kyrgyz pastors and evangelists. As the Master Plan states forthrightly, "the curriculum of UTS is to be primarily focused on fostering evangelists," especially through courses on discipleship and evangelism training. Again, the leadership of Rev. Kairbek as UTS's principal since 2010 has provided incentive to working with churches and having them promote outreach, and for UTS to provide national training thereby keeping foreign agents removed from interfacing with the Kyrgyzstan population as pastors and evangelists.

Both self-government and self-propagation are integrally related to the principle of self-support. It is widely acknowledged that self-support is the most difficult objective to achieve in mission situations. The chapter recognized finances as an ongoing issue for them because UTS is still dependent on outside support from individuals and churches. This foreign input always raises the specter of dependency and control in the national religious situation. However, UTS seems to have taken efforts to avoid this and in the last ten years has reduced foreign support by 50 percent. Nevertheless, substantial foreign support is still needed, mainly from Korean churches. Also, Kyrgyz church growth has plateaued thus providing a weak financial base for supporting UTS. In addition, a 2009 Kyrgyz government law put restrictions on religious finances. Again, this is a chronic issue in emerging Christian communities. However, UTS has confronted this matter in a straightforward manner, first by stipulating in the Master Plan that the local churches must "take ownership of the operations in the seminary and donate 5 percent" of their finances to the seminary. This goal has proved difficult to achieve. However, as principal, Rev. Kairbek initiated a move away from an emphasis on the full-day program to intensive courses and an evening program, both of which became very popular, and also students were obligated to pay a tuition fee providing needed income. Eventually, in 2019, the more expensive full-day program was terminated along with other economies. Also, the recent pandemic has demonstrated the feasibility and financial advantages in terms of cost savings of online education, especially for those in remote areas. In addition, the chapter recognizes the need for better auditing procedures, and this should probably be done by an outside agency, perhaps through the Euro-Asian Accrediting Association.

The matter of self-theologizing has important ramifications for a seminary education. The core issues for accomplishing this center around who does the theologizing, who determines the key issues, and where the process is located. The contextualization endeavor should be relevant and drawn from those in the cultural context and not transplanted wholesale from Korea, North America, Europe, or other culturally diverse areas. UTS recognizes this need. From its founding by Korean missionaries, it has focused on training and depending on Kyrgyz Christians for pastoring and outreach, as stipulated in its Master Plan. UTS sought and achieved recognition by the Ministry of Education of Kyrgyzstan and thus acquired government acceptance and integration into the national educational system. UTS's approach gained recognition "as an exemplary case of leadership transfer from foreigners to locals along with its development process." Rev. Kairbek seems instrumental in these achievements along with other local leaders. Challenges to UTS are relevant to self-theologizing, such as the need for "well trained theological educators in the Kyrgyz language" rather than Russian and the "need for high-quality theological literature in Kyrgyz." These are necessary for indigenizing Christianity in the culture and to "develop a Kyrgyz-speaking Christian academic society" as well as trained laypersons. In addition, the chapter makes an appeal for input from "cultural anthropologists" to provide guidance on cultural understanding relevant to Christian outreach. Very fortunately, some excellent studies pertinent to this endeavor already exist in the writings of Matteo Fumagalli (Senior Lecturer, School of International Relations, St. Andrews University, UK), Mathijs Pelkman (Professor of Anthropology, London School of Economics and Political Science), and David Radford (Senior Lecturer in Sociology, University of South Australia), all social scientists who analyze the role of religion, including Christianity, in Kyrgyzstan and Central Asia.[7] Illustrative of this is one of Radford's studies that analyzes through extensive fieldwork how Kyrgyz Christians have sought to preserve inherent Kyrgyz values "such as hospitality and respect for the elders, cultural expressions such as dress and music, and symbolic representations such as those associating the Kyrgyz with their homeland and with their nomadic origins [which] are all seen as binding the Kyrgyz together as a people regardless of religious affiliation."[8] This is a credit to the approach of those involved with UTS.

The authors of this chapter describing the origins, developments, and present stature of UTS deserve commendation for its clarity and transparency. It demonstrates a significant amount of self-awareness of where UTS has been and its plans and needs for the future. All of this maintains a clear focus on the Kyrgyz people and their culture and is in keeping with the traditional approach of the three-self model plus a strong contextual element.[9]

---

[7] Highly recommended are: Matteo Fumagalli, "'Identity through Difference': Liminal Diasporism and Generational Change among the Koryo saram in Bishkek, Kyrgyzstan," *European Journal of Korean Studies* 20, no. 2 (Spring 2021): 37–72; Mathijs Pelkman, "'Culture' as a Tool and an Obstacle: Missionary Encounters in Post-Soviet Kyrgyzstan," *Journal of The Royal Anthropological Institute* 13, no. 4 (Winter 2007): 881–899 and Pelkman, "Frontier Dynamics: Reflections on Evangelical and Tablighi Missions in Central Asia," *Comparative Studies in Society and History* 63, no.1 (January 2021): 212–241; and David Radford, *Religious Identity and Social Change: Explaining Christian Conversion in a Muslim World* (New York: Routledge, 2015) and Radford, "Kyrgyzstan," in *Christianity in South and Central Asia*, ed. Kenneth R. Ross, Daniel Jeyaraj, and Todd M. Johnson (Edinburgh: Edinburgh University Press, 2019): 70–82.

[8] Radford, *Religious Identity and Social Change*, 138.

[9] During my research numerous people shared their expertise with me and made recommendations. I would especially wish to thank William Yoder, Mark Elliot, Terri Taylor, Edward Sands, and Baktybek Abdrisaev. The views expressed in this chapter are solely mine.

Chapter 14
Church Missions in the Public Sphere with a Focus on Onnuri Church's Use of Public Funds

by Hong Joo Kim

Since its introduction to Korea, Christianity has played a significant role in reforming Korea's feudal society and modernizing public sectors such as education and healthcare.[1] However, Korean churches have since divided into progressive liberal churches and fundamentalist conservative churches. Many conservative churches, which make up the majority of Korean churches, prioritized salvation of souls and defense of doctrines over their social responsibilities, and the Korean church gradually lost its engagement with society.[2] When Onnuri Church was founded in 1985 in this divisive atmosphere, some evangelicals were starting a church movement that upheld both biblical truth and social responsibility.

Pastor Yong Jo Ha was one such evangelical who made efforts to unite evangelicals across denominations and founded Onnuri Church with a desire to present a new biblical model of a church in Korea.[3]

This chapter will demonstrate how Onnuri Church's evangelical philosophy of pastoral ministry is reflected in its structure, and examine the social benefits of the organizations established by Onnuri Church that utilize public funding from outside of the church to do missions in the public sphere. This chapter will argue that the significance of these projects that operate with "non-church" funding extends beyond the financial/economic benefits. Ministries that are connected to the public sphere through such funding will become the training grounds in which believers can practice social engagement, and important channels through which the values of Christian service and love can reach the world.

---

1 Joon Woo Lee, "Current Status and Direction of Korean Christian Social Welfare Foundations," *Journal of Church Social Work* 19 (August 2012): 75–76. Pastor Jae Hoon Lee also says that the mission of the church is to show the world that the Gospel is a universal truth, Jae Hoon Lee, *Looking for Good Christians* (Seoul: Duranno, 2019), 21–22.

2 Yong-Kyu Park, *The Evangelical Movement That Awakened the Korean Church* (Seoul: Duranno, 1998), 76–79.

3 Yong Jo Ha, *The Dream of an Acts-Like Church* (Seoul: Duranno, 2007), 9–10.

Onnuri Church's Establishment of NGOs and Social Welfare Foundations as Means of Participation in the Public Sphere

Pastor Yong Jo Ha, the founder of Onnuri Church, believed that parachurch can do what the church cannot, and that the church can do what parachurch cannot.[4]

Pastor Jae Hoon Lee, who currently serves as the second senior pastor of Onnuri Church, has inherited Pastor Ha's evangelical theology and philosophy of pastoral ministry. Onnuri Church now runs parachurch organizations that are engaged in various ministries in different fields.[5] Among these ministries, there are organizations that are involved in conventional church work, such as evangelism, but there are also organizations that serve neighbors in need and pursue public interests. This chapter will focus specifically on three ministries that are funded by the government and other secular institutions: A Better World, Onnuri Welfare Foundation, and Onnuri M Mission (Onnuri Migrant Mission), which serves immigrant communities in Korea. Examining these organizations will highlight the significance that the church's use of secular funding has on the church and the public sphere.

A Better World

In 2010, Onnuri Church celebrated its twenty-fifth anniversary and founded "A Better World," an international development NGO, with the vision to unconditionally share God's blessings with our neighbors. Even though A Better World is a relatively new NGO, only ten years old, it has grown to carry out projects in emergency relief, community development, healthcare, and education in twenty-nine regions of twenty-four countries suffering from poverty, disease, and natural disasters. The organization's secretary general, Chang Ok Kim, gave two reasons why A Better World was able to grow so rapidly—it is a church-based organization, and it partners with public institutions.[6]

Church-Based NGO

There are many Christian NGOs in Korea, but not many NGOs are based around local churches. However, A Better World has several advantages because it was founded and is run by Onnuri Church. First is its stable financial management. Every year, the members of Onnuri Church make donation pledges for A Better World. Currently, 11,166 members donate a total of $2.8 million every year. Moreover, $0.35 million of additional donations are collected annually, and most of the donors are members of Onnuri Church. These totals are equivalent to 48 percent of the organization's 2021 annual budget of $6.55 million. These regular donations from members of Onnuri Church play a significant role in the financial stability of A Better World, which in turn garners trust from public institutions.

The second advantage of A Better World being based around Onnuri Church is that it is able to partner with the network of nine hundred missionaries sent by the church. For instance, missionary Jeong Bung Jin of Onnuri Church had ministries based in South Sudan. When the civil war broke out again in 2016, he fled to Uganda along with numerous other Sudanese refugees. Then, he informed the church about the devastating situation of the refugees. After this report, A Better World registered as an official NGO active in Uganda in 2017, and started a full-fledged ministry for Sudanese refugees. Today, various projects are being carried out, including elementary and secondary school construction, distribution of meals, provision of drinking water through wells and water purifiers, and agricultural developments. Instances like these demonstrate the advantage of working with the network of Onnuri missionaries who are scattered around the globe.

The third advantage of A Better World operating around Onnuri Church is that it can utilize the abundant volunteers from within the church. A Better World has dispatched relief teams to eleven countries around the world affected by tsunamis, earthquakes, typhoons, and floods, on twelve different occasions. The majority of the emergency relief teams consisted of Onnuri Church members. For instance, when the 2015 earthquake occurred in Nepal, A Better World immediately recruited volunteers from the church, and was able to provide rapid emergency relief on two separate occasions. After the relief was provided, a recovery project was carried out in the village of Goredanda, which was located in a mountainous area where aid workers were struggling to reach. A Better World built seventy-two houses, new schools, and church buildings, repaired roads,

---

[4] Pastor Yong Jo Ha states that it was John Stott's London Institute in England that taught him the importance of parachurch. "There, I studied the balance between the gospel and gospel-led social responsibilities. The moment I saw London Institute, I had a vision of how to lead Duranno once I returned to South Korea. The Church is a church, and Duranno is a parachurch. I am still experimenting and trying to understand how churches and parachurches can coexist in Korean society" (Ha, 81).

[5] Organizations founded by Onnuri Church include Duranno Publishing, Tyrannus International Mission (TIM), A Better World, Onnuri Welfare Foundation, Onnuri Mission Foundation, Christian Medical Network (CMN), BEE Korea, CGN TV, and Onnuri M Mission. Partner organizations include Handong Global University, Father School, Worship and Praise, Ezer Mission, and Creation Science Society.

[6] Secretary General Chang Ok Kim, interview by author, January 31, 2021.

provided vocational training, and installed water pipes, completing all of the restoration and reconstruction projects in 2017.

Cooperation with Public Institutions

As A Better World gained experience, the organization actively promoted partnered ministries with multilateral organizations like the government or the UN.[7] In 2013, A Better World began to utilize the government's delegated Official Development Assistance (ODA) funds, and in 2017, the organization gained further credibility when it was awarded the UN ECOSOC (Economic and Social Council) Special consultative status for economic cooperation. The table below lists the projects that were carried out with matching funds from the government and other groups.

Many advantages have accrued to A Better World by carrying out projects using funds from the government and other external institutions. The first advantage is financial support. External subsidies account for 12.5 percent of A Better World's total budget for 2021. In addition, this ratio is projected to increase, and in 2021, the organization plans on requesting financial partnerships with UNHCR (United Nations High Commissioner for Refugees)[8] and GGGI (Global Green Growth Institute).

Another advantage of A Better World receiving outside support is the strengthening of its business capacity as well as improvements in the expertise and transparency of the organization. To receive external funds, A Better World is subject to higher accountability from the government. In other words, the organization is held to a higher standard of financial transparency, business performance, and expertise. As A Better World strives to meet these standards, its business capacity naturally improves.

The third advantage of A Better World cooperating with public institutions is the expansion of the scope of its projects. Since A Better World is a Christian NGO, there are many areas that would be difficult to access for religious reasons. However, because the organization works with the Korean government or local Korean embassies, it is able to carry out numerous volunteer services and development projects in Islamic, Hindu, and Buddhist areas regardless of the organization's Christian identity.

---

7 The experiences of the current CEO Kwang Dong Kim as a former diplomat were of great help in promoting these partnership projects.

8 UNHCR is also known as the UN Refugee Agency. "UNHCR protects and assists millions of displaced and stateless people around the world" ("What does 'UNHCR' stand for?," Frequently Asked Questions, UNHRC, 2021, https://www.unhcr.org/frequently-asked-questions.html#whatdoesUNHCRstandfor).

Table 14.1: ODA Matching Projects of a Better World and the Korean Government (Unit: $1 = ₩1,100)

No.	Target area	Duration	Project	Cost	Cost ratio (Agency support: A Better World)
1	Rwanda (Nkomangwa Village)	2013-10-01 to 2014-10-30	Maternal and child health mobile clinic	$72,727	5:5
2	Senegal (Bonnava Village)	2014-01-01 to 2021-12-31	Drinking water improvement, education, and agricultural development (1st and 2nd stages)	$2,659,091	8:2
3	Senegal (Lupisque County, Dakar)	2015-04-01 to 2018-12-31	Maternal and child health enhancement and environment improvement	$2,272,727	9:1
4	Nepal (Goredanda Village, Gorka)	2016-03-28 to 2017-01-31	Goredanda village early reconstruction	$181,818	10:0
5	Rwanda (Mugininya)	2018-05-14 to 2020-12-31	Maternal and child health and nutrition promotion (Wolby Consortium Project)	$963,636	7:3
6	Guinea-Bissau (Brom Village, Kinjamel)	2018-08-01 to 2018-10-31	Orphanage solar power and village drinking water improvement	$63,636	10:0
7	Uganda (Moyo, Obongi)	2018-08-13 to 2021-12-31	South Sudan refugees school meal distribution, education, and village drinking water support	$1,249,091	8:2
8	Moldova (Poguneshti)	2018-12 to 2019-12	Public health center remodel, capacity enhancement, and drinking water improvement	$109,091	10:0
9	Nepal (Guerali Dungerdy)	2020-07-20 to 2020-12-31	Emergency relief for residents of COVID-19 44 quarantine centers	$1,455,455	10:0

However, as a church-based NGO, A Better World also has difficulties when cooperating with public institutions. Above all, the field staff complains of the inability to engage in any religious activities. Therefore, the organization should correct the staffs' theology by sufficiently providing basic education on the holistic and universal nature of the Gospel. Furthermore, A Better World is a church-based NGO that minimizes central administrative costs[9] in an attempt to channel as much money as possible to local beneficiaries. Therefore, the organization usually ends up being run by volunteers and/or low-wage devotees. This can serve as an economic advantage, but on the other hand, it serves as a disadvantage when professional team members are not able to dedicate themselves long-term, with the unfortunate side effect of high turnover rates. Therefore, securing experts and members of younger generations with long term commitments is something that the organization needs to address.

Onnuri Welfare Foundation

Onnuri Welfare Foundation was founded on August 23, 1999 by Onnuri Church to implement professional social welfare programs based on the love of Christ. There currently are thirteen agencies that are delegated to or directly operated by Onnuri Welfare Foundation.

Korea's Government Organization Act of 1981 stipulates that "administrative agencies may entrust their affairs to a corporate organization that is not part of the local government, to its agency or an individual."[10] This is an official acknowledgement that the Korean government cannot provide all the services that people need, and that it is necessary to share the responsibilities in providing social welfare services between the government and private sectors.[11] Moreover, after the 1997 financial crisis, the Korean government developed this method further as a means of restructuring the public sector.[12]

Accordingly, Onnuri Church also established a welfare foundation in 1999 to help the aged, youth, and people with disabilities.[13] In 2001, community living facilities for people with disabilities, Bundong Koinonia House of Hope and House of Joy, were entrusted by the government for the first time. Experience and expertise have accumulated since then, and the number of entrusted institutions has increased. Today, funds from the government and outside organizations far exceed those provided by Onnuri Church. Onnuri Welfare Foundation spent a total of $280 million from 1999 to 2020, of which $22.75 million was sponsored by Onnuri Church, while the remaining $257.3 million (92 percent) was financed by government or outside support. The foundation's fiscal structure for 2019 is shown in table 14.2 on the following page.[14]

There are notable advantages to the church's participation in social welfare by utilizing the government's private entrustment system. First, the church has a duty to fulfill its social responsibilities, and managing government-entrusted social welfare facilities is a good way to do this. The church lacks the financial capacity for social welfare as compared to the government, but churches have the advantage of being deeply rooted in local communities and having dedicated volunteers who have experience in different areas of society. On the other hand, even though the government has the financial resources, its rigid bureaucracy limits its ability to provide comprehensive welfare services to the people. Therefore, if the government and the church share certain responsibilities, there are many areas where they can create shared synergy in the field of social welfare.

Young Beom Song, the CEO of Onnuri Welfare Foundation, also points to their sense of integrity and transparency as the strengths of the organization. He says that because it is a welfare foundation established in the name of the church, the organization always strives to operate with integrity and transparency in an effort to reveal the glory of God in their work.[15] Onnuri Welfare Foundation not only strictly complies with the legal standards required by the government, but also undergoes regular external audits by local governments and external accounting firms, as well as internal audits by the church.

---

9 A Better World currently uses only 5.6 percent of its total budget for domestic and abroad personnel expenses, which is a small amount compared to other NGOs.

10 [Act No. 3422, 1981.4.8., partially amended] Enforced 1981.4.8, https://www.law.go.kr/LSW//lsEfInfoP.do?lsiSeq=224249#. Here, private entrustment of affairs refers to the act of delegating the state's role to private sectors to perform.

11 Sang Pil Park, *NGO* (Seoul: Arke, 2005), 85–86.

12 However, in recent years, there is also a movement to expand the government's direct involvement in social welfare services. See Young Jong Kim, "A Study on Social Service and the Private Entrustment System in Korea," *Health and Social Welfare Review* 37, no. 4 (Dec 2017): 407.

13 Apart from the Welfare Foundation, Onnuri Church has a social missions department that helps the underprivileged through the church's internal finances. The budget for 2020 was $1.17 million.

14 Among them, the contracts for the Dongbu Municipal Specialized Senior Nursing Center and Dongbu Daycare Center were terminated in 2019, and instead, the Seocho 50 Plus Center was newly entrusted in 2020 to help educate people in their fifties or older in the second half of their lives.

15 CEO Young Beom Song, interview by author, February 2, 2021. CEO Song also serves as an elder in Onnuri Church.

Table 14.2: Fiscal structure of Onnuri Welfare Foundation (2019 Unit: $1 = ₩1,100)

2019	Government subsidies and support		Onnuri Church support fund (corporate transfers)	Self-payment, specific-purpose reserve, and carryover			Subtotal
	Subsidies	External fundraising projects		Self-payment	Specific-purpose reserve	Carryover	
Corporate Office	$262,247	$ -	$516,364	$ -	$387,167	$791,830	$1,957,608
Gunpo Hanaro Mid to Long-Term Male Youth Shelter	$404,996	$32,254	$101,818	$4,988	$ -	$94,183	$638,239
Southern Gyeonggi Youth Independence Support Center	$226,335	$ -	$18,364	$ -	$ -	$1,056	$245,755
Dream House Local Children's Center	$166,471	$6,727	$30,000	$ -	$ -	$25,645	$228,843
Onnuri Nursing Home	$62,699	$ -	$45,545	$3,442,742	$11,875	$252,905	$3,815,766
Yongsan Municipal Comprehensive Senior Welfare Center	$4,381,029	$142,666	$72,727	$242,294	$ -	$250,439	$5,089,155
Yongsan Daycare Center	$44,444	$ -	$ -	$285,279	$28,999	$25,445	$384,167
Yongsan District Cheongpa Senior Welfare Center	$702,198	$ -	$13,636	$20,324	$ -	$29,937	$766,095
Seochu-gu Central Senior Welfare Center	$2,146,264	$1,818	$45,455	$391,029	$ -	$121,686	$2,706,252
Seocho-gu Zelkova Shelter	$1,364,878	$ -	$27,273	$311,147	$ -	$977	$1,704,275
Bundong Koinonia Protection Facility for People with Disabilities	$397,400	$ -	$13,780	$663,824	$ -	$207,071	$1,282,075
House of Hope	$55,265	$ -	$ -	$4,845	$ -	$5,475	$65,575
Seoul Metro City Counseling Office in Seoul Station	$653,185	$18,182	$51,818	$171,167	$ -	$135,560	$1,029,913
Dongbu Municipal Specialized Senior Nursing Center	$133,822	$1,628	$82,274	$3,851,078	$ -	$662,348	$4,731,150
Dongbu Daycare Center	$41,847	$ -	$ -	$255,855	$ -	$34,216	$331,918
Total	$11,043,081	$203,275	$1,019,054	$9,644,561	$428,041	$2,638,775	$24,976,786

Table 14.3: Onnuri M Mission Government Subsidy Receipt Status (2020 Unit: $1=₩1,100)

Facility	Ministry	Church support	Government Subsidy	Subtotal
Ansan Onnuri Community Children's Center	Environment improvement project	$61,818	$141,033	$202,851
Hwaseong Multicultural Lifelong Education Center	Ansan City Korean Class	$82,727	$45,947	$128,674
	Gyeonggi Province Club			
	Ministry of Gender Equality and Family (Rainbow School)			
	Total	$144,545	$186,980	$331,525

The second advantage of Onnuri Welfare Foundation is its abundant volunteers. Onnuri Church is a megachurch with members living in various places near Seoul and Gyeonggi Province. Therefore, members can volunteer in local facilities in their regions. Sometimes, volunteers are placed in each facility based on their expertise, identified through facility management meetings and interviews. Welfare cannot be provided through financial support alone. People have complex social, cultural, and spiritual needs. Therefore, when the church community becomes an active member in welfare services, it can play a significant role in meeting people's diverse, complex needs.

Nevertheless, there are also areas in which the church must be cautious when running a welfare foundation. First, the church must guarantee the autonomy and independence of the organization in running its operations. In other words, the church must not attempt to privatize the welfare foundation as an affiliated institution of the church. Privatization is the thing that the government is most wary of when entrusting facilities to a private sector. Therefore, the trustee institution has a duty to build trust in society by constantly increasing its transparency and improving its service quality. Above all, a Christian welfare foundation will need to operate within its overall mission to reveal the universality of the Gospel and the goodness of God by providing better service and more efficient management than other secular private organizations.

Onnuri M Mission

Korean society is rapidly moving from a homogeneous culture to a multicultural society. Foreign immigrants, who began moving to South Korea in the early 1990s, now number 2.5 million.

Onnuri Church founded Onnuri M Mission, which has carried out numerous cross-cultural ministries since 1993. Along with its M Center located in Ansan where many immigrants reside, Onnuri M Mission also has M Centers in Gimpo, Hwaseong, Pyeongtaek, and Namyangju, and serves the population through worship services in fifteen different languages representing thirty-three countries, with five youth services and other multicultural ministries. Among them, the Hwaseong Multicultural Lifelong Education Center and Ansan Onnuri Community Children's Center, which were founded to help children from multicultural families and immigrants to adjust to Korean society, serve to fulfill a strong public interest. Therefore, they are now officially state registered and began to receive financial support from the local government. Although it is still a small amount, this government fiscal entrustment is expected to play an important role in expanding Onnuri M Mission's social responsibilities in the future.

According to data from the Ministry of Public Administration and Security, the number of children from multicultural families living in Korea had reached 237,506 as of November 2018. However, the *2018 National Multicultural Family Survey Study* by the Ministry of Gender Equality and Family revealed that these children were significantly less adapted to Korean society than other citizens.[16] This is because Korean society has maintained a homogeneous culture for a long time, making it difficult for people from outside cultures to integrate.

Since 2017, Onnuri M Mission has been assigning missionaries with cross-cultural experience to ministries that serve children of multicultural families. After these missionaries started serving in these ministries, Ansan Onnuri Community Children's Center was designated as an excellent service center since 2019, and the Hwaseong Multicultural Lifelong Education Center received the Minister of Gender Equality and Family Award in 2020.[17] These achievements demonstrate that missionaries are an important resource to carry out ministries that serve immigrants and multicultural families.

Today, immigrants and multicultural families are scattered all throughout Korea. It is also true that sixty-thousand churches are distributed across the nation, and these churches have the potential to become important platforms for ministries serving these populations. However, many Korean churches are unable to reach out to immigrants due to language and cultural barriers. If these can be overcome, ministries for immigrants and multicultural families can be expected to grow significantly. For this to happen, Korean churches must partner with missionaries as well as government entities in order to fulfill their social responsibilities of helping immigrants and multicultural families to successfully integrate into Korean society.

---

16 Research Institute of Policies for Korean Women, *2018 National Multicultural Family Survey Study* (Ministry of Gender Equality and Family, 2019), 57–60, www.mogef.go.kr/mp/pcd/mp_pcd_s001d.do?mid=plc503.

17 Pastor Gyu Seok Noh, who oversees all the ministries, Pastor Kyung Sook Lee, who served as the director of the Ansan Onnuri Community Children's Center, and Dr. Jeong Hee Kim, who founded the Hwaseong Multicultural Lifelong Education Center, are all former overseas missionaries.

Conclusion

Korean evangelicals have made efforts to extend the values of the Gospel from the private realm to the public sphere. However, Korean society still expresses serious doubts about the role of the church role in the public sphere. This is an indication that the Korean church is failing to testify about a universal God who brings salvation and restoration not only to the personal lives of individuals, but also to entire societies and to all of creation.

This case study of Onnuri Church's ministries has demonstrated that Onnuri Church founded parachurch organizations like A Better World, Onnuri Welfare Foundation, and Onnuri M Mission in order to extend the values of the Gospel to the public sphere. The chapter has also described how these organizations have collaborated with the government and other public institutions in order to serve their neighbors and pursue public interests. These kinds of organizations operate at the border between the church and the world, and the dangers of secularization as well as self-righteous attitudes are real threats for these organizations. Nevertheless, God's mission for the public sphere is a task that the church absolutely cannot overlook or give up on. The church must not hesitate to partner with governments and other outside organizations to solve social problems in the public sphere that impact our neighbors in need. The church is responsible for displaying the Gospel as a universal truth that has power in all areas of life. Therefore, the church must maintain its confidence in this Gospel, and commit to revealing its values and power in the public sphere.

Chapter 14 Response

by Atola Longkumer

With deep appreciation for the opportunity given to respond to the paper prepared by Hong Joo Kim, on the topic, "Church Missions in the Public Sphere with a Focus on Onnuri Church's Use of Public Funds," I read the paper with delight and interest. I was delighted for the privilege to learn about a new context, and I read with keen interest because the issue addressed by the writer is an urgent one for Christian mission. And indeed, I learned something new—about Onnuri Church and its history and vibrant witness to Christ through its multifaceted ministries. Incidentally, there is a successful ministry in my home church in Nagaland—Father School—and reading Kim's footnotes I learned that it has its roots in the ministry of Onnuri Church.[18] The central point that Kim presents is that the church's mission extends beyond the community of believers to the larger society—mission is not limited to the salvation of souls; it should also be concerned with the well-being of the whole creation. Undergirded by this notion of Christian mission, Kim presents the case of Onnuri Church and its engagement with the larger society through different focus areas often employing public funds.

Kim provides a brief history of Onnuri Church and explains the active participation of the church in the larger society, addressing the socioeconomic and cultural challenges both in Korea and in other parts of the world, particularly in the developing world. Onnuri Church was founded by Pastor Yong Jo Ha in 1985 in Seoul, with the purpose to teach and enable Korean Christians to engage in social responsibilities as a mark of Christian mission. This vision of evangelical social responsibility is carried out through a wide range of services provided by Onnuri Church, including publication, education,

---
18 In footnote #5 Kim lists the ministries of Onnuri Church, including Father School.

social welfare, migrant care, and broadcasting. In the paper, Kim presents financial records of Onnuri Church to demonstrate the constructive "utilization of public funds to do missions in the public sphere." Kim opines that "ministries that are connected to the public sphere through such funding will become the training grounds in which believers can practice social engagement, and important channels through which the values of Christian service and love can reach the world." Among the many areas of public engagement of Onnuri Church, Kim identifies three ministries that utilize public funds from the government and other secular organizations, such as the United Nations. The three ministries are: A Better World, Onnuri Welfare Foundation, and Onnuri M Mission (Onnuri Migrant Mission). Refugee resettlement, emergency relief during natural disaster, facilities for the disabled, maternity care, youth residences, developments such as drinking water and schools, and migrant care are some areas of ministry of Onnuri Church organizations.

Providing brief descriptions of these three ministries and their focus areas, Kim makes critical notes of both the advantages and disadvantages of church-based NGOs that collaborate with public organizations and resources. While accountability and transparency are high marks of performance for the organizations, retaining highly qualified personnel remains a concern due to low budget allocation for administrative purposes. Although supported by the church, as NGOs the organizations umbrellaed under Onnuri Church can participate in public areas, such as development. Kim, however, mentions the constrains felt by field workers to engage in "religious activities." Kim points out the critical need to train volunteers and workers in theological understanding of the Gospel as holistic. Furthermore, another challenge lies in ensuring the effective balance of the NGOs within the larger church mission and vision that reflects the marks of the Gospel while simultaneously maintaining the autonomy of the organizations under Onnuri Church.

As narrated and analyzed by Kim, the public engagement of Onnuri Church in social responsibilities through resourceful utilization of public funds makes an important point about the mission of the church that is holistic and life-affirming for all God's creation. Without going into the details and functions of the three organizations, which the paper adequately described, I will address three points that such a case study of the local church and its mission brings to our mission of faithful witness to the Gospel, the Good News as revealed in Jesus Christ—the love of God that desires all creation flourish. Firstly, Jesus of Nazareth manifests the triune God, whose nature is love expressed in immeasurable grace to all, including the most vulnerable and the marginalized. Secondly, the church as the community of God's people is called to participate in establishing God's Kingdom marked by justice and peace. Thirdly, the mission of the church begins and is sustained by joyful worship and the fellowship of God's people.

Firstly, God in Jesus Christ demonstrated his love for his whole creation. The triune God is the creator, redeemer, and sustainer of life. To confess the triune God as the source of life is to affirm life for all. A mission that ignores the flourishing of life is to deny the God of life. The mission document of the World Council of Churches reiterates this when it states, "God invites us into the life-giving mission of the Triune God and empowers us to bear witness to the vision of abundant life for all in the new heaven and earth."[19] A faith that is rooted in the fundamental tenet of belief in an all-encompassing God, whose nature and character is life-giving, cannot but be lived in active participation in mission that enhances life. Such a faith is marked by a profound commitment to the flourishing of life in all its aspects for all. To "prioritize salvation of souls and defense of doctrines," which is, as Kim explains, the understanding of many Korean Christians (and of many other Christian communities around the world), is therefore to neglect the comprehensive nature of the Good News as revealed and lived by Jesus of Nazareth. Conversely, creative and accountable collaborations by Christians with public organizations are affirmations of God's involvement in the whole of humanity for the good of all. To care for the public good is to proclaim God's intent of good for all. Serving the world around us as God's people is put eloquently in the following words attributed to the sixteenth-century mystic Teresa of Avila:

> Christ has no body now but yours. No hands, no feet on earth but yours. Yours are the eyes through which He looks compassion on this world. Yours

---
[19] Jooseop Kuem, ed., *Together Towards Life: Mission and Evangelism in Changing Landscapes, with a Practical Guide* (Geneva: World Council of Churches Publications, 2013), 6.

are the feet with which He walks to do good. Yours are the hands with which He blesses all the world. Yours are the hands, yours are the feet. Yours are the eyes, you are His body. Christ has no body now but yours. No hands, no feet on earth but yours.[20]

Secondly, the church as the community of God's people is called to participate in the mission of establishing God's Kingdom marked by justice and peace. The history of Christian mission has ample examples of God's people participating in establishing "the good life" as perceived by them in their specific time and contexts. To be sure, the history of Christian mission is more complex and dynamic, with many ambiguities; for instance, Christian mission's inevitable link with the operations of colonial empires. These complexities and ambiguities from the history of Christian mission provide insights for mission in contemporary times. Evangelical zeal for "saving souls" was not the only focus of mission; the zeal to preach the Good News as revealed in Jesus Christ also included sharing the facets of modern life that were perceived as life enhancing by the missionaries. In other words, Christian missionaries thought about the welfare of the natives and the converts they were evangelizing (despite their limitations and often inherent cultural biases). This concern found expression in the many social aspects of Christian mission, such as medical mission, education, and liberation of women from inhuman cultural practices, etc. The perspective of a Presbyterian missionary in India illustrates the social responsibilities included in Christian mission. Sam Higginbotham saw the connect between the Good News in Christ and the upliftment from poverty, as expressed in the following words: "There would be no Kingdom of God in India without an amelioration of poverty and this must be founded on a more productive agriculture."[21] In our own time, with so many insights from history as well as critical knowledge of socioeconomic structures, witness to Christ in seeking justice and peace requires critical concern about the structures and cultures we support and participate in. Put simply, equity, transparency, and common good continue to be urgent challenges in the world today.

Thirdly, the mission of the church begins and is sustained by joyful worship and the fellowship of God's people. Kim has aptly pointed out the need for education of field workers that helps clarify the holistic nature of the Gospel and its implications for practices of mission. To empower church members to carry out their social responsibilities in the public sphere, as participants in God's mission, it is important that worship and preaching include the concern for neighbors beyond the worshipping community. In my own evangelical upbringing, I observed a lack of worship elements that incorporate social issues. For example, in many churches the hymns that are sung are usually from the Euro-American mission period, which are filled with sincere calls for "saving the lost" and "rewards." The content of preaching is another area that feeds the division between concern for the salvation of souls and concern for social responsibilities. Preaching that is centered on individual edification and assurance only partially proclaims the Good News. The Good News in Christ is comprehensive and holistic, marked by compassion and thoughtfulness for our neighbors.

Conclusion

Kim's paper on Onnuri Church and its witness in the public sphere through the use of public funds presents a constructive example of the church's mission in today's world. Highlighting the need for social engagement by Christians and doing so by creative collaboration with public funds through transparent management illustrate the potential for the church to be an active participant in ushering in a just and compassionate world. The challenges of the world today on many levels—poverty, environmental crises, disparities, ethnocentrisms, fundamentalists of all stripes, and the impact of the coronavirus—continue to call on the church to be the prophetic, public, and pastoral community as people of the triune God.

---

20 DotMagis editor, "Christ Has No Body Now but Yours," IgnatianSpirituality, accessed July 14, 2021, Vimeo, https://www.ignatianspirituality.com/christ-has-no-body-now-but-yours/.

21 David A. Hollinger, *Protestants Abroad: How Missionaries Tried to Change the World but Changed America* (Princeton: Princeton University Press, 2017), 67.

Chapter 15
Evangelicals and Structural (In)Justice—What Are We Afraid Of?

by Justin Thacker

"For the LORD your God is God of gods and Lord of lords ... who executes justice for the orphan and the widow, and who loves the foreigners, providing them with food and clothing" (Deut. 10:17–18, NRSVA). In these words from Deuteronomy the two sides to our moral responsibilities to the economically vulnerable are highlighted. On the one hand, we are called to provide those who are destitute with "food and clothing." At the same time though, we are also required to implement God's missional concern for "justice." My contention in this article is that while we[1] have been relatively good in responding to the first of these aspects, we have, I would suggest, been woefully inadequate at addressing the second. Maggay perhaps sums this up most effectively when she says, "Evangelicals are unfortunately stuck in merely providing discrete services to the poor, without addressing the larger context of why people are poor. There is a reluctance to engage in advocacy, to create a public voice and insert the cause of the poor into political space."[2] Kingston-Smith goes further when she points out how engagement in acts of charity can actually further the mechanisms of injustice at work—"there is a very real danger that in our desire to show compassion and care for our neighbour, we can unwittingly become part of larger wheels already in motion in a machine which is not Kingdom-oriented in its mandate."[3]

In this essay, I want then to do two things. In the first place, I will lay out the biblical rationale for why we have a responsibility to address structural issues of economic justice. In their excellent work on this topic, Offutt et al. suggest that part of the reason for the lack of evangelical engagement in

---
[1] By "we" I largely mean the protestant church and even more specifically the white evangelical part of the protestant church.

[2] M. Maggay, "Justice and Approaches to Social Change," in *Micah's Challenge: The Church's Responsibility to the Global Poor*, ed. J. Thacker and M. Hoek (Milton Keynes: Paternoster, 2008), 125. The same point has been made by many other authors; cf. J. Thacker, *Global Poverty* (London: SCM Press, 2017), 156–157.

[3] C. Kingston-Smith, "Caring Wisely in a Globalised World," *Encounters Mission Journal* 35 (2010): 1.

structural issues is the lack of a sufficiently developed evangelical theology of sociopolitical engagement.[4] In the first part of this essay I therefore seek to make a modest contribution to that scholarship. I then go on to explore in the second part some of the reasons why we might be reluctant to engage in such issues. I conclude by drawing attention to Boesak's critique of the church that he described as the Reuben option and suggest that faithfulness to the task God has given us demands a different kind of response.

The Biblical Basis for Structural Justice

In order to set out the biblical basis for structural economic justice, I need to state precisely what I mean by this phrase. Dom Hélder Câmara is reported to have said, "When I give food to the *poor*, they call me a saint. When I ask why the *poor* have no food, they call me a communist." The association with communism is, of course, unfortunate, but the reason I have shared this quotation is precisely because it helps us to delineate the concept of structural economic justice to which I refer. What I mean by this phrase is simply this: structural economic justice represents the method and practice of addressing the root causes of material poverty. As such, it does not stop at noticing the poor have no food, or clothing, or shelter, but asks the question, "Why do such conditions exist?" Even then, it does not stop at a superficial answer such as, "They have no money," but continues to ask "Why?" until a sufficient end is reached. Consider this chain of reasons:

"Grace, a single mother of four in rural Tanzania, cannot feed her children."
"Why?"
"Because she has no income."
"Why?"
"Because she has no job, and the state provides no economic safety net."
"Why is there no economic safety net?"[5]
"Because her government has a major budget deficit due to its debt servicing."
"Why?"
"Because during the 1980s and 1990s her government was encouraged to take out loans they would never be able to repay."
"Why?"

"Because Western commercial banks were awash with petrodollars they needed to off-load, and lending to global south countries was the best way to generate a return."
"Why did they want to make more profit?"
"Because money is an idol that many worship."

Of course, other reasons could be added at various points. This explanation is not meant to be exhaustive, but illustrative. In addition, it is of course right that any such chain of reasons eventually concludes with a declaration of sin, in this case the sin of idolatry. Part of the way we tackle these issues is precisely by preaching the Gospel and seeking the personal transformation that only Christ can bring. However, the point I am trying to make is that a concern for structural economic justice takes us beyond responding to the immediate need, which in this case might mean provision of food aid, to also address some of those intermediate reasons that are the deeper and longer-term causes of Grace's poverty. In other words, it is about addressing the structural sins that keep the poor in poverty. Moreover, as I have suggested, such a concern is found throughout the Scriptures. There are many ways in which this could be shown but I want to illustrate this by focussing on two specific topics.

1. Justice in the Hebrew Scriptures

The first of these concerns the Old Testament refrain that we are called to offer care to the widow, the orphan, the stranger, and the poor. These categories occur in combination throughout the Old Testament (e.g., Exod. 22:22; Deut. 10:18; 24:17; Job 24:3; Ps. 94:6; Isa. 1:17; Jer. 7:6). For the purposes of this chapter, I analyzed every one of the references where at least two of them appear together. In that analysis, I scrutinized Scripture as to whether its injunction was that we directly help the relevant groups—for instance by providing food or shelter—or whether we should seek justice for the relevant groups by upholding their rights, pleading their cause, and so on. I have classified the first of these responses as that of "charity," and the second of these responses as that of "justice," and the results are shown below. The figures represent the number of verses where these groups occur and what kind of response the Old Testament advocates.[6]

---

[4] S. Offutt et al., *Advocating for Justice* (Grand Rapids: Baker Academic, 2016), 42ff.

[5] I appreciate that at this point I could have equally explored the question by following the chain of why there are no jobs available, but for reasons of space I have restricted myself to the safety net issue.

[6] To be clear the occurrences are not the number of times the words *hesed* (loosely, charity) or *mishpat* (justice) appear, but rather the number of times the concepts of charity, as direct provision of aid, and justice, as addressing the causes of material deprivation, appear.

	Charity	Justice
Widows, orphans, foreigners, and poor		1
Widows, orphans and foreigners	4	9
Widows, orphans, and poor		2
Widows and orphans	1	4
Poor and foreigners	3	2
TOTALS	8	18

It is worth noting that two of the verses suggested a response that could be classified as *both* that of charity and that of justice. The significant point from this analysis is simply that on balance the predominant response of the Old Testament to the challenges faced by the widow, the orphan, the foreigner, and the poor is that of justice. A couple of examples are provided here:

> You shall not withhold the wages of poor and needy labourers, whether other Israelites or aliens who reside in your land in one of your towns. You shall pay them their wages daily before sunset, because they are poor and their livelihood depends on them. — Deut. 24:14–15, NRSVA

> Ah, you who make iniquitous decrees, who write oppressive statutes, to turn aside the needy from justice and to rob the poor of my people of their right, that widows may be your spoil, and that you may make the orphans your prey!
> —Isa. 10:1–2, NRSVA

The sense we get in these verses (and others) is that while God does want us to respond to the situation of those who are poor by providing direct support in terms of food, clothing, and shelter, it is even more the case that we must not exploit them, that we must treat them fairly, and that we must defend their cause. In short, we must advocate for structural justice alongside our works of mercy.

2. Jesus and the Temple Bank

This idea is also evident in the life of Jesus. There are many examples we could give of where Jesus challenged the structural injustices of his day,[7] but perhaps the clearest is his actions on the Temple Mount:

> On reaching Jerusalem, Jesus entered the temple courts and began driving out those who were buying and selling there. He overturned the tables of the money changers and the benches of those selling doves, and would not allow anyone to carry merchandise through the temple courts. And as he taught them, he said, "Is it not written: 'My house will be called a house of prayer for all nations'? But you have made it a 'den of robbers'" (Mark 11:15–17, NRSVA).

There are, at least, four possible interpretations of Jesus's actions on this day. Some have suggested that his primary concern was the religious purity of the temple; others have concluded it was a statement of his authority over the Temple; another interpretation is that it was a prophetic act signalling the future destruction of the Temple; and finally there are those who believe it was a political statement about the economic system that operated in first-century Palestine.[8]

As with many theological debates, there is probably some truth in all four of these interpretations and I don't think we need to choose between them. Therefore, in what follows, I am not suggesting this is the only way to understand Jesus's actions on that day—but it is certainly one.

What we often fail to appreciate about the Jerusalem Temple was that it was not just a religious institution, it was also a bank. I mean this not just in the sense that it collected money from the population as they paid for their animals to be sacrificed, but also in the sense that it acted as a location to collect taxes (both Jewish and Roman), and that it received deposits from the people and gave out loans to those who wanted them. One estimate is that as much as the equivalent of $3 million was held on deposit in the Temple coffers in the first century.[9]

Hence, we can think of the Temple as not just a religious building, but also a commercial and economic one. When Jesus disrupted the business of this Temple bank he was not just challenging the sacrificial system of the priests; he was also challenging the whole economic system of Roman-occupied Palestine. What angered him so much was the way in which that system used taxes to exploit others, taking revenue from the poorest and funneling them up, through the Temple, to the rich and powerful. When Jesus called it a "den of robbers," he was referring to those who grew their wealth at the expense of the poor through this economic system.

---

7 See in particular J. H. Yoder, *The Politics of Jesus* (Grand Rapids: Eerdmans, 1994).

8 N. Hamilton, "Temple Cleansing and Temple Bank," *Journal of Biblical Literature* 83, no. 4 (1964): 365–372; W. Domeris, "The Enigma of Jesus' Temple Intervention: Four Essential Keys," *HTS Theological Studies* 71, no. 1 (2015).

9 Hamilton, "Temple Cleansing," 366.

Jesus's actions that day did not change the system overnight. Rather he was standing in the tradition of prophetic sign-acts in which God's judgement is signaled through action. The point was to do something visible and dramatic that drew attention to a structural injustice that plagued the people. The next day, the Temple bankers were back at their work. But in his speech and action on that day, Jesus was declaring that the economic system represented by the Temple bank was one to which God was opposed. In doing so, he also shows us that our responsibility is not merely to serve the poor through charitable giving, but also to call attention to and demonstrate against the structural injustices of our day.

Why Do we Ignore Structural Justice?

In light of this, the question we must now address is, "Why are we so afraid of structural injustice?" In addressing this, it is important that we recognize that some evangelical movements have been heavily engaged in the kind of structural transformation of society that I am advocating. The campaigns of Olaudah Equiano and William Wilberforce for the abolition of the slave trade are obvious examples, and so is John Wesley's encouragement of what today would be called a decolonization agenda.[10] We could of course add to this campaigns for reform of prisons, factories, and child labour, the fostering of education and health, and the eradication of slum dwellings, all of which were championed by members of the so-called Clapham Sect.[11] More recently, we could add to this list the Jubilee 2000 campaign to cancel Global South debt, Micah Global's work on corruption, Jim Wallis and the Sojourners movement, Bryan Stevenson and the Equal Justice Initiative, and even my own work on global tax justice.[12]

However, what is significant is the way in which, at least in the present time, such campaigns are marked by their relative marginality. In contrast to the campaigning evangelicals of the eighteenth and nineteenth centuries, the evangelicals of today who are concerned with social justice (and that is not all of them of course) are at risk of confining their activities to, in the words of Martin Luther King, "flinging a coin to a beggar."[13] There are many reasons for this including the sacred-secular divide, fear of association with communism and/or liberal and liberation theologies, an underrealized eschatology, or fear of losing our privilege,[14] but in this essay I am going to address two others that I consider to be of especial significance.

1. Individualistic Emphasis

It is noteworthy that the Roman Catholic magisterium does not appear to have as much of a problem with addressing issues of structural justice as the Protestant church, especially the evangelical protestant church. While at a local level Catholic churches are well known for engaging in discrete acts of charity in a way that parallels the efforts of many protestant churches, at a central level they have a much richer heritage of tackling socioeconomic problems in a way that puts the evangelical church to shame.

While one might disagree with particular conclusions, the fact is that since the first papal encyclical of 1891, *Rerum Novarum*, the papacy has produced a succession of incredibly well-thought-through statements concerning the issues of the day. Such pronouncements are marked by their deep analysis of the particular issue under consideration, their fidelity to the Catholic tradition, and their rich theological consideration. While there are individual exceptions, the same cannot be said of many evangelical attempts to address sociopolitical issues.[15] I do not think this is because the Catholic church has brighter minds or access to richer theological resources; I think it is because one of the unfortunate sequelae of the Reformation is that it has left us with an overemphasis on the individual as opposed to the corporate dimensions of life.[16] Clearly, the Reformation was sorely needed, but as

---

10 T. W. Jennings, *Good News to the Poor: John Wesley's Evangelical Economics* (Nashville: Abingdon Press, 1990), 80ff.

11 E. Howse, *Saints in Politics: The 'Clapham Sect' and the Growth of Freedom* (Toronto: University of Toronto Press, 1952).

12 "Church Action for Tax Justice," Church Action for Tax Justice, accessed January 9, 2021, https://www.catj.org.uk/.

13 Martin Luther King Jr., "A Time to Break the Silence," in *A Testament of Hope: The Essential Writings and Speeches of Martin Luther King Jr.*, ed. J. Washington (New York: Harper Collins, 1986), 231–244.

14 On this point, I have argued elsewhere that class divisions played a part in evangelical antipathy to social justice in the early twentieth century. See J. Thacker and S. Clark, "A Historical and Theological Exploration of the 1910 Disaffiliation of the Cambridge Inter-Collegiate Christian Union from the Student Christian Movement" (unpublished paper, last modified 2011). Available on request.

15 See in particular Sider's critique in R. Sider, *The Scandal of Evangelical Politics* (Grand Rapids: Baker Books, 2008), 25.

16 The internalized theocratic tendency of the Roman Catholic church may also play a part in this.

with many theological corrections, we seem to have lost something in the process. That something is an overemphasis on the individual as the unit of analysis. As evangelical protestants we have become so caught up with winning individual souls for Christ, and with democratizing our ecclesial structures (at least in the nonconformist traditions) that we now struggle to engage with anything apart from the individual.

What I am suggesting here is that there is a parallel between our focus on saving the individual soul and saving the individual poor person. In both cases, we think that if we work one-on-one as it were, we have discharged our responsibility. In saying this, I am not questioning the need for personal salvation, but I am saying that in the sociopolitical sphere not all problems can be solved by handing out a bowl of soup. We must, as Câmara reminded us, ask why they don't have their own bowl of soup in the first place.

2. Loss of Income

Figure 15.1: "Sauda Is One Day Old". Used with permission from Sarah-Jayne Clifton, Director of Jubilee Debt Campaign (1996 leaflet).

The second reason why I think we eschew getting involved in actions that address structural issues of injustice is simply that it does not pay so well. This might come across as cynical, but there is a reason why campaigns by international development organizations frequently use images of children in their fundraising efforts. Such imagery is more effective in prizing donations from otherwise reluctant givers. This effect has been well documented in the psychological literature as the "identifiable victim effect."[17] What that literature demonstrates is that if you are seeking to move the hearts, minds, and wallets of would-be donors, then you will be far more effective if you identify a single, named victim of some injustice rather than present a statistical overview of how many people are struggling with the injustice in the first place. This means that even when campaigners are addressing issues of structural injustice they tend to tell individual stories to illustrate the topic they are addressing. This is perfectly illustrated by the Jubilee 2000 campaign, which was a campaign in the late 1990s to highlight the issue of global south debt. The campaign's original and most successful leaflet was one that depicted a single newborn baby.

It is also for this reason that child sponsorship has become such an effective model for campaigning, and why so many international development agencies have adopted it.[18] The problem with giving to works that address structural issues of economic justice is that while you can easily identify those who are suffering the injustice, and can tell their stories, it is much harder, if not impossible, to identify those who benefit from your intervention. In contrast to child sponsorship, you cannot say that your ten dollars bought the blanket for that individual child. At most you can see that your ten dollars helped support a campaign that in the end ensured a fairer economic settlement for a particular country that in due course lifted thousands of unnamed people out of poverty.

At a human, psychological level, I can fully appreciate our desire to know the individual we have helped, but it strikes me that the biblical model is one where we do not let our left hand know what our right hand is doing—that we give not because of the blessing it brings to us, but for the benefit it gives to others—where the call upon us is to love the unnamed, unidentified victim as much as the named and known one. In calling us to invite for dinner those who cannot invite us back, in commanding us to love our enemies, in answering the lawyer's question about the nature of neighborliness by pointing to one who was ethnically and religiously other, Jesus is communicating to us that our moral responsibilities are categorically not demarcated by familiarity, but by calling and need. A realization of this fact would go a long way to fostering a greater concern for structural issues of justice.

Conclusion

In a famous sermon during the apartheid era, Allan Boesak challenged the church for too frequently taking "the Reuben option." When confronted with their brothers' desire to kill Joseph, Reuben broached a compromise to keep Joseph alive. In doing so, Reuben clearly knew what the right thing was to do but lacked the courage to follow it through and so

---

17 See my discussion in Thacker, *Global Poverty*, 153.

18 For a critique of child sponsorship cf. Thacker, 147–157.

pursued the easier path. Boesak lambastes the church for doing the same. Our problem he suggests is a fundamental lack of courage. Time and again we have known what the right thing was to do, but in the name of self-preservation we have followed the path of least resistance. His primary concern was the church's response to apartheid, but he goes on to say this:

> The Reuben option: Have a programme for hungry children, collect millions and spend them on the poor. "Give and feel good!" is the legend on a poster from one charitable organisation, with a picture of a little black child, arms grotesquely thin, protruding stomach, tears rolling down the cheeks. Yes, indeed. But to use all our energy, our resources, our ingenuity, to work honestly and openly to change an economic system that by its very nature cannot and will not give the poor a chance to become fully human? That we cannot do, because then we become "involved," and we have to look with new eyes at the system on which our budgets are based.[19]

Boesak's evocative description of poverty porn[20] in 1970s may no longer be relevant, but his broader point is still valid today. We remain guilty, I would suggest, of taking the Reuben option. We know that climate change is killing the global poor, yet we continue to resist the systemic changes that would truly generate a low carbon future; we know that the global economic system steals approximately $200 billion a year from the Global South through tax dodging, but we do precious little to campaign for a fairer global tax system; we know that Africa spends more in debt servicing than it spends on health or education, yet we fail to call our governments to account for the loans that we fostered upon Africa when it was at its lowest ebb; and especially for those of us in Europe and North America, we know that we impoverished many parts of the Global South through colonial exploitation and the slave trade, yet we refuse to have a serious conversation about the reparations that we owe. We have known what we should do, but we have taken the path of least resistance. We have taken the Reuben option. Or as Gutiérrez once said about aid, it has provided "at a cheap price, a good conscience to Christians, citizens of countries that control the world economy."[21]

Discussion Questions

1. To what extent are we complicit in propping up structures of injustice in and through our works of mercy?

2. In light of the Global North's contribution to climate change, its unfair global economic architecture, and its history of colonial exploitation should the churches in the Global North be framing their charitable giving to the Global South as reparations rather than donations? Theologically, what difference would that make?

3. How do we ensure that local communities are empowered to bring about structural change when the structures impoverishing them are designed and implemented in London, Paris and New York?

4. How do we integrate the call for reduced consumption in the Global North and an increase in living standards in the Global South? To what extent is there a tension between our desire to eliminate poverty and the need to tackle climate change?

---

19 A. Boesak, *Walking on Thorns* (WCC: Geneva, 1984), 39.

20 "Poverty porn" is the phenomena in which aid agencies use graphic images of poverty, especially of starving children, in order to elicit an emotional response from would-be donors.

21 G. Gutiérrez, "The Meaning of Development," in *In Search of a Theology of Development* (Geneva: SODEPAX, 1969), 152.

Chapter 15 Response

by Minyoung Jung

First of all, I would like to express my sincere appreciation and respect for this great chapter, which is both educational and thought-provoking. "Missions and money" in terms of justice, reflecting the merciful and righteous God whom we serve, has long been an enigmatic focal issue for me as a participant in *missio Dei*. In that regard, I am deeply indebted to the author.

The chapter maintains a healthy balance between its theological framework and practical suggestions thereof. Judging from what I have discovered, the author seems to walk the talk, practicing what he preaches instead of just being an armchair scholar or a keyboard warrior. The integrity of the writer surely enhances the authenticity of his chapter.

Since I didn't find any issues demanding a critique, rather than antitheses I present additional thoughts in line with the gist of the chapter. I hope these points will serve as food for thought for the author as well as readers on their continuing journey as reflective practitioners.

Countering the Wrong Reasons— More on the Biblical Basis

On top of what the author already delineated, I would like to add a couple more theological arguments for structural justice. We[22] can counter the wrong reasons that evangelicals give for ignoring structural justice—individualistic emphasis and loss of income—by reinforcing the biblical basis for it.

1. Community as the Basis of Structural Justice

The author points out that individualistic emphasis was "one of the unfortunate sequelae of the Reformation," and that "fear of association with communism and/or liberal and liberation theologies" is a reason for evangelicals ignoring structural justice. Historically, and even today, fear of being branded with "scarlet letters"[23] has been a strong deterrent against standing up to "continue in what you have learned and have become convinced of" (2 Tim. 3:14). As "a burnt child dreads the fire," many evangelical churches present with a symptom of post-traumatic stress disorder against totalitarianism,[24] leading to "an overemphasis on the individual as the unit of analysis." Individualistic perspective at the expense of community theology was "a baby thrown out with the bathwater" by many reformers, which we have inherited rather unwittingly.

The fundamental theological issue underlying the absence or lack of structural justice in the evangelical camp, I believe, is that of community. I don't have to go the extra mile here to defend the validity of the theological argument that community is at the core of the Christian religion. We are invited to join the Trinitarian fellowship collectively as the body of Christ rather than as unrelated individuals. The very concept of *church* is unthinkable apart from that of *community*. Missions is not something individual Christians do to help God, but about a communal journey toward becoming the true church, that is, the holy universal church. So the church, by its very nature, is a community characterized by inclusivity,

---

22 The author mentions in his first footnote that by "we" in the chapter he largely meant "the protestant church and even more specifically the white evangelical part of the protestant church." But I think his depiction of the protestant evangelical church will apply also to most, if not all, of the Korean church, as the latter has heavily copied the former in her theologies and practices.

23 Such as communism, socialism, liberalism, humanism, syncretism, pluralism, heresy, etc.

24 Such as the Dark Ages, chauvinism, fascism, Nazism, communism, military dictatorship, etc.

interdependence, mutuality, etc., and is an organism and commonwealth[25] reflecting the love and justice of her divine Head, which makes it impossible not to address the communal issue of structural justice.

Restoration or reinvention of a radical community theology is needed as the basis of structural justice and as an antidote to structural injustice. We should not forget that in the beginning the Triune God created us in their communal image and invited us to participate in their loving fellowship. We are here in this world temporarily as a missional community to invite others into that glorious fellowship characterized by love and justice.

2. Theology of the Cross Demanding Structural Justice

The second root cause the author points out for ignoring structural justice is fear of losing income. This phenomenon bluntly exposes the depth of the modern church's saturation, if not baptism, with the values of neoliberal capitalism. The author emphasizes the importance of raising "Why" questions, which unfortunately is lacking in many educational systems, including Korean schools and churches. Let me emulate the author's question and answer scheme:

Q1: Why do we fear loss of income so much?
A1: Because we in effect believe in materialistic values.
Q2: Why do we cave in to such worldly values?
A2: Because we are not truly rooted in the theology of the cross.
Q3: Why don't we live out what we confess, that is, the theology of the cross?
A3: Because it's too hard and countercultural to embrace. It is easier said than done.

No wonder many people, both religious and secular, stumble over the cross![26] Pursuing and acting on structural justice is so demanding and complicated that even goodwill evangelicals end up doing good only in the personal dimension of charity. The author borrows the concept of "the Reuben option" to define this tendency. Many Christians want to do good as long as it's relatively simple and easy. Like Reuben, we tend to prefer doing an easier but compromised good, thereby soothing our conscience, to standing up for much harsher truths and often risking our own safety, fame, and wealth. Even though most of us evangelicals may support structural justice in principle, we tend to change our mind when it actually demands our own share of the cost. That's the reason why the so-called NIMBY ("not in my backyard") phenomenon is prevalent in today's evangelical camp.

We should reestablish the theology of the cross that the reformers reclaimed, paying the cost dearly. Bearing the cross is the very essence of discipleship, which by no means is light or easy.[27] All three synoptic Gospels record Jesus's command to follow him by denying oneself and bearing one's own cross as the core qualifications of disciples.[28] To deny oneself and bear one's own cross is not just to "do good and feel good." Just as Jesus confronted and even overturned the unjust religious-political-economic tables at the Temple courtyard, which was a huge risk-taking that eventually led him to death on the cross, we his followers should willingly lay down our due rights (i.e., deny ourselves), including our wealth, status, comfort, security, etc., and take up the cross for the cause, including personal and structural justice.

Final Thoughts

On my recent trip back from an overseas event, I watched an in-flight movie titled, "Just Mercy." The film, based on the book of the same title,[29] is of a true story by/on Bryan Stevenson,[30] an American human rights lawyer and social justice activist who perseveres to overturn the conviction of a black prisoner, Walter McMillian, who was judged guilty based on perjury and fabricated evidence, and save him from death row. These lines from the film remind us of the importance of patiently pursuing structural justice:[31] "The enemy of justice is the learned sense of hopelessness leading to giving up. We should stand

---

25 The late John Stott defined the church as "God's new society," as against a group of individual Christians (John R. W. Stott, *Message of Ephesians: God's New Society* [Downers Grove: InterVarsity Press, 1984]).

26 1 Cor. 1:18, 23; 1 Pet. 2:8.

27 I believe this was the reason why Jesus didn't readily accept wannabe disciples who volunteered, but instead challenged them to count the cost (Matt. 8:19–22).

28 Matt. 10:38, 16:24; Mark 8:34; Luke 9:23, 14:27.

29 *Just Mercy*, directed by Destin Daniel Cretton (2019: Gil Netter Productions), Warner Bros. Pictures; Bryan Stevenson, *Just Mercy: A Story of Justice and Redemption* (New York: Spiegel & Grau, 2014).

30 Bryan Stevenson, also mentioned in Dr. Thacker's chapter, is the founder and executive director of the Equal Justice Initiative.

31 Since I am writing from my memory, the quotes may not verbatim.

up against injustice with hope;" and, "The opposite of poverty is not wealth but justice. The character of our nation is not reflected in how we treat the rich and those with power; it is reflected in how we treat the poor and the oppressed ... We all need justice, mercy, and unmerited grace."

Discussion Questions

1. Do you have any related theological insights and/or practical considerations to share?

2. The case of Jesus's Temple cleansing, I think, is worthy of further reflection:

    a) What is the appropriate time or occasion to overturn the tables?[32]

    b) Based on the following remark by the author, what issues and challenges do you find in today's church and capitalism?—"What angered him so much was the way in which that system used taxes to exploit others, taking revenue from the poorest and funneling them up, through the Temple, to the rich and powerful. When Jesus called it a 'den of robbers,' he was referring to those who grew their wealth at the expense of the poor through this economic system."

    c) What missional implications can you deduce from this incident, especially considering that transactions were made at the court of the Gentiles, which Jesus said should be called "a house of prayer for all nations" rather than "a den of robbers" (Mark 11:17)?

---

32 Compare Scott A. Bessenecker, *Overturning Tables: Freeing Missions from the Christian-Industrial Complex* (Downers Grove: InterVarsity Press, 2014).

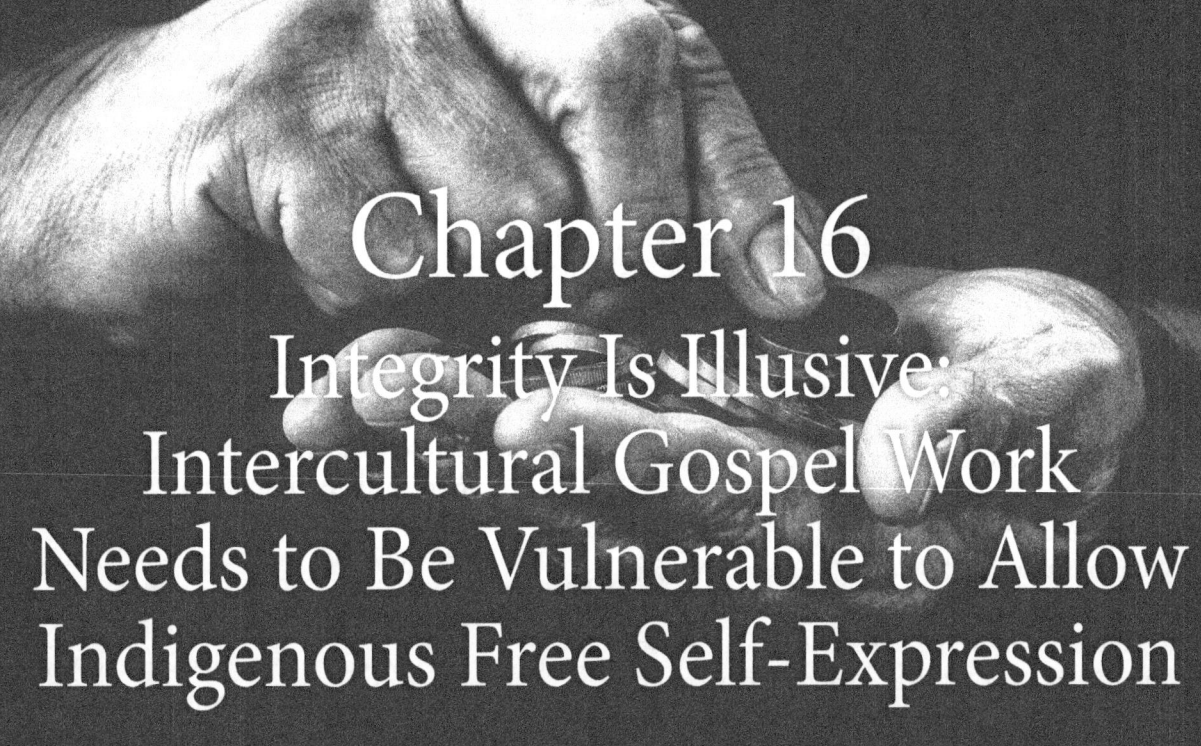

Chapter 16
Integrity Is Illusive: Intercultural Gospel Work Needs to Be Vulnerable to Allow Indigenous Free Self-Expression

by Jim Harries

>"'Thou shalt not speak the truth' is practically a commandment" Melland discovered one hundred years ago, in Africa[1]

I suggest that for Westerners to insist on integrity—"following your moral or ethical convictions and doing the right thing in all circumstances, even if no one is watching you … [being] … true to yourself and … [doing] nothing that demeans or dishonors you"[2]—in their relationships in Africa is to endeavor to dominate people from a position of understanding that is foreign. Insisting on the practice of one's concept of integrity being a universal value or measure can be a cultural imposition.

One example of differing cultural standards is the prime role of envy in African ways of life, which leads to the practice of witchcraft.[3] We should expect that people who have not been profoundly influenced by the Judeo-Christian biblical tradition will remain overtly more oriented to the practice of witchcraft. My research on this subject has contributed to my high valuation of the work of René Girard,[4] whose focus on mimetic desire was the foundation that led to him being considered one of the key thinkers of the twentieth century. Girard's finding that mimetic desire—the desire for what someone else has and even the desire for someone else's desire—is foundational to human living, and provides a helpful conceptual platform for understanding African engagement with witchcraft that is often ignored in the West. In African tradition envy easily results in openly despising wealthy people.

---

1 F. H. Melland, *In Witch Bound Africa: An Account of the Primitive Kaonde Tribe and Their Beliefs* (Philadelphia: J. B. Lippincott Company, 1923), 129. From my understanding, this discovery has wide application.

2 Your Dictionary, s.v. "Examples of Integrity," accessed December 5, 2020, https://examples.yourdictionary.com/examples-of-integrity.html.

3 Jim Harries, "Witchcraft, Envy, Development, and Christian Mission in Africa," *Missiology: An International Review* 40, no. 2 (2012): 129–139.

4 See Jim Harries, "A Foundation for African Theology That Bypasses the West: The Writings of René Girard," *Evangelical Review of Theology* 44, no. 2 (2020): 149–163.

Hence, poverty as a protective measure is widespread.[5] Christ's example, the Son of God who allowed himself to be the archetypal victim on the cross, despite his total innocence, is the globally known and uniquely effective counter to the horrors of witchcraft (scapegoating) attack and counterattack.[6]

A case study of a practice called *bulunda* among Kaonde people in Zambia seeks to illustrate how Western notions of integrity are not universal: *bulunda* integrity is very different to Western integrity. Frank Melland, an accomplished author and traveler who wrote an account of the Kaonde people in Zambia,[7] considers *bulunda*, an agreement between two people, to be "very ancient … [ranking] next to (possibly equal to) marriage as a civil contract and [having] definite obligations on each side."[8] *Bulunda* is entered into for "assistance in warfare, in times of famine, in litigation, … for … allies upon whom [someone] could rely in emergency."[9] *Bulunda* involves giving "a dowry gift just as [someone] would to a woman whom he was seeking as his wife … a shilling, a cup, or some other small article …[then] begin the serious obligations … [e.g., a] gift of a gun."[10] *Bulunda* is sealed through sharing of blood: "Each of the contracting parties makes a slight incision in the wrist or arm of the other, and drinks a drop of the blood therefrom."[11] *Bulunda* may "be dissolved by a civil suit brought by one of the parties … without … regret or animosity."[12] "Hospitality and friendship to a *mulunda's* relations are imperative," for example, through paying "the debts of one's brother's *mulunda*."[13] A *mulunda* may be given access to his fellow *mulunda's* wife.[14]

The term *bulunda* is today frequently translated into English as "friendship" (*mulunda*, "friend").

I assume that the above sentence, which I have set apart in its own paragraph for emphasis, has put my readers into a kind of "shock." *Bulunda* is very different from a Western understanding of friendship. Native English speakers value "disinterested friendship" that is unbiased, unselfish, mutually generous, and that does not seek personal advantage.[15] Even if the meaning of *bulunda* for the Kaonde has recently shifted, I suggest that it cannot have lost all of its original accruements. Friendship is commonly a foundation stone to *integrity*. Do Westerners entering into *friendship* with Africans know what they are signing up for?

My case study is of just one word, "friendship." Similar very revealing studies could be made of endless other words like community, insecurity, belief, etc.[16] How can one achieve integrity if one misunderstands every word one uses? How then can one create healthy relationships between Western missionaries and African people?

Working Together

When the universality of its integrity is threatened, the West draws on its superior financial strength. Financial generosity, combined with displays of technological prowess (e.g., motorcars, clothing, mirrors, etc., and lately phones and other gadgets) ensure African people's compliance with the West. This compliance is demonstrated by African countries' adoption of Western languages. Schools teaching in English have proliferated in what was previously Melland's territory. I taught at such a school from 1988–1991.[17] Use of indigenous languages within school compounds is punishable in many parts of Africa. The objective is, presumably, to immerse youth into desired prosperity through constantly forcing them into the use of a European tongue.[18] Using the language of a prosperous people is expected to result in prosperity.

---

5 I perceive envious hatred toward the wealthy among Africans in contemporary times being reflected in recent race riots following George Floyd's death in the US; some rioters sought to destroy or redistribute a lot of wealth (Rozina Sabur, Patrick Sawer, and David Millward, "Why are there protests over the death of George Floyd?," The Telegraph, UK, June 8, 2020, https://www.telegraph.co.uk/news/0/us-america-riots-george-floyd-death-protests/).

6 René Girard, *I See Satan Fall Like Lightning*, trans. James G. Williams (Maryknoll: Orbis, 2001).

7 Frank H. Melland (1879–1939) acquired his insights during twenty-five years serving as a magistrate in Zambia.

8 Melland, *In Witch Bound Africa*, 109.

9 Melland, 110.

10 Melland, 112.

11 Melland, 112.

12 Melland, 110.

13 Melland, 113.

14 Melland, 113.

15 Terms gleaned from Ron Belgau, "What Does 'Disinterested Friendship' Mean?," Spiritual Friendship: Musings on God, Sexuality, Relationships, accessed December 5, 2020, https://spiritualfriendship.org/2015/07/03/what-does-disinterested-friendship-mean/.

16 Hermen Kroesbergen, "Religion without Belief and Community in Africa," *Religions* 10, no. 4, 292 (2019):1–20.

17 Mukinge Girls Secondary School, Kasempa, Zambia.

18 There is much discussion in Africa on this issue, so certainly not all would agree with my reasoning here.

Unfortunately, borrowing other people's discourses (i.e., Africans appropriating the discourse of Europeans, specifically that of Brits) produces mixed results. Use of English reduces the precision with which Africans can describe and discuss indigenous issues. If listeners are not aware of which African original an English word translates, it can result in confusion. Let me take a custom referred to by Melland as *lubomboshi*. This custom, or game ("which it obviously is"[19]), involves a man approaching the hut of someone from his same totem during light rain, and waiting there until he is given a gift.[20] Using the Kaonde language, one merely has to say, "He (was doing) *lubomboshi*," to explain what was happening. No term in English encapsulates that meaning, or, I think, even comes close to doing so. Instead, a Kaonde man might say in English, "I went to someone's door in the rain," or "I did, you know, what not, at someone's door," or "I got a gift, you know!" Another Kaonde man may or may not quickly and easily realize, "Oh, of course he is talking about *lubomboshi*!" Either way, the statement will be less clear than if the term *lubomboshi* had itself been used. Someone not familiar with Kaonde customs, who does not have a clue about this game of standing at the door in the rain, will get confused very quickly. (The reverse scenario also applies: it is very difficult for an Englishman to articulate, say, the situation of the economy of his country using only Kaonde terms, since the Kaonde language incorporates no concept of "economy" as known in the West.)

Many of today's missionaries and cross-cultural workers greatly value being able to do things in a way that reflects familiar standards of integrity. Declaring this practice dubious may be very threatening to them. It would seem to require a missionary, in order to interact meaningfully with the people of another culture, to do what is morally questionable and beyond clear comprehension by supporters "back home." This reality of the communication situation of cross-cultural mission is an important reason why missionaries should strive to engage vulnerably. *Vulnerable mission*, mission or development work practiced by outsiders confining themselves to use of indigenous languages and resources in ministry, reduces a missionary's dependence on outside donors, and so enables practice of local rather than foreign integrity.

19 Melland, *In Witch Bound Africa*, 253.
20 Melland. 253.

To date, at least in part to achieve the appearance of integrity, the West has dominated in African mission contexts. In order to avoid unsightly clashes during engagement with Western donor-oriented mission, a widespread response from Africa has been to maintain a sharp distinction between its true cultural free expression, and its self-expression in engagement with Western mission. This can be illustrated diagrammatically:

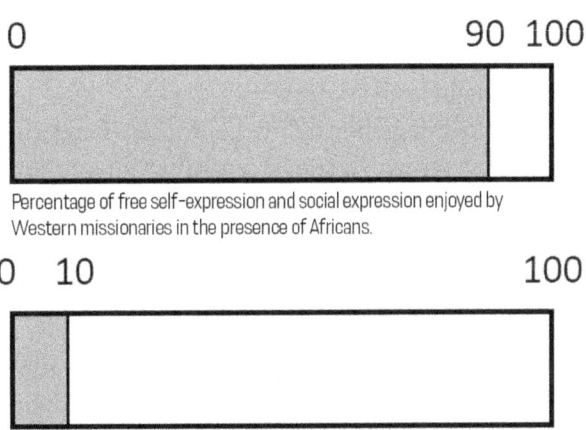

Figure 16.1:
"Free Expression" in Missionary/African Encounters

Percentage of free self-expression and social expression enjoyed by Western missionaries in the presence of Africans.

Percentage of free self-expression and social expression enjoyed by Africans in the presence of Western missionaries.

Westerners in mission try hard to include Africans in what they do and how they do it. This arises from a pro-secular bias in Western people's lives, often on the basis of what Westerners understand to be "integrity." Actually, the Gospel is interpreted by diverse people in many ways. Perhaps, in some cases, Gospel integrity is so wide as not necessarily to be considered integrity in modern terms. Contemporary modern integrity, I suggest, normalizes secularism interculturally: to avoid appearing to be racist, it must assume African people to be capable secularists. (It is considered racist, for example, to suggest that African people are innately not good at mathematics.) I believe Gospel integrity to be wider than this: the Gospel accepts people by grace, and not on the basis underlying anti-racism, that they are "equally good."

Issues alluded to above can be illustrated by clashes of understanding between different Christian denominations, such as the issue of women preaching. I do not consider it an appropriate response to clashes arising from these kind of differences to assume the other is "not Christian." These clashes may instead indicate multiple integrities. Some contemporary notions of integrity are not, I suggest, rooted in the Gospel, but in the Western assumption that secularism is a human universal.[21] Maintaining such secular integrity forces Africans to attempt to conceal the less than secular depths of their functioning, to maintain favor with their donors. Western types of integrity are likely to be sought through tried and tested expressions using Western languages such as English, even should such expression be a poor reflection of "reality" on the ground. (Western donors tend to evaluate projects they support by how they are described in English, rather than based on their actual functioning in local contexts.[22])

The above depiction of "free expression" in relation to integrity raises questions regarding intercultural engagement: To what extent should people doing outreach express themselves freely? To what extent should those being reached express themselves freely? Here are some "extreme" possibilities:

1. One hundred percent open expression by those doing outreach would be assuming those being reached to be culturally identical to them. In order to stay true to the way they are being addressed, responses by those being reached would have to take zero account of the peculiarities of their own languages and ways of life.

2. One hundred percent open expression by those being reached would be assuming those doing outreach to be culturally the same as them. Responses by those being reached would then take zero account of the peculiarities of the ways of life of those reaching them.

3. If both the reached and the unreached were to express themselves freely, 100 percent on both sides, this would amount to both sides ignoring the peculiarities of the culture of those they are interacting with.

Usually one presumes that a *visitor*, or visitors who are typically few in number, should adjust to native people, who are numerous. Sheer logistics would point in this direction—it is easier for a few visitors to learn an indigenous language and way of life than it is for many indigenous people to learn foreign ways. Colonialism reversed this, having indigenous people imitate outsiders, the aim apparently often being that this imitation should be lock, stock, and barrel.[23]

High levels of "free expression" by both sides will frustrate efforts at holding people together. Yet severe bending by Africans in receipt of mission and development, illustrated in figure 1 above, is cause for concern. I consider the cause of the peculiar shape of today's missionary versus African interreactions to arise from misplaced Gospel impact. Traditionally, African tribes tend to consider their own members to be bound by their laws and customs, and outsiders to be "enemies."[24] Westerners on the other hand, as a result of being historically impacted by the Gospel that claims to be universal, understand themselves as living according to standards to which everyone worldwide should submit. The understanding that what is "right" for them is "right" universally is, I suggest, where things get difficult. Westerners extrapolate the universality of the Gospel to their secular experience. But the Bible, the text from which the Gospel arises, is open to much wider interpretation than Western legal systems. Nowadays the West, often without realizing it, takes its own culture that was indeed deeply influenced by the Gospel, as if that culture is as universal as the Gospel itself. In other words, we could say the West has extended the biblical canon to include all of its secular stipulations, displacing God with Western people.[25] This situation needs urgent attention.

I propose that we need an alternative to Africans being judged, in the name of secularism, by every aspect of contemporary Western life (which happens when they borrow schooling in English). Western legal systems should not simply be universalized. A Western Christian missionary should aim to share the Gospel and not Western ways of life.

---

21 Jim Harries, forthcoming book that critiques contemporary practice of anti-racism (title undecided).

22 Illustrated using a theological example from Jim Harries, "Magic, Divine Revelation and Translation in Theological Education in the Majority World Today (with a Focus on Africa)," *Missionalia* 47, no. 2 (2019): 165–176.

23 The West increasingly sets global standards for others to follow, something graphically illustrated in educational systems and in the initial coronavirus crisis of 2020.

24 The English term "enemies" is not accurate in describing the identity of the "outsider."

25 This point is made by Oludamini Ogunnaike, "From Heathen to Sub-human: A Genealogy of the Influence of the Decline of Religion on the Rise of Modern Racism," *Open Theology* 2 (2016): 785–803.

A Westerner seeking to adjust to indigenous ways of life is preferable to bringing indigenous people into their secular realm. When indigenous people are, as a result, permitted to express themselves freely, Westerners are enabled to learn about and from them through indigenous categories of thought (though the learning curve is likely to be long and slow).

Many ongoing Western efforts at building morality on objectivity, I suggest, are spurious. This spuriousness is evident from within traditional Africa, where the roots and foundations of what the West calls "objectivity" may be totally invisible in the first place. How can something be objectively universally true if a billion Africans cannot even perceive it? When the West realizes this, instead of forcing its secularism on the rest of the world, it could concentrate on enabling others to benefit from its knowledge of God.

People cannot live "dual cultures" using one language. Adjusting to a vastly different culture, such as African culture relative to European, requires the use of a different "code" that must be learned in interaction with the way of life concerned.[26] I take intercultural translation to be in many ways impossible. Dual culture thinking, which implies that a Westerner living and working in Africa can adjust to Africa in major ways while using their own language, is misguided; so is the thinking that learning English results in African children functioning like Europeans.

To acknowledge the need for bi-integrity is to acknowledge that ways of life are different, and to respect those living out those differences. The universality of the Gospel and the fact that one God has created all lay the foundation for intercultural unity. Building on the universality of the Gospel with "secularism" is problematic. Achieving appropriate intercultural relationship and community requires listening to the other. A foreign "other" cannot effectively be listened to in one's own language. Similarly, a Westerner cannot effectively understand a foreign "other" who is making major efforts to "please" to retain funding. People being reached should be more able to freely express themselves than is commonly the case in contemporary mission.

Permitting Free Self-Expression, as Foundational to Intercultural Comprehension, to Enhance Effective Sharing of the Gospel of Jesus

Because English is the primary language of communication of many authoritative wealthy benefactors, use of English interculturally in mission builds, and typically must build, a platform that facilitates donor funds. If it does not, the transparency of English, which allows a diverse set of people, including those who are powerful, to assume they understand what is being communicated, will result in it being condemned by those associated with donors.

Let us go back to friendship. In theory, a church may well have a policy whereby people assist each other in a disinterested way. In practice, assistance may need to be paid for. If only English is in use, and payment for services by a church (e.g., healing or exorcism) is not a valued practice in the English world that is populated by many donors, fear of losing funding could result in such payments that are extant being concealed, or officially condemned. Use of an indigenous language would enable a church to communicate intelligently—overtly in the light of actual practice—in its evangelism and discipleship. Then either particular translation could be practiced (for example, giving a gift could be translated as "expressing appreciation") or particular issues could be obfuscated (the necessity of payment could simply be ignored) when the church presents itself to the English-speaking world.

The above illustrates how use of English restricts free expression, and so healthy intercultural relationships. A focus on a different approach to language and money is key to bringing improvements. Healthy gospel work is done, I suggest, by a missionary who uses the language of the people they are reaching, and who allows people to express themselves freely in that language by not using finances to draw them toward him. The question of appropriate levels of free expression is illustrated in figure 16.2:

---

26 Thorsten Pattberg, *Language Imperialism and the End of Translation* (New York: LoD Press, 2014/2015).

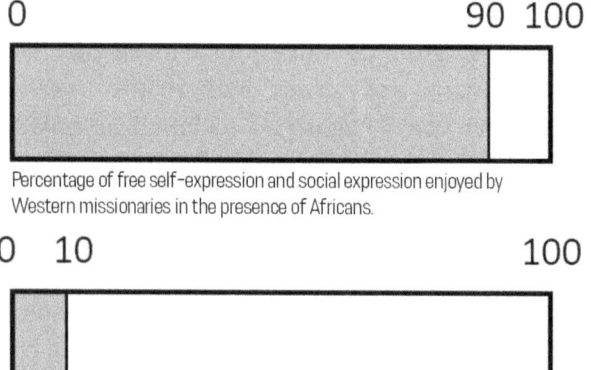

Figure 16.2: "Free Expression" in Missionary/African Encounters—As It Should Be?

Percentage of free self-expression and social expression enjoyed by Western missionaries in the presence of Africans.

Percentage of free self-expression and social expression enjoyed by Africans in the presence of Western missionaries.

Use of indigenous languages and resources in ministry by intercultural workers from the West has come to be known as "vulnerable mission."[27] By putting aside the two major factors that have resulted in Western domination—European languages and resources—vulnerable mission enables a Westerner to adjust to the African context rather than the other way around. Vulnerable mission does not need to be adopted by all Western cross-cultural workers. The few that follow it can enlighten their fellow countrymen, helping them to develop preferred mission strategies. However, learning from a vulnerable missionary requires a degree of sensitivity. Because one integrity is not universal, insights provided by vulnerable missionaries over and above those nonvulnerable missionaries hear in English from locals who are financially dependent on them, must be handled with great sensitivity. Lack of care could result in the ministry of a vulnerable missionary being undermined. For example, a nonvulnerable missionary wants to give a generous salary to a local person. He learns from a vulnerable missionary that the person is a thief. He withdraws the salary. This person can easily become an archenemy to the vulnerable missionary.

In anglophone Africa, the benefits of the use of English seem to stare you in the face at every turn. Economically and socially, in terms of prestige and advancement even in the church, English seems to be the way forward. As a result, a foreigner wanting to work in indigenous languages might have to set out from the beginning to heartily disagree with local people inumbrated by hegemonic neocolonial wisdom. These are the very kind of people who most likely want to be his "friends." We should listen to people, yes, but in their own language(s), while not posing an economic threat (or inadvertent bribe!).

For a foreign visitor to Africa, frankly, both personal observation and evaluation of the context one is confronted with, plus feedback from nationals, are likely to point to the advisability of the use of outside resources to promote a missionary's activities. As we saw in our discussion of *bulunda,* making friends in Africa, including those from foreign parts, is about searching for personal benefit (Maranz's whole book is about this[28]). Someone who is a source of money in a community ruled by envy ("mimetic desire," to use Girard's term) becomes a center of power, then a target of vicious attacks. This is particularly true when, as a result of their fear of witchcraft, others have not accumulated wealth.[29] These vicious attacks, often known as witchcraft, come from those who have become envious of you.[30] Vicious attacks result in many Westerners withdrawing from the "front line."

I here advocate for vulnerability for some missionaries. Confining my ministry to use of indigenous languages has left me working primarily among the poorer and more marginalized[31] members of a community. Familiarity and engagement with an indigenous language facilitates learning of local categories of meaning linked to indigenous terms, which can facilitate smooth communication.

A missionary's "financial" vulnerability (not wanting to be known for their money) may be achieved simply by delegating responsibility for provision of aid and funds to a colleague. Consistently not having resources available to share results in people in relatively "poor" contexts, as is the case in much of Africa, giving up on respecting you for what you have. This can result in a major shift in the nature of one's relationships, especially given how African people's friendships are oriented to what they can get (as seen in the example of *bulunda* above, and very widely the case). A Westerner's identity becoming normalized, "just a member of the community," can enable them to do ministry in locally sustainable ways.

---

27 "Mission Purpose Statement," Alliance for Vulnerable Mission, 2021, https://vulnerablemission.org.

28 David Maranz, *African Friends and Money Matters: Observations from Africa* (Dallas: SIL International, 2001).

29 The advent of colonialism has, by bringing means that blunt the pernicious impact of envy, contributed to enabling some African people to become wealthy.

30 Harries, "Witchcraft."

31 I.e., in global terms.

A final comment pertaining to African contexts, in which the expectation that a foreign missionary be very generous financially, is that any drop in one's popularity arising from not appearing generous may be tempered by a missionary's being charitable in a context other than that of their ministry. One example of this might be (as in my case) to care for orphan children in a way not related to the church leaders one works with.

Conclusion

Some Western missionaries to Africa ought to use indigenous languages and resources in their ministry(ies). This is a part of allowing bi-integrities or multi-integrities.

Discussion Questions

1. Explain some problematics of the use of European languages in the majority world.
2. What does bi/multi-integrity look like?
3. How would you describe "vulnerable mission" and how it works to a person unfamiliar with that term?
4. Comment on likely outcomes of allowing free expression by local people.

Chapter 16 Response

by C. S. Caleb Kim

Dr. Jim Harries has touched on a missiologically practical area essential to all cross-cultural or intercultural missionaries working in a cultural context different than their own. First of all, I highly commend him for his anthropological insights into a delicate issue among Western missionaries in African contexts, with missiological sharpness based on his hands-on missionary experiences.

Based on his own cross-cultural experiences, Dr. Harries suggests that the best way to avoid missionary imposition, whether intentional or inadvertent, is to become "vulnerable" by learning the local language of the people he serves and thus adapting himself to their local culture. His suggestion also goes along with the missionary's withdrawal from external resources so that the local people may be enabled to express themselves freely in the presence of Western missionaries. According to Harries, the missionary's financial strength and technologically superior prowess tend to hinder the indigenous people from sharing their honest views with foreign missionaries who have more financial strengths than themselves. "Vulnerable mission," then, allows the Gospel to be more purely communicated without any ulterior motives in both parties, the reaching and the reached.

My response to his article is as follows in light of my research and ministry experiences in East Africa. It includes:

1. an anthropological comment on Dr. Harries's analysis of different cultural concepts,
2. a missiological agreement with his emphasis on the fundamental requirement of the missionary's learning of the local language and cultural adaptation to the local community, and
3. a couple of questions for further considerations.

First, the examples he used to illustrate his main point are related to what cognitive anthropology calls "cultural models," which refer to "mental representations shared by members of a culture."[32] Elsewhere, I explain that all cultural models in society are derived from their cultural worldview,[33] which comprises cultural assumptions and values constructed through "enculturation" or traditional education.[34] Harries used the Kaonde customs of *bulunda* and *lubomboshi* to prove the improbability of the Westerner's comprehension of local cultural behaviors and their meanings unless he grasps the local language. Even the Western concept of "integrity" or "economy" has its cultural model, which people of other cultures can hardly understand even though some cultural values are common in humanity. For this reason, the definitions of many things made and carried by Western missionaries may not be universally objective and understandable. They can be reinterpreted and redefined in light of the cultural insiders' worldview and their experiences of the Gospel of Jesus. Otherwise, the missionary could even inadvertently impose his Western or home ideas upon his cross-cultural audiences without providing them adequate time and a fair chance to grasp the Gospel in their cultural context. Harries provides outstanding anthropological evidence for why the expatriate missionary needs to take the attitude of "vulnerable mission."

Secondly, Dr. Harries underscores a poignant fact in mission history that a power imbalance has emerged in African contexts due to the financial superiority that Western missionaries had. When people work together, the imposition of one's ideas or values often occurs if one group has more control over the other groups. Such an overpowering usually takes place when the power comes from financial strength. Harries sharply points out the malady of such one-sidedness between Western missionaries and Africans. Interestingly, he connects the financial disparity between the two to the language learning issue among Western missionaries in Africa. Linguistically and cognitive-anthropologically speaking, cultural assumptions and values are best expressed and communicated through one's heart language. Suppose the communicator imposes his language upon his audience because of financial superiority in communicating his religious conviction and values. In that case, it may be that the communicator deprives his hearers of their souls against his goodwill.

Hence, Dr. Harries proposes and encourages his fellow missionaries to consider opting for the attitude of missionary vulnerability through learning the indigenous language (or what I would call the "heart language"). The learning of a vernacular or heart language in a given locality tends to create missionary vulnerability. I concur with him that the missionary's use of a local language in communicating the Gospel is the most critical element that serves the hearers to experience the Gospel in their hearts. The imposition of English by British missionaries was not a wise option. As Harries pointed out, the missionaries tried to change local views of the world to that which they were carrying with them, as if theirs were universal and objective. Even though the missionary as a Gospel bearer presents a biblically truthful value to local people, it cannot automatically become a universal value people should adopt without processing it through their cultural filters and framework. If the missionary expects that to happen, his attitude or perception falls into the category of what missiologists call naïve realism.[35]

Dr. Harries illustrated this point with the African concept of witchcraft vis-à-vis the Western idea of integrity. These two concepts appear to be entirely unrelated. However, if one conducts thorough anthropological research into African worldviews, he would appreciate what Harries tries to show. The illustration of this point with some African customs such as *bulunda* and *lubomboshi* reveals that the communication of the Gospel in English as a foreign language is inadequate in Gospel presentation; in fact, it would be the opposite of the missionary model Jesus demonstrated through his Incarnation.

---

32 Giovanni Bennardo and Victor C. de Munck, *Cultural Models: Genesis, Methods, and Experiences* (Oxford: Oxford University Press, 2014), 3.

33 Caleb Kim, *Cultural Anthropology from a Christian Perspective* (Eldoret, Kenya: Utafiti Foundation, 2019), 71.

34 Kim, *Cultural Anthropology*, 26.

35 For example, see Paul Hiebert, *Anthropological Insights for Missionaries* (Grand Rapids: Baker Book House, 1985) and Charles Kraft, *Anthropology for Christian Witness* (Maryknoll: Orbis Books, 1996). History teaches us that human beings are intrinsically ethnocentric, which evidences the biblical truth about original sin. Thus, as seen in Herbert Spencer's social Darwinism, such an ethnocentric view of others is not only a problem with Westerners but also with all humanity, including the majority world.

Lastly, I would like to make my third point in the form of questions to Dr. Harries for further consideration and discussion. I would suppose that the missiological concept of missionary vulnerability that he has developed does not apply only to Western missionaries but also to non-Western missionaries like South Koreans, who also come with external financial resources. Plus, Korean missionaries also carry cultural and psychological baggage different from other Asians or Africans. Dr. Harries, you suggest that vulnerable mission is the most helpful way for cross-cultural missionaries to guard against becoming entrapped in the error of social or cultural superiority. Would missionary vulnerability based on the withdrawal from external resources and the learning of local languages be the only solution to such a human weakness among cross-cultural missionaries? As a genuine relationship between missionaries and local people results from missionary vulnerability,[36] can it also be built effectively through other ways among "nonvulnerable missionaries"? Can a missionary become a "righteous rich" person, as Jonathan Bonk and Christopher Wright elucidate,[37] even as he learns the heart language of the people whom he serves? In other words, can the vulnerability that breeds humility and enhances a total dependence upon the Lord as the only resource be experienced even when the missionary genuinely practices the "righteous rich" life?

Another question to Dr. Harries is about the localization of a foreign language. (In this case, it is English.) While I was working in East Africa for the past three decades, I saw many Kenyans speak English in a *Kenyan* way. Many Kenyans seem to have adopted English into their lingual culture and conveyed their African concepts in their localized English. In such a case, would you tend to recognize a different type of English adopted and used by Africans, probably mostly in urban situations, as a culturally functional means to carry indigenous concepts?[38] Consequently, the kind of English they are currently using is, in many ways, not the same English that its first native speakers had transmitted.

The last comment that I would like to add is about the relationship between missionary vulnerability and what I would call an "incarnational attitude." While the Incarnation is the unique historical event of our Lord's redemptive work for humanity, an "incarnational attitude" refers to what characterizes the mindset of the cross-cultural missionary, who makes efforts to follow his master's cross-cultural path (from heaven to earth, as described by Paul in Phil. 2:5–8). A cross-cultural missionary could sincerely learn the language (and culture) of the people he serves. However, language learning alone does not seem to be a full guarantee for the missionary's respectful attitude for them. I often hear my African students mention the lack of respect for their culture among foreign missionaries who speak local languages fluently. The Incarnation of the Son of God, who lived in human culture and spoke a human language, demonstrated how much God loves people unconditionally and respects human cultures,[39] including their languages.[40] In following his way, the cross-cultural missionary tries to love others as he makes efforts to understand and respect their culture and language. In doing these, the missionary rather naturally becomes "vulnerable" as he fights his inherent human weakness, that is, ethnocentrism. In other words, "vulnerability" results from an incarnational attitude. Hence, while watching out for the ever-lurking danger behind financial strength on which missionaries often lean to exert their influences upon their audiences, they should also constantly examine their inner attitude to maintain "incarnational vulnerability."

---

36 Harries says, "*Vulnerable mission,* mission or development work practiced by outsiders confining themselves to use of indigenous languages and resources in ministry, reduces a missionary's dependence on outside donors, and so enables practice of local rather than foreign integrity."

37 See Jonathan J. Bonk, *Missions and Money: Affluence as a Missionary Problem … Revisited,* rev. and exp. ed. (Maryknoll: Orbis Books, 2006), chaps. 7 and 8, Kindle.

38 Could "Sheng," which is the clever mix of English and Swahili, particularly among Kenyan youngsters, be such an example?

39 I use the term "culture" based on its missiological-anthropological definition by evangelical missiologists such as Hiebert, Kraft, etc., mentioned above. Also, see Kim, *Cultural Anthropology.*

40 The latter has been demonstrated in the translatability of the Word of God. Compare Lamin Sanneh, *Translating the Message: The Missionary Impact on Culture,* 2nd ed. (Maryknoll: Orbis Books, 2009).

Chapter 17
Mission, Power, and Money

by Paul Bendor-Samuel

Money is an integral element in the modern practice of mission: in individual support, development projects, external funding of pastors and churches, sustaining mission structures, churches "in partnership" with churches, etc. We might imagine a sequence where we discern how to participate in God's mission and then money is simply a resource to enable ministry. Not so. The ways we generate and distribute money not only serve ministry, but shape the way we conceive and practice mission.

The relationship between mission and money often reflects godly attitudes and behaviors, including dependence on God, faith, sacrificial generosity, trust, and integrity. Yet the challenges persist. We might see these primarily as the consequence of sinful human nature. Undeniably, this is part of the story. For others, the problems are those of supply and sustainability. Supply: How to fund those from less affluent contexts? Sustainability: How to ensure the sustainability of structures, when resources in the older mission contexts are drying up? While sin, supply, and sustainability are important issues, they are not the primary focus of this chapter. We live in a globalized, postcolonial, inequitable world of complexity and uncertainty. The issues addressed here, therefore, are primarily relational and systemic. All relationships involve power, and where money is involved, issues of power become more complex. This chapter will argue that we need to see under the surface of the systems that we are part of if we are to move to healthier partnerships in mission, where money is a servant to all.

Setting the Scene: Theological Reflections

Power: "the ability or capacity to do something, act in a particular way, direct, influence, or control the behavior of others or the course of events."[1] The Scriptures affirm that, as creator and sustainer of the cosmos, all power is derived from God. He has chosen to share power with humankind, seen in the first great commission, "Be fruitful, multiply, fill the earth, and subdue it" (Gen. 1:28).

---
1 Oxford Online Dictionary, s.v. "power," accessed February 2, 2021, https://www.lexico.com/definition/power.

The command to mastery of the whole earth is a consequence of Adam and Eve being made "in the image of God" (1:26–27). The phrase is interpreted variously by scholars.[2] Image bearing is understood structurally, indicating intrinsic, godlike qualities, such as reason; relationally, as our capacity for relationship with God and each other; eschatologically, as a pointer to the future when "we shall be like him, for we shall see him as he is" (1 John 3:2); and functionally, in relation to our role on the earth. We note that, just as kings of the ancient Near East placed statues of themselves in the farthest corners of their kingdom, so humankind bears the image of the creator to the utmost parts of his Kingdom, reflecting his authority over all creation.[3] For ancient kings, being made in the image of god obliged them to behave in ways that reflected their god. Thus, to be made in the image of God not only confers on each person the profoundest dignity, it obliges us to treat each other, and creation, as God would.[4]

Responsibility and authority to master the earth is given to the man and woman together. There was no power differential between the pair, a point emphasized in the second creation story. In Genesis 2, man is alone, which is "not good" (v. 18). There is no "suitable helper," so the woman is created out of the substance of man. Lest we imagine that "helper" assumes the idea of subservience, the Scriptures employ the same word (ʿezer) in reference to God as our helper (e.g., Ps. 46:1 [feminine form]; 89:19). Indeed, we now understand that, whether helping by, for example, giving directions, or in more formalized helping relationships such as consultant, therapist, or donor, the helper has significant social power.[5]

Oneness and equality are major themes in the earliest chapters of Genesis. This dynamic changes dramatically with Adam and Eve's rebellion. Relationships with God, the natural world, and all social relations are profoundly altered. The damaging dynamic of desire and domination (3:16) quickly leads to destruction and death (Cain and Abel, 4:6–8). Power in human relationships has changed fundamentally and, from this point on, issues of power will threaten to distort and damage all relationships. If not for Jesus Christ, the damage would be irreversible.

The work of Christ restores the possibility of oneness to all relationships. While much of the New Testament is preoccupied with issues related to oneness between ethnicities, the place of money features prominently in the teaching of Jesus and within the church, the community of restored relationships. The church in Jerusalem demonstrated radical generosity (Acts 2:45; 4:32–35), and a radical system for equitable distribution, allowing the marginalized minority to control the process (6:1–7). The power of money in the Kingdom lies not in how much you have but in the practice of radical generosity. The Gentile churches modeled the same behavior (2 Cor. 8:1–7). Paul considers the practical demonstration of oneness, through generous giving, so critical that it shaped his way of living (Acts 20:33–35), and he was willing to risk his life for it (Gal. 2:10; 1 Cor. 16:1–4). We also have incidents in the redeemed community where issues of power and money go badly wrong (Acts 5:1–11; 8:18; 16:19). Although the church is imperfect, a community on-the-way, it is called to pray for the Kingdom of God to come now and to model the Kingdom of oneness in its life together (John 17:20–23).

Question: Despite the work of Christ, his call to oneness, and the renewing power of the Holy Spirit, why do we struggle so deeply with issues of power and money in mission?

Context: Society, Church, and Mission

Any discussion of mission and money must take note of context. The COVID-19 pandemic has highlighted global realities (e.g., the impact of pre-existing inequalities within society or the need to reimagine economic assumptions given the damage of economies of consumption on climate change), while being experienced very differently in different contexts. The local is always "exceptional." Becoming open and vulnerable to others' stories is an important step in understanding power in the dynamics of money and mission. Here are some of the contextual issues impacting mission, money, and power.

Post- and neocolonialism. In 1914, 85 percent of the earth's landmass was controlled by European,

---

2 Michael Burdett, "Being Human in an Age of Technology: The Ethics of Artificial Intelligence," Human Flourishing in a Technological World: A Christian Perspective, Merton College, Oxford, May 29, 2019, Vimeo, https://www.christianflourishing.com/blog/2019/05/29/michael-burdett-being-human-in-an-age-of-technology-the-ethics-of-artificial-intelligence.

3 Gerhard von Rad, *Genesis* (London: SCM Press, 1961), 60.

4 Myrto Theocharous, "The image of God and Justice," in *Living Radical Discipleship: Inspired by John Stott*, ed. Laura S. Meitzner Yoder (Langham Global Library, 2021).

5 Edgar H. Schien, *Helping: How to Offer, Give, and Receive Help* (Oakland: Berrett-Koehler Publishers, 2011).

predominantly British, powers.[6] The impact of colonialism lives on in many ways: arbitrary national boundaries, alien forms of governance, powerful elites, unjust global economic systems, and cultural and psychological loss. It also lives on in the rhetoric and behavior of former colonizers and current empires. Globalization, when experienced as neocolonialism, provokes nationalism, often armed with religious intolerance, and demonstrates a profound struggle for identity and belonging. We are blind if we suppose it does not influence relationships in global mission communities.

Racism, whiteness, and intrinsic bias. While generally agreed that "race" is a socially constructed concept, reflection on our histories and continued inequalities reveals its ubiquitous power to shape human relationships, communities, and cultures. Just as the Bible has been used over time to justify genocide, ethnic cleansing, and colonialism,[7] we are becoming increasingly aware of the relationship between systemic forms of racism and mission. Johnny Ramírez-Johnson, writing in "Can 'White' People be Saved?," describes race as "a catchall term in Western English-speaking popular culture used as a synonym for nationality, ethnicity, skin-color-classifications (White, Black, etc.), [which] identifies members of a unique cultural group."[8] The book title plays on the disciples' question about the wealthy (Luke 18:26). While whiteness is deeply linked to prosperity and power, we should not dismiss the question. As I write, our mission agency newsletter appeared in my inbox with these opening lines: "I have just finished reading a letter written by a Namibian to his friends ... The pain that he has experienced in all sorts of ways, simply because of the colour of his skin, is heart-rending. His pain has not been caused by some white supremacist group, but by his everyday interactions with people who are passionate about God's Kingdom and His mission - people like you and me!"[9]

Edgar Schein, a leader in organizational development and culture, writes on the challenge of seeing what is around us. Our minds have been sensitized by prior experiences related to culture, gender, ethnicity, work, church, etc. He notes, "We do not passively register information. We select out of the available data what we are capable of registering and classifying, based on our language and culturally learned concepts as well as what we want and need ... we do not think and talk about what we see; we see what we are able to think and talk about."[10] I recall a recent exchange with a fine PhD student—white, female, and from the US south—in which she asserted very strongly that "there is no systemic racism in the USA." In mission systems, where white power, whether economic, educational, historical, or reputational, is so deeply embedded, it is a challenge for money and equitable, mutually life-giving, intercultural relationships to flourish together.

The enduring legacy of the modern mission movement. The legacy of the nineteenth century cross-cultural mission movement powerfully reverberates through the current understanding and practice of intercultural mission. Birthed when the world was neatly divided into "Christendom" and "Heathen," and reliant on special agents (missionaries), mission became the exclusive domain of a small portion of the church focused principally on establishing churches.[11] Without doubt, God blessed this sacrificial, faithful, courageous service, carried out in a spirit of obedience to the command of Jesus. The paradigm made sense in an environment of colonial expansion and was carried forward by North American evangelical mission in the second half of the twentieth century. More recently, newer mission movements from the majority world, whether Brazilian, Nigerian, Korea, or others, have adopted the powerful assumptions, expectations, approach, and systems of the movement.

The church's engagement in God's mission has not always been practiced as it is today. Studies, for example, in the growth of the early church

---

6 *Encyclopaedia Britannica Online*, s.v. "The new imperialism (c. 1875–1914): Reemergence of colonial rivalries," accessed February 2, 2021, https://www.britannica.com/topic/Western-colonialism/The-new-imperialism-c-1875-1914.

7 Michael Prior, "The Bible and the Redeeming Idea of Colonialism," *Studies in World Christianity* 5, no. 2 (1999): 129–155.

8 Johnny Ramírez-Johnson, "Intercultural Communication Skills for a Missiology of Interdependent Mutuality," in *Can "White" People Be Saved? Triangulating Race, Theology and Mission*, ed. Love L. Sechrest, Johnny Ramirez-Johnson, and Amos Yong (Illinois: IVP, 2018), 253, drawing on the work of Bill Ashcroft, Gareth Griffiths, and Helen Tiffin, *Post-Colonial Studies: The Key Concepts*, 2nd ed. (New York: Routledge, 2007), 20–21.

9 Bijoy Koshy, International Director's word in "Newslink," the internal *Interserve International Newsletter*, February 2021.

10 Edgar H. Schein, *Humble Inquiry: The Gentle Art of Asking Instead of Telling* (Oakland: Berrett-Koehler Publishers, 2013), 91.

11 Alan Krieder and Eleanor Kreider, *Worship and Mission after Christendom* (Milton Keynes: Paternoster, 2009), 16.

demonstrate a very different paradigm.[12] Indeed, to use the word "mission" prior to the sixteenth century is anachronistic.[13] This is not the place to discuss the ways in which the modern mission paradigm no longer fits today's contexts, but a few observations in relation to power and the role of money within the paradigm may be helpful.

Money has shaped many of the assumptions of the modern mission movement. For example, it is assumed that the primary human agent in mission is the "sent" disciple. This "missionary" needs finance. William Carey imagined missionary teams in which pairs (of men), ideally married, joined with a small team who went with them to provide for the needs of the group.[14] While Carey himself practiced this, the approach was not generalized and financial support from the sending churches and individuals became the norm. While denominational agencies supported missionaries from their collective means, interdenominational missions developed systems of personal support. Sending and money became joined in symbiotic embrace.

As the mission movement has globalized, great attention has been focused on how to finance missionaries from majority world contexts. The assumption is that mission is bound to sending because it developed in an economically powerful context, built on colonialism and empire.[15] A closer examination of how the church grew prior to Christendom and how it is growing today could help free us from a mission paradigm that weds sending with money.

Two other characteristics of the modern mission movement are worth noting: task and pragmatism. Since the 1950s, evangelicals in the USA have dominated global mission thinking and practice. The financial power of the US church has enabled specialist centers for the study of mission, with the development of mission theories, language, and praxis. Although developed in the highly individualized, competitive, managerial, white context of North American evangelicalism, these perspectives have been normalized in the global mission movement to the exclusion of other voices. Underlying assumptions include viewing mission as a task to be completed and that what works is right—pragmatism. These drivers, task and pragmatism, surface in the language of mission (e.g., "Finish the Task") and in an unrelenting search for the "right mission strategies." Money is a central driver in developing the capacity for mission theorizing and implementing "strategic" approaches to mission. One unintended consequence has been the failure to nurture other perspectives and the silencing of other voices, particularly where the church is fragile or lacks resources to develop its own mission theology and practice.

Pragmatic mission and "mission as task" are both heavily reliant on money, which becomes *the* critical resource for mission. In practice, we may minimize other resources: people, relationality, prayer, spiritual discernment, theology, creativity, etc. While each of these has their own power dynamic, the prioritization of money in mission gives those who control it a disproportionate degree of power within the mission system, to which we now turn.

Question: How can we best "own" the contextual issues raised above without letting them imprison us?

Human Systems Thinking

We now draw on the work of Barry Oshry.[16] Oshry, like many pioneers of organizational development, observed the horrors of the Second World War and asked, "Why"? His research focused on human systems, particularly on the dynamics of power within them. We all participate in multiple systems: families, neighborhoods, church communities, organizations, and networks. Just as the human body is made up of multiple systems (circulatory, immune, digestive, nervous, etc), so bigger systems are made up of multiple interrelated systems. The world of cross-cultural mission can be described as a mission ecosystem within which different agencies, churches, and networks function as systems within

---

12 See, for example, Carlos F. Cardoza-Orlani and Justo L. Gonzales, *To All Nations from All Nations: A History of the Christian Missionary Movement* (Nashville: Abingdon Press, 2013) and Alan Kreider, *The Patient Ferment of the Early Church: The Improbable Rise of Christianity in the Roman Empire* (Grand Rapids: Baker Academic, 2016).

13 Michael W. Stroope, *Transcending Mission: The Eclipse of a Modern Tradition* (London: Apollos/IVP, 2017).

14 William Carey, "An Enquiry into the Obligation of Christians to Use Means for the Conversion of the Heathen," facsimile of the original edition issued in 1792 (London: Baptist Missionary Society, 1942), 73.

15 Duncan Olumbe, "Dancing a Different Dance," *Connections: The Journal of the World Evangelical Alliance Mission Commission* 5, no. 2/3 (December 2006): 15–17.

16 For a brief introduction to Oshry's work on systems, see "What Lies Beneath - A Human Systems Perspective: A Conversation with Barry Oshry," Quality & Equality, accessed February, 5, video, https://www.quality-equality.com/what-lies-beneath-a-human-systems-perspective.

the whole. These "systems are not simply collections of individuals, they are patterns of relationships."[17]

Diagnosis. Power exists in all human relationships and money complicates the power dynamics further. When we encounter problems, we tend to see them as personal (issues of character, motivation, ability) and the story we tell ourselves is, "That's the way they (other people) are." When we encounter problems in our organizations, the story we tell is, "That's just the way we are."[18] We must take responsibility for personal failings. We also recognize that sin infects systems to the point that these systems can become strongholds of diabolic power.[19] Christian organizations can become places of systemic injustice based on gender, ethnicity, or social status. Systems thinking recognizes the place of personal characteristics but affirms that other dynamics are at work below the surface. Understanding these dynamics helps us work together for effective change. Oshry identifies five types of systemic blindness that stop us seeing what is below the surface: spatial, temporal, relational, process, and uncertainty.[20] Here we focus on the first three.

Spatial blindness:[21] the inability to see the whole system, seeing only the part we are in. To overcome this we must learn to put ourselves in others' shoes and see what they are seeing. When we do this, we grow in empathy. It takes openness and curiosity to look at the whole picture. Part of a leader's job is to see the whole system and create an environment that enable others to see too.

Temporal blindness:[22] the tendency to see the present without seeing the past and the way it shapes us now. Having delivered a workshop on the continuing influence of the Christendom model of mission, a leader assured me that his mission was unaffected by Christendom assumptions, "as it is only fifty years old." His spatial and temporal blindness was such that he failed to see how his organization, birthed and developed within the bigger mission ecosystem, was deeply shaped by the past. It's why, in this chapter, we have taken time to look at context from the perspective of history.

Relational blindness:[23] the central area in human systems thinking; we can only highlight a few concepts. Oshry identifies four main types of players in human systems: Tops, Bottoms, Middles, and "Customers." This is not a judgment on what should be or need be but an observation of "what is." Oshry demonstrates that, for example, Top and Bottom need not be hierarchical when the power of each part of the system is being used for the benefit of all. Oshry uses the terms in a nonprejudicial way and the roles are transferable to different kinds of systems, such as families or churches. Within mission, it is easy to recognize these roles in senior leaders, group leaders, and mission workers. "Customers" include sending and receiving churches, other organizations, and the people being served through the agency. The same person can occupy different roles at the same time. The international leadership of a multiorganizational structure may be Top, serving the whole, and at other times Middle, serving the demands of different organizations within the whole system. The four types of players develop their own predictable patterns of behavior within their groups and between the groups.

Oshry identifies three main types of intergroup relationships: Tops-Bottoms, Ends-Middles-Ends, and Provider-Customer. In each case, the main issue in play is one of responsibility. Consider the Top-Bottom relationship. Typically, Bottoms push responsibility to the Tops and the Tops suck this up. This results in overburdened Tops and marginalized Bottoms. How many times have we seen that pattern of relationship in Christian organizations? The same is true for Provider-Customer, where it can be assumed that the provider carries all the responsibility for delivery. The result is overburdened providers (donors) and "entitled" customers (beneficiaries). Oshry calls these repeated patterns of behavior the "dance of blind reflex"[24] because, repeatedly, human beings in any given system tend to default to this kind of behavior. The result is the same: the opportunity for genuine partnership is disabled through the shift in responsibility. Instead of harnessing the contributions of all players in the system, participants feel, depending on where they are in the system, burdened, unsupported, isolated, torn, oppressed, excluded, and unheard.

---

17 Barry Oshry, *Seeing Systems: Unlocking the Mysteries of Organizational Life* (Berrett-Koehler Publishers: San Francisco, 2007), 121.

18 Oshry, xiv.

19 See, for example, Walter Wink's extensive writing on "The Powers," including *The Powers that Be: Theology for a New Millennium* (Doubleday: New York, 1999).

20 Oshry, *Seeing Systems*, xxi.

21 Oshry, 14–19.

22 Oshry, 33–37.

23 Oshry, 63–80.

24 Oshry, 64–68.

Consider how the above plays out in mission systems. We have already noted that where money is prioritized as a resource, it gives disproportionate power to those who control it. They can easily assume the position of "Tops." Money for mission is unevenly distributed, still largely in the hands of richer churches and individuals of North America, Europe, Australia, and now parts of Asia. This sets up unequal relationships, made more complex by the contextual issues cited above. We have tried donor-recipient and patron-client relationships and these have failed. We try partnership models of ministry but still there is a struggle and old patterns of behavior surface. Little seems to change and we default to personalizing the problems, blaming "difficult people," cross-cultural miscommunication, or bad attitudes. Systems theory identifies the "dance of blind reflex" at work, in which senior leaders can become overburdened, and, with time, defensive and territorial. Those in the middle become torn by the competing demands placed on them from senior leaders and mission workers, while the mission workforce may feel ignored or marginalized. In relation to donors and recipients, as long as things are working, it's fine, but over time the donor can feel increasingly burdened to provide solutions while the recipient feels entitled and hard done by. Is there a way forward?

Question: In what ways might systems thinking help us move forward in our search for healthy partnership?

Choosing a Different Way

It would be dishonest to suggest simple solutions to problems that touch on deep issues of history, identity, and relationship. We depend on the Spirit of God at work within us and between us to shape us, and our communities, into the likeness of the Triune God. This is a journey. As we journey together, practicing hope and forgiveness, we do well to examine ourselves while at the same time paying attention to the systems we are part of.

Ourselves. How we choose to use ourselves, in any given situation, is critically important and will have more impact on the system than competency, techniques, and resources. To grow in the use of self, we learn to monitor our behavior and pay attention to our feelings. As we do this, we become aware of our anxieties and the assumptions and beliefs that feed them. We are then in a position for God to change the "mental tapes"; the stories we repeat that do not reflect his view of us or those around us. Because we exist in relationship, our feelings are not only clues about what is going on within us but also clues as to what is happening in the systems around us.[25]

Our systems. We might assume there is an inevitable power gradient within systems, with power concentrated in the Tops and with Bottoms marginalized and powerless. This need not be so. In fact, all players in the system have power.[26] Understanding and acting on predictable patterns of behavior between groups enables all actors within the system to own their power, including financial resources, for the health and fruitfulness of the whole system.

The better we understand the behavior patterns between different groups in our systems, the better placed we are to reject the toxic misuse of responsibility—taking too much or pushing it on to others. Partnership is "a relationship in which we are jointly committed to the success of whatever endeavour, process, or project we are engaged in."[27]

Choosing appropriate responsibility enables different groups in the system to partner and use their power in service of the whole.

Question: Is there anything you would like to change in the way you behave in the light of what you have read?

Conclusion

Power is a gift from God, a reflection of being made in his image, and the way we use power is intended to reflect the character and purposes of God. Issues of power shape all human relationships, often damagingly, too often destructively. As a people on-the-way, the church is not immune. While we often diagnose our problems in personal terms, we exist in relationships and these relationships are embedded in systems. Understanding patterns of behavior in systems can help us support one another to share responsibility, living and working together in ways that reflect the image of God and the reign of God.

---

25 Oshry, 125.

26 Barry Oshry, "Total System Power: Developers, Fixers, Integrators, and Validators," GovLeaders.org, accessed February 5, 2021, https://govleaders.org/total-system-power.htm.

27 Oshry, *Seeing Systems*, 85.

Chapter 17 Response

by Jongdo Park

First of all, I would like to thank to Prof. Jonathan J. Bonk and Dr. Jinbong Kim for presenting me with this wonderful opportunity to respond to Paul Bendor-Samuel, who is currently serving as executive director of the Oxford Centre for Mission Studies.[28] I have had the privilege of reading his chapter numerous times to fully understand it and to contemplate my response to it, in both positive and critical review. His chapter focuses primarily on relational and systemic approaches rather than the aspects of sin and the supply and sustainability issue of money for mission. The questions that we must consider are, Who has the power and who controls the money in the global body of mission? And going forward, How should we distribute power and money for a healthier mission ecosystem? These are some of the conundrums Bendor-Samuel presents in his theological reflections. They also occur within the context of post-colonialism and racism, so he employs Barry Oshry's "human system thinking" to diagnose problems in our mission "system." He suggests that Oshry's work on human systems will help us to see the subterranean current of the "mission ecosystem" and help to redistribute power and money for healthier relationships in the whole mission ecosystem.

Bendor-Samuel analyzes and diagnoses the main reason for unhealthy partnerships in mission within the constructs of power and money as original sin inherited from Adam and Eve. Human beings, who by nature are sinful, misuse power to distort and damage relationships. I am in total agreement with Bendor-Samuel's biblical and theological interpretation of original power, which is that God gave it to us with the purpose of "oneness and equality," that its subsequent misuse led to the fall of man, and that it was recovered and rejuvenated through the work and grace of Christ. As his theological reflection mentions, the power and money used by the church in Jerusalem during the first century "demonstrated radical generosity (Acts 2:45; 4:32–35), and a radical system for equitable distribution, allowing the marginalized minority to control the process (6:1–7)." Radical generosity characterizes life in the Kingdom of God, and Christian life in this present age should reflect the life of the age to come and its radical nature to some degree. Envisioning the Kingdom on earth entails (re)distribution of money and power, "allowing the marginalized minority to control the process."

The implementation of such a vision requires us to consider today's context of post- and neocolonialism and racism. As Bendor-Samuel incisively puts it, "Globalization, when experienced as neocolonialism, provokes nationalism, often armed with religious intolerance, and demonstrates a profound struggle for identity and belonging." In the neocolonial context, the modern mission movement has been supported by new economic powers such as Brazil, Nigeria, Korea, and other prominent countries along with North American countries. As the rise in the power of money and market dominates the global network under its homogenizing rule and shapes the path for mission by and large, ironically, the border walls of nations erected against incoming foreigners have been built higher than ever before. Identity conflicts have arisen and have raged across the world between ethnic groups, nations, and religions, and the world has stepped into a post-Christian era. Having those contexts in view, how can world mission respond and be reshaped? Bendor-Samuel introduces Barry Oshry's

---

28 Raynes Park Korean Church, London, in which I have been ministering for eighteen years, served the OCMS by hosting meals and barbeques for many years.

theory of human systems, which, roughly put, serves to identify the overburdened areas in a system and to redistribute the burden of responsibility to other parts of the system. For a system to operate successfully, no part of the system should be overstrained with responsibility or workload, as this will eventually lead to the total breakdown of the entire system. To prevent this, "habits," "patterned behaviors," or "mental tapes" of the system, which have long been buried deeply, need to be brought up to the surface. Spatially, temporally, and relationally conditioned blindness should be diagnosed, battled, and alleviated—if not eliminated. The solution is basically to change the "habits" or "patterned behaviors" that have long dictated and shaped the system.

To apply this theory to the present topic, the following questions can be raised: Which parts of the mission ecosystem have been infused with responsibility, power, and money? What habits or patterned collective behaviors in the system have controlled the whole system (overgrowing a part of the system with power and money)? How should they be redistributed over the mission ecosystem? To put this in the context of post- and neocolonialism and racism, these questions can be asked: How should responsibility, power, and money be redistributed to the marginalized and the "nonwhite" when most financial supports still come from North American white evangelicals and other prominent countries? What patterned behaviors in the eco-mission system should be changed for more equal distribution of resources and power or to counteract the new colonialism and increasing nationalism that affect the very system of our mission? They are the questions Bendor-Samuel puts forward in his introduction to Oshry's theory, and I deeply appreciate his questions and suggestions.

On the other hand, my personal feeling is that Bendor-Samuel could have made more explicit mention of money as power. In this capitalist society it is evident in most cases that the more financial power and influence an organization wields, the more respect it commands in a system, relationship, or strategy. While I understand the sensitivity of the notion of money, especially in the context of mission, I feel that Bendor-Samuel missed the opportunity to address the incongruities between doing mission out of love versus out of financial obligation. Megachurches have more opportunities for mission because they have more financial resources than smaller, poorer churches. Would this define power, and to what extent should it be recognized as such, particularly if it was for God's mission? I felt that Bendor-Samuel could have explained more explicitly the concept of money as power.

Perhaps the patterned behaviors that have structured our system have been dictated or shaped by our mental tapes or stereotypes about mission—the concept of mission as task and the symbiotic relationship between sending and money. Is mission a task to be completed? Does "sending" mean "giving money"? The deeply entrenched concepts of mission as task and of sending as giving money have become the norm and culture of the mission ecosystem. Restructuring that ecosystem may involve reevaluating our deeply entrenched notions of mission and sending. So construed, our attempts to view the whole system would lead to the reexamination of our own concepts of mission and sending, as these have been considerably determined by our mental tapes and mission behaviors (while it is also true that external environments have shaped and cultured our notions).

Libido dominandi[29] (the desire to dominate) still dominates the world and inhabits our hearts and desires. In our current society where the inequality gap is increasingly widening, we often lapse into romanticizing about those with power and thus constantly run the risk of succumbing to *libido dominandi*. This, in turn, can lead to further marginalization as we are gripped by such desires, unable to break free from this materialistic, capitalist societal evolution. Our sight is not only limited and conditioned by space and time and relation, as Oshry indicates, but also can be blinded by money and power. What should we do then? We need the Holy Spirit to help us recognize our *libido dominandi*, overcome it, and replace it with the desire to serve others in love.

As Bendor-Samuel suggests, by sharing responsibility and living and working together in ways that reflect the image of God and the reign of God, the church remains faithful to the Gospel. We usually understand that the church is merely an agent of mission or a constituent of a mission agency.

---

[29] Wikipedia, s.v. "*libido dominandi*," last modified November 3, 2020, https://en.wiktionary.org/wiki/libido_dominandi. The term is taken from the first book of Saint Augustine's *De civitate Dei* (426).

As for mission, we have a tendency to divide between the church and the missionary to be sent. But church and mission form an inseparable unity. Stanley Hauerwas suggests a new paradigm for the relationship between church and mission: "The church doesn't have a mission. The church *is* mission. Our fundamental being is based on the presumption that we are witnesses to a Christ who is known only through witnesses. To be a witness means you bear the marks of Christ so that your life gives life to others. I can't imagine Christians who are not fundamentally in mission as constitutive of their very being—because you don't know who Christ is except by someone else telling you who Christ is. That's the work of the Holy Spirit."[30] A paradigmatic shift occurs when we realize that the church is mission. The essence of mission and its task is to be church and a church wholly faithful to the Gospel.

In conclusion, most Christians understand that sending missionaries and doing mission work can only be done by large churches based in wealthy nations. The preexisting system dictates that small churches in poor countries simply do not have the capacity to send out missionaries. As Bendor-Samuel states, it is characteristic of the modern mission movement to focus on task and pragmatism. If mission is focused solely on achieving success rather than on being faithful to God's Word, money and power will be the dominant factors in mission and church activities. Contemporary churches do not even seem to attempt mission without money, compromised by worldly thinking that ultimately seems to ignore and forget this passage: "Then Peter said, 'Silver or gold I do not have, but what I do have I give you. In the name of Jesus Christ of Nazareth, walk'" (Acts 3:6).

Our model and paradigm of mission must focus on the teaching of Jesus Christ. According to Gospel of Matthew, Jesus sent out the disciples and told them, "Do not get any gold or silver or copper to take with you in your belts—no bag for the journey or extra shirt or sandals or a staff, for the worker is worth his keep" (Matt. 10:9–10). Being sent out into the world by Jesus can be a very dangerous and powerless mission from a worldly perspective: "I am sending you out like sheep among wolves" (Matt. 10:16). While there are no explicit guidelines mentioned in Jesus's and Paul's teachings to solve the problems of the relationship between mission, power, and money, it is good to see a debate evolving between modern Christianity and our ever-increasing capitalist society, and the fact that Bendor-Samuel recognizes this issue in his essay is extremely important for our conversations going forward.

---

30 Stanley Hauerwas, "Why Community Is Dangerous: An Interview," *Plough Quarterly*, May 19, 2016, https://www.plough.com/en/topics/community/church-community/why-community-is-dangerous. See also Stanley Hauerwas, "Beyond the Boundaries: The Church as Mission," in *Walk Humbly with the Lord: Church and Mission Engaging Plurality*, ed. Viggo Mortensen and Andreas Østerlund Nielsen (Grand Rapids: Eerdmans, 2010), 53–69.

Chapter 18
Global South Mission Is Possible!

by Andrew B. Kim

Contemporary missions is from everywhere to everywhere. Steve Hoke and Bill Taylor predicted a couple of decades ago that "as we move into the third millennium, the church of Jesus Christ [will] become truly globalized, and missions [will be] from all nations to all nations."[1] As the Global South churches enjoyed rapid growth, they began to assume a greater responsibility for world missions.[2] Thus, Paul Pierson described the remarkable growth of the non-Western missionary movement as "the greatest new fact of our time."[3]

Since the Great Commission was given to all Christians, all believers are expected to take their missional responsibility seriously, including those in the Global South. However, Global South churches have not been actively involved in missions and there may be several reasons why. We may assume that Global South churches struggle with lack of finances. Perhaps they have little to no exposure abroad and thus have no burden to reach out beyond their country. Churches may also have a poor understanding of their missional role and are experiencing difficulty in doing evangelism in their areas.

However, as a field missionary for almost four decades, I see these reasons as mere excuses. I would like to discuss Global South missions and financial issues in light of some cases that I have been greatly involved in.

Global South Churches Have Their Own "Five Loaves of Bread and Two Fish"

Global South churches have struggled with the chronic problem of dependency, which has rendered them weak. In reality, the problem of dependency is not a shortage of money or strategies because even the early churches took the initiative of missions though they were not affluent.

Reflecting on this overall gloomy picture of Global South churches, I tried to find reasons why churches in

---

1 Stephen T. Hoke, "Paradigm Shifts and Trends in Missions Training: A Call to Servant-Teaching, A Ministry of Humility," Evangelical Review of Theology 23 (October 1999): 19.

2 David Harley, *Preparing to Serve: Training for Cross-Cultural Mission* (Pasadena: William Carey Library, 1995), 4.

3 Paul Pierson, "Non-Western Missions: The Great New Fact of Our Time," in *New Frontiers in Mission*, ed. Patrick Sookhdeo (Exeter: Paternoster Press, 1987), 9.

the Global South remain dependent, and I found some good models of missional movement in the Global South that can encourage and even challenge other churches. I also learned that the local church will be healthier when it takes ownership of the Gospel and shares the Good News with the world. The following are some models of doing missions in the Global South churches:

- Mizoram Presbyterian Synod in Northeast India. The synod has deployed 2,280 cross-cultural missionaries though the state is one of the poorest and remotest in India. They offer firewood, a spoonful of rice per family member when they cook, and one out of every ten chickens for missions. Many churches cultivate their own banana plantations and give all the profit for missions. They are proud of being able to export the Gospel to other states and nations.
- Asia Vision Short-Term Missions Project in the Philippines. To encourage more believers to take part in the Great Commission through giving, the organization provided coin cans for missions. Church members, young and old, found it a joy to fill the cans for missions. Those who had more could give more (they put in bills instead of coins). Sunday School children were also encouraged to drop their missions offerings into the coin cans. Other church members who were not well-off still had the opportunity to share their resources through coins that accumulated over time. Some young people raised funds to support missionaries by washing vehicles and cleaning houses together. They also organized a "Sacrificial Dinner for Missions" and gave all the collected offerings for missions.
- Papua New Guinean Christians. They organized a "Mission Car Wash" and gave all the income for missions.
- An Ethiopian Local Church. Recently, an Ethiopian local church pastor told me, "We will support our missionaries through *enjira*. The local church members will cook *enjira*, sell that in the market, and give the income for missions." The church members are not rich, but they would like to share the Gospel with the Somalis and others through their own efforts. They try to find possible resources in their context to support their missionaries.

Jesus fed over five thousand in the wilderness with a small boy's simple lunch box of five loaves of bread and two fish. Once the Lord blesses our simple giving, there will be miraculous blessings. We all have our own "five loaves of bread and two fish" in our own contexts and there will be endless possibilities if we have the heart to proclaim God's glory among the nations.

I strongly encourage missionary candidates to proactively attempt great things for God, rather than passively waiting for great things from God. I always challenge missionaries, wherever I go, to put their faith in God and prove that their God is the living God. It is obvious that they should experience their God as the living God before they go and proclaim him among the nations.

Strategic Mission Models of the Global South

The Global South churches are located in the heart of major mission fields and are thus more effective in doing missions there. Several missional models arise from the Global South.

Brazilian Mission Models

Christian Vision in East Timor. Christian Vision of Brazil conducted a field survey in East Timor and developed a twelve-year master plan for East Timor missions. They deployed forty missionaries to the tiny nation in 2000. From the very beginning they had clear entrance and exit strategies for missions. They planted healthy churches in major cities/towns in the country, established a radio station in Dili and a pastors' training program in Baucau, and launched several evangelistic projects.

In 2012, thirty-seven missionaries completed their assigned ministries and withdrew from East Timor. Two more missionaries left in 2015. Finally, Christian Vision turned the leadership over to the East Timorean churches in 2017. Christian Vision of Brazil had a master plan for their mission from the beginning.

AMIDE (Associação Missionária para Difusão do Evangelho). Another missions agency in Brazil, AMIDE, also conducted a survey prior to deploying their missionaries to the field. They encouraged five churches to participate and support a field project together. They are new in missions, but they have strong prayers, practical training, and field-based surveys. They have even prepared for their missionaries' retirement, among other things.

Chinese Mission Model: The Five DNA and the Secret of Chinese Church Growth

When China fell under Communist rule in 1949, there were about half a million Christians in the entirety of China. It is estimated that this number has now grown to 135 million. Chinese churches experienced severe persecutions, but they have strengthened the churches through their five DNA: (1) Evangelism, (2) Prayer, (3) Infilling of the Holy Spirit, (4) The Cross (i.e., Suffering), and (5) Miracles. These made the Chinese church strong, and they have now started to send their missionaries out amid persecution and various other challenges. Some characteristics of Chinese missions are as follows:

- Humble beginnings. The church grew in agricultural states (i.e., the believers were not from rich backgrounds in general), so they fully trust in the Holy Spirit.
- Strategic gate cities. Key cities have been selected in mission fields to set up missional platforms and widely enhance their missions movement.
- Niche markets. They set up niche markets and concentrate on ministries that they can do well (e.g., Business as Missions [BAM]).
- "Just do it" spirit. They are not afraid of making mistakes.
- Rustication of leaders. Instead of encouraging others to do missions, leaders forge the way and present themselves as role models for missions.
- Field-oriented spirit. Missionaries live right where they work in the mission fields.
- Raising and investing in future leadership. They allot much of their finances and efforts to developing future leadership.
- Ministry-oriented and efficiency-oriented (like Mission Expo). When they have gatherings, they encourage church leaders, mission leaders, businessmen, and missionary candidates to come, participate, and interact with field missionaries so that they can share experiences, insights, and resources to maximize their abilities. They do have a Kingdom perspective on missions.
- Chinese way of missions. They know who they are, so they want to establish their own way of doing missions rather than copy from the West or others.

Northeast Indian Mission Model

The Council of Baptist Churches in Northeast India (CBCNEI) has six conventions with 113 councils under its umbrella. In 2014, CBCNEI launched a project dubbed "Adopt the 110 Districts by CBCNEI." The Mission Director of the CBCNEI, Dr. Jolly Rimai, led this project and completed the adoption of the 110 districts, which encompass about 400 million souls. The missions department of CBCNEI conducted a field survey of the 110 districts and encouraged all councils to adopt a district to saturate with the Gospel.

Ethiopian Mission Model

Ethiopia has a good number of evangelical Christians and in February 2020 they started a missions agency, GONEANAME (Good News to East Africa, North Africa, and Middle East), to reach East Africa, North Africa, and the Middle East with the Gospel. Just like Filipino churches, the Ethiopian churches will mobilize their diasporic Christians in the region and will extend their ministries to other parts of Africa, the Middle East, Asia, and beyond.

Some Factors to Consider in the Global South Missions Movement

The Global South churches do have their own strengths that they can harness in missions if they are committed to the Lord and cherish the Great Commission. We need to raise and deploy missionaries who can proclaim as Peter did, "Silver or gold I do not have, but what I have I give you. In the name of Jesus Christ of Nazareth, walk" (Acts 3:6). The Global South churches can learn from the mission models presented below.

1. Niche and Hinge Markets for the Global South. The Global South churches are new in missions; thus, it would be best to find their niche and hinge markets in missions where they can maximize their ministries with low cost but high efficiency.

2. Leaders' Field Exposures. Church or mission leaders and workers can visit various mission fields and see how others are working. Mission leaders can do a "vision trip" or lineup work on potential mission fields where they will deploy their missionaries. This sort of vision trip brings the heart for the area/s and embraces various possibilities of missions. In the vision trip, leaders can identify and select gate cities where they will establish missional platforms.

3. Missions Education. Missional conferences may be conducted regularly for key and strategic leaders. Contextualized missionary training programs may be developed. On-field education for missionaries and ongoing education for both home and field mission leaders and missionaries may be conducted in their context.

4. See the Big Picture. Churches can sit down to develop a master plan, with entry and exit mission strategies. Moreover, they can constantly evaluate and envision future missions.

5. Key Leaders' Role in Missions. From the cases of the Philippines, Brazil, China, India, and Ethiopia, I have learned that once national key leaders are deeply moved by the Spirit of God and become actively involved in missions, their missions grow well.

6. Mobilize National Christians. Many mission fields have a good number of Christians. They are the best missionaries to their own people, and must be mobilized in missions, rather than sending foreign missionaries and duplicating ministries.

7. Avoid Dependency. In general, money causes dependency, which must be avoided. Instead of offering "oxygen respirator" thinking in the fields, we should offer "priming the water" thinking. "Priming the water" enhances missions and leads to self-support, self-propagation, and self-government.

Challenges in the Global South Missions Movement

Christian missionaries are facing increasing challenges and hostility from Muslims, Hindus, Buddhists, and many other groups in various mission fields. Therefore, we need to find new avenues in missions and bring more mission forces into the fields.

We are living in a world that is constantly changing and becoming more unstable each day. Changes, big and small, are becoming more unpredictable—they are getting increasingly dramatic and are happening faster and faster. The COVID-19 pandemic, for instance, has created many interesting challenges and opportunities for churches and missionaries. We are not sure how we will cope on mission fields when the pandemic cools down.

This reminds me of the Choluteca Bridge in Honduras. Many other bridges were damaged by Hurricane Mitch in 1998, but the Choluteca Bridge survived in near perfect condition. However, roads on both ends of the bridge completely vanished, leaving no visible trace of their prior existence. More impressively, the Choluteca River had carved out a new channel during the massive flooding caused by the hurricane. The river no longer flowed beneath the Choluteca Bridge, which now spanned dry ground. The bridge quickly became known as, "The Bridge to Nowhere."

The lesson for us is that we often focus on creating the best solution for a given problem, but we often forget that the problem itself might change. Since the world is so unpredictable, we should highly value adaptive leadership in this VUCA—volatile, uncertain, complex, and ambiguous—world.[4]

Conclusion

Global South missions is possible if we are committed, filled with the Holy Spirit, and have a heart for the nations. Money is not and should never be an issue. There are many creative ways for us to do missions. I hope the Global South churches can leave their "comfort" and "fear" zones and move to the "growth" zone via the "learning" zone by faith in the Lord (see Gen. 12:1–3). Let's make great things possible!

Figure 18.1: The Comfort Zone[5]

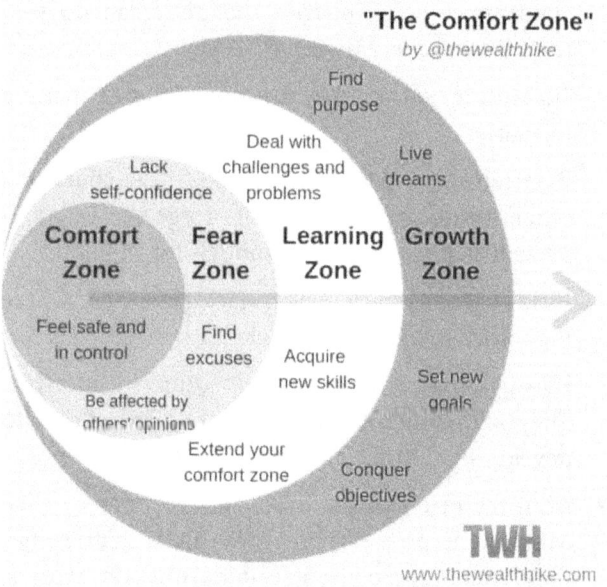

---

4 "VUCA is an acronym (artificial word), first used in 1987 and based on the leadership theories of Warren Bennis and Burt Nanus, and stands for Volatility, Uncertainty, Complexity, and Ambiguity. It was the response of the US Army War College to the collapse of the USSR in the early 1990s. Suddenly, there was no longer the only enemy, resulting in new ways of seeing and reacting" ("Leadership Skills & Strategies," VUCA-World, 2020, https://www.vuca-world.org/).

5 "The Comfort Zone," TWH, www.thewealthhike.com, accessed April. 12, 2021, https://i.pinimg.com/originals/f0/3a/cc/f03acc9fdba523e46841d9d6e362a6bd.jpg.

Chapter 18 Response

"We Are a Letter Of Christ"

by Wanjiru M. Gitau

Andrew B. Kim's key concern is that "Global South churches have not been actively involved in missions." Some reasons may be that the churches have financial struggles, have inadequate worldwide encounters, and have a poor understanding of their missional call. All true. More concerning is what he sees as the struggle with chronic dependency, although the details are left to the imagination. He outlines several helpful models of churches that have overcome dependency such as the Mizoram Presbyterian Synod in Northeast India, which has deployed some 2,280 cross-cultural missionaries, the Asia Vision Short-Term Missions Project in the Philippines, which funds missions using coin cans, and an Ethiopian church that sells their staple food to support missions.

The second issue he discusses is that Global South churches are more effective in doing missions in regions that resemble their own contexts. He cites case studies of Brazilian mission models that developed a sustained and successful master plan of mission to East Timor. He cites the humble Chinese model of mission with its fivefold DNA of evangelism, prayer, infilling of the Holy Spirit, suffering the cross of Christ, and miracles. He cites Northeast Indian mission models of the Council of Baptist Churches, and Ethiopian church models as well. The third and fourth issues concern factors and challenges faced in mission, including other world religions and the VUCA—volatile, uncertain, complex, and ambiguous—conditions of the contemporary world. He concludes with his main premise, that with commitment, creativity, and financial sacrifice, Global South missions is possible. Indeed.

In response, let me start by saying that my people have a saying: an elder sees more while inclining on his aged footrest under the tree than a boy sees when he is perched high in the branches of the same tree. There is wisdom from hard-won experience, and no amount of outsider observations can override the perspective a missionary such as Andrew Kim has from his many years of trying to mobilize insular churches to embrace the whole world as their parish, to do whatever it takes to spread the Gospel abroad. With more than four decades of mission field experience under his belt, Andrew Kim has a life school perspective on such challenges as dependency, reluctance, and lethargic mobilization. And broadly speaking, the waning of the fire for spreading the Gospel is a challenge that all churches must continually face, so his observations are relevant at anytime, anywhere.

Beyond Andrew Kim's chapter then, one has to read between the lines of the broad conversation about leadership in missionary mobilization. If there is a sense that Global South churches are not engaging in mission as well as they should, the examples in Andrew Kim's chapter in fact beg the question whether they are the exceptions to the rule. His examples here demonstrate that churches are in fact engaging in mission. Sharing the Gospel is an "innate" part of being a Christian. It turns out that most Christian communities have a sense that this must be so, locally, and abroad. It also turns out that our communicative capacities are inspired by such Old Testament scriptures as, "This is a day of good news, and we are keeping it to ourselves" (2 Kgs. 7:9), and "How beautiful on the mountains are the feet of those who bring good news, who say to Zion, your God reigns!" (Isa. 52:7). Not to mention New Testament verses such as the call of the Great Commission, and that "Christ's love compels us, because we are convinced that one died for all, and therefore all died. And he died for all, that those who live should no longer live for themselves but for him who died for them and was raised again" (2 Cor. 5:14–15), and "we are therefore Christ's ambassadors, as though God were making his appeal through us" (2 Cor. 5:20).

So the challenge is not the absence of inspiration, otherwise the church would not be as widespread as it is today. The late Lamin Sanneh, introducing a study on Pentecostalism, observes that the worldwide Christian resurgence has rendered Christianity the principal religion of the peoples of the world who once stood well outside the main orbit of the faith. The prophet Habakkuk long foresaw this day when "the knowledge of the LORD would fill the earth as the waters cover the sea" (Hab. 2:14). What is remarkable in our time is how quickly the faith has spread in new geographical areas, the diversity of cultures represented, and the upending of structural and theological forms that have long been dominant. As mission historians have observed again and again, although missionaries are often the catalyst to the process, it is local, indigenous people who are usually the true agents of mission as village or local evangelists, church planters, educators, and the ones doing works of compassion that testify to the presence of Christ in tangible ways. Furthermore, all around the world it almost goes without saying that it is almost always local Christian communities that are first to respond when there are catastrophes of disease, droughts or floods, or conflicts, and this too is witness to Christ, or mission to the local or regional culture. The rapid and obvious growth of Christianity across the Global South is testimony to the vibrancy of local and regional mission activity by local, national, and regional Christians.

There is a case to be made that Andrew Kim has cross-cultural, international frontier mission in mind. This is the main sense in which the word "mission" is used in conferential discourse. Missionaries are seen as those who cross boundaries of culture, nations, geography, and language to share the Gospel with foreign peoples. Now, if we are to charge Global South churches of not being involved in this kind of mission as well, it may be that we need to appreciate the altered parameters of international mission. The parameters of frontier mission were shaped by the influx of Western missionaries to all the regions of the Global South. Beginning the late eighteenth century, Western churches formed mission agencies and mobilized to take the Gospel to frontiers that had not hitherto had a first-time encounter with Christianity. The voluntary societies were a powerful, revolutionary idea, new for its time, and remarkable for its capacity to mobilize ordinary people to take interest in remote societies, with little to none of the geographical knowledge or none of the capacity for mobility that we have today. That project was also tied to a larger project—international mobility, which came to give us today's nation states everywhere. The capacity for international migration was at the time primarily open to Western people tied to the colonial project, which meant the world was by and large freely open to such Western people without much restriction. And throughout the twentieth century, Westerners retained that capacity to move with relative ease across nations. When we talk about mission mobilization today, we have to include a note of realism about conditions of modern geopolitical and international foreign policy restrictions on cross-border migrations. Global South residents cannot simply move at will without great expense. Subsistence and affordability of life in new spaces is not what it once was for Western missionaries. It is not that it cannot be done or that it is not being done, but mission leaders cannot talk naively about what it takes for Global South Christians to migrate, not only far and abroad but even in their own regions. This subject in of itself needs detailed treatment, which cannot be done here.

What we can note here is that cross-cultural, cross-border mission from everywhere to everywhere is indeed being conducted, just not within the same parameters of the earlier mission movement from the West. Mission is instead actively being carried out by forms of international migration that do not advertise themselves as mission work. Refugees, migrant labor workers, and international business executives, as well as young people pursuing higher education are the new, often unnamed missionaries. Coming from families, communities, and nations that are well evangelized, these are the new evangelists. In the words of Jehu Hanciles, who has studied this question of migration extensively, migrants are in fact discipling the next generations, in effect, Christianizing nations that in the moment may appear less Christian, but which in another generation will constitute new émigré populations.

To be sure, not every migrant is Christian or even actively shares their faith if they are. But this is the perspective to keep in mind when thinking strategically about new would-be missionaries. That the entire world is experiencing a great deal of mobility is a fact writ in modern life. Everywhere, people are moving from rural peasant life to townships, from towns to cities, to the metropolis, and to the wider cosmopolitan world. It is to be expected that the average person will move multiple times in their lifetime. Within this capacity for mobility is also the agency to carry the Gospel. Churches therefore need to change the conversation from imagining mission as only sending, to imagining mobility or movement as the vehicle for spreading the Gospel. The man or woman who is a follower of Christ is literally a letter of Christ, as Paul wrote: "You are a letter from Christ showing the result of our ministry among you. This 'letter' is written not with pen and ink, but with the Spirit of the living God. It is carved not on tablets of stone, but on human hearts" (2 Cor. 3:3, NLT). The issue is therefore not primarily about mobilizing for mission. The issue is discipling all those who are in the churches everywhere to embody this deep awareness that they are the bearers of Good News, no matter where they are and go: "How beautiful on the mountains are the feet of those who bring good news."

This underlines another vital point to be made here. "Mission" in the previous sense was also conceived of in terms of sending bodies, organizations, and formally constituted missional movements with the express purpose of *traveling* to share the Gospel. These kinds of organizations and institutions will continue to have their place, just as much as the church needs institutional scaffolding as a vessel for "the good deposit" of the faith (2 Tim. 1:14). Large-scale bodies that cultivate a global sensibility about Christ's mission, such as the Lausanne Movement that brings global evangelicals together, and focused groups that mobilize particular demographics, such as IFES (International Fellowship of Evangelical Students) among student movements, also have their place. Specialized mission organizations, such as World Vision, witness in particular ways as well. However, by and large the capital-intensive infrastructure of these kinds of organizations, the vestige of a previous generation of missions, makes them the exception rather than the rule. A great deal of mission activity emerging from the Global South cannot afford the kind of financial mobilization required.

To be sure, it is not that infrastructure is not needed. It is perspective that is needed. Here, one thinks of Paul and his fellow missionaries in the New Testament. They found themselves engaging in mission by using the Roman highways, Roman merchant networks like ships and nodal cities, and even Roman law for protection when necessary. Yet what strikes the careful observer is that they never seem to essentialize and overthink any of that infrastructure. Mission infrastructure is contingent and provisional, useful when available, irrelevant when not provided. That is why Paul can witness in prison, send letters when far away to beloved churches, send messengers when he cannot go himself, and even go to the belly of the beast, Rome, to face martyrdom as the ultimate witness, if that is what it takes. Through it all, the Gospel work took on traction. What we consistently find in Paul and his New Testament partners is an abiding and sincere conviction that Jesus, the Messiah of Israel, is also the Messiah of the whole known world, and that the whole world was the better off for believing and embracing this Messiah. And they wanted to communicate that, and they would take whatever means necessary.

It is good that we had the golden era of cross-cultural and geographic frontier mission, but if the conditions have changed, we need not saddle mission with sending agencies, expensive training institutes, heavily staffed networks, or even complex multiyear plans. Where God makes such provisions possible, so be it, but at the very least, let the churches of today create deeply committed disciples, "human letters of Christ" that will spread the message of Christ in today's mobile and VUCA challenged world.

Chapter 19
The COVID-19 Crisis and Opportunities for Increased Community: A Local Pastor's Recommendations

by Mongsik Lee

COVID-19 has brought tremendous pain and change in human life. With seventy million confirmed cases and over 1.5 million deaths worldwide, the pandemic has ravaged economies, societies, cultures, and educational systems. In Korea, over eighty thousand confirmed cases with over one thousand deaths occurred, transforming Korean society completely.[1] Because of this, the Korean church has faced an unprecedented crisis. Despite the church's efforts to prevent the spread of the disease, the public condemned the church as one of the centers of infection. Churches switched to offering online worship services and canceled many of their ministries and gatherings. Many churches were hit with financial difficulties. Some of them closed their doors, and some ministers were forced to leave. Debt-ridden churches struggled under the pressure of bankruptcy, while reports of church buildings being auctioned off circulated widely.

The situation on the mission field was no exception—the constraints in mobility affected many ministries. Missionary activities came to a halt as support from churches was cut off. Short-term mission trips, which so many Korean churches used to participate in, were canceled due to the pandemic. As a result, many ongoing ministries were called off. Also, the prolonged pandemic forced many missionaries to return to Korea.

According to Global Mission Society (GMS), the largest mission organization in Korea, 683 missionaries out of 2,574 GMS members temporarily returned to Korea since March 2020 due to COVID-19.[2] While some have gone back to the mission field, a significant number of missionaries have been forced to wait until the COVID-related situation improves. The loss of financial support from Korean churches is another reason for some missionaries not being able to return to the mission field.

---

1 See "Press Release," Korea Disease Control and Prevention Agency, updated daily (last update March 3, 2021 as of this writing), https://www.cdc.go.kr/board/board.es?mid=a30402000000&bid=0030.

2 Jung Han Kim, personal interview by author at GMS headquarters, January 20, 2021. See also GMS website, https://gms.kr.

The COVID-19 Era—A Time for Reflection

COVID-19 brought everything around us to a standstill. This pause naturally made us reflect on our ministry and mission. We prayerfully reflected on whether our ministry has been faithful to its essence. Such time for reflection was a gift from God. During those difficult times, local churches reviewed their identity as a church and reassessed their mission's direction. The missionary community is using this period as an opportunity to prepare countermeasures and establish new strategies during the crisis.

As a local church pastor, I heard much about the difficulties of local churches due to the pandemic. Listening to the stories, I pondered on how local churches should continue to serve missions during the pandemic. As a leader of a small missionary organization, I learned about the situation on the mission field through the missionaries and planned for risk management for the post-COVID era. In this article, I suggest the need for a change in the overall mission strategy during COVID-19. I also discuss two major issues regarding finance, from the perspective of a local church pastor.

Changes in Mission Strategy for the Post-COVID Era

A new mission strategy is required for the post-COVID-19 era. The world after COVID is likely to witness the rise of nationalism, isolationism, xenophobia, and liberalism, all of which will pose significant challenges to Christianity. Globalization is stagnating and there is a wave of localization that seeks only local interests. With the spread of the coronavirus, many countries are limiting the entrance of foreigners. This phenomenon is likely to continue for the time being. Many experts agree that we cannot go back to the pre-COVID era. In light of this, we might have to discard our former pattern of missionary work and proactively prepare for the impending changes.

The traditional way of mission was for missionaries to go to the ends of the earth to preach the Gospel and build churches. However, now there is a strong avoidance of foreigners in each country due to the pandemic. Thus, missions require a change of direction. In other words, the importance of scattered churches, as opposed to gathering churches, is emerging. Instead of a congregating church, the new emphasis is on a scattering church whose members continue to live as a church wherever they are. On the mission field, typical church planting involves constructing buildings. However, from now on family meetings and small group gatherings will qualify as churches on the mission field. There will be a significant shift in the paradigm of church planting, with its focus changing from buildings and regions to people.

In the COVID-19 era, construction-oriented project missions are difficult to achieve. Ministries are canceled due to reduced financial support from churches. Ministries that require large budgets are becoming more difficult to maintain. Therefore, an ongoing project ministry should seek cost reduction, and essential projects should find ways to become self-supporting. Furthermore, it is time to change direction toward local discipleship training and education ministries instead of pursuing projects that require a lot of money. Missionaries need to focus on building good partnerships with local churches and local ministers. If possible, it is time to set up dedicated local workers and prepare for the handover.

As the church mission budget decreases in the COVID-19 era, tentmakers, NGO missions, and business missions will increase significantly. As the church's support becomes difficult to secure, self-supporting missions will emerge. Young people today are more interested in business and professional missions than traditional pastoral missions. In particular, missions by lay professionals are expected to increase. We need to develop a mission plan for effective ministry in the field with a tentmaker's mindset. After the pandemic, mobilization for missions will become one of the key issues for churches and sending organizations to solve together.

The most evident change due to COVID-19 was the shift to online meetings. Instead of meeting face-to-face, we communicated remotely. Unable to gather, Korean churches held online worship services. This change is also important for the mission field. Although internet connectivity varies from country to country, we are left with no other option but to meet through the internet in most mission fields. The mission of communicating through the media and preaching the Gospel online is a task that we cannot delay any longer.

Missionaries have been aware of the usefulness and the possibilities of information technology (IT), but many of them did not actively use it until the coronavirus hit. Some were hesitant, thinking IT was difficult. In addition to technical barriers, missionaries avoided IT due to a negative view of grafting technology onto mission. Some thought that remote interaction using a video was theologically unsound or that it did not mesh well with the traditional missionary framework of relief ministry with the locals. But now, worship using IT has become a necessity, not an option. Korean churches and mission agencies should actively support missionaries so that they can use IT in the field. For instance, creating video content for missionaries might be helpful.

We must actively learn to use various information and communication technologies on the mission field. Some organizations are conducting videoconferencing and training on the mission field through Zoom. Training and nurturing can be done remotely without gathering in the same place. Young people all over the world are using YouTube. To support the younger generation in the field with the Gospel, we must be able to use YouTube as a tool. Excellent gospel-based content appropriate to the regional culture of each mission field would be enormously helpful. This task should not be entrusted to field missionaries alone but shared by all churches and organizations.

The Challenge to Restore Community

When COVID forced churches to close their doors, we regarded it as the crisis of ministry. But, in a deeper sense, it was a crisis of community. When we could not gather for worship on Sundays, we felt as if the whole church had stopped. People felt that way, understandably, because many Korean churches have considered the Sunday worship service as *the* church, focusing most of their energies and resources on that particular event. However, the unavailability of Sunday worship service does not mean that the church has disappeared. It only shows that the Korean church has yet to fully grasp the meaning of community. What we really need to restore in the COVID crisis is community.

The church is a community—not a building or a system, but a community connected by the Holy Spirit to become the body of our Lord. The early church believers presented themselves as a living church with genuine fellowship even though regular gathering was impossible under Roman persecution. A living community cannot stop being a church no matter what. Even if they could not worship together on Sunday, individual worship and fellowship within small group gatherings were possible. Just as family-based community survives despite the COVID crisis, church community withstands the threat from the pandemic. To think that the church has collapsed because there is no Sunday worship service is to misunderstand the very nature of the church as a community.

Community is the same on the mission field. Should missions really stop due to COVID? Of course, it is a reality that shutdowns or curfews during the quarantine have put some ministries on hold. Nevertheless, community-based churches were still alive and well on the mission field. Ministries that focused on relationships thrived even during the COVID crisis. In contrast, missions based on unilateral mass gathering ceremonies and organizational mobilization experienced interruptions. As we navigate the pandemic crisis, we must address the crisis of community in missionary work. The crisis only reveals what kind of relationships we have had with the people in our mission field. That is, the crisis exposes the differences between organic, people-centered community ministry and work-centered, project-oriented ministry.

We need to turn our ministry focus from projects to people, and shift toward relationship-centered community ministries on the mission field. We must create a community that embodies the values and the order of God's Kingdom, a living koinonia community. We should revitalize community ministries centered on small groups and build up local leaders. We should also recognize the importance of family ministry and enable small family communities to be established as strong ecclesial communities. Although digital technology seems to connect everyone, too many people are actually alienated. It is Christ's love that unites people, not the media. By switching from non-contact to deep contact, the Gospel will be preached, and the community of Christ will be established through personal relationships, even in a non-face-to-face era.

Recovering Stewardship in Missionary Expenses

The church's budget was also impacted by COVID-19. From May 28 to June 1, 2020, JI&COM Research conducted a survey on donations and attendance during COVID-19, with the participation of 1,135 senior pastors of the Presbyterian Church of Korea. According to 68.8 percent of respondents, offerings decreased due to COVID-19. The offerings might have declined even further in the ensuing months.[3]

From April 24 to May 7, 2020, The Korea World Missions Association (KWMA) investigated the effect of COVID on missionaries' financial support. Under the title of, "The Needs of Missionaries Due to COVID-19," they surveyed member organizations and mission officials in the association. The 470

---
3 See Yonhap News, "COVID-19 Reduces Both Donations and Attendance," *Maeil Business Newspaper*, June 15, 2020, https://www.mk.co.kr/news/society/view/2020/06/613077/.

respondents were composed of 372 missionaries on the mission field, eighty-five missionaries who temporarily returned to Korea for personal reasons due to the pandemic, and thirteen missionaries in other locations. When the missionaries remaining in the field were asked regarding changes in donations from Korean churches or sponsors, 55 percent (206) replied that there was no difference from before COVID-19, and 3.4 percent (twelve) said that there was an increase. On the other hand, 41 percent (154) said that donations had decreased. About half of the latter responded that donations were cut by 20 percent. Two missionaries said that their donations were almost totally cut off. Donations for temporarily returning missionaries were similar: 37 percent (thirty-one) said that donations were reduced.[4]

The church I serve rents a space in a commercial building. Due the pandemic, the offerings in 2020 fell by 20 percent from the previous year. But we kept the mission budget for 2021 at the previous year's level, while cutting the budget for other church expenses. It is encouraging to see that most churches are trying to keep their mission budgets intact while reducing other budgets. This is because each church upholds mission as the top priority, with a mindset of biblical stewardship. A steward is a person who manages the assets entrusted by the Master with integrity and according to his will. By implementing the mission budget, the church has acknowledged its stewardship and has sought to do the will of the Lord.

Due to the prolonged pandemic, church attendance is expected to fall, which will eventually lead to reduced mission budgets. If mission budgets are reduced, restructuring of missionary work will become inevitable. Ministry on the mission field may have to be reduced or stopped. In severe cases, missionaries may have to stop their work and return home. What are we supposed to do about mission when facing a financial crisis during the pandemic? We need to reflect on our philosophy and attitude toward the money that God gave us. How much importance does money have in mission? Obviously, mission is not about money, but without money, mission is impossible. Money and mission cannot be separated. Amid the COVID crisis, we cannot help but reflect on missionary work from the perspective of money.

Restoration of Trust through Communication between Churches and Missionaries

Amid the financial crisis under COVID-19, churches and missionaries should communicate with each other openly about the changes on the mission field caused by the pandemic. This is because an adequate response should be based on a proper understanding of the situation in the field. However, missionaries who returned to Korea due to COVID-19 reported that they found it difficult to communicate with churches. They had difficulty making appointments with the pastors or members of the sending or sponsoring churches. Although such difficulties apparently had to do with COVID, it is also hard to deny that when a church meets with a missionary, the issue of money usually comes up. A meeting with a missionary in which the issue of money is raised can be a burden, especially when a church is already suffering financial hardship due to the pandemic. However, now *is* the time that churches and missionaries should meet—to communicate and understand the situation on the mission field, and to pray about it. Churches and missionaries should work closely together to share difficulties and seek countermeasures regarding COVID-19.

Trust is important between churches and missionaries as partners in mission. However, there are cases where the trust between a church and a missionary is broken by the transaction of mission expenses. The first case is when a church promises to sponsor missionary expenses and then fails to keep its promise. The missionary prepares everything based on the assurance of the church's support, but trust falls apart when the church, without any explanation, cancels its plan to support the missionary. The church must have had a reason, but to do so without proper communication hurts the missionary.

The second case is when a missionary misuses the funds provided by the church. For example, a missionary presented a mission field's needs and requested a purpose offering from the church, which the church collected and gifted in response. However, when they later went to the mission field, they found out that the gift had not been used for the stated purpose. Upon investigation, they found out that the missionary redirected the funds for some other urgent need, but without consultation with the church. The trust between the church and the missionary might have remained intact had the missionary consulted with the church.

---

4 See Ji Hee Lee, "How Corona Affects Korean Missionaries," *Christian Daily*, May 24, 2020, https://www.christiandaily.co.kr/news/90462.

Third, when raising money for a project, missionaries usually do it not just from one church but from several churches. When fundraising is done in several churches, congregations are sometimes left in the dark about how their donations are being used, and they can feel suspicious. There would be no problem if the information on the fundraising and its implementation was reported transparently. More often than not, however, such communication does not happen. This often happens when missionaries raise money without an accurate explanation of its purpose, and churches donate nonetheless. Perhaps they do so because they trust each other so much, but difficulties often arise later. Accurate communication is a must. When a church and a missionary make a transaction for a mission budget, necessary detailed information should be shared to avoid complications later. The practice of extemporaneous fundraising and impromptu donation is another cause of such problems. Churches and missionaries need to recognize the importance of communication because they are partners in mission. As stewards of money, their communication must be transparent and ethical.

Reassessing Projects in Ministry

With shrinking mission budgets due to COVID, churches and missionaries working on projects should reassess their mission finances. Here, projects refer to building a church hall or a mission headquarters, or establishing educational institutions, hospitals, and schools. Typical activities include buying land, constructing buildings, and laying the foundations for missions. Since Korean missions have a short history, projects that lay the foundations on the mission field are necessary. Such projects are essential and effective for mobilizing local missions, especially in underdeveloped mission fields. However, projects cost a lot of money. When planning a project under financial pressure in a pandemic, it is essential to check the purpose, feasibility, and continuity of the ministry.

First of all, projects are expensive to execute. Although some may think that they only need to construct a building, the additional tasks of hiring locals to maintain the building and getting the system to work require continuous investment. We often see centers, schools, and hospitals that operate for a while and then shut down when they cannot afford the operating costs. Such ministries are even more vulnerable in the present COVID situation. If a church fails to maintain its sponsorship, an abrupt shutdown might be inevitable.

In addition, projects can make local churches dependent on external assistance while weakening the spirit of self-reliance. Although many investments in mission fields have yielded positive results, in many cases they also resulted in local churches becoming dependent on missionaries. Such projects created structures that call for endless financial aid. Even if a project is transferred later to a local church, a huge problem arises when the locals cannot operate it. When a transfer benefits only some of the local churches, it could stir up envy and jealousy among the rest of the local leaders who were left out, breaking the unity of the local churches.

When a mission budget cannot fully support a project's operating expenses, the ministry often loses focus on its purpose. For example, a missionary started his ministry by setting up a Christian school on the mission field. He started a kindergarten and then added an elementary school and a high school. Starting a school cost a lot of money, but running it also required a huge budget. Initially, the home country's mission budget covered the school's operating expenses. But as time passed, declining sponsorship resulted in a crisis in operation. To meet the costs, they raised the tuition fees, in the course of which they lost focus on their purpose of nurturing students as Christians through school ministry. This example shows the importance of checking in advance whether the purpose and the independence of the operation would be balanced and effectual. A ministry that fails to reap the fruits after a large investment is a burden to both the sponsoring church and the missionaries. We see how important it is to have sufficient prayers, plans, and stewardship, discussing mission spending together in advance.

Conclusion

The COVID-19 pandemic challenges all churches and mission fields with tremendous changes and trials. However, it is clear that our sovereign God still loves us and works within us. Churches and missionaries should not be afraid, but rather pray and reflect on the essence of mission during this period. The partners of mission must engage in honest and sincere communication. In doing so, we need to identify the essence of the crisis and establish effective countermeasures. Now is also the time to proactively develop missionary strategies for the post-COVID era.

The essence of the crisis is the loss of relationship-centered community. Its recovery should begin with the restoration of trust between churches and missionaries through close communication. Churches and missionaries should first restore trust in the transaction of mission expenses. This trust will be restored when both the churches and the missionaries acknowledge their stewardship regarding money. If we implement missionary spending without the spirit of stewardship, we will confuse the purpose and the means, and in the end, it will be a burden to everyone. When churches suffer financially during the pandemic crisis, we should overcome the challenge with the spirit of stewardship. Although the COVID-19 pandemic is a huge crisis for the church and the mission world, I want to proclaim that it is an opportunity for us to change.

Chapter 19 Response

by Sun Man Kim

The COVID-19 pandemic is an unprecedented epidemic. However, the Bible already warned that infectious diseases would be one of the signs of the last days (Luke 21:11). In light of this, it was appropriate for Pastor Mongsik Lee to raise the necessity of changing our overall mission strategy. Mongsik Lee is convinced that participating in missions and living a missional lifestyle ought to be the native language of all Christians and that it is necessary for the church and all Christians to do so for the completion of the Kingdom of God.[5] He wants to give meaning to the coronavirus pandemic as an opportunity to establish the identity of the church and change its mission strategy, while at the same time reflect on how faithful the church has been to the essence of missions.

Necessity of Change in Mission Strategy in the COVID Era

Ralph Winter said that the essence of the Great Commission is that the survival of an enormous number of people depends on its fulfillment. Nevertheless, he pointed out that the question of obeying the Great Commission has always been poisoned by affluence more than by anything else. However, he stressed that "affluence did not stop Francis of Assisi from moving against the tide of his time," and emphasized that the way out of this is "reconsecration."[6] Therefore, we must think about the lifestyle that churches and missions ought to pursue in the era of the coronavirus pandemic, while also considering our spiritual warfare with Satan.

In the 1990s when the Korean church was actively involved in missions, the need for an elaborate mission strategy had already been raised, and seminars and studies were conducted accordingly.[7] Even into the twenty-first century, the Korean church has covered a wide range of issues related to missions strategy and missions responsibilities, such as the establishment of missions theology, methods of raising missions expenses, upper and lower limits of missions expenses, education for children of missionaries, pension plans after sabbatical and retirement, and financial reporting

---

5 In the sermon that he gave on January 17, 2020, entitled "New Year for Missional Life" (Mt. 28:18–20), Pastor Mongsik Lee stressed that *missions* is a strategic word and that Christians were called and made to live a missional life for the completion of the Kingdom of God just as Jesus was incarnated and lived among people (Mongsik Lee, "New Year for Missional Life" [Mattt. 28:18–20], JesusHeart.org, January 17, 2020, YouTube, http://www.jesusheart.org/index.php?mid=juil_sermon&page=2&document_srl=1034162).

6 Ralph D. Winter, "Reconsecration to a Wartime, Not a Peacetime, Lifestyle," in *Perspectives on the World Christian Movement: A Reader*, ed. Ralph D. Winter and Steven C. Hawthorne (Pasadena: William Carey Library, 1981), 814.

7 Han Heum Ok, "Mission Strategies of Korean Church" in *Korean Church and the World Mission*, ed. Bong Ho Son (Seoul: Books Publication Emmaus, 1990), 72.

and audit of mission expenses.⁸ A change in missions strategy in the pandemic era is of course necessary. But the basic issue for the spiritual fruitfulness of the ministry must also be addressed, namely, what does it mean to live as a disciple of Jesus?

David Adney wrote, "As true disciples of our Lord Jesus, we should be learning more and more of what is involved in living and be able to adapt to different situations."⁹ He said that if he goes back to the mission field, he wants to share life with the people in house churches, and learn from the local people who have experienced numerous sufferings about what it means to suffer for Christ. In an essay entitled "Lifestyle for Missionaries," he concluded that the missional lifestyle that would accomplish God's purpose involved learning from the locals and giving himself up for them.¹⁰ We cannot underestimate the disadvantages and challenges caused by an unprecedented pandemic. However, our concern must be on how deeply the missionary's lifestyle is related to the principle of Jesus's incarnation. With regard to the lifestyle of a missionary, Jonathan Bonk wrote, "Christ came for the poor as one of the poor and put himself in the same position as the poor."¹¹ In some ways, the incarnate lifestyle may be an unwise missionary strategy. But what Jesus said and demonstrated should be the principle and foundation of the lives of those who preach Jesus.

Restoring Trust between the Church and Missionaries through Communication

The spiritual and financial responsibilities of mission agencies, churches, and missionaries must be reinforced.¹² A few years ago, my former senior pastor praised a certain missionary. He said that when the missionary returned from speaking at a church, he provided a list of the financial contributions he had personally received from the event. But when the same missionary spoke at my church, he did not provide such a list. I was expecting one and was puzzled to see him just leave. Consistency in fundraising must be maintained at all times.

Here is another example. Missionary C from Southeast Asia completed the construction of the Jesus Vision Center in January 2021 and gave a financial report to his supporters. The project had begun in April of the previous year when COVID-19 was in full swing. Missionary C's financial report demonstrated transparency and integrity. The report showed contributions from thirty donors, including three donations from the missionary couple themselves, five anonymous donations, and donations from the sending church, the evangelism group of local churches, partner churches, etc. It even reflected the division of living and ministry expenses.¹³

Professor Jong-Sung Kim pointed out that the priority in the publication of missionary property rights should be on the calling of missionary ministry, and that there should be honesty and transparency in ministry and financial reporting, raising the need for the verification of missionaries' private property.¹⁴

Reassessment of Project Ministry

Mongsik Lee suggests that the "Don't ask" style of carrying out construction projects in the mission field should be reevaluated in light of the economic crisis brought on by the COVID-19 pandemic. Project ministry is inevitable based on the needs of the mission field. However, he believes that an examination of the "purpose and continuity" of a project's ministry as well as a transparent financial plan are in order. A lack (or imbalance) of these increases the missionary's dependence on the sending countries or agencies, and more seriously, may provoke the envy

---

8   For example, each of the KGMLF forums has resulted in Korean and English publications: (1) Jonathan J. Bonk et al., eds., *Accountability in Missions: Korean and Western Case Studies* (Eugene: Wipf & Stock Publishers, 2011); (2) Jonathan J. Bonk and Dwight P. Baker, eds., *Family Accountability in Missions: Korean and Western Case Studies* (New Haven: OMSC Publications, 2013); (3) Jinbong Kim et al., eds., *Megachurch Accountability in Missions: Critical Assessment through Global Case Studies* (Pasadena: William Carey Library, 2016); (4) Jinbong Kim et al., eds, *People Disrupted: Doing Mission Responsibly among Refugees and Migrants* (Littleton: William Carey Library, 2018); and (5) Jonathan J. Bonk et al., eds., *Missionaries, Mental Health, and Accountability: Support Systems in Churches and Agencies* (Littleton: William Carey Library, 2019).

9   David H. Adney, "Lifestyles for Missionaries," in *Perspectives on the World Christian Movement*, ed. Winter and Hawthorne, 808.

10 Adney, 812.

11 Jonathan J. Bonk, *Missions and Money: Affluence as a Western Missionary Problem*, trans. Hu Chun Lee (Seoul: The Christian Literature Society of Korea, 2010), 260.

12 Ban-Seok Lee, "Accountability Issues in Korean Mission Agencies," in *Accountability in Missions: Korean and Western Case Studies*, ed. Jonathan J. Bonk, Sang-Chul Moon et al., trans. Sang-Chul Moon, Namyong Sung, and Yong-Kyu Park (Seoul: Word of Life Press, 2011), 259.

13 Missionary C in country M, "Financial Report of the Jesus Vision Center," email sent on January 19, 2021.

14 Jong-Sung Kim, "The Historical and Theological Significance and Reflection on Property Management," 2019 Korean Missions KMQ Forum, May 31, 2019, http://kmq.kr/forum/677.

and jealousy of local leaders, leading to divisions on the mission field, or even corrupt the missionary.[15]

I think that project missions should be carried out if they are necessary, even in the pandemic era. Even if there is no pandemic, project missions that focus heavily on performance or quantity should be refrained from. In June 1885, missionary Mary F. Scranton came to Korea and began her educational mission at her residence. Teaching English to a government official's concubine for three months was the beginning of her mission. The first student to enroll in her class was a girl from an extremely poor family, and the next was a small beggar girl whose mother was left out as diseased under a bridge nearby. Four months later, she bought some thatched houses and built a new house on a vacant lot and opened the Girls' Institute and Women's Center.[16]

Her son, Dr. W. B. Scranton, reported to their home country that, "We [Mrs. M. F. Scranton and I] take pleasure in making Koreans better Koreans only. We want Korea to be proud of Korean things, and more, that it is a perfect Korea through Christ and His teachings."[17] The first people she served and taught in Korea were concubines, poor girls, and beggar girls, not daughters of high-ranking officials. She tried to help them to have a true identity in Christ. This was the beginning of Ewha Womans University.

The key lies in the incarnate way of life. In this way, missionaries should make indigenous Christians themselves participate in missions projects and lead them to manage and to evangelize their people. Professor Yong-Kyu Park pinpointed that the essence of the Korean church and the Nevius methods are rooted in Bible study based on discipleship training.[18] The methods of self-support, self-government, and self-propagation were fruits borne when they applied what they learned from the Bible. Even if it takes time, we must demonstrate missionary leadership that makes people take ownership. Times and circumstances have certainly changed. However, if it fits God's will, missions projects can be conducted anytime, anywhere.

In conclusion, the Great Commission of Jesus is a task that must be fulfilled across all times and situations. It has been entrusted by the Lord and will be accomplished by him. However, we must apply the spiritual principles shown by the Lord to our lives and ministry. I cannot forget the words of a missionary I know who had a painful conflict with the sending church: "In a nutshell, it was all about money."

The spirit of true stewardship does not lie in what or how much is done, but in what kind of person one should be; "Since everything will be destroyed in this way, what kind of people ought you to be?" (2 Pet. 3:11). No one can be perfect, but what matters is the fact that I keep on going to "press on to take hold of that for which Christ Jesus took hold of me" (Phil. 3:12).[19]

True beauty is found in the life of a modest steward who makes disciples of Jesus, rather than in impressive projects. I would like to conclude with the words of Professor Jonathan Bonk—"After all, Christian stewardship is not something we do, but something we become. Not a technique but a way of living."[20]

---

15 For example, a mission center complex was built in country B of South America by a Korean immigrant church in the US, the buildings and land worth several million dollars. One of his predecessors had used local leaders as her private subordinates and caused trouble among those living around the mission center; she had to ultimately be released from her position. Missionary K sighed over the phone, saying, "Most missionaries begin missions out of simple faith and commitment, but as finances grow and properties are added, essentials become nonessential and nonessentials become essential to them" (phone interview on March 12, 2012, with former missionary K who served in country B). In sharp contrast, in 2010, fifty Korean missionary families serving in the Philippines declared a memorandum of renunciation of property in the mission field and executed a transparent property handover (Ji Hee Lee, "For Advisable Property Management and Transfer," *Christian Today*, July 29, 2019, http://www.christiantoday.co.kr).

16 George Lak-Geoon Paik, *The History of Protestant Missions in Korea: 1832–1910* (Seoul: Yonsei University Press, 1991), 133–134.

17 W. B. Scranton, "Notes from Korea," *The Gospel in All Lands*, August 1888, 373.

18 Yong-Kyu Park, *History of the Korean Church I: 1784–1910* (Seoul: Word of Life Press, 2004), 614.

19 "Until we all reach unity in the faith and in the knowledge of the Son of God and become mature, attaining to the whole measure of the fullness of Christ" (Eph. 4:13).

20 Jonathan J. Bonk, *Missions and Money: Affluence as a Western Missionary Problem* (New York: Orbis Books, 1991), 131.

Chapter 20
COVID-19 and Opportunities in Mission: An Ibero-American Case Analysis

by Levi DeCarvalho

This report represents a first attempt to analyze the impact of the crisis on churches and missionary agencies in the Ibero-American world caused by the spread of the COVID-19 virus and subsequent governmental and institutional measures in the first months of 2020.

In light of this unprecedented event, our sending structures (both churches and agencies) have been surprised by the effects of the crisis, especially in the economic sphere, but not exclusively. Its effects also extend to the management of different projects, training programs for candidates, and assistance to field workers, besides fundraising and field supervision trips. In parallel, both churches and agencies have lived and participated in the pain caused by the most negative effects of the virus, in the loss of precious human lives, whether or not they share the same kind of faith that motivates us to serve in missions.

God is not surprised by anything or anyone; he is sovereign over all our circumstances. However, taking advantage of the forced isolation that we have had to live in, we have asked the Ibero-American churches and mission agencies to share with us their reactions, impressions, and actions in the face of the present crisis. The goals of the present research are to (1) understand the immediate effects of the present crisis on their activities, and (2) learn together how God is leading us in his mission in these new times.

This research was initiated by the area directors of COMIBAM, at the behest of its Executive Director, Decio de Carvalho—whom we thank for allowing us to participate in the setup of the research tool and its analysis. We extend our gratitude equally to all the Ibero-American churches and agencies that responded to our survey as well as the research team, thus constituted:
- Edilson Renzetti
- Fabio Rocha
- Sonia Mendes
- Levi DeCarvalho, PhD, Coordinator

Our hope is that this analysis will serve the sending structures of Ibero-America as they strive to perfect their participation in the missionary task that God has entrusted to us.

The Research

The following questions and answers summarize the participation of eighty-five Ibero-American sending churches and missionary agencies in the survey, promoted by COMIBAM International, with the aim of understanding how the crisis caused by the COVID-19 virus has affected them, both in its positive aspects as well as the challenges it has presented to them.

A total of eighty-five Ibero-American churches/agencies participated in the survey, distributed as follows:
- Spanish-speaking respondents—sixty-one churches/agencies
- Portuguese-speaking respondents:
    Portugal—two churches/agencies
    Brazil—twenty-two churches/agencies
    Countries represented:
        Argentina
        Bolivia
        Brazil
        Chile
        Colombia
        Costa Rica
        Cuba
        Dominican Republic
        Ecuador
        El Salvador Guatemala
        Honduras
        Mexico
        Panama
        Paraguay
        Peru
        Portugal
        Puerto Rico
        Spain
        (Hispanic) USA

Answers and Analysis

(Note: The NA stands for "Not applicable to our situation/I prefer not to answer.")

Question 1. How Has COVID-19 Affected Your Sending Church or Agency? Indicate Three of the Most Relevant Aspects, According to Your Perspective.

What follows is a representative compilation of the majority of the comments received through the survey. Participants indicated how the crisis had affected them at first:

1. Scarcity of financial resources
2. Anxiety (workers and supporters)
3. Need to reallocate finances
4. More intense communication
5. Suspended face-to-face activities
6. Some missionaries had to be sent "home" (risk situations)
7. Fear of the future
8. Forced limitations on field workers (mobility)
9. Personal relationships limited
10. Food shortage(s)
11. Some events and field projects suspended
12. More inquisitive candidates (doubts)
13. Postponement of training programs
14. Postponement in sending missionaries
15. Mobilization in churches is affected
16. Suspended trips
17. Devaluation of the national currency
18. Laying-off of personnel
19. Relatives of workers seek more information
20. More focus on the church and less focus on mission
21. Uncertainty of reaching the least reached

In general, the impact of the crisis has been negative for most churches and sending agencies. However, there are also positive aspects to the crisis, as can be seen below.

The negative aspects have to do mainly with the decrease in financial support of the workers. Another negative effect has been the impossibility of keeping the commitments assumed before the crisis, especially regarding the residential training of candidates, the sending of new workers, and direct contact with the churches and supporters. The devaluation of the currency in some countries represents an additional burden on the finances of churches and sending agencies, in addition to the justified concern on the part of the workers' families in the "sending" countries of origin. It is a common fact that the finances designated for missionary work are the first to be affected in times of economic crises, which is the case right now. Adding to all this is the forced repatriation of some workers, in many cases against their will, which constitutes a complex but not hopeless situation, as can be seen below.

Question 2. What Measures Have Your Church or Agency Taken to Contain the Spread of COVID-19 among Workers? Indicate the Three Main Measures.

The following contagion prevention measures have been adopted by different churches/agencies, in different combinations:

1. Following health/government authorities' policies and regulations
2. Promote healthy eating habits
3. Donation of protective materials
4. Cancellation of all types of face-to-face meetings
5. Continuous contact with workers and administration personnel
6. Cancellation of all international travel
7. Formation of crisis relief teams
8. Group (cell) meetings through Facebook
9. Working from home
10. Online/video Bible study/training
11. Work shifts in the offices
12. Distribution of cleaning and protection materials
13. Restricted access to indigenous areas (due to the low immunity of indigenous populations)
14. Devising emergency plans
15. Education/training focused on protective measures and contagion prevention

Basically, governmental and organizational measures have been applied, with the aim of avoiding as much as possible the spread of the virus within the churches and agencies themselves, as well as among workers on the field.

Question 3. What Impact Has This Crisis Had on the Field Ministries? You Can Select More Than One Option.

Out of a total of eighty-five respondents—it was allowed to choose more than one answer—the following figures represent the diversity of problems encountered: (Note that the sum of the indices exceeds 100 percent, because the question admits more than one answer.)

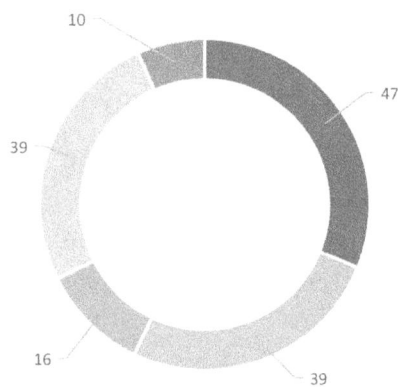

- Forty-seven respondents reported that they have been prevented from continuing their field ministries.
- Thirty-nine respondents are still seeking more information on the impact of the crisis on their fields of work.
- Sixteen respondents informed us that some of their workers have suffered discrimination for being foreigners.
- Thirty-nine respondents indicated that there is massive unemployment, including among national Christians.
- Ten respondents also indicated that health systems in the field have collapsed, with infections and deaths, including among missionaries and church leaders.

The fact that just over half (forty-seven churches/agencies) are unable to continue with their field ministries in itself indicates the seriousness of the situation that we all face in the current crisis. There are those who prefer not to advance specific reports (thirty-nine) because the data have not yet reached them, for various reasons. Although the news of infections and deaths (ten) is not alarming, it is worrying because it adds one more problem to those caused by massive unemployment (thirty-nine) and the collapse of health systems in some cases. Add to this the information that there are workers suffering discrimination for being foreigners (sixteen).

Question 4. How Have Your Field Workers Reacted to the Crisis?

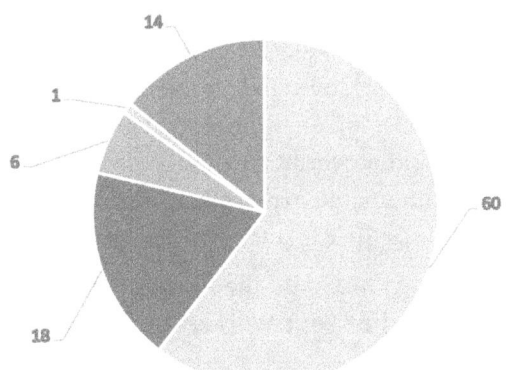

- Sixty percent indicated that the majority of their workers feel encouraged to continue in their field of work, even with limitations.
- Eighteen percent are still seeking information on their field situation.
- Six percent reported that some of their workers feel encouraged to continue working but others are discouraged and wish to return to their countries of origin.
- Only 1 percent indicated that the majority of their workers feel discouraged and are unable to work.
- NA = 14 percent.

It is encouraging that 60 percent of those surveyed reported a positive attitude of their workers to continue on the field. Apparently, 32 percent (18 + 14) do not yet have reliable information or prefer not to speculate on the matter.

Question 5. How Could This Situation Affect Your Church or Agency's Commitment to Support Field Missionaries?

Of the eighty-five agencies/churches surveyed, six do not have field workers. The remaining seventy-nine are found in one of the following situations:
- In good standing or using savings available for another two to six months: fifteen (19 percent)
- Still seeking information on the situation: thirteen (16.5 percent)
- In a bad financial situation: fifty-one (64.5 percent)

Nineteen percent of the sending structures are in a more or less balanced situation. On the other hand, the crisis has already negatively affected 64.5 percent of the sending agencies/churches. We anticipate more data from churches/agencies that are still seeking more reliable information on their current financial situation (16.5 percent).

Comments by some of the respondents:
- "Some workers have required support for an early return from the field, which had not been budgeted. Other workers have required additional support for emergency supplies and to be able to follow a required quarantine in place."
- "There is a lack of electronic money transfer services."
- "Our mission advertising has stopped."
- "Church members struggle with unemployment."
- "No full support could be sent; only minimal support has been made available. This has produced discouragement for some workers."
- "The value of the dollar is up, which affects the support of the churches and networks. Additionally, designated offerings for missionaries have decreased notably, due to the [initial] physical closure of the churches."
- "The churches have a lot of financial difficulties, because there are no resources to support the missionaries. They are prioritizing supporting the national pastoral teams."
- "Our income has dropped, and we may not be able to send out all the support we used to."
- "A major financial crisis has not yet been experienced in our country and in our fields, although this scenario may change in the coming [months], given that the government is anticipating a national financial crisis soon."

Candidates:
"At the moment, those who are studying have [sufficient funds] for the next few months, but they know that the economic crisis will hit later, when the church reduces their [offerings] or the emergency funds run out."

A dramatic case:
"[The present crisis] is already affecting us negatively in view of the fact that the churches are struggling to raise offerings, which in Argentina are made 80 percent in cash."

Positive comments:
- "The churches have done a good job in building the character of the workers. Furthermore, they are mature churches, so we are not being greatly affected in this area. Churches as well as workers and candidates have a positive outlook, just as before or even better now."

- "We believe that [our situation] will not be affected. We have enough savings for this year. However, we do not know the impact [the crisis will have] on the mission finances for next year."
- "Income for administrative and ministerial needs of our Missions Department have fallen between 50 and 60 percent approximately but we have begun to see God's provision in action."
- "The information we have and our analysis [of the situation] tell us that in the near future (May through July) our income may decrease. However, so far electronic transfers have increased, and people are sending in their offerings and tithes. We trust that [the crisis] will not stop us from honoring our financial commitments."

Question 6. In Case of a Drastic Economic Change, Does Your Agency or Church Have an Alternative Support Plan for Your Workers?

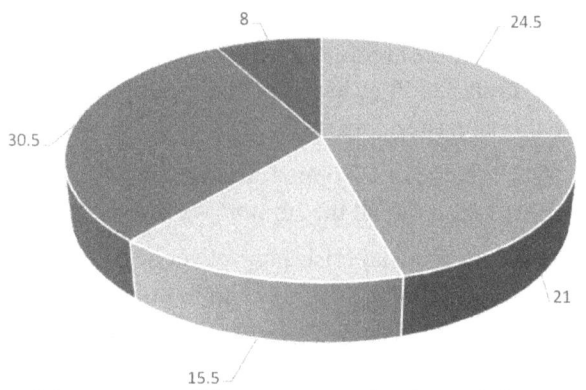

- 24.5 percent of those surveyed indicated that their finances are fine, because they have set up emergency funds.
- Another group declared that they are in a negative situation at the present time, either because they have not made alternative plans (21 percent) …
- … or because their emergency funds are insufficient (15.5 percent).
- Another 30.5 percent are looking for alternative sources of financing for their workers and projects.
- NA = 8 percent.

Of the total, 67 percent of the churches and agencies surveyed (adding 21 + 15.5 + 30.5 percent) are in a difficult situation, economically speaking. Critical situations require drastic amounts of reflection, planning, and action. Hence the importance of the following questions.

Note: The answers to questions 5 and 6 are equivalent. In question 5, a total of 64.5 percent of the respondents indicated problems in the area of finances, while in question 6 that total reaches 67 percent. In other words, two-thirds of those surveyed are facing an unanticipated situation due to the virus crisis, as far as their finances are concerned.

Question 7. How Could the Present Situation Affect the Stay of Your Workers on the Field?

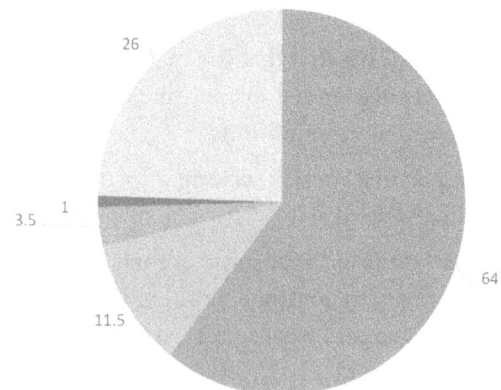

- Sixty-four percent of churches and agencies initially desire all their workers to remain in their fields of work.
- Another 11.5 percent say they may have to repatriate a small group of workers.
- 3.5 percent indicated that they will be able to repatriate or relocate their workers in other fields.
- One percent say they will have to repatriate most of their workers.
- NA = 26 percent.

The attitude of the majority of the churches and agencies surveyed is positive: 64 percent desire that their workers continue ministering in their fields of work. The possibility of repatriation of workers is small, if we add those who entertain this idea: 16 percent (11.5 + 3.5 + 1 percent). Repatriation can be balanced by relocating the workers elsewhere, until the crisis subdues in some of the fields at least. However, the NA group (which preferred not to answer the question) may tip the balance in favor of one or the other of the strategies mentioned here. The decisions of the churches and agencies must be monitored carefully even into the first months of 2021.

Question 8. What Are the Three Most Important Lessons Learned in Other Times of Crisis That You Think Might Apply to the Present Situation?

Respondents shared with us lessons learned from past experiences in various crises. Here is a condensation of those lessons:

1. Internal (in-group) fellowship is important
2. Communication is key
3. Crises are inevitable
4. Crises are opportunities (nationals/locals may open their hearts)
5. Crises teach us something
6. Crises foster intimacy with God
7. Dependence on God
8. Flexibility
9. Emergency funds [are a must]
10. Humility
11. Intercession is essential
12. Linking with other agencies is key
13. The worker is more important than the project
14. Do plan for emergencies ("plan B")
15. Being is more important than doing
16. God is sovereign
17. We must have peace of mind in the storm

Comments made by the respondents:

- "Constant and fluid communication is essential."
- "[Crises] are times to be in God rather than to do things for God."
- "Unity with other organizations [is essential] for mutual support."
- "Crises always bring new opportunities and provoke creative ideas to carry out the mission."
- "[We must be] flexible to promote drastic changes when confronted [with crises]."
- "Do not depend only on church offerings to stay on the field."
- "Spend more time in intimacy with God to more accurately understand the steps to follow."
- "The work is God's. [Crises] enable us to depend on God and not on our projects."
- "Field partners who care for and supervise workers are essential."
- "Field teams and workers with support nearby have greater stability [in times of crises]."
- "Having a bivocational profile is key for those who want to go out as missionaries."
- "To be proactive is essential in emergencies and circumstances with high volatility."
- "[We should be careful not to] overemphasize temple-based spirituality."
- "[The common man] has no hope in times of crisis."
- "Humility."
- "Gratefulness."
- "We can continue to serve the Lord in any circumstance."
- "Be faithful in sending [financial] support to the workers."
- We have plans to change the world, but God has the final answer."
- "God is in control, always."

The key issue in the measures adopted during the crisis has been communication—with workers, donors, and intercessors. Communication implies promoting dialogue, transparency, and open information about the needs and situations experienced by the workers and those who send them. Above all, obviously, there must be dependence on God, who is the Lord of the harvest and who sends and sustains his own people, whatever their situation. Here, too, communication is key, through prayer, supplication, and intercession.

Question 9. As an Agency or Church, What Plans Are You Making to Start a New Stage of Missionary Initiatives After the Present Time of Limitations? Indicate Your Three Main Ideas or Plans.

The main ideas or plans that have emerged as a result of the current crisis are the following:

1. Virtual Cross-Cultural Training School;
2. Emphasis on financial support by electronic means;
3. Development of high security software (communication);
4. Search for alternative health plans on the field;
5. Reduce operating costs for the central office;
6. Training of professional workers;
7. Virtual mission trips;
8. Webinars;
9. Intercession in virtual groups;
10. Sale of items to increase income (coffee, mugs, T-shirts);
11. Develop virtual discipleship in missions;
12. Emphasis on training a new generation of leaders;
13. Management via the internet;

14. Search for new models of missionary mobilization;
15. Biblical teaching focused on missions;
16. Broadcast interviews with missionaries through social media;
17. Enhance our comprehensive missionary care program;
18. Make the agency more visible (openness);
19. Join the social assistance programs set in place by our country as an agency;
20. Missions through the internet;
21. Ensure that all members have emergency funds for 2–3 months;
22. Create a "Work/Job Agency" for missionaries to carry out bivocational work;
23. Prepare candidates for extreme situations.

During the present crisis, churches and agencies have not been paralyzed in their ministry of recruiting, training, sending, and sustaining their workers. Rather, the crisis has prompted church and agency leaders to seek new ideas and strategies to expand missionary work, rather than shortening their activities and planning. The attitude has generally been realistic but positive.

Question 10. How Could COMIBAM Help You Achieve These New Missionary Initiatives? Suggest One or Two Ways of How We Could Help You.

The position of COMIBAM as a unifying movement and a catalyst of missionary efforts in the Ibero-American world is strategic, especially due to its capacity to serve according to the needs felt by the sending structures in each country. The present research has highlighted this supportive role, enhanced by the crisis we all face, locally and globally. The main requests for support shared by the respondents are as follows:

1. Carry out virtual training events.
2. Share resources or webinars.
3. Maintain an active dialogue among the entire missionary community.
4. Do not duplicate but multiply efforts ("strategic alliances").
5. Provide insurance information for workers—health, emergency evacuation, etc.
6. Provide training in managing digital networks and secure remote communication.
7. Provide training in comprehensive remote missionary care.
8. Compile and distribute sound agency policies, emergency plans, crisis responses (health, safety/security, etc.), financial matters, comprehensive care policies, etc.
9. Provide manuals as examples so that agencies can take them into account.
10. Carry out forums to exchange ideas.
11. Advertise and mobilize toward unreached ethnic groups.
12. Spread the work done by our missionaries to elicit more prayer.
13. Suggest an Ibero-American outlook regarding our potential and limitations in view of the changing times.
14. Present innovative strategies that are born from national movements.
15. Provide digital tools for these times.
16. Promote seminars/workshops to disseminate innovative initiatives to attract financial resources.
17. Help BAM initiatives to become more mature and more group oriented.
18. Intensify the message that the church is the great supporter of missionary work.
19. COMIBAM leaders could teach in our training programs.
20. Promote virtual meetings among mission leaders from various nations for the exchange of experiences, learning, and cooperation.
21. Promote research on churches to know their attitude regarding God's mission.
22. Create virtual spaces to share ideas on how to respond to the present crisis.
23. Facilitate virtual training for bivocational workers and community development projects.
24. Facilitate connection with ministries that hire professionals.
25. Facilitate contacts with investors interested in "businesses for the Kingdom" and community development projects.
26. Open a virtual space for missionary intercession.
27. Promote specific training in missionary administration and care.
28. Share contingency plans and security protocols.
29. Conduct surveys with field missionaries in light of the present crisis.
30. Carry out studies of missionary mobilization in times of pandemics.
31. Provide international channels and sources of information that could be useful for decision-making in crisis situations.

Notes

1. The research was limited to the perspectives of the leaders of the "sending structures"—churches and mission agencies. We are in the process of researching the perspectives of our field workers to understand the impact of the crisis on their lives and ministries.

2. The present survey measured the *initial* effects of the crisis on the sending structures. A second phase of the research will be necessary, so that we can understand how the structures have adapted to the "new normal" after the initial shock of the pandemic.

3. Furthermore, it will be necessary to compare the perspectives of both the senders and field workers in order to obtain a more realistic picture of the Ibero-American missionary movement at a global level.

4. Ideally, the Global South might consider dialoguing about our responses to the pandemic on the basis of similar research projects.

Chapter 20 Response

by Byung Soo Lee

What should be the Christian perspective on COVID-19? The Christian attitude toward COVID-19 should be twofold. First, we should see it as God's judgment and live a life of reflection and repentance. The reason is that when God's people sinned in the Bible, he gave them three types of punishment: the sword, the famine, and the plague. Second, we must view everything to be under the sovereignty and providence of God and take this pandemic as an opportunity to call for a new paradigm shift in missions. From such a viewpoint, DeCarvalho's chapter showed us how Ibero-American churches and mission agencies were navigating the crisis caused by COVID-19.

Main Thesis

DeCarvalho's chapter is a case study of the impact of COVID-19 on local churches and mission agencies in the Ibero-American community during the first months of 2020. Based on the surveys of those working in various churches and institutions, this chapter presented alternatives and measures to turn crises into opportunities. COVID-19's impact on the Ibero-American churches and missionary institutions is nearly identical to Christian communities worldwide. Thus, this report is also highly relevant and helpful to Korean churches and mission agencies.

A Summary of the Report

In this report, eighty-five churches and mission agencies participated in the survey composed of ten questions. The content of the report is summarized as follows: (1) the economic crisis and the response; (2) the importance of national, collective, and personal hygiene measures; (3) the importance of care for missionaries to relieve psychological and mental anxiety and fear of the present and future; (4) the importance of communication between churches and mission agencies and among missionaries to overcome the economic crisis and physical and mental difficulties; (5) the importance of people-oriented mission rather than project-oriented mission and the importance of focusing on fellowship and spirituality rather than on programs; and (6) utilization of virtual space and prayer over the internet. Also mentioned were strategy meetings, missionary retraining, leadership training, recruiting and educating missionary candidates, and alternative programs. Finally, this report emphasized that all crises and changes are within God's sovereignty and providence and that an active, flexible, and positive attitude is required to turn these crises into opportunities.

Strength

The report listed various problems faced by the churches and mission agencies and their respective solutions. In particular, the report approached the difficulties experienced by missionaries from an economic and psychological viewpoint and presented practical guidelines to deal with them. One of the recommendations for the restrictions on mobility and face-to-face meetings was to utilize virtual space. Missionary work in the online environment will be essential during and after the pandemic, but it also has its limitations. Thus, online missionary work should be balanced with a heightened focus on godliness and spirituality. In the future, a fusion of spirituality and technology will be deemed very important in missions.

This report highlights the importance of maintaining a balance between God's sovereignty and human responsibility concerning COVID-19.[1] It affirms that God is not affected by any circumstance or person and that God, the Lord of all things and history, is sovereign and works even in a pandemic in the ever-changing missionary context. As this is the biblical and theological foundation, we cannot stop doing mission but must continue to carry out our mission.

Therefore, prayer is the most crucial thing in the present situation for all of us in churches and mission agencies. We must reject the idea influenced by the Enlightenment mindset that we can do anything with our strength by mobilizing our reason, material means, and everything we have.[2] Instead, we must acknowledge that everything depends on God's sovereignty and pray with the power of the Holy Spirit— "Not by might nor by power, but by my Spirit" (Zech. 4:6).

---

1 J. I. Packer, *Evangelism and the Sovereignty of God* (Downers Grove: InterVarsity Press, 2008).

2 David J. Bosch, "Mission in the Wake of the Enlightenment," chap. 9 in *Transforming Mission: Paradigm Shifts in Theology of Mission* (Maryknoll: Orbis, 1991).

First, churches and missionaries need to pray for the mission field. Second, churches should pray for missionaries and mission agencies. Third, missionaries should pray for their families and their spirituality, and above all, for the church. The reason is that the church is also facing severe difficulties—spiritually, numerically, and economically—amid COVID-19. Apostle Paul as a missionary asks the Colossians to pray: "Devote yourselves to prayer, being watchful and thankful. And pray for us, too, that God may open a door for our message, so that we may proclaim the mystery of Christ" (Col. 4:2–3). We can do missionary work only when God opens the door for evangelism. In missions, we must pray with total dependence on God's sovereignty.

However, we should note that this report emphasizes not only God's sovereignty but also human responsibility. This is reflected in the two purposes of the report: (1) to understand the immediate effects of the present crisis on their activities, and (2) to learn how God is leading us in his mission during these times. In his book *A Study of History*, British historian Arnold Toynbee wrote that human history is the history of challenges and responses. This report described the responses of churches and mission organizations to the challenges of COVID-19 as human responsibilities. It also presented COMIBAM's role in helping Ibero-American churches and mission agencies fulfill their God-given missionary responsibilities. Finally, it shared the insights they gained in coping with the current crisis. In other words, it made an important contribution to the Eastern and Western churches, the universal church as the body of Christ.

Question

The financial impact of COVID-19 has been very significant on churches and mission agencies, as the responses from fifty-one churches and mission agencies indicate. Regarding the economic impact of COVID-19, I have several comments and questions. First, from a Korean perspective, Western missionaries' responses regarding finances are candid and straightforward. Second, from the missiological and sociocultural point of view of Koreans, it seems a bit excessive that Western missionaries should mention financial difficulties due to COVID-19. (If Korean missionaries would have responded similarly regarding these financial issues, they would also have been somewhat excessive.) Doesn't this show that they are influenced by a capitalist mindset? Jonathan Bonk also emphasizes this aspect in his book *Mission and Money*. What would be Dr. DeCarvalho's view in this regard? Reflecting on how the early church prevailed through extreme physical and economic difficulties with the power of the cross and the resurrection, we need to ask ourselves whether what we need in the COVID-19 crisis is to return to the mission of the apostle Paul and of the book of Acts and reclaim the essence of mission.

Conclusion

As a case study, "COVID-19 and Opportunities in Mission" is relevant to the Korean situation. It suggests ways to turn the difficulties, alternatives, and crises under the pandemic into opportunities. The practical insights in the chapter are beneficial and applicable to all churches and mission organizations in this land. I want to express deep gratitude and respect for the hard work of the researchers who have published this excellent case study.

Chapter 21
Mission, Fiscal Responsibility, and Care for the Environment

by Allison Howell

As a missionary with SIM Ghana, I was struck during my first trip to northern Ghana by the beauty of immense forests and the cleanliness of towns and villages that I passed through. Swimming in the clean ocean water was pleasurable. Over the years, however, the ancient tall trees of the forests rapidly disappeared. I observed beaches destroyed through rising sea levels. They also were polluted with litter, especially plastic waste, both on land and in the water. Discarded plastic products even lay around the grounds of some churches and Bible schools and littered open spaces.

Illegal mining in Ghana has exacerbated pollution of rivers and destroyed forests and farmlands. Christians and churches sometimes participated in these activities, and some churches directly profited from widespread environmental devastation with such monies going into church projects.[1]

Humanity's resource consumption is unsustainable. Beyond the economic impact, it has a profound ecological impact. Missionaries are part of the consumer culture wherever we are located. This culture invariably contributes to injustice not just towards the environment, but significantly, also towards the poor.

Dave Bookless argues that "biblically, the mission of God's people is incomplete, distorted and stultified if it does not include demonstrating God's care for all creation."[2] However, even though missionaries live in a world that increasingly is being exhausted, I have found that whenever these issues are raised in mission and church circles, a frequent response people give is that the work of the Gospel is preaching, saving people, individual redemption, and discipleship. Rather, "government or aid agencies should care for the environment." Some see investing resources in caring for the environment as an irresponsible use of mission finances.

---

1 Christopher Affum-Nyarko, "Theology, Human Need and the Environment: An Evaluation of Christian and Traditional Responses to Illegal Mining in Ghana" (MTh diss., Akrofi-Christaller Institute of Theology, Mission and Culture, Akropong-Akuapem, 2016), 56–57, 100–105, 115.

2 Dave Bookless, "Context or Content? The Place of the Natural Environment in World Mission," in *Missional Conversations: A Dialogue Between Theory and Praxis in World Mission*, ed. Cathy Ross and Colin Smith (London: SCM Press, 2018), loc. 397 of 5170, Kindle.

My purpose is to examine the biblical and missional basis for the care of creation, models of approach in associated activities, and some examples in mission history. Finally, I will examine how we as consumers can model responsible behavior while caring for the environment as a vital part of Gospel proclamation and discipleship.

Biblical and Missional Basis for Care for Creation

God's word moves from creation to new creation. In responding to the issue of care of the environment, people understandably begin with the story of God's creation in Genesis 1 and 2. God's creation was good. Humanity was created on the same day as the animals. They were all "living creatures" (*nephesh ḥayah*) and had the same breath of life. The distinction, however, is that humanity was created in God's image and given a responsibility reflected in Genesis 1:28. Connotations of the terms "dominion" and "subdue" have led some to accuse Christians of complicity in exploiting the environment.[3] A careful study of the words leads rather to an understanding of responsible care, especially when linked with Genesis 2:15 where God places the man in the Garden of Eden "to work it and take care of it." For many, this highlights humanity's responsibility for creation, hence the use of the term *stewardship* to describe the nature of this task.

A close reading of the story of Job and God's response, particularly in Job 38–41, gives a deeper perspective. Samuel Balentine suggests that God's speech from the whirlwind was not a rebuke but rather "a radical summons to a new understanding of what it means for humankind to be created in the image of God." God does not require silence and submission, but "steadfast lament and relentless opposition to injustice and innocent suffering, wherever it appears." Balentine describes Job as "a supreme model for humankind that God is committed to nurture and sustain."[4]

One key aspect of this model is drawn from the revelation concerning Behemoth. God told Job, "Look at Behemoth, which I made just as I made you" (Job 40:15, NRSV). This huge creature was a model for Job, and like Behemoth, Job was endowed with regal qualities, strength, and life-generating power.[5] God uses this creature to point to a model of worthy partnership between God and Job and, by implication, for humanity. In Job's response to God's revelation, we see a man who experienced undeserved suffering. Yet Job was not silenced. Rather, God gave him freedom and confidence to interact with him and be his partner. In any environment where human injustice occurs, this model goes beyond stewardship. It rather suggests a responsible *partnership* with God in creation care.

In both Genesis and Job, we see that God owns and sustains all creation. Within creation everything is interrelated including the relationship between humanity and creation. If something happens to one aspect of it, then all relationships are disrupted. When Adam and Eve disobeyed God, this opened the way for the abuse of creation. Evidence of creation suffering is depicted in Romans 8:18ff. Yet within the mission of God, the impact of Jesus's death and resurrection reaches beyond humanity, for "through him God was pleased to reconcile to himself all things, whether on earth or in heaven, by making peace through the blood of his cross" (Col. 1:20, NRSV). This reconciliation is for all of creation, including humanity being reconciled with God.

In partnership with God, humanity is to be involved in bringing reconciliation with and in creation, and in reconciliation with others. Not all humanity understands the call to reconciliation. Only those who understand it, accept the mandate, and actually work to carry it out are able to see the relationship between God's reconciliation of creation and the care of the environment. This is a profound message for those involved, as ambassadors, in the mission of reconciliation (2 Cor. 5:11–21). It also enables missionaries to respond to the perception that some Christians have that this earth will one day be destroyed, in which case, there is no point bothering about caring for creation. This, however, is an inadequate reading of the word "new," particularly in 2 Peter 3:10–13 and Revelation 21:1. The word "new" implies a new creation in the sense of "renewal" and "transformation," when the groaning of all creation stops, the waiting for the redemption of the sons of God ends, and God completes the reconciling of all things to himself.

---

3 Lynn White, "The Historical Roots of Our Ecologic Crisis," *Science* 155 (1967): 1203–1207.

4 Samuel Balentine, "What Are Human Beings That You Make So Much of Them?" in *God in the Fray: A Tribute to Walter Brueggemann*, ed. Tod Linafelt and Timothy Beal (Minneapolis: Fortress Press, 1998), loc. 3338-3344 of 5172, Kindle.

5 Walter Brueggemann, *Gift and Task: A Year of Daily Readings and Reflections* (Louisville: Westminster John Knox Press, 2017), 303.

It is therefore important to emphasize that in Scripture we have a biblical basis for the involvement of Christian missions in the care of creation through a model of partnership with God.

Mission Involvement with the Environment

Throughout mission history, churches and missions have been involved with environmental issues and care of creation. For centuries, the Ethiopian Orthodox Tewahedo Church has been preserving sacred forests in a context where deforestation has increased through competing land uses and climate change.[6]

Since the late 1970s, Christian missions and the church have been increasingly more concerned with caring for the environment. Pope John Paul II named Saint Francis of Assisi the patron saint of ecology and called Christians "to restore to creation all its original value."[7] This initiated activity in Catholic churches that has expanded since Pope Francis's 2015 encyclical, *Laudato Si': On Care for Our Common Home*.[8]

Churches working through the World Council of Churches (WCC) agreed in 1989 that "justice, peace and the integrity of creation"[9] were interwoven and required action from the Church. In 2004, American evangelical leaders pledged to "make creation care a permanent dimension of our Christian discipleship."[10] In 2010, at the Cape Town Lausanne III and Edinburgh 2010 conferences, participants made commitments related to creation care as part of Christian witness.[11] WCC Arusha Conference participants pledged in 2018 "to care for God's creation, and to be in solidarity with nations severely affected by climate change in the face of a ruthless human-centered exploitation of the environment for consumerism and greed."[12]

In the 1980s, individual Christians and small groups responded to environmental issues by founding organizations such as A Rocha, a Christian nature conservation organization,[13] and ECHO, a Christian organization focusing on community development and agriculture.[14] Christian relief and development agencies such as World Vision, Tearfund, and Christian Aid also began to address issues of climate change and the environment in their programs.

Increasing documentation is now emerging specifically on mission and church involvement in the care of creation and the environment, stemming from various global consultations.[15] The Lausanne Movement in partnership with the World Evangelical Alliance has established a creation care network.[16]

---

6   David K. Goodin, Alemayehu Wassie, and Margaret Lowman, "The Ethiopian Orthodox Tewahedo Church Forests and Economic Development: The Case of Traditional Ecological Management," *Journal of Religion and Society* 21 (2019): 1-23. See also Dana L. Robert, "Historical Trends in Missions and Earth Care," *International Bulletin of Missionary Research* 35, no. 3 (July 2011): 123–129; Lowell Bliss, "Environmental Mission: An Introduction," in *Creation Care and the Gospel: Reconsidering the Mission of the Church*, ed. Colin Bell and Robert S. White (Peabody, MA: Hendrickson Publishers Marketing LLC, 2016), 73–92, Kindle; and (Sam) R. J. Berry, "Creation Care: A Brief Overview of Christian Involvement," *Creation Care and the Gospel*, 140–159.

7   Quoted in Allan Effa, "The Greening of Mission," *International Bulletin of Missionary Research* 32 (October 2008): 171.

8   Pope Francis, *Laudato Si': On Care for Our Common Home*, encyclical letter, Vatican website, May 24, 2015, http://www.vatican.va/content/francesco/en/encyclicals/documents/papa-francesco_20150524_enciclica-laudato-si.html.

9   Effa, "The Greening of Mission," 172.

10 Effa, 173.

11 "The Cape Town Commitment," Third Lausanne Congress 2010, Lausanne Movement, accessed November 18, 2020, https://www.lausanne.org/content/ctcommitment; "The Common Call," Centenary of the 1910 World Missionary Conference, Edinburgh 2010, accessed November 18, 2020, http://www.edinburgh2010.org/fileadmin/Edinburgh_2010_Common_Call_with_explanation.pdf.

12 See "The Arusha Call to Discipleship," Conference on World Mission and Evangelism 2018, World Council of Churches, accessed November 18, 2020, https://www.oikoumene.org/resources/documents/the-arusha-call-to-discipleship. See also, Kenneth R. Ross, *Mission Rediscovered: Transforming Disciples, A Commentary on the Arusha Call to Discipleship* (Geneva: WCC Publications and Globethics.net, 2020), 59–68.

13 See "Projects," A ROCHA INTERNATIONAL: Conservation and Hope, accessed November 18, 2020, https://www.arocha.org/en/projects/. Further examples are in Bell and White, *Creation Care and the Gospel*; and Amy Ross, "Creation Care Around the World: Grounded Engagement," in *Missional Conversations: A Dialogue Between Theory and Praxis in World Mission*, ed. Cathy Ross and Colin Smith (London: SCM Press, 2018), loc. 617–640 of 5170, Kindle.

14 Bell and White, *Creation Care and the Gospel*, 217–218.

15 Bell and White. See also Andrianos Louk et al., *Kairos for Creation: Confessing Hope for the Earth*, The "Wuppertal Call"—Contributions and Recommendations from an International Conference on Eco-Theology and Ethics of Sustainability, Wuppertal, Germany, June 16–19, 2019 (Solingen: Foedus, 2019), 259–261, Vereinte Evangelische Mission (website), accessed January 31, 2020, https://www.vemission.org/fileadmin/redakteure/Dokumente/JPIC/Cairos_for_creation.pdf.

16 See "Creation Care," Lausanne Movement, accessed November 19, 2020, https://www.lausanne.org/networks/issues/creation-care.

A Movement of Farmer Managed Natural Regeneration

In the early 1980s, Christian missionaries with Serving in Mission (SIM) in Niger were confronted with badly deforested and degraded land due to decades of problematic attitudes and practices. In addition to projects that aggravated the land situation, drought led to famine. As a result, missionaries commenced an integrated response that included tree planting, energy-saving cooking stoves, small gardens, pit latrines, mulching, composting, cassava cultivation, and planting pits.

The reforestation program had little impact due to hostility and indifference from people in the communities and the sheer physical difficulties of achieving seedling survival in a harsh environment. Moreover, raising and planting seedlings was a costly process. Tony Rinaudo, a SIM missionary responsible for the reforestation in Niger at the time, realized that what they were doing would have little impact. He felt the situation was hopeless. However, once while driving to some villages with seedlings, he stopped to deflate his tires. Surveying the barren landscape, he prayed. "I asked God to forgive us for destroying the gift of his beautiful creation, knowing that much of the suffering and hunger people were experiencing directly related to environmental degradation, and I asked God to open my eyes and to show me what to do."[17] Rinaudo suddenly noticed a small bush growing nearby. On closer examination, he realized that it was in fact a tree that had been cut down. It was resprouting. And he knew he had discovered the solution. Millions of similar bushes testified to "the fact that a vast underground forest existed just beneath the surface of that seemingly barren landscape."[18] Actually, there was no need to plant trees.

Rinaudo began promoting "Farmer Managed Natural Regeneration" (FMNR). By working in partnership with the church and with farmers, he realized the need to be involved with the technical, social/cultural, and policy dimensions of reforestation. They encountered difficulties with getting people to change their practices and attitudes. More significantly, he discovered that a movement emerged that was not a "project." When enough farmers were convinced about the approach, it spread. Other organizations saw the benefits of the approach and encouraged it.

When Rinaudo relocated to Australia in 1999, he had not realized the full implications of the impact of this approach in Niger. It would take twenty years for him to see the vast changes that had occurred. By 2016, FMNR was being practiced on six million hectares across Niger. What occurred was not just reforestation—people also benefited in other ways. Independent studies show that widespread reforestation occurred in Niger because of the movement that began in the context of a Christian mission and a missionary's prayer. There have been other benefits such as: reclaimed land for crop production; improved soil fertility; return of some wild fauna; increased diversity of tree species; increased harvests; new food export markets; increased income and self-reliance, particularly for women; and improved social status for women.[19]

Rinaudo points out that "what happened in Niger was not a technological breakthrough and it was not reliant on enormous injections of money. It was a people's breakthrough."[20] He took up work with World Vision Australia where he introduced the approach and they began to promote it in various countries throughout the world.[21]

Although the approach depends on having living tree stumps and seeds in the soil, the movement itself has enormous potential within Christian mission, for it reflects Christians partnering with God. Although the materials currently produced on FMNR have no specific statement linking this approach with the Gospel, the spread of FMNR ideas provides a base for proclaiming the Good News of the Kingdom, nurturing believers in their faith, showing loving care to those in need, and transforming the unjust structures that hinder people's well-being. This is a model for Christian mission that cares for the environment.

---

17 Tony Rinaudo, "Discovering the Underground Forest," in *Tony Rinaudo—The Forest Maker*, ed. Johannes Dieterich (Zurich: Rüffer & Rub, 2018), 60–61.

18 Rinaudo, 60.

19 Manish Bapna, "Turning Back the Desert: How Farmers Have Transformed Niger's Landscapes and Livelihoods," in *World Resources 2008: Roots of Resilience—Growing the Wealth of the Poor*, UNDP, UNEP, World Bank and World Resources Institute - July 2008: 143, https://www.wri.org/publication/world-resources-2008, September 7, 2020.

20 Rinaudo, "Discovering the Underground Forest," 91.

21 See https://fmnrhub.com.au/resources/.

A Model for Christian Mission in the Twenty-First Century

In 1990, the Anglican Consultative Council expanded their definition of mission to include a commitment "to strive to safeguard the integrity of creation, and sustain and renew the life of the earth."[22] Their definition of mission became known as "The Five Marks of Mission,"[23] and provides the framework for a model for mission. These "Five Marks of Mission" are namely: "to proclaim the Good News of the Kingdom; to teach, baptize, and nurture new believers; to respond to human need by loving service; to transform unjust structures of society, to challenge violence of every kind and pursue peace and reconciliation; and to strive to safeguard the integrity of creation, and sustain and renew the life of the earth."[24]

Although presented as separate points, these "marks" are not necessarily definitive. Moreover, they are essentially interwoven within each other. For example, "striving to safeguard the integrity of creation, and sustaining and renewing the life of the earth," can be part of proclaiming the Good News of the Kingdom. Many Christians and churches do not seem to grasp the intersection of the two—proclaiming the Gospel and caring for the earth's natural resources—which actually form an integral part of God's creation. For some, "proclamation" means preaching a message that limits the Gospel to saving a human's soul from hell, crusades, deliverance sessions, all-night vigils, and large offerings. Jesus, however, is the Lord of all creation, and if Jesus came to reconcile to himself all creation, this is good news. Whether hearers accept the Gospel or not when this good news is proclaimed, they hear about their need to respond to the Lord Jesus Christ and their responsibility to care for creation.

In teaching and nurturing new believers, instructing on creation care is a vital aspect of discipleship training. People, however, cannot teach what they have not learned. New Christians often are not taught about care of creation because their teachers have not the slightest clue about it. In developing biblical teaching materials for all ages, it is important to include material that helps Christians grow in their understanding of God's view of creation and the ways in which humans can partner with God in caring for creation. For those in rural communities, this instructing and nurturing can incorporate teaching on farming practices that enhance productivity of crops, and show a caring awareness of land, vegetation, and water. In urban areas, churches can seek to revitalize polluted land or play an advocacy role in preserving the environment against misuse. Participating in practices that contribute to creation care thus becomes a formative part of growing as a disciple of Jesus.

Caring for creation also forms part of a loving response to human need that often arises because the environment a person lives in has been exploited by others. Following his experience in Niger, Rinaudo stresses the importance of caring when he states, "We will be successful at restoring the vast areas of the world's degraded farm and forest land when we learn to walk alongside those whose livelihoods depend on these areas, and together learn how to repair and maintain them, all the while restoring peoples' sense of pride and self-worth in the process."[25] This point is relevant whether it is in a rural area or a degraded urban environment.

This then means that caring for creation also has a role in transforming unjust structures in society. Willis Jenkins calls for "an ecology of mission."[26] One task includes critiquing inhumane environmental responses that lead to human suffering, such as when people are driven off their land to make way for a nature park without discussion or provision for their welfare. This contrasts with situations where affected groups are incorporated into the planning stages of such a development. Another task is connecting human dignity and environmental quality. Missions and the church have a role to play in confronting structures of sin that lead to polluted air and water, use of dangerous chemicals, and depleted and eroded soils that result in human/social degradation.[27] They also have a responsibility to respond to these problems in a way that restores human dignity. A further possible task is to be a prophetic voice to respond to governmental policies and corporate corruption that result in or cause environmental oppression. Rinaudo found in Niger that advocacy

---

22 Jesse Zink, "The Five Marks of Mission," *Journal of Anglican Studies* 15, no. 2 (June 2017): 145.

23 Andrew F. Walls and Cathy Ross, eds., *Mission in the Twenty-first Century: Exploring the Five Marks of Global Mission* (Maryknoll, NY: Orbis, 2008).

24 Zink, "The Five Marks of Mission," 145.

25 Rinaudo, "Discovering the Underground Forest," 91.

26 Willis Jenkins, "Missiology in Environmental Context: Tasks for an Ecology of Mission," *International Bulletin of Missionary Research* 32, no. 4 (2008): 178.

27 Jenkins, 178.

became necessary to change government laws to avert discrimination against those who practiced FMNR.[28]

From both biblical and missional perspectives, our role in mission is one of partnering with God in safeguarding, sustaining, and renewing creation. If we do not have all the skills to carry out the tasks, it means working in partnership with others and co-opting those who know how to assist us in formulating policies and implementing the tasks related to the care of creation and the proclamation of the Good News of the Kingdom of God.

Environment and Missionary Fiscal Behavior

The Gospel of Jesus Christ interacts with and impacts culture and the environment. When we as missionaries understand the extent of this spiritual engagement, we will realize that funds required for the training of personnel or the production of materials related to the care of the environment form part of a bigger picture. They are resources that can contribute to the effective mission of God in any context.

There are several issues with respect to missions, the environment, and fiscal behavior. The first one is when the lifestyle, residence or even children's education of missionaries portrays irresponsible consumerism as they live within a financially and environmentally struggling host community.[29] Personal and family behavior as consumers has consequences. It also impacts resources we use and how we consider even basic matters like the type of accommodation we reside in. Missionaries need to model responsible consumerism and embody an approach that shows they are "worthy missionary disciples"[30] who care for God's creation in a way that enables others to come to know God and adopt a modest lifestyle.

The second issue is the importance of missions and churches modeling responsible consumerism in the styles of buildings. They need to be environmentally friendly using materials that fit in with the creation around them. To create a prayer camp in a forested area by bulldozing off all the trees and topsoil, then building concrete structures and paths after trucking in new topsoil for a garden is irresponsible behavior and reflects a lack of creative planning.

The third one is that the missional call to sustain and renew the life of the earth does require financial resources. As Rinaudo has demonstrated, often resolutions of environmental problems do not require large amounts of money. Prayer is part of this process in the search for creative solutions as well as discussion with knowledgeable people.

Investment in training resources and courses to educate Christians about environmentally responsible behavior is a vital part of this process and of extending the Kingdom of God. This needs to be in the annual budget of a mission, church, or theological college.

Moreover, it is important to source for funds and employ personnel skilled in creation care issues to work with communities in which they live. Where Christians are highly motived to do something because they love the Lord and the world he has created, they will volunteer time and effort to clean, restore, and recreate the surrounding environment. Churches and missions can also partner with communities and people of other faiths, thus demonstrating God's love for them and his world to bring about reconciliation within creation.

Finally, in God's interaction with all creation throughout history and through the role of the Spirit of God, we see the growth of a movement in the lives of people in which reconciliation serves as the central purpose of Christian mission. This mission incorporates sustaining, renewing, and caring for all of God's creation.

---

28 Rinaudo, "Discovering the Underground Forest," 74.

29 Jonathan J. Bonk, *Missions and Money: Affluence as a Missionary Problem ... Revisited*, rev. and exp. ed. (Maryknoll: Orbis Books, 2006), 173–175.

30 Risto Jukko and Jooseop Keum, eds., "The Arusha Conference Report," in *Moving in the Spirit: Report of the World Council of Churches Conference on World Mission and Evangelism*, March 8–13, 2018, Arusha, Tanzania (Geneva: WCC Publications, 2019), 11.

Chapter 21 Response

by Bright Myeong-Seok Lee

I came to know Prof. Allison Howell as my PhD dissertation supervisor at the Akrofi-Christaller Institute of Theology, Mission and Culture (ACI). Howell had for a long time served as a single female missionary of SIM for the Kasena tribe in the northern part of Ghana in Africa, and her firsthand experience in the mission field shows through in her article. Most significantly, she witnessed for herself countless instances of environmental destruction persisting in Ghana every day, which drove her to pursue possible solutions and translate her convictions into action. Her extraordinary passion to care for God's creation has the power to draw people in.[31] The article she presented is no exception.

A New Understanding of What It Means to Partner with God in Creation Care

Howell lists three purposes for her article—"to examine the biblical and missional basis for the care of creation, models of approach in associated activities, and some examples in mission history." I will respond to each point in order.

The Scripture passages Howell sites as the biblical and missional basis are Gensis1-2 and Job 38-41. Challenged by the historian Lynn White's assertion that the Christian tradition caused today's ecological crisis, biblical scholars and theologians reexamined the original meaning of Genesis 1-2. There was a need to correct misunderstandings in the interpretation of the passage, which resulted in mistaken notions of ecology. They then rediscovered the call for stewardship of creation that differs from the traditional biblical interpretation.

Ecotheologians have devoted relatively less attention to Job 38–41. Howell cites Samuel Balentine's work that provides a new interpretation of the creature Behemoth and what God intended to teach Job through this creature. As Howell mentions, Balentine draws out a new sense of human responsibility by reading the passage through the lens of creation.[32] The Behemoth's characteristics described in Job are seen as a new model of creation care, a "model of worthy partnership between God and Job and, by implication, for humanity."

Ecotheologians have generally conceived of the human role in creation care as faithful stewards who recognize God's ownership of creation. But the new interpretation of the Behemoth in the book of Job calls humans to be more than stewards, even to partner with God. God's call to partnership is not unique to the passage in Job. God radically calls Abraham "my friend" in Isaiah 41:8. In John 15:15 Jesus does not call his disciples servants but friends.[33] This means humans are not simply God's lesser creation who should passively implement divine commands. The rediscovery of the function of the Behemoth helps us realize that the Trinitarian God gave humans the free will to make their own choices, thereby creating us as worthy partners of God. If the stewardship call emphasizes the vertical relationship with God, the Behemoth image emphasizes a more

---

31 For example, Howell used to live in Kuottam Estates in Oyarifa, Accra. It used to be covered with discarded waste, but it was transformed into a park surrounding a small lake, and was named Allison's Greens (Australian High Commissioner, Ghana, *Allison's Greens*, video, https://www.facebook.com/AustralianHighCommissionGhana/videos/2779250912092983).

32 Samuel Balentine, "What Are Human Beings That You Make So Much of Them?" in *God in the Fray: A Tribute to Walter Brueggemann*, ed. Tod Linafelt and Timothy Beal (Minneapolis: Fortress Press, 1998), loc. 3340-3415 of 5172, Kindle.

33 James 2:23 also says, "Abraham believed God, and it was credited to him as righteousness, and he was called God's friend."

active human role as partners with God.

This shift in perspective is significant in multiple ways. First, a Behemoth-like partnership with God emphasizes human agency and implies an even stronger sense of responsibility. But such a conception of Behemoth-like human identity would seem foreign in the East Asian cultural context where traditional vertical and hierarchical relationships remain strong. Whether the call to partnership or the call to stewardship works better for creation care in contexts like South Korea with a Confucian philosophical background remains to be seen.

Secondly, in the second section on mission involvement with the environment, Howell gives examples of interchurch organizations. These collaborations call for the church to not only carry out its directives as servants in God's vineyard but to take even more creative approaches in caring for God's creation.

Third, Howell introduces the former missionary of SIM, Tony Rinaudo, and his Farmer Managed Natural Regeneration (FMNR) movement. Rinaudo discloses how this new movement started with prayer. Up to that point in time, ecological movements and scholarships had had rarely been associated with the Christian spirituality of prayer. Rinaudo's prayer is significant because it shows how God's creation and human society are interconnected. Such Christian spirituality is in line with the ecospirituality of St. Francis of Assisi before the Enlightenment.[34] It also fits well with the Asian conception of ecology that pursues the coexistence of heaven, humanity, and nature.[35]

The challenge Rinaudo faced was "the tradition of free access to trees on anybody's property and a code of silence protecting those who cut down trees."[36] This local tradition can also be found in Korea during the Chosŏn Dynasty in the fourteenth century,[37] which served to prevent any exclusion from the use of natural resources, regardless of land ownership. Such a tradition works well when resources are plentiful. However, severe discord may follow when there is an imbalance between supply and demand. The challenge is to break the cycle of imbalance in supply and demand. The FMNR movement discovered a crucial principle in responding to this challenge—to motivate the local inhabitants to cooperate in the reforestation project, they had to be convinced of its real and material benefit. FMNR is minimally dependent on external financial aid. Operating a self-sustaining project in Africa without the support of external finances was also significant in another aspect, the sense of pride and self-respect it brought to the local inhabitants. Only as the partnering local inhabitants take pride in their own environmental movement can it be sustainable.

Howell cites a new dimension of Gospel proclamation. In the past, the conception of Gospel proclamation had neglected to preach the good news of ecological preservation and spurring responsible action for such cause. The Good News goes beyond individual spiritual salvation and includes our more vulnerable neighbors' salvation of their ecosystems.

On discipleship, Howell also significantly points out that "people cannot teach what they have not learned." In this regard, Howell has not only taught behind the lectern but has become a role model by her work on the urban environment. As the surrounding environment improves, the local inhabitants' sense of dignity is enhanced. This is not something the church community can achieve on its own. The issue is closely linked with government policies. In other words, the church's sustained cooperation with the secular government has become an essential part of the church's mission.

In the section on "Environment and Missionary Fiscal Behavior," Howell suggests increased partnership with the local inhabitants through prayer and discussions, investment in education, and human resource development for community volunteers. On this matter, I must point out that Howell neglects to mention conflicts between local indigenous governance and the national government on the usage of natural resources. For example, illegal gold mining by Chinese companies is a significant

---

34 Johannes Jörgensen and T. O'Conor Sloane, *St. Francis of Assisi: A Biography* (New York: Longman, Green and Co., 1957), 314–315.

35 Yo Han Bae, *The Divine-Human Relationship in Korean Religious Traditions* (Saarbrücken: VDM Verlag Dr. Müller Gmbh & Co. KG, 2010), 63–77.

36 Tony Rinaudo, "The Development of Farmer Managed Natural Regeneration," *Leisa Magazine* 23, no. 2 (June 2007): 33.

37 The Chosŏn dynasty instituted *Sanrimchuntaek Yeminkongji* (山林川澤 與民共之), which literally means the benefits of mountains, rivers, and reservoirs should be shared among people. The Chosŏn dynasty regulated people so that they would not privatize mountains, rivers, and reservoirs but belong to the government as the Commons (Sun-kyung Kim, "A Study of the Sajŏm of Sanlimchontack in the Late Chosŏn Dynasty" [PhD diss., Kyunghee University, 1999], 14–61).

problem in Ghana, resulting in severe environmental destruction.[38] The church community that has earned the trust of local indigenous governance must spread awareness in the local community that long-term harm from environmental destruction far outweighs short-term economic gains. On a larger scale, the church community must include the secular government as the target of mission and as a God-given partner in environmental protection. The church must play a key role in environmental policy-making in partnership with the government. This is the lesson the era of COVID-19 teaches us.

---

[38] James Boafo, Sebastian Angzoorokuu Paalo, and Senyo Dotsey, "Illicit Chinese Small-Scale Mining in Ghana: Beyond Institutional Weakness?," *Sustainability* 11, no. 5943 (2019): 1–18.

Conclusion

Even a perfect environmental protection policy cannot succeed without the cooperation of the local inhabitants. Howell makes the novel case for a self-directed and internally motivated movement rather than one dependent on external financial investment for sustainable environmental preservation in the majority world. To achieve this, a system should be put in place to prevent the exclusion of the local inhabitants from decision-making and to invite them to participate in discussions as cooperating partners and sharers in the benefits of protecting the Commons.

The church's role must now expand to include local indigenous governance and the national secular government in Gospel proclamation and discipleship, inviting them as partners in cooperation with God working toward peaceful coexistence with creation.

Chapter 22
Toward a Money-Missionary Relationship Model: A Grounded Theory Approach Based on the Empirical Data of Korean Missionaries

by Jooyun Eum

The purpose of this study is to theoretically explain the money-missionary relationship of Korean missionaries. To achieve this goal, this research attempts to discover the patterns of actions and interactions in the relationship between missionaries and money, and proposes a contextual model of the impact of money on missionary life and ministry.

The grounded theory methodology was adopted for this research because a conceptual framework suitable for the impact of money on the life and ministry of Korean missionaries has not yet been clearly identified. Furthermore, since Korea's missiological inquiry into this field has not been fully carried out, it is impossible to determine suitable and unsuitable variables. Therefore, the grounded theory methodology may be an appropriate research methodology for the purpose of this study.

Research Questions

The following research question and subquestions were set up for further research aimed at improving the abovementioned research problems.

Research Question

To what extent does money impact a missionary's life and ministry?

Research Subquestions

1. What are the problematic characteristics and dynamics of money under a set of perceived conditions among Korea missionaries and what are the underlying factors?

2. What are the strategies devised to manage, handle, carry out, and respond to the problematic characteristics and dynamics of money?

3. What factors shape, facilitate, or constrain the strategies that take place within a specific context?

4. What model of the relationship between money and missionaries can be derived that reflects the missionary's spiritual, emotional, relational, and practical reactions to money?

Research Methodology

Grounded theory methodology refers to an analysis method in which researchers derive general and abstract theories[1] about certain processes or actions based on the perspectives of participants.[2] The researcher classified and interpreted empirical data through the steps of open coding, axis coding, and selective coding.[3] Finally, the researcher proposes a context model that examines how contextual conditions (causal, contextual, intervening) affect outcomes through action/interaction.

Data Collection

In this research, participants were selected according to the theoretical sampling method.[4] Therefore, the researcher adopted the method of selecting the next interviewee to expand the theory based on the analysis of the first sample of ten participants.

The researcher selected a respondent who was expected to have considerable information on the subject as the first interviewee for the research. In order to confirm that the concepts, subcategories, and categories that emerged at this time could be truly representative, the researcher selected future interviewees based on the main characteristics of the participants.

Data Saturation

When conceptualization and categorization are saturated, the relationship between categories stabilizes so that data are no longer needed, and subcategories are no longer added. At this point, the researcher may conclude the interviews. After analyzing the data from interviews conducted with forty-seven participants, the researcher decided that this goal had been reached and discontinued further interviews.

Research Reliability and Validity

In qualitative research, reliability and validity are obtained by enhancing the trustworthiness, rigidity, and quality of the research. The researcher took the following steps to ensure the reliability and validity of this study: (1) individual discussions were conducted with related majors to avoid being buried in the subjective values of researcher and interview data. In this process, the researcher tried to find the weakness of the logic of the acquired empirical data; (2) the researcher reviewed the existing literature and made efforts to maintain sensitivity to the subject of analysis;[5] (3) from the initial stage of the analysis, memo and drawing were used to observe the entire analysis process; (4) in order to secure intersubjectivity, opinions of experts and scholars in the field were listened to and reflected on in the research. Specifically, to achieve this goal, two fellow missiologists and one theologian monitored the procedure and method of this study, as well as the data analysis and interpretation, and presented their views.[6]

---

1 Anselm Strauss and Juliet Corbin, *Basics of Qualitative Research: Techniques and Procedures for Developing Grounded Theory*, 2nd ed. (Thousand Oaks: SAGE Publications, 1998).

2 Melanie Birks and Jane Mills, *Grounded Theory: A Practical Guide*, 2nd ed. (London: SAGE Publications, 2015); Antony Bryant and Kathy Charmaz, "Grounded Theory Research: Methods and Practices," in *The SAGE Handbook of Grounded Theory*, ed. Antony Bryant and Kathy Charmaz (Thousand Oaks: SAGE Publications, 2007), 1–28; Kathy Charmaz, *Constructing Grounded Theory: A Practical Guide through Qualitative Analysis* (London: SAGE Publications, 2006); Anselm Strauss and Juliet Corbin, *Basics of Qualitative Research: Grounded Theory Procedures and Techniques* (Newbury Park: Sage Publications, 1990); Kathy Charmaz, "Grounded Theory: Objectivist and Constructivist Methods," in *Handbook of Qualitative Research*, 2nd ed., ed. Norman K. Denzin and Yvonna S. Lincoln (Thousand Oaks: Sage Publications, 2000), 509–535.

3 Noella Mackenzie and Sally Knipe, "Research Dilemmas: Paradigms, Methods and Methodology," *Issues in Educational Research* 16, no. 2 (January 2006): 193–205.

4 Barney Glaser and Anselm Strauss, *The Discovery of Grounded Theory: Strategies for Qualitative Research* (New York: Aldine de Gruyter, 1967); Strauss and Corbin, *Basics of Qualitative Research: Grounded Theory Procedures and Techniques*.

5 Jooyun Eum, "Does Money Promote Missions?: Paternalism and Dependence," in *Mission Research*, 84th ed., ed. Jinsuk Byun (Seoul: GMF Press, 2020), 17–29; Hwalyong Kim, "Paradigms on Mission Fund in the Korean Mission," in *Korea Missions Quarterly*, ed. Namyong Sung (Seoul: Mission Times Press, 2015) 55:15/1: 90–101; Hyojin Kim, "Mission Fund: Mission Fund Policy of the Missional Church," in *21st Century Mission*, ed. Editorial Department of Moksin (Seoul: Duranno Academy, 2010), 303–305.

6 Along with the researcher, Jinsuk Byun (PhD), Ulhee Cho (DMiss), and Hyochan Kim (PhD), who are professors at the Global Missionary Training Center (GMTC) in Seoul, South Korea, provided informative perspectives and insights for this study.

Ethical Guidelines

The researcher explained the purpose and method of the study, and informed the study participants that they were free to withdraw at any time. Each research participant signed a consent form. This form included a confidentiality agreement, a statement about safeguarding the privacy of each participant, and a statement that the researcher would be held responsible for disclosing personal information whether intentionally or negligently. All research participants were given pseudonyms to protect their privacy. Interviews were recorded with prior consent, and the parts of the transcribed interview data that were not related to the study were deleted.

Research Findings

Open Coding

Through the analysis of the grounded data, fifty-four concepts were obtained, and as a result of grouping similar concepts, twenty-eight subcategories and eleven categories were revealed.

Axial Coding

Axial coding is a recombination of data in a new way by linking concepts, subcategories, and categories to build a paradigm model. Table 22.1 summarizes the paradigm model for the relationship between money and missionary life and ministry.

Table 22.1: A Conditional Matrix of the Impact of Money on Missionary Life and Ministry

Concepts	Subcategories	Categories	Paradigm
Moderate scale of life	Ideal and reality	Dual aspects of money in missions	Causal conditions
Concern about unexpected spending			
Longing for an affluent life	Greed and contentment		
Pursuing a way of life of gratitude			
Goal-oriented ministry	Active fundraising and faith mission		
Relationship-oriented ministry			
Guilty feelings	Well-being life	Level of satisfaction with living expenses	Contextual conditions
Skepticism	Financial deficit		
Anxiety			
Incarnational spirituality			
Patron-Client dynamics	Superiority and inferiority		
Superiority complex			
Poor retirement measures	Insecurity		
Altruism	Sense of mission to practice charity	Level of satisfaction with ministry expenses	
Social engagement			
Power relationship	Longing for more ministry with more money		
Paternalism approach			
Living with a sense of satisfaction with the current economic situation	Positive outcome	Emotional ambivalence	Central phenomenon
Anxiety about the future	Negative outcome		
Cautious about luxury	Missionary values and beliefs	Missionary identity	Intervening conditions
Self-examining the missionary motive			
Duty of financial report	Policy and regulation		
Obligation to comply with organizational rules			

Trust in God	Prayer and contemplation	Spiritual response	Action/Interaction strategies
Seeking God's will			
Seeking God's providence			
Servanthood	Stewardship		
Frugality			
Managing resources for the glory of God			
Keeping a heart of gratitude	Emotional control	Emotional response	
Seeking for inner peace			
Self-reflection	Integrity	Relational response	
Clear conscience			
Righteousness and justice			
Readjustment of income and expenses	Self-evaluation	Practical response	
Tighten the budget	Readjustment		
Anger	Anxiety	Negative results	Results
Frustration			
Skepticism			
Vicious circle of dependency	Dependency		
Paternalism			
Materialism	Triumphalism		
Hypocrisy and pride			
Opportunism			
Loss of confidence	Defeatism		
Loss of self-esteem			
Trust in God's promises	Trust in God's provision	Positive results	
Plain living	Missionary life formation		
Low-cost and high efficiency lifestyle			
Information exchange	Smart spending		
Having professional advice	Missionary welfare		
Develop a retirement plan			
Exemplary Christian lifestyle	Exemplary life		
Exemplary Christian ministry			

The following (figure 22.1) is a schematic diagram of a paradigm model of a missionary's perspective on money. This paradigm model is an associative framework that links subcategories with their categories shown previously in table 22.1.

Figure 22.1: Paradigm Model of the Impact of Money on Missionary Life and Ministry

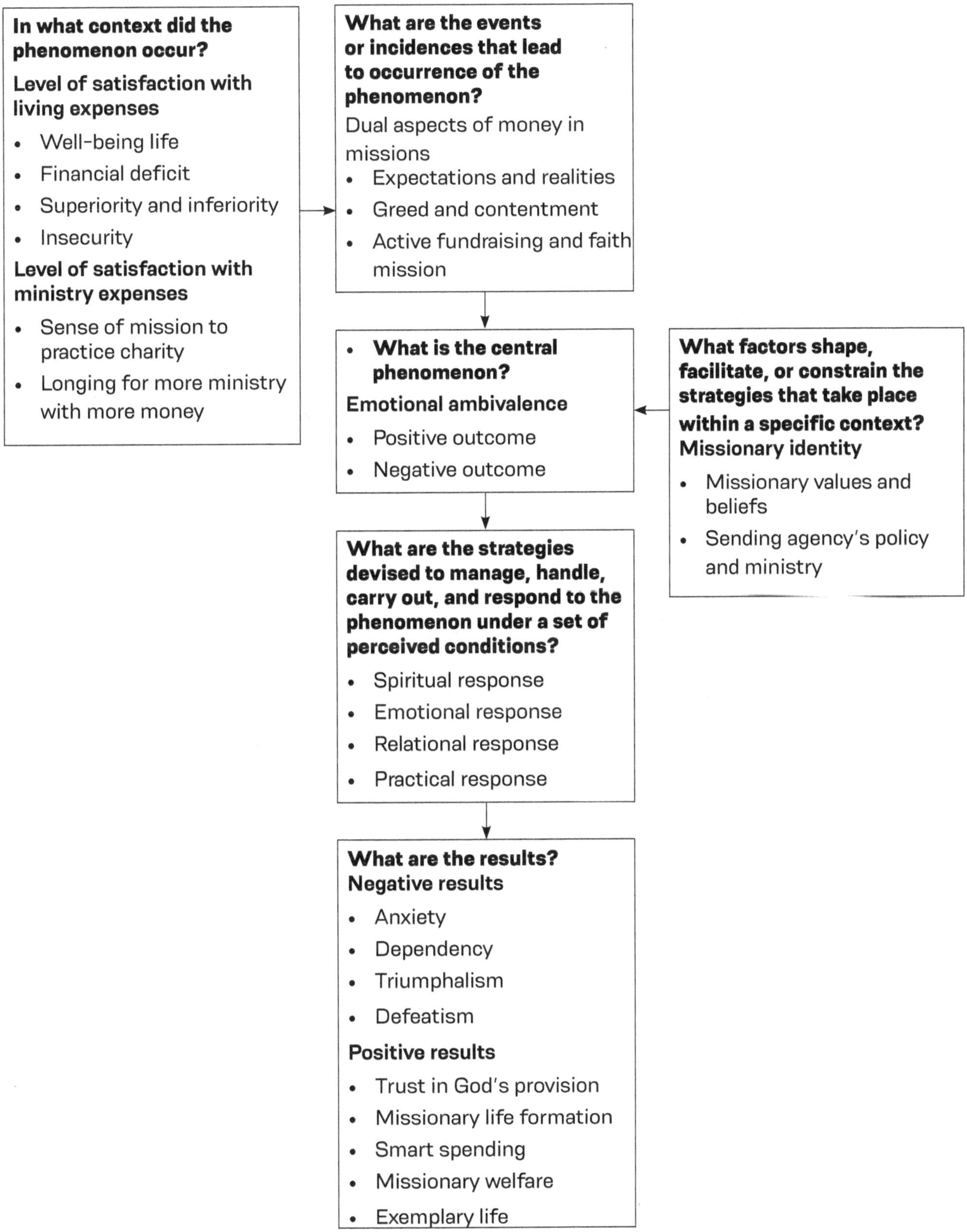

In what context did the phenomenon occur?

Level of satisfaction with living expenses
- Well-being life
- Financial deficit
- Superiority and inferiority
- Insecurity

Level of satisfaction with ministry expenses
- Sense of mission to practice charity
- Longing for more ministry with more money

What are the events or incidences that lead to occurrence of the phenomenon?

Dual aspects of money in missions
- Expectations and realities
- Greed and contentment
- Active fundraising and faith mission

- **What is the central phenomenon?**

Emotional ambivalence
- Positive outcome
- Negative outcome

What factors shape, facilitate, or constrain the strategies that take place within a specific context?

Missionary identity
- Missionary values and beliefs
- Sending agency's policy and ministry

What are the strategies devised to manage, handle, carry out, and respond to the phenomenon under a set of perceived conditions?
- Spiritual response
- Emotional response
- Relational response
- Practical response

What are the results?

Negative results
- Anxiety
- Dependency
- Triumphalism
- Defeatism

Positive results
- Trust in God's provision
- Missionary life formation
- Smart spending
- Missionary welfare
- Exemplary life

Selective Coding: Presenting a Grounded Theory on the Money-Missionary Relationship

Storyline. In the selective coding stage, a storyline was created about the relationship between money and the missionary in order to present a grounded theory for the impact of money on missionary life and ministry. After that, the conditional matrix (table 22.1) and the paradigm model (figure 22.1) were combined to present an integrated narrative outline and the researcher selected the core category.

The integrated narrative outline. Missionaries are generally satisfied with the regular missionary funds they receive. They have theological and emotional conviction that God has called them to participate in his mission. Furthermore, they have a firm belief that the God who calls missionaries will provide for their financial needs. Therefore, they are satisfied and grateful for the missionary funds that they receive regularly from their mission agencies as God's provision. In particular, they have a feeling of sympathy and even guilt for having a richer life than the common people in their mission contexts.

However, in real life and ministry, missionaries feel that the mission funds provided are insufficient. They recognize that the money they need for everyday life is sufficient, but rent for housing and education fees for children are insufficient. The biggest problems with money can be summed up into three things. First, there is not enough money reserved to cope with unexpected situations. Second, because the funds for living and ministry are not clearly separated, when the cost of ministry is covered by living expenses, they feel short of both. Lastly, although missionaries are satisfied with their current mission funds, they feel a considerable degree of concern and anxiety regarding retirement measures.

When it comes to money, the missionary does not feel completely happy or unhappy. Missionaries have feelings of satisfaction and gratitude, but are not completely free from anxiety and nervousness. Sometimes, even the feelings of satisfaction and gratitude they have are not purely their own, but attitudes that have been heavily influenced by theology or values.

However, missionaries implement a variety of response strategies to overcome negative emotions that arise in the face of these money-related challenges. Spiritually, the missionary strives to keep a heart of contentment and prayer for God's supply. Emotionally, missionaries try to counteract negative feelings with gratitude and inner peace. Relationally, they endeavor to reinforce the integrity of their relationships with supporters and churches through a clear conscience, consumption that reflects God's righteousness and justice, and self-reflection. And practically, they try to improve their awareness of money and spending habits by realigning their income and expenditure according to priorities and reducing the amount of their spending. Missionary identity influences the responses to overcome the multifaceted challenges related to money. Specifically, their responses reflect the values and beliefs they hold as missionaries, and the financial policies and rules of the sending agencies and churches.

Nevertheless, these various responses do not automatically produce positive results. A significant number of missionaries still live unfree of money concerns. Rather than relying on God himself to supply money, some missionaries live by relying on money. In addition, some missionaries become obsessed with triumphalism when money is abundant, and defeatism when it is insufficient.

The vast majority of missionaries responded in a variety of ways in the face of money-related challenges with positive results. Missionaries have more confidence in God's provision than in the past in their missionary careers, and they take on the role of stewardship of God's money in all areas of life and ministry. A plan for the future is also established through restructuring of the mission fund under the advice of experts. And they practice life and ministry that model an exemplary lifestyle for the common people they meet in their mission contexts.

From the above integrated narrative outline, the core category of the influence of money on missionary life and ministry is, "Epistemological and practical transformation of money and mission by spiritual, emotional, relational, and practical correspondence."

A Proposal for a "Money-Missionary Relationship Model"

The researcher intends to develop a "model of the relationship between money and missionary" by diagramming the factors derived from analyzing the evidence. To reach this goal, elements were identified among the various categories and attributes presented in empirical data, which were suitable for diagramming the relationship between money and missionary.

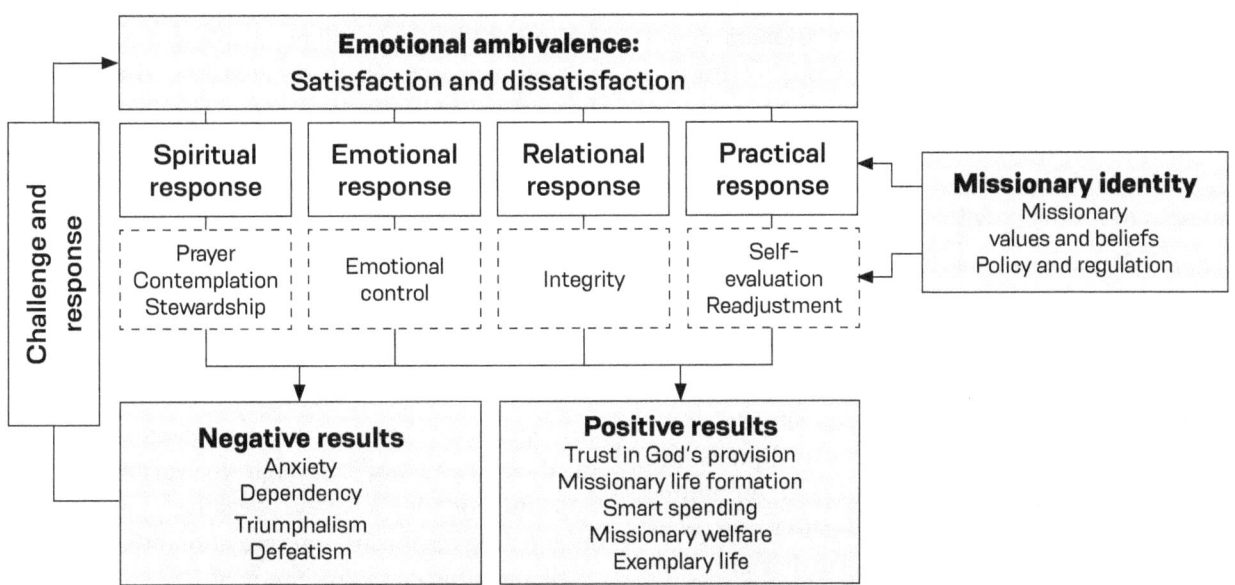

Figure 22.2: Money-Missionary Relationship Model

The researcher selected the ambivalence of satisfaction and anxiety as the central phenomenon of the missionary in relation to money, and placed it at the top of this model. In the middle of the model, missionaries' various responses were classified into four categories. The four subcategories in the broken line boxes differentiate specific practices that accompany each type of response. These responses with their specific practices are influenced by a missionary's identity. The researcher placed missionary identity on the right and used arrows to indicate the influence. The researcher divided the results of the four responses and practices into two broad categories and included them in a solid gray box at the bottom of the model. In addition, these results were again linked to the core category at the top by using an arrow, placed on the left side of this model, meaning that they repeatedly impact the missionary's ambivalence toward money.

A Provisional Grounded Theory Based on Empirical Data

The Inner Conflict between Satisfaction and Dissatisfaction

Missionaries have been taught to move away from greed for money and have a heart of gratitude for God's supply. In fact, according to the empirical evidence, they have a genuine appreciation for God's provision. At the same time, they have a sense of obligation to be content in any financial situation. The sincerity of satisfaction and the sense of duty are intertwined, leading them to emotional ambivalence that they must be satisfied without worrying about situations where they cannot actually be satisfied. This is the cause of many missionaries experiencing psychological stress, but having difficulty properly expressing or resolving it. There is a need for community support where it is acceptable for missionaries to be honest about their emotional state in relation to money.

Methodical Conflict in Financial Supply

Missionaries do not abandon the ideal expectation of God's provision for their daily living and ministry. However, when that expectation is different from reality, missionaries try to reconcile the tension between the two through active fundraising and/or waiting for God's answer through prayer. According to this grounded theory study, missionaries prefer to wait for God's supply in prayer or to review and readjust their current financial situation, rather than actively pursue additional fundraising activities to meet their financial needs. Some of the participants in this study believe that complete dependence on God's provision and faith in answered prayer was a more mature, spiritual approach than active fundraising. This trend reflects that Korean missionaries prefer to rely on irregular ministry funds rather than systematically supplementing them through fundraising initiatives by identifying specific goals, strategies, and financial needs in their ministries. It seems that the long-standing conflict and debate between fundraising through entrepreneurial promotion and faith missions is still causing confusion among Korean missionaries. This study has shown that confrontation and conflict also appear between missionaries over these two methods. To minimize this confusion, the community of missionaries, mission agencies, churches, and missiologists should come together to discuss theological, missiological, and strategic views and options for the provision of mission finance.

Dynamic Response to the Challenge

Missionaries respond dynamically in a wide variety of ways when faced with money-related challenges. The missionary attempts to overcome this challenge by responding to it with spiritual, emotional, relational, and practical dimensions. These multifaceted responses are focused on finding specific solutions through self-reflection as a party to solve money-related challenges. Furthermore, this trend implies that money-related challenges have a complexity and totality that includes theological, missiological, economic, and philosophical aspects that are difficult to solve with only one fragmentary response. The missionary does not use the four responses mentioned in figure 22.2 at the same time, but chooses some of them depending on the nature of the challenges posed by money.

Missionary Identity

Reinterpretation of money-related challenges based on missionaries' ontological and relational identities influences these multifaceted responses. Ontological reflection on identity includes interaction with the philosophy of ministry as a missionary, Christian values, moral responsibility as a spiritual leader, and theological beliefs. In addition, the relational identity as a church member who has been given a mission and sent by a church, and as a missionary who has the duty to comply with the financial policy of a mission organization, is one of the key intervening conditions leading to multifaceted responses. This study, based on grounded theory, shows that when missionaries have well-established ontological and relational self-identities, they can more effectively use the various responses in creative ways to overcome the challenges posed by money.

Variety of Results

Missionary responses to money-related challenges do not always lead to positive results. The results vary widely, depending on each missionary's beliefs and practices about the relationship between money and mission. In spite of the missionaries' various responses, they may still be unable to escape money-related concerns. These concerns can lead to anger, frustration, and a skeptical view of missionary identity. Some even show that the missionaries themselves have a significant degree of dependence on money. Further research is needed on how this dependence of missionaries correlates with the material dependence of others in mission contexts. Some missionaries become obsessed with triumphalism when they secure more funds than other missionaries, and vice versa, some fall into defeatism. Even with negative consequences, the majority of missionaries respond in their own way, although to varying degrees. Few missionaries respond negatively without any intervening responsive interpretation or action to the challenges that come from money.

Nevertheless, in the majority of cases, missionaries' responses to overcome the challenges posed by money have positive results. Missionaries generally have more confidence in God who supplies the material needs of the missionaries. Reflecting on this spiritual result, missionaries conduct self-evaluation to maintain a frugal and simple lifestyle. In addition, information on low-cost and high-efficiency lifestyles is collected and implemented in everyday life. Missionaries establish specific retirement measures by reviewing expert advice or related information to relieve anxiety about their life after retirement. In addition, the missionary's response process and results to the challenges that come from money set an example to follow for those involved in mission contexts.

Circulation Structure

Money-related challenges have continued throughout my life as a missionary; the challenges from money and the missionary's response form a circular structure and lasts for a lifetime. Even for missionaries who have been through money-related trials or who have an established theological view of money, there is no complete escape from this circulation structure. Nevertheless, this structure can be further simplified as a missionary's self-reflection increases its depth.

Summary of the Implications of This Research

1. As the world's economic structure is reshaping faster than ever before, research on the relationship between mission and money must also reflect this changing situation. Considering these

characteristics, research on this subject should focus on context-oriented mission, participant-centered research, and phenomenological inquiry.

2. Considering the impact of money on human emotions, lifestyles, ways of thinking, culture, economy, and values, this study should be conducted through collaboration across interdisciplinary boundaries such as missiology, biblical theology, sociology, and economics.

3. Regarding missionaries as a homogeneous group in establishing the model of the relationship between money and missionaries cannot completely rule out the risk of falling into an overgeneralization error. This requires a multifaceted study that includes elements such as the temperament and beliefs of each missionary, ethnic characteristics, perspectives and expectations of mission organizations and churches, and sociocultural settings of mission contexts. Such a study will be able to come closer to the real truth about the relationship between money and missionaries only when in-depth participatory observational research on individuals and small groups and a large-scale survey are combined.

4. Being both a Christian and a human being, it is a normal emotional response for a missionary to have both satisfaction and dissatisfaction with the money-related challenges that are constantly affecting the missionary. No one can demand or force a missionary, either implicitly or explicitly, to respond transcendentally to a money-related challenge. Rather than expecting a missionary facing such a challenge to respond positively by relying entirely on individual capabilities, support from a community of stakeholders is required.

5. The model of the relationship between money and missionaries presented in this study is the result of analysis and interpretation of only forty-seven Korean missionaries' grounded data. In addition, due to the limitations of the time and space given to the researcher, it was difficult to carry out other complementary studies. Therefore, this model cannot be generalized as a universal phenomenon. Missionaries' responses to money-related challenges are so diverse that this model cannot effectively reflect them all. The researcher hopes that this model will be constantly modified and supplemented through future studies.

6. Mission education that deals in depth with the dynamic relationship between money and missionaries should be strengthened. This missionary education should include an effective discussion of questions such as: What challenges can missionaries face with money? How can a missionary respond to these challenges? What are the expected outcomes? How can challenges and responses form a virtuous cycle?

7. There is a need for a missional community that encourages and revitalizes research on missions and money, taking into account various types of missionaries and mission contexts around the world.

Concluding Remarks

The study of money and mission should focus on the transformation and maturity of the Korean missionary community, not on the study itself. Therefore, such research should be carried out through close interaction and collaboration between researchers and missionaries. Furthermore, it is hoped that this study can make a small but meaningful contribution to future discussion and research on the missionary community.

Chapter 22 Response

by Ruth Maxwell

Thank you, Dr. Eum, for your excellent research on this important topic, and for designing the missionary-money relationship model. Both the research and the model reveal the ebb and flow of the challenges of financial stress. Those facing this stress certainly need to be understood and supported.

The Research Question

The question, "To what extent does money impact a missionary's life and ministry?" was examined carefully in this chapter.

The Methodology

The question was addressed using grounded theory, and looked at systematically, inductively, and qualitatively in order to develop a working theory and model. Insiders in this story have been listened to, heard, and understood. Their experience was studied so that the relationship between missionaries and money could be diagrammed.

The Research

Forty-seven Korean missionaries were interviewed for this research. The data gathered through interviews uncovered a realistic list of different kinds of responses. These were synthesized into categories, and then further grouped into larger categories that unpacked how the responses/factors are interconnected. These larger categories were then shaped into the model.

The Narrative

The categories were woven into a narrative, which brought in many different factors and reflected the breadth of responses financial stress can elicit. How one person or family responds to financial stress, while doing their best to be truly faith-based and service-oriented, will differ from others. The underlying contributing factors may also differ.

The Working Model and Provisional Grounded Theory

The model is dynamic and portrays the interactive ebb and flow that inevitably occurs, depending on the various perspectives that each individual might take. The provisional grounded theory section of the chapter explains the dynamics imbedded within the model.

The Recommendations

Dr. Eum's chapter concludes with several recommendations for further research and study. Although the research for this chapter was understandably limited in scope, the analysis provides a basis for discussion. Each recommendation is worth considering. The foundation for further work exists.

"What Now?"

I am focusing the remainder of my response on "What now?" There is an obvious need for those living with emotional ambivalence caused by stress while in ministry to be helped. Hopefully, affirmative steps of action can come from combining the research, the model, the question, "What now?," and your group discussions. You are the experts on your culture.

After studying this research, I found myself asking one question: "How do we, as those who are concerned about the welfare of missionaries in relation to money, adequately support and care for them as they face the inevitable financial challenges and the ambivalence that will come?" Research is necessary. But deciding what to do with research requires wisdom. I believe God has brought wise people to this forum. And so, I gladly place my question before you.

The principles in the model, the provisional theories, and how Scripture frames this very important topic intersect with other aspects of our faith journey. How we respond to financial stress overlaps with, how we respond to other challenges in our faith journey. This makes the "What now?" question even more urgent.

I appreciate Dr. Eum's concluding statement that "the study of money and mission should focus on the transformation and maturity of the Korean missionary community, not on the study itself. Therefore, such research should be carried out through close interaction and collaboration between researchers and missionaries." Transformation and maturity within relationships point to the "What now?" question as well.

In order to move from credible research to creative resourcing for those living with these realities, the following categories of questions and thoughts, I trust, will generate new thinking and wise responses:

1. The central phenomenon—emotional ambivalence between satisfaction and dissatisfaction or anxiety—needs to be given serious consideration.

   - How can cross-cultural workers facing this storm be strengthened and supported?
   - What kinds of perspective and support make it possible for Korean cross-cultural workers to survive, thrive, and possibly become resilient through the storm of ambivalence?

2. There is a larger context in which the model and its dynamics take place. In what way are the challenges stated in the model not about money, but about something much deeper? How do these larger categories impact this challenge?

   - The theology of suffering, prosperity, faith, and community practiced in the local church shapes the person the missionary is as they head into missions.

3. What does a healthy blend of faith and work look like in the model? How could that be taught, encouraged, validated, demonstrated, and supported in the context of community?

   - Is it possible to build into the ethos of fundraising the concept that fundraising is a beautiful expression of faith? If so, how?
   - Is it possible to build into fundraising the concept that faith might best be expressed through the humble process of inviting others to be part of the team?

4. What is the larger context of our identity? Missionary identity in this model is defined in light of values and beliefs about money and combined with organizational procedures and policies. Identity must be included in Dr. Eum's chapter in some form. Is there another level of identity that offers a larger anchor for the stress of all the storms?

   - How does who we are as believers in Christ impact these challenges?
   - How can our identity in Christ be used, not as a hammer, but as a context in which we are invited to safely struggle with ambivalence, challenges, responses, growth, and imperfection?

5. There is a great deal of information in this research. How else can this information be mined as it is, even if no further research is conducted? What are we already being "told" by the concepts and categories in the research?

   - How could the concepts and subcategories information be utilized for determining support structures needed now?

6. Dr. Eum provided a compiled narrative. We each have a story. What is your story? My story surfaces when I consider retiring after more than forty years of full-time ministry. Thankfully, it pushes me toward God. One resource God blessed me with was conversations with a friend who watched his missionary parents retire on limited resources. He told me their story. They had lived simply all their lives, so they needed very little. That awareness sparks hope in me—part of my readiness is in a lifestyle, not a bank account. My very real challenge has also been helped by a wise friend and his wife, relationally connecting with me, sharing a relevant story, and encouraging me that God is caring for me—partly through what he has already built into me … a simple lifestyle.

   - What if stories of honest struggling, or of growth in including others, or of feeling inadequate as a faith missionary could be compiled so that those who are dealing with these challenges could be encouraged?
   - What if the stories weren't only "great stories of faith," but instead were "great stories of journeying with God" in the area of money, ministry, and missions?
   - What if it was okay to not have an answer and to be able to live well and to know God's peace when there seems to be only ambivalence?

7. The model reveals the cyclical nature of this challenge. This isn't a "deal with it once and for all" journey. It isn't linear and final. It is a repeating challenge.

    - How could we create an atmosphere that grants permission for missionaries to struggle, for personal imperfection, for a journey that isn't straightforward, for bumps along the way?
    - How could we reframe this as an opportunity for growth, and not as an indication of failure to grow?
    - How can we normalize this dynamic?

8. Dr. Eum stated, and I agree, that there is a need for a supportive community if any person is facing this challenge. What stands in the way of creating supportive communities?

    - What cultural tendencies might support or hinder this?
    - How might these be addressed?
    - How could missionaries be prepared in advance to ask for help in a crisis?
    - What might a supportive community within a multicultural team look like, where differences in culture, style, economics, and personal finances may be accentuated and more obvious?

Conclusion

You know that feeling—one day you feel you have faith that can move mountains. Another day you feel, no, you know, that God is hearing and answering. Another day all is silent, and questions and doubts hover at the fringes of your mind. The storm can come from anywhere, around any topic.

Who is equal to this task of helping someone navigate these storms? The answer, I suspect, lies in some of us offering grace-filled spaces to those in our circle caught in a storm, and then watch God abundantly multiply it into the lives of others. Will it start with you?

Chapter 23
The Role of Patron as Father (*GAP*) in Church Planting Efforts in Cambodia

by Robert Oh

My PhD's primary research question is, "How does the patron-client dynamic between Korean missionaries and Cambodian church planters offer an alternative understanding of aid dependency within the discourse of mission studies?" While the patron-client relationship has been a popular concept in social anthropology studies, its value and effects have not been sufficiently explored within mission studies; specifically, aid dependency, particularly between Korean missionaries and Cambodian church planters, has not been the subject of focused research. The critical effects of patron-client dynamics are explored in my thesis through a case study methodology, examining the Cambodia Bible College (CBC)[1] church planting projects in Cambodia.

The aid dependency issue—both healthy and unhealthy—was identified as one of the significant effects in patron-client dynamics from initial research data. In the CBC church planting process, the findings show that the patron takes on three unique diachronic and progressive roles: first, the patron as a father; second, the patron as a sponsor; and third, the patron as a partner. Similarly, the client also takes on three roles: first, the client as a child; second, the client as sponsoree (client); and third, the client as a partner.

Although social studies currently express patron-client dynamics primarily in material and political terms, in the case between the CBC founder and the CBC pastors, an intangible relational asset, that is, "the patron as a father," was observed. This chapter argues that "the patron father" plays a significant role in developing CBC pastors as church planters, helps them access the necessary resources to establish their churches during the initial stages, and offers an alternative reading of aid dependency as a relational concept rather than an economic one.

---
1 As requested by the research participants, all names are pseudonyms to protect their identity.

Patron as Father (*GAP*)

The data from interviewing the CBC church planters point to three different roles that Ted, the CBC founder, and the CBC pastors played. This chapter will discuss Ted's playing the role of a father, both with patron-client relationship literature and data. I argue that the Korean hierarchical *Gap* (갑) and *Eul* (을)[2] exists in the relationship between Ted and the CBC pastors, with Ted as a potential *Gap-jil*.[3] The roles they play are complex, dynamic, and transitional. Both the benefits and the adverse effects of the patron playing the father role are presented, highlighting the aid dependency issue as the primary effect.

Ted as Patron (*GAP*)

Ted playing a father's role was accepted, especially during the beginning stage of his mission, and somewhat welcomed by overall CBC students. However, many scholars, both Cambodian and Western, negatively view the hierarchical aspect of a patron-client relationship.

In the case of CBC, this hierarchical social ranking was observed between Ted and the CBC pastors, and among the CBC pastors themselves based on the time of their entering CBC and their age and gender. However, the Cambodian pastors' preference for hierarchical relationships between themselves and Ted was also observed. According to an American missionary in charge of the Bible College in Phnom Penh, many of his Cambodian students felt uncomfortable when he approached them as a "friend" and wanted to keep the social distance by calling him "teacher."

Eisenstadt and Roniger state that in the Southeast Asian context "there is an emphasis on reciprocity and mutually beneficial exchange rather than on personal commitment and personal significance as basic constitutive elements of clientelistic attachments."[4] However, in the CBC context, personal commitment is emphasized more during the first two stages. Then, from the third stage, a mutually beneficial exchange is stressed. Eisenstadt and Roniger also argue that in Buddhist settings "there is ambivalence in attitudes towards authority—an ambivalence to be overcome only if superiors show merit, by being (however strong) benevolent and indulgent father-surrogates."[5] This is the case at CBC, where Ted plays a kind and indulgent father-surrogate in the first and the second stages of the CBC students.

GAP & EUL

This chapter addresses *Gap* and *Eul* relationship issues in the context of Ted's playing the role of father to the CBC students. In an interview, Ted mentioned the *Gap* and *Eul* relationship issue seven times, using the exact terms. He stated that *Gap* and *Eul* represent and express "a dynamic which happens in the mission field (referring to Cambodia) quite well. I feel it is a good term. If there is another term, I will use it, but it would be true even in my case." He argued that "there are many other Korean missionaries who would agree with him," and even confessed that he has potential to become a *super-Gap*, "since I personally taught them ever since they were young children—providing everything—and even treated their physical illness."

Ted admits that Korean missionaries playing *Gap* is "causing many problems in Cambodia and is a major source of irritation, yet many are not aware of the issue." He claims that "someone has to address this topic. I talk to them (other Korean missionaries) from time to time, arguing that this has to be corrected."

Ted is aware of the Cambodian pastors' complaints (including those of the CBC pastors) about Korean missionaries playing *Gap*. However, he states, "I wish it was only a part of the process, and unless Korean missionaries recognize this and sincerely change, the problem with *Gap* will not end." He feels that because Korean missionaries are conditioned to materialism and because Korea has "more material and education and national power that [they] are playing the role of *Gap*."

A similar *Gap* and *Eul* relationship was observed in Japan as *oyabun-kobun* (Boss-follower) in Japanese. Eisenstadt and Roniger state that within the Japanese patron-client relationship, "the *oyabun-kobun* link may be characterized as a highly emotional and diffuse dyadic arrangement. A 'superior' adopts an 'inferior,' and the latter recognizes the long-term authority of the former, both partners maintaining a long-term, personalized mutual concern with each other's public

---

2 *Gap* and *Eul* is a general term used to indicate "first" and "second" in the order of priority. It is also used to indicate the first of the list of ten—*Gap, Eul, Byong, Jung, Moo, Ki, Kyong, Shin, Im, Kye*, as in the alphabetical list order of a, b, c.

3 The abuse of power by *Gap* is known as *Gap-jil*, which means "doing the *Gap*" in Korean.

4 S. N. Eisenstadt and L. Roniger, *Patrons, Clients and Friends: Interpersonal Relations and the Structure of Trust in Society* (Cambridge: Cambridge University Press, 1984), 122.

5 Eisenstadt and Roniger, 122.

and private affairs."[6] This Japanese term is accepted and used in Korean society, especially describing the relationship between the boss and his followers in the Korean criminal world.

John explained his experience of *Gap* and *Eul*, saying that "Christians need the foreigner to be the partner and then the foreigner should behave like they are missionaries. They are called 'missionary,' but they are not a missionary; they are the boss." "Any foreigner that comes teaches Cambodia to be the leader and then they are ready to go out. No, they come to be the boss!" John argued that foreigners, including missionaries, do not want to leave Cambodia even after Cambodian pastors have matured as leaders and are ready to take over the ministries. "It is the formula—their formula that they come to Cambodia to be the boss and the Cambodian is the slave to their work."

He addressed the problem he faced when his church's name, Bright Church, was chosen by a Korean donor, although it had no meaning for him and his church members. He added that "the worker cannot deny the boss. If you are the sponsor, we cannot say 'no' to you." He argued that when the church planting effort is not producing the kind of fruits missionaries demand, often only Cambodians are blamed, saying, "Cambodia is still weak as a baby, an immature baby, I say baby in Christ. We are still weak, and then you blame Cambodians. If the staff commits wrongdoing, a boss is also 50 percent wrong." John also argued that many times missionaries tried methods not conducive to the Cambodian culture, adding, "And the missionaries come to help us, they bring their own culture, and they practice their own culture so when they practice their own culture, we need to follow that culture, depending on their boss, and then the missionary or the foreigner that comes to Cambodia."

The Korean Christian C-Channel presented similar examples in a two-part documentary it produced.[7] In this documentary, many Cambodian pastors were waiting for their turn to be paid by the Korean missionary Um, and he explained why such a practice was necessary: "This is ministry funds the mother church in Korea is giving to these Cambodian staff." "We planted churches in 148 villages, and the reason why we have to be accurate in keeping these records is that sometimes these pastors, after receiving their funding, claim that they never got their portion." He was indirectly admitting that their church planting Cambodian pastors could not be trusted when it comes to financing.

Cho argues that, "It seems to be a case of *Gap* and *Eul*, but a *Gap* and *Eul* relationship has existed in Korea since the *Joseon* dynasty," but these days, "depending on the shifting of power, sometimes *Eul* becomes *Gap*." In his experience, he has observed that Cambodian pastors who played the role of *Eul* became *Gap* as they became more powerful, became the First Order Brokers (FOB), and played the role of patron to their people.

Cho also holds that Korean missionaries are *Eul* to their sending churches, who play the *Gap*, and that "the entire system is built on the wishes of the individual church and its senior pastor or director of the mission department, [and] they (Korean missionaries) have to follow their direction." As an example, Cho shared about a Korean missionary who we both knew was treated as *Eul*. Cho explained, "You know about him, including the name of the church from Korea, but the fact is, when he refused to name the Cambodian church in Korean, identical with the sponsor's Korean church name, he was cut from the support at once." The client's powerless and voiceless dynamic is played out as *Eul*, similar to that of the CBC pastors as *Eul* when they could not confront Ted's primary patrons, the *Gap* players.

Cho makes the following argument regarding the hierarchical patron-client relationship between missionaries and Cambodians:

> Wouldn't it be better to keep Cambodia's current hierarchical patron-client relationship since it is already part of their social structure? Although a Western missionary insists on "friendship," in reality it isn't a relationship between friends. It is only in terms they use. Why don't we use the Cambodian patron-client relationship more positively so this form of *Gap* and *Eul* dynamic and abuse will not occur? It should not be an entirely negative experience.[8]

In the CBC case, because *Gap* and *Eul* are based on a father/parent and child relationship, the relationship remains and endures.

---

6 Eisenstadt and Roniger, 146.

7 T. Um, *Shining Hope in Cambodia*, Part 1 (Vision! World Mission, Episode 12, C Channel, 2014), accessed August 21, 2015, http://tinyurl.com/jx4p2bo; T. Um, *Shining Hope in Cambodia*, Part 2 (Vision! World Mission, Episode 13, C Channel, 2014), accessed August 21, 2015, http://tinyurl.com/z4zt6gq.

8 Cho, interview by author, July 28, 2015 (Interview 85 in research participant data).

Effects of Ted as Father and the CBC Pastors as Children

I observed both the positive and negative effects of Ted as a father and the CBC pastors as children. As Chan and Chheang argue, the patron-client relationship's adverse effects can occur when clients feel that the patrons benefit much more than the clients.[9] Accordingly, I examined the data and compared and contrasted what Ted said with what the CBC pastors said during the interviews. By analyzing the research data, I found significant adverse effects resulting from Ted's playing the role of patron father to the CBC pastors: 1) prolonged dependency, and 2) lack of client motivation. These effects are mixed and complex in range. I will discuss in more detail each of the effects and factors involved in the relational dynamics.

Relational Dependency and Prolonged Dependency

CBC was built on a parent and son relationship as Ted and his wife loved and cared for young people at the mission house, relating to them like parents to children. Especially in the mission house stage, most Cambodian boys living there had been displaced from their families. For example, Tom spoke frankly of his desperate situation at that time, saying, "I ran away from home and had no place to go." The mission house became his home, the mission house members his family, and Ted his father. His tone of voice and facial expressions reflected his sincere feelings of appreciation and gratitude to Ted.

Luke, another mission house student, also spoke frankly: "I was on the street when Ted shared the Gospel with me and asked me to come to his house." He had a family but they could not send him to school, so he spent the day wandering around the village. Walking down the main road of the village, he met Ted, who was doing street evangelism. Once he moved to the mission house, he was trained to become a pastor.

Next, John, another mission house student, shared, "I was a secondary (school) boy, and I was a poor boy." He initially joined the mission house to be educated in English. He said he eventually finished his BA degree in Singapore, supported by Ted and his Singapore sponsors. However, Ted later verified that John did not finish his BA degree in Singapore because of a visa complication. However, he did complete his BA in Theology from CBC. He and his wife are still involved with CBC work as staff members.

As a mission house student, Daniel emphatically praised Ted and stated, "I respect him as my pastor, my teacher. I was born from him. He imparts me all these spiritual gifts." He is now the president of an FBO in Cambodia. He began feeding needy children and educating them, similar to what Ted did at CBC. His way of expressing his gratitude for Ted is by saying that, "I was born from him."

Out of such a personal and long-term father and child relationship, the CBC students and Ted formed a dependent relationship in the beginning stage of CBC ministry. It resulted in the positive effects of Ted's playing the role of a father. However, out of such a personal relationship, the tendency for prolonged dependency may develop. My definition of an unhealthy aid dependency is, "a psychological and financial situation where the church leader cannot set the agenda and plan for the church, and the church cannot provide for its staff and ongoing ministry without external assistance and continued funding. This difficult cycle appears not to contribute significantly to the church's becoming self-sustaining." As of 2016, none of CBC's twenty-one church plantings was self-sustaining, which Ted called a significant drawback in his church planting.

Even for the mission house students, signs of prolonged dependency were observed. For example, after finishing a bachelor's degree in Singapore and qualified to seek a career anywhere, Tom worked at the CBC to pay back his "debt." He was not legally responsible for it, but emotionally, he sought Ted's approval. The extra time that Tom spent at the CBC delayed his career advancement for several years. It stopped only when the CBC no longer could support his role as a professor there.

Moreover, although Luke was a pastor over a CBC church, he pursued an MA degree in English in the evening. During the interview, it became clear that he did not want to be in ministry. When he moved into the mission house, everyone in that community was being trained to become pastors, and he, too, was taught that. However, he did not have any other choice. After graduating and being in ministry for several years, he realized that he was not cut out to be a local church pastor, so he trained himself, supported by another NGO, toward finding another job opportunity.

Next, John and his wife are still technically CBC staff because Singaporean churches through CBC's financial structure support John's ministry. At the time of the interview, he was trying to become independent from

---

9 R. Chan and V. Chheang, "Cultural Challenges to the Decentralization Process in Cambodia," *Ritsumeikan Journal of Asia Pacific Studies* 24 (2008), 9.

CBC, but using unethical means. He was trying to get support from others without going through CBC, neither cooperating with nor reporting this process to CBC.

Ted is aware of this unhealthy dependency issue and stated, "In Cambodia, they are so used to just receiving—because we are poor we have to receive. From the leaders to everyone, they have become experts at receiving." He was not accusing the CBC pastors, since self-sustainability was not part of church planting objectives in the beginning stage of CBC's church planting project. Ted is now tackling this unhealthy dependency with his CBC church planters.

Some CBC pastors addressed prolonged dependency concerns as well, especially among the older and more established church planters. Peter stated, "To get the support does not mean they will support a hundred years, at first they teach us how to walk, but after we know how to walk, will they be able to build to support us more, to sustain or to check the balance of walking? No, we have to walk by ourselves." Although he was emphatic about this point, many younger pastors in the group interviews avoided commenting on it or joining the conversation. They did not seem to be ready to participate in the discussion since it was unfamiliar to them because they had not reached Peter's church development stage. Calvin concluded that to overcome their financial dependency he had to preach about tithing: "So I preach about the tithe, at least once a month. Preach about the tithe because we need to explain to the Cambodian how to do the tithe." He and his wife, both CBC graduates, have a church in the Kampong Cham area with over one hundred members. However, due to his congregation's lack of giving, his church still needs monthly support from outside. Both he and his wife were vocal and energetic about the possibility of becoming independent from any foreign aid in the future.

Lack of Motivation

Although there are some exceptions from the research data, I observed lack of motivation in many CBC pastors. We need to ask, "Is it due to the relational dynamic structure between the CBC pastors and Ted?" Bosch argues that in Cambodia, questioning the local authorities has yet to be transformed into reality due to the hierarchy's deeply embedded structure, which remains sacrosanct.[10] Most of the significant decisions about church planting—location, timing, staffing, and even naming the church—were decided by Ted as their sponsor or by an FOB of either Korean or Singaporean churches.

According to Ledgerwood and Vijghen, understanding the patron-client relationship in Cambodia provides a helpful insight into decision-making dynamics between a community's leader and his/her people in the country. "Like other Southeast Asian countries, Cambodia is a society embedded with a very strong patronage system regulating all social relationships."[11] Chan and Chheang also agree with Ledgerwood and Vijghen and argue that understanding this Cambodian patronage model explains how people in Cambodian villages reach a decision.[12]

Alex is an example of a CBC church planter with a lack of motivation. He is pastoring one of the original seven churches. In my view, based on visiting all seven church sites, his church has the best quality building as the entire church building materials were shipped from Korea in a container and assembled in that village. It is located in one of the best parts of a large village on a large plot of land. From the beginning of the interview to the end, however, he seemed discouraged. He complained about everything, from the lack of a fence to not having enough funds to give to newcomers (mostly little children), who were not even part of the CBC church planting strategy.

During the interview, I noticed the land the church was built on and I asked about the possibility of growing mango trees to support his church. He immediately stated that there were no funds to build fences around such a large property. He argued that when mango trees are young, neighborhood cows and other animals eat the leaves and subsequently kill the trees. However, I noted that other Cambodian neighbors overcame such problems by just putting up localized screen fences around the mango trees. This inexpensive method does not require imported materials. Since students built most of these localized fences, they should be very familiar with such a method of protecting fruit trees. However, I had an insight into a possible cause for Alex's reluctance when he stated that it was not his choice to be in that church location but that Ted had solely decided. He has moved around to many church plant projects. In this case, Alex's lack of motivation may have stemmed from not making his

---

10 D. J. Bosch, *Transforming Mission* (Maryknoll: Orbis Books, 1994), 11.

11 J. Ledgerwood and J. Vijghen, "Decision-Making in Rural Khmer Villages," in *Cambodia Emerges from the Past: Eight Essays*, ed. J. Ledgerwood (DeKalb: Center for Southeast Asian Studies, Northern Illinois University, 2002), 143.

12 Chan and Chheang, "Cultural Challenges," 4.

own decisions about the location and method of doing his ministry.

Similarly, in another interview, Luke stated that all decisions regarding his church ministry and kindergarten business were made "all under Ted and his wife, Sarah," emphasizing the word "all." He argued that Ted and Sarah make all the outreach events and financial decisions and they do not participate in any decision-making processes. Once again, the reason for Luke's lack of motivation and reluctance in initiating his own ministry was because he did not feel that he had control over these matters.

Ted also stated that once CBC was established and the student body exceeded one hundred, he could no longer get intimately involved in his students' lives. Ted's role needs to shift from a patron as a father to a sponsor or an FOB to meet the demand of the growth and organizational change of the CBC church planting project. By making significant life decisions, for example, vocational choices and locations of church planting sites, Ted stepped into a *super-Gap* role and may have engaged in the form of *Gap-jil* without knowing it.

Summary

In this chapter, I first discussed Ted's playing the father's role from patron-client relationship literature. Then I discussed *Gap* and *Eul* issues in the context of relational dynamics between a father and his children. I presented, out of the research data, the overall effects of a few patrons playing the father role and defined healthy relational dependency versus unhealthy dependency.

I noticed that once the CBC student body grew in number, CBC church planting reached a different stage—Ted could no longer play the father's role, his involvement and personal care was insufficient, and this combination resulted in CBC pastors' lack of motivation. However, by making major life decisions for them without having a good relationship, for example vocational choices and locations of church planting sites, Ted stepped into the role of a super-*Gap* and may have engaged in the form of *Gap-jil* without knowing it.

Discussion Questions

1. Do you observe *Gap and Eul* relationships in your context?

2. Have you been subject to *Gap-jil*? If so, how did you respond?

3. How can we safeguard *Gap and Eul* relationships from developing into *Gap-jil*?

Chapter 23 Response

by Sokreaksa Himm

I am not an academic, so I will write a practical response to Dr. Oh's chapter.

As soon as the government opened the door for Christian ministry in Cambodia, Korean, American, Canadian, Singaporean, and other missionaries brought their own methodologies and church planting strategies to implement throughout the country. These might have brought them success elsewhere, but not in Cambodia. Missionaries injected thoughts and ideas from their church planting strategies into Cambodia, but they lacked understanding of and sensitivity to the culture. In the course of their work, most foreign missionaries in Cambodia introduced unhealthy dependencies to varying degrees. I will list some of these in random order, although they are also interconnected:

Pay Dependency

When missionaries arrived, they wanted to plant churches quickly. One strategy used to meet this goal was to pump in a lot of money to attract local people to church, for example, hiring locals to build churches and other centers. Whoever spent the most money usually gained the most attention from local people. Many Korean missionaries used money to motivate local people to work for them. They created a system that made local leaders dependent upon Korean financial support. This guaranteed dependency. Missionaries were also seen as competing against each other to gain or maintain popularity. From a local perspective, working with Korean missionaries is a guarantee of better pay. Therefore, among the several nationalities of missionaries serving in Cambodia, Korean missionaries are the most popular.

Foreign Leader Dependency

Missionaries need to understand the history of foreign influence in Cambodia. The local people regarded foreigners as much better than themselves or their leaders, and more worthy of respect. This history is repeating itself again and again in the missionary and church scene in modern Cambodia. Missionaries are seen as intellectually and economically superior. The big boss from outside is much better than the local boss. The big boss gets the job done, and local leaders are not respected. Therefore, missionaries are more influential than the local leaders they are training. From a cultural perspective, local leaders must do what their missionary bosses tell them to do. But since missionaries fail to contextualize their behavior and structures within Cambodian culture, they fail to empower the local leaders they are raising in Cambodia. Missionaries gain respect from local people, but the pitfall is that they are robbing local leaders of their social influence.

Outside Funding Dependency

Missionaries are actually stealing the social influence of local people. This raises the question of whether the church can survive after the missionaries pull themselves out of Cambodia. Most of the missionaries who have worked in Cambodia have pumped a lot of funds into the churches. At this stage, local churches cannot be sustained by local offerings. Most local leaders need funding from outside supporters, and it will be hard to stop depending on outside funds. It is a vicious cycle. The more they receive in funding, the more funding they need as their ministry projects expand. I might be wrong, but I am very much concerned about this dependence on outside funding. If outside funding is cut off, the local church will eventually die. Can local churches survive if all foreign missionaries are asked by the government to leave the country the next day? That is the question.

Aid Dependency

When missionaries went to Cambodia, they created aid dependency for the local people. It is healthy and unhealthy. It is good when aid gets attention of the local people. Local people or local leaders in Cambodia see the aid as a blessing. They are first drawn by the aid, not so much by the Gospel of salvation in Jesus Christ. They have no idea what is meant by salvation. Everyone wants to get a share of the aid—whether it be money, materials, educational opportunities, etc. Without aid, missionaries cannot establish anything. Local churches depend on outside aid, and without such support, the local churches will never survive in the long run.

Poverty in Cambodia influences people to look for something to meet their physical needs. It is a natural human instinct. What is bad is that missionaries do not know how or when they can cut aid or stop supporting the local churches. When aid is introduced into the community, there is no way to stop it. In fact, more money is needed for growing numbers of community projects. Local leaders and churches totally depend on financial support from the outside. Missionaries create this unhealthy dependency.

Building Maintenance Dependency

Missionaries often define ministry success in terms of the construction of a church building. However, a common pitfall is building one too early. Most missionaries start to erect a church building before local believers clearly understand the concept of building maintenance. Church buildings attract people to the church. They look impressive. But within a few years, churches need maintenance, and local resources are simply not there. In the long run, there will be major problems with foreign funded church buildings. This means that Cambodian Christians and their leaders will need missionaries or short-term visitors to come and help them. For countryside churches, it is unlikely that local believers will ever be able to afford to maintain these missionary-constructed church buildings. They, too, will rely almost entirely on funding from the outside.

I am not suggesting that building a church is wrong. I simply point out that missionaries need to clearly teach local people to take responsibility for maintaining their church buildings without depending on outside financial support. It will take time for local church leaders and believers to understand the concept of building maintenance. I used to take missionaries to visit many churches in many different places. I often heard local church leaders complain about the lack of money for maintenance of church buildings. Generally speaking, they asked for more money to help maintain their churches. When they could not find money to maintain them, they become depressed and discouraged. I would encourage missionaries to be cautious about erecting church buildings. The success of a ministry is not based on a church building, but on solid biblical training of local church leaders. If these leaders want to have their own churches, let them develop their own strategies for erecting and maintaining buildings. It will take time. Please note that not many Cambodian church leaders know how to plan for the future. Most of them are not long-term visionaries.

Teacher Dependency

Missionaries are often called *teachers*. In Cambodian culture, when missionaries are addressed as teachers, they are likely becoming second parents to the students. This means that some local people highly respect missionaries as their second parents, and they may become overly dependent on them.

As teachers, missionaries may have a hard time getting close to the local leaders. While in some cases their relationship may be very close, like brother to brother, in other cases a teacher-student relationship creates a social distance between them, and local leaders may not feel comfortable getting close to missionaries. Missionaries have a hard time understanding what is going on here. When a mistake is made that needs to be addressed by the missionary, the local leader may have a hard time accepting it. The local leader may be unhappy with the missionary. If the relationship is falling apart, the church will split or the local leader may walk away and begin an organized attack on the missionary. Forgiveness will be hard to handle from both sides. There is a question—how does the local missionary establish a relationship with the local leader?

It is hard to find a good solution. Building up trust with local church leaders is the most important factor for the missionary. However, a missionary as a teacher may need to draw a clear boundary with the local church leader that is clearly understood by both sides. It is vitally important that a local church leader not be seen as utterly dependent on the foreign missionary. Such dependency creates an endless need for outside financial assistance and resources. When a missionary fails to deliver, in a worst-case scenario local leaders may look for another supporter or missionary to help them. Cambodian church leaders may be loyal only to the missionary who provides the most money. This is very sad.

Denominational Dependencies

There are many conflicts among missionaries serving in Cambodia. Instead of finding common solutions to serve the same Master in this country, they compete against each other. It is not a healthy situation. Missionaries have also introduced many different denominations into Cambodian society, creating a big problem for church planting in Cambodia. The Cambodian church is very young and fragile. The sudden introduction of scores of different denominations created a lot of confusion in the society. This generates distrust and disunity among local Cambodian leaders. I am not saying diversity does not work in Cambodia, but I want to point out that the church in Cambodia is too young to understand the concept of different denominations and denominational divisions.

In closing, I would like to make a small suggestion for missionaries who have been working in Cambodia. One issue that most missionaries fail to recognize from a Cambodian psychological perspective is the unresolved grievances among the local leaders that missionaries are raising up to be church leaders. Some of these leaders carry unresolved grievances in their lives. There are a lot of unseen wounds among local leaders and they harbor many hidden emotions. Congregations led by these wounded leaders will be vulnerable to significant weakness and failure.

Chapter 24
Can Any Good Be Done on a Short-Term Mission Trip? Opportunities and Pitfalls in Athens, Greece

by Darren M. Carlson

It has become popular to write about the ills of short-term mission, and for good reason. While missiologists have written about it at length, one wonders whether any impact has been made on the nearly $2.4 billion industry. Curriculum continues to be produced, and popular books like *When Helping Hurts* have been modified to address short-term mission. The youthful zeal and inexperience of most participants, coupled with issues of cross-cultural communication and expectations, has led to an incongruence between what is often reported by participants and those who professionally study short-term missions.

Are short-term mission trips primarily for those who go or those who are served? Does a desire to serve and the ability to fundraise essentially qualify someone to go? Would mission organizations see a drop in long-term goers and senders if short-term mission trips were canceled? Do the lives of those who go on short-term trips appreciably change? When a never-ending stream of short-term teams are sent to partner with long-term missionaries, are we aiding or inhibiting the missionaries work, and how would we even know if we were? These types of questions are where the dividing lines are found. The answers are elusive.

This chapter has a narrow focus. It will highlight some specific challenges in one of the most popular destinations for short-term missionaries—Athens, Greece. While researching migrant faith communities and those serving them between 2015–2018 I often interacted with short-term teams.[1] On any day I could walk through Athens and find a short-term team without much effort.

Greece's history and culture make it even more attractive to evangelical short-term teams. Christian colleges shape spring break trips to study Greek history and the New Testament, while adding a service element. Teams can stand on Mars Hill in Athens or at

---

1 For a fuller discussion see D. Carlson, *Christianity and Conversion among Migrants: Moving Faith and Faith Movement in the Transit Area* (Boston: Brill, 2021) and *Jesus in Athens*, directed by Peter Hansen (2019: Hansen Productions), Amazon Prime Video.

the Bema Seat in Corinth. It is also a popular place for college musical groups as well as American Christian bands to hold concerts. These groups often stay with Greek-led parachurch ministries, who charge them rates that help fund their overall ministry.

Athens was at the center of a world crisis in 2015. During the first nine months, 487,000 people arrived on Europe's shores, twice the number of migrants that came in all of 2014.[2] This and other factors led the European Commission to call this the "largest global humanitarian crisis since World War II,"[3] while German chancellor Angela Merkel stated that the crisis would define the decade.[4] Greece accounted for 92 percent of all arrivals of migrants into the EU, with 924,105 refugees arriving on Greek islands between January 2015–March 2016. In 2016, the International Organization of Migration estimated that the daily arrival of migrants to Greece increased to two thousand a day, ten times more than the previous year.[5] The flow of migrants and refugees into Greece is not new. Its proximity to Turkey, with multiple islands just a few kilometers away, make it the preferred entry into Europe.

Evangelical Christians have taken notice and been very active. Evangelical ministries, refugee centers, and churches have been started. Greek evangelicals, long labeled a cult by Greek Orthodox Christians, are viewed with suspicion by Greeks. Yet, while the Orthodox Church dwarfs evangelicals in number, the efforts of evangelicals to reach and provide assistance to refugees far exceed any work of the Orthodox Church.

Greek evangelicals have been joined by various long-term missionaries, predominantly from Western countries and Korea. Some of these missionaries work within Greek parachurch ministries, while others work with no connection to Greek Christians. Refugee centers provide food and services for mainly Muslim migrants, some of whom have converted to Christianity. Groups of converts have planted churches. Some Greek evangelical churches run their own programs to reach Muslims and plant Greek-speaking churches in refugee communities. These ministries and churches are not making Athens an Orthodox city but an evangelical and charismatic one.

Into this context enter short-term teams, with a strong desire to herald the Good News of Jesus while serving Christian and Muslim refugees. These include seminary and college students on school sponsored trips or on break, teams sent by churches, mission organizations who sent people to Athens to recruit them for long-term work, and ministries like YWAM, who often have teams around the city. What they think they are experiencing and what is really happening is not always the same.

Baptizing People in the Name of Jesus

Christians in Athens attempt to express hospitality to Muslims in a number of ways. One of those ways is by sharing the Gospel with them, and many of them convert as a result. Baptizing a new convert from Islam is not something many people in the United States or Korea get to witness In Athens, it is normal occurrence, and when teams come with their Gospel presentations, they are happy to baptize these converts. Putting aside whether this is theologically appropriate, there is still a complicating reality. Migrants realize that converting to Christianity heightens the probability of being granted asylum. It is a contradictory reality of sorts: while many Muslims fake conversion, the actual cost to convert is significant and often means putting oneself in physical danger, for these "converts" still live with Muslims coming from cultures who believed in honor killing and that the punishment for apostasy should be death. Still, people take the risk. One Persian woman explained:

> These two Iranians had a brother in England who would call them and tell them, "When you get to England, you have to tell them that you're Christian so they let you stay. You have to tell them that Jesus is your savior, and Jesus saved you, and all that." I was listening in all these conversations, so when I saw the Korean lady I lied and said, "I'm a Christian too, can I have a Bible?" I got the Bible,

---

[2] N. Banulescu-Bogdan and S. Fratzke, "Europe's Migration Crisis in Context: Why Now and What Next?," Migration Information Source, Migration Policy Institute, September 24, 2015, http://www.migrationpolicy.org/article/europe-migration-crisis-context-why-now-and-what-next.

[3] *Syrian Crisis* (Brussels: European Commission Humanitarian Aid and Civil Protection, 2016).

[4] W. Hutton, "Angela Merkel's Humane Stance on Immigration Is a Lesson to Us All," *The Guardian*, August 29, 2015, International edition, https://www.theguardian.com/commentisfree/2015/aug/30/immigration-asylumseekers-refugees-migrants-angela-merkel.

[5] "Mediterranean Migrant Arrivals in 2016 Pass 76,000; Deaths Top 400," UN Migration, International Organization for Migration, press release February 9, 2016, http://www.iom.int/news/mediterranean-migrant-arrivals-2016-pass-76000-deaths-top-400.

but I was only doing it because I thought it would get me to England.⁶ ⁷

Short-term teams, especially those working outside any ministry in Greece, were nearly always unaware of this reality. To be fair, some long-term workers were as well. One leader put it bluntly, laying the blame on needing to report numerical success to donors:

> One of the things I'm very thankful for is that we don't have to raise our support. What that means is I don't like to give numbers. I don't feel that same pressure. I'm not saying that is what people are doing, but our guys that work in some of these other ministries, they will just tell you that the majority of people who get a certificate are not Christians."⁸

But short-term missionaries, with pure intentions and excitement, were happy to head down to the Aegean Sea and baptize people. In some cases, they would bring migrants to churches to ask pastors to baptize the new converts, but when pastors would follow up, the migrants were never heard from again.

Short-term teams would return home with powerful stories. This would then help recruit more young people to go on trips. Stories of conversions and baptism make good fundraising letters. Facebook pages of people who had traveled to Athens were filled with pictures of blurred-out faces, celebrating conversions and baptisms. But the reality of the people being baptized was different. To just give one example:

> I only wanted them to give me a baptism certificate, which is why I said I was a Christian. When they were doing the baptism in the church, it was freezing cold, and the water was freezing. When the guy said, "Who wants to get baptized?" I wanted to go first, because I didn't want to go in the water that all the other people went in. I thought it was gross, so I quickly put my hand up. The guy said, "Repeat after me." I repeated his prayer, whatever he said, and said yes to whatever questions he asked, because I wanted to get it over and done with. I was angry at my husband for bringing me to the church.
>
> I went to their lessons for two weeks and then they baptized me. After that I never went again. All the Iranians that got baptized on the same day as them, they were all doing it just for the documents, and they were all telling me that you have to do it here, because Greece is the only country that the Christians will give you a baptism certificate so quickly. All the Iranians that came with us to get baptized, all the people there, they lied and said they were believers. We were mocking. I couldn't believe I was getting baptized. After the baptism, they went out and got drunk.⁹

Could all this be avoided? Not "all." There is a dynamic in the world that when the Spirit acts, the devil undermines and often apes the Spirit's work. "He knows his time is short" (Rev. 12:12). With that knowledge, we should not be surprised that deception is occurring or that desperate migrants are doing whatever it takes in order to survive.

Still, this highlights a significant issue for short-termers—should they be sharing the Gospel at all on their short-term trip? They know they cannot share the Gospel with people without heavily relying on translators. By using Christian translators, they are taking time from people who are already sharing the Gospel with migrants and refugees in their own "heart language." It does not seem wise or necessary for short-term teams to ask them to stop that in order to translate their own presentation, which in reality would be half as much content, spoken by a stranger. Some leaders related that they often would not translate what was being said because of how unnecessarily offensive the naïve short-term missionaries were in the words they chose.

Some teams were introduced to the Muslim friends of long-term missionaries, as an opportunity to understand Islam and receive hospitality from Muslims. These types of decisions made for much more meaningful interactions and are often helpful to long-term workers. The overall ministry of long-term missionaries, who are already in relationship with Muslims and sharing the Gospel with them throughout daily life, was enhanced when their Muslim friends were given the opportunity to show hospitality to the short-term team and tell them about their faith and life.

These types of encounters had a tremendous impact on short-term teams, especially in dismantling their ethnocentrism. Muslims were no longer a foreign

---

6 A note about all quotations: I have decided to not correct the grammar of speakers so that their voice can be heard.

7 Persian Woman 1, interview by author, March 21, 2017.

8 Western Leader 1, interview by author, date withheld. I withhold the date and gender in some cases to preserve the person's anonymity.

9 Persian Migrant 1, interview by author, date withheld.

threat to be scared of, but someone to share a meal with. Americans, with a significant political debate over immigration waging at home, are confronted with the needs of real people. Many short and long-term missionaries would tell stories of returning home excited to tell about God's work in Athens, only to have the Christians in their churches deride them for helping Muslims and speak of how Muslims would destroy Europe. Receiving hospitality from Muslims helped short-term team members, but more importantly, the efforts of long-term missionaries to lead their Muslim friends to Christ.

Money

Migrants and refugees often find themselves in a desperate situation in Athens. If they are not registered with the government, they have no access to any money except what they may have brought with them or what might be wired to them via Western Union. If they do register, the UN gives them a small stipend to buy meals. By visiting refugee centers throughout the city, people try to survive on what they have. Some migrants get jobs. They can make twenty euros a day for passing out fliers. Some beg. Some become caught up in sex trafficking, especially unaccompanied minors. Migrants with jobs can't work in one place for too long because Greek companies must report their income and pay taxes on it if it surpasses a certain level.

Knowing this, evangelical Christians have responded in a variety of ways and some disagreements have arisen among the Christian ministries on how to best help migrants. The bibliography on the topic of missions and money is long—and people will continue to write about this important topic. Jonathan Bonk states what many feel, that "the independence, segregation, and isolation that come with wealth translate into an unbridgeable social gulf between rich and poor."[10] Is it really this stark or even worse given the cross-cultural barriers between Western short-term teams and refugees from the Middle East?

Passing out money often feels right when on a short-term mission trip. The people often being served seem desperate and in significant need, and a quick fix is to give them money, something that most participants would never consider doing in their home country without giving it a lot of thought. Short-term teams are notorious for doing this. Well-meaning college students in their twenties see migrants in need and give them money. Or they may meet a migrant in a refugee center that tells them a harrowing story, and they feel compelled to give. They are not thinking broadly about the implications for the long-term workers or the potential duplicity of the person telling them a story, but narrowly of how they can immediately help the person in front of them.

These issues are not limited to short-term teams. There are times when long-term workers get involved in passing out money as well. Having one ministry give money directly to migrants often endangers ministries that are trying to serve people in other ways. It creates an expectation that not everyone can fulfill:

> Recently, a ministry here has been giving loaded Visa cards to refugees, and it's caused a huge problem for us. What we do is not enough when people are giving money. Last week I took a Swiss team out. I had two guys who were there and they went to about seven Afghans and said, "Hey, we're here, we're here to help you. Here's what we're doing. Here's our program." They stopped them and said, "Do you have those cards? Do you give money?" And they said, "What are you talking about?" The Swiss team then turned to me and said, "We have to give them money like the other church does." I told them [the Afghans] we don't do that. They got angry and said, "Go, we don't want to talk to you. Go."[11]

In Athens, short-term team members think they are helping persecuted Christians by giving them money. They end up going home reporting how they served the persecuted church in Athens. Nearly every ministry center worker I interacted with agreed that it rarely helped the Christian migrants and often the short-term teams were duped by people posing as Christians. Refugee center leaders reported that many migrants ended up spending the money on drugs and brothels. On some occasions, Christian money donated from the West has even facilitated the sex trade.

In 2016, an American male arrived in Athens outside of any partnership with established organizations and churches with a plan to start a refugee center on his own during his three-month stay, which would then turn into a base where

---

10 Jonathan J. Bonk, "Missions and Mammon: Six Theses," *International Bulletin of Missionary Research* 13, no. 4 (October 1989): 176.

11 Western Leader 2, interview by author, date withheld.

short-term teams could come and serve. He did not consult with any other organization but used donated money to buy a large building that he planned to use for a meeting space as well as to house migrants. But for some migrants, this was an opportunity to make money off a naive Western Christian. According to those I interviewed, these migrants were former members of other centers who had caused problems. They began to bring people to the missionary that were willing to be baptized. He would then take pictures and raise more money, eventually even hiring some of the Muslims posing as Christians. The American never knew, or at least seemed to not want to know. Money could be raised, and the American could pay the migrants more money. As one more pessimistic Afghan told me, "If I were to start a ministry here, I'd be a rich man because there's a good market here."[12]

Here we find many cultural dynamics in play—power, money, and deception. Nearly every leader at a refugee center and many Persian and Afghan leaders spoke of lying as a regular practice. Many had been taught to lie from childhood. Some saw it as a virtue. Many reasoned that if Allah deceives people, so they should as well. The practice was referred to as *Tarof*, which was as simple as saying you did not want to eat a meal with someone when you did, or as blatant as stating something that was false. Faking conversion and fooling people proved how smart one was. Raising support from multiple sources without disclosing where all the money was coming from was not a problem.

There was a Youth with a Mission (YWAM) team in Athens that went to Victoria Park, holding up signs in Greek stating: "We will interpret your dreams." It was common for former Muslims who had converted to report having a dream of Jesus. After an afternoon in Victoria Park, the team stopped by a Greek evangelical church and told the pastor they had led fourteen people to faith in Christ by interpreting dreams and that the migrants would be coming to the church to be baptized. The team left with a great story for fundraising appeals, but the Muslims never came to the church. The Greek pastors believed migrants took advantage of the young Americans who were enthralled with dream stories.

How is it possible for short-term teams to wisely enter into a situation where they come from positions of power (they can leave anytime they want) and wealth (they have money they can give away without any pain) into a place where they are targets of desperate people trying to make a living The solutions are easy to write down but hard to put into practice. It means serving in the background. It means longer preparation. It means long-term missionaries taking the time to pass down wisdom to eager believers, providing some basic discipleship and alerting them to the complexities money brings and how migrants view the teams coming in and out of refugee centers. By placing short-term teams behind the "front lines" of work, they can be protected from being taken advantage of and instead support the work of missionaries living in Athens.

God Still Works

If short-term workers focus on simple acts of service under the direction of long-term missionaries, rather than speaking, they can make a significant impact. Even "simple acts" communicate differently in various cultures, but I have seen various examples of service that led to Muslims becoming Christians. If short-term teams would embrace service over words, support over front lines, and receiving hospitality from those they desire to serve, they may find themselves surprised by the lasting impact of their work.

A young Western missionary in his twenties told a story of a Muslim man who verbally assaulted him for being a Christian, only to find out the Christian was cleaning his toilets. The Muslim was shocked and became open to hearing about Christ. The Muslim could not conceive of an American Christian cleaning the public toilets of refugee men.[13] Consider how a short-term team's acts of humble service might open the door for the long-term missionaries to have meaningful conversations later.

In another instance, a young Afghan told a story of needing dental care. One day he met a Korean dentist in Victoria Park serving as a short-term missionary to Greece.[14] Getting his teeth cleaned was the first time he had met a Christian. There were many ministries that used highly skilled workers with great success. One short-term team met a refugee who was a dentist

---

12 Afghan Migrant 1, interview by author, April 13, 2017.

13 Refugee Center Leader 1, interview by author, March 8, 2017.

14 Afghan Man 1, interview by author, April 3, 2017.

that had fled his home country. "I came because all of my clients were dead." Instead of serving this dentist, they had him join their team and connect with the Greek parachurch ministry they were working with. The result, according to a Greek missionary: "It was the first time I saw him smile."[15] The dentist eventually started coming to church with them, and when he was relocated to Ireland, he thanked the Greek evangelicals profusely for the opportunity to work. He told them they were not what he expected Christians to be like.

A Persian couple told the story of receiving shoes from a Christian as the first point in their turn from Islam:

> When we were in Turkey, I had the shoes that I was wearing, and in my backpack, I had sneakers. When we were in a hotel in Turkey the boy, the Iranian boy that was staying with us, his shoes were completely soaked. My husband told me to give the sneakers to that boy. We got on our boat and got to Greece and were completely soaked because the boat— We were nearly drowning. The boat was halfway full of water.
>
> The boy's feet were really big, so he just flattened the trainers out and he wore them. He was on the boat with us, and when he got to the camp, because he was soaking wet he put my trainers next to the heater for them to dry and he went to sleep. I said to my husband, "I want my trainers back." He saw that the guy was asleep, so he took my trainers from the heater and gave them back to me. It was freezing and I was completely soaked too. This guy woke up and he went barefoot outside of the camp to get soup from these Christians.
>
> My husband was outside eating soup and he saw this boy coming, tiptoeing because everywhere was wet, and he saw him tiptoeing to the people who were serving soup. He said he wanted to take his soup back inside, but the people, the guards of the camp wouldn't let him, because they said you have to eat it outside. He was showing them that he was barefoot and it was cold.
>
> I saw the Christian guy who was holding the rubbish bin started untying his own shoelaces. The Christian who was holding the rubbish bin took his shoes off, gave it to the guy, and then he went back and he was just standing there barefoot. My husband said to me, "Look, we couldn't even give up a pair of trainers to do good to somebody else, but this guy, this Christian, who doesn't even—He's not even from our country, he doesn't even know our language—These Christians have something special about them." That's the first time we saw God's love in people.[16]

To be fair, there were also instances where Muslims became Christians due to the work of short-term missionaries. There was a short-term missionary and pastor from Chicago whom the police had allowed into the prison to speak to anyone who knew English. On one of his visits, he led a Persian man to Christ. Eight months later the missionary returned to find the Persian convert still in prison. The church in Chicago began to pray for his freedom. Two years later he was free.

In another instance, an Afghan woman had a dream during her journey that became a primary reason for her conversion:

> When I come to the island, I had a dream. In the dream, someone stayed behind me and gave me an envelope. Later when I was crossing the border between Greece and Macedonia, someone came up to me and gave me an envelope with the same design. When I opened it, I found a copy of the gospel here.[17]

In the dream no one spoke. Only a gift was given. The gift, an envelope, was designed in a specific way so she remembered what it looked like. Months later, when leaving Greece, a Korean Christian approached her on the border and handed her a Gospel tract in an envelope that was identical to the one in her dream. That tract eventually led to her conversion.

The Lord is pleased to use short-term missionaries, especially when they serve in the background, have been prepared to understand the limit of their impact, and have had a long-term missionary or national leader disciple them. We who are primarily critical of these teams sometimes need to step back and appreciate that in the midst of our criticism eternally good things are being accomplished. This is no small thing, and it should not be ignored by researchers, and should push us all the more to help Christians who eagerly desire to serve Christ in cross-cultural settings on short-term trips.

---

15 Greek Missionary 1, interview by author, April 5, 2017.

16 Persian Woman 2, interview by author, March 21, 2017.

17 Afghan Women 3, interview by author, March 30, 2017.

Chapter 24 Response

by Cheol Kang

Two things motivated me to begin my short-term missions ministry: first, my view of the church bought with the blood of Jesus Christ, and second, my perspective on true faith—as I witnessed too many Christians failing to practice Christ's love in their daily lives, notwithstanding their confession of faith. The Korean church is in crisis today because many believers are pursuing their greed and selfish desires. In that context, I started planning for short-term missions with a view to strengthening the role of the church in secular Christians' lives, to restoring the essence of what it means to be a Christian, and to fulfilling our responsibilities as believers in Jesus.

Darren Carlson's chapter challenged me from the very beginning when he wrote, "Are short-term mission trips primarily for those who go or those who are served? Does a desire to serve and the ability to fundraise essentially qualify someone to go? Do the lives of those who go on short-term trips appreciably change? When a never-ending stream of short-term teams are sent to partner with long-term missionaries, are we aiding or inhibiting the missionaries' work?"

Apparently, 924,105 refugees landing on Greek islands does cause lots of issues.

Baptize Them in Jesus's Name

Thousands of refugees in Athens are baptized for "hospitality and salvation."[18] However, many of them receive the baptism in order to secure their asylum applications, not necessarily to confess Jesus as the Christ and God. As such, Muslims can easily fake conversions. As quoted in the chapter, "the majority of people who get a certificate are not Christians."

The Usefulness of the Money Needed for Missions Witnessing the desperate situation of the refugees, short-term mission teams often hand out money out of goodwill. Although it looks like a quick solution, long-term missionaries are aware of how such impromptu donations would undermine their ministries: the refugees would turn to the long-term missionaries for money. But when their request is denied, the backlash will be even worse. Carlson shares a story of a ministry handing out loaded Visa cards to refugees, only causing more problems. The story reminds me of the incidents in Korean churches when young participants in short-term missions return and complain that all they did was have a tour and give some money to the locals.

A direct donation by a short-term mission team does not benefit long-term missionary work. It is wiser to donate to the missionaries. If a short-term mission team distributes money to attract more people, takes pictures with them, promotes their superficial achievements to raise more money, and boasts about their missionary accomplishment while the people who received the money spend it on alcohol, drugs, and sex trafficking, it will not result in the expansion of God's Kingdom. It will only enlarge Satan's evil domain.

While Carlson's chapter is on international short-term missions, my pastoral ministry involves short-term missions serving weak churches in the rural regions of Korea. I was amazed, however, that the sentiments were similar whether the ministry was international or domestic.

On the purpose of the church Otto Weber wrote, "The church is in the dispensation of God's eternal choice, not based on individual or collective decisions. And the church is in expanding the Kingdom of God through the reign of Christ and the renewal of the Holy Spirit, and for this the church exists."[19]

Stanley J. Grenz asked, "Why did Christ initially institute the church? And for what end does the Spirit continue to constitute the churches today? Our final answer to this question can only be, for God's glory.

---

18 Joshua W. Jipp, 환대와 구원 [Hwandae-wa Guwon, Hospitality and salvation], trans. Il Song (Seoul: 새물결플러스 [Saemugyeoul-Puleos], 2019), 20.

19 Otto Weber, 칼빈의 교회관 [Kalbin-eui Kyohoekwan, Calvin's church], trans. Young Jae Kim (Suwon, Korea: 합신대학원출판부 [Hapsindaehakwonchulpanbu, Hapshin Graduate School of Publishing], 2008), 40.

The church in all its expressions exists ultimately for the sake of the glory of the triune God."[20] To the question, "What should we do to glorify God in order to fulfill the purpose of the church's existence?," our answer was, "Let us go to the field where we can serve the least with the word proclaimed from the pulpit. Let us first set our foot on the field, and find out what we can do to serve, and then do it."

The next perspective of faith was related with "fellowship." The Bible says, "Our fellowship is with the Father and his Son, Jesus Christ" (1 John 1:3). I questioned whether this fellowship is within us and whether our fellowship with God is being made perfect. I asked myself if I, a pastor, had been teaching my congregation to love, but with words only. "If we claim to have fellowship with him and yet walk in the darkness, we lie and do not live out the truth" (1 John 1:6). I questioned whether we were only saying that we believed and had fellowship with God, but were still deceiving ourselves.

"Fellowship" in Greek is "koinonia" (κοινωνία), originating from an adjective meaning "common." Thus, fellowship is about finding common ground, sharing common emotions, and living toward a common goal, which starts with knowing God and what God has done for us.[21] What has God done? God sent his Son into the world to save us (John 3:16), and God "loved us and sent his Son as an atoning sacrifice for our sins" (1 John 4:10). Therefore, the commonality, the common emotion, and the common goal for everyone, especially Christians, should be the Heavenly Father and his Son, Jesus Christ.

I then contemplated on how to perfect our fellowship with God and his Son, Jesus Christ. Jesus said, "Whatever you did for one of the least of these brothers and sisters of mine, you did for me (Matt. 25:40)."

The Lord said through John, "Dear children, let us not love with words or speech but with actions and in truth" (1 John 3:18). In Carlson's chapter, a refugee couple witnessed such love when a Christian took his shoes off and gave it to a barefoot refugee. The refugee couple realized that "these Christians have something special about them."

In light of the words of the Bible, I wondered what we, a small church, could do with our small budget. We, Uijeongbu Dongbu Church, decided to serve churches that are even smaller than us as a ministry to Jesus. In order to love "with actions and in truth," we reached out to the churches on the islands and coastal areas of Korea.

Many churches in the rural areas of Korea are mainly composed of members aged seventy-five or older. As a result, many chapels are left in their tattered state. So we dedicated our efforts to renovate their church buildings by adding rooms, waterproofing the walls, installing heated floors and shower booths, and preparing quarters for the single elderly members.

Such volunteering ministry has continued for a decade. The guiding principles of our ministry included the following: serve anonymously; do not let your left hand know what your right hand is doing; do not expect anything in reward; and do not add any burden to the church, even by accepting a meal as a sign of their gratitude for our hard work.

When we hit a financial roadblock, we learned that the lack of money does not necessarily mean that the mission is over. We experienced that if we abide in Christ and have fellowship with God, God will provide us with whatever we ask and open up new paths for us. If we restore the purpose of the church and the essence of our faith in short-term missions, we will experience the miracle of the five loaves and two fish among us today in short-term missions.

The Lord knows about our efforts at long-term and short-term missions and he is pleased with us: "It is true that some preach Christ out of envy and rivalry, but others out of goodwill. But what does it matter? The important thing is that in every way, whether from false motives or true, Christ is preached. And because of this I rejoice. Yes, and I will continue to rejoice" (Phil. 1:15, 18).

I close by quoting Carlson's words:

> The Lord is pleased to use short-term missionaries, especially when they serve in the background, have been prepared to understand the limit of their impact, and have had a long-term missionary or national leader disciple them. We who are primarily critical of these teams sometimes need to step back and appreciate that in the midst of our criticism eternally good things are being accomplished.

---

20 Stanley. J. Grenz, 조직신학 [*Jojiksinhak*, Systematic theology], trans. Ok Soo Shin (Paju, Korea: 크리스챤 다이제스트 [Keuliseuchyan Daijeseuteu, Christian Digest], 2003), 696.

21 Disciples' Publisher, ed., 옥스퍼드 원어성경대전 [The Oxford Bible Interpreter] (Seoul, Korea: 제자원 바이블네트 [Jejawon Baibeulneteu, Disciples' Publisher & Bible Net], 2006), vol. 128, 352.

Chapter 25
Paul Mission Training Center and Jeonju Antioch Church Mission Fund

by Seung-Il Lee and Dong-Whee Lee

This study asserts that the sender's missionary DNA and ethos sculpt its fiscal policies, and that these policies determine the quality and the vision of the missionaries they send. This assertion is based on the fiscal policy of Jeonju Antioch Church (hereafter JAC), which founded The Paul Mission International (hereafter TPMI) and the Native Missionary Training program it runs. It will clearly show that money should flow horizontally through the organic relationship built from mutual trust among churches in his Kingdom, not through a vertical movement from the missionary to the mission field. It will be argued that apportioning of integral values as well as "organic trust and responsibility" should be the major elements behind this organic horizontal flow. As this is a case study of JAC and TPMI, the primary sources for it are the periodicals published by the two organizations.

Jeonju Antioch Church and The Paul Mission International

History of Jeonju Antioch Church and The Paul Mission International

JAC is a missionary church founded in March 1983, and TPMI is an indigenous Korean mission agency established in 1986. Both organizations were pioneered by Rev. Dong-Whee Lee (hereafter Lee). Initially, TPMI was part of JAC, but since has grown into an interdenominational mission agency, with mission partners from 921 churches and thirty-one denominations.[1] Lee retired from his position as senior pastor of JAC in 2006, but is currently serving as a missions pastor, and is the chairman of TPMI's board of trustees.

---
1 The Paul Mission International, "2020 Annual Report" (unpublished).

Organic Relationship between Jeonju Antioch Church and The Paul Mission International

Lee comments that JAC's and TPMI's interdependence is like bone and muscle, and their separation would lead to a mutually assured destruction.[2] This organic relationship can be explained in four ways.

First, a unified understanding of missions. Lee understands mission as "the work of saving people by saved Christians through delivering the savior Jesus Christ."[3] While emphasizing that mission does not exist for the church but rather the church for mission,[4] Lee claims that evangelism and mission are the only means to achieving salvation,[5] followed by the natural establishment and growth of the church. This church, both institutional and the individual body of Christ, plays an outpost role in expanding God's Kingdom.[6] Lee's understanding of God's Kingdom correlates with Ladd's, who identified it as "God's sovereign reign."[7] However, Lee takes a more militant and radical approach in expanding God's Kingdom: "We are an army dedicated to his Kingdom. There is no question of this when one completely understands the Great Commission as a royal command to us. We are to deliver rescue breaths to souls that are comatose, separated from God."[8] While encouraging JAC members and TPMI missionaries to live a wartime lifestyle where they are, Lee identifies the mindset Christians need to be equipped with, and prioritizes the ultimate authority and power of God. Lee's definition of mission as "the work of God's people to expand his Kingdom through saving souls" became the ideological foundation for TPMI and JAC.

Second, the presence of organic cooperation and symbiosis. JAC and TPMI have achieved spiritual and ministerial symbiosis. At the core of spiritual symbiosis exists the twenty-four-hour prayer room, established in 1995. In the assigned hour of a month, a JAC member prays for prayer requests, updated constantly by TPMI, in a prayer room located in JAC. This symbiosis allows spiritual cooperation to take place in the physical reality.[9] Regarding the ministerial symbiosis, JAC named each church department as the name of a mission field. For example, each grade in Sunday school is named after a different country; they pray for the missionaries within the country, and their offerings are set apart as mission funds for that country. TPMI continuously provides JAC with mission information, conducts the mission-related seminars in JAC, and guides short-term missions. Reliability and transparency are two key factors attributed to the thirty-five-year interdependence. JAC's trust in TPMI is reciprocated through TPMI's financial accountability, its reporting back to JAC, and its commitment to help JAC's mission work. The partnership is maintained under the joint council between JAC's mission committee and TPMI headquarters.

Third, the presence of the mutual core value, "Faith Mission." Lee defines "Faith Mission" as a "missionary ethos convicting us that God is the source of everything for mission; it is a missionary principle activating God's sovereignty, Jesus' authority and power, and the Holy spirit's creativity where we are."[10] Lee's definition seeks to confer a missional spirit on all Christians, emphasizing an intimate relationship with God, service to the world, and intentional humility for salvation in one's life. This concept of faith mission has become part of the daily lives of JAC members and TPMI missionaries, who experience spiritual and physical miracles by continuously acknowledging the Trinity.

---

2 Dong-Whee Lee, 불편하게 삽시다 선교하며 삽시다 [*Bulpyeon-hage sabsida. Sungyo-hamyeo sabsida*, Let's enjoy discomfort in life for mission] (Jeonju: Paul Mission Press, 2007), 126–27.

3 Dong-Whee lee, "바울선교회 7대정신" [*Baul-songyohoi childae-jeongshin*, The Paul Mission's sevenfold spirit], *Baul Sungyo* (July/August 2002): 1.

4 Dong-Whee lee, "하나님의 팔 길이, 결코 짧아지지 않았다" [*Hananim-ui-pal-giri, Gyeolko-jjalbaziji-anatta*, god's hand, still powerful and effective], *Baul Sungyo* (March/April 2020): 1.

5 Dong-Whee Lee, 천국은 가득차고 지옥은 텅텅비어라 [*Chunkook-un kadeug-chago jiog-un tungtung-biera*, Let heaven be full, let hell be empty!] (Jeonju: Paul Mission Press, 2007), 199.

6 Dong-Whee lee, "필리핀 100개 교회 개척" [*Philippine bagge gyohoi-gaechuk*, Let's plant one hundred churches in the Philippines], *Baul Sungyo* (September 1987): 1.

7 G. E. Ladd, *The Gospel of the Kingdom: Scriptural Studies in the Kingdom of God* (Grand Rapids: Eerdmans, 1959), 22.

8 Dong-Whee lee, "총사령관의 군령을 따르라" [*Chong-saryungan-ui kunryung-eul darura*, Let's follow our commander's order], *Baul Sungyo* (January/February 2008): 1.

9 Dong-Whee Lee, 깡통교회 이야기 [*Kangtong-gyohoi iyagi*, The story of Jeonju Antioch Church, the so-called Tin Can Church], 17th ed. (Seoul: duranno, 2004), 53–60.

10 Seung-Il Lee, 바울선교회 미래준비위원회 기획보고서 [*Baul-sungyohoi mirae-junbi-wiwonhoi kihoik-bogosuh*, Report on the future of The Paul Mission International] (Jeonju: Paul Mission Press, 2013), 46.

Fourth, JAC and TPMI share a missionary identity—"all Christians as missionaries." Lee sees Acts 1:8 as a missional command for all Christians, arguing for "the missionaryization" of all believers as follows:

> Acts 1:8 is the last command Jesus gives on this earth before his ascension to heaven. The fact that these are his last words, his last will on this world, and his great command makes accomplishing his command an "absolute necessity." The four mission fields (Jerusalem, Judea, Samaria, and the ends of the earth) signify the "essence" of mission. The call for a concurrent evangelization stresses the "nowness" of this commission. His priority on sending witnesses to the ends of the earth over the disciples' wish for Israel's political restoration communicates the "urgency" of this mission. This is a definite royal command. When one accepts Jesus as their savior and the Holy Spirit lives in them, their identity as witnesses (missionaries) is established, and they automatically receive the Great Commission. Therefore, his people should proclaim, "I am a missionary. I am a missionary." Jerusalem is a central city, signifying the place one lives. Judea symbolizes national evangelization. Samaria symbolizes the marginalized. The ends of the earth signify foreign missions … It is time for all Christians in the world to identify themselves as MISSIONARIES.[11]

While encompassing the necessity, essence, nowness, and urgency of missions, Lee stresses the simultaneous evangelization of Jerusalem, Judea, Samaria, and the ends of the earth. Lee further developed the "understanding of eight categories of missionaries." This proclamation calls all Christians to live with a missionary identity. They are (1) commissioned missionaries who are sent abroad, (2) parent missionaries who dedicate their children to become missionaries, (3) prayer missionaries who pray for a revival in mission fields and missionaries, (4) financial missionaries who dedicate their finances and belongings to world missions, (5) vocational missionaries who show a Christian lifestyle in their workplace, (6) family missionaries who focus on ministering to their unsaved family members, (7) cultural missionaries who share Christian ideals through their artistic talent, and (8) lifestyle missionaries who clearly live out their identity as his people in all areas of life, having a significant, positive affect on others through his/her character.[12] The concept of the "missionaryization" of all believers lays the foundation for an active and dynamic missionary lifestyle in locations where TPMI missionaries operate.

As shown above, JAC and TPMI have successfully maintained an organic interconnectedness in ideological, relational, and structural ways, being tied together with mutual transparency and trust, presenting an example of symbiosis between modality and sodality.[13]

Fiscal Philosophy of Jeonju Antioch Church

JAC's fiscal philosophy is presented in a set of written policies and a set of lifestyle policies.

Written Policy

The written policy is stated in the "Seven Codes of Conduct" (hereafter SCC) of JAC, which aim to present the vision and mission set in stone from its establishment:

1. JAC congregation dedicates themselves and their lives to become a true *worshiper*.
2. JAC congregation becomes a *disciple* following Jesus Christ.
3. JAC congregation acts as *missionaries* commissioned to international, native, marginalized, and educational ministries.
4. JAC congregation becomes a *giver*, delegating over 60 percent of church finances for missions.
5. JAC congregation volunteers to be a *participant* of the missional structure present in the church.
6. JAC congregation takes the role of a *servant* in various service opportunities.
7. JAC congregation participates in *all ministries and meetings* with a sense of agency.

The SCC state the purpose of JAC as missions: a JAC member's identity as a disciple, missionary, giver, and servant allows one to rightfully view themselves as worshipers aiming to expand the Kingdom of God.

---

11 Dong-Whee Lee, "사도행전 1장 8절은 어명이다" [*Sado-haengjeon iljang-paljeol-un umyeong-ida*, Acts 1:8 is the Royal Command], *Baul Sungyo* (May/June 2004): 1.

12 Dong-Whee Lee, "선교사가 되는 8가지" [*Sungyosaga-doinun yeodul-gaji*, Eight categories of missionaries], *Baul Sungyo* (March/April 1998): 1.

13 Chul-Yong Kim, "A Critical Evaluation of the Two Structures Theory of Ralph Winter" (PhD diss., William Carey International University, 2013), 62-63.

The fourth article specifically declares its financial commitment, by "delegating over 60 percent of church finances for missions." Lee explains the reasoning behind the 60 percent as follows:

> Zacchaeus' first commitment to Christ is to "give half of my possessions to the poor." This is the lifestyle of a truly saved person. I believe that the church should follow this commitment. The offering set apart for the Lord is not mine, not the church's, but the Lord's. It should be used for his will. His biggest concern is for global salvation. Therefore, he would ask us to use it accordingly, using at least half of it for others. When Jesus comes back on this earth, he will ask church leaders, "How have you used your finances?" We need to prepare for an adequate answer.[14]

Taking Zacchaeus's example as the basis of fiscal policy reflects the passion to make God's Kingdom work a priority.[15]

Currently JAC's mission can be categorized by domestic, marginalized, and overseas missions. Domestic missions focus on planting churches in rural areas without one, and conducting periodic seminars for church leaders from the provinces. Marginalized mission includes caretaking for the elderly and orphans, and ministries in North Korea. Overseas missions consist of financing over 500 missionaries in over one hundred countries, including TPMI missionaries.[16] The table below shows JAC's finances for selected years.

Table 25.1: Use of JAC's Finances

Particulars/Year	2001	2004	2007	2011	2019	2020	Avg.
General operating expenses	24.4%	23.1	38.8%	33.8%	29.99	37.1%	31.3%
Mission expenses	75.6%	76.9%	61.2%	66.2%	70.01	62.9%	68.7%
Total	100%	100%	100%	100%	100%	100%	100%
Senior pastors	Dong-Whee Lee		Jin-Koo Park		Sung-Jun Oh		

The table clearly shows that general operating expenses averaged 31.3 percent,[17] while mission expenses averaged 68.7 percent. This indicates the continued financial commitment of spending more than 60 percent on their mission funds, despite JAC's change of senior pastors.

Lifestyle Policy

Compared to the written fiscal policy, the lifestyle fiscal policy exists in the form of a slogan or motto in the heart of JAC leaders and members.

Firstly, the church does not assign a budget. During Lee's ministry (1983–2006), JAC did not set an annual budget.[18] Although operating without a budget could be a hard transition for a traditional church, it was possible for JAC through the church congregation's unanimous approval and Lee's philosophy.[19] Lee says:

> In my previous church, the board meeting rejected the idea of helping a rural church due to insufficient budget. As this constrains the work of God to a yearly budget, I have decided to pastor without a yearly budget to fully respond to God's commandments with an "Amen" ... Only a monthly financial statement exists ... Since JAC has handled finances based on Faith Mission, God continued to increase his provision, with mission funds growing month after month. This would have been impossible if we had a yearly budget.[20]

This system, relying on faith in God's complete and perfect provision, allows flexibility in sending help to mission fields in need. The chart below graphs the mission expenses JAC has spent over the past years.

Figure 25.1: JAC's Mission Expenses

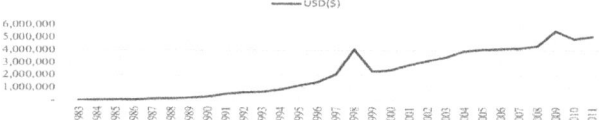

As the chart shows, JAC spent $10,305 in 1983, while spending $5,105,433 in 2011. The growth in mission spending, despite the stagnant growth of the church in 2006, allows one to see JAC's battle-like, active perspective toward missions.

Secondly, the call to welcome discomfort. As mission became the priority of JAC, Lee encouraged Christians to enjoy discomfort to benefit ministries and to educate the native Christians in mission fields.

---

14 Lee, 깡통교회 이야기 [The story of Jeonju Antioch Church], 54.

15 Lee, 54. Lee comments that JAC uses all its tithes for missions, which makes up over 60 percent of offerings.

16 "Introduction to JAC's overseas missions," JAC's Overseas Missions Committee, updated January 24, 2021, http://antiochia.org/main/sub.html?mstrCode=3.

17 Lee, 깡통교회 이야기 [The story of Jeonju Antioch Church], 82.

18 Dong-Whee lee, "믿음선교" [Midum-sungyo, Faith mission], Baul Sungyo (March 1989): 1.

19 Dong-Whee Lee, "하나님의 시각으로 세계를 응시하라" [Hananum-ui sigakuro segyerul ungsi-hara, See this world from God's perspective], Baul Sungyo (March/April 2001): 1.

20 Lee, 깡통교회 이야기 [The story of Jeonju Antioch Church], 55.

Just like Jesus who was born in a manger and grew up in a poor carpenter's home,[21] the church should stop investing in their facilities and use the money for global salvation. This led to JAC's philosophy of only "obligations, rather than rights."[22] This philosophy is still evident within JAC, where the main auditorium is a makeshift tin storage building, even with a congregation of five thousand.

Thirdly, the offering of JAC is of the Lord, not the church. In the thirtieth anniversary service of TPMI (taking place at JAC), Lee urged not to be proud of JAC's mission funds increase, as it was merely giving back what is his, not the church giving what is theirs.[23] This reflects the idea of stewardship, which traces offerings back to its rightful owner and honors his will. JAC presents offerings with a pure heart, prays that they would be used in accordance to his will, and calls missionaries to conserve and be frugal with their resources.[24]

As we observed, JAC's fiscal policy has consistently reflected JAC's DNA. In addition, it contains the desire for JAC members to live their lives as missionaries not only in the area of giving, but also in all other areas.

Native Missionary Policy

In this part, the study focuses on how missionary DNA within JAC and TPMI is applied in native missionary policies.

Current Status of Native Missionaries

As of January 2021, TPMI has sent 496 missionaries to over ninety-two countries. Korean missionaries take up 82 percent of the commissioned missionaries, while native missionaries, sent to four continents—Asia, America, Europe, and Africa—comprise the remaining 18 percent.

Figure 25.2: Categories of Missionaries in TPMI

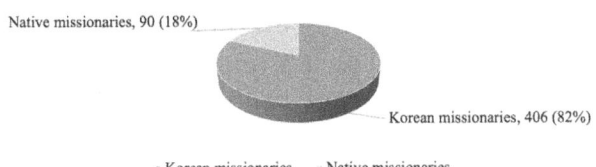

---

21 Dong-whee Lee, 사람을 내놓아라 [*Saramul naenoara*, Wanted!] (Seoul: Amen, 1996), 211–12.
22 Dong-Whee Lee, "권리는 없고 의무만 있는 사람들" [*Kwonrinun upgo uimuman-itnun saramdul*, Obligations, rather than right!], *Baul Sungyo* (September/October 2020): 1.
23 Dong-Whee Lee, "세 겹줄 선교" [*Segyupjul sungyo*, Threefold missions], *Baul Sungyo* (July/August 2018): 1.
24 Dong-Whee Lee, "수도사적인 선교사" [*Sudosa-jogin sungyosa*, Monastic missionary], *Baul Sungyo* (November 1995): 1.

Native missionary training within TPMI takes place in the Philippines and Brazil, and native missionaries work under Frontier Mission Headquarters (hereafter TPMI-FMHQ), a part of TPMI.[25] Starting in 2022, TPMI plans to set up other native missionary training centers, focusing on the major language groups such as French, Spanish, Russian, Arabic, and Chinese.

Mission Policies for Native Missionaries

The core of native missionary policy can be divided into three categories: organic partnership with kingdom workers, sharing of core values, and dual membership with local agencies.

Figure 25.3: TPMI-FMHQ's Partnership Mechanism

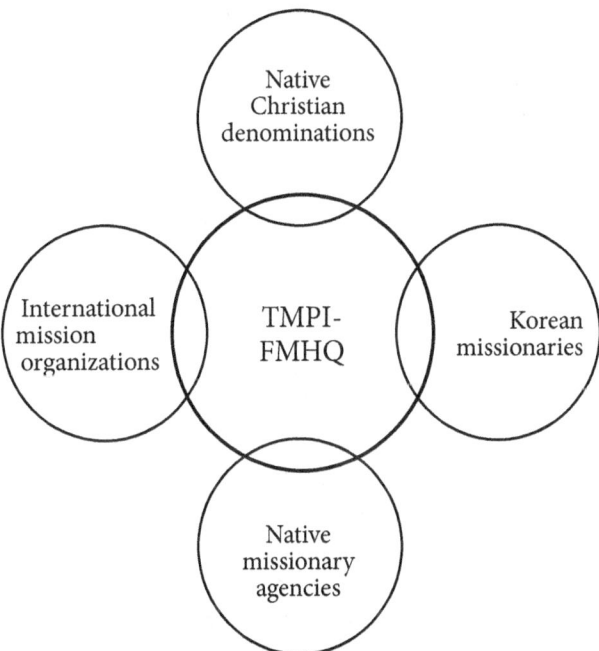

First, organic partnership with Kingdom workers. TPMI-FMHQ aims to hold mutual partnerships with local denominations, international mission agencies, and Korean missionaries. TPMI-FMHQ has set up a Memorandum of Understanding (MOU) with Filipino denominations, including One Sending Body (OSB) and the mission department of the Southern Baptist Convention. OSB sends potential missionary candidates to be trained in TPMI-FMHQ, and the missionary is co-sent to a mission field OSB commissions them to. TPMI-FMHQ cooperates with international mission agencies including OM,

---

25 TPMI-FMHQ is located in Antipolo, Philippines, while TPMI Headquarters is located in Jeonju, Korea.

YWAM, CEF, NTMP, and others, exchanging speakers and conducting missionary training programs. TPMI-FMHQ also partners with Korean missions associations in the Philippines, accepting and co-commissioning missionaries. TPMI-FMHQ is also a member of the Philippine Missions Association (PMA) and receives their endorsement for activities. Through partnership with various mission agencies and denominations in the Philippines, TPMI-FMHQ achieves synergy in mobilizing, training, commissioning, mentoring, and supporting native missionaries.

Second, the sharing of core values. TPMI-FMHQ shares spiritual, life, and strategic values with its partners.

"Faith mission" serves as a spiritual value.[26] This is demonstrated through "Faith Trip," a training program designed for missionary candidates to experience God's provision and protection. The candidates are dropped off at Baguio city, located seven hours away from TPMI-FMHQ, without money or food, and are asked to return in six days, ministering along the way. This allows trainees to experience God who perfectly provides food, transportation, lodging, and ministry opportunities in his timing.

"The sevenfold spirit" acts as a life value: absolute assurance of salvation, absolute divine calling, absolute prayer, absolute thanksgiving, absolute obedience, absolute commitment, and absolute love.[27] As the Gospel is realized through the one who spreads it,[28] the sevenfold spirit codifies the holistic missionary life a missionary should assume.

"Indigenous missionary church planting" is shared as a strategic value. This strategy focuses on equipping indigenous Christians as missionaries through continuous emphasis on the Great Commission in Christian churches.[29] While teaching Acts 1:8 as the biblical reference to "the missionaryization of all believers," the understanding of the eight categories of missionaries is used as a practical reference by TPMI-FMHQ missionaries in their mission fields.[30] TPMI-FMHQ rejects the dualistic view that differentiates between "missionary sending countries" and "missionary receiving countries"; rather, it views natives as potential missionaries who migrate across their cultural borders to spread the Gospel.[31]

Third, dual membership with local agencies. Both TPMI and their mission partners established systemic cooperation, in which the former is responsible for fundraising, disciplining, and ministry, while the latter provides missionary training, field entry and settlement, language learning, cultural adaptation, and mentoring. Commissioned missionaries under dual supervision are required to send a bimonthly newsletter and financial statement to both TPMI and their denomination. Mission funding is provided through a matching fund, with the sending denomination providing 50 percent. The denomination first receives funds from TPMI and sends it along with their own to the missionaries. This allows the native church to be accountable in supporting their missionaries. After a three-year term, missionaries return to the Philippines for a six-month debriefing period with the two organizations. The denomination and the missionary determine whether he/she will be recommissioned or will undergo a career change. After the debriefing period, a recommissioned missionary becomes a member of the local denomination and an associate member of TPMI. Even though TPMI discontinues the financial contributions to missionaries, TPMI continues to provide ethical and spiritual support through mentoring.

Figure 25.4:
Missionary Training and Commissioning Process

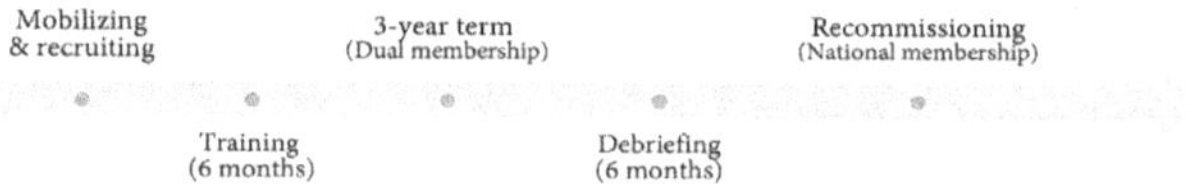

Mobilizing & recruiting — 3-year term (Dual membership) — Recommissioning (National membership)

Training (6 months) — Debriefing (6 months)

As shown above, cooperation based on "mutual responsibility" is present at every step, leading to the nourishment of indigenous missionaries who will serve their own institution and commission their own native missionaries.

---

26 See TPMI's definition of "faith mission" above.

27 Lee, "바울선교회 7대정신" [The Paul Mission's sevenfold spirit], 1.

28 Dong-Whee Lee, "바울선교의 성서적 조명" [*Baulsungyo-ui sungsojuk jomyung*, Biblical foundation of apostle Paul's Mission], *Baul Sungyo* (May 1986): 1.

29 Seung-Il Lee, "Mission Planting Beyond Church Planting," in *Globalization and Mission*, ed. Timothy K. Park and Steve K. Eom (Seoul: EWCMRD, 2017), 575–584.

30 I noted the eight categories of missionaries above: (1) commissioned missionaries, (2) parent missionaries, (3) prayer missionaries, (4) financial missionaries, (5) vocational missionaries, (6) family missionaries, (7) cultural missionaries, and (8) lifestyle missionaries.

31 Dong-Whee Lee, "식민주의적 선교를 중단하라" [*Shikmin-juijeog sungyorul jungdanhara*, Stop Christendom mission], *Baul Sungyo* (May 1996): 37.

The Positives of TPMI's Native Missionary Training Program

First, increase of long-term missionaries with TPMI DNA. In the case of Filipino missionaries, there has been an increase in long-term missionaries who returned to their mission fields. The chart below analyzes the career path of Filipino missionaries after the initial three-year term.

Figure 25.5: Career Paths of Missionaries after Three Years in Ministry

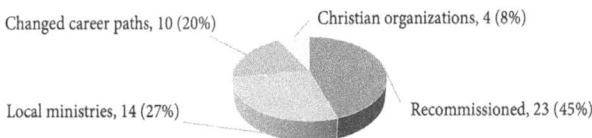

Among the fifty-one Filipino missionaries commissioned by FMHQ from 2006 to 2018 (batches 1–9), 45 percent (23 people) were recommissioned. It shows that for Filipino missionaries, financial difficulties did not hinder their missionary work. On top of that, long-term Filipino missionaries who are in mission field start sending their own native disciples to TPMI-FMHQ as missionary candidates. In addition, 27 percent of missionaries (fourteen people) dedicated themselves to local ministries in the Philippines. Although they are not commissioned missionaries, they are actively engaged in mission-oriented ministries. Having a close relationship with TPMI, they send their disciples as missionary candidates and support the Filipino missionaries financially. This is a sign that TPMI DNA is being passed on through generations. This shared vision and ethos allowed missionaries to remain in the mission field, even when their financial support was cut off after three years. Ultimately, the missionary ethos vitalizes and activates the ministry, leading to reproducibility. This system allows one to anticipate more dynamic mission movements through Filipino missionaries.

Second, increased capability as professional tentmakers. It is encouraging to see the diversity of ministries in recommissioned missionaries. Contrary to popular belief that Filipino missionaries minister only as English teachers, their professions have broadened, working as pastors, BAM (Business as Mission) practitioners, teachers, ministers within international organizations, and seminary professors.

Figure 25.6: Ministries of Recommissioned Missionaries

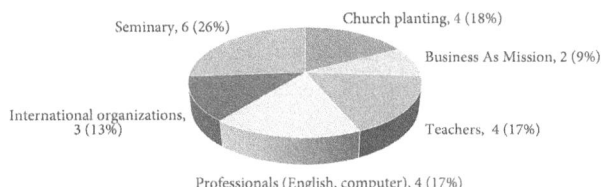

This is a result of the Holy spirit opening doors to effectively utilize Filipino missionaries, and is a sign that other native missionaries would also be fully capable of being tentmakers. For example, a missionary in country L is ministering to the unreached people groups through a restaurant, while missionaries present in country C are working in international schools as computer engineers, English teachers, and social developers along with the local churches. The most encouraging aspect is that these Filipino missionaries are teaching the native Christians to take part in world mission and are training their disciples as missionaries no matter what ministry they do.

Thirdly, the potential for diasporic mission. Among the numerous advantages, diasporic missions is the most unique aspect. For example, two Vietnamese missionaries who were trained in TPMI-FMHQ are currently ministering to Vietnamese international students in Korea. While discipling Vietnamese students in Korea and leading Vietnamese service with a Korean local church, these Vietnamese missionaries have a vision to train Vietnamese students as cross-cultural missionaries. A Filipino missionary in country L has started a church community for Filipinos residing in that country, while a missionary couple in country B started an English service, which has now grown into a multinational international church. In the era of multiculturalism and migrants, utilizing native missionaries proves to be an effective mission strategy.

Conclusion

This case study demonstrates that a mission organization's financial spending aptitude can be traced back to its missionary ethos. The sender's missionary DNA and ethos determines its fiscal policy, and this policy shapes the vision and quality of a missionary's ministry. JAC and TPMI present mission planting in which native Christians recognize their identity as missionaries and live not only as local missionaries, but also as cross-cultural missionaries. To achieve this goal, TPMI shares its core values with native Christians. This allows TPMI to engage in ministries along with the native church and leads to a horizontal fiscal policy. Horizontal flow of funds eliminates the dualism between missionary sending and receiving countries, leading to a sense of community that TPMI defines. TPMI's native missionary training policy not only effectively realizes the "missionaryization of all believers," but also provides a model to establish his Kingdom on earth through cooperation with native churches.

Response

by David S. Lim

This chapter is the personal testimony of Rev. Dong-Whee Lee, the founding pastor of Jeonju Antioch Church (JAC) and founding president of its The Paul Mission International (TPMI) that supports Paul Mission Training Center (PMTC), which is presently led by Dr. Seung-Il Lee. Rev. Lee describes how their missionary DNA and ethos shape their fiscal policies and how these policies determine the quality and the vision of the missionaries they send, and Dr. Lee describes the Native Missionary Training program that PMTC runs.

In the first paragraph, he states that they envision that "money should flow horizontally through the organic relationship built from mutual trust among churches in his Kingdom, not through a vertical movement from the missionary to the mission field." Was this validated in this chapter? I will use SWOT analysis (strengths, weaknesses, opportunities, and threats) to give my assessment.

Positive Aspects

There are many positive aspects (strengths and opportunities) in their given financial policies:

Strengths

I would like to highlight four strengths:

1. *Visionary and passionate leadership.* Their greatest strength is the visionary and passionate leadership of Rev. Lee. His call for radical obedience to Christ and a "wartime lifestyle" has resulted in sacrificial commitment and giving to missions. He creatively outlined eight categories for his church members to act on his teaching that "every believer is a missionary." To continue using a makeshift tin storage building as the sanctuary of a five thousand member congregation helps the members to experience the "feeling" of frontier missions regularly. This has resulted in their confidence to allocate 60 percent of their regular church collection to missions!

2. *Prayer mobilization.* Much of the credit for the success of missions mobilization in the church was given to setting up a prayer room in 1995. Through the consistent program of providing timely prayer requests, the members were encouraged to keep up-to-date with the situation of their supported missionaries, which would also help raise more human and financial resources for their missions program.

3. *Separate mission structure.* I think it was very wise of Rev. Lee to create a mission structure separate from the church. The traditional approach of having a denominational mission board within the church structure put pressure on their supported missionaries to follow age-old conventions, which usually needed contextualizing on the mission field, especially in the postmodern age of rapid change. Having a separate governance board that specializes in missions will help develop a more culturally sensitive leadership team that will allow more freedom and flexibility to frontline missionaries—without cutting their support when they differ from church policies—while also welcoming contextual and creative activities and programs on the mission field.

4. *Self-supporting missionaries.* Excellent policies for self-support were taught and practiced by the trainees in PMTC. They were trained to not expect long-term financial support, with three years as the maximum limit. This has led to creative and varied economic livelihoods and vocations for these missionary trainees. (Hence the culture of dependency has been avoided, unlike on many mission fields.) I'm most glad that almost half of them have chosen the tentmaker (self-supporting missionary) option, which allows easier access to restricted areas and is cost-effective.

Opportunities

I see two opportunities:

1. *Native missions.* It's wonderful to see that as of late, 18 percent of the budget has been used for "native missions." In a globalized world where people are seeking to affirm their sociocultural identity in order not to feel lost in the crowd, "nationals reaching nationals" has been a more effective way of evangelizing and discipling peoples, communities, and nations, besides being cost-effective. Their plan to set up new training centers beyond the Philippines and Brazil to train native missionaries promises a more strategic use of their missions budget.

2. *Local mission outreaches.* In our world of mass migration of peoples due to globalization of the world's labor and business markets, cross-cultural ministry has brought missions to our doorsteps. I'm glad that TPMI has begun to minister among the Vietnamese students and Filipino workers in their region, and is starting to reach people of other faiths in their vicinity. May the outreach to the diaspora peoples, like international students, businesspeople, and foreign workers, increase, and may it strategically disciple the new converts to Christ to share him (with some training in contextualization) with their relatives and friends back home.

Challenging Aspects

There are a few gaps or problematic areas (one weakness and two threats) in the financial policies shown in this chapter:

Weakness

I can only point to one weakness:

Strategic planning. Based on my experiences in mobilizing churches to send missionaries to share the Gospel of the Kingdom of God among unreached peoples (particularly in China, Buddhist, and Muslim majority countries), I have discovered that determining the right mission strategy for our missionaries to use in the frontiers is most important. Missions today continue to misallocate God's resources in two ways: most missionaries continue to work without direct contact with the unreached;[32] and many denominational missionaries to the unreached do not plant churches effectively, in spite of the relatively large amount of financial support given for the purpose. Is our Lord's plentiful harvest really so illusive that we cannot aspire to harvest a hundredfold, or at least thirtyfold?

I published an article ten years ago entitled, "Effective Partnerships for Church Multiplication and Insider Movements,"[33] in which I described how different missionaries from various churches and agencies can work and finance their frontline ministries with these four main points: 1) key substance: commonality of strategy; 2) key relationship: friendship of equals; 3) key objective: empowerment of locals/nationals; and 4) key attitude: servanthood of expatriates. Native missionary training seems to follow the last three points, but it seems to miss my first major point—finding and funding the best mission strategy for effective multiplication of disciples and churches for "saturation evangelism" of whole villages and tribes among the unreached.

Thus, I hope Dr. Lee will write a subsequent chapter describing the best church planters and the best practices of the more than five hundred missionaries who they have supported through these thirty-eight years (especially those who lived and served among the unreached), and how they were supported financially. This would be most helpful for those of us who are strategically planning to fulfill the Great Commission by focusing our deployment and support of missionaries

---

32 As of February 2021, Joshua Project reports that much less than 10 percent of missionaries work among the unreached, 81 percent of the unreached do not know a Christian, and while Christians of all types make up about one-third of the world's population, the absolute number of non-Christians is increasing ("Status of World Evangelization 2021 from Various Perspectives," Joshua Project, *Operation World, World Christian Encyclopedia*, BEE World, Jesus FilmProject, progress.bible, *Status of Global Christianity*, January 2021, https://joshuaproject.net/assets/media/handouts/status-of-world-evangelization.pdf).

33 In *Complexities of Money and Missions in Asia*, ed. Paul De Neui (Pasadena: William Carey Library, 2012): 121–190.

toward effectively reaching the truly unreached. Perhaps conversations or visits with other mission leaders, especially the Korean Society of Frontier Missions, could generate new insights that would enrich the more strategic budgeting of their mission funds.

Threats

And I can see two major threats:

1. *No annual budgets.* This has resulted in an average of 31 percent allotted for operating expenses. The usual allotment for administrative expenses in various kinds of organizations, including mission agencies, is 20 percent. Efforts should be made to reduce the 31 percent allotment to as close to the "normal" as possible, especially as we face the "new normal" of our post-COVID-19 world.

2. *Youth mobilization.* With the accelerating prevalence and influence of postmodern thinking (deconstruction of all absolutes and all institutional authorities) and the dominant use of social media (almost anything goes on the internet and smartphones), all churches are seeing a mass exodus of youth from their congregations. Who will win in capturing the vision and mission of our younger generations, who share a common global pop culture promoted via YouTube and TikTok? Allocating a part of the mission budget to research and development of new programs to reach Korean youth—and global youth!—may be the most strategic way to sustain and expand our churches and missions programs.

Conclusion

Let us be thankful to God for this stimulating story of how a Korean church with its sister mission agency creatively modeled an excellent partnership arrangement of horizontal relationships of equals, amid the many models of so-called "partnerships" that have a more vertical (hierarchical/top-down) arrangement. May the positive aspects that I highlighted be practiced more in our churches, mission agencies, and missionary training centers. And may the challenging aspects that I raised stimulate our prayerful search for better ways of stewarding mission funds for reaping God's plentiful harvest among the unreached in all nations.

Discussion Questions

1. Could your church or mission agency follow the financial policies of JAC and TPMI? How would you modify them in your context?

2. Do you agree with the positive assessments of the financial policies mentioned in this response chapter? What else could you add?

3. Do you agree with the challenging aspects mentioned in this response? What else could you add? How can these be overcome?

SECTION C: Testimonies

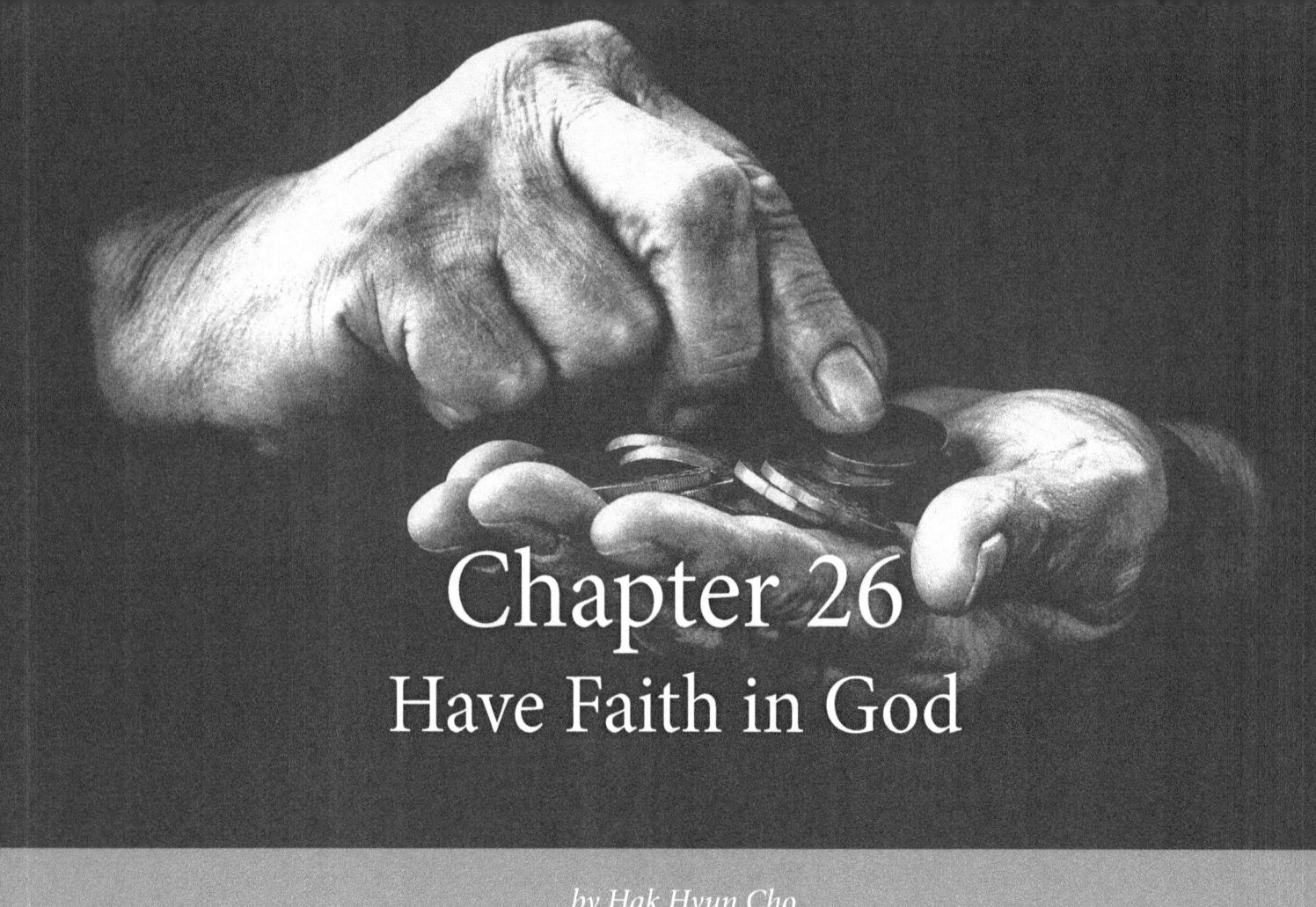

Chapter 26
Have Faith in God

by Hak Hyun Cho

When I was trained as a missionary candidate I read the autobiography of Hudson Taylor, which impressed and encouraged me a lot, especially "depending upon God alone for supplies."[1]

One important thing that I found in his autobiography was the financial principle he practiced—he believed that all his needs were met only by God, not by men. Hudson's faith principle of trusting in God for financial support presented a strong challenge to me, and at the same time it led me to apply to the mission he founded, Overseas Missionary Fellowship (OMF). But as I was living as a missionary, I learned that it was not easy to apply this principle concretely.

My wife and I had a commissioning service in May 1998 at my home church in Gwangju, S. Korea. Because OMF is an international organization that uses English as its primary language, and our English was not good enough, we needed English training. So, after the commissioning service we went to Australia to study English instead of going straight to Cambodia as our mission field. At that time, South Korea was facing a major economic crisis that had never been seen before. In 1997, the Asian economic crisis had finally impacted Korea, causing many Korean companies to go bankrupt and workers to be laid off. In addition, the exchange rate was so bad that it was necessary to double or triple the amount of money needed to remit money abroad. The economic crisis in Korea also affected us, as some churches and others who had promised to support us were not able to. So, we trained in English with very little financial help.

One day while we were studying hard, we got a letter from the OMF office in Korea. It said that we were required to reach at least 80 percent of our total amount of supporting income to go to Cambodia. But at that point, we had only reached 60 percent. I was concerned and worried about our financial situation.

---

[1] J. Hudson Taylor, *Hudson Taylor: The Autobiography of a Man Who Brought the Gospel to China* (Baker Publishing Group: Michigan, 1987), 124.

If our required support was not met, should we go back to Korea and start fundraising again? But even if we asked the churches for more support, I was certain that they would not be able to because they were also struggling with their own financial shortages.

During that time, I was reading the Bible with a feeling of being heavily weighed down. One day I read 1 Kings 19, and a verse caught my heart strongly: "Yet I reserve seven thousand in Israel— all whose knees have not bowed down to Baal and whose mouths have not kissed him" (1 Kgs 19:18). When Elijah looked around and complained to God that he had no one to help him, God gave him this answer. Before reading these words, my heart was just like Elijah's. But I knew that God who listened to Elijah's prayer and answered would listen to me and answer my prayer as well. The Lord first gave us the word of his promise and solved our difficulties in his own way. A few months after that a Korean church in Sydney contacted us and said that they wanted to start supporting us. This happened just before we left for Cambodia. In fact, we didn't know the church very well and we had not formed a relationship with it. That church became one of the very faithful supporting churches up till now.

As soon as we arrived in Cambodia, the mission started giving us language and culture orientation and training. One of the core values in the *OMF Field Handbook* was living an incarnational life— living more practically and following the lifestyle standard of local high school teachers as much as we could. According to the financial guidelines of the mission, we were not to buy new furniture or household appliances, but to use the ones left behind by other missionary colleagues when they went away on furlough or for other reasons. For the house we rented, OMF set a limit on the amount we could pay so we would not live in a big house.

In order to follow the guidelines presented by the mission, for a while I did not purchase a car but rode a motorcycle and public transportation, same as the local people, and I lived in a Cambodian-style wooden house for ten years, without a washing machine and air conditioner. However, despite our efforts to live minimally and simply, there was still a huge economic disparity between me and our Cambodian brothers and sisters. Comparing the GDP per capita of Korea and Cambodia in 1999, the magnitude of the difference was about fifty times (Cambodia $294 vs. S. Korea $10,667). We were pretty much the only ones in our neighborhood with a refrigerator, and to the many people who didn't even know what a computer was, we were rich because of the expensive stuff we owned. In comparison to the poverty of our Cambodian neighbors, I felt that our wealth was sometimes shameful, and even condemned.

For the last twenty years, Cambodian living standards have significantly improved as the Cambodian economy continued to develop. Indeed, many people in Cambodia just barely escaped from extreme poverty. However, the unfair redistribution of wealth has intensified the polarization of Cambodian society, and the poor are unable to even protect their rights. The new area we moved to for our second church planting ministry is close to the Thai border, and most of the residents and their family members are working as migrant workers in Thailand. People we meet every day to share the Gospel with are the families of migrant workers remaining in Cambodia. Comforting our neighbors, who have no choice but to be separated for the sake of their economic prosperity, with the word of God and becoming their new family and friends are still the way we live out the incarnation.

My wife and I started planting a church in a small town in the southeastern part of Cambodia in 2001. Our primary goal in church planting ministry was to build up the local churches, by teaching and training, and help them to become self-reliant—to hand over leadership to them and then let us as missionaries be phased out. For the church to become financially self-supporting, it had to reduce its dependence on missionaries or outsiders. Sometimes it was difficult to apply OMF's financial policies to our ministries because they were stricter and more detailed than we expected. OMF's policy regarding church planting work was that missionaries could not employ local evangelists or pastors. Therefore, three missionaries from my church planting team, including myself, directly evangelized, taught, and trained people in order to equip them to teach and train others. From the beginning of the church plant, although there were a small number of members, the missionaries encouraged members not to depend on them for even the smallest expenditures but to use the finances they were offered.

We have done several things to reduce financial dependence as much as possible. For example, we did not overdo the offerings of missionaries at every Sunday's worship meeting compared to the offerings of the locals. This was because if the offerings of missionaries took up a large portion of the total offerings, it would cause dependence of local members and hinder the financial independence of the church. At first, however, it was not easy for both missionaries and local believers to understand and practice this. Even though the missionaries were able to offer more, there was a concern that the local church members might think that the missionaries were stingy people by giving only a tiny part of the offerings. On the other hand, local believers thought that the church would not have difficulty covering expenses if missionaries gave more offerings.

We always needed wisdom on how to share the greater resources we had while protecting the local churches from relying financially on missionaries. We encountered instances where it threatened our financial principles, and also, as the number of members increased little by little, we needed a larger church building to accommodate them. In the meantime, the church had rented a small room for meetings, but it started to think of the need for a building just for our church. However, the church's size and the financial ability of its members did not allow them to buy a big enough building or to build a new one. Nevertheless, missionaries and the local church members started praying together and formed a committee to prepare the building project. Not long after the committee was formed, we saw that a building situated on a large piece of land was put up for sale and we looked up the price, but it was a too much for the church members to afford on their own. The cost of the building was too high, but the church did not want to give it up. They needed help from outside the church. Missionaries didn't want to give up on OMF's financial policy, but thought that compromise would be needed. At the same time, we had tried to get the most out of the local congregation. Church members had offered about 12 percent of the total budget, or $6,000, to purchase the church building. Considering that one of our church members was a schoolteacher at that time, and his monthly salary was about $60, we could calculate how much the sacrifice of the Cambodian church members was. The local church members did their best to offer, but I learned that their continued financial dependence on missionaries was due to the wrong motivations (including greed) and impatience of the missionaries themselves.

Fourteen years have passed since missionaries started planting the church, and we have handed over leadership to local leaders. Although the members received most of the money for purchasing the church building from outside sources, they have been trained to take ownership and have grown and matured enough to support the pastor and the church's necessary finances themselves.

Adhering to these financial principles is still a major challenge, but also a core value to the life and ministry of missionaries. I have learned and experienced new lessons from several past mistakes. And I believe that healthy principles make healthy ministries. I give thanks and praise to God for faithfully providing our needs in my life and ministries.

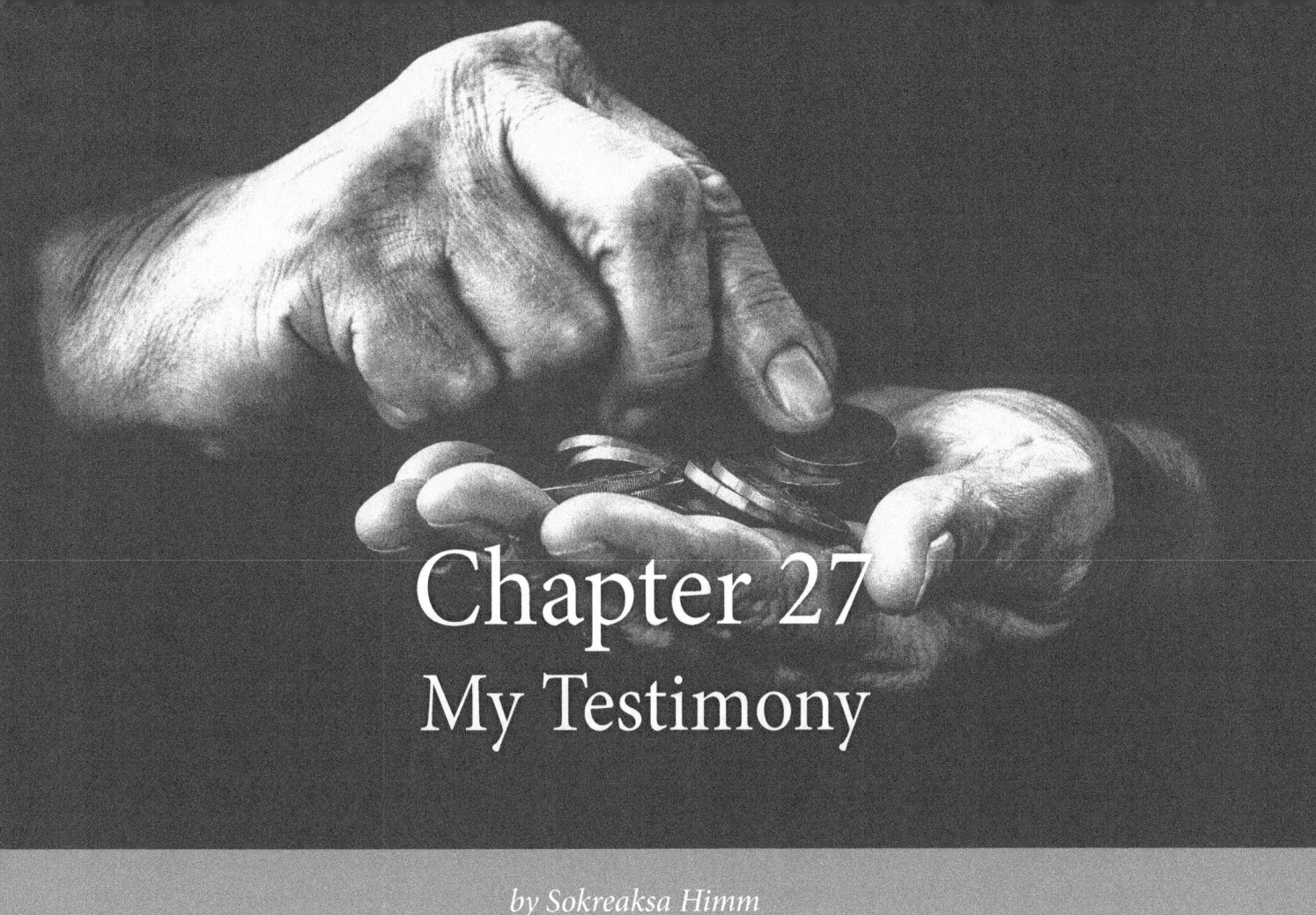

Chapter 27
My Testimony

by Sokreaksa Himm

Greetings. My name is Reaksa Himm. It is a special privilege for me to be with you this evening. I was born in a big family of eleven siblings in the small district of Pouk, Siem Reap Province, Cambodia. I was brought up in a Buddhist culture where I learned to observe all ritual practices in the Buddhist context. Life was so happy for us. But this kind of happiness did not last long—only until April 17, 1975, when the Khmer Rouge captured the whole of Cambodia. A few days after they captured the country they turned it upside down.

All city people were forced to live in the countryside; we were forced to do hard work with not enough food to eat. If someone opposed them, they would be "sent to school"—which literally meant, "to execution." When I was thirteen years old, I was assigned to take care of water buffalo and cows for the whole day, and I was paid with only two meals. "No work, no food to eat" was the Khmer Rouge's policy. Every morning before I left the village to take care of the water buffalos and cows, I had to pack my own lunch—basically rice and dried fish wrapped in banana leaf. One afternoon when I was by myself sitting under the shade along a river, a stranger came up to me and asked, "Will you share your lunch with me?" My lunch was just enough for myself. If I shared it with him, I'd go hungry for the whole day. But then, not sharing it would be selfish, and my parents had taught me not to be selfish. I couldn't bring myself to say yes right away. I looked at him and then at my lunch, and I knew I couldn't refuse such a gentle request. "You can have some of it," I said, "but please keep some for me." Then I handed over my lunch. I sat down and watched him eat.

I could see he was very hungry. When he'd finished half of it, I thought he might give the rest back to me, but he showed no sign of slowing down. After he'd finished every last bit of my lunch, he said, "You're a good boy. It's nice of you to give up your lunch for me. You're so kind." By this time, I wasn't interested in his compliments; I was too angry. "If he's so grateful, at least he might have saved a bit for me," I thought. He didn't seem to realize that I was actually very angry with him. Then he said, "I want to tell you a story." I calmly listened. He said, "In the next six months, your family will be killed, but you'll survive in the jungle. You won't die, but you will have to endure a lot of pain …" I was very upset with him.

I wasn't interested in listening anymore. Nothing he was saying made any sense, and I thought he must be crazy. At first I'd felt sorry for him, but now I was just angry. He ate all my lunch, and then he told me bad things about my life, as if it was some sort of horrible curse. I turned my back on him and walked away as fast as I could. I tried to look back at him one more time, but he had already disappeared. When I got home that evening, I wanted to tell my father, but I was afraid to tell him because it was not a good story to tell.

Sometime after that, one early morning I saw the local soldiers gathering in a group, sharpening knives, axes, and hoes. I knew something dreadful was about to happen to us, and a thousand butterflies started up in my stomach. I felt weak. Fear took over in my life.

A young teenager came to my house inviting my father for a meeting: "Comrade brother, *angkar loeu* (higher organization) invites you to meet in the meeting shelter now." My father replied, "I will be there in a few minutes." My father left the house. I trailed behind him to see what would happen. As soon as he reached the meeting shelter, a soldier arrested my father and bound his arms behind his back and said, "You are the enemy of the *angkar loeu*. You are CIA. You served the American government. You betrayed the country. We will destroy you today." Then I knew that the day had finally come. I ran home and told my younger brothers and sister that our father had been arrested, but I didn't know what to do. My hands and legs were shaking uncontrollably, I couldn't stand, and I couldn't sit still, though I felt as if all the strength had drained from my limbs. I tried to embrace my brothers and sister, and they started to tremble like me too. I never knew that the fear of execution was so terrible. Then the soldiers dragged my father to the house and they called to us to come out. They bound my hands behind my back, but then realized that there was no one to carry my little brother, so they untied me. Then they told us, "We will send you to school, because you are the enemies of the *angkar loeu*. Go with your father!" They put the six of us in an oxcart and drove us out of the village, dragging my father and two professors on foot.

I looked ahead and saw another group of city children on an oxcart, but none of their mothers were there —all the women had left early to go out to their work in the fields. I could tell they were frightened like me. I held on to my youngest brother, but my arms wouldn't stop trembling.

About twenty minutes prior to the execution, we had to wait because they were digging the grave. I got off the oxcart and carried my youngest brother to my father, who knelt to kiss him and the rest of us. I hugged him but he couldn't hug me back because his arms were bound. He couldn't speak because of the tears that poured down his face. I said, "Papa, I would like to thank you so much for being my father." I couldn't say any more; my tears were choking my voice. Then I heard him say, "Reaksa, my heart is torn in pieces. I've lived my life, but you children are too young to die."

When they finished digging the grave, the soldiers came and pushed us forward toward it. I choked out, "Goodbye, Papa! I love you." He nodded to me, then he called back, "It's time for us to die. I love all of you!" My younger sister began to scream. "Papa, please help me! I'm scared, Papa!" My father didn't answer; he was a helpless man about to be executed. I reached out and held her tightly against my side.

My father was standing and facing the grave. They kicked his legs from behind, so he fell onto his knees; as he turned his head to look at me, I saw them club him with a hoe. He fell forward into the grave with a scream. I was screaming too, a pointless, futile scream: "Help us, God, help us." Then one of the soldiers jumped into the grave and turned him over to finish him off. Then it was our turn. They made us kneel in front of the grave, and as I knelt, I felt a blow on my neck and I fell into the grave on top of my father. He was still alive, and I heard his last few breaths. Then there was nothing. My younger brothers and sister and the other children tumbled into the grave too, on top of me. Finally, they clubbed my baby brother. The first three times they clubbed him he screamed loudly, then they clubbed him one more time and I didn't hear him again. I was still conscious but I couldn't move. I knew that the other children were not yet dead, for the soldiers jumped into the grave to finish everybody off. There was a sound of hacking blades, and I felt their warm wet blood pour over my body.

When they'd finished butchering, slashing, and axing, they climbed out of the grave.

I heard one of them say, "I think that one's not dead yet." One soldier jumped down into the grave again and pulled a body off me, and hit me with the hoe one more time. It was a heavy blow, but not hard enough to end my life. I knew enough then to lie still. If I had moved at all, they would have finished me off. Someone began to throw earth on top of us, but then I heard a voice say, "Don't bury them yet; we've still got some more enemies to be destroyed." They left the grave open and went off to pick up my mother, my older sister, and other women who were reaping rice in the fields. I had only one sensation then—the taste of death. Blood flowed out through my nose and mouth and choked me, and I was covered with the blood of my family and friends. I wanted to escape, but I knew I mustn't move a muscle until all the soldiers had gone. Face down on my father's body, pain and panic took hold of me.

I had to force myself to calm down. They weren't going to bury us immediately, and once the killers were out of sight I could get away. I couldn't see what was happening, so I listened; there were no more voices, either from the living or the dead. I waited ten minutes after everything was quiet, and then cautiously started to move. I tried to disentangle myself from the dead bodies; it took me almost half an hour to climb out from under their heavy weight, because I was so weak. I crawled out onto the dusty ground and turned around to look at the grave. Everyone was lying dead; some of their throats had been slashed. My three younger brothers' brains had spilled out. My baby brother's head had been clubbed until it was pulpy, and one of his eyes was hanging out. As for my father, his throat was slashed, and his ribs were sticking out. His eyes were open as though he was looking at me. Slowly I climbed back into the grave, reached down, and gently closed his eyes. I checked everybody in the family in the faint hope that someone had been left alive like me, but no one had.

Then I saw my beloved mother, my older sister, and some women stumbling toward the grave. Their faces were covered with *kramas*, the scarves they always wore. I opened my mouth but no sound came out; it was as though I was paralyzed. Some power came over me and shut off my voice. The soldiers killed all the women, and closed the grave and went back home.

When the sun had almost set, I crept out to the grave. I pounded my head on it, "Mother, please take me with you, take me with you. I don't want to live." I called to my mother, but she couldn't hear me. I screamed and cried and lamented, but no one answered. In that jungle there was no one left alive to hear.

I bowed before the grave and made three promises to my family: "Mother, father, brothers and sisters, as long as I live, I will avenge your deaths. If I fail in this, then I promise that I'll become a monk. If I can't fulfil these two promises, then I won't live in Cambodia anymore." After I had made these promises, I sat down and cried until thirst and hunger overcame me. Now it was getting dark. I'd never been alone in the jungle before, and I was afraid. I knew that wild animals would be drawn to the grave by the smell of fresh blood, so I couldn't sleep nearby. So I knelt by the grave and said, "Spirits of the thirty-three innocent victims, please protect me tonight from wild animals. I will remember all of you, and as long as I live I will pay my respects and show my gratitude to all of you." I made a final bow, and left the grave.

Life after such terrible tragedy is full of psychological trauma and emotional crises. Not only did I lose my family; I also lost my mind. It was a double tragedy for me. The first tragedy was my family being taken away forever. The tragedy struck me when I was a teenager. I was not mature enough to handle the ongoing psychological trauma. A moment after I regained consciousness, as a young teenager lying on the dead bodies of my family, I could not understand what was going on in my life. Emotionally, psychologically, intellectually, and spiritually I was dead—I could not feel, think, or reason. I was like a zombie. How could any young teenager handle such tragedy? To make a long story short, I survived ...

In early 1979, Vietnamese soldiers took over Cambodia. In late 1979, I went back to live in the city with my auntie and I went back to school. In early

1983, I joined the police force in Siem Reap city. By the middle of 1984, I escaped to Thailand and stayed at Khao-I-Dang refugee camp for five years. On May15, 1989, I was accepted by Canadian Immigration and sent to Toronto, Canada. One year later, I received Jesus Christ as my personal Lord and Savior, and spent more than ten years studying in Canada.

In May 1999, I returned to Cambodia and lectured on counseling and psychology at Phnom Penh Bible School. In late 2002, I went back to live in my hometown in Siem Reap to build up the Khmer Christian Center. In early March 2020, I left Cambodia and returned to Canada to live with my family.

Allow me to ask you a question: If you were in my shoes, would it be possible for you forgive your family's killers? Forgiveness was not easy to accomplish. It required strong emotional energy and personal determination to accomplish this almost impossible mission.

It had to come from my pure and sincere heart. I should not live my life anchored in the root of unforgiveness. I should not waste my time pursuing my family honor by taking revenge. My hope in Christ is for a brighter tomorrow. My sins are forgiven. I am no longer chained by the deep dark pit of the past.

I had enough bitterness in my life, and I needed to move on because Christ had given me a new purpose. I could no longer allow myself to be infected by the cancer of my soul or it would soon destroy me. Life should be a joyful journey in Christ, so I had to remove all the negative emotions that had made me so miserable. I believe that the Lord spared my life from the grave and gave me the ministry of forgiveness and reconciliation with my family's killers. In June 2003, more than twenty years after my family was killed,

I decided to return to the village to express my forgiveness to the two surviving killers. I went there to proclaim a living testimony of the grace of Jesus Christ in my life.

When I got to about a mile from the village, I could feel the sharpness of painful memories intensifying in my heart. My heart started to pound faster and faster. My lips began to freeze, and my face became red. Inside my heart, I was filled with mixed emotions—fear, sadness, anger, and pain. I could tell that my nervousness started to kick at my soul.

Finally, I met the two men who killed my father and mother. I offered each one of them a Cambodian scarf as a symbol of my forgiveness for them, a shirt as a symbol of my love for them, and a Bible as a symbol of my blessing for them. I read Luke 23:34: "Father, forgive them; for they do not know what they are doing." I read this passage aloud and declared, "I forgive you." It gave me power over my family's killers. I hugged the man who killed my father; I could feel that he was very shaky. I told him that twenty-eight years ago when you took my family into the jungle, this is how I felt, "but today I come back as an ambassador of Jesus Christ to set you free." In that moment, I actually set myself free. Forgiveness was very difficult, but, by the grace of my God, I had accomplished my mission of forgiveness in my life.

Forgiveness was not to gain back what was initially lost, but to live with the loss by relying on the grace of God to overcome the hurt and pain in my life. I chose to start over again by canceling what I actually wanted to do to them many years ago. I chose to replace hate with love. The message of loving our enemies is the most fundamental teaching of Jesus Christ. He said, "Love your enemies, do good to those who hate you, bless those who curse you, pray for those who mistreat you" (Luke 6:27–28). This is a hard road to travel, and not many people are willing to travel it. Forgiveness gives me the freedom to move on. The message of love for my enemies transforms my life—from being paralyzed by the power of hatred, now I am free in Christ.

Thank you so much for giving me an opportunity to share my story with you.

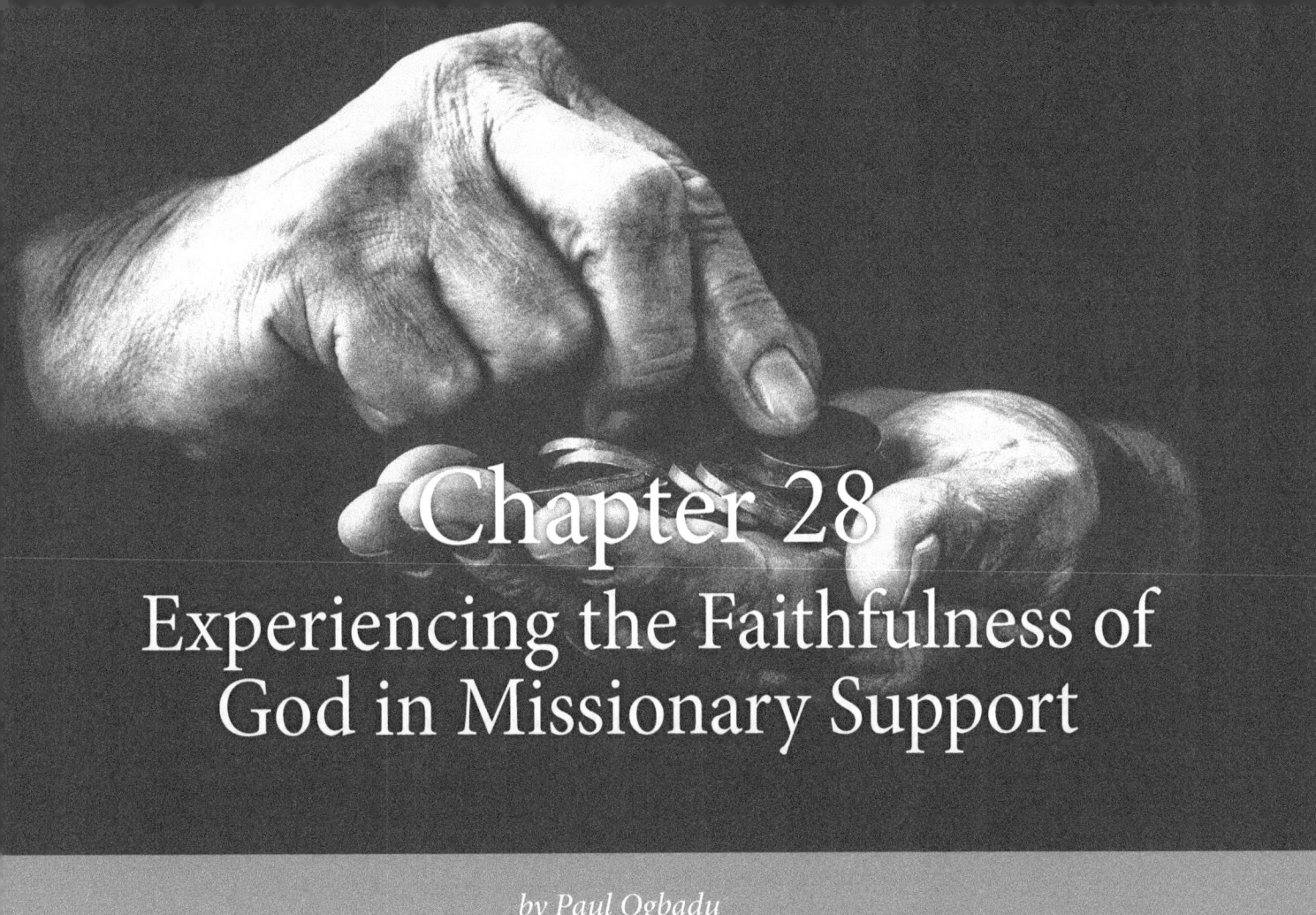

Chapter 28
Experiencing the Faithfulness of God in Missionary Support

by Paul Ogbadu

The Journey Begins

"Come, follow me," Jesus said, "and I will send you out to fish for people."

—Matthew 4:19

When I informed my parents of my call to missions, little did I know that the Lord had gone ahead of me to prepare the way, especially with my dad. He related an experience he had shortly before I was born. He had a dream that he didn't understand. He shared it with an Anglican pastor friend, who attempted to interpret the dream. He told him that one of his children was going to serve the Lord. My dad kept it in his heart, and was watching to see whom among his children the Lord had chosen to serve him. He told me that he was not surprised that I was the one. He had been watching closely my commitment to Jesus. He prayed with me and assured me of his support and encouragement. It was a great joy that my dad identified with the call of God upon my life. He continued to pray for my wife and I until he went to be with the Lord in March 1994.

The Call and the Mandate

The LORD will guide you always; he will satisfy your needs in a sun-scorched land and will strengthen your frame. You will be like a well-watered garden, like a spring whose waters never fail. Your people will rebuild the ancient ruins and will raise up the age-old foundations; you will be called Repairer of Broken Walls, Restorer of Streets with Dwellings.

—Isaiah 58:11–12

In July 1987, just after I rounded up the one year compulsory National Youth Service Corps program with the Nigerian government, the Lord confirmed to me that he was calling me to serve him as a cross-cultural missionary. He instructed me to go to a particular city in Nigeria and wait for further instructions. As soon as I arrived there,

I looked for the chapter members of Calvary Ministries (CAPRO)—the Sending Arm of CAPRO, a group of missions-minded Christians who meet regularly to pray and to send some resources to missionaries on the field, as much as possible, now known as CAPRO Sending Teams (CAST)—and started meeting with them to pray for missions. This kept me abreast of what was happening in missions, and in CAPRO in particular. While waiting for further instructions from him, he opened a door for me to start working as an educational and sales representative for an international publishing house, coordinating the activities of the company in two states in Nigeria.

In December of 1989, the Lord reminded me that it was time to take a step of faith into the mission field. It was therefore natural for me to join CAPRO. At that point, CAPRO had been in existence for fifteen years as a faith mission agency. I had already been a part of this group for more than two years, as a member of its Sending Arm.

Exhausted, Yet Pursuing

So Gideon came to the Jordan and crossed over [the river], he and the three hundred men who were with him—exhausted, yet [still] pursuing [the enemy].

—Judges 8:4 (AMP)

The day before I resumed study at the CAPRO School of Missions in January 1990, some of my friends spent time praying with me all through the night. That morning I picked up my luggage, boarded a bus, and resumed classes. One of my friends who prayed with me that night shared Judges 8:4 as a word he received from the Lord for me. In the midst of some tiredness, frustration, and discouragement on the field, the Lord has used this verse to encourage me. The call of God upon our lives to declare his glory among the nations is a legacy we have received from him, which we are expected to defend at all times and under all circumstances.

While in training at the CAPRO School of Missions, it became clear to me that the Lord would have me start my missionary journey among the unreached people groups in the Francophone West Africa. I therefore joined a few students who were interested in learning the French language for their future ministries, attending some classes with one of our trainers who studied French at the university. Even though after my training I was initially sent to work among the Hausa people of Katsina State, Nigeria, I knew it was a stepping-stone into the larger vision that the Lord had set before me.

How Are You Supported?

The one who calls you is faithful, and he will do it.

—1 Thessalonians 5:24

When I joined CAPRO, one of the questions that I was asked during my initial contacts with the leaders was how sure I was that God was calling me to work with this organization. This question was asked to remind me (and many others) of the financial policy of the mission agency. CAPRO is a faith mission agency; both the ministry and its missionaries depend on God's provision through the generous gifts of his people. None of the missionaries are salaried. All gifts that come into the ministry are used as designated.

When people ask me, "How are you supported?," it is always a difficult question to answer. When I respond by telling them that "It is God who supports us," in most cases it leads to a series of more, difficult questions. The truth is that it is the Lord who has been supporting us all these years. Sometimes he uses people we don't know, or may not meet for a very long time, or may never meet on this side of eternity. He also uses others we know closely. Some of our family members, close friends, the CAST that I was a part of, and friends of the ministry have been there for us in some ways. In the course of our ministry over the years, God also raised some missionary colleagues from time to time to meet some of our needs.

When we arrived in Guinea-Conakry in October 1992, I didn't renew my driver's license since we didn't have a car at that point. A missionary couple with whom we worked closely was returning to their home country. They gave us their car. The car served us for a period of eleven years before we gave it to another missionary couple when we relocated to the Republic of Cameroon in 2004.

Strategic Partnership for Kingdom Advance

I must work the works of him that sent me, while it is day; the night cometh, when no man can work. As long as I am in the world, I am the light of the world.

—John 9:4–5 (KJV)

Around 1985, Guinea-Conakry opened up for missionaries to return and work in the country. WEC International and CAPRO missionaries separately undertook a survey to determine what they would do in the land. In comparing notes, they discovered that the Lord was showing them basically the same direction of ministry—to focus first on the coastal region, the Susu people group, and especially on the youths. The strategies were similar—start a youth center in the city of Conakry and engage the people group in evangelism and discipleship, leading to indigenous, viable, and self-propagating churches.

The two mission groups decided to join hands together in Guinea and serve the Lord as a team. A formal partnership agreement already existed between the two groups at the international level, which could cover the national joint operation. It was a multinational and multicultural team showing forth the glory of the Lord among the unreached peoples of Guinea, supporting and encouraging one another in advancing his Kingdom. We had missionaries from Australia, New Zealand, Nigeria, United Kingdom, Switzerland, United States, France, South Korea, Brazil, Ivory Coast, and Guinea who served on the team at various points. My wife and I served on this team along with some of the missionaries from these countries.

The work that started in earnest in late 1987, under the umbrella name of "Mission Évangélique Internationale en Guinée" (MEIG), was a testimony of what God can do with ordinary people from different backgrounds and upbringings who choose to be totally yielded to him. Though the national joint operation was set aside much later, out of this strategic partnership was born a youth center in Koloma, Conakry, a mini youth center in Dubreka, Tabitha Center in Fria, and some churches among the Susu people and the Fulani people of Futa Djallon, which continue to flourish till today. WEC and CAPRO continue their partnership at the international level, operating as brethren with a kindred spirit at the national level. It suffices to say that the whole work was later left in the hands of CAPRO missionaries, who continue to serve in various locations around Guinea.

Refreshed to Advance

... So Jesus said to his disciples, "Come, let's take a break and find a secluded place where you can rest a while."
—Mark 6:31 (TPT)

After serving in Cameroon for several years, it became obvious that we needed a rest. We applied to and were accepted by the Overseas Ministries Study Center (OMSC), New Haven, CT, USA, as part of the missionaries and scholars in residence for 2018/2019. The Lord miraculously made a way for us to get our visas in the midst of many refusals at the American Embassy in Yaoundé. Being residents at OMSC in 2018/2019 was quite a refreshing moment. It afforded us the opportunity to spend more time to pray, read and study Scriptures, and commune with the other missionaries in residence as well as the staff of OMSC. We had lectures and courses that enabled us to reflect on our past field experiences and to prayerfully plan for the days ahead. While at OMSC, we reconnected with a South Korean missionary couple, Jinbong Kim and Soon Young Jung, with whom we served in Guinea-Conakry several years back. It was indeed a beautiful and pleasant surprise. At the end of our stay at OMSC, we were convinced that the Lord wanted us to return to Cameroon to consolidate the work there before finally disengaging and taking up another assignment.

Conclusion

But my God shall supply all your need according to his riches in glory by Christ Jesus.
—Philippians 4:19 (KJV)

Over the years, God has continued to raise up young men and women who were willing to step out of their comfort zone, willing to abandon everything and go out without any assurance of financial and material support. They have continued to serve sacrificially till this very day among unreached people groups and in very difficult terrain. Some of them came out of our labor in Guinea and in Cameroon.

Even though needs abound, we have continued to experience the faithfulness of God in supplying our needs according to his riches in glory. We are very grateful to God and to all the brethren he has used over the years to meet our needs and make our stay on the fields possible. Their kneeling in prayer and offering of material support kept us standing to proclaim the love of Christ among the nations:

For God is not unrighteous to forget your work and labour of love, which ye have shewed toward his name, in that ye have ministered to the saints, and do minister.
—Hebrew 6:10 (KJV)

Chapter 29
Testimony of Smyrna Church

by Hakkyoon Shin

On July 31st, 2009, I was discharged from the army, ending my fifteen years of service as a military chaplain. Although several Christian friends were encouraging me to start a new church, I had no intention of planting a church.

For two years I sought ministerial positions at existing churches, but to no avail. Then a pastor who prayed for me nudged me to join "Seven Days of Fasting and Prayer." So I went to a fasting and prayer center at Yangpyeong. I might say I experienced "heaven" there. That is, I did not feel hungry at all for the whole week. I even went into the cafeteria to test myself. I could smell the food, but it did not stimulate my appetite.

While feeling God's presence and his empowerment, I took a walk and saw a bird coming down about ten meters ahead of me and then quickly fly away. Then, I heard a voice saying, "Will he not much more clothe you?" I did not believe that it was God's voice. Since I had memorized the verses of Matthew 6:26–34 since my early childhood, I thought it must be just that and kept on walking. After several minutes of walking, I saw a different bird coming down about ten meters away and quickly fly away. The same voice rang in my ears, saying, "Will he not much more clothe you?" This time, I interpreted the message as, "Plant a church." It was the voice of God telling me to plant a church.

After fasting and praying, an intense trial was awaiting me. I was thinking, "Well, since it is God's calling, I guess I'd have to plant a church." Then a senior pastor I knew offered me the position of associate pastor at his church. *Why now?* His offer included salaries, seasonal bonuses, and housing subsidies. I was confounded, thinking, "The temptation of the tree of the knowledge of good and evil must have been something like this." The pastor spoke with good intentions, but to me, it was like the temptation in the garden of Eden. It was all the more tempting because my family's bank account was down to almost zero. Two years after my discharge from the army, my severance pay and savings on which we lived were nearly all gone. The cost of high school education for my two sons was high, especially with our younger son's vocal lesson fees amounting to ₩1.5 million per month.

I thought to myself, "Having heard the voice of God, I have no other choice. If I do not obey, I am of no use as a pastor." I said to the pastor who gave me the offer, "Thank you, but I have to plant a church." He said, "Let's pray about it for a month." That one month was a period of agony for me. Everyone around me, even my family members, criticized me for turning down such an offer.

On the day before I planned to give my final words of refusal to the pastor, my wife came to me in tears. In an agitated voice, she asked me to accept the offer. "You know our situation. We need to survive. The kids need to go to school. Let's serve as the associate pastor for several years and then plant a church." My wife's face looked like that of a devil, so to speak. It was tormenting.

While I stood there speechless, my wife's phone rang. It was from our younger son. I heard his voice over the phone, "Mom, I'm sorry ..." My son was playing catch during recess. The baseball hit him in the face, and two of his front teeth were cracked but not entirely broken. After hanging up, my wife's face looked like that of an angel. She said, "Let's plant a church." She later told me that our son's words, "I'm sorry," echoed in her mind as, "God, I'm sorry." She thought, "If I disobey God's will, this child might die."

The next day I told the senior pastor that I would plant a new church. And thus, my new journey began.

One of the elder pastors I knew introduced me to a shelter for the homeless where he served. I used the building for worship service on Sundays. The first service of Smyrna Church took place on the first week of September 2011, with the attendance of two persons—my wife and me. But we offered the worship service with joy. The membership increased to four by the next month when God sent a family I knew. Some people would come and go, but the membership stayed at four.

A spiritual warfare went on as soon as we planted the church. I somehow kept thinking, "Since God has told me to do this, he would take care of me." I never asked anyone for a financial gift. I never wrote a letter asking for financial sponsorship. As a pastor, I was gifted with a strong body, but I did not think of working for money. My wife was the same. She majored in piano, but she did not think of earning money. All we did was kneel before God and pray. We maintained this position with firm faith, but the situation got worse.

In late 2011, our elder son was admitted to a college in Daejeon. The joy of being accepted did not last long. We were barely surviving. How were we supposed to pay for college and living expenses in Daejeon? We were also paying for our younger son's music lessons. We tried all we could to scramble up some money, but to no avail. We could do nothing but pray.

My wife went out to get some cash the day before the tuition deadline, but she returned empty-handed. In her desperation, she cried out to God in the car, "Oh, God, now that our son received admission, shouldn't he attend college? If you granted him the admission, shouldn't you also provide us with the tuition?" She was screaming and wailing in the car. It was at that moment when her phone rang. It was from a dentist whom we were mentoring spiritually. The dentist said, "God had stirred my heart several days ago to send money to you, but I was too busy. God stirred my heart again a moment ago, ever so strongly, so I transferred the money just now. Please do check." Surprised, my wife went to the bank and found ₩10 million in the bank account. God had called us with the message, "Will he not much more clothe you?," and he faithfully kept his promise. Sometimes, though, the timing was off a bit because the crows he employed were somewhat slow to act. (Our younger son was also admitted to a college as a music major in late 2012; God provided for us that time too.)

During the early days of starting the new church, one of the difficulties was receiving overdue messages from our credit card company. Thrifty as we were, we used a credit card when we were desperate. But we ended up missing the payment date. Then, without fail, a message would pop up, "Your credit card payment is now overdue. Please make the payment as soon as possible. Otherwise, your credit card may become unusable." Then we would fall before God, praying, "God. It is so difficult." God would then touch our hearts with the following message: "You haven't been in debt in your whole life, have you? Among your congregation, there will be many people with various kinds of debts. You need to understand how they feel deep inside." When I found out God's intention, the peace in my heart was restored. And we were able to make the payment within a few days.

After a year, the four of us had to move out. This time, God provided us with the classroom of an alternative school for worship gatherings. And then another year passed by. One day in November 2013, God sent us ₩40 million from one person and ₩3 million from another person. The ₩40 million was from my wife's friend. God's extraordinary providence was behind all this. While we were still serving in the army, my wife and her friend had a discussion on tithing. My wife's friend was married to a successful businessperson. This couple tithed to their church and helped other people with an additional 20 percent of their income. For some reason, however, they had to stop helping other people. So they consulted with my wife on this issue. My wife suggested, "Why don't you save 20 percent of your income for the time being? God might show you what to do with the savings when the time is right." Upon hearing this, the couple started saving 20 percent of their income. Then several years passed.

One day my wife's friend was praying when God stirred her heart, prompting her to send the saved money to Smyrna Church. So she called my wife and wired the money. It was November 2013. God had plans for Smyrna Church for years ahead. Then an additional ₩3 million was sent from a brother whom we had mentored spiritually several years ago. He wired the money with a simple "Thank You," without any further explanation. It was also November 2013. God's timing is amazing.

Now with ₩43 million in our hands, we prayed for God's guidance on what to do with it. Then God impressed upon our hearts that it was for establishing the church. So we began to look for a church site. On January 11th, 2014, we contracted an office space, furnished the interior, and placed a signboard with Smyrna Church's name. God's calculation is so precise. "Why ₩43 million?" we had wondered. After we completed the contract and the furnishing, we had only a small amount of money left. God has his plans. We certainly had difficult moments. One day, we complained to God in desperation; his answer was, "So, did you even miss a meal?" I was startled. We had difficulties, but we always had something to eat. Sometimes rice and kimchi were all we had, but we did not go on an empty stomach. So we thanked God and kept hanging on, with our eyes only on God, until this day.

Our church celebrated our tenth anniversary. As of May 2021, 45 percent of our monthly budget is for fixed expenditures, including rent and maintenance. The congregation is small, but God takes care of each family's finances so that we can keep going. As a result, Smyrna Church has no debt. We don't have to worry about the rent payment. All we are concerned about is to be pleasing to God.

A few years after we started Smyrna Church, I asked my wife what she thought of our decision to plant the church. My wife replied, "We did well to start a church. Otherwise, we would not have experienced so much of the living God and his working among us!" I am so thankful. When God called me to plant the church, he made one thing very clear: "I am the owner of Smyrna Church, and you are my servant." I fully admit that God is the owner of Smyrna Church, and I can only obey him. When I responded to his calling in obedience and persevered in faith, God made me a happy minister. So my ministry is a happy ministry. The members at Smyrna Church hear my confession all the time: "No other minister can be happier than I." God is still at work within us.

"Blessed are you, Israel! Who is like you, a people saved by the LORD?" (Deut. 33:29). I understand this verse this way: "Blessed are you, Pastor Shin!" Hallelujah!

SECTION D: Conclusion

Chapter 30
Concluding Summary

by Timothy Kiho Park

Money is essential in missionary work. But where and how a mission spends its money has far reaching consequences. When money is used well it helps missionary work, but the wrong use of money can become an obstacle. Unwise financial support from foreign churches to churches in the mission field does more harm than good, more often than not.

Modern missions were mainly carried out by missionaries sent from rich countries to poor countries, and the paternalism of the missionaries from rich countries resulted in local churches becoming dependent, which hindered them from becoming truly indigenous. In contrast, today's mission has become one in which all global churches participate.

It is necessary to examine how money has affected the missionary work of the churches that have participated in the mission movement so far, and to consider how money should be used for healthier mission in the future. A total of twenty-two various articles were presented at the 2021 KGMLF forum held under the theme of "Missions and Money." Each presenter has a different point of view on mission and money. In this concluding summary, I will comment on the main points of each article and share my own thoughts on missions and money:

In "Faith-Based Organizations and Investments in Mission: The Case of the All Africa Conference of Churches," **Bright G. Mawudor** says that African churches tend to depend on external resources, which is a violation of the principles of self-government, self-support, and self-propagation. It calls for a "new way of thinking" about how churches receive foreign financial aid, "new theological thinking, and growth strategies on maximizing internal strengths and resources" in order to continue their mission.

The tendency to depend on external resources is not only a problem for African churches, but also for churches on other continents. This dependence on external resources is hindering local churches from becoming truly indigenous churches. Charles Troutman called paternalism the "most despicable curse" that we could put on the national church.[1] William J. Kornfield said, "Increasing financial paternalism and accompanying Westernization of the gospel are the two most critical issues facing us in world missions today. We have a choice to make: either push these issues under the rug and hope they will go away by maintaining the status quo, or face them honestly with confession, repentance, and the search for better ways."[2] I fully agree with Mawudor's assertion that strategies to maximize internal strengths and resources are needed to build self-governing, self-supporting, and self-propagating healthy, reproducing indigenous churches.

In "Fundraising Practices of the Mizoram Presbyterian Church," **Zosangliana Colney** talks about how the Mizoram church has been carrying out local and cross-cultural missionary work, without relying on outside help. Mizoram, located in northeast India, is a poor state with an average annual income of $150, but the local church has become a self-governing, self-supporting, and self-propagating indigenous church, and a missionary church supporting 2,741 missionaries both inside and outside India, without external funding. How could such a poor church support so many missionaries? As soon as the Mizoram people embraced Christianity, they quickly assumed the responsibility of spreading the Gospel across their borders. They give tithes and rice, run farms, raise chickens, and collect firewood to cover their missionary expenses, doing the best they can.

In today's era of mission that goes from "everywhere to everywhere," the biggest obstacle to the participation of Global South churches in missions is the idea that they are poor. The donation practices of Mizoram church members are a great challenge not only to Global South churches today, but also to the churches of the Global North that put too much emphasis on money. If the members of the Mizoram church can do missionary work, what church cannot participate in the missionary movement? We thank God for the members of Mizoram church and for their leading example.

---

1 Charles Troutman, "Paternalism," in *Everything You Want to Know about the Mission Field but Are Afraid You Won't Learn until You Get There: Letters to a Prospective Missionary* (Downers Grove: InterVarsity Press, 1976), 72.

2 William J. Kornfield, "What Hath Our Western Money and Our Western Gospel Wrought?," *Mission Frontiers* (January 01, 1997), http://www.missionfrontiers.org/issue/article/what-hath-our-western-money-and-our-western-gospel-wrought.

In "Missions and Money: Christian Finance in Global Perspective," **Gina A. Zurlo** says that "a basic resource in any Christian activity is money, which plays an important role in denominations, churches, missions, and evangelism." And "there exists a deep inequality in the global Christian family as it relates to money, since Europe and North America are home to only 33 percent of the world's Christians, with the majority living in Asia, Africa, Latin America, and Oceania. That is, the North has the money, but the South has the Christians." Money in the North, but Christians in the South.

The churches of the northern hemisphere have their own unique assets, including financial resources, but so do the churches of the southern hemisphere. The churches on earth are members of one body of Jesus Christ. Paul says in Ephesians 4:16: "From him the whole body, joined and held together by every supporting ligament, grows and builds itself up in love, as each part does its work." Just as there are many members in our body, and each member performs a unique function to grow the body, so if each church would cooperate with their own assets, a synergistic effect of mission will appear. The church on earth is a member of one body. Northern and Southern churches with different gifts should use their gifts to work for a common purpose.

In "Jesus Abbey: A Case Study in 'Faith Financing,'" **Ben Torrey** says that "the concept of faith financing is generally understood by the members of Jesus Abbey to be a way of life that trusts God for material provision without seeking help from others or any sort of fundraising. Faith financing does not prohibit individuals or businesses from earning money or receiving gifts. Funds received by members go into the community's common fund, and gifts can be kept privately."

The lifestyle of the community of Jesus Abbey, trusting God for material provision without seeking help from others, is a good model for all Christians, particularly for cross-cultural missionaries. I believe that "faith financing" will make us more completely dependent on God, make our lives and work more godly, and bring glory to God.

In "The Structure and the Financial Management Policy of GMS from the Perspective of Credibility, Transparency, and Accountability," **Jinbong Kim** discusses the financial management problems of the Global Mission Society (GMS) and how to solve them.

GMS is the largest missionary-sending agency in Korea (with 2,574 missionaries to 101 countries), and the second largest missionary-sending organization in the world. However, 53 percent of GMS missionaries do not trust in the management of its finances. In order to carry on missionary work successfully, GMS must be credible, transparent, and accountable in the management of its finances. Rev. Dr. Kim suggests that GMS include the representatives of missionaries on the board of directors because 75 percent of GMS missionaries believe that their opinions are not properly reflected in policy making. GMS should maintain transparency throughout the entire process of decision, execution, and settlement of the organizational bylaws, and the third-party expert audit report should be open to all missionaries to gain credibility, transparency, and accountability.

As the Korean mission agency that has sent the largest number of missionaries, GMS is directly or indirectly affecting Korean missions in many ways. For the bright future of Korean church missions, GMS should set a good example for other Korean missions, especially in the area of financial management. As a point of disclosure, I also belong to GMS along with missionary Jinbong Kim. As Jinbong Kim suggested, GMS should include missionary representatives on the policy making board to reflect the opinions of missionaries and ensure the transparent use of finances.

In "Missions and Education," **Allison Howell** says that "today's missions and churches continue to establish and manage educational institutions." However, a mission or missionary's sudden departure or retirement from the field "can have numerous complications that controvert the viability, sustainability, and usefulness of the educational establishment." For any institution to be viable it needs to be sustainable, which "depends on its setup, longevity, and capacity to be financially autonomous."

Although not a small number of missionaries set up educational institutions on the mission field, the scale is generally not what the locals can afford. When the missionaries who established these educational institutions retire or leave the field, the chances of survival of those educational institutions become slim, and even if they do survive, they experience difficulties in operation. Missionaries should consider this issue carefully and establish a viable educational institution that even the locals can operate from the beginning.

In "Registration of Real Estate: A Pivotal Factor in a Collaborative Effort to Establish a Seminary in Postwar Japan," **J. Nelson Jennings** talks about the schism between the church and seminary in Japan, mainly attributed to theological differences and registration of the properties.

There are too many problems caused by the matter of ownership of property acquired by missionaries in the mission field. When funds are raised exclusively by missionaries who eventually claim their ownership, it causes conflicts with locals. If missionaries, from the beginning, serve as advocates to raise local leaders and let them take the leadership in fundraising, registering property, and running programs, and missionaries remain as helpers, churches and schools would not be divided and would run better.

In "Money and Self-Support: A Challenging Principle of the Nevius Method for Korean Protestant Churches and Missions," **Sung-Deuk Oak** introduces the various genealogies of the Nevius Method applied to Korea. He points to the temporary and immutable principles of the method, emphasizing the need to vary from situation to situation. Self-reliance has become the basis of indigenous local churches, but he points out that today, more than 80 percent of small churches (with less than fifty members) in Korea "are struggling for survival and it is one of the most serious 'church-centric' problems today. Like Nevius in 1880s, we need to invent a new 'mission-centered' church method that promotes a healthy ecosystem where missions and churches are interdependent, and the small churches and megachurches are in the relationship of coexistence and co-prosperity."

Oak's introduction to the various genealogies of the Nevius Method applied to Korea provides us with good insight into the establishment of indigenous churches. I myself have taught on church planting in other cultures for a long time, but I was not flexible in teaching the principles of planting indigenous churches. However, Dr. Oak's presentation, which talks about the temporary and unchanging principles of the Nevius method and emphasizes the need for flexibility depending on the situation, will be helpful in developing the relationship between missions and the church in which they are interdependent and live together.

In "Optimizing Missions through Organizational Financial Accountability," **Valentine Gitoho** says that "the face of an organization to the world is its leadership and governance. So, when they are not faithful in their roles there is loss of credibility of the organization." She warns that the conscious or unconscious use of designated offerings for other purposes poses a risk to a mission's reputation and credibility and has a negative impact on missionary work. For proper financial management and transparency, it is necessary to have a good accountant, even if it costs a lot.

Gitoho's words are very true. Who would support missionaries or mission agencies that are misusing their finances or are not transparent about their use of finances? Mission supporters look for integrity and accountability in the mission agencies they support. Therefore, it is important to select the right leaders and to have a system in place to ensure that the leaders use their agencies' finances correctly and transparently.

In "The Core Elements of the Establishment and Development of United Theological Seminary in Kyrgyzstan," **Joohyung Lee, Emil Osmonaliev**, and **Sungbin Hong** talk about how to efficiently operate the United Theological Seminary, established by foreign missionaries in Kyrgyzstan. It is proposed to develop online programs to educate people in and outside of Kyrgyzstan, to translate theological books into Kyrgyzstan, and to encourage local people to write theological books in their own language. Raising local leadership for the seminary and having students pay tuition would be a sustainable way to go.

I also set up a seminary, in the Philippines, and have experience in theological education for Filipino and other Global South church pastoral candidates. I had a similar experience to the one the authors had in Kyrgyzstan. Developing online programs to cost-effectively educate ministerial candidates and pastors not only in Kyrgyzstan but also in neighboring countries, translating theological books into Kyrgyz, and encouraging locals to write theological books are all very good ideas. Getting students to pay tuition for a sustainable education without relying on foreign funding is also very good. Missionaries should be able to provide sustainable theological education at the local level, not their own.

In "Church Missions in the Public Sphere with a Focus on Onnuri Church's Use of Public Funds," **Hong Joo Kim** says that "the church absolutely cannot overlook or give up on God's mission for the public sphere" and that "the church must not hesitate to partner with governments and other outside organizations to solve social problems in the public sphere."

It is not common in Korea for the church to use church funds directly with the government and external agencies to solve social problems. However, Onnuri Church has become a good model for Korean churches in this area. In order to successfully carry out these tasks, the church must act with integrity and accountability.

In "Evangelicals and Structural (In)Justice—What Are We Afraid Of?" **Justin Thacker** emphasized that there are "two sides to our moral responsibilities to the economically vulnerable. On the one hand, we are called to provide those who are destitute with 'food and clothing.' At the same time though, we are also required to implement God's missional concern for 'justice.'" He staked his claim on the words, "For the LORD your God is God of gods and Lord of lords … who executes justice for the orphan and the widow, and who loves the foreigners, providing them with food and clothing" (Deut. 10:17–18, NRSVA). Evangelicals should love orphans, widows, and strangers in their work of evangelism, providing them with food and clothing and seeking justice for them.

For a long time, I considered it the mission of the church to preach the Gospel and save the lost, and I devoted myself to the ministry of preaching the Gospel. Of course, this is very important. However, the practice of loving neighbors is also very important (James 2:8; Gal. 5:14). I also realized that loving people by meeting their needs, as well as doing justice for the poor and weak, is a very important part of God's missionary work. Solomon says in Proverbs 21:3: "To do what is right and just is more acceptable to the LORD than sacrifice." Thank you, Justin Thacker, for reminding us of the importance of not only practicing love but also justice.

In "Integrity is Illusive: Intercultural Gospel Work Needs to be Vulnerable to Allow Indigenous Free Self-Expression," **Jim Harries** says that "healthy gospel work is done by missionaries who use the languages of the people they are reaching, and who give people the freedom to express themselves in those languages," without using finances as a draw. "We should listen to people, yes, but in their own language(s), while not posing an economic threat (or inadvertent bribe)."

It is very important for missionaries to learn the local language and culture in order to establish a good relationship with the locals and to communicate properly. And they must have a servant heart and attitude. The financial support of missionaries to the locals may sometimes deprive them of their freedom of expression. While I was working in the Philippines I observed that when missionaries provided financial support to the locals, they were not able to freely express their opinions to the missionaries, but after the financial support ended, the locals freely expressed their opinions. Foreign money should not deprive local people of freedom and dignity.

In "Mission, Power, and Money," **Paul Bendor-Samuel** says that just as the systems in our body interact with each other, "different agencies, churches, and networks function as a mission ecosystem." Though "money is an integral element in the modern practice of mission," there are other elements in missions such as "people, relationships, prayer, spiritual discernment, theology, and creativity. While each of these has their own power dynamic, the prioritization of money in mission gives those who control it a disproportionate degree of power within the mission system. We must give the same emphasis on the other elements as we do on money."

Bendor-Samuel's point is perfectly valid. It is true that money is needed to carry out missionary work, but perhaps factors such as prayer and the work of the Holy Spirit are more important than money. We know that the mission of the apostles was not dependent on money, but on the power of the Holy Spirit. We need to remember what Peter said to the beggar who was sitting at the temple gate begging for money: "Silver or gold I do not have, but what I do have I give you. In the name of Jesus Christ of Nazareth, walk" (Acts 3:6).

In "Global South Mission Is Possible!," **Andrew B. Kim** argues that even poor Global South churches can carry out missionary work if they have a right understanding of mission and give what they have to the Lord. Although the Global South churches are in poverty compared to the Western churches, they have their own unique assets. As Jesus fed more than five thousand people in the wilderness with a boy's simple lunch of five loaves of bread and two fish, miracles can happen when the Lord blesses their own "five loaves of bread and two fish." He quotes Acts 3:6, "Silver or gold I do not have, but what I do have I give you. In the name of Jesus Christ of Nazareth, walk." If we are filled with the Holy Spirit and give what we have to the Lord, money is not and should never be an issue.

When the Korean church started its missionary work in other cultures, it was just a young church, under Japanese colonial rule, and in one of the poorest countries in the world. If the Korean church performed missionary work under such circumstances, and if the Mizoram church in India can do missionary work in such a poor state, no one has the excuse that they cannot do missionary work because of poverty. In the final analysis, the work of God cannot be accomplished with money; it can only be done by the power of the Holy Spirit.

In "The COVID-19 Crisis and Opportunities for Increased Community: A Local Pastor's Recommendations," **Mongsik Lee** says that the COVID-19 pandemic, spread across all churches and missions, is a huge crisis, but "it is clear that our sovereign God still loves us and works in us. Churches and missionaries should not be afraid of the pandemic, but meditate on the essence of mission and pray. Now is the time to proactively develop mission strategies. When churches struggle financially during a pandemic crisis, they must overcome the challenges with a spirit of stewardship."

Our God is a missionary God. As Jesus said, "With man this is impossible, but with God all things are possible" (Matt. 19:26) and as Paul wrote, "All things work for good" (Rom. 8:28), nothing is impossible with God and God will work all things together for good. God is working even in a crisis such as the COVID-19 pandemic, and he will turn this crisis into a missionary opportunity. Missionaries who had no other alternative than face-to-face ministry and thought that they could not work without relying on money in the past should come up with creative ways to do non-face-to-face ministry without money.

In "COVID-19 and Opportunities in Mission: An Ibero-American Case Analysis," **Levi DeCarvalho** analyzed "the impact of the crisis on churches and missionary agencies in the Ibero-American world caused by the spread of the COVID-19 virus." He argued that while "both churches and missions agencies suffered and participated in the most negative effects of the virus, God was not surprised by anything or anyone, and he is sovereign over all our circumstances." He said that "during the current crisis, churches and institutions were not paralyzed in their ministries of recruiting, training, sending, and sustaining their workers; rather, the crisis prompted church and agency leaders to seek new ideas and strategies for expanding missionary work rather than shortening their activities and planning."

We praise and thank our sovereign God for reigning and working during this crisis, as he continues to work for the coming of his Kingdom and the fulfillment of his will. We must trust in the Lord and be bold. We must seek and pray for the guidance of the Holy Spirit, who is the leader of mission.

18. In "Mission, Fiscal Responsibility, and Care for the Environment," **Allison Howell** cites Dave Bookless, who argues that "biblically, the mission of God's people is incomplete, distorted and stultified if it does not include demonstrating God's care for all creation." But missionaries consider "the work of the Gospel is preaching, saving people, individual redemption, and discipleship. Rather, 'government or aid agencies should care for the environment.' From biblical and missiological perspectives, our role in mission is one of partnering with God in safeguarding, sustaining, and renewing creation."

Evangelicals have traditionally raised funds to preach the Gospel and plant churches, to establish schools to educate people, and to establish hospitals to heal people, but generally they did not raise money to care for the environment. That work was considered to be the government's job. However, our mission is to work with God in destroying Satan, saving the lost, and renewing the world.

In "Toward a Money-Missionary Relationship Model: A Grounded Theory Approach Based on the Empirical Data of Korean Missionaries," **Jooyun Eum** says that "missionaries are generally satisfied with the regular mission funds they receive, but in real life and ministry they feel that the mission funds provided are lacking. They have been taught that they should not be greedy for money and should have a heart of gratitude for God's provision." Therefore, there is a conflict about whether they should raise money to meet their needs or be satisfied with God's provision. "To minimize this confusion," Eum advises that "the community of missionaries, mission agencies, churches, and missiologists should come together to discuss theological, missiological, and strategic perspectives and options for financing missions."

The Apostle Paul says in 1 Timothy 6:6: "But godliness with contentment is great gain." I believe that the basic necessities of life for missionaries must be met and that the commissioning church must provide them. However, there is no limit to people's desire. I believe that God will provide for all the needs of missionaries who he called to do his work (Matt. 6:33; Phil. 4:19).

In "The Role of Patron as Father (*Gap*) in Church Planting Efforts in Cambodia," **Robert Oh** discusses the relationships between a foreign missionary and local pastors in a church planting ministry from a patron-client perspective. On the mission field, missionaries and local people form patron-client relationships. There are forms of healthy and unhealthy dependency in these relationships. The relationships between missionaries and local pastors are healthy when loving care with humility and a sacrificial spirit is given to the clients, but they can become unhealthy when patrons try to control clients.

Missionaries need to look after local pastors with love, humility, and a spirit of sacrifice, rather than controlling them with the power of money.

In "Can Any Good Be Done on a Short-Term Mission Trip?: Opportunities and Pitfalls in Athens, Greece," **Darren M. Carlson** "wonders whether any impact has been made on the nearly $2.4 billion industry." He emphasizes that short-term missionaries should not pass out money indiscriminately to refugees as their mission, and that they must work in cooperation with field missionaries and agencies with an attitude of discipleship and humble service.

Short-term missionary work is necessary in today's mission environment. Short-term missions, if well operated, are very beneficial not only to the ongoing missions, but also for new mission leadership development. Christians who participate in short-term missions should, first of all, use it as an opportunity to learn rather than do fieldwork, and then work in cooperation with field missionaries and help in their ministries. I believe this is a healthy short-term mission.

In "Paul Mission Training Center and Jeonju Antioch Church Mission Fund Case Study," **Seung-Il Lee and Dong-Whee Lee** talk about how The Paul

Mission International and Jeonju Antioch Church worked to help locals carry out their missions in partnership with local churches by training and supporting them. They not only train and mentor the local missionaries, but help them financially with matching funds, which is one of the ways to encourage locals to get involved in missions.

Jeonju Antioch Church is a good model for the missionary movement of local Korean churches. More than half of the church's total budget is used for overseas missions. The missionaries belonging to The Paul Mission International, which is led by Jeonju Antioch Church, are not only engaged in cross-cultural missionary work, but also in established missionary training centers in the fields to raise locals as missionaries. Using a matching fund method to encourage the missionary movement of the economically weak field churches has proven beneficial.

Conclusion

We need money to carry out our missionary work. But where and how we spend our money matters. In missionary work, external funds should be used within the scope of helping local churches to become healthy indigenous churches, without fostering dependence on foreign churches.

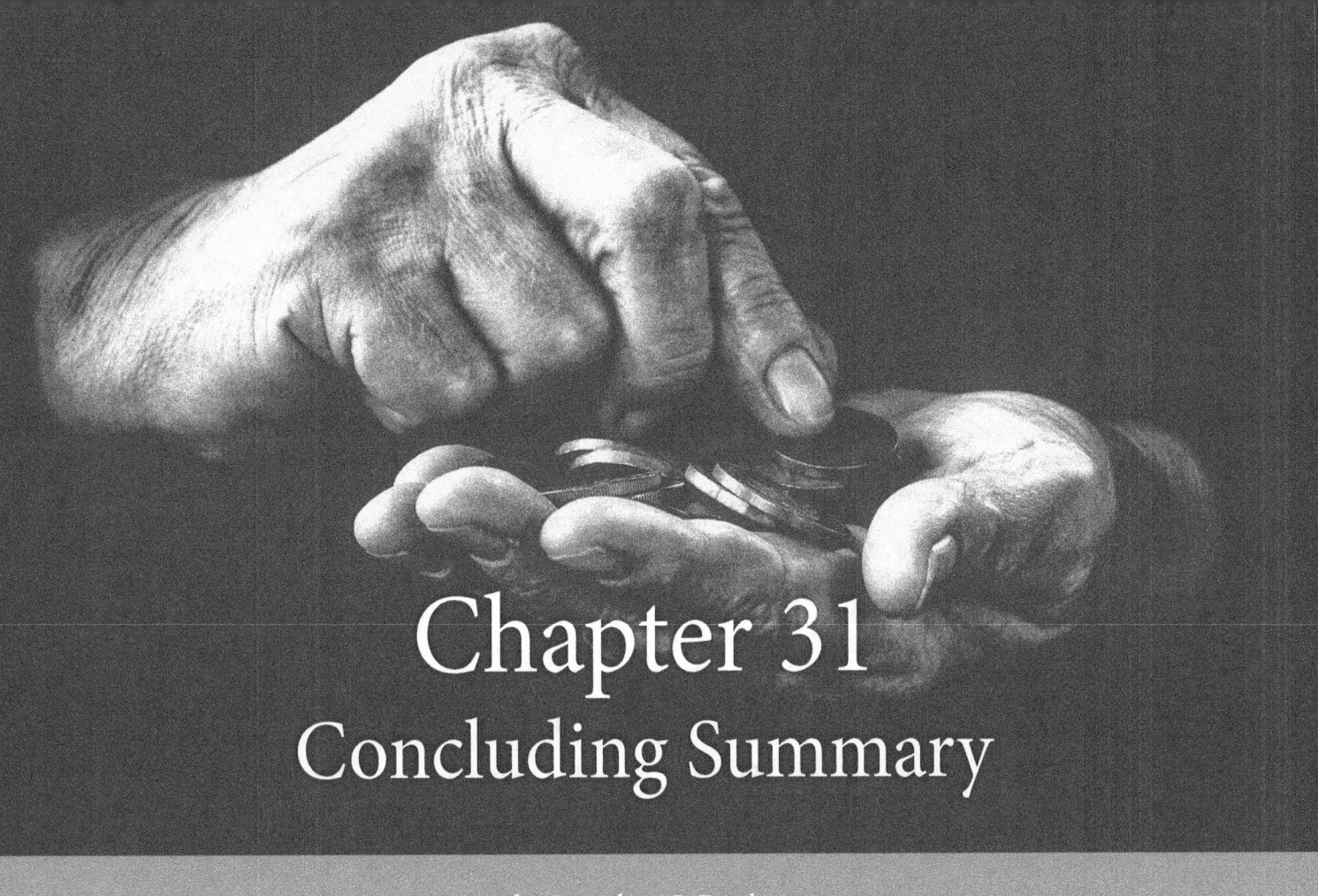

Chapter 31
Concluding Summary

by Jonathan J. Bonk

To write an adequate summary conclusion to a book such as this one within the compass of a few thousand words is extraordinarily difficult, and yet Dr. Timothy Kiho Park has done this for us. Thanks to Dr. Park's good work, I will focus my concluding remarks on Dr. Wright's excellent teaching, and then on several themes that either *have been* touched upon, or which *should have been* more substantially addressed, or which *might have been* missed altogether. I will not restrict myself to missiological comments per se, but to historical, political, ethical, and economic frameworks within which the Protestant missionary movement of the twenty-first century has carried on its work. But first, the Bible studies.

In Dr. Wright's message from Chronicles on the "integrity of our funding in the eyes of God," we were reminded of the inspiring case of David whose example generated a kind of tsunami of generosity in support of the construction of a temple, for which David's son Solomon would receive credit. David reminds us that selfless generosity can inspire and foster generosity in those around any giver, whether king, missionary, or pastor!

But beyond the immediate details of this inspiring story is the tragedy of David's son who actually built the temple and whose eventual fame was launched by that extraordinary achievement. We should be sobered when we recall the story of Solomon, whose theoretical wisdom could not spare him or his people from the internal decay that was increasingly evident as he became tyrannical and self-aggrandizing. While he impressed powerful peers and rulers in "the whole world," among his own subjects he became an oppressive dictator, and his obsession with prestige and women turned his citizens into slaves. His son Rehoboam simply applied the coup de grâce that destroyed an already staggering nation and scattered its peoples (1 Kings 11–12). As missionaries, we can understand from this story that auspicious beginnings, good opportunities, and spectacular accomplishments do not guarantee righteous outcomes or enduring results. We do well to remember that what David dared to dream for, pray for, and sacrifice for could be frittered away and destroyed because of the infidelity, greed, and negligence of his successor, King Solomon himself "in all his glory."

We in Christian leadership do well to think carefully about the wise observations put in the mouth of Archbishop Thomas Beckett by T. S. Eliot in his epic masterpiece, "Murder in the Cathedral":[1]

> The last temptation is the greatest treason;
> To do the right deed for the wrong reason …
>
> … Ambition comes when early force is spent
> And when we find no longer all things possible.
> Ambition comes behind and unobservable.
> Sin grows with doing good …
>
> … To become servant of God was never my wish.
> Servant of God has chance of greater sin
> And sorrow, then the man who serves a king.
> For those who serve the greater cause may make the cause serve them,
>
> Still doing right: and striving with political men
> May make that cause political, not by what they do
> But by what they are …
>
> I know that history at all times draws
> The strangest consequence from remotest cause.
> But for every evil, every sacrilege,
>
> Crime, wrong, oppression and the axe's edge,
> Indifference, exploitation, you, and you,
> And you, must all be punished. So must you.[2]

Dr. Wright's second Bible study addressed the importance of "accountability in our stewardship of the grace of God" (2 Cor. 8:16–9:5). Paul was an effective fundraiser. But he never raised funds for himself or for his own ministry. He worked with his own hands to support himself and his colleagues. His reminder to the elders of the Ephesian church as they exchanged tearful farewells should be pondered deeply by missionaries today: "I have not coveted anyone's silver or gold or clothing. You yourselves know that these hands of mine have supplied my own needs and the needs of my companions. In everything I did, I showed you that by this kind of hard work we must help the weak, remembering the words the Lord Jesus himself said: 'It is more blessed to give than to receive'" (Acts 20:33–35).

Paul's lifelong practice of self-support and generous sharing of whatever he earned gave him immense integrity as a fundraiser and as a steward of the Gospel. People trusted him because he was not one of those who "peddled the word of God for profit" (2 Cor. 2:17). One of the most cumbersome ethical burdens borne by missionaries for the past 150 years has been the flow of support from foreign sources. This has made missionary insistence on self-support for indigenous churches difficult to comprehend, since they themselves are clearly not self-supporting, and they cannot show by example just what this means in the local situation. Paul was not similarly handicapped. He could speak about money with profound and evident integrity. Several of the case studies and workshops in this forum presented the unique challenges associated with "faith financing"—notably the case studies presented by Ben Torrey, Zosangliana Colney, and Sung-Deuk Oak and the workshop presented by Andrew Kim.

Paul's practice is among the several good reasons why we today should pay close attention to the five Pauline principles for stewarding donations identified by Dr. Wright. Financial scams across the Christian world are not a new phenomenon. According to estimates based on research published by the Center for the Study of Global Christianity, by realistic estimates more than $68 billion in financial fraud was perpetrated by and within Christian organizations worldwide in 2019. This is more than the total amount—$60 billion—given by churches to support mission work during the same time frame.[3] One principle is especially needful for us who are church and mission leaders today: downward accountability is our primary accountability, and the only authentic way of being accountable to Jesus, who identifies with "the least of these brothers and sisters of mine" (Matt. 25:40). Intentional administrative downward accountability might have spared the organization featured in Dr. Jinbong Kim's workshop on GMS financial management from many ongoing worries.

Dr. Wright's final study was on the *viability of ministry* (Eccles. 11:1–6). Wisdom is the perspective that comes from a broad and deep grasp of oneself, one's environment, one's history, and one's community.

---

1 Beckett had been appointed by King Henry II of England as government chancellor. The duplicitous monarch then arranged to have him brutally murdered by four of his knights in Canterbury Cathedral in 1155.

2 T. S. Eliot, "Murder in the Cathedral," in *T. S. Eliot: The Complete Poems and Plays, 1909-1950* (New York: Harcourt, Brace & World, Inc., 1971): 196–197.

3 "Fraud against Churches Exceeds What Churches Give to Missions," Brotherhood Mutual, October 10, 2019, https://www.brotherhoodmutual.com/resources/safety-library/risk-management-articles/administrative-staff-and-finance/finances/fraudsters-target-churches/#:~:text=According%20to%20the%20current%20Status%20of%20Global%20Christianity,worldwide%20mission%20work%20during%20the%20same%20time%20frame.

Concluding Summary—Jonathan J. Bonk

As Dr. Wright's teaching reminded us, just as something as common as a fly can ruin excellent ointment, so "small" matters can upset the best laid plans and reputations, and money's voice can drown prudence and pervert justice. We know from experience and from observation that this is true in ministry—perhaps *especially* in ministry—where *looking good* can displace actually *being* good. "Godly opportunism" as described and lauded in Ecclesiastes and as appropriated and utilized by entrepreneurs to justify exploitation of the weak for personal profit is not only wrong but spiritually deadly.

How many professing Christians on this lucrative path have found their spiritual lives choked by the deceitfulness of riches and the cares of this world? And yet, there can be no gain without awareness, timeliness, and effort, whether one is a resourceful entrepreneur, a dedicated pastor, or a visionary mission executive. This practice—an echo of what the writer has said in Ecclesiastes 9:10—is central to New Testament teaching as well, not because we all die so we might as well live with all possible gusto, but because we are working for God, whether we are business tycoons or lowly servants: "And whatever you do, whether in word or deed, do it all in the name of the Lord Jesus, giving thanks to God the Father through him" (Eccles. 9:10; Col. 3:17). Each of us is part of God's epic creation and redemption story—a story that is much, much bigger than our lowly or lofty, invisible or conspicuous stations in this life.

A few comments relating to Dr. Gina Zurlo's masterful overview of global Christian finance will serve as a segue to my concluding remarks. Against the backdrop of the infinitesimal little planet known to us as "the earth" within its solar system—just one of numberless similarly incomprehensively vast solar systems—we humans do not even rise to the level of microscopic specks. And yet the world as we understand it revolves around the notion that we as persons, cultures, nations, races, or species are at the center of everything. Gina Zurlo provides a helpful overview of the demographic and linguistic shifts within global Christianity away from Europe and North America and European languages to the continents of Africa, Asia, and Latin America. These shifts are impressive, even if Christianity as a percentage of the total world population has apparently declined from an estimated 34.5 percent in 1900 to 32.3 percent in 2021.[4]

---

[4] Gina A. Zurlo, Todd M. Johnson, and Peter F. Crossing, "World Christianity and Mission 2021: Questions about the Future," *International Bulletin of Mission Research* 45, no.1 (2021): 15–25, https://journals.sagepub.com/doi/pdf/10.1177/2396939320966220.

But there is another reckoning that is beginning to take shape—hinted at by Dr. Zurlo in her final question about the staggering inequality of access to material resources within the global community of Christians. Mr. Daeshik Jo remarks on this inequity in his response. What are the factors that gave rise to and perpetuate these profoundly troubling inequities? Please be patient with me if I seem to meander into my limited understanding of this and related questions.

As missionaries and church leaders we are not exempt from being shaped, limited, compromised, and enabled by great systems (events, fabricated memories, dead-end political dreams, exploitations, etc.) so all-encompassing that we live largely unaware of them. Much of this falls into the category of what Peter referred to as "the empty way of life handed down to you from your forefathers" (1 Pet. 1:18, NIV, ESV). We cannot avoid inheriting and incarnating the values, beliefs, and lifeways of the cultures in which we are born and educated. We are all aware that since the Gospel is both the prisoner and the liberator of culture, our cultural material inheritance becomes a part of whatever Gospel we share—the "jar of clay" in which God's treasure is carried wherever we go (2 Cor. 4:7). Fortunately, while we carry this treasure in human vessels, through the Spirit of God we can be redeemed from the empty ways we have inherited, and seeing them for what they are, redirect our own lives by renewing our minds (Rom. 12:1ff.).

Today, as in the days of our Lord, prophets do not often come from the ranks of the religious establishment. In North America at least, many of those who occupy evangelical pulpits and command a hearing are false prophets, advocating a kind of "America first" idolatry based on glamorization of a fictionalized past that never existed—glossing over the racist, genocidal, unjust, and violent realities of conquest, dispossession, and slavery and in its place elevating the "little house on the prairies" occupied by a poor but law abiding family whose very existence is threatened by savage "Indians"—the people from whom the land on which their little farm is located was forcibly taken.

Profound lessons relating to the use and abuse of money have been shared in the case studies and workshops of this forum, and we are much the better for having read and discussed them. But the world that we have inherited, participated in, and bequeathed to our children, grandchildren, and great grandchildren is a deeply troubled one. Justin Thacker, Jim Harries, and Allison Howell touch on aspects of this world in their essays. Whether we want it or not, all missions and money discussions and policies from now on will take place within the contexts of existential crises of humanity's own making.

Over the past several decades it has become increasingly clear that the civilization often referred to as "the West" was built on foundations of racial genocide. *Exterminate All the Brutes!* is the title of a book written by Sven Lindqvist, who argues that these words are at the heart of modern civilization.[5] They summarize the means and the results, so far, of Europe's racist "civilizing mission" (in which Christian mission has played its part), its emissaries compassing land and sea to make the rest of the world feed into our frantic wealth-swelling hamster wheel vision of life. Western civilization's relentless mission to dominate the world has been characterized by racial genocides on an unprecedented scale, enslavement, bombs, wars, hyperconsumption of nonrenewable resources, and the creation of environmentally disastrous products that—when harnessed to rapacious consumer appetites—have destroyed species, vast bodies of water, the soil, and the atmosphere.[6]

Grappling with the complexities of mission-related money matters going forward will require revisiting and recasting our understanding of at least three verities of the Western civilization out of which the modern missionary movement emerged:

1. First is the question of how we in the West came to be where it is. Economically and socially, the West has become accustomed to being in the driver's seat of the world's economies, innovators, envied exemplars, and purveyors of a way of life that has often been exhibit A in our arsenal of proofs that our way of life is superior to others, and that our way of life was possible because it was rooted in the Bible. This is a partial truth at best, and should be seen for what it is: a lie. Going forward, Western missionaries along with those who have taken their cue from the West cannot be so sanguine about this comfortable way of life. We now recognize that the planet cannot survive the avarice that lies at its root—the "continual desire for more" ethos built into its DNA is stripping the planet of nonrenewable resources, contaminating rivers and oceans, exterminating species, and guaranteeing an atmosphere that will suffocate life forms such as human beings.

2. Second, the idea that the Western way of consumption can be and should emulated by others around the world who subscribe to our way of life is a dangerous one. The world cannot afford a human population that consumes and pollutes at the same level as do the nations who have adopted capitalism or Marxism or some other economic model of infinite economic growth through ever increasing human consumption of goods, services, and nonrenewable raw materials. North America in its present political and social forms, it must never be forgotten, was born and sustained through great evils—the greatest genocide in the history of human genocides, followed by the most egregious form of human slavery ever practiced—all justified and sustained to this day by a system of laws and practices that obliterate or disenfranchise the vanquished and the once enslaved. Which other nation in the world today can adopt such practices as they embark on their path to so-called "development"? And yet genocide and slavery are foundational to the stories of the United States and Canada. And we who live in the West or who are its economic and military satellites are beneficiaries of evils that can never be undone and should never again be emulated.

Is there any sign of repentance for this in the most "Christian" nation in the world? On the contrary, there are many who do not want to even talk about this past, which is still visibly present. I recently read a disturbing but unsurprising report on the suppression

---

[5] Sven Lindqvist, *"Exterminate All the Brutes": One Man's Odyssey into the Heart of Darkness and the Origins of European Genocide* (New York: New Press, 2007).

[6] The roots of the European "discovery" and forcible occupation of entire continents and the dispossession and sometimes obliteration of indigenous inhabitants was economically driven, racially based, and religiously rationalized. In the nineteenth century, scientific racism was a part of the emerging evolutionary model of understanding how life came to be and where life was going. Intellectual giants such as Arthur de Gobineau (1816–1882—*The Moral and Intellectual Diversity of Races* [1856]), Charles Darwin (1809–1882—*On the Origin of Species* [1859]), William Winwood Reade (1838–1876—*The Martyrdom of Man* [1872]), and Herbert Spencer (1820–1903—*Social Statistics* [social Darwinianism]) began to break the stranglehold that religion had on Western thinking, suggesting that the great purpose of life was best explained by evolution and the survival of the fittest. The weak would die out and the strong would survive. These theories were applied as both evidence and justification of white supremacy. The extinction of weaker races was inevitable. The meaning of life was evolution itself: the fit would survive, the weak would die off. One of the best documented chronicles of this genocide is the book by David E. Stannard, *American Holocaust: The Conquest of the New World* (New York: Oxford University Press, 1993).

of truth in schools across the southern United States in *The Guardian*: "Black Educators Silenced from Teaching America's Racist Past."[7]

How ironic that lies and half-truths are being promoted and funded across the "Bible Belt," as though the truth does not matter in God's moral universe and God can be mocked with impunity! This is hardly unprecedented, of course. Isaiah described this phenomenon in his day this way: "They say to the seers, 'See no more visions!' and to the prophets, 'Give us no more visions of what is right! Tell us pleasant things, prophecy illusions. Leave this way, get off this path, and stop confronting us with the Holy One of Israel'" (Isa. 30:10–11). Key political leaders from the southern states—most if not all of them "Christian"—echoed this distant message from Isaiah when they urged the federal government to shelve efforts to integrate critical race theory into school curricula so that the nation's centuries-long experience with slavery and systemic racism could be recognized and addressed: "Families did not ask for this divisive nonsense," a well-known conservative senator wrote, "voters did not vote for it. Americans never decided our children should be taught that our country is inherently evil."

He was certainly telling the truth about conservative white voter sentiment! But God is not mocked. What nations and people sow they must reap, whether or not they deny, suppress, or conceal the truth (Gal. 6:7). The white religious leaders and politicians who promote and laud this kind of truth suppression are bequeathing to their children the judgment that comes upon any social or physical edifice that is nothing more than a glitzy facade stretched over an internal frame and foundations of rot and deceit: "The prophets prophecy lies, the priests rule by their own authority, and my people love it this way. But what will you do in the end?" (Jer. 5:31, and through to 7:8).

3. Third is the impact of overconsumption on the planet's environment. We are entering a period of instability and unpredictability as the planet warms, the glaciers and ice caps melt, the oceans acidify and rise, and entire populations either migrate or die. The empty way of life that we have inherited from our forefathers has produced this inevitable result.[8] Dr. Howell in her workshop addresses this significant but often ignored reality. Icelander Andri Snaer Magnason helps us to grasp the immensity of the problem:

> Scientists have shown us that the foundations of life, of Earth itself, are failing. The principal ideologies of the twentieth century considered the Earth and nature as sources of inexpensive, infinite raw material. Humans assumed that the atmosphere could continually absorb emissions, that oceans could endlessly absorb waste, that soil could constantly renew itself if given more fertilizer, that animal species would keep moving aside as humans colonized more and more space.[9]

He explains why we have such difficulty grasping, let alone addressing, the huge climate changes that are due, in good part, to the avaricious brilliance of Western civilization and its ability to amplify or multiply every human impulse for evil or for good:

> When it comes to discussing issues that affect all water on Earth, all Earth's surface, the planet's entire atmosphere—the issue's enormity absorbs all the meaning. The only way to write about the subject is to go past it, to the side of it, below it, into the past and the future, to be personal and also scientific, and to use mythological language.[10]

What effect should this inescapable reality have on mission finance, mission modus operandi, or on the very idea of mission? Like fish who cannot live without being in water, but who are not capable of comprehending the nature of their environment beyond that it is an indispensable condition of life, so we as human beings today live and move in an environment that we barely understand and which is beyond our capacity to control, even when we become aware of the fatal impact of our way of life on our own survival. So we do not have an answer to the question. But whether or not we find answers, the questions arising from this dawning reality will remain. It is a gloomy story, as we see oceans rising, deserts forming, ice melting, species extinguishing. And make no mistake: Christian mission in its

---

7 Melinda D. Anderson, "'These are the Facts': Black Educators Silenced from Teaching America's Racist Past," *The Guardian*, September 14, 2021, https://www.theguardian.com/education/2021/sep/14/black-us-teachers-critical-race-theory-silenced.

8 One of the most poignant recent publications that I have read is by the Icelander Andri Snaer Magnason, *On Time and Water*, trans. Lytton Smith (Windsor, ON: Biblioasis, 2021).

9 Magnason, *On Time and Water*, 8, Kindle for PC.

10 Magnason, 10.

Western manifestations and models is very much a part of the problem, not part of the solution.

But let me conclude on a more positive note! The good news is that God's redemptive purposes in our world remain. They do not rely upon any human discovery of how to save the planet from their own carelessness and greed! Nor do his purposes rely upon the generosity of wealthy churches and individuals. This is evident in Zosangliana Colney's inspiring case study from Mizoram. Sanctified ingenuity—what missiologists like to refer to as "strategy"—is a characteristic common to individuals and communities who are infused with a passion for Jesus. As one reflects on this case study, one is reminded that here are the Macedonian brothers and sisters of our day, whose extraordinary generosity was recognized by Paul as "the grace that God has given … [for] in the midst of a very severe trial, their overflowing joy and their extreme poverty welled up in rich generosity" (2 Cor. 8:1–2). Paul's reminder that "Whoever sows sparingly will also reap sparingly, and whoever sows generously will also reap generously" (2 Cor. 9:6) is beautifully demonstrated in the churches of Mizoram!

Whatever I have written in this chapter—the human-devised "thorns in the flesh" that we have such difficulty extracting from our bodies ecclesiastical or politic—our weakness opens the door for God's grace (2 Cor. 12:9).

"May the grace of the Lord Jesus Christ, and the love of God, and the fellowship of the Holy Spirit be with you all" (2 Cor. 13:13).

Appendix

KPM's Missionary Leadership Structure and Responsibilities for Financial Policy (Accountability and Reliability)

by Young Gee Park, General Director of the KPM

The Kosin Presbyterian Mission (KPM), the official organization in charge of missionary work for the Kosin Presbyterian Church in Korea, began its work in 1956. Since sending the first missionary to Taiwan, 660 missionaries have been dispatched, and currently there are about 500 missionaries serving in fifty-six countries. KPM's clear purpose is "to glorify God by sending missionaries around the world to obey Jesus's Great Commission and to establish Reform churches in all possible ways." In order to achieve this goal effectively, the Kosin Presbyterian Church in Korea entrusted the responsibility to KPM. In this article, I would like to introduce KPM's leadership structure and financial policy.

Leadership Structure of KPM

KPM has a uniquely structured board responsible for overseas mission. Every three years, the General Assembly appoints seventeen board members consisting of the Missions Sponsorship Association, missionary experts, elders, and pastors as synod representatives. The chairman of the Missionary Society, the chairman of the Mission Policy Committee, and the director of the KPM headquarters become the ex officio members of the board of directors. In KPM's leadership structure, related organizations within our denomination, various experts, and missionaries at headquarters and on the field play vital parts.

Board of Directors. The board of directors is responsible for:

1. Mission strategy and policy decisions of KPM articles of association and regulations,
2. Appointment and dismissal of directors, approval of project plans, and implementation performance,
3. Approval of the budget, settlement of accounts, and financial management,
4. Ministry supervision, oversight of human resources, and determination of research, training, forums, conventions, etc. for missionary development,
5. selection, dispatch, and redispatch of missionaries,
6. cooperation with other mission organizations,
7. obtaining, disposing, exchanging, donating, and managing of properties,
8. Supervision of the Mission Policy Committee, the Member Care Committee, the Missionary Society, and the Local Leader Training Committee.

The board of directors oversees almost every aspect of KPM's work and is responsible for implementing God's intentions, plans, purposes, and strategies. The board has a bimonthly meeting to tend to these obligations. Whenever issues are too difficult to judge straightaway, they are settled later based on the studied recommendations of standing policy committees. The current KPM board of directors serves both the roles of managing and governing. KPM's leadership structure—a structure in which the entire denomination is in mission together—has built in accountability and reliability.

KPM Headquarters. The KPM established a mission headquarters for the smooth performance of its duties, which are conducted according to articles of association and implementation rules. The general director administers the Kosin Presbyterian Mission, represents the mission headquarters, and directs and supervises employees, regional mission departments, and missionaries. It was established to divide the administrative affairs of the headquarters, training center, member care center, administrative bureau, ministry support bureau, research bureau, and mobilization bureau, and each office and bureau serve according to KPM articles, enforcement rules, and manuals.

How can we accomplish the mission of the triune God? The answer to this is the incarnation. The incarnation is the only way the Father is revealed to the world as the subject of all mission work. Therefore, incarnational mission is the mission theology of KPM. The principles of incarnational ministry are embedded in all mission spirituality, mission purposes, and policies of KPM. The greatest principle of incarnational mission is to serve others. The headquarters has sixteen missionaries and nine employees working together and emphasizes that serving each other is its most important ministry. First of all, in order to foster a joyful, homelike atmosphere, all ministry employees greet each other, talk, and pray daily. All the families of the headquarters pray together during early morning devotions and share graciously with one another. Second, the sixteen missionaries gather at weekly meetings on Fridays to report on the ministries of the councils and states, to check with each other's plans for the week, and to discuss and decide on various issues from each council, state, and regional department, seeking grace from the Holy Spirit. Finally, once a month all the families, including those of employees and missionaries of the headquarters, gather in an expanded meeting to fellowship, celebrate birthdays, and share meals, all of which promotes happiness in the mission headquarters.

The leadership team at headquarters makes it clear that its ministerial duty is to serve missionaries in the field and churches. KPM is implementing a matching synod system to enhance mutual trust and accountability in its relations with churches. It is a system that matches each synod with local departments on the mission field so that missionaries and churches in the field understand and get to know each other more deeply. Through this system, the churches of the synod visit the matched missionary field more frequently. Exchanges of human and physical resources thus naturally occur. This results in increased mutual trust between missionaries and churches, as well as greater transparency in ministry and finance reporting.

In addition, KPM has been working for several years toward transferring leadership responsibilities to the field in order to increase mutual trust between headquarters and field missionaries. KPM's ultimate goal is to be transformed from headquarters-centered to regional-centered administration, from centralized to regional autonomous operation, from headquarters's financial decision-making authority to regional government financial decision-making authority, and from position-oriented to function-oriented regional leadership. This is consistent with our belief that headquarters should not administer unilaterally but pursue a leadership structure that trusts and therefore includes missionaries on the field.

Among its leadership structures, the headquarters manages a Member Care Center to fulfill its responsibilities to care for missionary families. The center's ministry includes supporting missionary kids (MKs), retired missionaries, children in military service, and parents with medical support, marriage and funeral support, emergency support (such as for COVID-19), and preparation for redispatch of missionaries during their sabbatical and retreat programs. Practically, this means that:

1. Approximately 560 MKs will receive tuition support to attend schools.
2. Elementary school students receive $200, middle school students $300, and college students $500 per month; graduate students receive $2,000 per year.
3. Some receive special scholarships worth $1,000 per year.
4. MKs are encouraged to connect with each other via SNS (social networking services).
5. MKs go on retreats to cheer one another, and they are encouraged to become future missionaries.
6. Gifts are regularly sent to MKs who have joined the army.
7. Gifts on behalf of missionaries are regularly sent to their parents so that they can be proud of their missionary kids.
8. Parents of missionaries are invited to each region where they are given time to learn about the ministries of their children and encouraged to be proud of them as missionaries.
9. The center helps the immediate family of missionaries in hosting family occasions and attending consolation events.
10. Before sending missionaries back to the field, the center provides expert psychological counseling so that leadership at headquarters can discern whether it is possible for them to continue ministry, or whether they need readjustment of the ministry or missionary field.

11. Retreats for rest and recharge are arranged for missionaries on sabbatical.
12. Missionaries' letters are read, answered, and forwarded to sponsoring churches.
13. Struggling missionaries are cared for.
14. There is an emergency manual that outlines emergency measures for situations such as COVID-19. In particular, the center operates a web-based telemedicine system in cooperation with Kosin Gospel Hospital for those in need of on-site medical support. The coronavirus has infected about thirty KPM missionaries, and this system has proven very useful in their cases.
15. The center organizes the S65 meeting for a group of senior missionaries to prepare for their approaching retirement.
16. Construction of a memorial hall for missionaries who have passed away is currently in the planning stage.

Fiscal Policy: Transparency, Reliability, and Accountability

Missionaries have a duty to faithfully follow the guidance of the Lord in their lives and ministry. In addition, every missionary bears the responsibility to clearly reveal his or her life and ministry before God and before a sending organization or sponsoring church. This is very important for each individual and for the history of the mission. The headquarters of missionary organizations have similar responsibilities. They must establish fiscal policies, develop and operate financial management systems, mobilize material resources, allocate funds effectively, evaluate missionary expenditures, audit boards of directors, and report on all of these publicly.

KPM's Financial Policy: Mutual Financial Responsibility among Missionaries Enlisted in the Semi-Pooling System

The principles of incarnational mission apply to financial policy as well. The inner relationship of the Trinity (perichoresis) is most clearly revealed to the world through the incarnation of Jesus Christ (John 14:9). Perichoresis is a very special concept in which the three persons of the triune God open up space for each other to reside and work. The principles of mutual trust and mutual cooperation between the triune God are also manifest in the incarnation of the Son, Jesus. According to the reciprocal principle so integral to incarnational ministry, KPM members share financial resources through a semi-pooling system. Through this system, mutual trust and comradeship between members are maximized.

Due to the increasing number of deficit financing missionaries, KPM was once asked by the denomination to quit the semi-pooling system and implement a private fundraising system (YGWYG system: you get what you get). The YGWYG system is based on the principle of survival of the fittest, encouraging further competition among missionaries for raising funds. In the end, KPM missionaries opposed the YGWYG system, and the semi-pooling system remains in place. The average number of missionaries in deficit accounts reaches about 40 percent of the total, but missionaries with surplus accounts voluntarily redirect their funds to deficit account missionaries through the "love account movement." We are experiencing the touch of God that fills KPM entirely, with no shortage every year when we settle the accounts of surpluses and deficits. The headquarters likewise implements an enhanced semi-pooling system to maintain the financial solvency of missionaries with deficits. Missionaries with large deficits are encouraged to take early sabbaticals in Korea to raise support. In addition, missionaries with deficits of more than a certain amount are limited to 70 percent of their living expenses, and restrictions are imposed on the remittance of ministry expenses when reviewing their resending.

For transparency, the headquarters operates a financial management computer system. For accountability, it works with related agencies on budgeting, settlements, and audits. The budget is jointly established by the missionary society and the board of directors, and matters concerning the finances of missionaries must be submitted to the headquarters's electronic payment system through consultation with regional leadership. At the end of the year, each missionary's financial report is evaluated by regional leadership and reported to headquarters. A missionary's locally owned property must be registered under the name of the regional department, and after retirement, a missionary's financial interests will also be transferred to the local department. The system of financial settlement and reporting through regional departments enhances the financial transparency of individual missionaries. In addition to each missionary's fundraising accountability rules, the additional bank accounts allowed at headquarters are not permitted for individual missionary sponsorships. Nevertheless, when it comes to financial transparency and reliability, KPM relies primarily on the spirituality of missionaries living in the presence of God (*Coram Deo*), the core of our missionary spirituality.

Implementation of Public Financial Responsibility with the Matched Synod

The principles of incarnational ministry require that KPM engage in universal church (catholic) mission. As an official missionary organization of the church, KPM endeavors to manifest catholicity in its financial responsibilities. In addition, each missionary has a communal financial responsibility for the church's finances, far removed from the notion that "the finances I raised are for my missionary expenses." KPM also administers its catholic missionary duty by matching the synods under the Kosin General Assembly with regional departments. This method prevents overlapping investments in missionary fields. Another major benefit is that small churches belonging to a synod can easily participate in missionary work. When a church's catholic consciousness disappears, churches give way to unseemly competition, even in their missionary work. The sad result is that missionary work is carried out only in medium to large churches that have the required human and physical resources, while small churches are excluded from missionary work, which is the very essence of being a church. In the end, this results in the weakening of mission work across the entire Kosin denomination.

Matched synods visit the mission fields of the local departments more frequently and they become aware of the needs of the missionaries, so they are also financially responsible. In addition, KPM and matched synods will join in selecting, training, and sending new missionaries within the associated synod. And it also has a policy for matched synod fundraising for new missionaries to fulfill their responsibilities together.

Selected Bibliography

Atkins, Margaret and Robin Osborne, eds. *Poverty in the Roman World*. Cambridge: Cambridge University Press, 2006.

Blomberg, Craig L. *Neither Poverty nor Riches: A Biblical Theology of Possessions*. Downers Grove: InterVarsity Press, 1999.

Boerma, Conrad. *Rich Man, Poor Man—and the Bible*. London: SCM, 1979.

Bonk, Jonathan J. "Economic Development and Christian Mission: A Perspective from History of Mission." In *Mission and Money: Christian Mission in the Context of Global Inequalities*, edited by Mari-Anna Auvinen-Pöntinen and Adelin Jørgensen, 145–170. Leiden: E. J. Brill, 2016.

———. "Following Jesus in Contexts of Power and Violence." *Evangelical Review of Theology* 31, no. 4 (2007): 342–357.

———. "The Gospel and Ethics." *Evangelical Review of Theology* 33, no. 1 (2009): 47–61.

———. "The Mission of Money: Toward a Theology of the Righteous Rich." In *Intercultural Living*, vol. 1, edited by Lazar T. Stanislaus and Martin Ueffing, 258–275. New Delhi: Steyler Missionswissenschaftliches Institut/ISPCK, 2015.

———. *Missions and Money: Affluence as a Missionary Problem ... Revisited*. Rev. and exp. ed. Maryknoll: Orbis Books, 2006.

———. "Missions and Money: Affluence as a Western Missionary Problem ... Revisited." *International Bulletin of Missionary Research* 31, no. 4 (October 2007): 171–174.

———. "Money as Power in Mission." In *Mission and Power: History, Relevance and Perils*, edited by Atola Longkumer, Jørgen Skov Sørensen, and Michael Biehl, 298–313. Oxford: Regnum Books, 2016.

Brown, Peter. *Through the Eye of a Needle: Wealth, the Fall of Rome, and the Making of Christianity in the West, 350-550 AD*. Princeton: Princeton University Press, 2012.

Brueggemann, Walter. *Money and Possessions*. Louisville: Westminster John Knox Press, 2016.

Chrysostom, Saint John. *On Wealth and Poverty*. Translated and introduced by Catharine P. Roth. Crestwood, NY: St. Vladmir's Seminary Press, 1984.

Cone, Orello. *Rich and Poor in the New Testament*. New York: The MacMillan Co., 1902.

Countryman, L. William. *The Rich Christian in the Church of the Early Empire: Contradictions and Accommodations*. Lewiston: Edwin Mellen Press, 1980.

Daly, Lew. *God's Economy: Faith-Based Initiatives and the Caring State*. Chicago: University of Chicago Press, 2009.

Davis, Mike. *Planet of Slums*. New York: Verso, 2006.

Dommen, Edward. *How Just Is the Market Economy?* Geneva: WCC Publications, 2003.

Eskridge, Larry and Mark A. Noll, eds. *More Money, More Ministry: Money and Evangelicals in Recent North American History*. Grand Rapids: William B. Eerdmans, 2000.

Finn, Richard, OP. *Almsgiving in the Later Roman Empire: Christian Promotion and Practice, 31–450*. Oxford: Oxford University Press, 2006.

Geisst, Charles. *Collateral Damaged: The Marketing of Consumer Debt to America*. New York: Bloomberg, 2009.

Glanville, Mark R. and Luke Glanville. *Refuge Reimagined: Biblical Kinship in Global Politics*. Downers Grove: IVP Academic, 2021.

Gnuse, Robert Karl. *You Shall Not Steal: Community and Property in the Biblical Tradition*. Maryknoll: Orbis Books, 1985.

González, Justo L. *Faith & Wealth: A History of Early Christian Ideas on the Origin, Significance, and Use of Money*. New York: Harper & Row, 1990.

Graeber, David. *Bullshit Jobs: A Theory*. New York: Simon & Schuster, 2018.

———. *Debt: The First 5000 Years*. New York: Melville House, 2014

———. *The Utopia of Rules: On Technology, Stupidity, and the Secret Joys of Bureaucracy*. New York: Melville House, 2015.

Hengel, Martin. *Property and Riches in the Early Church: Aspects of a Social History of Early Christianity.* Philadelphia: Fortress Press, 1974.

Holman, Susan R., ed. *Wealth and Poverty in Early Church and Society.* Grand Rapids: Baker Academic, 2008.

Hoppe, Leslie J. *There Shall Be No Poor among You: Poverty in the Bible.* Nashville: Abingdon Press, 2004.

Huffington, Arianna. *Pigs at the Trough: How Corporate Greed and Political Corruption Are Undermining America.* New York: Crown Publishers, 2003.

Johnson, Luke T. *Sharing Possessions: Mandate and Symbol of Faith.* Philadelphia: Fortress Press, 1981.

Lindqvist, Sven. *"Exterminate All the Brutes": One Man's Odyssey into the Heart of Darkness and the Origins of European Genocide.* New York: The New Press, 2021.

Longenecker, Bruce W. *Remember the Poor: Paul, Poverty, and the Greco-Roman World.* Grand Rapids: William B. Eerdmans, 2010.

Magnason, Andri Snaer. *On Time and Water.* Translated by Lytton Smith. Windsor, ON: Biblioasis, 2019.

Mansfield, Stephen. *The Search for God and Guinness: A Biography of the Beer That Changed the World.* Nashville: Thomas Nelson, 2009.

Mawudor, Bright Gabriel. *Financial Sustainability of Church Related Organizations: An Empirical Study on Kenya.* Geneva: Globalethics.net, 2016.

McTevia, James T. *The Culture of Debt: How a Once-Proud Society Mortgaged Its Future.* New York: MB Communications, 2010.

Mullin, Redmond. *The Wealth of Christians.* Maryknoll: Orbis Books, 1983.

Pilgrim, Walter E. *Good News to the Poor: Wealth and Poverty in Luke and Acts.* Minneapolis: Augsburg, 1981.

Razu, Indukuri John Mohan. *Global Capitalism as Hydra: A New Look at Market, Money and MNCs. Ethical Dilemmas between the Idols of Death and the God of Life.* Delhi: ISPCK/BUILD, 2006.

Reinhart, Carmen E. and Kenneth Rogoff. *This Time Is Different: Eight Centuries of Financial Folly.* Princeton: Princeton University Press, 2009.

Rempel, Henry. *A High Price for Abundant Living: The Story of Capitalism.* Scottdale: Herald Press, 2003.

Rosner, Brian S. *Greed as Idolatry: The Origin and Meaning of a Pauline Metaphor.* Grand Rapids: William B. Eerdmans, 2007.

Schweiker, William and Charles Mathewes. *Having: Property and Possession in Religious and Social Life.* Grand Rapids: William B. Eerdmans, 2004.

Sheils, W. J. and Diana Wood, eds. *The Church and Wealth.* Papers read at the 1986 Summer Meeting and the 1987 Winter Meeting of the Ecclesiastical History Society. Oxford: Basil Blackwell, 1987.

Stearns, Richard. *The Hole in Our Gospel.* Nashville: Thomas Nelson, 2009.

Stückelberger, Christoph, William Otiende Ogara, and Bright Mawudor, eds. *African Church Assets Handbook: Good Stewardship for Sustainable Impact.* Geneva: Globalethics.net, 2018.

Trout, J. D. *Empathy Gap: Building Bridges to the Good Life and to the Good Society.* New York: Viking, 2009.

Wheeler, Sondra Ely. *Wealth as Peril and Obligation: The New Testament on Possessions.* Grand Rapids: William B. Eerdmans, 1995.

Wilkinson, Richard and Kate Pickett. *The Spirit Level: Why Greater Equality Makes Societies Stronger.* New York: Bloomsbury Press, 2009.

Wright, Christopher J. H. *Old Testament Ethics for the People of God.* Downers Grove: IVP Academic, 2004.

Wright, Christopher J. H. with James Cousins. *The Shortfall: Owning the Challenge of Ministry Funding.* Includes "The Grace of Giving" by John Stott. Carlisle, UK: Langham Global Library, 2021.

Wolff, Edward N. *Top Heavy: The Increasing Inequality of Wealth in America and What Can Be Done About It.* A newly updated and exp. ed. New York: The New Press, 2002.

Zinbarg, Edward D. *Faith, Morals, and Money: What the World's Religions Tell Us about Ethics in the Marketplace.* New York: Continuum International Publishing Group, 2005.

Participants

Dr. Bendor-Samuel, Paul
Executive Director,
Oxford Centre for Mission Studies
Director, Regnum Books Oxford, UK

Dr. Bonk, Jonathan J.
President, Global Mission Leadership Forum Inc.
Founding Director Emeritus, DACB
Research Professor, Boston University School of
Theology Winnipeg, Manitoba, Canada

Dr. Carlson, Darren M.
President, Training Leaders International
Minneapolis, Minnesota, USA

Rev. Cho, Hak Hyun
Missionary, OMF International
Siem Reap, Cambodia

Rev. Chung, Jimoon
Missionary, OMF International
Yokohama, Kanagawa Ken, Japan

Rev. Colney, Zosangliana
Former Finance Officer, Mizoram Presbyterian
Church Synod Aizawl, Mizoram, India

Dr. DeCarvalho, Levi
Research Area Director, COMIBAM
International Sao Paulo, Brazil

Dr. DiStefano, Michel G.
Independent Scholar
Homewood, Manitoba, Canada

Dr. Eum, Jooyun
Professor, Global Missionary Training Center
(GMTC) Seoul, South Korea

Dr. Gitau, Wanjiru
Assistant Professor, Palm Beach Atlantic
University Florida, USA

Mrs. Gitoho, Valentine
Chairperson, African Council for Accreditation
and Accountability Nairobi, Kenya

Dr. Harries, Jim
Missionary and Chair, Alliance for Vulnerable
Mission Andover Baptist Church, UK
Near Kisumu, Kenya

Mr. Himm, Sokreaksa
Former Missionary in Cambodia
Toronto, Ontario, Canada

Rev. Hong, Hyunchol
Executive Director, Korea Research Institute for
Mission (KRIM) Seoul, South Korea

Dr. Hong, Sungbin
Missionary, WEC International
Bishkek, Kyrgyzstan

Dr. Howell, Allison
Associate Professor, Adjunct Staff, Akrofi-
Christaller Institute of Theology, Mission and
Culture Akropong-Akuapem, Ghana

Rev. Dr. Jennings, J. Nelson
Mission Pastor, Consultant, and International
Liaison, Onnuri Church
Editor, *Global Missiology—English*
Connecticut, USA

Mr. Jo, Daeshik
Secretary-General of the Korea NGO Council for
Overseas Development Cooperation (KCOC)
Elder, Onnuri Church Seoul, South Korea

Mr. Jung, Dae Su
Officer and Treasurer, Lausanne Committee Korea
CEO and Chairman, GMD Korea
Elder, Onnuri Church Seoul, South Korea

Mr. Jung, Minyoung
Mission Consultant Seoul, South Korea

Dr. Jung, Soonuk
Translator, Independent Researcher
Seongnam, South Korea

Dr. Kang, Cheol
Senior Pastor, Dongbu Presbyterian Church
Uijeongbu, South Korea

Dr. Kim, Andrew B.
Consultant, Missions Department, CBCNEI (Council of Baptist Churches in North East India)
Director, Global Connections for Advancement, Korea
Director, GDI (GMP Development Institute), Korea Seoul, South Korea

Dr. Kim, C. S. Caleb
Director of Institute for the Study of African Realities, Africa International University
Nairobi, Kenya

Rev. Kim, Hong Joo
Director, Department of Missions, Onnuri Church Seoul, South Korea

Dr. Kim, Insoo
Founder and Representative, Dandelion Community Sancheong-Gun, South Korea

Rev. Dr. Kim, Jinbong
Managing Director, GMLF Inc.
Coordinator, KGMLF
Shelton, Connecticut, USA

Rev. Kim, Sun Man
Senior Pastor, Choonghyun Presbyterian Church
Dallas, Texas, USA

Rev. Dr. Kwon, Sung-Chan
Executive Director, Global Missionary Fellowship (GMF) Seoul, South Korea

Dr. Lee, Bright Myeong-Seok
Visiting Faculty, Presbyterian University &Theological Seminary Seoul, South Korea

Dr. Lee, Byung Soo
Professor, Kosin University
Director of International-Multi Cultural Institute
Busan, South Korea

Rev. Lee, Dong-Whee
Chairman, The Paul Mission International
Gimje, South Korea

Mr. Lee, Jeffrey J.
CEO of SfK Network
Greer, South Carolina, USA

Rev. Lee, Joohyung
Senior Pastor, Sasang Presbyterian Church
Busan, South Korea

Rev. Lee, Mongsik
Senior Pastor, Juhyanghan Church
Président, Communauté Coréenne des Missions pour la Francophonies (CCMF)
Seoul, South Korea

Dr. Lee, Seung-Il
Director, The Paul Mission Human Resource Development Center Cainta, Rizal, Philippines

Dr. Lim, David S.
President and CEO, Asian School of Development and Cross-Cultural Studies (ASDECS)
Paranaque, Philippines

Dr. Longkumer, Atola
Visiting Faculty, SAIACS Bengaluru, India

Dr. Mawudor, Bright Gabriel
Deputy General Secretary-Fin. and Admin, All Africa Conference of Churches
Nairobi, Kenya

Dr. Maxwell, Ruth
Leader Care and Pastoral Care Provider, SIM
Abbotsford, British Columbia, Canada

Dr. Oak, Sung-Deuk
Associate Professor of Korean Christianity, UCLA
Los Angeles, California, USA

Rev. Ogbadu, Paul
Missionary, National Director of Calvary Ministries
Yaoundé, Cameroon

Dr. Oh, Robert
Co-Founder, Cambodia Research and Resource Center Phnom Penh, Cambodia

Dr. Osmonaliev, Emil, MD, BBS
Pastor, Rector, United Theological Seminary
Bishkek, Kyrgyzstan

Participants

Rev. Dr. Pachuau, Lalsangkima
J.W. Beeson Professor of Christian Mission
Dean of Advanced Research Programs
Asbury Theological Seminary
Wilmore, Kentucky, USA

Rev. Dr. Park, Jongdo
Senior Pastor, Raynes Park Korean Church
London, United Kingdom

Dr. Park, Timothy Kiho
Senior Professor of Asian Missions, Fuller
Theological Seminary Pasadena, California, USA

Rev. Park, Young Gee
Shinsapporo Bible Church
Sapporo City, Hokkaido, Japan

Dr. Shaw, Karen L. H.
Missionary and Author, SIM/MECO Australia
Glendenning, Australia

Rev. Shin, Hakkyoon
Senior Pastor, Smyrna Church
Yongin, South Korea

Dr. Thacker, Justin
Research Fellow, Cliff College, UK
Just Scripture Advisor, Christian Aid
Chesterfield, United Kingdom

The Rt. Rev. Dr. Torrey, Ben
Executive Director, The Fourth River Project, Inc.
Taebaek, Gangwon, South Korea

Dr. Weber, Charles
Emeritus Professor of History, Wheaton College
Wheaton, Illinois, USA

Rev. Dr. Wright, Christopher J. H.
Global Ambassador and Ministry Director,
Langham Partnership
London, United Kingdom

Dr. Zurlo, Gina A.
Co-Director, Center for the Study of Global
Christianity, Gordon-Conwell Theological
Seminary South Hamilton, Massachusetts, USA

Contributors

PAUL BENDOR-SAMUEL was appointed the executive director of the Oxford Centre for Mission Studies (https://www.ocms.ac.uk/) in 2016. Prior to this, Paul lived and worked in a wide range of contexts. He spent his early childhood in Brazil and West Africa and trained as a medical doctor in the UK. Following two years of theological training, he, his wife, and four sons then spent twelve years in Christian development and church planting ministry in North Africa. Between 2003–2015, based in Malaysia, Paul led the work of Interserve, an interdenominational, global mission agency focused on Kingdom growth among the peoples of Asia, the Middle East, and North Africa (https://www.interserve.org/). Paul is passionate about seeing discipleship at the heart of personal life and mission, about exploring what it means for individuals and groups to participate in God's mission today, and about building healthy organizations and organizational spirituality.

JONATHAN J. BONK is research professor of mission at Boston University and founding director emeritus of the *Dictionary of African Christian Biography* (www.dacb.org). He is executive director emeritus of the Overseas Ministries Study Center (www.omsc.org) where he served from 1997 until his retirement in July 2013. He was editor of the *International Bulletin of Missionary Research* (www.internationalbulletin.org) from July 1997 until June 2013. He has authored five books, has edited nine collaborative volumes, and published more than one hundred scholarly articles and book chapters and numerous reviews and editorials. His best-known book is *Missions and Money: Affluence as a Western Missionary Problem*. He is president of the Korean Global Mission Leadership Forum and has been actively involved with the KGMLF since it began in 2010. He and his wife are active members of the Fort Garry Mennonite Fellowship in Winnipeg, Manitoba, Canada. He was raised in Ethiopia by missionary parents.

DARREN CARLSON is the president of Training Leaders International, which he founded in 2009, and now serves with a staff of over fifty people around the world providing theological training in underserved and undertrained areas. He is the executive producer and creator of *Jesus in Athens*, a movie telling the story of the work of God in the midst of a refugee crisis in Athens. He is currently a pastor at the Evangelical Free Church of Bozeman. He is also the general editor of the *Journal of Global Christianity*. Darren holds two master's degrees from Trinity Evangelical Divinity School and a PhD from the London School of Theology. He has been married to his wife Amy for eighteen years, with whom he has five children.

HAK HYUN CHO has served as a missionary since 1999 with OMF International. He and his wife have been church planting in rural Cambodia for the past twenty-two years. After handing over the church that they planted to local leaders, they moved to near the Thai border and are now doing another church plant.

JIMOON CHUNG, Korean, is now involved in church planting at Yokohama. After receiving training at Chongshin Theological Seminary and MTI, GMTC in Korea, he and his wife, EunOck Kim, joined OMF International in 1989. They served the Lord with Japanese pastors at Hokkaido and Chiba. He and his wife are blessed with one daughter and one son, and four grandchildren.

ZOSANGLIANA COLNEY is a retired presbyter of the Mizoram Presbyterian Church Synod (a unit of the Presbyterian Church of India). He was the mission secretary of the MPC Synod (2001–2006) and later the synod executive secretary and finance officer (2007–2012). He was also the secretary of the PCI General Assembly (2010–2014) and vice president (2012–14) and president (2014–16) of the North East India Christian Council (NEICC). After retirement from church service he joined the State of Mizoram government as a member and later the chairman of the Mizoram Public Service Commission. He retired from the government in November 2019. Since April 2020 he has been engaged by the church as the principal of the "English Congregation School" in Aizawl, Mizoram, India.

LEVI DeCARVALHO is research area director of COMIBAM International. He studied and worked at the School of Intercultural Studies, Fuller Theological Seminary. Levi does research in cultural anthropology, missiology, intercultural communication, linguistics, Bible translation, and theology (New Testament and Greek). His current project is "Strengths and Weaknesses of the Ibero-American Missionary Movement" (Fortalezas y debilidades del movimiento misionero iberoamericano) with COMIBAM (www.comibam.org).

MICHEL G. DISTEFANO got his master's degree in Old Testament and Semitic languages before his doctoral studies were interrupted for a decade. So in the 1990s he quickly studied nursing and worked as a neonatal intensive care nurse. In the 2000s he got his PhD at McGill and taught ancient Near Eastern religions and Hebrew Bible there. Now he is an independent scholar. He conducted a workshop at the last forum and is the copyeditor for this one. He has known Prof. Jonathan Bonk (Dad) for forty years, and he was often reminded of Dad's thoughts and writings on missions and money. It has been a great privilege to work with him and the rest of the executive on this project. Michel and his wife, Heather, have three adult children, a son and daughter-in-law, and a granddaughter.

JOOYUN EUM is a professor at the Global Missionary Training Center (GMTC), an evangelical missionary training institution established in 1986 in Seoul, South Korea. He holds a PhD in missiology from the Oxford Centre for Mission Studies (OCMS) in Oxford, England, and has long devoted himself to Korean missionary training. His wife, Kyungg-Hwa Son, is the representative of the Women Leadership Focus (WLFocus), a division of the Global Leadership Focus (GLF), and has been involved in strengthening the leadership competency of Korean women missionaries. She is also a certified Korean instructor for the Taylor-Johnson Temperament Analysis® (T-JTA®).

WANJIRU M. GITAU is a global research professional. She looks for the good stories about how contemporary religious communities support upwardly mobile young adults as they navigate a world in flux. She connects stories of local communities with national, regional, and global histories. Wanjiru is assistant professor of World Christianity and Practical Theology at Palm Beach Atlantic University. Her IVP-published *Megachurch Christianity Reconsidered: Millennials and Social Change in African Perspective* has drawn rave reviews and has raised awareness of vitally important social dynamics associated with both African young people and megachurches worldwide. Gitau was born and educated in Kenya, but she has lived in quite a few places and traveled for service and research on every continent, including four countries of the Pacific Rim. She studied a bachelor's degree in linguistics and literature (University of Nairobi), a Masters in missiology (NEGST), and a PhD in world Christianity (Africa International University/University of Edinburgh).

VALENTINE GITOHO, FCA (ICAEW), FCPA(K), CPS (K), MBA, BCom, a Kenyan living in Nairobi, is a financial and management professional with over forty years of experience, with over twenty years board experience in for-profits and nonprofits. The first fourteen years were in for-profits with Binder Hamlyn (chartered accountants) in England (1979–1983), Price Waterhouse Kenya (1983–1989), and Diners Club International Limited and Diners Finance Limited in Kenya (1989–1993). The next eighteen years were in nonprofits, joining multidisciplinary teams of professionals— CORAT Africa (1993–1995), the World Council of Churches (1995–2002) across Africa, and the World Bank in Pakistan (1997–2002), India (2004), and Eastern Africa (2006–2010). She is a cofounder and director of three companies with a pan-African organizational discipleship mandate in accountability and sustainability—

LEEDS Foundation (2012), LEEDS Consulting (2014), and African Council for Accreditation and Accountability (2015). Valentine is married to James, and they are blessed with two married children and two grandchildren.

JIM HARRIES is British-born, earned his PhD in theology at the University of Birmingham, UK, and has served in theological education in Zambia, then Kenya, predominantly using African languages, since 1988. He is currently serving under the umbrella of the Coptic Orthodox Church in Kenya. Jim is sent by Baptist Union churches in the UK, and he is adjunct faculty at William Carey International University, Pasadena. He chairs the Alliance for Vulnerable Mission. His published writing includes eleven books (three fiction) and numerous articles.

SOKREAKSA HIMM is an author, teacher, and church planter in Cambodia. He came from a large family in Siem Reap City, Cambodia when the country fell to the Khmer Rouge on April 17, 1975. Forced to join the exodus to the jungle villages, the whole family was marched to a mass grave and killed one by one. Young Sokreaksa, gravely wounded, was covered by the bodies of his brothers and sisters. In time, he escaped the killing fields and fled to a Thai refugee camp. He eventually made his way to Canada. Later, he received Jesus Christ as his Lord and Saviour. He went back to plant churches in Cambodia from 1999–2019. He is the author of The *Tears of My Soul*, which describes his journey to freedom, faith, and purpose, and *After the Heavy Rain,* which tells of his journey of forgiveness and reconciliation to the people who killed his family. His last book, *Shepherd of My Soul*, which chronicles his journey through PTSD through the healing grace of the Good Shepherd, will be released this year.

HYUNCHOL HONG, a former missionary in China, is executive director of the Korea Research Institute for Mission, Seoul, as of January 1, 2020. He is a graduate of Korea Aerospace University, Hapdong Theological Seminary, and Alliance Bible Seminary, Hong Kong. He taught biblical hermeneutics to Chinese ministers while serving in China from 2005 to 2018.

SUNGBIN HONG is married with two children and associated with WEC International. He and his wife, Eunjung, served and reached out to Muslims in Kyrgyzstan, working on a multicultural church planting team. Sungbin Hong earned an MDiv from Chongshin Theological Seminary, Korea, an MA in intercultural studies from Columbia International University, South Carolina, and a doctorate in intercultural studies at Fuller Theological Seminary. He has been serving expats, church planters, and multicultural church planting teams in leadership roles and will be serving as an area director from 2022. He is passionate about reaching out to Muslims in Central Asia and training local church leaders and expat workers.

ALLISON HOWELL is an associate professor and adjunct staff member with the Akrofi-Christaller Institute of Theology, Mission and Culture in Ghana, and is now based in Australia. Allison also currently coordinates a group of Kasena pastors who are writing a Bible commentary on the Gospel of John in Kasem. Prior to working at the Akrofi-Christaller Institute, she served as a missionary with SIM Ghana in the Upper East Region among the Kasena. Earlier in life she spent time working with UNICEF in Switzerland and on projects in India and Nepal. An Australian, Allison was born in the Democratic Republic of Congo (formerly the Belgian Congo), where her parents were missionaries with Christian Mission to Many Lands (CMML).

J. NELSON JENNINGS (PhD, Edinburgh University) is vice president of the Korean Global Mission Leaders Forum. He is mission pastor, consultant, and international liaison with Onnuri Church, Seoul, South Korea. He is also editor of *Global Missiology – English*. He and his family served in Japan for thirteen years (1986–1999), first in church planting then in teaching at Tokyo Christian University. Jennings next taught World Mission for twelve years at Covenant Theological Seminary, then served as director at the Overseas Ministries Study Center (2011–2015). He has published numerous books and articles, and he has also served as editor of *Missiology: An*

International Review and *International Bulletin of Missionary* [now *Mission*] *Research*. Jennings and his wife, Kathy, are both US-Americans and live in Hamden, Connecticut, USA.

DAESHIK JO is a secretary-general of the Korea NGO Council for Overseas Development Cooperation (KCOC). KCOC is a nongovernmental council of 140 or so Korean CSOs (Civil Society Organizations) specializing in international development cooperation. KCOC represents 140 NGOs with 4.4 million members in Korea. Before he joined civil society, he was a career diplomat. He served as ambassador of the Republic of Korea to Canada and deputy minister for planning and coordination of the Ministry of Foreign Affairs (MOFA). With a profound interest in poverty and development in developing countries, he has extensive experience in both the public sector and private sector, including CSOs. He is serving as an elder of Onnuri Church in Seoul. He holds a master's degree in sociology from USC (University of South Carolina, USA) and a BA in sociology from Korea University. He is married with two sons. The ROK government awarded him the Order of Service Merit twice, in 2008 and 2013.

DAE SU JUNG was born in 1952, during the Korean war. He graduated from Seoul National University in 1975, majoring in economics. He then served in the Korean Air Force in 1975 and 1976 and worked for the Korean Air and Dongnam Securities for fifteen years (1974–1990). In 1992 he graduated from the MIT Sloan School of Management, Cambridge, MA. In 1992 he was baptized in the Cambridge Korean Church, Cambridge, MA. He has been CEO and chairman of GMD Korea since 1992, an elder at Onnuri Community Church, Seoul, Korea since 2006, director of BEE Korea since 2015, and officer and treasurer, Lausanne Committee Korea, since 2017 (all to the present). He has been happily married to Hae Joung Jung for forty-two years, and they have two married daughters and three granddaughters. He is committed to family ministries, especially couples counseling, and to the global mission, with emphasis on Japan and Indonesia. He is also presently the oldest first-year student at Torch Trinity Graduate University of Theology.

MINYOUNG JUNG, along with his wife Jaejin, participated in a Bible translation project for a tribal group in Papua, Indonesia in the 1980s and 1990s before joining the leadership team of Wycliffe Global Alliance, where he served until his retirement at the end of 2017. He is now a freelance consultant. He and his wife have three grown-up children living in three countries.

SOONUK JUNG, PhD in chemical technology and MBA, served as a translator for KGMLF since 2019. Married, with three teenage daughters, he lives in Seongnam, Korea.

CHEOL KANG graduated from the College of Ocean Sciences, Jeju National University, and worked as a ship navigator at a Korean shipping company for five years. After receiving God's call, he entered Presbyterian University and Theological Seminary Graduate School and began pastoral ministry in 1993, serving at various churches. Since 2004, he has been serving as a senior pastor at the Uijeongbu Dongbu Church. In 2008, he received a ThD in ministry at Presbyterian University and Theological Seminary Graduate School.

ANDREW B. KIM is missions consultant of the Council of Baptist Churches in North East India (CBCNEI), India. He joined missions in 1984, and pursued mission studies at Fuller in Pasadena, CA (ThM in Intercultural Studies) and at Asia Baptist Graduate Theological Seminary in Hong Kong–Philippine Branch (ThD in Missiology). Andrew and his wife joined a Korea-based mission agency, Global Missions Pioneers, in 1991, and he served as co-director of the mission (1999–2000). He taught at Philippines Baptist Theological Seminary and Asia Baptist Graduate Theological Seminary (2000–2012), then moved to China where he and his family lived till 2018. Nowadays, Andrew is serving as a missions consultant for some emerging mission agencies in the Philippines, China, Indonesia, Ethiopia, and Djibouti. Andrew and Lydia are blessed with two grown-up children.

C. S. CALEB KIM is a Korean missionary serving in East Africa since 1989. He joined the faculty of Africa International University (AIU, then NEGST, i.e., Nairobi Evangelical Graduate School of Theology) in Nairobi, Kenya, in 2002 after earning his doctorate at Fuller Theological Seminary in 2001. Kim's authored books include *Islam among the Swahili in East Africa* (Acton Publishers, 2004, 2016), *Cultural Anthropology from a Christian Perspective* (Ufafiti Foundation, 2019), and 선교학총론 [*Introduction to missiology*] (GMS, 2020). He currently serves as the director of ISAR (The Institute for the Study of African Realities) at AIU. Kim has recently taken up the responsibility to direct the Institute for Mission Research and Development (IMRD), the research center under his mission organization (Global Mission Society), as a home assignment during his sabbatical leave from AIU in 2021. He is married to Manok with two daughters.

HONG JOO KIM, a mission pastor at Onnuri Church, has been director of the missions department since 2014. He completed an MDiv and ThM at Chongshin Theological Seminary and is now pursuing a doctor of missiology (DMiss) at MBTS (Malaysia Baptist Theological Seminary). He first came to Onnuri Church in 2002 to oversee migrant ministries, after having served Indonesian migrants for four and a half years (1998–2002) in Korea. In 2004, he traveled to Indonesia with his wife and two children and served as a missionary for ten years. There, he served the Komering tribe, an unreached Muslim people group in southern Sumatra.

INSOO KIM is the founder and director of Dandelion Community, established in 1991 for rural mission. After graduating agricultural study, Gyeongsang National University, he got a PhD in rural adult education from Seoul National University and an MDiv from ACTS (Asian Center for Theological Studies and Mission) in Korea. He has rich experience in church planting and community development mission-related activities. Dandelion Community supports Himalaya Mission and Cambodia (ISAC), runs Dandelion School, and pursues mission-centered, sustainable village formation. He and his wife are blessed with two sons and one daughter and six grandchildren.

JINBONG KIM, the coordinator of KGMLF, proposed its creation in 2008 and is now the managing director of the umbrella organization, Global Mission Leadership Forum. After training in theology and missiology at Chongshin Theological Seminary, Korea, and All Nations Christian College, England, and interning at a church in France, he went to Guinea in West Africa to work among Fulani Muslims as a member of WEC and GMS. After moving to the United States, Kim served for six years as the director of international church relations at OMSC. He's been blessed working with Dr. Jonathan Bonk and Dr. Nelson Jennings for the KGMLF since 2011. He and his wife are blessed with two sons

SUN MAN KIM is the founding pastor of the Shalom Presbyterian Church of McKinney, McKinney, Texas. He also preaches through the radio program, "Today's Meditation," on Dallas Korean Network Radio Broadcasting. From 2012 to 2015, he served at the Overseas Ministries Study Center, New Haven, Connecticut, as a member of its board of trustees. In 2014, he served as president of the Korean Church Council of Connecticut. He also served at the First Korean Presbyterian Church of Greater Hartford, Manchester, Connecticut (2006–2016), and served at the Reformed Presbyterian Theological Seminary of the East, Flushing, New York, as professor and a member of its board of trustees (2010–2015). He is the author of *Expository Preaching on the Book of Revelation* (in Korean—Seoul: CLC Publication, 2014).

SUNG-CHAN KWON, the executive director of GMF, started his missionary journey in 1992 by joining Global Bible Translators (Wycliffe Organization). He served in a Muslim country for six years as a translator and community worker. Then he moved back to Korea to serve as the executive director of GBT for two terms. After moving to Singapore, Kwon served as the director of Wycliffe Asia-Pacific Area. He got his PhD at OCMS (Oxford Centre for Mission Studies) in 2019, researching a missional reading of John's Gospel. He and his wife, Jahwa Kim, have two sons.

BRIGHT MYEONG-SEOK LEE served as a missionary in Ghana, providing ICT knowledge among Ghanaian youth for about twenty years. He earned his PhD in Korean ecotheological history at the Akrofi-Christaller Institute (ACI), Ghana. Lee currently leads the Korea IAMS Fellowship as co-president and serves as administrator of AMRIConnect (an online platform created by the Alliance of Mission Researchers & Institutions), while teaching at Presbyterian University and Theological Seminary and Torch Trinity Graduate University. He and his wife, Grace Mi-Ae, have one son, Enoch.

BYUNG SOO LEE was born in Busan, South Korea. He studied at Korea Theological Seminary as an MDiv student and continued to study systematic theology and missiology at Reformed Theological Seminary, Jackson, MS, USA. He married a Chinese wife of Taiwan nationality and has three sons and three grandchildren.

DONG-WHEE LEE, the founder of Jeonju Antioch Church and The Paul Mission International, ministered as a senior pastor in several churches in Korea from 1961 to 2006. Since his retirement, Lee has been serving as the chairman of The Paul Mission International Board of Trustees as well as a mission mobilizer nationwide and worldwide. The Lee family was one of the first families in Honam province who accepted Jesus, and Rev. Lee is the third generation of Christian belief. Lee received theological training at Hanshin Theological College and Asian Center for Theological Studies and Mission. Lee has been married to Young-soon for sixty years and they have four grown children, who are all missionaries, and ten grandchildren.

JEFFREY LEE is founder and CEO of SfK Network, consisting of twenty-one entities in sixteen countries. SfK aims to equip and empower aligned missional businesses in Asia and Africa with three types of capital—intellectual, financial, and value chain. Previously, Jeffrey was in banking for thirty-seven years, including seventeen years as CEO for three banks in the US and Rwanda. He also taught at University of Colorado, Denver and Handong Global University in Korea as an adjunct professor. He is a financial entrepreneur, teacher, trainer, coach, and mentor in various areas of business management, leadership, and transformation. He and his wife, Kristin, have two daughters and one grandson.

JOOHYUNG LEE is the senior pastor of Sasang Presbyterian Church in Busan, South Korea, since 2020. After studying at Korea Theological Seminary (MDiv), he founded a church and then went to Kyrgyzstan as a missionary with his wife and two daughters in 1993. He planted three churches and, in 1997, founded the United Theological Seminary. He devised the "Master Plan 2010 for Handover to Locals," and served as rector (1998–2002, 2008–2010) and lecturer (until 2020). He began the master's program (ThM) in the United Seminary and served as a director (2011–2020). He also served as a missionary in Afghanistan from 2003 to 2007. He studied at Midwestern Baptist Theological Seminary (DMin). He is happily married to his wife and has been blessed with three children.

MONGSIK LEE is currently serving as the senior pastor of Juhyanghan Church. He also serves as the president of Communauté Coréenne des Missions pour la Francophonies (CCMF), the Korean French-speaking mission. He was educated at Chongshin University and Chongshin University's Graduate School of Theology. He saw a vision of the French-speaking region, which is an underprivileged region of missions, and in 1992 he established a French-speaking mission to mobilize missions in French-speaking regions and serve missionary churches. He has three children.

SEUNG-IL LEE, the director of Human Resource Development Center in The Paul Mission International, is a missionary trainer. Lee received theological training at Hapdong Theological Seminary, Asian Center for Theological Studies and Missions, and Wales Evangelical School of Theology, and earned his PhD degree at the University of Wales, UK. In 2005, Lee and his wife, Sharon Haewon, joined The Paul Mission International, and they are involved in mission planting, pastoral training, theological education, and missionary training for missionary candidates who come from Korea, Philippines, Nigeria, Cote d'Ivoire, Vietnam, Bangladesh, and USA. He and his wife are blessed with three kids. Donghyuk, his eldest son, contributed to this presentation in data collection and translation.

DAVID S. LIM is a Chinese Filipino who resides in MetroManila, Philippines. He is the president of the Asian School for Development and Cross-Cultural Studies (ASDECS), which provides graduate degrees and training programs for transformational missions. He is also the president of China Ministries International-Philippines, which has sent more than 120 tentmakers to China. He also serves as the board chairman of Lausanne Philippines, an executive council member of Asia Lausanne and Asian Society of Frontier Missions, and a steering group member of SEANET, the global network to reach the Buddhist world. He earned his ThM from Asian Center for Theological Studies in Seoul, Korea, and his PhD in theology from Fuller Theological Seminary. He has recently coedited the compendium of Asian Society of Missiology's conference, *Christian Mission in Religious Pluralistic Society*.

ATOLA LONGKUMER is a Naga, from northeast India. She has taught in seminaries in mainland India for over fifteen years in the areas of world religions and mission history. Longkumer received her theological education in India and the USA. Currently, she resides in Imphal, Manipur, where her husband, Rev. Khayaipam Khamrang, pastors a church. Apart from teaching, Longkumer has contributed papers on missions, gender, and indigenous Christianity.

BRIGHT GABRIEL MAWUDOR is the deputy general secretary (Finance and Administration) of the All Africa Conference of Churches, and part-time lecturer in public finance and business related subjects at various institutions. He serves on the Daystar University Council, Kenya, chairs the Council Sub-Committee on Investment and Resource Mobilization, and serves on the boards of several Christian organizations. He obtained his professional accountancy qualification from the London School of Accountancy and Business Studies, his MBA (Finance) from the University of Manchester Business School, and his PhD (Business Management) from the Open University of Tanzania in Dar es Salaam. He is also a senior fellow/visiting professor in business related subjects at the Institute of Diaconic Science and Diaconic Management, Protestant University Wuppertal/Bethel, Germany.

RUTH MAXWELL provides leader care, pastoral care, and coaching in SIM. She grew up in Nigeria and witnessed her parents compassionate care for fellow workers. Her childhood included village life and boarding school. The loss of her parents in a car accident was very difficult but gave her the opportunity to experience God's comfort and compassion personally. During Bible school at Prairie College (Canada), God developed her love for him and for discipleship. Five years on faculty at Prairie College gave her invaluable experience in teamwork, discipleship, and leadership. During thirty-six years with SIM, Ruth has been engaged in member care, leader care, mentoring, discipleship, coaching, training, hospitality, and supporting others as they care for Christian workers. Ministry has taken her to Canada, Liberia, Kenya, South Africa, Asia-Pacific, and many places beyond via the internet. During COVID she joined SIM's Pastoral Care Alliance Team supporting SIM personnel around the world.

SUNG-DEUK OAK studied at Seoul National University and Presbyterian Theological Seminary. He served at Onnuri Community Church as an evangelist/intern minister from 1988 to 1992. Just after his ordination as a minister of PCK in 1993, he came to the USA with his wife, Hye Kyung Jin, and three children and studied the ThM program at Princeton Theological Seminary. He pursued doctoral study at Boston University School of Theology. Since 2002, he has been working at UCLA, teaching the history of Korean Christianity, Korean religions, modern Korean history, and Korea-West encounters. He manages the Dongsoon Im and Mija Im Program of Korean Christianity and the Calyx Program of Korean/Korean American Christianity of the UCLA Center for Korean Studies. He and his wife reside in Simi Valley, California.

PAUL OGBADU is a Nigerian cross-cultural missionary, who served in Guinea-Conakry for about twelve years before relocating to the Republic of Cameroon in 2005. He currently serves as the national director of Calvary Ministries (CAPRO) in the Republic of Cameroon, Central Africa. From Yaoundé, the capital city, he leads a team of missionaries in evangelism, discipleship, mobilization, training, and church planting among the Fulanis and the Mbuméré people groups of Cameroon.

ROBERT OH is the director of Life Giving Ministry USA. After receiving his BA in philosophy at UC Berkeley and MDiv at Fuller Theological Seminary in the USA, he and his wife planted five Asian American churches in the Los Angeles area for twenty years. From 2000 on, they pursued mission work in Cambodia and in 2009 he started his PhD research at the Oxford Centre for Mission Studies. They have established the Oasis House Counselling Centre and the Cambodia Research & Resource Centre in Cambodia—living six months a year in Cambodia and in the USA. He and his wife are blessed with three grown-up children and two rabbits.

EMIL OSMONALIEV is currently serving as the senior pastor at the "Great Grace" Church and the rector of United Theological Seminary in Bishkek, Kyrgyzstan. His church is a part of the worldwide Greater Grace World Outreach and his seminary is a nondenominational, local religious educational institution. He received his secular training as a medical doctor in the Kyrgyz State Medical Academy and his theological training in the local Bible college affiliated with Maryland Bible College & Seminary. He and his wife both have been serving in the local church for twenty years. He was ordained to be the senior pastor fifteen years ago and became the rector of the seminary two years ago. They are blessed with five children - two daughters and three sons.

LALSANGKIMA PACHUAU is the John Wesley Beeson Professor of Christian Mission and dean of advanced research programs at Asbury Theological Seminary. An ordained minister of the Presbyterian Church of India (Mizoram Synod), he previously taught at the United Theological College, Bangalore, India. He is a member of the Center of Theological Inquiry (Princeton, NJ, USA), and previously served as the editor of *Mission Studies: Journal of the International Association for Mission Studies*.

JONGDO PARK is currently serving as the senior and founding pastor at Raynes Park Korean Church (2003 to present). He received his training at Chongshin Theological Seminary after studying philosophy at Pusan University. He then proceeded to study under Dr. Iain Torrance in Aberdeen University, where he received his PhD in 2001. His wife, Sook Hee Park, and he both became members of the Global Mission Society and are both active members in the UK. They have both been serving at Raynes Park Korean Church for eighteen years, having established many mission programs to Greece, Ukraine, Syria, Burkina Faso, and the Central Africa Republic. They are blessed with two children (one daughter and one son) as well as Tofu (dog).

TIMOTHY KIHO PARK has been on the faculty of the School of Intercultural Studies at Fuller from 1996 until 2020, teaching Asian missions. He also served as director of the Korean Studies program until 2015, when he became director of Global Connections. As an Asian missiologist he makes unique contributions to the development of Asian missions. Before coming to Fuller, Park served as a cross-cultural missionary in the Philippines for fifteen years and was involved in church planting in Metro Manila and various locations on Luzon Island. He helped found the Presbyterian Theological Seminary in the Philippines (now PTS College and Advanced Studies), where he served as professor and president. Park also founded the Institute for Asian Mission (IAM) and Asian Society of Missiology (ASM), through which he works with other Asian missiologists to help Asian churches and missions through research, publication, consultation, and education. He also serves as president of East-West Center for Missions Research and Development (EWCMR&D) and as head chairman of Asia Missions Association.

YOUNG GEE PARK graduated from Korea Theological Seminary (MDiv) and studied at Tokyo Christian Theological Seminary (completion). He served as a co-chairman of the Korean World Missionary Fellowship from 2016 to 2020. Also, he was general director of Kosin Presbyterian Mission from 2018 to 2021. He went to Japan as a missionary thirty-seven years ago and planted "Shinsapporo Bible Church" in Sapporo City, which now has seven branch churches.

KAREN L. H. SHAW is the author of the book, *Wealth and Piety: Middle Eastern Perspectives for Expat Workers*. Formerly an associate professor of cross-cultural ministry at Arab Baptist Theological Seminary in Mansourieh al-Metn, Lebanon, Dr. Shaw is now engaged in cross-cultural ministry in Sydney, Australia. She is married to Dr. Perry Shaw, and they have two adult children.

HAKKYOON SHIN comes from a third-generation Christian family. He graduated from Kosin University (BA) and Kosin Graduate School of Theology (MDiv) in Korea. He served as a Korean military chaplain from 1994 to 2009. In 2011, after much prayer and consideration, he planted Smyrna Church. Since 2014, he, together with his wife, a prayer warrior, and two sons has been pastoring a storefront church with about thirty seats capacity, in Yongin city, Gyeonggi-do, Korea. He describes himself as the happiest minister in the world with total dependence on God. Also, he is an avid tennis player and multi-instrumentalist.

JUSTIN THACKER is the Just Scripture advisor for Christian Aid, UK, and a research fellow at Cliff College, a Methodist training institution in the UK. Previously, he served as the College's academic director as well as at different times its undergraduate, postgraduate, and research lead. His first career was as a medical doctor, training in pediatrics. He worked in Kenya as a pediatrician before embarking on theological studies. He was formerly the head of International Operations for the Royal College of Paediatrics and Child Health, head of Theology for the Evangelical Alliance, and executive director of the World Evangelical Alliance Theological Commission. His most recent book is *Global Poverty: A Theological Guide* (SCM Press, 2017).

BEN TORREY is the director of the Fourth River Project in Taebaek. Ben grew up in Korea, where he joined with his parents, Jane and Archer Torrey, in pioneering Jesus Abbey, a community of prayer, high in the Taebaek Mountains in Kangwon Do. Participating in the original construction work at Jesus Abbey, he also designed and worked on some of the original buildings at the Three Seas location. He is missionary bishop for Korea of the Syro-Chaldean Church of North America (https://syrochaldeanchurch.wixsite.com/syrochaldeanchurch, https://www.facebook.com/syrochaldeanchurch). He graduated from Sarah Lawrence College in 1975. In 2003, he was appointed director of the Three Seas Center and launched the Fourth River Project. Ben and his wife, Liz, are members of Jesus Abbey and live at the Three Seas Center. They also maintain an office and residence in the US.

CHARLES W. WEBER is emeritus professor of history at Wheaton College, Illinois. His MA and PhD are from The University of Chicago. During his forty-five years at Wheaton, he specialized in teaching and research related to modern Asian and African history and cultures, especially the role of Christianity in relation to their national identities and the impacts of European colonialism. He has researched, published, presented papers, and taught internationally on these topics. Presently he is a lifetime member of the American Historical Society and is active in the Conference on Faith and History, the Chinese American Museum of Chicago, the heritage commission of the Baptist World Alliance, and the initiation of Cornerstone International University. He and his wife, Linda, live in Wheaton, Illinois, and share concerns for religious liberty and human trafficking worldwide.

Contributors

CHRISTOPHER J. H. WRIGHT is a missiologist, an Anglican clergyman, and an Old Testament scholar. As international ministries director of Langham Partnership International, he represents and promotes the vision and work of Langham around the world through his international travel and speaking and his writing ministry as a Christian scholar and author, and shares in the spiritual and strategic leadership of the organization. An ordained pastor in the Church of England, Chris spent five years teaching the Old Testament in India, and thirteen years as academic dean and then principal of All Nations Christian College in England. He is an honorary member of All Souls Church, Langham Place in London, UK. A prolific author, he has published scores of books and articles and is probably one of the most widely read and influential authors in the world of evangelical and mission scholarship.

GINA A. ZURLO, PhD, is co-director of the Center for the Study of Global Christianity at Gordon-Conwell Theological Seminary. Her research focuses on the intersection between the demography of religion, world Christianity, and the history of the social scientific study of religion. She is also a visiting research fellow at Boston University's Institute on Culture, Religion and World Affairs, where she is coeditor-in-chief of the *Journal of Religion and Demography* and works on the *World Religion Database* (Brill). She is the coeditor of the *World Christian Database* (Brill) and coauthor of the *World Christian Encyclopedia*, 3rd edition (Edinburgh University Press). She has two forthcoming books, with Zondervan (*Christianity Around the World*) and Wiley-Blackwell (*Women in World Christianity*).

Indices

Subject

A

AACC. *See* All Africa Conference of Churches

accountability, in stewardship
See also financial accountability
biblical principles of 7–12
downward, to the least 11, 242
mutual/relational 10, 61, 75
relational, with Christ 12

AfCAA. *See* African Council of Accreditation and Accountability

African Council of Accreditation and Accountability 94–96, 100

All Africa Conference of Churches 21–28

Asian Mission, support for KGMLF forum x–xi

B

BAM. *See* Business as Mission

board of directors, missions
AACC SBU, as separate entity 25
GMS, with no missionary representation 59–63, 65
KPM, with missionary representation 247
TPMI, as separate structure, specializing in mission 216

Business as Mission 30, 55, 149, 155, 168, 215
See also business models, missional

business models, missional
AACC 23
AfCAA 95
SfK 29
See also BAM; CRO; FBO; NGO

Better World, A 112–114, 117
awarded ECOSOC Special consultative status 113

Bible Training Class 87

C

calling and mission finance 55–57

church related organization 21–22, 95, 97–98
See also business models, missional; FBO; NGO

CRO. *See* church related organization

climate change 244–245
as existential crises 244
and missiology 244

colonialism 22, 46–47, 119, 125, 132, 134n29, 140–141, 140nn6–7, 152, 238, 264
neo 134, 139–141, 144–145, 264
post- 138–139, 140n8, 144–145
and white power 140

COVID-19
effects
on church giving 59, 154, 156
crisis of community 156
on global inequalities 48
on guests at Jesus Abbey 54
on mission budgets 155–157, 163
on missionary mobilization 154, 163, 165–166, 168, 170
and new mission strategies
online Gospel preaching 155
online learning 69, 107, 109, 164, 167–68
reassessment of project ministry 155–156, 158
self-supporting missions 155
time for reflection 155, 169
transparent fundraising 157
responses to
exemplary response by GMS 62
God is sovereign 158, 162, 167, 169–170
prayer 170

creation care 172
and Asian conceptions of ecology 179
biblical basis of 173–174
ecology 3, 176n26, 244
ecospirituality 179
Farmer Managed Natural Regeneration 175
in Cape Town Commitment 4
in church history 174
in educational mission curriculum 71
in expanded definition of mission 176
and mission 117
in partnership with God 173–174
in partnership with government 179–180
and responsible consumerism 177
and transforming unjust structures 175–176

curriculum 82, 84
Bediako's African model 70

D

Dandelion Community 55, 254, 260
    self-reliance in five areas 56

dependency
    historical
        a chronic issue 109, 147
        a form of bondage 29
        as most despicable curse 235
        in paternalism 234
        in patron-client relationships 193
        as toxic charity 30
    in present-day churches
        Africa 21
        Cambodia 196, 198–200
        project maintenance 199
        project ministry 80, 158

diasporic mission 202, 215
    and short-term teams 202

double entry bookkeeping system 99–100

E

education. *See* curriculum; missions and education

ethnocentrism 75

F

faith-based organization 25–26, 30–31
    See also business models, missional; BAM; CRO; NGO

faith financing 50, 186–187
    at CAPRO mission 228
    and dependence on God 50, 52–53, 55
    practitioners of 55
    Jesus Abbey 50–53, 56
    testimony of Hak Hyun Cho 220
    testimony of Hakkyoon Shin 230–232
    testimony of Paul Ogbadu 227–229

faith living
    in cooperative community 56
    and labor 56–57
    practiced at Jesus Abbey 57
    and prophetic guidance 56
    and self-reliance 56
    without debt 56

FBO. *See* faith-based organization

financial accountability
    biblical principles of 95
    definition of 95
    of leadership and governance 95
    standards of AfCAA 95

financial independence 23
    essential to promote public interest 26
    as a facilitative approach 23
    as first principle of self-support 89
    of small churches 89

financial management
    as an apostolic honor to Christ 11, 61
    biblical concepts of 99
    as a sacred trust 7
    safety in numbers 9, 61

financial mismanagement
    and mission drift 96
    and poor stewardship 96

financial sustainability 23
    via asset development 24

fiscal policies
    affected by sender DNA and ethos 209, 213, 215

foreign donor funds
    and control of boards 79–80
    and control over purchasing decisions 79
    and influence on registration of real estate 78–79
    as a threat to indigenous churches 79–80

fraud
    in churches 46
    exceeds global foreign missions expenditures 46
    in nonprofits 45

fundraising *See also* missionary fundraising, traditional
    appeals 8–9
    contextualization 38
    ethics 5
    leadership setting example 2, 102, 241
    practices 22, 34–37, 148, 235
    projects, biblical 1, 7

G

Gap and *Eul* 193–195, 198

Gap-jil 198

generosity 2–3, 5–6, 8, 82, 138–139, 144, 241, 246

giving
    biblical principles of 2–3, 5–6
    biblical motivations of 1–4, 8

global Christian finance 40–47
    financial inequalities 40, 43–44, 47

global Christianity
    demographic shifts 40, 46
    environmental concerns 46
    different readings/experiences of Bible 42
    linguistic shifts 42
    lower quality of life in South 42, 46
    war and conflict zones 46

global inequalities
- frameworks of 243-245
  - integrated UN response to 48
  - reparations for 125
  - repentance for 244-245

Global Mission Society 58-64, 236, 260, 263
- administrative expenses 59
- board of directors 59-63, 65
- headquarters 59-60, 62-63
- history of 59
- missionary welfare finances 60
- recommendations for credibility, transparency, and accountability 61-63
- and similar financial management at MECO 64

GMS. *See* Global Mission Society

Great Commission, the 4, 95, 147-149, 151, 159, 161, 210-211, 214, 217, 247

H

human systems thinking
- dynamics of power 141
- intergroup relationships 142
- responsibility 142, 145

I

immigrants 116

Improper Solicitation and Graft Act 60

Incarnation, the 136, 160
- attitude of 137
- lifestyle 160-161, 221
- ministry 248-250
- spirituality 183
- and indigenous languages 136-137
- and vulnerability 137

integrity 129-135
- bi and multi-integrities 132-133, 135
- biblical principles of 1-6
- definition of 6, 129
- differing cultural models of 136
- differing notions of 130, 132-134
- related to the Gospel 131

J

JAC. *See* Jeonju Antioch Church

Jeonju Antioch Church 209-218
- fiscal philosophy of 211-212
- history of 209
- no assigned budget 212
- relationship with TPMI 210-211

Jesus Abbey 50-57, 235, 264
- establishment of 51-52
- as example of faith mission 57
- original calling 53, 55
- primary calling 53, 55
- in a transition period 53

jubilee
- to cancel debt of the poor 56
- Jubilee 2000, to cancel Global South debt 123-124

justice
- missional concern 119-120
- structural 120-125
  - biblical basis of 120-121
  - and community 126-127
  - definition of 121

K

Kim Young-ran Act 60

Korea's Government Organization Act of 1981 114

Kosin Presbyterian Mission 247-250
- finances and the semi-pooling system 249
- leadership serving field missionaries 248
- matched synod method 250
- transfer of power to the field 248
- uniquely structured board 247

KPM. *See* Kosin Presbyterian Mission

M

MECO. *See* Middle East Christian Outreach

Middle East Christian Outreach 64

migrants
- fake conversions of 202, 203, 205
- ministries to 202, 221
- short-term teams giving money to 204-205

migration 42, 105
- and diaspora 46, 217

missionary
- cross-cultural, frontier as 152
- after deconstructing "-isms" 47
- and diaspora blurring the lines 46
- eight categories of 211
- first millennium cross-cultural model of 47
- local, indigenous people as 152
- national cross-cultural workers as 42, 217
- self-supporting, bivocational as 48, 167-168
- as sent disciple 141
- shifting concepts of 42, 48, 152

missionary fundraising, traditional
- at GMS 59
- history of 141
- at MECO 64

missionary mobilization 151
    eighteenth century history of 152
    present-day realities for Global South 152–153
    in traditional sense of traveling 153

missionary receiving
    by countries with most Christians and resources 45
    in predominantly Christian countries 43

missionary sending
    long-term from West in decline 42
    sending and money in symbiosis 141
    sharp increase in short-term 42
    shift from Global North to South 40, 46
    special agent paradigm 140
    without contacting the unreached 217

missions
    five DNA of 148, 151
    five marks of 176

missions and education
    autonomy and sustainability of 67, 74, 105, 107
    in community relationships 74
    financing educational missions 67–69
    in the money-missionary relationship 189
    and philosophy of education
        consumerist model 67, 71
        Gospel as loving service 68, 72
        non-consumerist 70
    preparing for indigenization 73
    sustainability of after "owners" leave 67
    viability of and government regulations 67

missions and justice. *See* justice

missions paradigms *See also* missionary sending: sending and money in symbiosis
    of the early church 141
    Global South mission models 148–149
    international migrations 152, 217
    mobility as agency versus sending 153
    modern 141

missions strategies 149–150

missions, traditional
    impacted by public sector social welfare 48
    impacted by UN integrated approach 48
    Western, in decline 42, 46, 48

Mizoram 33–34

Mizoram Presbyterian Church 33–34, 37–39, 148, 235, 253, 256

money
    basic resource for mission 43
    critical resource for mission 141, 157
    nonessential in some models 47, 56–57, 146, 150

money and power 65, 136, 138–143
    disproportionate control of 141, 143
    in human systems 141
    in mission ecosystems 141
    in the modern mission paradigm 141
    related to task and pragmatism 141
    related to task and sending 145

money-missionary relationship model 181–189
    ambivalence and anxiety 187
    ambivalence and support 190–191
    missionary identity in 187–188, 191

MPC. *See* Mizoram Presbyterian Church

N

Nevius Method, the 37, 84
    academic interpretations of 88–89, 91–92
    adopted by Korean Mission of the PCUSA 86
    four major points of 90
    genealogies of 84–85, 90n24, 236
        NM in Shandong 84, 89–92, 236
        Ross method Manchuria and NRM 84–91
        Underwood NM 85–87
        Moffett NM 86–87
        as unified entity 91–92
    and growth of Korean church 87, 108
    modeled by UTS 108
    temporary and immutable principles of 236

NGO. *See* nongovernmental organization

NM. *See* Nevius Method, the

nongovernmental organization
    church-based 48, 112, 114
    as instrument of mission 48, 155
    partnering with public institutions 113
    social welfare foundations 112, 114
    See also business models, missional; CRO; FBO

O

Onnuri Church 111–112, 114, 116–117
    founding 111
    organizations founded 112n5, 114
    philosophy of pastoral ministry 111–112, 114, 116–117
    social responsibilities 111–112, 114, 116–117, 114n13
    support teams for KGMLF 2021 ix–xii

Onnuri M Mission 112, 115–117

Onnuri Welfare Foundation 112, 114–117

P

paternalism 75, 183–184, 234–235

patron-client relationships 193–198
- diachronic roles in 193
- economic versus relational dependency in 193
- in human systems 143
- and lack of motivation 196–198
- and prolonged dependency 196–197

Paul Mission International, The
- history of 209
- native missionary training program 209, 213–214
- relationship with JAC 210–211
- wisdom of separate boards 216

power and money. *See* money and power

power and responsibility, in human systems 143

prosperity gospel 6

public funding and missions 111–114
- *See also* NGO

R

Reuben option, the 121, 124–125, 127

reverse mission 40, 46–47

righteous rich, the 137

Rule of St. Benedict 54

S

self-support
- a church-centered mission method 86–87, 89
  - in early Cambodian church plant 221
  - early Korean examples of 86
  - during early stages of Korean church growth 83
  - and rules of the Korean mission 86
- as the cornerstone of indigenization 87
  - for Christian Presbyterian Church of Japan 79
  - as difficult to comprehend by indigenous peoples 242
- and present-day emerging missions 155
  - taught by Paul Mission Training Center 217
- principles of
  - *See also* self-sustenance; three-self principles
  - as enduring principle 84
  - financial independence as first principle of 89
  - in Nevius method 84
  - in Underwood's Nevius method 86
- as tentmaker 55, 155, 215, 217, 242
  - Paul's example of 55, 242
- of UTS 101–103, 107
  - modeled after three-self principles 108

self-sustenance *See also* self-support
- of AACC 23, 25, 29, 31
- in missional business models 31
- one of three-self principles 26

self-theologizing 39, 108–109

SfK. *See* Synergy for the Kingdom Network

short-term missions
- in Athens, Greece 201–206
- of Uijeongbu Dongbu Church 207–208

social responsibilities 117
- for the common good 118–119
- as compassion for our neighbors 119
- and holistic nature of the Gospel 118–119
- as mark of missions 117–119

sovereignty of God
- leads to opportunism in mission 17
- *See also under* COVID-19: responses to

stewardship 7–12
- in creation care 173, 178–179
- and financial management 96
- of mission budgets 157
- as a way of living 161, 186–187, 213 *See also* accountability, in stewardship

structural justice. *See under* justice

Synergy for the Kingdom Network 29, 261

T

TCTS. *See* Tokyo Christian Theological Seminary

tentmaking. *See* self-support: as tentmaker

three-self principles
- as fruit of Bible study 161
- and autonomous indigenous churches 108, 150, 234–235
- and Mizoram Presbyterian Church 33, 37, 235
- modeled by UTS master plan 108, 110
- of moral philosophy 26
- in the Nevius method 84
- in the Ross method 85
- *See also* self-support; self-sustenance

Tokyo Christian Theological Seminary
- establishment of 76
- real estate registration of 78, 80–81, 83
- ruptures between founding entities of 78–80
- and mistrust between colleagues 82

transfer of leadership to locals
- in Cambodia 221–222
- in East Timor 148
- of UTS 103, 109

transparency
- of AACC business dealings 25
- biblical principles of 10–11
- definition of 61
- demand to strengthen 49
- of individual missionaries 65
- of leadership 10

transparency, lack of
  and misappropriation of funds at GMS 61
  results in low confidence and lack of trust 48–49

U

UN Refugee Agency. See United Nations: UNHRC

United Nations
  A Better World partnering with 113
  and integrated response to inequality 48
  UNHRC 113, 113n8, 204

United Theological Seminary 101–110, 237, 254, 261, 263
  establishment of 101
  partnership with MITS 103
  and self-support 101–104, 107
  in its sociopolitical context 108

UTS. See United Theological Seminary

V

viability of mission work
  biblical principles of 13–19
  in educational institutions 68

vulnerable mission 129–137, 134n27
  definition of 131, 134

W

Western civilization and mission
  consumption and the desire for more 244
  overconsumption's effect on the environment 245
  and the racist civilizing mission 244

World Missionary Conference
  1900–1910 88
  1910 58

NAMES

A

Abdrisaev, Baktybek 110n9
Adei, Stephen 67n1
Alkire, Sabina 48n8
Allen, Horace N. 86
Anderson, Rufus 87, 108
Arthington, Robert 33
Avison, Olive R. 87

B

Baek, Jeonghoon 61n10
Baird, William M. 88
Balentine, Samuel 173n4, 178, 178n32
Ban, Peter xii

Becker, Arthur L. 87
Beckett, Thomas (archbishop of Canterbury) 242, 242n1
Bediako, Kwame 66, 70, 70nn2–3, 72, 75
Bendor-Samuel, Paul 138–146, 238, 253, 256
Bessenecker, Scott A. 128n32
Boesak, Allan 121, 124–125
Bonk, Jonathan J. ix–xi 32, 32n1, 35, 35n17, 58n1, 60n9, 61n13, 62nn17–18, 63, 65n22, 107, 107n2, 137, 137n37, 144, 160n8, 160nn11–12, 160–161, 161n20, 171, 177n29, 204, 204n10, 241–246, 251, 253, 256–257, 260
Bookless, Dave 172, 172n2, 239
Bosch, David J. 170n2, 197, 197n10

C

Câmara, Dom Hélder 121
Carey, William 123, 141n14
Carlson, Darren M. 201–206, 201n1, 207–208, 239, 253, 256
Chan, R. 196, 196n9, 197, 197n12
Ch'ang-ho, Ahn 88
Chapman, Donald 34n11, 34–35, 35n16
Chheang, V. 196, 196n9, 197, 197n12
Ch'iho, Yun 89
Cho 195, 195n8
Cho, Hak Hyun 220–222, 253, 256
Chun, Chun Sung 88, 88n19
Chung, Jae Chul x–xi
Chung, Jimoon 81–83, 253, 256
Ch'un-gyŏng, Ro 86
Clark, Charles A. 88, 88nn16–17, 90, 90n25
Colney, Zosangliana 32–38, 235, 242, 246, 253, 256–257
Cousins, James 7
Cretton, Destin Daniel 127n29

D

David H. Adney 160, 160nn9–10
DeCarvalho, Levi 162–169, 171, 238, 253, 257
Distefano, Michel G. xii, 253, 257

E

Eisenstadt, S. N. 194, 194nn4–5, 195n6
Eliot, T. S. 242, 242n2
Ellinwood, F. F. 86, 86n9
Elliot, Mark 110n9

Equiano, Olaudah 123
Eum, Jooyun 181–192, 239, 253, 257

F

Floyd, George 130n5
Foxwell, Jane 77
Foxwell, Phil 77–78, 80
Francis of Assisi, Saint 159, 174, 179
Freire, Paulo 65, 65n20
Fumagalli, Matteo 110, 110n7

G

Gale, James S. 86–87
Girard, René 129, 130n6, 134
Gitau, Wanjiru M. 151–153, 253, 257
Gitoho, Valentine 94–100, 237, 253, 257
Gordon, Henry D 87
Grenz, Stanley J. 207, 208n20
Gutiérrez, G. 125, 125n21

H

Ha, Yong Jo 111–112, 112n4, 117
Han, Sookyoung xii
Hanciles, Jehu 152
Harries, Jim 129–135, 129nn3–4, 132nn21–22, 134n30, 135–137, 137n36, 237, 243, 253, 258
Haruo, Omura 78
Hauerwas, Stanley 146, 146n30
Hepburn, James C. 86–87
Heron, John W. 86
Hickman, Albert W. 45n3, 45n5
Hicks, Melissa xii
Hiebert, Paul 39, 39n21, 108, 136n25, 137n39
Higginbotham, Sam 118
Himm, Sokreaksa 198–200, 223–226, 253, 258
Hoek, M. 120n2
Hoke, Stephen T. 147, 147n1
Holdcroft, J. Gordon 77–79
Hollinger, David A. 118n21
Hong, Hyunchol 73–75, 253, 258
Hong, Sungbin 101–107, 253, 258
Hong-jun, Paek 86
Howell, Allison 66–75, 172–180, 178n31, 236, 239, 244–245, 253, 258
Hrangkhama, Mr. 35

J

Jenkins, Willis 176, 176nn26–27
Jennings, J. Nelson x–xi, xiii–xiv 76–83, 236, 253, 258–260
Jin, Jeong Bung 112
Jo, Daeshik 47–49, 243, 253, 259
Johnson, Todd M. 40n1, 43n2, 45n3, 108n4, 110n7, 243n4
Jones, David Evans 33
Jung, Dae Su 99–100, 253, 259
Jung, Minyoung 126–128, 253, 259
Jung, Soon Young xii, 62, 62n17, 229
Jung, Soonuk xii 253, 259

K

Kairbek, Rev. 103, 109
Kang, Cheol 207–208, 254, 259
Kang, Wijo 88, 88n21
Kapezya, Bethany 67n1
Kim, Andrew B. 147–152, 238, 242, 254, 259
Kim, C. S. Caleb 135–137, 136n33, 254, 259
Kim, Chang Ok 112, 112n6
Kim, Hong Joo xii 111–119, 237, 254, 260
Kim, Insoo 55–57, 254, 260
Kim, Jeong Hee 116n17
Kim, Jinbong x–xii 58–64, 58n1, 60n9, 61n11, 62n18, 65, 144, 160n8, 229, 235–236, 242, 254, 260
Kim, Jong-Sung 160, 160n14
Kim, Jung Han 62, 62n15
Kim, Kwang Dong 113n7
Kim, Sun Man 159–161, 254, 260
Kim, Young Ok 62, 62n18
Kim, Young-Ok 62, 62n18
King, Martin Luther 123
Kingston-Smith, C. 120, 120n3
Kornfield, William J. 235, 235n2
Kupoe, Francis 67n1
Kwon, Florence xii
Kwon, Sung-Chan 37–39, 254, 260

L

Ladd, G. E 210, 210n7
Ledgerwood, J. 197, 197n11
Lee, Bright Myeong-Seok 178–180, 254, 261
Lee, Byung Soo 169–171, 254, 261

Lee, Dong-Whee 209–216, 210nn2–6, 210nn8–9, 211nn11–12, 212, 212nn14–15, 212nn17–20, 213nn21–24, 214nn27–28, 214n31, 216, 239, 254, 261
Lee, Graham 86, 88
Lee, Jae Hoon ix, xi–xii, 111n1, 112
Lee, Jeffrey J. 29–31, 254, 261
Lee, Joohyung 101–107, 237, 254, 261
Lee, Kyung Hee xii
Lee, Kyung Sook 116n17
Lee, Mongsik 154–159, 159n5, 160, 238, 254, 261
Lee, Sang Joon xi
Lee, Seung-Il 209–216, 210n10, 214n29, 216–217, 239, 254, 261
Levy, Annette 67n1
Lim, David S. 216–218, 254, 262
Lindquist, Brent 60n9
Lindqvist, Sven 244, 244n5, 252
Lloyd, J. Meirion 34n10, 34n14, 35, 35n15
Long, Zeb Bradford 53
Longkumer, Atola 117–119, 251, 254, 262
Lorrain, James Herbert 33, 33n5
Lupton, Robert D. 29–30, 29n7

M

Maggay, M. 120, 120n2
Magnason, Andri Snaer 245, 245nn8–10, 252
Mallary, Francis Lorain 51
Maranz, David 134, 134n28
Mawudor, Bright G. 21–28, 234–235, 252, 254, 262
Maxwell, Ruth 190–192, 254, 262
McMillian, Walter 127
Melland, Frank H. 129–131, 129n1, 130nn7–14, 131nn19–20
Mendes, Sonia 162
Merkel, Angela 202, 202n4
Moffett, Samuel A. 84–88, 86n11, 87n13, 90–92
Moon, Steve Sang-Cheol 58n2, 73, 73n5, 74n6, 160n12
Mueller, George 51, 55

N

Neill, Stephen 90m26, 90
Nevius, Helen S. C. 85n2
Nevius, John Livingston 37, 84–92, 85n1, 85nn3–5, 88nn16–17, 90n25, 108, 108n5, 161, 236
Noh, Gyu Seok 116n17

O

Oak, Sung-Deuk 84–89, 87n15, 90–92, 236, 242, 254, 262
Offutt, S. 120, 121n4
Ogbadu, Paul 227–229, 254, 263
Oh, Robert 193–198, 239, 263
Oh, Sung-Jun 212
Oshry, Barry 141–142, 142nn17–18, 142nn20–24, 143nn25–27, 144–145
Osmonaliev, Emil 101–107, 237, 254, 263

P

Pachuau, Lalsangkima 90–92, 255, 263
Park, Albert L. 89, 89n22, 161
Park, Chung-shin 88, 88n21
Park, Jacqueline 88, 88n21
Park, Jin-Koo 212
Park, Jongdo 144–146, 255, 263
Park, Timothy Kiho 214n29, 231, 234–240, 255, 263–264
Park, Yong Kyu 160n12, 161, 161n18
Park, Yong-Kyu 111n2
Park, Young Gee 247–250, 255, 264
Pelkman, Mathijs 110, 110n7
Pwakechega, Vasco 67n1

R

Radford, David 110, 110nn7–8
Ramírez-Johnson, Johnny 140, 140n8
Reese, Robert 108, 108n6
Reiji, Oyama 82
Renpei, Watanabe 76–78, 80, 82
Renzetti, Edilson 162
Rho, Kyu Suk xii
Rimai, Jolly 149
Rinaudo, Tony 175n17–18, 175n20, 175–77, 176n25, 177n28, 179, 179n26, 179n36
Rocha, Fabio 162
Roniger, L. 194, 194nn4–5, 195n6
Ross, John 84–86, 85n6, 90–92
Ross, Kenneth R. 43n2, 110n7, 174n12
Roy. See Shintaro, Hasegawa

S

Saiaithanga, Rev. 34, 34n8
Sands, Edward 110n9
Sang-nyun, Sŏ 86
Sanneh, Lamin 137n40, 162
Savidge, Fredrick William 33
Schein, Edgar 130, 140n10
Scranton, Mary F. 161
Scranton, W. B. 161, 161n17
Severance, Louis H. 87
Shaw, Karen 64–65, 65n22, 255, 264
Shaw, Perry 64, 264
Shigeaki, Fujii 80
Shin, Hakkyoon 230–232, 255, 264
Shintaro, Hasegawa 76–80, 80n26, 82–83
Shintaro, Roy 77–79. *See* Shintaro, Hasegawa
Siamkungi, Mrs. 35
Soh, Canon Chye Ann 37
Song, Young Beom 114, 114n15
Sŏnju, Kil 87
Stevenson, Bryan 123, 127, 127nn29–30
Stokes, Charles D. 88, 88n18
Stott, John 5, 112n4, 127n25, 139n4
Sung-chun, Chun 88, 88n19

T

Taylor, Bill 147
Taylor, J. Hudson 55, 220, 220n1
Taylor, Terri 110n9
Teresa, of Avila 118
Thacker, Justin 120–125, 120n2, 123n14, 124nn17–18, 127n30, 237, 243, 255, 264
Torrey, Ben 50–55, 235, 242, 255, 264
Torrey, Deberniere 51n3
Torrey, Jane 50–53, 52n11, 264
Torrey, Liz 50, 264
Torrey, Reuben Archer, III 50–55, 50n1, 51nn4–6, 52nn7–8, 53nn12–13, 53n15, 54n16, 264
Torrey, Reuben Archer, Sr. 51
Toynbee, Arnold 170
Troutman, Charles 234, 235n1
Tutu, Desmond 24

U

Underwood, Horace G. 84–87, 85n8, 86n9–10, 89n23, 90–92

V

Venn, Henry 87, 108
Vijghen, J. 197, 197n11

W

Wallis, Jim 123
Walls, Andrew F. 58, 58n1, 72n4, 176n23
Weber, Charles 108–110, 255, 264
Weber, Otto 207, 207n19
Wells, J. Hunter 86n12, 88
Wells, John D. 87
Wesley, John 123, 123n10
White, Lynn 173n3, 178
Wilberforce, William 123
Williams, William 33
Winchester, James 33
Winchester, Mary 33
Winter, Ralph 159, 159n6, 160n9, 211n13
Wright, Christopher J. H. 1–19, 61, 61n13, 137, 241–243, 252, 255, 265

Y

Yoder, William 110n9
Yohan xii
Yoichi, Yamaguchi 76n1–3, 77n8–10, 78n11–17, 79n19–20, 80n22, 80n24–25
Yŏngik, Min 86
Yoseph xii
Young, Jean 77
Young, John M. L. 77n6–7, 77–80, 80n23, 80n26, 82

Z

Zairema, Rev. Dr. 35, 35n18
Zurlo, Gina A. 40–47, 40n1, 43n2, 45n3, 45n5, 47n6, 48–49, 108n4, 235, 243, 243n4, 255

SCRIPTURES

Old Testament

Genesis 173
  1–2 13–14, 173
  1:27 97
  1:28 138, 173
  2 139
  2:15 30n9
  2:18 139
  3–11 13–14
  3:16 139
  4:6–8 139
  6:5 6
  12:1–3 150
  13 83

Exodus
  7:16 30n10
  22:22 121
  33:16 1
  35 1

Leviticus
  25:23 5

Deuteronomy
  8:17–18 5
  10:14 3
  10:17–18 120, 237
  10:18 121
  17:17 2
  24:14–15 122
  24:17 121
  33:29 232

Joshua
  24:15 30, 30n11

Judges
  8:4 228

1 Samuel
  12:3 61
  12:4 61

1 Kings
  19, 221
  19:18 221

2 Kings
  7:9 151
  12:1–16 95

1 Chronicles
  17:16 4
  28:2 2
  29:1–19 1–6

Job
  24:3 121
  38–41 173, 178
  40:15 173

Psalms
  24:1 3, 98
  46:1 139
  89:19 139
  94:6 121

Proverbs
  1–9 18
  21:3 237

Ecclesiastes
  9:10 18, 243
  11 19
  11:1–6 13–19

Isaiah
  1:17 121
  10:1–2 122
  30:10–11 245
  41:8 178
  52:7 151
  58:11–12 227

Jeremiah
  5:31 245
  5:31–7:8 245
  7:6 121
  17:5 7, 95

Hosea
  4:6 96

Habakkuk
  2:14 152

Zechariah
  4:6 170

New Testament

Matthew
  4:19 227
  5:16 94
  6:26–34 230
  6:33 51, 239
  8:19–22 127n27
  10:9–10 146
  10:16 146
  10:38 127n28
  16:24 127n28
  19:22 61
  19:26 238
  24:45–50 98
  25:14–30 95
  25:19–21 95
  25:40 11, 208, 242
  28:18 4
  28:18–20 95, 159n5

Mark
  6:31 229
  8:34 127n28
  11:15–17 122
  11:17 128

Luke
  6:27–28 226
  9:23 127n28
  12:13–14 65n19
  12:33 51
  12:35–48 17
  14:27 127n28
  14:28–30 95
  16:10–13 95
  18:26 140
  21:11 159
  23:34 226

John
  2:22 95
  3:16 208
  5:17 30, 30n12
  9:4–5 228
  14:9 249
  15:15 178
  15:16–17 95
  17:20–23 139

Acts
  1:8 211, 211n11, 214
  2:45 139, 144
  3:6 146, 149, 238
  4:32–35 139, 144
  5:1–11 139
  6:1–7, 139 144

  8:18 139
  15 82
  16:19 139
  20:33–35 139, 242
  20:35 98

Romans
  8:18ff. 173
  8:28 82, 238
  8:32 4
  12:1ff. 243
  15 7
  16:7 12

1 Corinthians
  1:18 23, 127n26
  10:31 30n14
  12:25 96
  12:26 96
  15:3–4 95
  16 7–8
  16:1–3 8
  16:1–4 95, 139
  16:3–4 9

2 Corinthians
  2:17 242
  3:3 153
  4:7 243
  5:11–21 173
  5:14–15 152
  5:20 152
  8:1–2 246
  8:1–5 3
  8:1–7 7, 139
  8:4 5
  8:5 2
  8–9 7
  8:16–9:5 7–12, 242
  8:16–24 9
  8:18–19 11
  8:20–21 11, 95
  8:21 11, 95
  8:22 9
  8:23 12
  8:23–24 11
  9:1–5 8
  9:6 246
  12:9 246
  13:13 246

Galatians
    2:10 139
    5:14 237
    6:7 245

Ephesians
    4:13 161n19
    4:16 9, 235
    5:15–16 17

Philippians
    1:15 18, 208
    2:3–5 83
    2:25 12
    2:25–30 12
    3:12 161
    4:19 229, 239

Colossians
    1:15–20 4n1
    1:20 173
    3:11 97
    3:17 18, 243
    3:23 18
    3:23–24 96
    4:1 96
    4:2–3 170

1 Thessalonians
    1:3 56
    5:16–18 18
    5:24 228

1 Timothy
    5:18 96
    6:6 239
    6:10 98

2 Timothy
    1:14 153
    3:14 126
    3:16 95
    4:2 17
    4:10 10
    4:11 82
    4:16 9

Titus
    1:7–9 95

Hebrews
    1:2–3 4n1

James
    2:8 237
    2:23 178n33

1 Peter
    1:10–12 95
    1:18 243
    2:8 127n26
    5:1–5 96

2 Peter
    3:10–13, 173
    3:11 161

1 John
    1:3 208
    1:6 208
    1:7 98
    3:2 139
    3:18 208
    4:10 208
    4:19–21 97

Revelation
    12:12 203
    21:1 173

www.ingramcontent.com/pod-product-compliance
Lightning Source LLC
Chambersburg PA
CBHW082207090526
44583CB00021BA/2811